BARRIER-BREAKING BANQUET

*An Exegetical Study of Jesus' Meal with Zacchaeus (Luke 19:1-10)
In the Background of the Hellenistic Banquet Traditions*

BARRIER-BREAKING BANQUET

*An Exegetical Study of Jesus' Meal with Zacchaeus (Luke 19:1-10)
In the Background of the Hellenistic Banquet Traditions*

Joseph Lourdusamy

2020

Barrier-Breaking Banquet: *An Exegetical Study of Jesus' Meal with Zacchaeus (Luke 19:1-10) In the Background of the Hellenistic Banquet Traditions* — published by the Indian Society for Promoting Christian Knowledge (ISPCK), Post Box 1585, Kashmere Gate, Delhi-110006.

© Author, 2020

All rights reserved. No part of this book may be reproduced or transmitted in any form or by any means, electronic, mechanical, photocopying, recording, or by any information storage and retrieval system, without the prior permission in writing from the publisher.

The views expressed in the book are those of the author and the publisher takes no responsibility for any of the statements.

Online order: http://ispck.org.in/book.php

Also available on amazon.in

ISBN: 978-81-946569-0-6

Cover picture: Anna-dhaanam (community meal) at a village festival in Tamilnadu.

Laser typeset by

ISPCK, Post Box 1585, 1654, Madarsa Road, Kashmere Gate, Delhi-110006
• Tel: 23866323

e-mail: ashish@ispck.org.in • ella@ispck.org.in
website: www.ispck.org.in

Dedicated

To my parents who instilled in me

the interest to read the Holy Scriptures

and find answers from them for the questions of life!

Contents

Dedication	...	v
Preface	...	ix
Abbreviations	...	xi
Introduction	...	xiii

Chapter - 1
    Table Fellowship of Jesus: Socio-Cultural Context ... 1

Chapter - 2
    Table Fellowship and the Gospel of Luke ... 106

Chapter - 3
    The Story of Zacchaeus:
    An Exegetical Analysis (Luke 19:1-10) ... 183

Chapter - 4
    Casteism in the Light of Zacchaeus Story ... 347

General Conclusion ... 376

Bibliography ... 403

Preface

"How you eat, reveals your character!" My mother used to say this to us her children time and again, as she was trying to teach us table etiquette. In different cultures, not only how we eat but also what and with whom we eat define who we are and how we are perceived by others. The Gospel traditions too deal with these questions. It is fascinating to see in the Gospel of Luke, how often Jesus is portrayed to be invited to dinner parties, from people of different walks of life – the rich and the poor, ´saints´ and sinners alike. This fascination is the impetus for the present work. It is not an exaggeration if we say that different narratives about the Table Fellowship are the one thread that binds the third Gospel together as a whole. One cannot understand the Gospel of Luke, when one overlooks the importance of Table Fellowship. Dinners, diners and their Table Talks at frequent intervals in the third Gospel suggest to the readers that not only the historical Jesus felt at home at dinner parties, but also that the Lukan Jesus made use of these Table Fellowships as occasions to impart the ideals of the new evolving community. The present work, resulting from the Doctorate studies, attempts to decode the nuances of Table Fellowship and Table Talk in the Gospel of Luke and its message not only for the audience of Luke at the time of his writing but also to the Indian community at present.

Many have been instrumental and inspirational in the formation and completion of this work. I am thankful to his Excellency Rev. Dr. Susaimanickam Jebamalai, the Bishop of Sivagangai, who allowed me to pursue my Doctoral Studies in Germany. The amount of time he spends for writing books and articles of academic excellence is an inspiration for many. My sincere thanks goes to the Arch Diocese of Freiburg for their fraternal and financial support in my years of study in Freiburg im Breisgau. I am indebted to Rev. Dr. Anandam Lourdu who helped me find a place in the esteemed Albert-Ludwigs-Universität, Freiburg. His constant guidance in the academic as well as personal life deserves utmost admiration and gratitude. The different professors in the Faculty of Theology, specially in the field of Biblical Theology were at their best, whenever I knocked at their doors for help. Dr. Mark Grundeken read through my paper and gave valuable corrections and guidance. Dr. Carola Diebold-Scheuermann was ever ready to correct and polish my German presentations. The Franciscan Sisters of Erlenbad, with whom I lived in Freiburg took care of my every day needs with so much of love and motherly concern. The priests and the faithful of different parishes in the Arch Diocese of Freiburg where I have been going to for weekend and holiday ministry have been very much supportive and encouraging. My sincere thanks to every one of them!

If the work has come to its completion it is because of my Guide and well-wisher, Dr. Ferdinand Prostmeier, to whom I owe my deepest gratitude. I was lucky to have found this meticulous guide and wonderful human being. Conversations with him gave me not only answers to many of the unsolved questions; they evoked new questions which beckoned an answer. Not only the research was important to him but also the researcher. The respect which he showed to my standpoint and arguments at different discussions, taught me many things not only in the academic but also in personal life. I sincerely thank also my second Guide Dr Thomas Johann Bauer, the Dean of the Faculty of Catholic Theology, in the University of Erfurt, Germany, who helped me go beyond my limits and push the work to higher standards. Thanks to the ISPCK and its readiness, the years of academic endeavor have emerged into a wonderful book!

Joseph Lourdusamy

Abbreviations

CSI	Church of South India
AE	*American Ethnologist*
AJS Review	*Association for Jewish Studies Review*
Aristoph. *Wasps*	Aristophanes, *Wasps*
Ath.	*The Deipnosophists*
BBR	Bulletin for Biblical Research
BSAS	British School at Athens Studies
Contempl.	Philo, *On the Contemplative Life*
DSD	Dead Sea Discoveries
Fam.	*Epistulae ad Familiares*
Hom. *Od.*	Homer, *The Odyssey*
Hor. S.	Horace, *Satires*
J. *BJ.*	Josephus Flavius, *The Jewish War*
JSHJ	*Journal for the Study of the Historical Jesus*
LSP	*Letter & Spirit*
NIBC	*New International Biblical Commentary*

Petr.	Petronius, *Satyricon*
Philo. *Hypoth.*	Philo, *Hypothetica*
Plat. *Laws*	Plato, *The Laws*
Plat. *Sym.*	Plato, *Symposium*
Plut. *Brut.*	Plutarch, *Brutus*
Plut. *Quaes. Conv.*	Plutarch, *Quaestiones Convivales*
Plut. *Septem.*	Plutarch, *Septem Sapientium Convivium*
Theog. Fr.	Theognis Fragments
WA	World Archaeology
Xen. *Sym.*	Xenophon, *Symposium*

Notes

Other Abbreviations cited in the book are taken from S. M. Schwertner, *IATG²: Internationales Abkürzungsverzeichnis für Theologie und Grenzegebiete*, Walter de Gruyter, Berlin, 1992.

For the Footnotes and Bibliographical references, this work follows the methodology of the Turabian, 8th Edition (Notes).

The Greek passages of the New Testament are cited from Nestle, E., B. Aland, and K. Aland, eds. *Novum Testamentum Graece*. 28th ed. Stuttgart: Deutsche Bibelgesellschaft, 2013. English passages of the Bible cited here, are taken from *The Holy Bible, The New Revised Standard Version (Catholic Edition)*. Bangalore: Theological Publications in India, 2010.

Source references for the citations from the classical authors like Homer, Plato, Plutarch, etc., are given at the first time when each classical work is quoted. For further citations, the exact occurrence of the quote is stated in the main text itself with chapter and the verse(s) within brackets.

Although the paper is written in English, the German quotes are used liberally throughout, with the hope that the use of German quotes would not hamper the flow of the reading but enhance it. Inconvenience, if any, is sincerely regretted.

Introduction

Food is an everyday necessity. By the very fact of one's existence, one needs to eat. The oft-quoted verse from Odyssey states succinctly: "There is nothing more shameless than a hateful belly, which bids a man perforce take thought thereof, be he never so sore distressed ... yet ever does my belly bid me eat and drink, and makes me forget all that I have suffered, and commands me to eat my fill" (Hom. *Od.* VII. 216-18).[1] Millions of children, women and men all over the world, especially in Africa and other developing countries, are unsure, whether or not they would have something the next day, to satisfy this primary biological need; getting a daily meal for more than half of the people of the world is then a nightmare. In this sense, food is an individual affair.

Food and Society
Food, however, seems to be something more than personal. There is more to food than just an individual, satisfying his biological need. Sharing of food would have played a vital role in the formation of societies in the early times of human evolution. Since food helps bring people together, It could then be viewed as a "highly condensed social act."[2] Food is shared in different ways at different times, with the family members, friends, acquaintances, with people superior or inferior in rank and at times even with strangers. When shared, food creates bonds between individuals and has a certain influence on our relationship with others. In all these instances, food brings one closer to others in a society. Thus, questions like, what we eat, with whom we eat, how and where we eat

are very important in a society. Answers to these questions define the identity of individuals and groups in a society. For people in some part of the world, for example, dog meat is a delicious dish, which is looked upon by others as nauseating. Pork for Jews and beef for some groups of Hindus are, in the same way, an anathema, whereas for others they have nutritious value. Examples such as these confirm the fact that food indeed plays a double role. It builds bridges, bringing people together to form a society; at the same time, it creates barriers between different groups, cultures and societies.

Within a particular culture itself, food plays the role of including some and excluding others. Banquets eaten together show the outside world, who is in and who is out of a particular group. The invitation to a banquet implies the social bond between the partakers. There is a sense of *we* as against *they* who are not invited. Apart from enhancing social relations, banquets may also be looked at as "the social component of display - usually of success, social status or power."[3] Hence with all its cultural and social implications, food is vital for individuals as well as groups for creating and maintaining their social identity.

Food in the Old Testament

From the first book of the Old Testament till the last, we are able to see the vital role played by food. The sin of Adam and Eve was that they ate what was forbidden to them by God (Gen 3:1-7). The first Passover Feast celebrated by the enslaved people of Israel in Egypt becomes a symbol of freedom (Exod 12:1-28); this Passover meal signals the formation of a new people and becomes the characteristic feature of the new nation of Israel. Hence we could say that food, namely the Passover meal is one of the characteristic features of the Jews as a race apart from circumcision and the observance of Sabbath. Further in the Old Testament we also see the strict rules regarding what an Israelite should eat and what food he should avoid (Lev 11:1-47). This classification of clean and unclean food shows how Israel as a nation was preoccupied with the theology of holiness and ritual purity. Whether it could be understood as God-given rule for his people or a rule that aims to make a difference between the Jewish people against other races, the rules of clean and unclean food have been characteristic features of the Jewish people. In the post-exilic period the people of Israel are forced to go against these dietary rules and forced to eat pork which is forbidden. The resistance shown by Eleazar, the seven children and their mother are examples of how some Jews were vehemently against the Hellenization of the Jewish land (2 Mac 6–7). Hence food in the Old Testament plays the role of unifying the Israelites as a nation over against the people of other races and cultures.

Synoptic Gospels and Table Fellowship

Food plays an important role not only in the Old Testament, but also in the New Testament, especially in the Gospels and in the Acts of the Apostles. Our study is around the banqueting table of Jesus, as portrayed in the synoptic Gospels. When we think of food in the New Testament, specially in the Gospels, the first thing that comes into our minds is the Last Supper of Jesus, wherein he instituted the Eucharist. This is rightly so, because the Last Supper of Jesus has become the characteristic feature of Christianity. Apart from this important meal, the Gospels of Mark and Matthew do narrate that Jesus was at times hungry (Mk 11:12; Matt 4:2; 21:18). One notices, however that there are not many instances in Mark and Matthew, which portray Jesus sitting / reclining at dinner with others. Although Mark does use words like φαγεῖν, ἐσθίειν,[4] these words do not carry weight in the texts, where they are placed. Matthew too follows Mark closely in taking the scenes of table fellowship of Jesus. Although we see the meal scenes of Jesus in Matthew, we do not see in Matthew a deliberate emphasis on the theme of Meal. Apart from the Last Supper, there are only two narratives in the Gospels of Mark and Matthew, showing Jesus sitting at dinner (at Levi's house Mk 2:13-17; Matt 9:9-13 and at the house of Simon the Leper Mk 14:3-9; Matt 26:6-13). Even in these instances the actual banquet scenes seem to be only of secondary importance for Mark and Matthew. For example at the anointing at Bethany (Mk 14:3-9 and par.) the importance is not given to the very aspect of the banquet itself; the banquet is actually sidelined just "*in einem kurzen Genitivus absolutus.*"[5] Markan and Matthean interest and focus in the narration of this incident are directed not on the meal but on the act of anointing, which is shown to be an anticipation of the anointing of Jesus after his death on the cross (v. 8). In their entirety the Gospels of Mark and of Matthew do not display a consistent interest in the theme of meal.

Theme of Food in the Third Gospel

Fellowship meal is a theme dear to Luke in contrast to Mark and Matthew. As one reads the Gospel of Luke, one clearly sees the numerous narrations, which have something to do with a meal. Right at the beginning, the newly born child Jesus is placed in a manger, a place of food for the cattle (Luke 2:7); this goes on till the last chapter where Jesus breaks bread with the Emmaus Disciples (Luke 24:30) and later eats with the eleven apostles in the upper room (Luke 24:41-43). Time and again we are able to see the interest of the evangelist of the third Gospel for the theme of food; Jesus is reclining at table at regular intervals. Karris, who gives as many as forty three instances of food-related texts in the third Gospel[6] sums up succinctly when he says, Jesus is "either going to a meal, at a meal, or coming from a meal."[7] The food imagery in Luke has been scattered in many literary forms. Meal imagery is seen in pronouncement stories (Luke 6:1-5), in miracle stories (Luke 9:10-17), in the form of the parables (Luke 15:1-32, 16:19-31), etc.

Jesus who Reclines

Apart from numerous parables of Jesus in which a banquet scene occupies the central stage, Luke narrates numerous instances where Jesus is shown to be partaking at different banquets. The following table shows the number of banquet narratives in the Gospel of Luke, which show Jesus either hosting a banquet for others, or being invited to partake of a banquet:

Luke 5:27-32	Levi the tax collector hosts Jesus a great banquet (δοχὴν μεγάλην)
Luke 7:34	Jesus is criticized as a glutton and drunkard, a friend of tax collectors and sinners
Luke 7:36-50	Simon the Pharisee hosts Jesus a dinner
Luke 9:10-17	Jesus gives food to over 5000 people in the desert
Luke 10:38-42	Jesus accepts hospitality at the house of Martha and Maria
Luke 11:37-54	A Pharisee invites Jesus for a dinner (ἄριστον)
Luke 14:1-24	A leader of the Pharisees invites Jesus for a Sabbath meal
Luke 15:1-2	Jesus is criticized to be welcoming the tax collectors and sinners and eating with them
Luke 19:1-10	Jesus goes to the house of Zacchaeus the chief tax collector and receives hospitality
Luke 22:7-38	In Jerusalem Jesus celebrates Last Supper with his disciples
Luke 24:13-35	The Risen Lord breaks bread with the Emmaus disciples
Luke 24:36-43	The Risen Lord eats fish in front of the terrified, but joyful disciples.

The salient elements found through these meal narratives are the following:

a. In comparison to Mark and Matthew, Luke has more instances of Jesus having a meal. Bösen classifies these narrations into four categories:[8] i. Meal scenes taken from Mark [banquet with Levi in Luke 5:27-32 (Mk 2:13-17); multiplication of the loaves in Luke 9:10-17 (Mk 6:30-44)]; ii. Criticism against Jesus from the Q Source [criticism of Jesus as a glutton and drunkard in

Luke 7:34 (Matt 11:19)]; iii. Texts unique to Luke (Luke 19:1-10); and iv. Other meal scenes attributed to the Lukan redaction (Luke 7:36; 11:37; 13:26; 14:1; 15:1). We see from the abovementioned classification of Bösen that Luke's Gospel has more banquet stories (nos. iii, iv), which are unique to him and due to his redactional efforts, than those banquet narrations, which Luke takes from Mark and Q. Moreover, the redactional work of Luke within each of these stories are clear to be seen. The theme of table fellowship thus has a unique place in the third Gospel.

b. Apart from the feeding of the five thousand, practically every banquet narrative in which Jesus is said to have partaken before his Jerusalem entry, seems to be loaded with a controversy. Practically at every meal of Jesus, there seems to be a controversy; the controversy is either due to some event that happens during a particular meal or due to the table companions of Jesus – 'the tax collectors and sinners.'

c. In these meal narrations, the groups of tax collectors and Pharisees appear time and again. In fact, the banquets of Jesus in the third Gospel are thoughtfully placed in such a way, that the beginning and the end of the banquet narrations, apart from the Last Supper are told to be the banquets that take place in the houses of tax collectors (Luke 5:27-32; 19:1-10). They are located right at the beginning and at the end of Jesus' ministry in Galilee. In between them are the fellowship meals of Jesus at the houses of the three Pharisees (Luke 7:36-50; 11:37-54; 14:1-24). Hence we could say that apart from the Last Supper, the narration of fellowship meals of Jesus with the two tax collectors serves as an inclusion for the narration of Jesus' banquet with the Pharisees.[9] This inclusion heightens the interest in the study of the story of Zacchaeus, specifically because Luke 19:1-10 stands as the final part of this inclusion and since this seems to be the last banquet narration before Jesus' entry into Jerusalem, where the banquet *par excellence*, the Last Supper would take place. Both texts (Luke 5:27-32; 19:1-10) betray a similar structure: the initial invitation of Jesus both to Levi and Zacchaeus (Luke 5:27; 19:5), table fellowship or hospitality given to Jesus (Luke 5:29; 19:6), the controversy it evoked among the opponents of Jesus (Luke 5:30; 19:7) and finally the mission statement of Jesus that proclaims the purpose of his coming (Luke 5:31-32; 19:9-10): these nuances help one to recognize the similar structure of both the texts. The above-mentioned similarity of the structure is the starting point of this research.

Focus Book

The interconnection of the story of Zacchaeus (Luke 19:1-10) with the foregoing banquet narrations in the Gospel of Luke and the significance of its placing right before Jesus' entry to Jerusalem and its possible implications for the Lukan community are the *foci* of this study. This book attempts to understand the story of Zacchaeus from the background of other meal narratives, which involve Jesus' meal encounters with the tax collectors as well as the Pharisees (Luke 5:27-32, 7:36-50, 11:37-54, 14:1-24, 19:1-10). This is because of two reasons:

1. The meal narratives of Jesus with the tax collectors and the Pharisees seem to complement each other in giving a vital message for the audience of Luke. Placed at important locations of the Gospel, they seem to be the pillars on which the central section of the Gospel is placed.

2. These narratives of Jesus' fellowship meals with the tax collectors and Pharisees are modelled after Hellenistic *symposia*. In order to concentrate on Jesus' relation to these two groups, this book however sidelines the study of the Last Supper. This chapter also excludes Martha's hospitality to Jesus, during his informal stop at her house in Bethany (Luke 10:38-42). In other words, the study of Luke 19:1-10 aims to answer the following questions:

In a broader context of the third Gospel

- Why is the story of Zacchaeus placed at the location, where it stands now?
- How does the placement of the Zacchaeus story impact the rest of the Gospel?
- How is the story of Zacchaeus linked to the rest of the banquet stories of the third Gospel?

As an independent text

- What can we surmise from Jesus' encounter with Zacchaeus in the 'city' of Jericho about the community to which Luke addresses?
- What do the character of Zacchaeus, his profession and his attitude towards Jesus, have to offer to the Lukan community?

In today's context

A scientific study of the Holy Scripture becomes complete when it attempts to address and challenge our lives here and now; hence the paper aims to look at Luke 19:1-10 from the present context and asks,

- In what way is Zacchaeus' attitude towards Jesus and Jesus' response to Zacchaeus relevant to the present-day Indian context?
- What are the similarities between the Lukan community back then and the Christian community now, especially in India?
- How does Luke 19:1-10 challenge the Indian society as a whole and Indian Christians in particular?

Limitations

In its effort to comprehend the nuances of Zacchaeus encountering Jesus, this work does not make an exhaustive study of each and every narrative in the third Gospel that is connected to the theme of food. The parables and miracles in the third Gospel which are pepped up with food imagery are not touched upon in this book. The author's focus is only on those banquet narrations in the third Gospel in which Jesus partakes. Even among those banquet materials in which Jesus is shown to be partaking, the texts of the Last Supper (Luke 22:7-38), the breaking of the bread at Emmaus (Luke 24:13-35) and his eating before the eleven apostles (Luke 24:36-42) are omitted. This book also does not deal with Luke 10:38-42, where Jesus is shown to be enjoying hospitality at the house of Martha and Maria. This is done with a purpose of looking at Jesus' relation to the two major groups that come time and again in the third Gospel – the Pharisees and the tax collectors. The interweaving of the Lukan narrations of Jesus' banquet involvement with these two specific groups (tax collectors on the one hand and the Pharisees on the other) in Luke, has been the background for the study of Zacchaeus' encounter with Jesus (Luke 19:1-10).

Methodology and Structure of the Book

Although the exegetical study of Luke 19:1-10 will be done with the help of the traditional tools like textual criticism, source criticism, redaction criticism and form criticism, it transcends the strict adherence to the historical critical method, in order to understand the cultural world view which is the background of any given text. Hence in order to obtain answers to the above mentioned questions our research is complemented with the background study of the social world of the Hellenistic Palestine with the help of different social science models – sociological, cross-cultural and religious, because the culture of the Jews of Palestine at the dawn of the new era was similar to the rest of the Greco-Roman world and even tried to adapt itself to the cultural elements of the Hellenistic world. Hence the first chapter tries to understand the meal practices of the Greco-Roman world between the first century BCE and the first century CE.[10] The chapter concentrates particularly on the institution of *symposium*, a practice that was very much prevalent in the Hellenistic world. We look at the characteristics of a Hellenistic banquet setting, how the institution of *symposium* was performed, what roles were played by the partakers of this special meal. We also look at whether such a sympotic setting was accepted and absorbed by Jews at the time of Jesus. If so, what are the differences between a Hellenistic *symposium* and the so-called '*symposium*' celebrated by Jews in general and the different groups of Judaism in particular? We come to know from the first chapter that the Hellenistic sympotic practice was gladly accepted and modified by the Judaic world. And the literary *symposium* already well-known in the elite circles of the Greco-Roman world, was well embraced by the authors of the books of both the Old Testament as well as the New Testament.

The second chapter looks at the importance of banquet scenes in the Gospel of Luke. We confine ourselves to those banquet narrations, in which Jesus is invited by the two different groups to dine in their house, as we have hinted earlier – the banquet of Jesus with the tax collectors on the one hand, and with the Pharisees on the other. These banquet narrations are modelled after Greek literary *symposia*. This is seen in the light of the recurring criticism of the Pharisees and scribes that Jesus is the "friend of tax collectors and sinners" (Luke 7:34) and he and his disciples "eat and drink with the tax collectors and sinners" (Luke 5:30; 15:2; 19:7). These criticisms serve as the pillars on which the banquet narrations stand.

The third chapter makes an exegetical study of the story of Zacchaeus. The preliminary studies will focus on the form, source and the redaction of the text which would be followed by the word analysis of Luke 19:1-10; this should shed light on how Luke connects the encounter of Zacchaeus with other literary *symposia* in the Gospel. The chapter will also elucidate how Zacchaeus, through his actions, has become a paradigm for the rich in the Lukan community, who could enter the Kingdom of Heaven, even when they have not left everything in order to follow Jesus. The chapter will also try to seek an answer to an important question, whether Zacchaeus repented and thus assured of salvation or whether his act of giving half of his property to the poor and compensating fourfold is a gesture of gratitude for the salvation already received from Jesus. We will also see that the self-invitation of Jesus to Zacchaeus, the intended table fellowship with him, the controversy it evoked among all those nearby and the mission statement of Jesus that states the purpose of Jesus' coming etc... bring back the basic themes of "conflict, forgiveness and inclusion of sinners"[11] which come again and again in the central section of the third of Gospel. Through the fellowship meals of Jesus, Luke also seems to project the post Easter believing community for which celebrating such *symposia* would have been a significant event of the community.

These chapters show how Luke has used the theme of food to interconnect three different eons. Fellowship meals of Jesus bring to the mind of the readers the different *symposia* (including literary *symposia*) of the Hellenistic times; they shed light on how the historical Jesus might have enjoyed sympotic meal gatherings. They also impart the readers how the Lukan community should host and partake at Christian symposia. We shall complete the analysis of the story of Zacchaeus with an attempt to read and understand Luke 19:1-10 in the present day context. Hence, the fourth chapter tries to comprehend the meaning of the encounter of Zacchaeus with Jesus in the light of the present situation of the Tamil society in India. This chapter tries to make it clear that Jesus' willingness to defy the then known barriers between pure and the impure 2000 years ago, and his keenness to seek, embrace and save the lost, is still a fresh challenge to the Indian, and especially to the caste-ridden Tamil society, which is rigidly structured around the unbreakable walls of caste system, whereby a large group of people are stigmatized as untouchable and hence live their lives as social outcasts, suffering in every sphere of life - economic, social and religious.

Endnotes

[1] Homer, *The Odyssey: trasl. A. T. Murray; G. E. Dimock*, The Loeb Classical Library (Cambridge, Mass: Harvard University Press, 1995).

[2] A. Appadurai, "Gastro-Politics in Hindu South Asia," *American Ethnologist* 8, no. 3 (1981), 494.

³ M. van der Veen, "When Is Food a Luxury?," *World Archaeology* 34, no. 3 (2003), 414.

⁴ In fact, of all the New Testament books only in the Gospel of Mark the word *symposium* occurs. This comes in Mk 6:39, καὶ ἐπέταξεν αὐτοῖς ἀνακλῖναι πάντας συμπόσια συμπόσια ἐπὶ τῷ χλωρῷ χόρτῳ. The double use of the noun in plural however has not been used here in the sense of a drinking party; rather it is used to refer to participants. We also find the verb ἀνακλίνω in the same verse. The combination of ἀνακλίνω (reclining) and the συμπόσια suggests for Collins, that Jesus is here hosting a banquet for the people. Cf. A. Y. Collins and H. W. Attridge, *Mark: A Commentary*, Hermeneia (Minneapolis: Fortress Press, 2007), 324.

⁵ W. Bösen, *Jesusmahl, Eucharistisches mahl, Endzeitmahl: Ein Beitrag zur Theologie des lukas* (Stuttgart: Katholisches bibelwerk GmbH, 1980), 80.

⁶ R. J. Karris, *Eating Your Way Through Luke's Gospel* (Collegeville, Minnesota: Liturgical Press, 2006), 16-20; cf. also his other book R. J. Karris, *Luke, Artist and Theologian: Luke's Passion Account as Literature*, Theological inquiries (New York: Paulist Press, 1985), 49-50; also J. P. Heil, *The Meal Scenes in Luke-Acts: An Audience-Oriented Approach*, Monograph series (Atlanta, Ga.: Soc. of Biblical Literature, 2004), 5.

⁷ Karris, *Eating Your Way Through Luke's Gospel*, 15.

⁸ W. Bösen, *Jesusmahl, Eucharistisches mahl, Endzeitmahl*, 82-83.

⁹ R. C. Tannehill, *The Narrative Unity of Luke-Acts: A Literary Interpretation* (Philadelphia: Fortress Press, 1986), 107-108; D. A. Neale, *None But the Sinners: Religious Categories in the Gospel of Luke*, Journal for the study of the New Testament. Supplement series 58 (Sheffield: JSOT Press, 1991), 100.

¹⁰ In this book, the terms B.C. and A.D. (meaning "Before Christ" and "*Anno Domini*" respectively), are avoided in sensitivity to non-Christians who form the majority in India. In their place the secular terms BCE and CE are used (meaning "Before the Common Era" and the "Common Era" respectively) throughout this book.

¹¹ D. A. Neale, *None But the Sinners*, 110.

Chapter - 1
Table Fellowship of Jesus: Socio-Cultural Context

As a prelude to our study of Jesus' meal with Zacchaeus, it is worth looking at the meal culture of the Hellenistic world of which Palestine was a part. We look, in particular, at the practice of *symposium* – the table fellowship of elite male members of the Mediterranean world. This would help us in our attempt to unravel the nuances of table fellowship scenes of Luke. Hence this chapter aims at understanding how a *symposium* was performed, the place, the socio-economic status of the partakers, the process of inviting guests and the entertainment enjoyed during the *symposium* and the importance of *symposium* for different groups and cultures of the Hellenistic world. We also try to look at the impacts of this practice in the society at large – both positive and negative. We then move on to see whether Greco-Roman banquets, especially sympotic meals have influenced the Jews before and after the time of Jesus, and if so, how it has shaped the meal culture of the Jews of Palestine and beyond. Looking at some of the Old Testament texts, in which allusions of *symposium* are scattered, we try to investigate, whether the fellowship meals of different Jewish sects have borrowed from the ideals of *symposium* genre of food sharing. Studying *symposium* would also help to observe the Hellenistic sympotic traits in the Passover Seder in the light of Hellenistic culture.

Our focus in this work is on the time period from 800 BCE onwards, since it is from here we begin to see the traces of sympotic culture in ancient Greece. The timeline of Hellenistic world that is followed here is taken from Watson.[1] The concepts 'Greco-Roman' or 'Hellenistic' are used interchangeably in this work to mean "the combined culture of the Mediterranean world of circa 300 BCE. (Alexander the Great) to circa 300 CE (Constantine)."[2]

Banquet Tradition in the Greco-Roman Society

During the archaic period we could find three different types of meals: „ἄριστον »*normale Frühmahlzeit*«; δόρπον »*Abschlussmahlzeit des Tags*«, *also normaleweise die Abendmahlzeit*; δεῖπνον *ist nach der Charakterisierung eher mit Lunch als Mittagessen wiederzugeben und kann erste und zweite Mahlzeit in sich vereinen*."[3] As the lunch, δεῖπνον was the major meal of the day at the time of Homer. Around the sixth and fifth centuries BCE in the classical period however, we see a shift in the meal time; we find that ἄριστον, which was the breakfast, moved from morning and was taken at midday or forenoon, and as a result the δεῖπνον the lunch was transferred to the evening. The meal, which was taken immediately after getting up was called ἀκράτισμα – which, from the very name, could be recognized as "a piece of bread dipped in undiluted wine."[4] Ἄριστον the midday meals was also very light, usually some of the leftovers from the last day's δεῖπνον, with a little wine. Hence we see that the major meal of the day is shifted from midday to evening. We find also other names given for these meals like ἑσπέριμα and δορπηστός. In *The Deipnosophists* Athenaeus talks about four different meals, ἀκράτισμα, ἄριστον, ἑσπέρισμα, and δεῖπνον (Ath. I. 11).[5]

> Now the *akratisma* they called *breaking the fast*, the *ariston* ("luncheon") they called *deipnon*, the evening meal *dorpestos*, the dinner *epidorpis*... The fourth meal is mentioned by Homer in these words, "Go thou when thou hast supped," referring to what some call *deilinon* which comes between our *ariston* ("luncheon") and *deipnon* ("dinner").

The Romans had three meal program a day – *Ientaculum, prandium* and *cena*.[6] In the olden times there were *ientaculum* the breakfast, the *cena* the midday meal and *vesperna* the evening meal. As it was with δεῖπνον for the Greeks, *cena* came to be eaten late in the afternoon and so "it dispossessed the evening meal (*vesperna* in Rome…) for which there was no longer any need and at the other end it created a gap which required to be filled by a new meal, *prandium* …"[7] Marquardt says it was normal for some Romans to have four meals a day. He considers *comissatio*, the after-dinner drinking as a separate meal. However, he also says that some men normally ate only twice a day. He gives the example of Galen, the Roman physician in the second century CE who had an *ientaculum* in the fourth hour and a *cena* in the 10th hour.[8] *Ientaculum*, the breakfast was "the lightest of meals."[9] Although *prandium* was followed by *cena* in three hours' time, it consisted normally of meat or fish, together with fruits and figs and a little wine.

Δεῖπνον / Cena

The major and the leisurely meal of the day for the Greeks was the δεῖπνον. It usually took place after sunset. Either one eats with his family or invites friends to his house or he gets invited. "It became not only the one formal meal of the day but also potentially the social highlight of the day as well."[10] The meal proper had two courses, δεῖπνον which is followed by the drinking party, called συμπόσιον, to which we shall return shortly. In the Roman times, there was also an appetizer course, which as the historians think, might have been modeled after the *gustatio* of the Roman meal.[11] Besides, it looks as if, the terms are sometimes interchangeably used. *The Deipnosophists* attests to this: "*Deipnon* in Homer is sometimes synonymous with *ariston*; for of the morning meal he somewhere said, 'They then took their *deipnon* and after that began to arm for battle; that is, immediately after sunrise and the *deipnon*, they go forth to fight'" (Ath. I. 11).

The major meal of the day for the Romans was *cena*. While among the Greeks δεῖπνον began shortly before or after sunset, *cena* started in summer at the 9th hour, around 3.45pm or in winter around 2.15pm. It was divided into three courses, appetizers (*gustatio*), the main meal (*cena*) and the dessert course (*mensae secundae*).[12] Salad, boiled eggs and other vegetables were served in *gustatio*. The *cena* proper was a multi course meal and consisted of variety of meat and in the *mensae secundae* one would get cakes and fruits.

From Ordinary Evening Meal to Dinner Party

The ordinary evening meal consisted only of one course, i.e. the *cena* without *gustatio* and *mensae secundae*;[13] in course of time, δεῖπνον for the Greeks and *cena* for the Romans became the solemn meal, and was "the climax of daily eating and a respite from daily business."[14] From an ordinary personal evening meal with the family, it came to be a dinner party. More than an occasion to quench the biological needs of the body, food came to be a social act. In Plutarch's *Moralia*, we hear about a person who says after his lonely meal in his house "I have eaten, but not dined to-day" (*Table Talk* VII. 697 c),[15] implying thereby dinner parties or banquets gave an opportunity to create and maintain a social bond and status. For the Greeks too, δεῖπνον became so elaborate and pompous that it was "probably the only meal at which elaborate cooking and serving was provided and which company was usually entertained."[16] The social impact of δεῖπνον was so high, that as Vössing points out "eating at home only with the family was either socially meaningless or a sign of demonstrative self-isolation."[17] In such a context *symposium* and *convivium* obtain their significance.

Symposium / Convivium

The two constituent parts of the word συμπόσιον (σύν – *with*, and πόσιον – *drink*) render the literal meaning of the word - drinking together. It was "a night-time drinking, a luxurious wine party with a highly ritualized ceremony, in which a very restricted group of males participated on equal terms, and which was dominated by the egalitarian and at the same time competitive spirit of the aristocratic participants."[18] Participation of family women was prohibited. If women were present for the δεῖπνον, they left the room as the συμπόσιον began. As Murray points out, "of all the Greek social institutions known to us, more evidence exists for the *symposion* than for any other."[19] For Murray and other historians, *symposium* is the "defining characteristic of Greek culture and society."[20] Although συμπόσιον was a separate event in itself[21] one could say it was part of the formal meal and slowly came to symbolize the table fellowship and the shared meal.[22] Similarly the Latin word *convivium*, literally meaning 'living together' came to symbolize the *cena* proper as well as the *comissatio,* the after-meal event in the Roman circles. Romans understood communal dining as "an established social and cultural institution at Rome, part of the normal routine of life. This was a formal meal at a set time, dividing the Roman day between 'business' and 'leisure' (*nogotium / otium*)."[23] The word *convivium* has a great significance. Cato in Cicero's *Letter to His Friends* says, it is fitting that the Romans chose the word *convivium* for the practice of reclining at the banquet. "Our country men …are wiser therein than the Greeks; *they* call them συμπόσια or σύνδειπνα which is to say, 'drinkings together' or 'dinings together'; *we* call them 'livings together'; for then, more than ever, do our lives coincide" (*Fam.* 9. 24. 3).[24] In this work, for the sake of clarity, ease of use, the terms *'symposium'* and its plural *'symposia'* are employed as general terms to denote the *social institution* that covers the entire dinner party including δεῖπνον and συμπόσιον – as the equivalent of *convivium;* the word συμπόσιον is used to specifically denote the after-dinner drinking party.

Evolution of *Symposium*

Already in the eighth century BCE we could smell the fragrance of sympotic banquets in the archaic Greece. Odysseus upon entering the house of Alcinous sees that at the house the leaders of the city cozily eating and drinking at a banquet while slave boys hold torches for light and slave girls work at the house (Hom. *Od.* VII.80-105); Homer says further "I mark that in the house itself many men are feasting: for the savour of meat arises from it, and therewith resounds with the voice of the lyre, which the gods have made the companion of the feast" (Hom. *Od.* XVII.264).[25] These exclusive all-male banquets might have had their origin in the sacrificial banquets in the ancient societies, which were more inclusive in nature, in that all male members of the community could partake in it. The more exclusive banquets of aristocratic leaders and their "warrior elite at its leisure"[26] are perhaps proofs for the existence of communal banquets in the Homeric period, which got molded into *symposium* in course of time.[27] By hosting such banquets, the military and social elite tried to ascertain its influence in the society and get outside support. The relationship created in the "feast of merit served to enhance the status of the noble *basileus* within the community and in particular provided him with a band of *hetairoi* obligated to follow him in military and naval exploits."[28] At these Homeric feasts the participants sat while banqueting; strict separation between eating and drinking was not yet made. Through the archeological finding of 'the Cup of Nestor' at the grave of a male teenager in *Pithekoussai*[29] and through the prophetic utterances of the prophet Amos against those reclining at couches, one could sense a gradual evolution of communal banquets from warrior feasts of Homeric period towards a more refined type of private banquets.

Archaic *symposium* evolved from such Homeric warrior feasts. Once the warrior elite lost its significance, and with the emergence of the *polis* "the aristocracy of warriors had become an aristocracy of leisure … and … the aristocratic *symposion* developed into a refuge from the real world, a way of life aimed solely at *euphrosyne* (delight)."[30] Entertainment in such occasions became very important and various innovations were introduced, the most important of which was the eastern way of reclining at banquets instead of sitting. In the classical period between 5-4th centuries BCE, as democracy set in, tension could be seen between democracy and the various *hetaireia* of the aristocracy over the control of the *polis*. Garnsey cites the example of the democratic leader Cleisthenes who promulgated strict norms against late night *symposia* in Athens and other cities.[31]

By the end of the 5th century BCE we see that the *symposium* emerged as a literary genre. Philosophers of Greco-Roman world used *symposium* as an instrument to bring together entertainment and education, wine and philosophy. Plato's *Symposium* would be the best example for it. Besides, various philosophical schools used the actual *symposium* setting for their philosophical education. As we proceed to the Hellenistic period, we see that *symposia* were organized by wealthy benefactors not just for a select few but for a large number of people. In this way *symposium* as a social institution and as a literary form continued to influence not only the people and culture of ancient Greece but practically all the cultures throughout the Mediterranean world.

There were also however voices against the excesses of luxurious living and extravagance of the wealthy at *symposia*. Already from the third century BCE we find Roman satirists using banquet motif in their works against gluttony and overindulgence. The interest continued in later centuries with Horace in his *Banquet of Nasidienus* and Petronius in his *Cena Trimalchionis* and Lucian of Samosata in *The Carousal or the Lapiths* all the way up to the work of the Roman emperor Julian in 4th century CE.

This brief overview shows that *symposium* remained from the beginning onwards as a social institution responsible for creating and maintaining the social bond of men outside the family circle. The setting of *symposium* served not only as a platform for entertainment but also gave the group a particular identity as against the society at large. As a social institution, *symposium* had its own set of norms, as to how it should be performed and what roles the participants had to play. In the following pages we shall see some of the norms of *symposium* in detail.

Sympotic Space

Ἀνδρων

Symposia were conducted in a typical room called ἄνδρων, which was devoted for the purpose of the formal dining of men. Such specifically designed rooms could be seen in the Greek world as early as the 7th century BCE.[32] But the earliest literary reference to ἄνδρων is from the fifth century Herodotus, who uses this word six times. "In each of these examples ἄνδρων appears to be a private space rather than a sympotic space. It is an area used by men rather than a dedicated dining space."³³ We could say that any room that was not used by women of the household could have been used by men to entertain the guests. The archeological excavations of houses in cities like Olynthus, Athens, Corinth show that wealthy houses had specially designed dining rooms. This helps us understand that in course of time, ἄνδρων emerged as a specific place at houses, designated specifically for the dining of male members of the society.

The placement of the room was at the front corner of the house, so that guests who came for dinner had easy access to the room and did not disturb the household as they came to and went from ἄνδρων. There is also evidence for an 'ante-chamber' which was used for receiving the guests and for initial welcome and service to them.³⁴ The construction of ἄνδρων was identical in its form, mostly of rectangular shape.³⁵ But there were also other dining rooms with structural differences.³⁶ But most of them were similar in their size. A standard ἄνδρων was built so as to contain minimum of seven couches. Each couch could easily accommodate two or three guests, depending on its size. There stood before each couch a small table on which food was served for the diners. The guests reclined on the couches which were placed along each side of the wall and one couch was placed on another side of the wall and the door of the room was not in the middle of the room but was a little away from the center. The diners "form a continuous ring, interrupted only by the door. This arrangement both emphasizes and reinforces the unity of the group, a sense of common fellowship within the circle, which is so fundamental to the ethos of the Greek *symposion*."³⁷ There were also broad dining rooms to be seen at *Agia Pelagia*, which were not of rectangular shape and which had door at the center. Bergquist suggests that such rooms accommodated two subgroups of diners who were reclining on the either side of the door.³⁸ With its precise construction and well decorated walls and floors with pebble mosaics, the ἄνδρων was the central focus of a wealthy house. But some houses could contain more than one ἄνδρων. Hellenistic period saw changes in the structure of ἄνδρων. Instead of having a typical ἄνδρων, rich houses of the elite had a large room, which was used for dinner parties as well as for other purposes. This room was larger than all other rooms and was better decorated than others, implying thereby that public and "social display"[39] was the main aim of the existence of such rooms at the houses of the rich.

Triclinium

In the Roman world too, in many of the wealthy houses, there were two dining rooms – *cenatio* and *triclinium*; *cenatio* was an ordinary dining room, which was small and was used for dining with family members or for small number of guests whereas *triclinium* was used for dinner parties. As the word suggests, *triclinium* had three couches. The couches were arranged in 'Π' form and each couch could accommodate three diners. Hence originally the *triclinium* was aimed at hosting nine diners at a time.[40] There was one single table at the center for all the diners. As it was with ἄνδρων, *triclinium* could be easily distinguished from other rooms of the house because of the extensive decorations in the walls and in the pavements of the rooms, especially with mosaics of fruits, flowers, landscapes, birds and animals, even mythological scenes and portrayals of vessels normally used at *convivia* and gifts offered to Dionysius, the god of Wine.[41] The large front part of the room was reserved for reception of the guests and entertainment. At the end of each couch, benches were placed so that wives, children or other inferior persons could sit.

Garden *Triclinium*

Banquets were organized not only in *triclinia*, specially designed rooms at houses. In fact "any space can be used for a *symposium*. It is the presence of the individuals, their behaviors and the use of artifacts which give the space its meaning."[42] Excavations at Pompeii attest to the fact that it was normal in the Roman world to have *convivium* outdoors in gardens during summer. Some of the luxurious garden *triclinia* had also "special water effects, where the diners reclined with fountains splashing around them or jets of water in the middle of the table."[43] Provisions for garden *triclinia* were also available for hire in the inns.

Stibadium

In the late antiquity there was another development in the structure of the dining room. In these rooms the couches were made in semicircular form. These were called *stibadium*. The front portion of the room and the floor was richly decorated so that the diners could see the beautiful mosaics and admire them. The back portion of the room was marked with a semicircle, obviously for the couches and another smaller semicircle at the center, for the table. The *stibadium* was used for a smaller group of diners as compared to the *triclinia*. However there are also evidences of houses, which, apart from a large *triclinium*, contained also a *stibadium* which had seven apses, which could accommodate as many as fifty guests.[44] Although the structure of *stibadium* continued to exist for some time, it was *triclinium* which dominated the Roman world and that the dinner party in sigma couch was used for banquets more in the open air rather than inside the house. It was a matter of social prestige for a house in the Greco-Roman world to have possessed an ἄνδρων or a *triclinium*. While most houses of the wealthy had such a special room for entertaining guests, it was also not uncommon for moderate families which did not have ἄνδρων or *triclinium*, to use larger rooms of the house for entertainment of the guests.

Participants at a *Symposium*

The people in the Greco-Roman world were a folk that loved sociability. Hence they invented occasions to come together. Whether it was *agora* in the morning, the *gymnasium* in the afternoon and *symposium* in the evening, everything served the purpose of coming together. With its own set of rules and rituals, *symposium* remained as an "alternative society."[45] Every one of the participants had a role to play in a *symposium*. These roles had to be faithfully carried out so that proper order was kept at *symposia*. This is why we find serious discussions in the *symposium*, regarding the roles played by the participants of a *symposium*.

The Host

Of all the institutions, *symposium* gave an individual the opportunity to display "the cultural ideals of generosity, grace and manliness."[46] Hence wealthy aristocrats who had time and money for sympotic activity invented occasions to organize a *symposium*. Anything could be an occasion for a *symposium*. Prodicus is shown by Hesiod to host the dinner for his friend Hermogenes who was going on a journey to the satrap of Mysia.[47] In Xenophon's *Symposium* Callias hosts a banquet in honor of his young friend Autolycus for his victory at *pancratium* (Xen. Sym. I.2). Agathon hosts a *symposium*, as Plato describes, for his victory in the drama contest (Plat. *Sym*. 173 a). The occasion for Aristaenetus to host a *symposium* for philosophers and others was the wedding of his daughter Cleanthis (*The Carousal or The Lapiths* 5).

A host also made it a point to call the learned men of the society for the *symposium* so that the *symposium* hosted by him was not only a time for enjoyment but also an occasion for learning and philosophical debate. Socrates is shown to be present in the *symposia* by Xenophon and Plato. Lucian's Aristaenetus calls philosophers of various schools for the wedding *symposium*. Plutarch shows Laurentius as a host who frequently invited philosophers to dine with him. Apart from sociability, another important reason for hosting a *symposium* was to show off one's wealth and social status and thereby influence and enhance one's stand in the society. Perhaps, the main intention of the host in organizing *symposia* was to gain favor among the elite members of the society. Hence the host would discuss politics with his chosen friends and "project an image of importance and power."[48] This is true also of the public banquets thrown by kings of the Greco-Roman world.

The Duties of the Host

There were many things that the host must look into before the guests arrived. Horace narrates in his Satire about 'the trials of being a host.' "To think that, in order that I may have lavish entertainment, you are to be racked and tortured with every anxiety" (Hor. *S*. II. VIII. 67-68).[49]

After inviting his guests, the host had to make sure everything was properly arranged for the occasion. He went to the Agora and hired a professional cook for *symposium* and necessary utensils, if he did not have them. Professional cooks were available in the agora and could be hired for a feast.[50] Then he double-checked that his house and the room for the *symposium* were cleaned and decorated, that each slave was properly dressed and well trained to serve guests, and that the dishes were cooked properly. In the evening when it was time for the *symposium*, the host, clothed in his best attire, stood at the entrance of his house to welcome the guests. When someone came uninvited, the host was polite enough to invite him too. During the banquet he made sure that the seating arrangement was done to the fullest satisfaction of each of the guests, and that no one was hurt for having been ill-treated. When no leader was selected for the occasion, he took up the leadership of the gathering and decided how much wine would be served to the guests.

Guests

In the Greco-Roman world, banquets were understood to be an "interchangeable currency."[51] Those who were invited by someone for dinner now had the obligation to return the favour later. And only those who could reciprocate the favor got invited to a *symposium*. This would mean that only the wealthy aristocrats who had enough resources to host a *symposium* and had enough time for leisure, were the participants at a *symposium*. The number of participants could vary depending on the generosity of the host and the availability of resources.

Similarly the Roman literature suggests, that extravagant *convivia* were hosted in Rome by kings, sometimes even for thousands of people.[52] But in the private *convivia* the number of participants would be moderate. It could be as small as three and could go up to any number. In the Roman circle five to eight was considered to be the preferable number for *convivium*.[53] Athenaeus tells in *The Deipnosophists* that the number of the participants at a marriage *symposium* in Macedonia was twenty (Ath. IV. 128 c). Because of participatory nature of the private *symposia* the number was not more than thirty as it was in *The Deipnosophists*.

Plutarch's *Table Talk* in its chapter "Concerning those that invite many to a supper" advises against inviting too many guests for a *convivium*:

> For the size of a party ... is right so long as it easily remains one party. If it gets too large, so that the guests can no longer talk to each other or enjoy the hospitality together or even know one another, then it ceases to be a party at all. For at a social gathering there should be no need for *aides-de-camp*, as in an army, or boatswains to set the stroke, as in a trireme, but people should converse directly with one another; even as in a chorus the end man is within earshot of the leader. (*Table Talk* V. 678 d).

It was also normal for an invited guest to inquire about the names of other guests. Some decided whether they would attend the *symposium* or not, only after having known the names of the rest of the invited guests. This is attested in Plutarch's *Septem Sapientium Convivium* where Chilon does not immediately accept the invitation for the dinner, "until he had learned the name of every person invited" (Plut. *Septem*. 148 A). This implies that the host had to be careful in selecting "the right kind of guests" (Plut. *Septem*. 147 E); otherwise the guests might get offended or even not turn up for a *symposium*.

Among the guests, the host could also invite someone as a guest of honor for a *symposium*. This chief guest had the honor of reclining adjacent to the host. In the words of Erdkamp, "The more status a guest had, the closer he sat to the host."[54] In the Greek world the most honored position was to the right side of the host, which was called πρῶτος. In Plato's *Symposium* Socrates is the guest of honor and occupies the πρῶτος until Alcibiades comes and sits in between Agathon and Socrates. If a foreign dignitary was present at a *symposium*, he was preferred to be the guest of honor. All the other guests were seated according to their ranks.

Invitation to the Guests

The host gave a formal invitation to the guests for a *symposium*. The invitation could be oral, or, in case of a formal banquet, in written form. Chan-Hie, analyzing the papyrus invitations found in Egypt, says the invitations for *symposia* had a common structure. They comprised of "(1) an invitation-verb, ἐρωτᾶν or καλεῖν, in the 3d pers. sing. pres. indic. act.; (2) the invited guest in the acc. of the pers. pron. σέ; 3) the identity of the host; (4) the purpose of the invitation in the aor. infin. δειπνῆσαι; (5) the occasion of the feast; (6) the place; (7) the date; and (8) the time."[55] The invitation is said to be in the third person, indicating thereby that the servant of the host would go to the houses of the guests and would read out the written invitation for the *symposium* on behalf of the host. In specific cases the invitation was sent out one year in advance. The time gap between the invitation to the dinner and the dinner proper had practical purposes. First of all, the kitchen staff should know how many persons were coming to the dinner. Besides, "for formal banquets, guests needed sufficient time to arrange for suitable apparel and jewelry; for dinner time was show time."[56] But normally the invitation was given a few days in advance and in extreme cases, on the same day. Callias in Xenophon's *Symposium* for example invites Socrates the same day in the afternoon. In Plato's *Symposium*, Agathon too invites Aristodemus on the same day of the party. "Aristodemus … if you came on some other errand, put it off to another time. Only yesterday I went round to invite you, but failed to see you" (Plat. *Sym.* 174 e).[57] Prodicus in *Hesiod* invites his guests as he goes in the morning to the Agora. Those who passed by without having seen him and greeted him, were given a twitch by one of his slaves and then invited for his *symposium*.[58]

An invited guest could accept or refuse an invitation (cf. Luke 14:15-24). But having accepted the invitation if a guest did not turn up for a *symposium*, it was considered to be an insult for the host. Ammianus Marcellinus in the fourth century BCE says, "It was better to murder a man's brother than to refuse his invitation to dine."[59] It was also normal that a guest was invited for more than one *symposium* on the same day. When an invited guest does not turn up for a *symposium*, then the host tried to fill up the dining room by inviting someone else at the last moment. In Lucian's work we have an example for this: Eucrates invites Micyllus in this way: "'Micyllus,' said he, I am giving a birthday party for my daughter today, and have invited a great many of my friends: but as one of them is ill, they say, and can't dine with us, you must take a bath and come in his place, unless, to be sure, the man I invited says, that he will come himself, for just now his coming is doubtful" (*The Dream or the Cock* 9).⁶⁰ The invited guests made sure to arrive at a *symposium* not early, so as to be judged by the host as an avaricious person who was longing for an invitation and not too late so as to make other guests wait.

Συμποσίαρχος – the King of *Symposium*

In the opinion of Plato, without an organizing principle, a drinking party could easily turn into a chaos and disorder. Since, "a gathering, if accompanied by drunkenness, is not free from disturbance," it always needed a leader to take care of the proceedings (Plat. *Laws* I. 640 c). The leader of *symposium*, who was called συμποσίαρχος (the *symposiarch*) or the ἀρχόν, the ruler or the ΄king of *symposium*,΄ was chosen from among the participants for the smooth running of the drinking party. His role is similar to that of "a general, without whom it is dangerous to go to war."⁶¹ In Plato´s *Symposium*, there was no one selected as a *symposiarch*; but Eryximachus behaves as a self-appointed *symposiarch* and proposes the topic of the discussion (Plat. *Sym*. 176 d – 177 d); even after the arrival of Alcibiades who elects himself to be the master of the feast (Plat. *Sym*. 213 e), Eryximachus is able to assert his authority as the master of the feast. In a similar way, a person was selected to guide the proceedings of the Roman *comissatio*, the after-dinner drinking ritual. He was called the *magister, arbiter bibendi* or *rex*. Sometimes he was chosen by casting lots.⁶² Plutarch parallels the symposiarch with a king and says that a symposiarch is the one who "may bring the natural dispositions of the guests from diversity into smooth and harmonious accord" (*Table Talk* I. 620 f), just like a king is able to govern and bring together diverse groups of people. The symposiarch wore a special cloak and *kidaris*, an oriental hat which "indirectly alludes to the king."⁶³ Just like a crown for a king, this oriental hat was to be a symbol of the one who takes control over the entire proceedings of συμπόσιον, similar to the ΄*basileios*΄ who has the control over the entire nation.

Duties of a *Symposiarch*

The *symposiarch* or the *arbiter bibendi* had various duties to perform. He was responsible for the mixture of water and wine. He made sure how much wine the participants should take so that "each of the guest was in the best possible condition throughout the whole event, that is to say, half-way between sobriety and drunkenness, so that all could enjoy liberty and ease of speech."[64] Hence he ordered servants how much wine each guest should be served. In that way he might "neither allow them to misbehave nor deprive them of their pleasures" (*Table Talk* I. 620 d). He raised toasts and proposed the topic for the discussion, as we see in Plato´s *Symposium*, where Eryximachus suggests they make an *encomium* in honor of *eros*. Sometimes diners at a *symposion* would be asked to make a praise on the neighbor on their right. Each participant took the cup of wine that was passed around, sipped a little wine and said, "it behooves me to praise my neighbor on my right," (Plat. *Sym.* 222 e) and should say positive qualities about his neighbor and passed the cup to another. The *symposiarch* also made sure that the conversation went lively, because he was the 'guardian of their friendship' (Plat. *Laws* I. 640 d); when the conversation went dry he introduced other entertainments. Sometimes the *symposiarch* gave special prizes for someone who invented a new game, provided it did not hurt the sentiments of other participants. Plutarch in his *Table Talk* shows the example of the Assyrian king who promised a reward on anyone who invented a new sort of pleasure and says, the 'king of the συμπόσιον' should also do the same for the *symposiasts* (*Table Talk* I. 622 a).

The Qualities of a *Symposiarch* / *Arbiter Bibendi*

Plato in his *Laws* and Plutarch in his *Table Talk* narrate about the qualities of a *symposiarch* (Plat. *Laws* 640 b-e; *Table Talk* I. 620 a – 622 b). First of all, a *symposiarch* should be prudent, kind hearted and wise, also alert and diligent. He should be someone who "has the skill and ability to train and mold" the souls of the fellow-banqueters (Plat. *Laws* 671 c). This means that mostly not a young but an elderly person in his sixties was selected to be the *symposiarch*.[65] He should also be a strong man who should be able to overcome the temptation to drink more wine. He should not suppress any unruly uproar of a drunken guest but try to control it through his efforts. He should not give equal amount of wine to all, but give everyone "the amount which is a proper and suitable measure for each man's temporary condition or permanent capacity" (*Table Talk* I. 620 f). He should also be a humorous person and should make the conversation lively and also see to it no one is hurt by the anger or the comments of another. When the *symposiarch* was successful in maintaining the order and the decorum of the party, he was praised and was given rewards for his leadership at the συμπόσιον.

Uninvited Guests: Ἄκλητοι and *Umbrae*

It was not uncommon at a *symposium* that the host received guests whom he had not invited. In the opinion of Węcowski the participants at a *symposium* could well be put under three categories, "the full members (called *hetairoi* or *philoi*), the 'uninvited ones' (*aklētoi*), and the so-called 'shadows' (*skiai*) who came invited not by the host or by common consent of the full members, but by one of the diners."[66] In Plato's *Symposium* Aristodemus is an uninvited guest, since he is not invited by Agathon but Socrates takes him along. When he comes alone without Socrates to the house of Agathon, the host is polite in inviting him, saying that he was looking for him in the market place to invite him (174 b). Similarly, in the Roman *convivia*, we have *umbrae*,[67] or the shadows. Shadows were the "lucky clients of a powerful patron"[68] who was invited for a banquet. Davis cites the example of the host Prodicus who had to invite the two 'shadows' of the guest of honor Hermogenes with a "polite lie"[69] stating that he was actually looking for them in the agora.

Ἄκλητοι

It was possible that the invited guests did not turn up for the dinner party, or they had a better offer somewhere else. In this case, last minute invitations were given to some others. There were also people who were waiting for such a last minute invitation. Balsdon gives the example of

Horace who was vainly expecting a last minute invitation and at last ⊠swallowed his pride and hurried off to his patron's - Mae*cenas*' - table 'when it was already getting dark' - which means that Mae*cenas* dined late, or had waited a long time for his defaulting guest."⁷⁰ Such men were called ἄκλητοι (the uninvited) and in later times as παράσιτοι (parasites). In Odyssey, we find an ἄκλητος in the person of Odysseus. He comes as an ugly person and a stranger to the banquet of the suitors and begs for food. An uninvited person could be tolerated to the banquet only when he was able to entertain the group with his performance or jokes (Hom. Od. XVII.380-388; cf. also Ath. VI. 236 e-f).ē "During the banquet the *aklētos* displays his ugliness, weakness, voracity, or whatever by chance and unintentionally, thus making the invited guests laugh as they felt their superiority. Secondly the physical and moral inferiority of the *aklētos* is revealed consciously and on purpose: the *aklētos*, as it were, performs himself."⁷¹ In Xenophon Philippus comes as an ἄκλητος, tries to entertain the group through his wits. After realizing no one laughs for his wits, he tries later to imitate the dance of a girl deliberately imperfectly, so that the group laughs (Xen. *Sym.* 2.22).

The sixth and the seventh books of Athenaeus' *Deipnosophists* are dedicated to the explanation of parasites and flatterers as they were sometimes called. We see here a parasite introducing himself:

> Dining with him who desires me (he needs only to ask me), and alike with him who desires me not (and there is no need to ask); at dinner there I am a wit, and cause much laughter and praise my host. And if anyone wants to say something hostile to him, I revile the upstart and so get myself hated. Then after eating heartily and drinking heartily I take my leave; but no slave carries a lamp ahead for me. I skulk along the slippery way and am all alone in the darkness, if I meet the watchmen anywhere... the patrol wants no more of me than a flogging. And when I at last get home, done to death, I go to sleep without any bedding and never heed the first thing so long as the neat wine holds and befuddles my senses. (Ath. VI. 236 a-b).⁷²

In return for his free meal, a parasite was the first to praise the host at the slightest given chance, especially for the quality of the food served. He briefed his patron time to time about the gossips of the city. When he was mocked at by the benefactor or the group, the parasite was very gracious to accept it lightly and joins them in their laughing. Furthermore, a parasite was loyal to his benefactor. In *The Deipnosophists* Athenaeus again gives the example of Cleisophus, a parasite of Philip the king of Macedonians. "When Philip had his eye knocked out, Cleisophus went along with him with his own eye bandaged in the same way. Again when Philip was wounded in the leg, Cleisophus marched limping along with the king. And whenever Philip tasted any food that was bitter, Cleisophus also made a wry face as if he had eaten it too" (Ath. VII. 248 f - 249 a).

Parasites were at the risk of getting insulted in a gathering and regarded as avaricious eaters and drunkards. Athenaeus shows how the character of ἄκλητος is first introduced by Epicharmus: "another came stalking in here, at the heels of the first - one whom… you will easily … find ever ready to assist the feast. (However poor he may be) this fellow can none the less quaff life in a single breath as he would a cup." (Ath. VI. 235 f). Węcowski is of the opinion that those aristocrats who became economically poor and were no longer able to host a *symposium* were no longer invited, but at the same time were tolerated in a drinking party as ἄκλητοι.[73] There were also other examples of uninvited guests seen in the literary *symposia*. These men who took part in a *symposium* elsewhere and at the end of it tried to enter into the houses where *symposium* was still on. For example Alcibiades in Plato´s *Symposium* comes fully drunk after having attended a *symposium* elsewhere. He was nevertheless not only welcomed but also was allowed to lead the course of the *symposium* as the *symposiarch*.

Seating Arrangements
The community gathered at a *symposium* was nothing but a society in its miniature. Hence the rules applied to the society at large, applied also to a banquet. The seating order of the guests reflected the social order outside. In this sense one of the important characteristics of a good host was to respect the status of the guests in the society and to seat them according to their social ranks and honor. Plutarch in his *Table*

Talk brings in the discussion whether the host should seat the guest according to their age, honor and social status, or the guests should take their own place. The context of the discussion was a *symposium* where a well dressed foreigner gets offended at the seating arrangement, is infuriated that he did not get his rightful place to recline, and so goes away indignant without attending the *symposium* (*Table Talk* I. 615 d). Based on this incident, the discussion is carried on about the seating arrangement at a *symposium*, where three suggestions are given for the best seating arrangement. First, the father of Plutarch and of Timon the host, gives the suggestion, that good order has to be kept at the dinner parties. A dinner party which does not value the age, the financial status of the banqueter or his rank or his social position, fails to give respect to the banqueter; because setting everyone in his proper place changes "chaos into order" (*Table Talk* I. 615 e – 616 b). Secondly, the host Timon proposes that the seating arrangement based on the social status has to be abolished at a *symposium* (*Table Talk* I. 616 c-f). Third, a mediatory position is proposed by Plutarch: when one invites intimate friends and fellow citizens, it is better to allow the guests to choose their places; when the guests include elderly men and foreign dignitaries, one should assign to them places according to their ranks, lest they be embarrassed. Sometimes the host could also place the guests according to their interests, "men who like to drink, - and lovers too, not only those who feel the bite of love for lads, as Sophocles says, but also those bitten by love for women and for girls" (*Table Talk* I. 619 a).

Romans too had used banquets as an occasion to reiterate the social order and status of the banqueters. But they had evolved the system further.[74] The seats (*lecti*) in the Roman *triclinium* were named as *lectus summus*, *lectus medius* and *lectus imus* - the highest, middle and lowest couches respectively. The *lectus imus* was occupied by the host with his wife or other family members. The *lectus medius* - the couch in the middle was the couch of honor. It was the *locus consularis*, where the guest of honor was seated. Each couch had its own highest position; the person who reclined at the head of the couch was the distinguished person on that couch. This place was filled first. Other places in the couches were filled once the seat of honor was filled. In the *lectus medius* the guest of honor reclined not at the head of the couch but at the tail end. Plutarch says, it is because he reclined next to the host who reclined in the *lectus imus*. It was also because he had enough space to deal with any important and urgent situation. (*Table Talk* I. 619 e-f). We also find occasions in the literary *symposia*, where an uninvited guest insisted on reclining on the *lectus medius*, the *locus consularis,* as it is portrayed about Favonius in Plutarch´s ´Brutus´ (Plut. *Brut.* 34. 2).[75]

The Custom of Reclining

One of the most important characteristics of sympotic meals was the custom of reclining. The origin of such a practice was adopted perhaps from the Near Eastern customs. For nomadic people who lived in tents without much furniture, the custom of reclining was suitable for eating.[76] Later the custom could be seen in the royal houses. The garden party of the Assyrian king Ashurbanipal reclining with his queen could be an evidence to it.[77] The Greeks who were accustomed to sit for their meals took upon this Near Eastern custom of reclining, which was later absorbed by the Romans who considered sitting at formal meals as an "old fashioned simplicity."[78] It is difficult to pin point the exact time when Greeks changed their position of the formal meal from sitting to reclining on couches. While for some it could have begun in the eighth century itself, for others it might have been a century later.[79] Only the adult male citizens were allowed to recline. Women, if at all they were present for a formal meal, and free adolescent boys, sat at a *symposium* while men reclined. When a Greek aristocrat came for a formal meal, he reclined on his left elbow on the couch and his right hand was free for eating.[80] Based on Greek arts, Evans points out that there were at least more than one model of couches. "One was a simple chaise lounge: a chair with an extended seat so that a man could sit on it and stretch out his legs horizontally in front of him. Another was a sofa with a large pillow or bolster at one end where a diner could recline on his elbow."[81] Apart from being a symbol of luxury, the custom of reclining was a symbol of manhood too. Evans points out the custom in Macedonia, where a man who wanted to recline in a banquet needed to have first proved his manhood "by killing a wild boar without trapping it first in nets."[82] Evans gives the example of Casssander, one of the military generals, who could not recline at a *symposium* although he was thirty five years old. This is why adolescent boys who partook at a *symposium* did not recline but sat, just like Autolycus sat in Xenophon's *Symposium*. By the end of the archaic period, this aristocratic custom of reclining "became the characteristic mark of a wider social class, all those, with wealth to spare and leisure to enjoy"[83] and the custom later spread also to the lower rungs of the society. At the feast of Saturnalia, at which the normal order of the society was reversed, even the slaves were allowed to recline.

Originating from a custom of nomadic people who did not have furniture to sit down, the practice of reclining became more than a physical posture; it came to be the characteristic mark of an aristocratic society. Reclining at a banquet had become very important because, in the opinion of Węcowski the very essence of the institution of *symposium* was this custom of reclining.[84] When one wanted to follow an aristocratic life style, then one should have learnt how one should elegantly recline at a *symposium*.[85] It was the symbol of social status, luxury and wealth. It "marked a greater degree of social privilege and autonomy than any other dining posture."[86] To be asked to sit at a *symposium* was considered to be womanish, and a sign that the person was of a lower rank. Alcidamas the Cynic who comes uninvited in Lucian's *symposium* is asked to sit on a chair. He protests against it saying, ⊠a soft womanish trick, to sit on a chair or a stool! One might as well loll at one's food half on one's back, like all of you on this sofa couch with purple cushions under you. As for me, I will take my dinner standing and walking about the room. If I get tired, I will lay my old cloak on the ground and prop myself on my elbow like Heracles in the pictures" (*The Carousal or The Lapiths* 13).[87]

Rituals of Δεῖπνον *and* Συμπόσιον

Symposium as a formal meal was a highly structured event, with rituals to be observed. The participants of a *symposium* prepared themselves for a heavy meal by going to *gymnasium* for exercise. This was followed by a public bath. One made sure to groom his body with perfume and wore special dining clothes. The same was also the practice in the Roman circle.

Δεῖπνον / *Cena*

As the guests arrived at the house of the host, they were welcomed by the host; in Xenophon the host Callias has a eunuch doorkeeper to welcome the guests. As the guests entered the ἄνδρων, the slaves attended to them, took off the shoes of the guests and washed their feet, picked their nails. Once the guests reclined on their respective couches, cool water was poured on their hands for washing. Then tables were brought in – small moveable tables for each couch. In the earlier times ἄνδρων had permanent tables made of stone. But in later times moveable wooden tables were preferred, since it was easy to clean the room after the meals were over.[88] The first part of the menu was served. The guests ate with their fingers. They used pieces of bread to clean their hands in between and threw them on the floor for dogs.

In contrast to that of the Romans the menu of the Greeks for δεῖπνον was moderate. In private dinner, δεῖπνον would include bread in many varieties and vegetables like beans, olives and onions and fish. At *symposia* meat was a necessary part of the meal.[89] However for the Greeks the importance was given more to συμπόσιον than to δεῖπνον. In the words of Hobden, "there is a cultural selectivity at work in the Greek imagination that prioritizes drinking together, over eating together. It is the συμπόσιον, with its generic potential for social and political interaction through conversation and song within a framework of shared music, pleasure and wine that captures the imagination."[90] This was the opposite for the Romans. The Romans took the *cena* more seriously than the *comissatio*. Their evening dinner parties were heavy which were abound with a variety of meat items. Balsdon quotes Seneca, "Men eat to vomit, and vomit to eat; their dishes are fetched from every corner of the earth, and then they do not even deign to digest them."[91] The *Cena* proper was divided into three courses (*cena prima, cena secunda, cena tertia*). Sometimes it was extended even up to seven courses. The highlight of Trimalchio's dinner party was the 'Trojan pig' into which preparations of meat of different kinds were stuffed. The menu in his *Cena* was so "extravagant and lavish to the point of ludicrous."[92] As a parody the *Cena Trimalchionis* of Petronius could be assumed as an attempt to pinpoint the malady of the society, wherein the extravagance of dinner was a point of concern for the author.

Συμπόσιον / *Comissatio*

After the δεῖπνον was over, ritual actions took place to mark the beginning of συμπόσιον. The tables were removed, the floor was cleaned by the slaves and water was poured over the hands of the guests. Garlands of flowers were gifted to them and perfumes were offered. To begin the συμπόσιον, a libation of undiluted wine was passed around. The guests took a sip in it in honor of 'the Good Divinity' (ἀγαθοῦ δαίμονος). This Good Divinity was considered to be Dionysius the god of wine. (Ath. XV. 675 b). After this, wine was mixed in a formal way in front of the guests, which was poured in three *kraters*. After the mixing of wine in three *kraters*, libation was offered from each of the *krater*, first to the Olympian gods, then to the heroes and then to Zeus the savior.[93] The host took up the first cup dedicated it to the Olympian gods and poured a little wine onto the floor, took a sip from the cup and passed it to other guests who took a sip dedicating the cup to the Olympian gods. This was done with the other cups too. This religious ritual was also accompanied by the singing of 'paean' a solemn song or chant in praise of Dionysius the god of wine, which went as follows:

> "In mighty flagons hither bring,
> the deep red blood of many a vine,
> that we may largely quaff and sing,
> the praises of the God of wine!"[94]

This song was accompanied with the playing of flute by flute girl. After this the tables were brought again and the dessert course was served to the participants, which would consist of cakes, nuts, olives, figs and sweetmeat as side dishes for the drinking. Salt also would be provided in order to induce thirst and more drinking.

Mixing of Wine

The ancient Greeks drank wine always mixed with water. Wine was understood to be medicinal if it was drunk mixed with water; it was considered poison when it was drunk without mixing it with water. For Greeks to drink wine *akratos* – undiluted, was "to drink like a Scythian"[95] namely, an act of barbarians. Mixing was therefore understood to be a symbol of civilized men. Greeks as well as Romans thought they distanced themselves in this way from the barbarian culture. Lissarrague narrates the custom in ancient Sparta to force the young helot slaves to drink too much undiluted wine and let them free afterwards. Heavily drunk, these youths coming from the lower ranks of the society went into the city and behaved in an uncouth manner, singing indecent songs and dancing lewdly. Such a scene was to be a lesson for the Spartan young citizens to teach them the dangers of drinking wine undiluted.[96] Mixing was done in a solemn way. The wine was brought in a goatskin and was mixed with water in the *krater*. *Krater* was an indispensable element in any sympotic event. One can find the presence of *krater* in almost all the attic vases of the archaic period, in which *symposium* is portrayed. In some vases the slaves enter the ἄνδρων with a procession carrying the *krater*. In others, *krater* is even garlanded just like the *symposiasts* were garlanded.[97] Such images show that the *krater* had a prominent place in the mixing and the distribution of wine. Joanna Luke is of the opinion that the very possession of a *krater* shows that the owner was civilized.[98]

The amount of water to be mixed with wine was also carefully looked into. For example, in the Alcaeus Fragment (346), Alcaeus of Mytilene wrote "Let's drink! Why are we waiting for the lamps?…Friend, take down the large decorated cups. For the son of Semele and Zeus gave men wine to make them forget their sorrows. Mix one part of water to two of wine, pour it in brimful, and let one cup jostle another."[99] Plutarch's *Table Talk* proposes various suggestions like three cups of water mixed with two cups of wine, or two cups of water mixed with one cup of wine or a more sober kind of drinking in which three cups of water is mixed with one cup of wine. His final proposal is two cups of water should be mixed with three cups of wine. This mixing is "most harmonious, a complete inducer of sleep and relaxer of care, a protecting and soothing governess." (*Table Talk* III. 657 d). The mixing of water into wine also helped the *symposiasts* prolong their enjoyment of drinking.

In the Roman circle wine was already served during the *cena* itself; it was extended to the *comissatio*. During the *comissatio*, the mixing of water was done in the *krater* as was the case with the Greeks. The Romans drank wine "in the Greek manner"[100] mixing it with water. For the wine they had together with their *cena*, they mixed the water in their own cups. The elderly men drank wine mixed with hot water; others preferred cold water, sometimes they mixed wine with ice.

Symposium and Entertainments

The very aim of *symposium* was εὐφροσύνη. As a place of social interaction and relaxation, the entire event of *symposium* was understood to be a social entertainment.[101] Entertainments varied, depending on the interest of the guests. Looking at the Attic vases, one could see the interest of the participants for the entertainments during the *symposium*. When the elite guests had interest over philosophical discussions, the host brought philosophers in the banquet, so that the banquet had a philosophical taste in it. When the group consisted of guests who liked music and dance, then the host made sure that the guests had varieties of entertainment ranging from music, poetry, dance, games and so on. The following are some of the possible entertainments at a sympotic gathering:

Sympotic Music and Poetry

An intimate connection could be seen between sympotic banquet setting and Greek music and poetry. As a "place of performance"[102] *symposium* was one of many occasions in which poetry was performed and songs sung. In the words of Griffith "music, with its repetitive rhythms, combinations and juxtapositions of voices and limbs and strong emotional effect, has always been one of the strongest promoters of social cohesion and fellow-feeling."[103] This was very true in the context of the *symposium*. Singing was an important and indispensable part of a dinner party. Plutarch talks about the presence of the flute in a sympotic gathering. A flute "is as essential to our libations as the garland and it helps impart a religious tone to the singing of the *paean*" (*Table Talk* VII. 713 a) and therefore one "ought not to dissolve an intimate association of such long standing" between flute and banquets (*Table Talk* VII. 712 f). More than poems about war and military battle, poems of love were encouraged at a *symposium*. The following were some of the genres, which were frequently sung at a *symposium*:

Παιάν

At the beginning of a *symposium*, it was customary that the participants sang together a *'paean.'* Paean was a short religious singing, "a cry addressed to Apollo as the god of healing."[104] It was a song of joy and was sung in various contexts. It is sung sometimes before the battle in order to give hope to the soldiers; it is also a victorious song after the battle, or a religious song, sung at a shrine. Besides addressing to various gods, in the Hellenistic period it was addressed also to a victorious general.[105] Singing a *paean*, does not mean that one sings an entire song. "Merely to utter the ritual word *le paean* – or some metrical variations of them – was to sing a *paean*."[106] *'Le paean'* was like a refrain for the song; it was repeated at regular intervals. There is a dispute in *The Deipnosophists*, whether Aristotle's song to the dead Hermias was a *paean* or not. For Democritus, Aristotle's song is not a *paean* because it does not have the refrain in it, which is the characteristic of a *paean* (Ath. XV. 696 e). It is important for our study to note that it was a ritual to sing a *paean* along with the libations at the beginning of a *symposium*. In the sympotic setting it was addressed to Dionysius, the god of wine. Plato´s *Symposium* narrates, when dinner was over, "they made libation and sang a chant to the god and so forth, as custom bids" (Plat. *Sym.* 176 a). We see something similar in Xenophon´s *Symposium*: "…the tables had been taken away and they had poured a libation and sung a *paean* (hymn)" (Xen. *Sym.* 2.1). Later in *The Deipnosophists*, Athenaeus takes from Xenophon to say "men of good cheer should first of all praise the god with pious stories and pure words; they should pour libations and pray for the power to do the right…" (Ath. XI. 462 d).[107] Looking at these texts, once could say in a nutshell that *paean* was a ritualized hymn that gave the sympotic gathering a perfect start for the *symposion*.

Σκόλια

There were two other types of songs, performed by the participants, which scholars call σκόλια. Σκόλια were songs that were popularly sung at dinner parties. After the *paean*, it was the turn of the guests to sing individually; the guest who sang, held a myrtle branch in his hand and began a song or a particular part of a song from a renowned poet and gave the branch to another guest, who had to continue the song and complete it. Such practice was called capping.[108] Such an ability to cap verses is a sign of a ´civilized´ symposiast. The young Bdelycleon in Aristophanes´ *Wasps* tries to teach his father Philocleon how to cap verses from the poet Harmodius (Aristoph. *Wasps*. 1222-1250). Such singing went on from one participant to another and from one couch to another, either in a random order or in a ´crooked´ way. In this way the name *skolion* is etymologically explained. The other mode of performance of σκόλια was that the guests sang parts of songs, created by great poets of the past; this was "sung to the lyre not by all the guests, but by those who were able, οἱ συνετώτατοι."[109] This custom of guests singing to the lyre slowly died out from the time of Aristotle in the fourth century BCE; instead of composing new σκόλια a few lines of renowned poets were taken over and reused. A guest could also add some new verses of his own to the existing *skolion*.

Athenaeus at the end of *The Deipnosophists* has a collection of twenty-five σκόλια, which must have been composed around the sixth to fifth centuries. The first four σκόλια are dedicated to different gods, the fourth of which is offered to the god Pan.

> "O Pan, ruler over glorious Arcadia
> Dancing attendance with the reveling Nymphs,
> Smile joyously on these merry songs of mine!" (Ath. XV. 694)

Pan was considered to be "the god of ecstatic merriment and joy."[110] This *skolion* was sung in sympotic gatherings because the god was understood to increase the happiness of the evening. There were also other themes that were touched upon in σκόλια. Marchinus divides these σκόλια according to major themes: songs for gods (1-4), human affairs such as the trustworthiness of friends, health, youth and wealth and merriment (5-9), remembering the heroes of the past (10-16) as well as erotic themes (17-22).[111] Hence we could say that after songs in praise of God were sung, the stage was set for singing songs in praise of one another especially the host or even others who were not present at the *symposium*. There are also evidences of songs in praise of wine in *Theognis Fragments*:

> Wine, in some respects I praise you, but in others I blame you:
> Nor can I ever either wholly hate you or wholly love you.
> You are a blessing and a bane.
> Who could blame you, who could praise you,
> If he had any measure of wisdom? (*Theog. Fr.* 873-876)[112]

Different genres of poetry could be heard to be sung at a *symposium*, varying from Elegy to *Iambus*. West says that *symposium* was one of the many occasions in which elegy was sung.[113] For Bowie "elegy in its shorter form is closely associated with the *symposium*"[114] which was normally sung accompanied by *aulos*. Theognis the sixth century poet foretells that his elegies would remain immortal, because they would be sung over and over in the sympotic meals:

> No meal or feast but thou'lt be there, couched 'twixt the lips of many a guest, and lovely youths shall sing thee clear and well in orderly wise to the

clear-voiced flute. And when thou comest to go down to the lamentable house of Hades in the depths of the gloomy earth, never, albeit thou be dead, shalt thou lose thy fame, but men will think of thee as one of immortal name, Cyrnus (*Theog. Fr.* 237-43).

Iambus was another genre that found its place in a sympotic setting. As a literary form it originated in the seventh century BCE. In this genre mockery and explicit narrations of sex were prominent. In Carey's opinion, "most of the *iamboi*, like most small-scale archaic poetry, were performed in the *symposion*."[115] This is why iambic poetry was eagerly accepted in sympotic gatherings, wherein sexual entertainments were order of the day.

Philosophical Discussions

Apart from poetry, philosophical discussions also had an important place at a *symposium*. This is why the focus of a literary *symposium* was much more on the philosophical dialogue than on the description of the food items. In Plato's *symposium* Eryximachus, the self-appointed *symposiarch* suggests that the flute girl departs and shows her talents to the women of the house, so that the participants could dedicate their time for a higher level of entertainment – *encomium* on love (*Plat. Sym.* 176 e). In Xenophon's *Symposium* after a wonderful performance by the flute player and the singers and the dancer, Socrates guides the guests towards a philosophical conversation and says only such a conversation would 'heighten the festivity' of the *symposium* (Xen. *Sym.* III. 2). Trimalchio wants to show off not only his wealth, but also his wisdom, when he says, "We must not forget our book-learning even at our table." (*Petr.* VI. 39).

In this way the setting of *symposium* was seen very appropriate for the transmission of the sayings of famous philosophers. Plutarch's *Table Talk* and Athenaeus's *Deipnosophists* are the best examples of such a transmission. In his desire to report the tradition about the legendary seven sages Plutarch creates a banquet setting and brings together his ideas on government, family and universe. In *Table Talk* he says, "it is worse to take away the pleasures of conversation at table than to run out of wine." (*Table Talk* V. 679 a). As Lukinovich puts it, for Athenaeus, the "true passion is not for the banquet itself but for everything having to do with the theme of 'the banquet' *in literature* and *in conversation*."¹¹⁶ Not only in the food that is served but also in the conversation of the *symposiasts,* one could see "ποικιλία, καινότης, πολυτέλεια, 'variety, novelty and expense'."¹¹⁷ Since for Plutarch a *symposium* should be a place for "philosophical discussions, combining fun with serious effort" (*Table Talk* VI. 686 d), the themes dealt in the *Table Talk* are both serious ("whether philosophy is a fitting topic for conversation at a drinking-party" [*Table Talk* I. 612 e] and "Whether the host should arrange the placing of his guests or leave it to the guests themselves" [*Table Talk* I. 615 d]), as well as funny and light ("Whether the hen or the egg came first" [*Table Talk* II. 635 e]).

Ἑταῖραι

There were also hired entertainers at a *symposium*. One such important entertainment of a sympotic gathering was the performance of ἑταῖραι. As the word means, ἑταίρα is a woman 'associate' at the *symposium*. The term refers to "any woman of questionable reputation … who is defined first and foremost by the mere fact that she is seen to spend time in the company of, or who associates with, men to whom she is not related."¹¹⁸ In the context of *symposium* ἑταίρα was a woman "common to anyone who wished … She, in opposition to the wife, was shared among men like the food or wine, falling under the sympotic rule of equal shares."¹¹⁹ Sometimes she could be shared by two or more men at a *symposium*. Aristophanes says the war between Spartans and Athenians was partly because of the abduction of a *hetaira* named Simaetha by Athenians.¹²⁰

Although the role played by *hetairai* shows them to be "the highest class of prostitutes,"¹²¹ there is a difference between a ἑταίρα and a πόρνη. A πόρνη is a sex worker on the street, offering sex for anyone who gives her money. A ἑταίρα on the other hand is not a street side prostitute, but a courtesan, who has her own clients and has a long-term partnership with some of the rich men of the society; she goes along with them as their sexual companion to *symposia*. Apart from her physical beauty, she "had acquired some intellectual training and possessed artistic talents such as singing and playing musical instruments. Some of these *hetairai* were as educated as or more educated than their upper-class male clients. The *hetairai* were known to have actively participated in the intellectual, artistic and musical life of the period."[122] We have references in the *symposium* literature to flute girls (αὐλητρίς), harp players (ψάλτριαι)[123] and dancers (ὀρχηστρίδες), who had the role of "entertaining the guests with music at the beginning, and with sex at the end of the party."[124] From many vase paintings we could infer that the presence of the flute girl was as important for the *symposium* as the *krater*. Although in Plato's *Symposium*, the sympotic gathering of Agathon sends away the flute girl so that the gathering could focus on an elevated conversation on love, the flute girl is sent away only after the *paean* is sung and after libations are poured (Plat. *Sym.* 176 a). Hence, it is very rare that a *symposium* took place without the presence of the flute girl.

The flute girls who played instruments and entertain guests at dinner parties were of the lower strata of the Greek society and were far below in social and economic standards. They were either slaves of a master (for example Syracuse in Xenophon), or hired from other free men who own them or they were even "self-employed."[125] Although there was much demand for such women in the ancient Greece, although because of their musical and artistic talents they were paid high,[126] they were not considered to be socially respectable. Plato in his Protagoras and Aristotle in his Athenian Politics differentiate the flute girls from domestic female musicians who learnt music and were poets and singers. Polygnota the daughter of Socrates who played harp and received prize of five hundred Drachmas is not a *hetaira* but a domestic female musician.[127] Apart from these women there were also other entertainers such as acrobats and fire-eaters who were hired to entertain the *symposiasts*.

Games at Symposium
Sympotic entertainment also included variety of games; the most loved game of the *symposiasts* was κότταβος. Originating from Sicily, this

game was played in different ways. Either a bowl, a disc or a bird with a phallus symbol was delicately balanced and was set up on the top of a stand at a distance. With the last drops of wine in their bowls, the participants aimed at hitting at the bowl or disc on a pole or a little saucer that was kept floating on the water. As they flung the wine at the target, each player called a toast to someone he loved.[128] A sixth century Attic vase painting shows the *hetaira* Smikra attempting to fling the wine at the target and saying "I am flinging this for you Leagros."[129] The *symposiast* who was able to hit the target in such a way as to make it fall down and to produce a clear sound, was declared the winner. Various prizes like eggs, fruits and cakes, including sexual favors were awarded to the winner. This game is represented in many vase paintings. It was so popular that there was even a saying that the "Greeks wasted most of their wine playing *kottabos* rather than drinking it."[130] Another game was the game of balancing. From the vase paintings, where this game is portrayed vividly, we see that the participant tries to balance the cup or vase on his hand, his mouth or his stomach.[131] Game of dice too was favorite during the *symposium*. The guests also tried out riddles as their entertainment at the *symposium*.

Symposium and *Convivium*: Differences

As we have already seen, Cicero is of the opinion that *convivium* and *symposium* are identical - there is only a change of name involved. However, scholars say that differences could be seen between the *symposium* of Greeks and the *convivium* of the Romans. The major ones are as follows:

Gender

The ancient Greeks considered women as the second-class citizens. The world of a woman in ancient Greece revolved around her house of her father, if unmarried and around the house of her husband, if married. It was uncommon to see women walking alone in the streets or in the agora. Even if she went outside, she mostly went out accompanied by others. Their place in the house too was limited to γυναικωνῖτις, or γυναικεῖον – the women's chamber.[132] Entering into the woman's chambers by an outsider is punishable. Evans gives a case in the fourth century Athens, in which a man is accused of entering into the women's chamber.[133] An exception could be seen in Sparta, where women enjoyed more freedom than their counterparts in other cities. There a girl was allowed to involve in sports and in learning; otherwise women had a very private life. Even at house, women rarely ate together with their husband even for private meals.[134] If they ate together in private, the man reclined while the woman sat. As regards the institution of *symposium*, it was an all-male event. Domestic women had no place in it. The only women who were present in the *symposium* were the *hetairai*, - women of low status – flute girls, dancers and those who satisfy the sexual needs of the participants. Their presence at a *symposium* was purely for entertainment.

In the Roman *convivium* however, wives were allowed to participate together with their husbands. Scholars point out the evidences from the paintings at the Etruscan tombs in which women are portrayed to be partaking at a *symposium*; they are not nude but fully dressed. This shows that they were not flute girls or slaves but members of the family. The Hellenistic literature too alludes to the Etruscan custom of including women in the *symposium*, but terms this practice as the custom of "the barbarians of the West."[135] This Etruscan custom was absorbed by the Romans. It was a normal custom in Rome to see women partaking in the *convivium*. At an earlier date a woman sat at her husband's feet during the banquet. Later she reclined with her husband.[136] Cornelius Nepos says in the first century,

> There are numerous actions decent by our standards which are thought base by them (the Greeks). For what Roman would hesitate to take his wife to a dinner party? … But this is all very different in Greece; for there she is only invited to dinners of the family and sits only in the inner part of the house, which is called 'the woman's quarters' (*gynaeconitis*); no one enters unless bound by ties of kinship.[137]

Cicero when talking about the corrupt governor Verres says that he and his men compelled a Greek host in the Greek city of Lampsacus to bring his daughter in the ἄνδρων to which the Greek host replied that it was not the custom of the Greeks to bring women in the ἄνδρων.[138] In *Cena Trimalchio* we see that Fortunata, the wife of Trimalchio reclines with her husband, also Scintilla the wife of the late-comer Habinnas recline with other participants (*Petr.* 67). In Lucian´s Wedding *Symposium* women occupy their couches along with the bride (*The Carousal or the Lapiths* 8).

For some Roman authors however the presence of women at a *convivium* was not a welcome change. Livy talks about the contest among the princes at a banquet, as to whose wife is the best among them. One Tarquinius Collatinus says boastfully that no wife could be better than his wife Lucretia. Upon the desire to check their wives unexpectedly as to what they would be doing at present, they come to know that all the daughters-in-law of the king were seen in heavy banqueting, while "Lucretia, though it was late at night, was busily engaged upon her wool, while her maidens were toiling about her in the lamplight as she sat in the hall of her house" (Livy I. 57).[139] And for some, when women partook at a *convivium*, the posture of women sitting rather than reclining exhibited an 'orderly conduct', and the "postural shift marks a moral decline."[140]

Hierarchy

Equality (ἰσονομία) was the aim of the Greek *symposium*. This equality between the participants was symbolized through the common drinking and the equal distribution of wine and equal portions of meat. The same was said to be the ideal in the Roman *convivium* too. Just as Cicero says about the ´co-living´ character of the Roman *convivium*, thereby implying social equality, Pliny the younger speaks in one of his Letters (II. 6) about the proper conduct in *convivia*: According to him, the right practice is to give everyone of the guests an equal share. "when I make an invitation, it is to sup, not to be censored. Every man whom I have placed on an equality with myself by admitting him to my table, I treat as an equal in all particulars."[141] In *Table Talk* Plutarch also stresses this point, when it says, it is wrong to "transfer(s) empty fame from market-place and theatre to social gatherings," and when a diner enters the banqueting hall, vanity is "much more fitting for men to have washed from their soul than the mud from their feet" (*Table Talk* I. 616 d); therefore banqueters should realize "as soon as they enter the door that the dinner is a democratic affair and has no outstanding place like an acropolis where the rich man is to recline and lord it over meaner folk" (*Table Talk* I. 616 f). This ideal of equality however could not be seen in the actuality. The first argument in Plutarch's above-mentioned *Table Talk* is that proper order should be maintained at table and due respect must be given to the person's age honor and social rank. As Donahue puts it, beginning with the seating of the guests, "Hierarchy, not equality was the central organizing principle of Roman commensality," so much so that, these dinner parties "served the dual function of brining the community together on important occasions and on reinforcing class distinctions through differences in the amount or in the quality of the fare offered to the assembled diners." Further D'Arms narrates an instance at a *convivium* in which Pliny the younger is shown to be present, where the host and some others enjoyed better food than the rest.[142] Especially in the client *convivium*, humiliation and abuse of clients was common and was understood by the patron as entertainment.

Equality of Participants
The participants of the Greek *symposium* were thought to be friends and social equals. They were aristocrats who influenced the day to day activities of the city. As we have already seen, a host invited only those who could invite him back. Hence they were equal in their social status, wealth and political influence. The situation was different in the Roman *convivium*. A Roman threw banquets not only for his social equals but also for his subordinates. In the client dinner, the host entertained his social inferiors, the *clientela*. Clients in the Roman Empire were people "on the fringe or beyond the fringe of good society, unsuccessful men who, at the cost of whatever personal humiliation, hoped for gain, favor or advantage…"[143] One of the characteristic features of the *clientela*

according to Green is that "the patron and the client were not of equal social status and different types of goods and services were exchanged between them."¹⁴⁴ It was more of ´give-and-take´ between the patron and the client. Through such *convivia* that he had with his clients who were far below his standards, a host or a patron made sure of their support to him.

Drinking Versus Eating

In the *symposium* of the Greeks the *symposiasts* could see a clear cut difference and separation between the δεῖπνον and the συμπόσιον.¹⁴⁵ However the focus was given to the latter among the Greeks. This importance given to the συμπόσιον is evident in the vase paintings of ancient Greece. It is at the συμπόσιον where the *symposiasts* had more elaborate rituals. While δεῖπνον was light and short, the συμπόσιον went on endlessly. Sometimes the guests were invited just to the συμπόσιον alone. While this was not the opposite in the Roman *convivia*, the Romans had blended both together. Gowers explains the difference well when he says, the difference between the Roman *convivium* and Greek *symposium* is that "the *symposium* was a drinking party padded out with sweetmeats and relishes, while the Roman *cena* was inescapably weighed down by food."¹⁴⁶ The *comissatio* part of the *convivium* did not play such an important role in the Roman *convivium* as συμπόσιον did for the Greeks. The best example would be Petronius´ *Cena Trimalchio*nis, where Trimalchio is presented to be giving his guests a variety of food items. Although drinks were passed on, it was food that played an important role in the work of Petronius. This could be seen from the very title of his work - *Cena*.

Other Types of Symposia

Public Banquets

It could be surmised from the preceding pages that private banquets were the focal point of the social life of the Greco-Roman world. Apart from private banquets organized by individuals, there existed also public banquets either organized in a city level thrown to all the people or those organized by kings on important occasions. In the public banquets offered by kings the number might go up to thousands. In *The Deipnosophists* Athenaeus gives the number of participants at the banquet of Alexander as 'sixty or seventy men.' He also talks about some fifteen thousand men who feasted with the king of Persia (Ath. IV. 146c). The baggage that Alexander the Great took with him in his campaign against the Persian Empire consisted of a great banqueting tent that could accommodate as many as 100 couches.[147] Julius Caesar threw a public banquet for the entire people of Rome after his series of military victories in 45 BCE.[148] By hosting a *symposium*, the king not only aimed at renewing his relationship with the noble men of the society, but he did so, also with the aim of getting their support for his policies.

Banquets of κοινόν / *Collegium*

Just as the modern society has clubs of different nature, the Hellenistic world too witnessed people of a common goal or of common tastes coming together to form clubs of different kinds. Ancient literature attests to numerous such clubs. These associations and clubs (κοινόν) played an important role in the Greco-Roman society. Already in the sixth century BCE, we find the existence of clubs that flourished in ancient Greece.[149] The primary purpose of formation of such clubs was religious. People came together to form a club so that they could offer sacrifice to a deity common to them. It was their god and the reverence to their deity that gave the club a social identity. Hence many associations were named after a deity around which they gathered. Smith gives the names of various religious clubs that existed. "'The *Asklepiasts'* or devotees of the god Asclepius, the 'Dionysiasts' or devotees of the god Dionysus, and the 'Sarapiasts' or devotees of the god *Sarapis*"[150] are some of them. These religious clubs were called by a general name θίασος or ὀργεῶνες (sacrificing associates). Sometimes the members of these clubs were also called ἑταῖροι (companions).

People also came together to form a club on the basis of their occupation. Especially in the cities where different industries flourished, merchants, purple dealers, artists, ship owners and many other skilled laborers had their own associations. These men "were cut off from the social and cultural life of the senatorial and equestrian class. Devoting themselves to their crafts and small businesses these people discovered the benefits of gathering together on holidays."[151] Community bond and recreation together with the religious worship were the main aims of these groups.

These clubs met at regular intervals having their own set of rules to be followed. The literary evidence of the statutes of one such club that existed around the third century renders many details about its organization, for example the information about the conditions for joining a club, how many times the association gathered, how a member had to behave in meetings, the penalties for a bad conduct, the duties of the leader of the association and the portions of the meat, allocated to different members of the association, etc.[152] The important result of having such clubs was that the participants had a familial bond, a sense of belonging and self-identity as against the society at large.[153] To sum up, one could say that the Greek associations had two important functions. They were formed by a voluntary group of men to perform religious rites to a particular deity. Through the common meals and relaxation, the association also served to enable the self-identity of a particular group, be it religious or of particular occupation.

The Romans too had their *collegia*. *Collegia* were formed for the main purpose of social protection for the men of same occupation, like shopkeepers, firefighters or tax collectors. Since "Roman society was deeply divided along class lines, and most of the occupations of freedmen were despised by the ruling class… The *collegia* gave men a sense of identity and comradeship, a social unit larger than the family and smaller than the state where they could meet together with friends, eat and drink, worship, play and share common experiences."[154] *Collegia* functioned also as funerary societies.[155] They gave a decent burial to all those members who paid their membership and monthly fees regularly without due. Many of the *collegia* had their own burial sites. This is why *collegia* was popular even among the poor and slaves who, in their desire to have a decent burial, wanted to be members of a *collegium*. There were also *collegia* which came together purely for the enjoyment of drinking.

Symposia of the Clubs

Eating and drinking was an integral and essential part of the Greco-Roman clubs and so the climax of these club gatherings was banquet and wine. Banquets in clubs served as an advertisement and a "self-promotion" of particular associations.[156] They feasted together once a year after offering sacrifices for their deity, and many times during the year, mainly on the birthdays of the patron or benefactor of the club. The membership fees was mainly spent for extravagant banquets, The names of some of the clubs indicate that these clubs were formed for no other particular reason and the members came together just for the sheer pleasure of feasting together.[157] The rules of conduct during such banquets are the same as in the private sympotic gathering. In the statutes of the Association of *Orgeones*, which we have mentioned earlier, as well as in other Greco-Roman clubs, we have evidences of rules for the leader of the feast who was to lead and take care of the order and conduct of the feast. Improper behavior was to be punished severely either with a penalty or with a temporary expulsion.[158]

Sometimes this very self-identity of the clubs was the cause for unrest in the Greek society. As we had seen earlier, in the late sixth and early fifth century Greece, it was the *heatairoi* of the aristocrats that tried to overthrow the democracy, which was later suppressed by Cleisthenes.[159] There were also other clubs whose very names show that they have disregard for gods and men. Murray notes that the young citizens of Greece formed clubs, which were not educational but perverted in nature. For example Murray cites the existence of a club called κακοδαιμονισταί, a club whose very name sets them in direct contrast to those clubs who come together in honor of ἀγαθοῦ δαίμονος. This club came together on the days of ill omen.[160]

In Rome there were similar unrests created by *collegia*. MacMullen shows the different unrly behaviors of some *collegia*, the protests and strikes organized by some of the trade associations which were the reasons for different emperors to ban them.[161] However as we look at the history of associations, we see that ἑταῖροι / *collegia* have been evolved over the centuries, from being an aristocratic political club to a multi ethnic group, where people of different races could interact with each other, an institution through which different workers could fight for their rights, also a place where sometimes even slaves could be members.

Marriage Banquet

As in any culture, banquet is an integral part of a wedding in ancient Greece. Even before marriage took place, there was a *symposium*, in which girls were betrothed to the suitable bachelors. This took place during the spring festival. After various games were conducted, wherein young men showed their valor and ability, there took place a drinking party where the young men proposed to a girl for marriage and asked for the permission of her father or her brothers, which was either accepted or rejected. We hear how Adrastus of Argos made the betrothal of his two daughters in the setting of *symposium*.[162] The wedding too was marked with a dinner party. This wedding feast and banquet took place in the house of the bride or the groom or sometimes also in a temple sanctuary. It was an occasion where the families showed off their wealth and made an extravagant dinner. Such marriage banquet was similar to a *symposium*; but this time, women too participated in it along with the bride, as we see this in Lucian's *Symposium* (*The Carousal or the Lapiths* 5).

The Funerary Banquet – *Das Totenmahl*

The connection between death and *symposium* is very evident from the different archaeological findings at different tombs. We had already pointed out a fourth century urn in an Attic tomb where the dead man is portrayed to be reclining with his wife sitting next to him. Archaeological findings also show different vases that portray κλίνη that was used to carry the dead bodies to the burial sites and either cremated or buried together with the dead.[163] Boardman cites a sixth century tomb in Lycia where the dead man is buried in a κλίνη made of stone and the walls filled with two types of painting – on one, the man on a battle and on the other the man reclining and feasting. This portrayal of the dead reclining is a phenomenon commonly called by scholars as the *Totenmahl*, the feast of the dead. Such portrayals betray the common belief of the Near Eastern world that "the life below is one long drinking party"[164] and the dead were said to be enjoying an eternal *symposium*.

The tomb paintings of men reclining and feasting could also be understood differently. First, as Smith points out, they could be a representation of what the dead has enjoyed in his earthly life.[165] Second, the portrayal of the dead reclining could also mean that the dead person participates with his relatives in the funerary banquet (περίδειπνον) that was held after his burial and on the days of his remembrance. To this meal it was believed that the dead person himself was present.[166] In fact wine was literally offered to the dead and poured on his remains through a system called "feeding tubes."[167] The Romans also had such feeding tubes in their burial sites. More than Greeks the Romans believed that the dead could still enjoy such pleasures of eating and drinking. Hence, they went to the burial sites at the days of remembrance of the dead to have banquets.

Symposium and the Values of the Society

With its own set of rules, *symposium* was understood to be a society in miniature. Though "identities are constructed through the differences"[168] with the society at large, though there was a sense of 'we' among the *symposiast*s as against the 'they' meaning the outside society, the required set of values demanded from the participants of a *symposium* were similar to those of the citizens of *polis*, namely, respect for one another, peace and harmony, obedience to the ruler, moderation and temperance in words and actions. Hence the society at large and the participants at a *symposium* were guided by the same principles and in a special way affect each other for better or for worse. The celebration of a *symposium* and also its after-effects affected the lives of not only the participants, but extended to the outside society as well. In this connection it would do well to learn what set of values a sympotic group incorporated from the society at large and how an actual *symposium* participated by a dozen men affected the entire society.

Equality or Hierarchy?
Those who invited others for a *symposium* made sure that it was their social equals that were invited – members of equal social and economic status. Grignon terms such fellowship meals as 'segregative' commensality, meaning thereby that the very idea of coming together for a meal was "a way to assert or to strengthen a 'We' by pointing out and rejecting as symbols of otherness, the 'not We,' strangers, rivals, enemies, superiors or inferiors."[169] Hence, the norm of *symposium* is egalitarianism. People who came together to participate in a common meal aimed at achieving a sense of solidarity. "Those who chose to eat together, tacitly recognize their fellow eaters as saliently equal."[170] It is to promote and emphasize this idea of equality that wine was mixed in one *krater* and wine was distributed in equal proportion to the participants. Hence the diners understood themselves as belonging to a community of equals against outsiders as subordinates. Murray goes to the extent of saying that a drinking party is to be seen as "an antithesis of social organization. Confronted by its power all men are equal. The social order disintegrates."[171] To create gradations within the sympotic group meant to bring in enmity between members. "The marks of honor are usually temporary and the result of general consent: they consist merely of special portions of food or extra wine, not the more formal and potentially permanent special seat."[172] Hence there is a deliberate attempt to emphasize the equality of the members.

In Roman *convivia*, hierarchy was an important factor but sharing together the common meal with the members of different classes of the society meant leaving behind, at least for a short period of time, the social barriers that separated them, Hence as D'Arms states, equality between the diners was the characteristic of "*convivia* of the truly civilized."[173] Balsdon renders the example of the emperor Hadrian; when the emperor threw a banquet, he tried to make sure that all diners had similar food in quality as well as quantity by ordering for himself the food that was served at the lowest table.[174] We could sum up this discussion on equality with a quote from Plutarch´s *Table Talk*, where Timon says banqueters form a new society within the banqueting hall. Inside the banqueting space they are all equal, for "they have not entered a contest, but have come for a dinner" (*Table Talk* I. 616 c-d). Hence the washing of the feet at the entrance is to be a symbolic gesture for washing of the status, one has been enjoying in the outside society. Hence the ideal of a sympotic feast was the equality of all the participants.

Evidences, however, point to the fact that egalitarianism remained merely in ideal. A tension between this ideal and the actual social differences could be seen both in Greek *symposium* as well as in the Roman *convivium*.[175] The presence of the parasites in the Greek *symposium* is the best example for it. As a person who is "uninvited and empty handed" but "showing up at the hospitably open front door of any house in which a party was underway,"[176] a parasite was considered to be a person who did not deserve to be invited to the *symposia*, unless he entertained the gathering. This is why Philippus in Xenophon´s *Symposium* does not eat, until he could make the guests laugh through his wits.

In Rome too, strict observance of hierarchy was vivid not only in the public banquets but also at private *convivia*. The very names given to the couches (*summus, medius* and *imus*) show how allocation of seats were done according to the social status of drinking partners. The discussion of the placement of the participants acquires its context and significance in the above-mentioned Plutarch´s *Table Talk* from the fact that a dignitary felt offended and left the sympotic gathering, since he did not get his rightful place at the room. This shows that the seating arrangement according to their social rank of the banqueters was the rule of the day and served "to legitimize and reinforce the existing social order, not to emphasize political equality, but precisely 'to register and naturalize the inequalities of the social system'."[177] The gradations at banquets meant, that some guests were identified as personal friends of the host while others were his less important friends and others were just freedmen.

Not only the quality but also the quantity of the food was different for people at different couches. Balsdon brings in the case of a banquet where Julius Caesar partook. There were three different tables set before the guests. The people at the lower table had lesser quantity than those who sat at the higher table.[178] The fact that the Emperor checks whether the food in the lowest table was of the same quality shows that hierarchy of food was the order of the day. Pliny the Elder attacks those who drink the best wine available and offer cheaper wine for those of lesser social status at a *convivium*.[179] Horace informs that while all the guests at the *symposium* of Nomentanus enjoyed wine to the full, the guests at the lowest couch had to drink very sparingly (Hor. S. II. VIII. 41). Humiliations too were common at a *convivium*. Emperor Caligula was seen laughing out loud at a *convivium* for no apparent reason. Asked about why he laughed, he seemed to have said that he was thinking how it would have been to have all the heads of the guests, participating at the *convivium* cut off.[180] Hence we see that although the ideal of equality among the drinking partners is emphasized in different literature, the actuality saw varied gradations at the sympotic gathering.

Friendship or Drunken Brawl?
One of the basic aims of sympotic gathering is cultivating friendship. The leader of the *symposion* according to Plato is that "he has both to preserve the friendliness which already exists among the company and to see that the present gathering promotes it still further" (Plat. Laws 640 d).[181] The institution of *symposium* was to lead the group towards φιλοφροσύνη. This is why Plutarch in the *Table Talk* talks of the "friend-making character of the dining-table." (*Table Talk* I. 612 d). In the Roman *convivium* too the primary aim of *convivial* gatherings

was friendship, and the "atmosphere appropriate to good *convivia* (is) *hilaritas*."[182] There are however, many vase paintings that show that not friendship and φιλοφροσύνη, but drunkenness and revelry were the norm of the day at different sympotic gatherings.

Although in the *Laws*, Plato writes about an idealized *symposium* where friendship is cultivated, he points out a little later that at the present time, *symposium* has become a place where enmity is created. "If such was the character of the drinking and of the recreation, would not such fellow-drinkers be the better for it, and part from one another better friends than before, instead of enemies as now?" (Plat. *Laws* 671 e - 672 a). In his advice to drink moderately Theognis tells of what would happen when someone drinks too much. "He that overpasseth the due measure of drinking is no longer master either of his tongue or his mind, but telleth reckless things disgraceful to sober ears, and hath no shame in what he doeth in his cups, a wise man once, but now a fool." (*Theog. Fr*.477-487).

Such misbehavior was not limited to the ἄνδρων alone, but extended also outside in *komos*, the after-drinking revelry. The revelers went out into the streets singing, shouting and sometimes burning the houses of the poor on the way side with their torches that were used to guide them to their houses, beating the public and damaging religious statues. Especially in the classical period the *komos*, the drunken riot was performed by the aristocrats with a deliberate intention of upholding and demonstrating their power over in the society. The broad minded acceptance of the value, 'right to live as one pleases' was not tolerated for long. In the year 415 as the phallic statues of Hermes denoting fertility and luck were mutilated by the drunken revelers, these acts were understood as an attempt of revolution to overthrow the *Demos*[183] and hence strict laws were enacted to control and suppress such indecent behavior of the revelers. This is why Plato writes in his *Laws* through a banqueter from Sparta, that drunken misbehavior was less common in Sparta because unlike in Athens strict control was observed in Sparta with extra penalties especially for drunken behavior:

> The rules about pleasures at Sparta seem to me the best in the world. For our law banished entirely from the land that institution which gives the most occasion for men to fall into excessive pleasures and riotings and follies of every description; neither in the country nor in the cities controlled by Spartiates is a drinking-club to be seen nor any of the practices which belong to such and foster to the utmost all kinds of pleasure. Indeed there is not a man who would not punish at once and most severely any drunken reveler he chanced to meet with (Plat. *Laws* 637 a - 637 b).

Convivium and the *comissatio* are also said to have been marred by notorious gluttony and drunken behavior in Rome.[184] Carcopino quotes from Seneca who describes how gluttonous the Romans were in the *convivium*: "*Vomunt ut edant edunt ut vomant*"[185] - this was the principle which the diners followed in order to be able to eat the whole time during a *convivium*. In his *Wisdom of Nigrinus* Lucian calls such banquets of the rich as the "vulgar thing, the source of many evils." He further narrates the drunken behavior of the diners: "At last they go away either finding fault or nursing a grievance, either abusing the dinner or accusing the host of insolence and meanness. They fill the side-streets, puking and fighting at the doors of brothels, and most of them go to bed by daylight and give the doctors a reason for making their rounds" (*The Wisdom of Nigrinus* 22).[186] Still worse is the case in Lucian's *symposium*, which was attended by the philosophers of various schools (Stoics, Peripatetics, Epicurians and Cynics). Heavily drunk these philosophers engage themselves in all kinds of verbal and physical abuse (*The Caraousal or the Lapiths* 19, 33, 44-45). At the end of it all, the bridegroom is severely injured and is whisked away in the same chariot, which was supposed to be the vehicle for the bridal procession (*The Carousal or the Lapiths* 47).

Evidences of stealing too have been mentioned about the *symposiasts* in the satirical works. Alcibiades comes late to the *Symposium* offered by Anytus, and instead of entering into the ἄνδρων, he orders his slaves to steal half of the gold and silver cups of the host. In another instance, a diner stole the golden cup of emperor Claudius.[187] In Aristophanes' *Wasps*, Philocleon goes a step further. He comes home after a sympotic gathering heavily drunk and bringing along with him a stolen flute girl (Aristoph. *Wasps 1341-1360*). Hence, *symposium* was a place where unrest could erupt at any time. In the words of Smith, "a sanitized *symposium* where behavior is universally harmonious, seems almost a contradiction in terms."[188]

Elevated Dialogues or for Sexual Indulgence?

The works of Plato, Xenophon and Plutarch show that a *symposium* is a space for serious philosophical discussion and learning. At the *symposium* the guests could get acquaintance with various poets and philosophers and get to know the literature of the time. Hence the time of *symposium* was considered to be educational.[189] This is why Xenophon concentrated on the conversation part of the *symposium* and this is why the flute girl in Plato's *Symposium* is sent away so that the diners could engage in serious discussion. For Plato "the convivial gathering, when rightly conducted, is an important element in education" (Plat. *Laws* 641 d). Hence a sympotic gathering could be a blending and "kinship of intoxication and inspiration."[190] Plutarch detesting those people who remember the details of what they ate and drank at the sympotic meal, tells that at a dinner only the philosophical discussions "give pleasure by remaining ever present and fresh to those who actually recall them" (*Table Talk* VI. 686 c) and are better than "the pleasures of eating and drinking." (*Table Talk* V. 673 a). According to Gellius the student of Plutarch, it was not the food or money but various topics, which were to be the contributions of each diner to a *symposium*.[191] *Symposium* was supposed to serve for the young and free male members of the society to be an "informal extension of teaching"[192] - as a platform for learning the etiquette, social life and the world. This is why boys were encouraged in Sparta to attend public banquets where men reclined. They could ask the adult males questions regarding life and many topics were discussed at such parties, like important events of history, heroic deeds of great men, charitable deeds, philosophy, piety and so on (*Table Talk* I. 614 b). Through such educational discussions, the young could be molded.[193] The fragmented poetry of Alcaeus, "wine, beloved boy and truth ..."[194] is understood to be some kind of exhortation given to a boy in the context of a *symposium*. At a *symposium* boys could learn great works of important poets. It is where they came to know about the different military activities of heroes of the past.

The question remains, however, whether and how far we could take the evidences of philosophical discussion and education described in the literary *symposia* to be historically true. For, Plato, Xenophon and Plutarch seem to give the *symposiasts* of their time, an ideal of how *symposium* had to be conducted. But mosaics and iconographies elucidate that this ideal was not followed many times. *Symposium* was more often a place of sexual indulgence than a place of learning and education. In the words of Corner, "the symposium brought the brothel into the *oikos* - in the sense, that is, of taking a man out of his family and bringing him into the community of non-kin men who share in the enjoyment of an extramarital, anti-productive, anti-domestic sexuality."[195] There were beauty contests among the flute girls, sometimes auction among the *symposiasts* for a particular flute girl. A *symposiast* could have fight over the possession of a flute girl, another could dispute over the possession of a young boy, and another could ask a flute girl for a favor of sex.[196] In such a context, young boys who attended sympotic gatherings were only negatively influenced. For example Verres's son who was present at his father's *convivium* was an observer of a nude man dancing and of prostitutes sexually engaging with diners.[197] This leads one to the conclusion that *symposia* were more of erotic nature than of normative character.

Summing up our discussion on the effects of the sympotic gatherings on the societal values, we see that on the one hand the ideals of sympotic gathering were equality, friendship, education and learning. This is expressed by the literary *symposia* of Plato and others. On the other, hierarchy, drunken misbehavior and sexual indulgence were normal at *symposia*. This is evidenced by numerous vase paintings, mosaics, erotic poems and satirical plays. Either Plato and others were trying to give an idealized picture of how a *symposium* should be organized and not how it actually happened, or it could also be possible that the satirists exaggerated the behavior of the *symposiasts* in order to instill in the readers, modesty of behavior at *symposia*. The tension between the ideal and the actual is what could have been the reality at every *symposium*.

Literary Symposium versus Actual Symposium

Having learnt about the sympotic culture of the Greco-Roman world, from the authors like Plato, Xenophon and Plutarch, the question that needs an answer is how much of it was real. Was philosophy really discussed in an actual sympotic setting, as Plato and Plutarch and Athenaeus point out? Or did these authors take up the motif of banquet and use it to inject their ideas of the society and philosophy? While having confirmed through the archaeological evidences that the sympotic culture did actually exist in the Greco-Roman world, we learn that these authors tried to impart their ideals using the framework of this sympotic culture and have thereby invented a new literary genre of *symposium*. "A literary *symposium* is a dialogue that takes place at some time in the course of that ancient ritual of dining, drinking and conversation known as the *symposion*. In other words, it is by form a dialogue."[198] Plato is said to be the first to use this genre in his *Symposium*, others inspired by his work, have followed and improvised the literary form. Martin informs, how well-structured this literary genre was, with preordained set of persons who participated in it, like the host, the chief guest, the entertainer, the doctor, the guest who comes late to the dinner and the guest who cries during the banquet.[199] The important distinction between the actual and the literary *symposia* is that in the literary *symposium* words play a greater role than food and drink. The participants speak more than they eat and drink. By doing so, the author of a particular *symposium* wants to show that "this *symposion* is superior to a real *symposion* because words and speeches stand in for food and drink. This proud attitude will have a long history; it will become common place for guests to arrive at a literary *symposium* with words and riddles and debate as their share."[200]

Characteristics of the Literary *Symposium*

Every work in the literary genre of *symposium* follows a particular style of writing. The work begins with the description of the place of *symposium*, the reason for coming together, the witness who narrates the events of the *symposium*, participants going to the house of the host, some intriguing or disturbing events that take place that give the occasion for the initial table talk, libations and at last an abrupt and sudden end.[201] For Relihan one of the main characteristics of the literary *symposium* is that "the *symposiac* genre must violate sympotic norms in order to function as literature."[202] If flute girl was the normal custom of a *symposion*, it is decided that the flute girl be sent out in Plato´s *Symposium*. Further the main character should be *unsympotic*. Socrates himself is the example for it. When everyone reclines for δεῖπνον, he is lost in his thoughts and nowhere to be found. When everyone makes an *encomium* on *eros*, Socrates admits that he does not know the method of making an *encomium* on *eros*. Furthermore, the conversational rules at a *symposium* should be that the participants are to be polite to one another when they discuss. The way Socrates discards Agathon´s view point by asking impolite questions one after another, is against the rule of the *symposium*. Hence Socrates is presented more *unsympotic* in Plato´s *Symposium* than any other character.

The Host as a Character of Ridicule?

Another important characteristic of the *symposium* as a literary genre concerns the host. We find in the sympotic literature that the host is often portrayed as character to be ridiculed.[203] The best example for it would be *Cena Trimalchionis* of Petronius. The very first appearance of the host in the scene relieving himself brings laughter not only to the guests but also to the readers. The way he is carried by the slaves into the *symposium* room brings hushed laughter among his invited guests (*Petr.* V. 32).[204] Each time he boasts about his wealth and shows himself as a man of learning, the guests are forced to applaud the cleverness of the host but they try to hide their laughter (*Petr.* VII. 47) and his wisdom is considered by them to be a nonsense (*Petr.* VIII. 49). The author ends the story with laughing out 'loud and long' at the conceit of the host. Nomentanus in Horace is also being laughed at by his guests secretly, although he is applauded openly (Hor. S. II. VIII. 60-79).

The silly portrayal of the host is not only in the satirical works of Petronius, Horace and others; Martin enumerates how this model of ridiculous portrayal of the host could be seen right from Plato's *Symposium*.[205] Agathon has won the prize for his first tragic play, and is considered by the guests as a genius. Socrates too praises the host for wonderful words of wisdom that came forth from him before thirty thousand Greeks (Plat. *Laws* 175 d). But Agathon himself knows that the praise of Socrates is ironic (Plat. *Laws* 175 e). Later Agathon is applauded by other guests for his excellent exposition on *eros*. But after initially praising him ironically for a wonderful oration, Socrates goes on to ridicule the arguments of the host in such a way that Agathon is forced to say at the end that he did not know what he was talking (Plat. *Laws* 201 c). The fact that the uninvited Alcibiades took away the wreath he offered to the host and placed it on the head of Socrates is once again a proof, as Martin puts it, for the host's *'niederlage.'*[206]

The ludicrous portrait of the hosts in the literary *symposia* goes perfectly well with the portrayal of the hosts in the Gospel of Luke. The hosts, in whose houses Jesus reclines are almost always portrayed as characters of ridicule, either by Jesus or by anyone within the narrative. Levi and Zacchaeus who hosted Jesus at their house are paired together with sinners, by the onlookers. Furthermore, the physical shortness of Zacchaeus and his struggle to climb up a tree to see Jesus are once again features which would make the readers giggle at the character of the host. On the other hand the three host Pharisees who host *symposium* for Jesus are rattled by the chief guest Jesus himself. Just like Socrates rattles the pride of Agathon, the Lukan Jesus demolishes the character of the host Simon the Pharisee, and lists out everything which, he as a host, has not done for his guest (Luke 7:44-46). But Luke goes a step further in breaking the norms of literary *symposia*; in his Gospel, the Lukan Jesus takes upon himself the role of the host in inviting himself to the house of Zacchaeus (Luke 19:5)[207] Later he once again usurps the role of the host by breaking the bread and sharing with the two disciples of Emmaus (Luke 24:30). The reason for it remains to be answered.

Another characteristic of the literary *symposium* is the "anticipated death of the main character."[208] The best example would be the Trimalchio, who makes a rehearsal of his own funeral at his *symposium*. *The Carousal* of Lucian too narrates that the bridegroom is terribly wounded during the *symposium*. This anticipation of death is similar to the *symposium*-like Last Supper of Jesus. As Jesus and his disciples celebrate the Last Supper, the death of Jesus looms large in the background of the banquet. This helps to confirm the hypothesis that Luke, who structured his Gospel around various meal events, employs the well-known *symposium* genre in his Gospel and in this way projects Jesus as a philosopher like Socrates.

Jewish Banquet Tradition and its Response to Greco-Roman *Symposium*

With his idea that a common language and culture could unite different parts of the world into one, Alexander the Great sowed the seeds of Hellenization of the entire Mediterranean world. Already before him, inroads had been made into Palestine towards a cultural interchange through commerce. In this short section we try to ascertain, how far Palestine was hellenized, whether the Hellenistic culture influenced the people of Palestine so completely in every area of their lives, that Hengel could call Palestinian Judaism as "Hellenistic Judaism,"[209] and what the reaction to such a thorough Hellenization of Palestine was by the different groups within Judaism. We begin by analyzing the Biblical texts that look similar to the Hellenistic meal customs; we try to surmise whether these Biblical texts have something in common with the Hellenistic sympotic culture. We then look at the meal traditions of different Jewish sectarian movements as attested by some of the non-biblical Jewish literature in order to understand the mindset of both the Palestinian and the Diaspora Jews regarding their view on Hellenistic sympotic culture.

Old Testament Meal Tradition

The tension between the Hellenistic culture and Judaism is vividly portrayed in the Books of the Maccabees. The forced imposition of some of the Hellenistic meal practices like eating of pork, has led many Jews to give up their lives rather than yield to it (2 Mac 7). It was this imposition that had forced Jews towards war. But the question like whether there was only opposition against the intrusion of Hellenistic culture, whether one finds attestations of the accommodations of Hellenistic eating habits in the Old Testament and how far such absorptions of Hellenistic banqueting culture are portrayed in the Old Testament would be answered in the following pages.

A *Symposium* at the Wedding of Samson?

The historical time period of the Judges could be placed between the twelfth and eleventh centuries BCE. Biblically this was the time that the Jews had to dwell among the inimical Canaanites and Philistines. Samson goes to Philistine to marry a girl in Timnah. He hosts the marriage dinner for seven days. Thirty young men participate in it as bridegroom's friends. As it was the custom at a normal *symposion*, Samson puts a riddle before the participants and a reward is announced for the answer of the riddle. The banquet setting, participation of friends at the banquet and the riddle placed at the banquet and the prize for it - all these point to Burkert, that here we are looking at an earliest form of a *symposium*.[210] Burkert is of the opinion that the Philistines would have borrowed this custom of a *symposium*-like banquet from the Mycenaean Greeks whom they conquered in 1200 BCE.[211] Perhaps the wedding banquet of Samson reflects the crudest form of *symposium* at its earliest stage. The date of the composition of the Book of Judges perhaps could help us. If the Book of Judges was written in the second part of the seventh century BCE, as Hamlin points out,[212] then already at this time we have a faint glimpse of a *symposium* in the book (14:1-19). The fact that materials about the twelfth century Judges were collected and compiled and redacted at the eighth century BCE, and that the book was added into the Deuteronomical collection of books only by the seventh century[213] when the Mediterranean world might have been aware of *symposium*, would help to find frail traces of a *symposium* in wedding banquet of Samson.

Marzēaḥ in Amos

The term *marzēaḥ* occurs in the Old Testament only twice (Amos 6:7; Jer 16:3), although it has been quoted implicitly in some other texts of the Bible without using the exact word.[214] *Marzēaḥ* was a social institution with a religious overtone, attested in many parts of Ancient Near Eastern world. "A *marzaʼu* at Ugarit is an important social organization, an exclusive club consisting of ʼthe men of the *marzaʼu*ʼ headed by a president (*rb*), owning a ʼhouseʼ and other property; …the men meet for ceremonial feasts, including heavy drinking, in the worship of a specific god."[215] *Marzēaḥ* had unique characteristics: "specific location, appointed leader, elite membership, alcoholic consumption and religious connection."[216] The word is also used to denote the extravagant feastings that these clubs organized.

Resemblance with Hellenistic *Symposium*

As we look at the specific features of *marzēaḥ*, we could see clearly a close link between the *symposium* and *marzēaḥ* as a social institution. First of all the practice of ceremonial banquets with religious overtones and the consumption of alcohol with a leader elected for such an occasion show the link of *marzēaḥ* with Hellenistic *symposium*; Just as the Hellenistic *symposia*, *marzēaḥ* was a closed celebration of the social elite. Looking at the *marzēaḥ* text of Amos 6:4-7 we are able to see the close resemblance of the banquet traditions of the different Ancient Near Eastern cultures. The text shows in a striking manner how the banquet narration of the eighth century Palestine closely resembles that of the Hellenistic *symposia*:

> Alas for those who lie on beds of ivory, and lounge on their couches, and eat lambs from the flock, and calves from the stall; who sing idle songs to the sound of the harp, and like David improvise on instruments of music; who drink wine from bowls, and anoint themselves with the finest oils, but are not grieved over the ruin of Joseph! Therefore they

shall now be the first to go into exile, and the revelry of the loungers shall pass away (Amos 6:4-7).

The text demonstrates how the social upper class society of Samaria enjoyed luxurious and sumptuous banquets as in the Hellenistic *symposia* of later times. The banqueters do not sit for their meal; they recline in their well decorated couches. Their table is filled with different meat items "which was not part of the ordinary diet and thus a luxury."[217] Their banquet does not finish with eating. It is extended into wine. The fact that the banqueters do not drink wine from cups or glasses instead from bowls, shows that it was a lavish, unending and unrestrained drinking party. This drinking party is combined with music and entertainment. Hence the *marzēaḥ* in Amos closely resembles the sympotic banqueting behavior of the Greeks. We are able to see, though, that in *marzēaḥ* there was no distinct separation between the eating and the drinking, as it was in *symposium*.[218] The second use of *marzēaḥ* in the Old Testament is seen in Jer 16:5. The word is translated in LXX as θίασος. Here, however the word is seen in the funerary context, since בֵּית מַרְזֵחַ is translated in NRSV as the house of mourning. Fabry translates it as *"Haus des Festmahlhaltens."*[219] For him, an ordinary cultic meal was perhaps later combined with *"Trauer und Götzendienst."*[220]

There are also other banqueting texts in the prophetic literature which closely resemble the Hellenistic *symposia*. For example in Hos 4:16-19 we have the combination of excessive drinking of wine and sexual promiscuities, which was the case in the Hellenistic *symposia*. In Isa 5:11-13, the drinking guests are entertained with music. In Isa 28:1-4, the elite drinking group shows its financial power. Besides the banqueting guests are crowned with flower garlands, a custom practiced also in the Hellenistic *symposia*; All these instances in the prophetic literature attest to the adoption of the banqueting culture of the Ancient Near Eastern world by the Jewish upper class.

Book of Sirach and Banquets

The Book of Sirach gives answers to questions like, how much of influence the Greek culture had in Palestine and in Jerusalem at the second Temple period, what sort of response the Jews gave to the Greek culture, whether the Jews were resisting to the intrusion of the Greek practices and values in their daily life or whether they were welcoming such changes. It has been suggested that the Book of Sirach has been written in the early years of the second century BCE, somewhere around 200–180 BCE in Jerusalem, which was later translated into Greek in Egypt.[221] As a scribe and a teacher (cf. Sir 38:24–39:11) Jesus Ben Sirach must have had a school of his own, where he taught young pupils of Jerusalem about successful moral living according to the Torah. Although the book places the Temple cult and the priesthood in high pedestal, it does not seem to be in war with Hellenism;[222] rather the author shows himself as the one who has travelled far and wide to many countries and learnt from the wisdom of other cultures. Hence, the Wisdom that he imparts his pupils is not only 'Jewish' but universal; this wisdom, however, has its roots in the fear of the Lord and in keeping His commandments (1:26).

Clear Pointers to Hellenistic *Symposium* in Sirach

Apart from other practical teachings about the daily living, Sirach also teaches his students how to behave oneself at a banquet. The context is always *symposium* of the Greco-Roman world. The detailed narrations of the banqueting culture of the elite Jews in the book strongly suggests that the practice of *symposium* was well known to the aristocrats of Jerusalem in the Second Temple period. In Sir 11:29, Sirach advises that one should invite only friends for a banquet at home. When one is invited by a powerful person, one should show himself humble and reserved, so that he could be invited with more respect (Sir 13:9). Sirach must have been aware of many instances in the Greek literature where people had been portrayed as waiting to be invited for a *symposium*. On the contrary he advises his pupils not to be longing to be invited for a *symposium*, not even to immediately accept the offer of invitation to a banquet. Rather he has to be reserved so that he finds respect from the benefactor who invites him. The advice "Do not put him next to you, or he may overthrow you and take your place. Do not let him sit at your right hand, or else he may try to take your own seat" (Sir 12:12) informs the readers how the Hellenistic idea of seating arrangement of the guests was well known to the aristocracy of Palestine. Sirach's advice to his pupils was that they should not invite a stranger or an enemy to the banquet, even if he is invited he should not be selected to be the guest of honor, sitting at the right side of the host.

Just as Bdelycleon advises his ignorant father how to behave at a *symposium* (Aristoph. *Wasps* 1208-1264), Sirach imparts his students what behavior would earn them respect at a sympotic banquet and what would not. The entire section of Sir 31:12-32:13 deals with the *symposium* setting. Skehan divides the section into three; showing moderation in eating (Sir 31:12-21); the uses and abuses of wine (Sir 31:22-31); and right behavior at a *symposium* (Sir 32:1-13).[223] Every advice of the author suggests how well the author as well as his pupils and readers are acquainted with the proceedings of the Hellenistic *symposia*.

In the first section (31:12-21) Sirach advises his disciples to avoid greediness at meals and to be sensitive to the needs of the neighbor. Against the normal custom of Romans in the *convivia* to vomit so that one could eat well once again, Sirach advises here to eat moderately. Eating moderately and in a good manner and being the first to stop eating does not only help one gain respect among others but also does good to one's health (Sir 32:20; cf. *Prov* 23:1-6). He does however suggest his pupils to make use of the custom of vomiting in order to relieve oneself (Sir 31:21). In the second section (Sir 31:22-31) Sirach talks about the uses of wine which, if taken moderately, is 'life to human being.' Sirach says wine is the gift of God to humans to gladden their hearts (cf. Ps 104:15). But excessive drinking leads only to hatred and violence. As a well-read man in the ancient literature Sirach must have been aware of many such incidences of drunkenness and violence narrated in the literary *symposia*. He has also support for his saying in the Jewish Scriptures which condemn excessive drinking (Amos 6:6; Hos 7:5; Isa 5:11-12; 28:1; Prov 20:1; 23:29-35; 28:7). Through this advice against excessive drinking, "*Ben Sira* cannot be used to postulate a specifically Jewish modesty, because his advices are no more related to practical behavior."²²⁴ In the third and final section (Sir 32:1-13) Sirach talks about the duties of the *symposiarch*, the power of music at a *symposium*, and about how one should behave during the table talk. He caps the entire section with the advice of praising God who is responsible for all goods; this praising could be linked with the libation offered to the gods at a *symposion*.

We could see in all these verses a familiar acquaintance of Sirach with Hellenistic sympotic culture. This acquaintance could be the result of his extensive travelling that he attests in his book (Sir 34:12). The book also attests to the fact that the Hellenistic spirit and especially the spirit of sympotic culture was not foreign to the aristocracy of Palestine at the time of Sirach. Hence we could say that the Palestinian Judaism in the second Temple period was not antagonistic towards the Hellenistic culture. In this sense Sirach "is entirely open to Hellenic thought as long as it can be Judaized."²²⁵ Sirach is the best example of how Jewish moral and religious values could be successfully expressed in Hellenistic world view and how Hellenistic culture could be accommodated in Judaism without disturbing the Jewish religious tradition.

Symposium and the Meal Traditions of Different Jewish Sects

Just as sharing the common meal gave an identity for the sympotic groups of Greco-Roman world, different Jewish sects derived their identity through their partaking in a common meal. In the following we try to look at the meal traditions of some of the Jewish sects in the light of Hellenistic *symposium* and try to look at the commonalities as well as the differences between the banquets of Jewish sects and the Hellenistic sympotic banquets.

Meal Ideology of the Pharisees

Apart from the Gospel attestations, we come to know about Pharisees from Josephus Flavius. Both Josephus and the Mishna, a post 70 CE. text, confirm the picture that is given in the Gospels about the Pharisees. Pharisees are known for their strict observance of the Torah, the tithing and for their purity laws. They tolerated the foreign rule of Palestine, provided Torah was accepted to be the guiding principle of the lives of Jews. Neusner sees Pharisees as "Jewish mode of a common international cultural 'style' known as Hellenism,"[226] since their lifestyle and actions were similar to those of Greek philosophers. "Not only was the theory of the Pharisaic school like that of a school of Greek philosophy, but so were its practices. Its teachers taught without pay, like philosophers, they attached to themselves particular disciples who followed them around and served them, like philosophers; they looked for gifts for support, like philosophers..."[227] Above all their meal culture was similar to the Greek banqueting culture.

As a group, Pharisees held the view that a Jew should keep the purity laws even outside the Temple. Though they were not priests, they show their superior status by faithfully observing the temple purity in their daily lives. This applied very specially to everyday meal they took. "One must eat his secular food, that is, ordinary everyday meals, in a state of purity as if one were a Temple priest... (Hence) the table of every Jew in his home was seen to be like the table of the Lord in the Jerusalem Temple."[228] This is why the Pharisees are called a "society of table-fellowship"[229] which had more than half of their purity rules directly or indirectly related to their table fellowship. Those eating everyday meals in a state of purity are paralleled to the Temple priests eating the Temple sacrifices in a state of purity. This idea of every Jew as a priest, his home as the Temple and his table as the altar of Jerusalem Temple gained influence after 70 CE, once the Temple was no more. A rabbinic text points to this view clearly: "As long as the Temple stood, the altar atoned for Israel, but now a man's table atones for him."[230]

Symposium and the Table Fellowship of the Pharisees: Similarities

The comparison between the Pharisaic table fellowship with sympotic table fellowship shows that first of all, both Pharisees and Hellenistic *symposiasts* made use of food to strengthen their group identity. The way they viewed their table fellowship brought them together as a separate community within the larger society. While at Hellenistic *symposia* there was mainly an economic exclusivism of the participants based on their social and economic status, for the Pharisees there was a religious exclusivism of participants, based on the value of purity. Only those who strictly followed their standards of purity could participate in their fellowship meals.[231] Food for both Hellenistic *symposiasts* and Pharisees was 'ritualized.' For Pharisees, as it was for the elite participants of the Hellenistic *symposia*, partaking of this fellowship meal was understood to be a sign of confirmation of their social status in the society, a sign of "we" against "they." As it was in the Hellenistic *symposia*, the participants were to wash their feet, oil should be poured on their heads, and they should be kissed as a sign of welcome (cf. Luke 7:1-36). In the Pharisaic meal too, there was a hierarchy of the participants. Jesus' participation in the Pharisaic *symposia* shows that there were places of honor for the guests (Luke 14:7); As in the Hellenistic *symposia* there was a presence of 'sinful women' also in the Pharisaic *symposia*. Only the actions of this sinful woman towards Jesus and the action of Jesus allowing her to touch and kiss his feet were a cause of scandal for the Pharisees, while her actual presence in this elite group of the Pharisees seems to be tolerated. In short, one could say that the Pharisaic fellowship meal was something which was very similar to the Hellenistic *symposia*; the one point of departure however could be the religious motif of their fellowship meals – their preoccupation and striving towards purity of the group and of Israel.

The Gospel accounts portray Pharisees in a negative light; they are described as a group which always opposed Jesus and his message. Apart from the issue of observing Sabbath and tithing, the conflict between Jesus and Pharisees emerges especially with regard to the purity laws which they expected Jesus to follow during his meal time. While a Pharisee will never share his table with a tax collector who did not care to follow the law, Jesus eats happily with tax collectors and sinners; his disciples too do not observe the purity laws which the Pharisees held high; they do not wash hands before they eat and so do not have any regard for ritual purity. It is mainly in the aspect of meal and its purity and separation from everything and everyone unclean, that the schools of Pharisees and of Jesus differ and stand against each other.

The Essenes and their Meal Tradition

Essenes (Εσσαίοι or Ἐσσηνοί) are one of the sectarian groups that had lived from 2ⁿᵈ century BCE to the first century CE till the destruction of the Temple. Together with the Pharisees, they are said to be a group emerging out of the *Hasidim*, the Jewish group that was vehemently opposed to the influence of Hellenistic culture. Deeply dissatisfied with the affairs of the Hasmonean priesthood in Jerusalem, they withdrew from the mainstream of the society and started living together as a close knit community, first in different villages and cities and then at the caves near the Dead Sea. The destruction of the Qumran due to an earthquake in 31 BCE forced them to come back to the cities like Jerusalem. At this time the Essenes seem to have had the benevolence of Herod. Josephus talks about the Essene Gate and about their settlement in Jerusalem.[232] Once again they seem to have moved back to Qumran after the death of Herod.

To the question as to whether the Essenes and the Qumran Community are one and the same, many scholars are in the affirmative, saying they are the same community. According to Pliny the Elder the Essenes lived among palm trees. Archaeology proves that the place Khirbet where the community of Qumran flourished, had in fact plenty of palm trees. De Vaux has this to say regarding the identity of the Essenes and Qumran. "If Pliny was not mistaken and if we are not mistaken, the Essenes of whom he speaks are the community of Qumran."[233] Besides, the time of their existence, the internal organization of the community as narrated by Josephus about the Essenes, the findings from the excavations of the Dead Sea Scrolls and the importance given by them for the ritual purity are very similar.

Community Meals of the Essenes

In his works, especially in *The Jewish War*, Josephus narrates about how the Essenes lived as a table fellowship community.[234] The longest section is found in *the Jewish War* (J. BJ. 2.8.130-134) which presents a clear picture of the sect of the Essenes and their communal meals:

> Girding their loins with linen cloths, (they) bathe their bodies in cold water. After this purification, they assemble in a private apartment which none of the uninitiated is permitted to enter; pure now themselves, they repair to the refectory, as to some sacred shrine. When they have taken their seats in silence, the baker serves out the loaves to them in order, and the cook sets before each one plate with a single course. Before meat the priest says a grace, and none may partake until after the prayer. When breakfast is ended, he pronounces a further grace; thus at the beginning and at the close they do homage to God as the bountiful giver of life. Then laying aside their raiment, as holy vestments, they again betake themselves to their labours until the evening. On their return they sup in like manner, and any guests who may have arrived sit down with them. No clamour or disturbance ever pollutes their dwelling; they speak in turn, each making way for his neighbour. To persons outside the silence of those within appears like some awful mystery; it is in fact due to their invariable sobriety and to the limitation of their allotted portions of meat and drink to the demands of nature.[235]

The text shows how similar the practices of the Essenes were to the Hellenistic *symposia*. Just as the Hellenistic *symposiasts* took bath together, before attending a *symposium*, the members of the Essene community bathe themselves in cold water before attending the fellowship meal. Every meal of the Essenes (two meals a day) is narrated to have preceded by a bath. This was however not an ordinary bath but a ritual purification. The fact that only those members with a year of probation were permitted to participate in this purificatory bath, proves that it was a ritual bath. One required a special white robe for the meal and not all members could participate in it. Through the traditional white dress for the banquets and through the entering into the hall as if it was a holy shrine, we could find the sacredness of the meal. The meal was eaten in silence. If they spoke, they spoke one after another, so that the decorum of the community was kept. By portraying the fellowship meals of the Essenes in a so solemn way, Josephus might have aimed at contrasting the fellowship meals of the Essenes with the Hellenistic *symposia* where much noise and chaos were the rule of the day.[236] This is why Josephus states that such silence was for the outsiders an awful mystery. Hierarchical order was strictly kept in the Essene meals and the baker served the food according to the order; at the same time there was equality. Unlike in the Hellenistic sympotic gathering, where the guest of honor might receive better food, each one in the Essene community received the same portion from the cook.

Purity was the most important characteristic of the Essenes. Even if a senior member of the community was touched by chance by a novice, he had to wash himself. Such purity was strictly maintained also in the food. An Essene was not allowed to eat any food which was not prepared by his own community, for the fear of impurity. This is why, when an Essene was expelled from the community, he sometimes starved to death.

Dead Sea Scrolls on the Community Meal

"They shall eat together, together they shall bless and together they shall take counsel." (1 QS 6:2-3).[237] This statement from the Rule of the Community states how the fellowship meal was important for the Qumran Community. Archaeological findings attest to the custom of dining together. De Vaux narrates his findings of two huge dining halls and an adjacent room filled with thousands of pottery vessels of plates, bowls, cups and other serving vessels.[238] Such preservation of dining utensils shows that fellowship meal was central to the existence of the Qumran Community. That, which is narrated by Josephus, is corroborated by the Scrolls: the importance of the priest, the seating arrangement of the members according to the rank, blessing over the food and wine are some of them. The members entered the dining room in a procession according to their rank. The Rule of the Community explains how the community meal was celebrated:

> In every place where there are ten men of the Community council, there should not be a priest missing amongst them. And when they prepare the table to dine or the new wine for drinking, the priest shall stretch out his hand as the first to bless the first fruits of the bread or the new wine for drinking (1 QS 6:3-6).

Two things are striking. First, the Rule of the Community points out that the Qumran Community did not recline for its meal. Although there is a suggestion that the archaeological findings of bench-like objects could very well have been reclining couches at the dining rooms,[239] the clear statement of members sitting for the meals contrasts it from the sympotic setting. Secondly there is the presence of "new wine" which was not attested in Josephus. Pfann mentions that there was a wine press at the Qumran site.[240] The word used here for wine could refer to unfermented wine or grape juice. If so, the drinking of wine was not for enjoyment as it was the case in Hellenistic sympotic gatherings. Immediately after the explanation of the community meals comes the rule for the study of the Torah (1 QS 6:6-8). This reminds one of the Hellenistic literary *symposia,* where together with sympotic affairs, philosophical discussions or debates on *eros* took place. The members of the Qumran use the table talk not for philosophical discussion but for learning the Torah.

The Fellowship Meals of the Essenes - A Refined *Symposium*?
The contrasts between the Greco-Roman sympotic meals and the community meals of the Essenes are quite evident. At the very outset Josephus tells that the members "shun pleasures as a vice and regard temperance and the control of the passions as a special virtue ... riches, they despise" (J. *BJ.* 2.8.120, 122). Having self-control and overcoming passion were considered virtues, which was just the opposite of the sympotic gatherings, which were occasions created for the sheer purpose of satisfying sensual pleasures. Besides there was no presence of women in the Essene community as we hear from Philo "no Essene takes a wife" (Philo. *Hypoth.* 11:14).[241] This sets their fellowship meal clearly in contrast to the Greco-Roman *symposiasts* who used their fellowship meals for sexual licentiousness. Further the Essenes pooled all their properties together and so considered every one equal. This equality is shown in the distribution of equal portion of food. The hierarchy in the community was based not on the economic or social status as in the *symposia* of the Greeks and Romans, but on the gradation of their training (J. *BJ.* 2.8.150). There were other rules in the Qumran Community that contrast them from the Hellenistic *symposiasts*. 1 QS

6:8-13 commands that there should not be chaos in a discussion. First the man of higher rank is allowed to speak and then others. Every one speaks in turn. And when someone wants to convey something, he should not interrupt others but should let the community know it that he has something to say. Only then he is allowed to speak. In this way the author makes the community meals of the Essenes similar to the ideal scene in Plato's *Symposium*, where the participants take turns to speak in praise of *eros*. He also tries to contrast the community meals of the Essenes with the chaotic and unruly behavior at the sympotic settings which could be seen in different satires.

Banquet of the *Therapeutae*

Another sect whose important characteristic has something to do with banquets is the group of the *Therapeutae*. They are a group narrated in Philo's work *'On the Contemplative Life.'* The group is called so, because as Philo says, they were a people who knew the art of healing not just the body but also the soul. Since one of the meanings of θεραπεύω is "to serve a divinity,"[242] Philo calls them as those who serve and worship God (*Contempl.* 2). The word was commonly used in the Egyptian cults for those who consecrated themselves to the service of gods. Hence Philo might have used the term to denote the Jewish group who devoted themselves for the study and the service of God.[243] This was a group of people from the affluent class which abandoned everything it had, and came to a deserted place to lead a life of contemplation. Philo tells that this group lived "above the Mareotic Lake" (*Contempl.* 22). They did not live so near to the villages as to be disturbed by them, nor did they live so far from the villages fearing their safety, lest they be looted by robbers. Some consider that the *Therapeutae* are just a creation of Philo.[244] While it is difficult to convincingly prove the existence of the group, we do not go into the historicity of the *Therapeutae*; our concern in this work is only to look at Philo's texts and understand their banqueting behavior in relation to the Hellenistic *symposia*.

The Therapeutae and the Essenes

The fact that Philo elsewhere uses the same word Θεραπευταί θεοῦ for the Essenes, as the servers of God, leads to a discussion whether both the *Therapeutae* and the Essenes are linked to each other.[245] Both the groups abandoned the city life and came together to live a community life of solitude and contemplation. Both gave special attention to community prayer and worship; their special identity is shown by their fellowship meals. The food they ate was simple in contrast to the sympotic meals of the Hellenistic culture around them. During their meals both the groups had the exposition of the Scripture by the leaders.

There are, however, striking dissimilarities between the Essenes and the *Therapeutae*. The Essenes sold their property and brought the money to the community, whereas the *Therapeutae* did not need to sell their properties to enter into the community and so left it with their relatives. Their dwelling place was most suitable for an upper-class elite, which was not only safe from robbers but also most pleasant to live (*Contempl.* 23). The Essenes apart from their life of prayer also worked the whole day before they came together for fellowship meals, whereas the life of the *Therapeutae* was more contemplative than active. "The interval between early morning and evening is spent entirely in spiritual exercise. They read the Holy Scriptures and seek wisdom from their ancestral philosophy" (*Contempl.* 28). At times the elders are not said to have come out of their little houses for three, sometimes even six days at a stretch, having no desire or longing for food; for "they have become habituated to abstinence like the grasshoppers who are said to live on air" (*Contempl.* 35). Another important difference is that the Essenes were a male society; even if it were to be that there was a discussion about the presence of women in the Qumran Community, the coming together for praying and for the fellowship meal was strictly a male event whereas the *Therapeutae* included women in their community activities of singing, praying and fellowship meals (*Contempl.* 32, 69). On the whole in comparison to the *Therapeutae*, "The Essenes come across as more egalitarian and communalist but also more sexist, in that only males are included as members."²⁴⁶ These striking differences clarify to the readers that Philo wanted to make a contrast between these two groups rather than linking them together.

The *Symposium* of the *Therapeutae*

In his detailed description of the community meal of the *Therapeutae*, Philo informs on the one hand how the group had very much in common with the sympotic meal culture of the time, and on the other, he narrates how the procedures of the *symposium* of the group is in contrast with the drunken and violent banquets of the other societies (*Contempl.* 40, 64).

Before expounding on the banquet of the *Therapeutae*, Philo explains in detail how nauseating the situation at the Hellenistic *symposia* has been (*Contempl.* 40-56). The Greco-Roman *symposiasts* recline in couches decorated with costly materials. They are provided with every kind of meat available under land, sea and sky that one could possibly imagine. After they satisfy their senses of seeing and smelling they devour the food like barbarians. "When they are quite exhausted, their bellies crammed up to the gullets, but their lust still ravenous, impotent for eating (they turn to the drink)" (*Contempl.* 55). Heavily drunk and overpowered by wine, "those who but now came to the party sound in body and friendly at heart leave soon afterwards in enmity and with bodily mutilation - enmity in some cases calling for advocates and judges, mutilation in others requiring the apothecary and physician and the help that they can bring." (*Contempl.* 44). According to Philo even the literary *symposia* of Plato and Xenophon in which Socrates is shown to have taken part, were ridiculous in comparison with the pure *symposia* of the *Therapeutae* (*Contempl.* 58). For, the one (Xenophon's *Symposium*) is filled with the entertainments that induce the sense pleasures and the other (Plato's *Symposium*) is filled with discussions on "common vulgar love, which robs men of the courage" (*Contempl.* 60).

Over against this background Philo explains how the *Therapeutae* conducted themselves in their fellowship meals (*Contempl.* 64-89). The elders who resided within their cells for six days in solitude and prayer, came together for the community meal on the seventh day of the week and at the end of the seventh week (50th day) they made a great feast. Such fellowship meals of the community were in some ways similar to the *symposia* of the time. The participants reclined as was the case in any other *symposia*. Strict order and hierarchy was maintained in the seating arrangements. Women too were present in the fellowship meal. But in many other ways the *symposia* of the *Therapeutae* was completely different from the '*symposia* of the others.'

After praising God, the elders begin their fellowship meal, men on the one side and women on the other. The women who were present there, were not prostitutes as was the case in the *symposia* of the Hellenists; they were free members of the group and maintained purity in their body and soul. The couches they were in, were not costly ones but were made of rugs and papyrus of very ordinary quality, prepared by the younger ones in the community. There were no slaves present in the community. Those who served the elders were "freemen, who perform their tasks as attendants, not under compulsion nor yet waiting for orders, but with deliberate goodwill anticipating eagerly and zealously the demands that may be made" (*Contempl.* 71). Instead of wine the *Therapeutae* drank purest water – "cold for most of the guests but warm for such of the older men as they live delicately." (*Contempl.* 73). The food was simple and their table talk consisted of expounding the Scriptures, which was done by the head of the community. There was no interruption from the part of the hearers who "listen with ears pricked up and eyes fixed on him always in exactly the same posture, signifying comprehension and understanding by nods and glances, praise of the speaker by the cheerful change of expression which steals over the face, difficulty by a gentler movement of the head" (*Contempl.* 77). After applauding the speaker for his words of wisdom, they started singing Psalms or other hymns one after the other, praising God. Instead of drunken revelry the members of the *Therapeutae* made a festive vigil that night and celebrated till the dawn of the day singing in turns, men on one side and women on the other. At sunrise after having thanked God they went back once again to prayer and solitude (*Contempl.* 89).

Although Philo was not the first to attack the drunkenness and avariciousness and violence found at the Hellenistic *symposia,* by contrasting, "the ascetic *symposium* of the Jewish philosophers being opposed to that of the Greek Other, who lose control and indulge in beastly pleasures,"[247] Philo wants to idealize the banqueting culture of this Jewish group over against the Hellenistic *symposiasts*. By fulfilling the norms of Jewish ethics, the *Therapeutae* are portrayed completely in contrast to the uncontrolled behavior of the Hellenistic upper-class.

Symposium Motif in Other Jewish non-biblical Literature

An important question that arises on the banqueting culture of the Jews is about their openness to dine with people of other races. If the Jews of Palestine and the Diaspora Jews frequently engaged in *symposium,* were they open enough to recline at a banquet together with gentiles? How far could a Jew of the Second Temple period could balance between his observance of the laws of purity and his social interaction with the people of other cultures especially with regard to the meal customs? Smith writes, "even when the scholars argue that rabbis from the backwaters of Palestine were not affected by Greek ideas in any significant way, they nevertheless acknowledge that other aspects of culture did infiltrate."[248] Hence questions such as these were raised not only today but already in the second Temple Period. Attempts were made to answer these questions already in the Jewish non-biblical literature. Here we look at the *Letter of Aristeas* and the *Book of Joseph and Aseneth* and try to understand their stand on the sympotic culture and its impact on the Jewish milieu.

The Letter of Aristeas

The *Letter of Aristeas* contains the oldest written information about the origin of the LXX; it is considered to have been written by a Hellenistic Jew who must have probably lived in Alexandria. His work, written around the second half of the second century BCE,[249] shares the same feeling with the Book of Sirach, informing the readers about the importance of the Hellenistic culture and the Greek language for the Jews, not only for the Diaspora Jews but also for those living in Jerusalem.

What concerns this paper is the seven days' *symposium* which the Jewish sages had with Ptolemy and his gentile philosophers (*Arist.* 187-300). Six leaders from every tribe (altogether seventy two of them) are selected and sent by the High Priest Eleazar to Alexandria for translating the Torah into Greek. On the anniversary of Ptolemy's naval victory over Antigonus they are invited for the *symposium* with the King and the philosophers of the court. The seating arrangement is made by the overseer Dorotheus. "He set out the couches in two lines, in accordance with the royal command, because the king had ordered that half should sit at his right hand, and the rest behind his royal couch, leaving no stone unturned in his desire to do these delegates honor" (*Arist.* 183).[250] The place of honor is given to the eldest of the sages. Instead of praising the gentile gods, the Jewish banqueters praise Yahweh. During the table talk after the meal the King poses various questions on the kingship and the successful living, for which every one of the sage answers very wisely.[251] Amidst other entertainments, the King toasts to the health of the guests (*Arist.* 273). Banquet here as in *The Deipnosophists* serves to be an occasion where philosophical exchange takes place.

We learn from the author of the *Letter of Aristeas* that it was not wrong for the Jews of Palestine to participate in a *symposium* together with the gentiles. Not all the Jews considered eating with the gentiles as defiling. Sharing fellowship meals with the gentiles seems to be a problem only to those Jews who were rigorous in observing the Law. While for many diaspora Jews, it must not have been a problem to partake at a meal with the gentiles, since the book shows that Jews from Palestine including priests (*Arist.* 184), reclined here with gentiles. Hence in the words of Klawans, "it is an error to assume that Jews in ancient times generally considered Gentiles to be ritually defiling and it is even more of an error to assume that such a conception would have been an impediment to Jewish-Gentile interaction."[252] If Sirach was to advise Jerusalem youth to behave properly at a *symposium*, the Letter of Aristeas is about how well the Jews were regarded in the eyes of the Hellenists at *symposia*. As an apologetic work, the book aims at showing the greatness of the Jewish worldview and philosophy over against the Hellenistic philosophy, so much so that even the king and his philosophers admire greatly the wisdom of the Jews. In other words, the very purpose of the elders to go down to Alexandria is that the king lacks the much needed wisdom in his country. The gentile king and his philosophers (gentile philosophy altogether) lack the wisdom of the Jews, which consists in keeping the Lord above everything else, keeping him as the final answer for all the questions of the king.[253] Here we are able to see the purpose of the author in showing that although Jews could very well assimilate the culture of the Hellenists, they nevertheless keep their unique identity.

Joseph and Aseneth

If food had brought the Jews and gentiles together in the *Letter of Aristeas*; the same food would serve as a line of demarcation between a Jew and a gentile family in another book, again from Alexandria - *Joseph and Aseneth*. The date of its composition is still debated. With conversion as the main purpose of the book, it was earlier taken to be a fifth century Christian work;[254] although some put the work as early as 100 BCE – 115 CE,[255] together with Burchard and others, we assume that the work would have come to existence in the second century CE, and written in a Hellenistic background of Alexandria to woo the proselytes.[256]

Concept of Meal in *Joseph and Aseneth*

Apart from the marriage *symposia* which lasts for seven days, on which every man in Egypt is ordered by Pharaoh not to go for work (*JosAs* 21:6-7), there are other references to food, which stands as a barrier between *Joseph and Aseneth*. Aseneth is seen by Joseph as an 'untouchable' who ⊠with her mouth blesses dead and dumb idols, and eats of their table the bread of anguish, and drinks of their libations the cup of insidiousness" (*JosAs* 8:5)[257] and hence not worthy to kiss a Jew "who worships God, who will bless the living God with his mouth and eat the blessed bread of life, and drink a cup of immortality" (*JosAs* 8:5). After having received the honeycomb from the angel and eaten it, Aseneth tells Joseph later, "all the idols I have thrown away from me and they were destroyed. And a man came to me from heaven today, and gave me bread of life and I ate, and a cup of blessing and I drank." (*JosAs* 19:5). This reference to Bread of Life which comes very close to John´s description of Jesus as the Bread of Life (*Jn* 6:33, 41, 51),[258] does not however refer to some kind of a ritual meal like that of the *Therapeutae* or of the Essenes,; it rather refers to "to the totality of Jewish eating in contrast to heathen meals defiled by idolatry, and more generally to the entire Jewish way of life in contrast to heathen conduct."[259] Hence the meal that is presented in *Joseph and Aseneth* does not say much about the table fellowship that the Jews of Alexandria might or might not have had with the gentiles. The use of meal in this book is only to show the superiority of the Jews over against the gentiles, which could be seen not only here but in other instances as well such as Levi forgiving the gentile son of Pharaoh who wanted to kill Joseph (*JosAs* 23:2, 27:6).

The Passover Seder: A Jewish Symposium?
The festival of the Passover is one of the most important festivals of the Jews, in which they remember and celebrate how their ancestors were miraculously delivered by Yahweh from the bondages of Egypt. It was a festival of freedom and was the passing over of God through the houses of Israelites and striking the houses of Egyptians. It was the passing over of the Jews from their slavery to freedom. The feast took place on the 14th day of the first month of the year, *Nissan or Aviv*. The festival comes to the climax with the festive meal that begins at the twilight of the 14th of *Nissan*. In the biblical narrations however we are able to see at least two important differences in the ordinances for the celebration of the festival and the festive meal.

Celebration of the Passover: Biblical Instructions

The festival of the Passover and the festival of the unleavened bread is linked in the Bible. Hence while the Passover is celebrated on the 14th of Nissan, the festival of unleavened bread is done on the next day. The festival continues for seven days and the rules of celebrating the feast of the Passover is presented in *Exod* 12:1-13: On the tenth of the month the Israelites should select a one year old lamb; the head of the family slaughters it on the 14th evening, its blood is put on the doorposts and the lintel of the houses. The flesh is roasted in the fire and eaten with unleavened bread and bitter herbs; nothing of the sacrifice should remain for the next day and so the rest should be burnt.

We see that this first instruction manual teaches the Israelites to celebrate the festival at the households. The festival at this level has nothing to do with the Temple. Rather, the head of each family acts like the priest offering sacrifice and instructing the children about the redemption the forefathers received at the hands of Yahweh from the bonds of the Egyptians (Exod 12:26-27; 13:8). But in the Book of Deuteronomy we see a change in the celebration. The festival of Passover was to be celebrated and the meal eaten not at the houses of each Israelite nor within any other cities that God gave them, but only in the holy place where "God will choose" (Deut 16:2, 5). Only the next day they are supposed to go home (Deut 16:7). Besides, in this passage there is no mention of sprinkling of the blood on the doorposts.

In Ezra the festival is celebrated by those who returned from the exile. But "the duties of every householder, is transferred in Ezra to the tasks of the priests and Levites."[260] For it is not the heads of the household but the priests who slaughter and offer the sacrifice, which is eaten by all the people. The same is seen also in 2 *Chr* 30 and 35 where Hezekiah and Josiah invite all the Israelites to come to Jerusalem to celebrate the Passover. This suggests the evolution of the festival and the centralization of the sacrifice in the second Temple period by the priestly author, who institutes Passover as one of the three major feasts of Israel in which all the Israelite males are obliged to come to Jerusalem to offer sacrifice (*Deut* 16:16-17). This is why Jesus celebrates Passover in Jerusalem on the eve of his arrest.

The situation is different after 70 CE. Once the Temple is no more, the rules of celebrating the Passover are described in detail in the Passover Seder of Mishnah. The reasons for such an elaborate *order* of the Passover ritual could be "the general increase in midrashic exegesis since the beginning of the Christian era, the amalgamation and harmonization of a great variety of these rabbinic traditions, eschatological expectations side by side with the attempt to organize national resistance against Rome, and the tendency to stress the antiquity of the Jewish people."[261] What concerns this paper the most is the close link that we could see between the Passover Seder and the rituals of Hellenistic *symposia* which is strikingly evident in the description of the *Mishna Pesachim*:

Mishna Pesachim 10

1. On the eve of Passover, from about the time of the Evening Offering, a man must eat naught until nightfall. Even the poorest in Israel must not eat unless he sits down to table, and they must not give them less than four cups of wine to drink, even if it is from the [Paupers'] Dish.

2. After they have mixed him his first cup, the School of Shammai say: He says the Benediction first over the day and then the Benediction over the wine. And the School of Hillel say: He says the Benediction first over the wine and then the Benediction over the day.

3. When [food] is brought before him he eats it seasoned with lettuce, until he is come to the breaking of bread; they bring before him unleavened bread and lettuce and the *haroseth,* although *haroseth* is not a religious obligation. R. Eliezer b. R. Zadok says: It is a religious obligation. And in the Holy City they used to bring before him the body of the Passover offering.

4. They then mix him the second cup. And here the son asks his father (and if the son has not enough understanding his father instructs him [how to ask]), 'Why is this night different from other nights? For on other nights we eat seasoned food once, but this night twice; on other nights we eat leavened or unleavened bread, but this night all is unleavened; on other nights we eat flesh roast, stewed, or cooked, but this night all is roast.' And according to the understanding of the son his father

instructs him. He begins with the disgrace and ends with the glory; and he expounds from *'A wandering Aramean was my father . . .'* until he finishes the whole section.

5. Rabban Gamaliel used to say: Whosoever has not said [the verses concerning] these three things at Passover has not fulfilled his obligation. And these are they: Passover, unleavened bread, and bitter herbs: 'Passover' - because God passed over the houses of our fathers in Egypt; 'unleavened bread' - because our fathers were redeemed from Egypt; 'bitter herbs' - because the Egyptians embittered the lives of our fathers in Egypt. In every generation a man must so regard himself as if he came forth himself out of Egypt, for it is written. *And thou shalt tell thy son in that day saying, It is because of that which the Lord did for me when I came forth out of Egypt.* Therefore are we bound to give thanks, to praise, to glorify, to honour, to exalt, to extol, and to bless him who wrought all these wonders for our fathers and for us. He brought us out from bondage to freedom, from sorrow to gladness, and from mourning to a Festival-day, and from darkness to great light, and from servitude to redemption; so let us say before him the *Hallelujah*.

6. How far do they recite [the *Hallel*]? The School of Shammai say: To *A joyful mother of children*. And the School of Hillel say: To a *flintstone into a springing well*. And this is concluded with the *Ge'ullah*. R. Tarfon says: 'He that redeemed us and redeemed our fathers from Egypt and brought us to this night to eat therein unleavened bread and bitter herbs.' But there is no concluding Benediction. R. Akiba adds: 'Therefore, O Lord our God and the God of our fathers, bring us in peace to the other set feasts and festivals which are coming to meet us, while we rejoice in the building-up of thy city and are joyful in thy worship; and may we eat there of the sacrifices and of the Passover-offerings whose blood has reached with acceptance the wall of thy Altar, and let us praise thee for our redemption and for the ransoming of our soul. Blessed art thou, O Lord, who hast redeemed Israel!'

7. After they have mixed for him the third cup he says the Benediction over his meal. [Over] a fourth [cup] he completes the *Hallel* and says after it the Benediction over song. If he is minded to drink [more] between these cups he may drink; only between the third and the fourth cups he may not drink.

8. After the Passover meal they should not disperse to join in revelry. If some fell asleep [during the meal] they may eat [again]; but if all fell

asleep they may not eat [again]. R. Jose says: If they but dozed they may eat [again]; but if they fell into deep sleep they may not eat [again].

9. After midnight the Passover-offering renders the hands unclean. The Refuse and Renmant make the hands unclean. If a man has said the Benediction over the Passover-offering it renders needless a Benediction over [any other] animal-offering [that he eats]; but if he said the Benediction over [any other] animal-offering it does not render needless the Benediction over the Passover-offering. So R. Ishmael. R. Akiba says: Neither of them renders the other needless.[262]

The Passover Seder and Hellenistic *Symposia*: Some Similarities

Bahr and others give an elaborate description of how the festive meal went on, and how the similarities between *symposia* and Passover Seder are very obvious.[263] At first the participants of the Passover meal are seated in a room adjacent to the main room for meal – just like the ante chamber adjacent to the Greek ἄνδρων. The *Mishna Pesachim* commands that the Passover meal should not be eaten unless it is dark and "even the poorest in Israel must not eat unless he sits down to table." (*m. Pes.* 10:1); reclining thus becomes mandatory for the Passover meal as it was in the sympotic gatherings. The participants too were male, as it was in the Hellenistic *symposia*. Stein says, "Women take no part in the Seder liturgy. Apparently they did not even serve upon their guests and the members of their household. The Mishnah knows only of the paschal lamb prepared by husband or father for wife or daughter respectively."[264] To these men who recline for the Passover meal, four cups of wine are to be served. Just as it was in the Hellenistic sympotic gatherings, in the Passover Seder too initial rituals of washing are done to the diners. When all are present, hands of the guests are washed[265] and the first cup of wine is served. The use of waiters who serve upon the guests is also similar in both the cases. Each of the diners said a benediction over the first cup. The benediction goes thus, "Blessed are you O Lord our God, King of the universe and Creator of the fruit of wine." One could immediately remember the libations that were offered to the deities as the wine was drunk at every *symposium*. The first course of meal containing bitter herbs, eggs, fruits and nuts are brought and blessing is said over the food.

After the first course of meals, the diners went to the dining room proper, where they reclined for their main course of meals. As we have seen in the M. *Pesachim*, it is mandatory that the diners reclined during the Passover meal. Once they reclined the second cup of wine is brought and the wine is mixed, just like at a sympotic meal. The mixing however is done not in a *krater* but individually in each cup of the diner. Over the second cup one said the benediction for all present. The meal was brought by the servants over which the host said the blessing for which the diners responded with Amen. The meal contained unleavened bread, bitter herbs and fruits and in Jerusalem paschal lamb (*m. Pes.* 10:3). In the *Tosefta Pesachim* one finds the blessing over the Passover: "What is the blessing of the Passover-offering? 'Blessed who sanctified us with his commandments and commanded us to eat the Passover-offering'⊠ (*t. Pes.* 10:13).²⁶⁶ During the main meal the child asks questions about the rituals and the history of redemption is narrated. The father gives answer beginning from 'disgrace' and ending it with 'glory.' Such conversation could be very well compared to the table talk that took place in the Hellenistic *symposia*. Stein sees a clear link between these *mah nishtanna* questions of children and the sympotic questions in Plutarch's *Table Talk*.²⁶⁷ As it was in the sympotic gatherings there were games to entertain and occupy the attention of the diners and to keep the children awake commands that the diners grab unleavened bread of each other to astonish the children so that they do not fall asleep (*t. Pes.* 10:9b).

At the end of the main course the diners in the Passover meal sing the first part of *Hallel* (beginning with Ps 113). Then similar to the sympotic gathering after δεῖπνον, the floor is swept, the table is cleaned, and the third cup of wine and the dessert are brought. The fourth and the final cup of wine is served which is blessed and the final part of *Hallel* is sung (Ps 118). Mishna is very particular to say that the diners do not end the festival with *afiqimon* (*m. Pes.* 10:8). Whether *afiqimon* is to be understood as a dessert course[268] or as the after drinking revelry of the Hellenistic *symposia*[269] this specific admonition might indicate to the readers that the Seder makes a deliberate attempt to distinguish the identity of the Passover from that of *symposia*.

Symposia and the Passover Seder - Differences

There are also differences between the festive meals of *symposia* and the Seder. Bokser provides many instances in which the Seder is distinct from *symposia*.[270] The *symposia* was a gathering for the rich elite of the society and it was for a limited group of equal status. But Mishnah instructs and invites all to participate regardless of one's economic background. Bokser sees the drinking of wine in both the festive meals as different from each other. While *symposiasts* drank for the sake of pleasure the participants of the Seder drank wine in a purely religious context. The ritual dipping of bitter herbs twice is also different from the sympotic customs of the Hellenists. Besides, the drinking of wine and singing in the Seder are made sure not to degenerate into immorality; this is done by the command not to drink between the third and the fourth cup, when the climax of *Hallel* is sung (*m. Pes.* 10:7). The distinction between the Seder and the *symposia* is made very clear by the admonition in the Seder not to involve in *afiqimon* – the drunken revelry that often took place after the Hellenistic sympotic gatherings. All these show for Bokser the distinct characteristics of the Seder.

One is however able to see clear the links between the two, when one looks at the way both the festive meals are celebrated. The command to recline, the equality of the persons reclining regardless of the fact whether one is poor or rich (*m. Pes.* 10:1), ritual washing of hands, saying benediction over wine, singing during the meal and above all intellectual discussion over the meal... all these rituals of the Passover Seder are striking parallels to the Hellenistic *symposia*. Though the rules of *Mishnah* and *Tosefta Pesachim* take pains to distinguish the *Seder* from *symposia* through different sets of rules, we learn that the very attempt itself shows how Passover Seder was seen similar to the Greco-Roman *symposia*. Though we could resist the temptation to say that the Passover Seder is a Jewish *symposium*, we cannot outrightly reject the fact that the order of Passover Seder, the festive meal of the Jews is very much influenced by the order of the *symposia* which was the most prevalent norm of festive meals of the Hellenistic world. Sympotic meals would have already become the norm of festive meals of every culture at that period. Jews were no exception to this.

To sum up this part on the Jewish response to the sympotic culture, we could say that as a country that was under foreign rule for hundreds of years, Palestine was forced to accommodate itself to different cultural elements of the time. In the Old Testament as well as among different groups of people, we could see both standpoints – one that fiercely opposed such cultural accommodations as well as the other that welcomed it, provided, the Jews retained their unique identity. While on the one hand Amos pronounces judgments against those who 'recline' for banquets, Sirach on the other is at home with it. While on the one hand members of the Qumran Community and the *Therapeutae* portray their fellowship meal as unique and different from the sympotic culture, on the other the people in general and the Jewish political leaders in particular seemed to be at home with it. The successful Maccabean revolt against the imposition of the Hellenistic culture could not stop the intrusion of the sympotic culture. The tension between these two world views characterize the response of Judaism towards the sympotic culture of Greco-Romans. Hence as a society that adapted itself to other cultures of the time, Judaism benefitted from the sympotic culture and its meal rituals of the time. It tried to take from it what was beneficial to it, while rejecting from *symposium* what it found to be immoral and frivolous.

Overview

We began this chapter with a brief outline of the meal customs of the Greeks as well as Romans. We saw how δεῖπνον was transformed from being an ordinary meal at home, to a dinner party with friends. With its elaborate rituals and definite set of regulations around it (for example, how one has to be invited, how one has to behave at a *symposium*, what sort of role is to be played by the host, the guest and the leader of the *symposium* and how the drinking guests should be entertained), *symposium* has made the participants a microcosm of the larger society. With a unique place for such a banquet gathering - ἄνδρων, built in a unique way, with unique sets of furniture and utensils especially used for such table fellowship, with unique set of games played especially at such gatherings and with unique type of poetry, performed at these gatherings, *symposium* has occupied and fascinated the minds of the elite as well as the learned of the Hellenistic world for centuries, so much so that philosophers like Plato, Plutarch and others made out of it a literary genre with which they could impart their ideals to the society. Hence without the mention of *symposium / convivium* one cannot comprehensively talk of Hellenistic culture.

We have also seen that Jewish meal culture has to be looked at in a broader perspective and how *symposium* has affected the world view of Palestine, its different sectarian groups, its festivals and above all the very Scripture of Judaism. This takes the paper forward to the first century Paestinian world, in which the historical Jesus lived and worked.

What did the cultural set up of Galilee in which Jesus grew up teach him? If he had gentile contact, how far did it affect his world view and his teachings? Was he at home with Hellenistic practices, especially with meal customs like *symposium*? Where did the Lukan Jesus stand in this tension between attraction towards Hellenistic culture and unadulterated practice of Jewish culture? Did the historical Jesus (as well as the Lukan Jesus) ever participate at *symposia*? In short, can the Lukan Jesus be called a *symposiast*? These are the questions that catch our attention now. Perhaps the next chapter will throw light on these questions.

Endnotes

[1] Watson designates c. 800 BCE – 500 BCE as archaic period, during which city states were established and ruled by aristocrats. During the classical period, c. 500 – 338 BCE philosophy and literature and architecture flourished. In the

Hellenistic period, c. 338 – 146 BCE, Greek culture spread far and wide, thanks to the military expeditions of Alexander the Great. With the steady emergence of Rome as powerful empire 146 BCE onwards the term Greek was understood to denote more the Greek culture than a nation._D_. F. Watson, "Greece and Macedon," in *Dictionary of New Testament Background*, ed. C. A. Evans and S. E. Porter, *The IVP Bible Dictionary Series* (Downers Grove, Ill: InterVarsity Press, 2000), 421-426. More or less a similar chronology of ancient Greece is given by Murray in D. Sacks, O. Murray, and L. R. Brody, *Encyclopedia of the Ancient Greek World* (New York: Facts On File, 2005), xviii-xx.

² D. E. Smith, *From Symposium to Eucharist: The Banquet in the Early Christian Wrld* (Minneapolis: Fortress Press, 2003) 18-19.

³ G. Bruns, "Kuchenwesen und Mahlzeiten," in *Archaeologia Homerica*, ed. F. Matz and H.G. Buchholz (Göttingen: Vandenhoeck & Ruprecht, 1967-) Q, 57-58.

⁴ E. A. Gardner and D. Litt, "Food and Drink, Meals, Cooking and Entertainments," in *A Companion to Greek Studies*, 4th ed., ed. L. Whibley (Cambridge Eng: Cambridge University Press, 1931), 641; we do not find the usage of this word κράτισμα in Homer. This signifies the later development of this meal time; cf. G. Bruns, "Kuchenwesen und Mahlzeiten." Q, 58; also G. Hotze, *Jesus als Gast: Studien zu einem Christologischen Leitmotiv im Lukasevangelium* (Würzburg: Echter Verlag, 2007), 190-191; W. S. Davis, *A Day in Old Athens* (Boston, New York etc: Allyn and Bacon, 1914), 175. D. E. Smith, *From Symposium to Eucharist*, 20.

⁵ Athenaeus, *The Deipnosophists: With an English translation by Charles Burton Gulick*, [Loeb Classical Library.] (London, New York: William Heinemann; G. P. Putnam's Sons, 1957). Dio Cassius also talks about four ~~meal times~~mealtimes: κράτισμα, ριστον, δεÖπνον and μεταδόρπιον. Cass Dio 65. 2, as cited in J. Marquardt, *Das Privatleben der Römer* (Darmstadt: Wissenschaftliche Buchgesellschaft, 1975), 257.

⁶ J. Marquardt, *Das Privatleben der Römer*, 258-259.

⁷ J. P. V. D. Balsdon, *Life and Leisure in Ancient Rome* (London: Bodley Head, 1969), 25; along the similar line, J. Carcopino, *Daily Life in Ancient Rome: The People and the City at the Height of the Empire*, Peregrine Books (S.l: Penguin, 1964), 287.

⁸ Cf. J. Marquardt, *Das Privatleben der Römer*, 257.

⁹ J. P. V. D. Balsdon, *Life and Leisure in Ancient Rome*, 20.

¹⁰ D. E. Smith, *From Symposium to Eucharist*, 21.

¹¹ D. E. Smith, "Social Obligation in the Context of Communal Meals: A Study of the Christian Meal in 1 Corinthians in Comparison with Graeco-Roman Communal Meals" (Harvard University, 1980), 10.

¹² D. Matz, *Daily Life of the Ancient Romans*, The Greenwood Press "Daily life through history" series (Indianapolis IN: Hackett Pub. Co, 2008), 24; in early Roman period there is no mention of *gustatio* – only the main course and the dessert; cf. J. Marquardt, *Das Privatleben der Römer*, 323.

¹³ On normal days the evening meal was served, not at a *triclinium*, which was set apart for big occasions, but in a small room called *cenatio*. Cf. J. P. V. D. Balsdon, *Life and Leisure in Ancient Rome*, 33.

¹⁴ E. Gowers, *The Loaded Table: Representations of Food in Roman Literature* (Oxford: The Clarendon Press, 1993), 25.

¹⁵ Passages from the two parts of *The Table Talk* of Plutarch are quoted in this paper from Plutarque, P. A. Clement, and H. B. Hoffleit, *Plutarch's Moralia*, The Loeb Classical Library (London, Cambridge: Heinemann; Harvard Un. Press, 1986) and E. L. Minar, JR., F. H. Sandbach, and W. C. Helmbold, *Plutarch's Moralia: With an English Translation*, 15 vols., LCL 9 (Cambridge, Massachusets, London: Harvard University Press; William Heinemann, 1961).

¹⁶ E. A. Gardner and D. Litt, "Food and Drink, Meals, Cooking and Entertainments." 642.

¹⁷ K. Vössing, "Family and Domesticity," in *A Cultural History of Food in Antiquity*, ed. P. Erdkamp, 6 vols., 1 (London: Berg, 2012), 143.

¹⁸ M. Wκcowski, "Homer and the Origins of the Symposion," in *Omero Tremila Anni Dopo*, ed. P. Ascheri and F. Montanari, 210 (Roma: Edizioni di Storia e Letteratura, 2002), 626. Cf. also H. G. Liddell and R. Scott, *A Greek-English Lexicon* (Oxford: Clarendon Press, 1968), 1685.

¹⁹ O. Murray, "The Greek Symposion in History," in *Tria corda*, ed. E. Gabba and A. Momigliano, *Biblioteca di Athenaeum* 1 (Como: Ed. New Press, 1983), 257.

²⁰ Ibid., 258; others authors with a similar opinion are J. Székely, *Structure and Theology of the Lucan 'Itinerarium': (Lk 9,51-19,28)* (Budapest: Szent Jeromos Katolikus Bibliatársulat, 2008), 141; P. Garnsey, *Food and Society in Classical Antiquity*, Key themes in ancient history (Cambridge: Cambridge University Press, 1999), 129.

²¹ Cf. K. M. D. Dunbabin, *The Roman Banquet: Images of Conviviality* (New York: Cambridge University Press, 2003), 19; Smith states that guests were sometimes invited only for the συμπόσιον and not for the δεῖπνον; D. E. Smith, *From Symposium to Eucharist*, 16-18; O. Murray, "Sympotic History," in *Sympotica: A Symposium on the Symposion*, ed. O. Murray (Oxford: Clarendon Press, 1990), 6.

[22] W. Bauer, *Griechisch-Deutsches Wörterbuch: Zu den Schriften des Neuen Testaments und der übrigen Urchristlichen Literatur* (Berlin, Newyork: Walter de Gruyter, 1965), herausgegeben von Kurt Aland und Barbara Aland, 1556-1557.

[23] P. Garnsey, *Food and Society in Classical Antiquity*, 134.

[24] W. G. Williams, *Cicero: The Letters to His Friends: With an English Translation*, 3 vols., LCL 2 (London, Cambridge, Massachusetts: William Heinemann; Harvard University Press, 1952). Similar differentiation between *symposium* of the Greeks and the *convivium* of the Romans could also be seen in J. D´Arms, "The Roman Convicium and the Idea of Equality," in *Sympotica: A Symposium on the Symposion*, ed. O. Murray (Oxford: Clarendon Press, 1990), 311; K. M. D. Dunbabin, *The Roman Banquet*, 13; E. Gowers, *The Loaded Table*, 25; P. Garnsey, *Food and Society in Classical Antiquity*, 136.

[25] A. T. Murray, *Homer: The Odyssey: With an English Translation*, 2 vols., LCL 2 (Cambridge, Massachusetts, London: Harvard University Press; William Heinemann, 1919).

[26] O. Murray, "Histories of Pleasures," in *In Vino Veritas*, ed. O. Murray and M. Tecuşan (Oxford: The Alden Press, 1995), 8.

[27] For further evidences in Homer, O. Murray, "The Culture of the Symposion," in *A Companion to Archaic Greek World*, ed. K. Raaflaub and H. Wees, *Blackwell Companion to the Ancient World* (Malden, MA: Blackwell, 2006), 546; also O. Murray, "The Greek Symposion in History." 250-260. M. Węcowski, "Homer and the Origins of the Symposion." 625-637.

[28] O. Murray, "The Greek Symposion in History." 260; ταὖρος is understood by Danker to be a "person who has something in common with others and enjoys association, but not necessarily at the level of a φwλος or φίλη, comrade, companion," F. W. Danker and W. Bauer, eds., *A Greek-English lexicon of the New Testament and other early Christian literature*, 3rd ed. (Chicago, London: University of Chicago Press, 2000), 780.

[29] For Murray, the Cup of Nestor signifies a transition between the Homeric feasts and the new form of conviviality, the συμπόσιον with its specific characteristics - the custom of reclining and the clear separation between eating and drinking. Cf. O. Murray, "Nestor´s Cup and the Origin of the Greek Symposion," in *Annali di archeologia e storia antica* (Napoli: [s.n.], 1994), 48; also M. Węcowski, "Homer and the Origins of the Symposion." 633-634.

[30] O. Murray, "The Greek Symposion in History." 263.

[31] P. Garnsey, *Food and Society in Classical Antiquity*, 130; O. Murray, "The Affair of the Mysteries: Democracy and the Drinking Group," in *Sympotica: A Symposium on the Symposion*, ed. O. Murray (Oxford: Clarendon Press, 1990), 151.

³² F. Hobden, *The Symposion in Ancient Greek Society and Thought* (Cambridge: Cambridge University Press, 2013), 9; O. Murray, "The Culture of the Symposion." 511.

³³ J. Morgan, "Drunken Men and Modern Myths: Reviewing the Classical Andron," in *Sociable Man: Essays on Ancient Greek Social Behaviour in Honour of Nick Fisher*, ed. S. D. Lambert, N: R. E. Fisher and D. L. Cairns (Swansea: Classical Press of Wales, 2011), 269; In Herodotus, the νδρων in the palace of Croesus was a room where weapons were stored; cf. M. Jameson, "Private Space and the Greek City," in *The Greek city: From Homer to Alexander*, ed. O. Murray and S. R. F. Price (Oxford: Clarendon, 1990), 188; also D. E. Smith, *From Symposium to Eucharist*, 25-26; J. A. S. Evans, *Daily Life in the Hellenistic Age: From Alexander to Cleopatra*, Daily life through history series (Westport, Conn: Greenwood Press, 2008), 101.

³⁴ The reference to the *ante-chamber* is also found in the practices of the Jewish festive meals. In the Tannaitic texts like T. Berakoth, we find the following rules for the festive meal. "What is the order of the meal? The guests enter [the house] and sit on benches, and on chairs until all have entered. They all enter and they [servants] give them water for their hands. Each one washes one hand. They [servants] mix for them the cup; each one says the benediction for himself. They [servants] bring them the appetizers; each one says the benediction for himself. They [guests] go up [to the dining room] and they recline, and they [servants] give them [water] for their hands..." as quoted in G. J. Bahr, "The Seder of Passover and the Eucharistic Words," *NT* 12, no. 2 (1970), 182.

³⁵ B. Bergquist, "Sympotic Space: A Functional Aspect of Greek Dining-Rooms," in *Sympotica: A Symposium on the Symposion*, ed. O. Murray (Oxford: Clarendon Press, 1990), 37-65; cf. also K. M. D. Dunbabin, *The Roman Banquet*, 36-37.

³⁶ For further studies on the shape of νδρων in different cities of ancient Greece, cf. B. Bergquist, "Sympotic Space: A Functional Aspect of Greek Dining-Rooms." 37-65; F. Cooper and S. Morris look at the archeological evidences for round buildings which were used for the purpose of *symposium*; F. Cooper and S. Morris, "Dining in Round Buildings," in *Sympotica: A Symposium on the Symposion*, ed. O. Murray (Oxford: Clarendon Press, 1990), 66-85.

³⁷ K. M. D. Dunbabin, *The Roman Banquet*, 38.

³⁸ B. Bergquist, "Sympotic Space: A Functional Aspect of Greek Dining-Rooms." 45-46.

³⁹ J. Morgan, "Drunken Men and Modern Myths: Reviewing the Classical Andron," in *Sociable Man: Essays on Ancient Greek Social Behaviour in Honour of Nick Fisher*, ed. S. D. Lambert, N R. E. Fisher and D. L. Cairns (Swansea: Classical Press of Wales, 2011) 267.

⁴⁰ J. Marquardt, *Das Privatleben der Römer*, 302; J. P. V. D. Balsdon, *Life and Leisure in Ancient Rome*, 35; D. E. Smith, *From Symposium to Eucharist*, 26; J. Carcopino, *Daily Life in Ancient Rome*, 288; E. LaVerdiere, *Dining in the Kingdom of God: The Origins of the Eucharist in the Gospel of Luke* (Chicago, IL: Liturgy Training Publications, 1994), 17.

⁴¹ For the details of the decorations in a Roman *triclinia*, R. Ling, "The Decoration of Roman Triclinia," in *In Vino Veritas*, ed. O. Murray and M. Tecuşan (Oxford: The Alden Press, 1995), 239-251.

⁴² Morgan, "Drunken Men and Modern Myths: Reviewing the Classical Andron." 273.

⁴³ K. M. D. Dunbabin, "Triclinium and Stibadium," in *Dining in a Classical Context: Symposium on Symposia*, ed. W. J. Slater (Ann Arbor: University of Michigan Press, 1991), 124.

⁴⁴ Ibid., 130.

⁴⁵ R. L. Hunter, *Plato's Symposium*, Oxford approaches to classical literature (Oxford, New York: Oxford University Press, 2004), 6.

⁴⁶ C. Moulton, ed., *Ancient Greece and Rome: An Encyclopedia for Students* (New York: Scribner, 1998) vol. 2, 67.

⁴⁷ Cf. W. S. Davis, *A Day in Old Athens*, 181.

⁴⁸ C. Moulton, *Ancient Greece and Rome*, vol. 4, 55; cf. also F. Moscato, "The Symposium," in *Symposion: La Cultura del Vino nei Valori Della Conoscenza Storica e Nelle Strategie di Mercato*, ed. S. Menghini (Firenze: Firenze Univ. Press, 2012), 65; J. A. S. Evans, *Daily Life in the Hellenistic Age*, 92.

⁴⁹ Passages from the writings of Horace are taken in this paper from Horace, *Satires, Epistoles, Ars Poetica: trasl. H. R. Fairclough*, Loeb Classical Library 194 (Cambridge, Mass, London: Harvard University Press; W. Heinemann, 1978). The mistress of the host also helped out in the foreseeing of the arrangements. Cf. W. S. Davis, *A Day in Old Athens*, 181-182; E. A. Gardner and D. Litt, "Food and Drink, Meals, Cooking and Entertainments." 642;

⁵⁰ J. Wilkins and S. Hill, *Food in the Ancient World*, Ancient Cultures (Oxford: Blackwell Publishing, 2006), 46; W. S. Davis, *A Day in Old Athens*, 181-182.

⁵¹ E. Gowers, *The Loaded Table*, 8.

⁵² Cf. K. M. D. Dunbabin, *The Roman Banquet*, 72.

⁵³ Marquardt cites the famous quotes about the desired number of participants in a *Convivium*: "*Septem Convivium, novem vero convicium*" meaning 'Seven makes a dinner, nine makes a brawl' which is a saying found in a *stibadium* mosaic. J. Marquardt, *Das Privatleben der Römer*, 307, cf. also J. Rositter, "Convivium and Villa in Late Antiquity," in *Dining in a Classical Context: Symposium on Symposia*,

ed. W. J. Slater (Ann Arbor: University of Michigan Press, 1991), 203 and 211; also J. P. V. D. Balsdon, *Life and Leisure in Ancient Rome*, 35.

[54] P. Erdkamp, "Introduction: Food and Commensality in the Ancient Near East," in *A Cultural History of Food in Antiquity*, ed. P. Erdkamp, 6 vols., 1 (London: Berg, 2012), 12.

[55] K. Chan-Hie, "The Papyrus Invitation," *JBL* 94 (1975), 392; Chan-Hie at the end of the article says that the rarity of such written invitations could be a proof for the fact that mostly invitation was given orally; cf. also J. F. Gilliam, "Invitations to the Kline of Sarapis," in *Collectanea papyrologica: Texts publ. in honor of Herbert Chayyim Youtie*, ed. A. E. Hanson, *Papyrologische Texte und Abhandlungen* 19 (Bonn: Habelt, 1976), 315-324; D. E. Smith, *From Symposium to Eucharist*, 23.

[56] W. Braun, *Feasting and Social Rhetoric in Luke 14*, Monograph series / Society for New Testament Studies 85 (Cambridge: Cambridge Univ. Press, 1995), 102; Balsdon talks about ´dinner suits´ in the late republic and early Empire period, which a guest of a noble society wore when he went for a *symposium*. This suit "consisted of a tunic and a smallish cloak (*palliolum*), both made of very light material for use in summer and of heavier stuff for use in winter. Both garments were of the same, usually very bright in color." J. P. V. D. Balsdon, *Life and Leisure in Ancient Rome*, 34. Jesus´s mention of a man without the wedding garment in the Parable of the Wedding Banquet acquires its significance from this background (Matt 22:11-12).

[57] W. R. M. Lamb, *Plato: Lysis, Symposium, Gorgias: With an English Translation*, LCL (London, New York: William Heinemann; G. P. Putnam´s Sons, 1925).

[58] W. S. Davis, *A Day in Old Athens*, 181.

[59] As quoted in J. P. V. D. Balsdon, *Life and Leisure in Ancient Rome*, 33.

[60] A. M. Harmon, *Lucian: With an English Translation*, 8 vols., LCL 2 (London, Cambridge, Massachusetts: William Heinemann; Harvard University Press, 1960).

[61] F. Lissarrague, *The Aesthetics of the Greek Banquet: Images of Wine and Ritual; translated by Andrew Szegedy-Maszak* (Princeton, N.J., Oxford: Princeton University Press, 1990), 9.

[62] C. E. Robinson, *Every Day Life in Aniceint Greece* (Oxford: The Clarendon Press, 1934), 77; also J. Marquardt, *Das Privatleben der Römer*, 331-332; J. P. V. D. Balsdon, *Life and Leisure in Ancient Rome*, 49; W. S. Davis, *A Day in Old Athens*, 186.

[63] M. Miller, "Foreigners at the Symposion?," in *Dining in a Classical Context: Symposium on Symposia*, ed. W. J. Slater (Ann Arbor: University of Michigan Press, 1991), 67. Miller gives in his article other interpretations, why a particular

diner at a *symposium* wore a *kidaris* hat. For example, the one wearing a *kidaris* hat could imply that the participant was a foreigner, since the hat was foreign to Greek culture.

⁶⁴ E. Pellizer, "Outlines of a Morphology of Sympotic Entertainment," in *Sympotica: A Symposium on the Symposion*, ed. O. Murray (Oxford: Clarendon, 1990), 179.

⁶⁵ M. Tecuşan, "Logos Sympotikos: Patterns of the Irrational in Philosophical Drinking," in *Sympotica: A Symposium on the Symposion*, ed. O. Murray (Oxford: Clarendon Press, 1990), 252; A. Lill, "The Social Meaning of Greek Symposium," in *Studien zu Ritual und Sozialgeschichte im Alten Orient: Studies on Ritual and Society in the Ancient Near East: Tartuer Symposien, 1998-2004*, ed. T. R. Kämmerer (Berlin, New York: Walter de Gruyter, 2007), 177.

⁶⁶ M. Węcowski, "When did the Symposion Rise?: Some Archaeological Considerations Regarding the Emergence of the Greek Aristocratic Banquet," *ΑΡΧΑΙΟΓΝΩΣΙΑ*, no. 16 (2012), no. 13, 21.

⁶⁷ J. P. V. D. Balsdon, *Life and Leisure in Ancient Rome*, 35.

⁶⁸ A. Dalby, *Empire of Pleasures: Luxury and Indulgence in the Roman World* (London, New York: Routledge, 2005), 255; client's relation to his patron could also be seen in J. Carcopino, *Daily Life in Ancient Rome*, 191-193.

⁶⁹ W. S. Davis, *A Day in Old Athens*, 183.

⁷⁰ Cf. J. P. V. D. Balsdon, *Life and Leisure in Ancient Rome*, 34

⁷¹ B. Fehr, "Entertainers at the Symposion: The Akletoi in the Archaic Period," in *Sympotica: A Symposium on the Symposion*, ed. O. Murray (Oxford: Clarendon Press, 1990), 186; an κλητος could be paralleld to a *parasitus* of the Roman satires. There are many classical texts, where the relation between a parasite and the host is parallel to the relation between a dog or any other house animal and his owner. Cf. C. Damon, "Greek Parasites and Roman Patronage," *Harvard Studies in Classical Philology* 97 (1995), 181-195.

⁷² C. B. Gulick, *Athenaeus: The Deipnosophists: With an English Translation*, 7 vols., LCL 204 3 (London, Cambridge, Massachusetts: William Heinemann; Harvard University Press, 1967).

⁷³ M. Węcowski, "When did the Symposion Rise?" 21.

⁷⁴ For details about the Roman seating arrangements, J. Marquardt, *Das Privatleben der Römer*, 303-305; J. P. V. D. Balsdon, *Life and Leisure in Ancient Rome*, 35, 41; J. Carcopino, *Daily Life in Ancient Rome*, 289-290; K. M. D. Dunbabin, *The Roman Banquet*, 39-40; Dunbabin, "Triclinium and Stibadium." 123.

⁷⁵ Cf. Plutarque and B. Perrin, *Plutarch's Lives*, The Loeb Classical Library 98 (London, Cambridge (Mass): W. Heinemann; Harvard University Press, 1970), 203.

[76] D. E. Smith, *From Symposium to Eucharist*, 17-18; Heidel suggests that already in the Sumerian Epic Gilgamesh it is said that in the banquet which Gilgamesh hosted for his friends, "the heroes lay down, resting on their night couches." (Tablet VI. 190). Cf. A. Heidel, *The Gilgamesh Epic and Old Testament Parallels*, Phoenix books (Chicago: University of Chicago Press, 1967), 55; also A. Rathje, "The Adoption of the Homeric Banquet in Central Italy in the Orientalizing Period," in *Sympotica: A Symposium on the Symposion*, ed. O. Murray (Oxford: Clarendon Press, 1990), 284.

[77] Albenda raises a doubt whether it was because of his illness that Ashurbanipal reclined. She further says that the king's continuation of such reclining habit, although for reasons of health, which "continued for a period of time, ... could have precipitated a new custom that had a lasting effect upon court life, as reflected in the *symposium* scenes of later date." P. Albenda, "Landscape Bas-Reliefs in the Bit Hilani of Ashurbanibal," *The American Schools of Oriental Research* 224 (1976), 65.

[78] K. M. D. Dunbabin, *The Roman Banquet*, 81.

[79] Murray, "Sympotic History." 6; B. Bergquist, "Sympotic Space: A Functional Aspect of Greek Dining-Rooms." 43-44; R. A. Tomlinson, "The Chronology of the Perachora Hestiarorion and its Significance," in *Sympotica: A Symposium on the Symposion*, ed. O. Murray (Oxford: Clarendon Press, 1990), 99; A. Rathje, "The Adoption of the Homeric Banquet in Central Italy in the Orientalizing Period." 283. From the archaeological finding of a seventh century Corinthian *krater* and through the portrayal of couches in the works of Alcman, the seventh century Poet of Sparta, Murray assumes that the custom of reclining could have fully established by the seventh century BCE. O. Murray, "The Culture of the Symposion." 514.

[80] Curiously enough Davis says, that the guests at a *symposium* reclined with their right arm resting on the couch and their left arm was free for eating. W. S. Davis, *A Day in Old Athens*, 184.

[81] J. A. S. Evans, *Daily Life in the Hellenistic Age*, 95.

[82] Ibid., 101.

[83] K. M. D. Dunbabin, *The Roman Banquet*, 11.

[84] M. Węcowski, "When did the Symposion Rise?" 22.

[85] In the 5th century BCE *Wasps*, Aristophanes brings in the character of Bdelycleon who is teaching his father in a mock *symposium*, how to recline at a *symposium* (*Wasps* 1208-1215); B. B. Rogers, *Aristophanes*, [Loeb Classical Library.] (3 vol. William Heinemann: London; G. P. Putnam's Sons: New York, 1930), 522-525. This means that in the archaic period there were also many free

citizens who did not know how to recline at meals; cf. F. Cooper and S. Morris, "Dining in Round Buildings." 77.

[86] M. Roller, "Horizontal Women: Posture and Sex in the Roman Convivium," in *Roman Dining*, ed. B. K. Gold and J. F. Donahue (Baltimore (Md): The Johns Hopkins university press, 2005), 52.

[87] A. M. Harmon, *Lucian: With an English Translation*, 8 vols., LCL 1 (London, Cambridge, Massachusetts: William Heinemann; Harvard University Press, 1961).

[88] Such moving tables could be attested in the archaeological findings of the large dining rooms at the temple precincts of *Asklepeios*. Cf. C. Roebuck, *Corinth: Vol 14, The Asklepioion and Lerna* (Princeton, N.J: The American School Classical Studies at Athens, 1951), 54. It is also possible that such changes could have taken place in the private houses too. Cf. D. E. Smith, "Social Obligation in the Context of Communal Meals: A Study of the Christian Meal in 1 Corinthians in Comparison with Graeco-Roman Communal Meals." 11.

[89] For the dishes served at a *symposium*, cf. C. Moulton, *Ancient Greece and Rome*, 77; W. S. Davis, *A Day in Old Athens*, 184; D. E. Smith, *From Symposium to Eucharist*, 31-32; J. Marquardt, *Das Privatleben der Römer*, 324-325; J. P. V. D. Balsdon, *Life and Leisure in Ancient Rome*, 42. J. A. Evans says that in comparison to the Greeks in other cities the Macedonians had lots of meat in their deipnon; J. A. S. Evans, *Daily Life in the Hellenistic Age*, 101.

[90] F. Hobden, *The Symposion in Ancient Greek Society and Thought*, 14.

[91] J. P. V. D. Balsdon, *Life and Leisure in Ancient Rome*, 42; also E. Gowers, *The Loaded Table*, 29.

[92] C. Moulton, *Ancient Greece and Rome*, 58.

[93] Cf. E. A. Gardner and D. Litt, "Food and Drink, Meals, Cooking and Entertainments." 643; also D. E. Smith, *From Symposium to Eucharist*, 28-29.

[94] W. S. Davis, *A Day in Old Athens*, 187; for songs at a *symposium* cf. also E. A. Gardner and D. Litt, "Food and Drink, Meals, Cooking and Entertainments." 643; D. E. Smith, *From Symposium to Eucharist*, 30.

[95] Lissarrague narrates the Spartan King Cleomenes who died like an insane person, because he drank wine undiluted together with the Scythian envoys. F. Lissarrague, *The Aesthetics of the Greek Banquet*, 7; K. M. Lynch, "More Thoughts on the Space of the Symposium," *British School at Athens Studies* 15 (2007), 243, D. E. Smith, *From Symposium to Eucharist*, 32; J. Carcopino, *Daily Life in Ancient Rome*, 293.

[96] F. Lissarrague, *The Aesthetics of the Greek Banquet*, 7.

[97] For a detailed study of some of the attic vases in which *krater*s are prominent, check F. Lissarrague, "Around the Krater: An Aspect of Banquet Imagery," in

Sympotica: A Symposium on the Symposion, ed. O. Murray (Oxford: Clarendon Press, 1990), 196-209; also K. M. D. Dunbabin, *The Roman Banquet*, 20.

[98] J. Luke, "The Krater, 'Kratos,' and the 'Polis,'" *Greece and Rome* 41, no. 1 (1994), 22.

[99] As quoted in, D. A. Campbell, ed., *Greek Lyric: Sappho and Alcaeus*, The Loeb Classical Library 142 (Cambridge Mass, London: Harvard Univ. Press; W. Heinemann, 1982), 379-380.

[100] K. M. D. Dunbabin, *The Roman Banquet*, 20; J. Marquardt, *Das Privatleben der Römer*, 332-333.

[101] P. Garnsey, *Food and Society in Classical Antiquity*, 136; D. E. Smith, *From Symposium to Eucharist*, 48.

[102] P. S. Pantel, "Sarificial Meal and Symposion, Two Models of Civic Institutions in the Archaic Society?," in *Sympotica: A Symposium on the Symposion*, ed. O. Murray (Oxford: Clarendon Press, 1990), 20. Poets like the sixth century Anacreon have composed their poetry specifically in the context of *symposium*. Cf. O. Kirk, *Controlling Desires: Sexuality in Ancient Greece and Rome*, Praeger series on the ancient world (Westport, Conn: Praeger, 2009), 33.

[103] M. Griffith, "Greek Lyric and the Place of Humans in the World," in *The Cambridge Companion to Greek Lyric*, ed. F. Budelmann (Cambridge, New York: Cambridge University Press, 2009), 85. Poets like the sixth century Anacreon have composed their poetry specifically in the context of *symposium*. Cf. O. Kirk, *Controlling Desires*, 33.

[104] W. H. Race, "Paean," in *Princeton Encyclopedia of Poetry and Poetics*, 3rd ed., ed. A. Preminger and T. V. F. Brogan (Princeton: Princeton University Press, 1993), 874.

[105] Ibid., 874.

[106] A. E. Harvey, "The Classification of Greek Lyric Poetry," *The Classical Quarterly* 5 (1955), 172.

[107] C. B. Gulick, *Athenaeus: The Deipnosophists: With an English Translation*, 7 vols., LCL 5 (London, Cambridge, Massachusetts: William Heinemann; Harvard University Press, 1963).

[108] D. Yatromanolakis, "Ancient Greek Popular Song," in *The Cambridge Companion to Greek Lyric*, ed. F. Budelmann (Cambridge, New York: Cambridge University Press, 2009), 274; also D. A. Campbell, "Monody," in *The Cambridge History of Classical Literature: Vol 1. Greek Literature*, ed. P. E. Easterling and B. M. W. Knox (Cambridge: Cambridge University Press, 1985), 220; F. Lissarrague, *The Aesthetics of the Greek Banquet*, 129.

[109] A. E. Harvey, "The Classification of Greek Lyric Poetry." 162; Taking from the fifth century Dicaearchus, Harvey says there are three modes of performing σκόλια; he includes the *paean*, as part of the σκόλια, in which all the guests sing together and second mode of performance is the singing by individual guests as the myrtle twig is passed around and the third is performance by those guests who are able to sing well. D. Yatromanolakis, "Ancient Greek Popular Song." 274.

[110] M. Van der Valk, "On the Composition of the Attic Scolia," *Hermes* 102 (1974), 3.

[111] Ibid., 13.

[112] The passages from the *Theognis Fragments* that are quoted in this paper are taken from http://www.perseus.tufts.edu/hopper/text?doc=Perseus%3Atext %3A2008.01.0479%3Avolume%3D1%3Atext%3D11%3Asection%3D2, accessed on 15.10.2013.

[113] M. L. West, *Studies in Greek Elegy and Iambus* (Berlin, New York: De Gruyter, 1974), 11

[114] E. L. Bowie, "Early Greek Elegy, Symposium and Public Festival," *The Journal of Hellenistic Studies* 106 (1986), 34; further on Elegy cf. also A. Aloni, "Elegy: Forms, Functions and Communication," in *The Cambridge Companion to Greek Lyric*, ed. F. Budelmann (Cambridge, New York: Cambridge University Press, 2009), 168-188.

[115] C. Carey, "Iambos," in *The Cambridge Companion to Greek Lyric*, ed. F. Budelmann (Cambridge, New York: Cambridge University Press, 2009), 160.

[116] A. Lukinovich, "The Play of Reflections between Literary Form and the Sympotic Theme in the Deipnosophistae of Athenaeus," in *Sympotica: A Symposium on the Symposion*, ed. O. Oswyn (Oxford: Clarendon Press, 1990), 265.

[117] Ibid., 267.

[118] J. Davidson, "Making a Spectacle of Her(self): The Greek Courtesan and the Art of the Present," in *The Courtesan's Arts: Cross-Cultural Perspectives*, ed. M. Feldman and B. Gordon (New York: Oxford University Press, 2006), 36; cf. the earlier book from the same author J. N. Davidson, *Courtesans & Fishcakes* (London: Fontana Press, 1998), 73-108; also L. Kurke, "Inventing the "Hetaira": Sex, Politics and Discursive Conflict in Archaic Greece," *Classical Antiquity* 16, no. 1 (1997), 107-108; N. Robertson, "The Betrothal Symposium in Early Greece," in *Dining in a Classical Context: Symposium on Symposia*, ed. W. J. Slater (Ann Arbor: University of Michigan Press, 1991), 59.

[119] S. Corner, "Bringing the Outside In: The Andrτn as Brothel and the Symposium's Civic Sexuality," in *Greek Prostitutes in the Ancient Mediterranean*,

800 BCE-200 CE, ed. A. Glazebrook and M. M. Henry (Madison, Wis: University of Wisconsin Press, 2011), 70.

[120] Cf. B. A. Sparkes, "Kottabos:: An Athenian After-Dinner Game," *Archaeology* 13, no. 3 (1960), 202.

[121] D. Touliatos, "The Traditional Role of Greek Women in Music from Antiquity to the End of the Byzantine Empire," in *Rediscovering the Muses: Women's Musical Traditions*, ed. K. Marshall (Boston: Northeastern University Press, 1993), 114. For the differences between ἑταίρα and πόρνη cf. also L. Kurke, "Inventing the "Hetaira."" 108 ff; J. Davidson, "Making a Spectacle of Her(self)." 36. Corner says the ἑταίρα and πόρνη could be used interchangeably. Because ἑταίρα plays the same role in the *symposium* as the πόρνη does in the brothel." S. Corner, "Bringing the Outside In: The Andrôn as Brothel and the Symposium's Civic Sexuality." 72.

[122] D. Touliatos, "The Traditional Role of Greek Women in Music from Antiquity to the End of the Byzantine Empire." 114.

[123] Boys were also chosen to play such instruments. In Xenophon´s *Symposium* (2), it is a boy who plays the harp and dances.

[124] J. N. Davidson, *Courtesans & Fishcakes*, 81.

[125] L. Kurke, "Inventing the "Hetaira."" 108; cf. also R. Harmon, "Plato, Aristotle and Women Musicians," *Music & Letters* 86, no. 3 (2005), 353; D. E. Smith, *From Symposium to Eucharist*, 35; Davidson says that by the end of the fourth century BCE, these flute players were understood to be cheap street prostitutes. J. N. Davidson, *Courtesans & Fishcakes*, 82.

[126] Davidson and others say that sometimes the charge for an *aulos* girl is so expensive that the magistrates and town officers fix their price for two *Drachmas*. J. Davidson, "Making a Spectacle of Her(self)." 37; R. Harmon, "Plato, Aristotle and Women Musicians." 353.

[127] R. Harmon, "Plato, Aristotle and Women Musicians.", 351; Polygnata is also mentioned in D. Touliatos, "The Traditional Role of Greek Women in Music from Antiquity to the End of the Byzantine Empire." 115.

[128] More on κότταβος could be found in C. E. Robinson, *Every Day Life in Anicient Greece*, 80; G. Bruns, "Kuchenwesen und Mahlzeiten." 643; L. Adkins and R. A. Adkins, *Handbook to Life in Ancient Greece*, Facts on File Library of World History (New York, Oxford: Oxford University Press, 2005), 456; F. Lissarrague, *The Aesthetics of the Greek Banquet*, 80-85; W. S. Davis, *A Day in Old Athens*, 188.

[129] Cf. B. A. Sparkes, "Kottabos::" 202; F. Lissarrague, *The Aesthetics of the Greek Banquet*, 83-84.

[130] As cited in D. E. Smith, *From Symposium to Eucharist*, 34. But this "pouring" of wine during the *kottabos* was compared by Athenaeus to the pouring of wine during the libation.

[131] F. Lissarrague, *The Aesthetics of the Greek Banquet*, 76-80.

[132] D. Sacks, O. Murray, and L. R. Brody, *Encyclopedia of the Ancient Greek World*, 133; C. E. Robinson, *Every Day Life in Anicient Greece*, 82; C. Moulton, *Ancient Greece and Rome*, 57; O. Kirk, *Controlling Desires*, 48.

[133] J. A. S. Evans, *Daily Life in the Hellenistic Age*, 66-67.

[134] K. E. Corley, *Private Women, Public Meals: Social Conflict in the Synoptic Tradition* (Peabody, Massachusetts: Hendrickson, 1993), 26.

[135] As cited in S. Menghini, ed., *Symposion: La cultura del vino nei valori della conoscenza storica e nelle strategie di mercato* (Firenze: Firenze Univ. Press, 2012), 67; cf. also K. M. D. Dunbabin, *The Roman Banquet*, 28; P. Garnsey, *Food and Society in Classical Antiquity*, 136.

[136] J. Carcopino, *Daily Life in Ancient Rome*, 289; M. Roller, "Horizontal Women: Posture and Sex in the Roman Convivium." 49; K. E. Corley, *Private Women, Public Meals*, 26.

[137] As quoted in Vössing, "Family and Domesticity." 134-135; cf. also D. E. Smith, *From Symposium to Eucharist*, 43; Wilkins and Hill, *Food in the Ancient World*, 74.

[138] Cf. K. M. D. Dunbabin, *The Roman Banquet*, 22.

[139] B. O. Foster, *Livy: Books I and II: With an English Translation*, 13 vols., LCL 1 (London, Cambridge, Massachusetts: William Heinemann; Harvard University Press, 1939).

[140] Valerius as quoted in M. Roller, "Horizontal Women: Posture and Sex in the Roman Convivium." 50.

[141] W. Melmoth, *Pliny: Letters: With an English Translation*, LCL 55 (London, New York: William Heinemann; Macmillan, 1931), 111.

[142] D'Arms, "The Roman Convicium and the Idea of Equality." 315.

[143] J. P. V. D. Balsdon, *Life and Leisure in Ancient Rome*, 22; similar view on clients could also be found in P. G. W. Glare, *Oxford Latin Dictionary* (Oxford, New York: Clarendon Press; Oxford University Press, 1982), 337.

[144] G. L. Green, *The Letters to the Thessalonians*, Pillar New Testament commentary (Grand Rapids, Mich: W.B. Eerdmans Pub.; Leicester, 2002), 24.

[145] Murray, "Sympotic History." 6; E. Gowers, *The Loaded Table*, 29; K. M. Lynch, "More Thoughts on the Space of the Symposium." 243. Smith argues that we should not separate *symposion* from the meal preceded by it. *Symposion* for

him is part of the total meal. D. E. Smith, "Table Fellowship as a Literary Motif in the Gospel of Luke," *JBL* 106, no. 4 (1987), 16.

[146] E. Gowers, *The Loaded Table*, 29; K. M. D. Dunbabin, *The Roman Banquet*, 21.

[147] Cf. J. A. S. Evans, *Daily Life in the Hellenistic Age*, 101-102.

[148] Cf. K. M. D. Dunbabin, *The Roman Banquet*, 72.

[149] The Athenian Lawmaker Solon gives various names for the clubs like φρατρίαι, @ργεόνες, θιασ}ται, —ρανοι. For a detailed reference of such clubs, cf. D. E. Smith, *From Symposium to Eucharist*, 87-95.

[150] Ibid., 90; notes on various clubs could also be seen in C. Moulton, *Ancient Greece and Rome*, 53.

[151] S. Benko and J. J. O'Rourke, eds., *The Catacombs and the Colosseum: The Roman Empire as the Setting of Primitive Christianity* (Valley Forge: Judson Press, 1971), 280; for a similar view cf. O. Murray, "The Greek Symposion in History," 267.

[152] For the statutes of the third century *Orgeones* in Athens, cf. D. E. Smith, *From Symposium to Eucharist*, 91-92.

[153] A. D. Nock says, that the associations functioned as a family outside one's own family. A. D. Nock, "The Historical Importance of Cult-Associations," *The Classical Review* 38, 5/6 (1924), 105. Some of the childless members of such associations did not leave their property to their close relatives but they left their entire property to these associations so that the club held banquets frequently in their honor after their death. For the report from the second century historian Ptolybibius about these cults, cf. J. A. S. Evans, *Daily Life in the Hellenistic Age*, 47.

[154] S. Benko and J. J. O'Rourke, *The Catacombs and the Colosseum*, 281; MacMullen puts the purpose of *collegia* very clearly: "Their objects were simple: summed up in the phrase '"social security"': to have a refuge from loneliness in a very big world, to meet once a month for dinner, to draw pride and strength from numbers, and at the end of life (if one's dues were paid up) to be remembered in a really respectable funeral." R. MacMullen, *Enemies of the Roman order: Treason, Unrest, and Alienation in the Empire* (London: Routledge, 1992), 174; cf. also C. Moulton, *Ancient Greece and Rome*, 54.

[155] D. E. Smith, *From Symposium to Eucharist*, 96; A. D. Nock, "The Historical Importance of Cult-Associations," 105; S. Benko and J. J. O'Rourke, *The Catacombs and the Colosseum*, 280.

[156] W. Braun, *Feasting and Social Rhetoric in Luke 14*, 25; cf. also C. Moulton, *Ancient Greece and Rome*, 53.

[157] Smith gives names of such clubs: "Late-night Drinkers" (*Seribibi*), "Society of Diners" (*Collegium comestorum*), "Table-companions of Concord" (*Convictor*

Concordiae), "Comrades of the *Symposium*" (*Sodales ex symposia*), "Banqueters of Elvenia" (*Triclinium Elvenanum*) are some of them. D. E. Smith, *From Symposium to Eucharist*, 96.

[158] Fighting or using abusive language against another member, striking another member and encroaching the couch of another person are some of the improper behavior of the members. ibid., 101-102, 120-121, for further reference on derisive behavior of the clubs, cf. Wilkins and Hill, *Food in the Ancient World*, 86.

[159] Cf. C. Moulton, *Ancient Greece and Rome*, 53; O. Murray, "The Greek Symposion in History." 265-266.

[160] Murray, "The Affair of the Mysteries: Democracy and the Drinking Group." 157; O. Murray, "The Culture of the Symposion." 515. Clubs were also formed with perverted aims. The names of clubs like ἰθύφαλλοι (erections) and aPτολυκυθοι (the wankers) show the perverted aim of some clubs.

[161] R. MacMullen, *Enemies of the Roman order*, 176-178; D. E. Smith, *From Symposium to Eucharist*, 97.

[162] Cf. Robertson, "The Betrothal Symposium in Early Greece." 27-29; D. E. Smith, *From Symposium to Eucharist*, 39-40.

[163] J. Boardman, "Symposion Furniture," in *Sympotica: A Symposium on the Symposion*, ed. O. Murray (Oxford: Clarendon Press, 1990), 128.

[164] R. Garland, *The Greek way of death* (London: Duckworth, 1985), 70.

[165] D. E. Smith, *From Symposium to Eucharist*, 41.

[166] R. Garland, *The Greek way of death*, 39.

[167] *Cena Trimalchionis* presents the custom of pouring wine over the dead man's tomb (65). But there is also another viewpoint that says that the dead cannot enjoy the pleasures of *symposium* anymore. In *Theognis Fragments, for example, we read*: "No mortal man so soon as he is covered with the earth and goeth down to the house of Persephone in Erebus is rejoiced any more with the sound either of lyre or piper or with receiving the gifts of Dionysus." (*Theog. Fr.* 973-977). Further Murray cites the *Anon. Fragments*, where it is stated that the dead man "will lie in the deep-rooted earth sharing no more in the *symposia*, and the lyre or the sweet cry of flutes." Based on this Murray thinks that "there existed in the Greek world a polarity, a more or less absolute distinction between the world of the *symposion* and the world of the dead." Cf. O. Murray, "The Greek Symposion in History." 264; cf. also D. E. Smith, *From Symposium to Eucharist*, 41-42.

[168] P. Scholliers, "Meal, Food Narratives and Sentiments of Belonging in Past and Present," in *Food, Drink and Identity: Cooking, Eating and Drinking in Europe since the Middle Ages*, ed. P. Scholliers (Oxford, New York: Berg, 2001), 5.

[169] C. Grignon, "Commensality and Social Morphology: An Essay of Typology," in *Food, Drink and Identity: Cooking, Eating and Drinking in Europe since the Middle Ages*, ed. P. Scholliers (Oxford, New York: Berg, 2001), 29. sSimilar view about the ´outsiders´ in a *symposium* and the 'insiders' is given also by P. Scholliers, "Meal, Food Narratives and Sentiments of Belonging in Past and Present." 8; J. F. Donahue, "Toward a Typology of Roman Public Feasting," in *Roman Dining*, ed. B. K. Gold and J. F. Donahue (Baltimore, Maryland: The Johns Hopkins university press, 2005), 104.

[170] P. Scholliers, "Meal, Food Narratives and Sentiments of Belonging in Past and Present." 9.

[171] O. Murray, "Histories of Pleasures." 4.

[172] O. Murray, "The Symposion as Social Organization," in *The Greek Renaissance of the Eighth Century B C: Tradition and Innovation*, ed. R. Hägg (Stockholm: Skrifter utgivna av Svenska Instituten i Athen, 1983), 197.

[173] D´Arms, "The Roman Convicium and the Idea of Equality." 312 ff; J. F. Donahue, *Epula Publica: The Roman Community at Table During the Principate* (Ann Arbor, MI: UMI, 2002), 1.

[174] Cf. J. P. V. D. Balsdon, *Life and Leisure in Ancient Rome*, 43.

[175] Wilkins and Hill, *Food in the Ancient World*, 73; P. Garnsey, *Food and Society in Classical Antiquity*, 137; K. M. D. Dunbabin, *The Roman Banquet*, 40; D´Arms, "The Roman Convicium and the Idea of Equality." 312.

[176] C. Damon, "Greek Parasites and Roman Patronage." 181-182.

[177] W. Broekaert and A. Zuiderhoek, "Food and Politics in Classical Antiquity," in *A cultural history of food in Antiquity*, ed. P. Erdkamp (London: Berg, 2012), 92.

[178] Cf. J. P. V. D. Balsdon, *Life and Leisure in Ancient Rome*, 42.

[179] As seen in J. Carcopino, *Daily Life in Ancient Rome*, 293-294.

[180] Cf. C. Moulton, *Ancient Greece and Rome*, 70.

[181] R. G. Bury, *Plato IX: The Laws: With an English Translation*, 2 vols., LCL 1 (Cambridge, Massachusetts, London: Harvard University Press; William Heinemann, 1961).

[182] D´Arms, "The Roman Convicium and the Idea of Equality." 314; the verb within brackets is not in the original.

[183] Murray, "The Affair of the Mysteries: Democracy and the Drinking Group." 149-161, 151; O. Murray, "The Greek Symposion in History." 268; also J. Luke, "The Krater, 'Kratos,' and the 'Polis.'" 29; W. Broekaert and A. Zuiderhoek, "Food and Politics in Classical Antiquity." 90. It is to be noted that some of those who were accused of vandalizing the statues were Alcibiades, Phaedrus and

Eryximachus, who were the characters in Plato's *Symposium*. Cf. P. Garnsey, *Food and Society in Classical Antiquity*, 6.

[184] E. Gowers, *The Loaded Table*, 25; K. M. D. Dunbabin, *The Roman Banquet*, 20-21.

[185] J. Carcopino, *Daily Life in Ancient Rome*, 295.

[186] The passage from the Wisdom of Nigrinus is taken from Harmon, *Lucian*.

[187] G. Paul, "Symposia and Deipna in Plutarch's Lives and in Other Historical Writings," in *Dining in a Classical Context: Symposium on Symposia*, ed. W. J. Slater (Ann Arbor: University of Michigan Press, 1991), 159.

[188] D. E. Smith, *From Symposium to Eucharist*, 140.

[189] T. Morgan, "Ethos: The Socialization of Children in Education and Beyond," in *A companion to families in the Greek and Roman worlds*, ed. B. Rawson, *Blackwell companions to the ancient world* (Malden, Mass. [u.a.]: Wiley-Blackwell, 2011), 508.

[190] O. Murray, "The Greek Symposion in History." 270.

[191] Cf. D. E. Smith, "Social Obligation in the Context of Communal Meals: A Study of the Christian Meal in 1 Corinthians in Comparison with Graeco-Roman Communal Meals.", 41.

[192] T. Morgan, "Ethos: The Socialization of Children in Education and Beyond." 509; W. Rösler, "Wine and Truth in the Greek Symposion," in *In Vino Veritas*, ed. O. Murray and M. Tecuşan (Oxford: The Alden Press, 1995), 109.

[193] J. M. Bremmer, "Adolescents, Symposion, and Pederasty," in *Sympotica: A Symposium on the Symposion*, ed. O. Murray (Oxford: Clarendon Press, 1990), 137; also T. Morgan, "Ethos: The Socialization of Children in Education and Beyond." 509.

[194] As cited in Bremmer, "Adolescents, Symposion, and Pederasty." 137.

[195] S. Corner, "Bringing the Outside In: The Andrôn as Brothel and the Symposium's Civic Sexuality." 66.

[196] E. Pellizer, "Outlines of a Morphology of Sympotic Entertainment." 183.

[197] Cf. F. Dolansky, "Celebrating the Saturnalia: Religious Ritual and Roman Domestic Life," in *A Companion to Families in the Greek and Roman Worlds*, ed. B. Rawson, *Blackwell companions to the ancient world* (Malden, Mass. [u.a.]: Wiley-Blackwell, 2011), 495.

[198] J. C. Relihan, "Rethinking the History of the Literary Symposium," *Illinois Classical Studies* 17, no. 2 (1992), 218; also B. R. Voloshin, "Literary Banquets," *Pacific Coast Philology* 45 (2010), http://www.jstor.org/page/info/about/policies/terms.jsp, 5, accessed on 03.03.2014.

[199] J. Martin, *Symposion. Die Geschichte einer Literarischen Form* (Paderborn: Verlag Ferdinand Schöningh, 1931), 296. Already in the second century CE *symposium* was accepted to be a specific literary form, by Hermogenes of Tarsus; cf. R. McKeon, "Symposia," *Proceedings and Addresses of the American Philosophical Association* 25 (1971), 19.

[200] J. C. Relihan, "Rethinking the History of the Literary Symposium." 220.

[201] J. Székely, *Structure and Theology of the Lucan 'Itinerarium'*, 142.

[202] J. C. Relihan, "Rethinking the History of the Literary Symposium." 216.

[203] For a detailed discussion J. Martin, *Symposion. Die Geschichte einer Literarischen Form*, 36-53.

[204] Petronius Arbiter, *Satyrica: trasl. R. B. Branham; D. Kinney* (London: J.M. Dent, 1996).

[205] J. Martin, *Symposion. Die Geschichte einer Literarischen Form*, 37-38; R. L. Hunter, *Plato's Symposium*, 10.

[206] J. Martin, *Symposion. Die Geschichte einer Literarischen Form*, 38

[207] F. R. Prostmeier, "Symposion - Begegnung - Rettung: Lukas und Seine Narrative Theologie," in *Jesus als Bote des Heils: Heilsverkündigung und Heilserfahrung in Frühchristlicher Zeit*, ed. C. Georg-Zöller, F. R. Prostmeier and L. Hauser, *Stuttgarter biblische Beiträge* 60 (Stuttgart: Katholisches Bibelwerk, 2008), 97.

[208] J. C. Relihan, "Rethinking the History of the Literary Symposium." 216.

[209] M. Hengel, *Judaism and Hellenism: Studies in their Encounter in Palestine During the Early Hellenistic Period*, 1st ed. (Philadelphia: Fortress Press, 1974), 103.

[210] W. Burkert, "Oriental Symposia: Contrasts and Parallels," in *Dining in a Classical Context*, ed. W. J. Slater (Ann Arbor: University of Michigan Press, 1991), 15-16.

[211] Burkert parallels the wedding banquet of Samson to be related to the *symposium* of the Greeks. Just like the Hellenistic *symposia* was for the "nonmonarchic and aristocratic" community, so too is the Book of Judges about the nonmonarchic tribes and their customs. The similarity between the banqueting custom of the Philistines (at the wedding of Samson) and the Greek *symposium* is for Burkert due to the "Nordic" connection of the Philistines with Mycenaean civilization. Cf. ibid., 16.

[212] E. J. Hamlin, *At Risk in the Promised Land: A Commentary on the Book of Judges*, ITC (Grand Rapids, Michigan: W. B. Eerdmans, 1990), 3.

[213] R. G. Boling, *Judges*, The Anchor Bible v. 6A (New Haven, CT, London: Yale University Press, 2008), 30.

[214] E.g. Amos 2:7b-8; 4:1; Hos 4:17-19; 9:1-6; Isa 5:1 1-13; 28:1-4; 28:7-8; 56:9-57:13; Ezek 8:7-13; 39:17-20; cf. J. L. McLaughlin, *The Marzēaḥ in the Prophetic Literature: References and Allusions in Light of the Extra-Biblical Evidence*, Supplements to Vetus Testamentum v. 86 (Leiden, Boston: Brill, 2001), 2; also S. Ackerman, "A Marzēaḥ in Ezekiel 8:7-13?," *The Harvard Theological Review* 82, no. 3 (1989), 275.

[215] W. Burkert, "Oriental Symposia: Contrasts and Parallels." 9; in the words of Fabry, *marzēaḥ* is „*eine religiös-kultische Institution, deren Ziel es ist, die Gemeinschaft mit einer Patronatsgottheit ... zu suchen und zu realisieren ... Der Zentralritus dieser Kultgemeinschaft war also das Kultmahl ... Diese religiöse Verbundenheiit wurde zu einer Sozialen weiterentwickelt.*" H.J. Fabry, "מַרְזֵחַ," in *ThWAT*, ed. G. J. Botterweck, G. W. Anderson and H. Ringgren, 10 vols., 5 (Stuttgart: W. Kohlhammer, 1986), 5, 12; also O. Murray, "The Culture of the Symposion." 514; D. E. Smith, *From Symposium to Eucharist*, 170.

[216] P. S. Johnston, "Marzēaḥ," in *The New Interpreter's Dictionary of the Bible*, ed. K. D. Sakenfeld, 5 vols. (Nashville: Abingdon, 2006-2009), 3, 828; with regard to the question, whether marzēaḥ in the Near Eastern culture had a funerary banquet connotation, McLaughlin answers in the negative. J. L. McLaughlin, *The Marzēaḥ in the Prophetic Literature*, 66-71; contra H. L. Bosman, "Marzēaḥ," in *New International Dictionary of Old Testament Theology & Exegesis*, ed. W. A. VanGemeren, 5 vols. (Grand Rapids, Michigan: Zondervan Publishing House, 1997), 2, 1102-1103.

[217] J. L. McLaughlin, *The Marzēaḥ in the Prophetic Literature*, 97-98.

[218] A. J. Nijboer, "Banquet, Marzeah, Symposion and Symposium During the Iron Age: Disparity and Mimicry," in *Regionalism and Globalism in Antiquity: Exploring their Limits*, ed. F. De Angelis, *Colloquia Antiqua* 7 (Leuven: Peeters Publishers, 2013), 95-126.

[219] Fabry, "מַרְזֵחַ." 15.

[220] Ibid., 15; the evolution of marzēaḥ into cultic festival of the dead is also narrated in J. L. McLaughlin, *The Marzēaḥ in the Prophetic Literature*, 180.

[221] P. W. Skehan and A. A. Di Lella, *The Wisdom of Ben Sira*, Anchor Bible. 39 (New York: Doubleday, 1987), 16.

[222] Cf. M. Hengel, *Judaism and Hellenism*, 138; R. J. Coggins, *Sirach: Guides to Apocrypha and Pseudepigrapha* (Sheffield: Sheffield Academic Press, 1998), 50; Nickelsburg also writes that Sirach seems to be lacking polemics against Hellenism and so "it would be an exaggeration to portray Ben Sira simply as a polemicist against the alien elements in his environment." G. W. E. Nickelsburg, *Jewish Literature Between the Bible and the Mishnah: A Historical and Literary Introduction*, 2nd ed. (Minneapolis: Fortress Press, 2005), 62-63. For a similar

view J. J. Collins, *Jewish Wisdom in the Hellenistic Age*, The Old Testament library (Louisville, Ky: Westminister John Knox Press, 1997), 33.

[223] P. W. Skehan and A. A. Di Lella, *The Wisdom of Ben Sira*, 388.

[224] B. Eckhardt, "Meals and Politics in the Yahad: A Reconsideration," *Dead Sea Discoveries* 17, no. 2 (2010), 190.

[225] Sanders as quoted in R. J. Coggins, *Sirach*, 53; for a similar view cf. M. Hengel, *Judaism and Hellenism*, 134.

[226] J. Neusner, *From Politics to Piety: The Emergence of Pharisaic Judaism* (New York: Ktav Pub. House, 1979), 9; also J. Neusner, *Formative Judaism: Religious, Historical, and Literary Studies: Fifth Series: Revisioning the Written Records of a Nascent Religion*, Brown Judaic studies 91 (Chico, Calif.: Scholars Press, 1985), 54.

[227] J. Neusner, *From Politics to Piety*, 9; J. Neusner, *Formative Judaism: Religious, Historical, and Literary Studies*, 55.

[228] J. Neusner, *The Idea of Purity in Ancient Judaism*, The Haskell lectures, 1972-73 1 (Leiden: Brill, 1973), 65; cf. also B. M. Bokser, *The Origins of the Seder: The Passover Rite and Early Rabbinic Judaism* (Berkeley: University of California Press, 1984), 55; G. M. Soares-Prabhu, *The Dharma of Jesus*: ed. F. X, D´Sa (Maryknoll, N.Y.: Orbis Books, 2003), 120-122; D. E. Smith, "Table Fellowship as a Literary Motif in the Gospel of Luke." 150-152.

[229] J. Neusner, *Formative Judaism: Religious, Historical, and Literary Studies*, 76.

[230] As quoted in J. Neusner, *The Idea of Purity in Ancient Judaism*, 70.

[231] G. M. Soares-Prabhu, *The Dharma of Jesus*, 121; , 364.

[232] Cf. J. Frey, "Essenes," in *The Eerdmans Bible Dictionary*, ed. A. C. Myers (Grand Rapids, Mich.: Eerdmans, 1987), 599-602.

[233] T. S. Beall, *Josephus' Description of the Essenes Illustrated by the Dead Sea Scrolls*, Society for New Testament Studies monograph series 58 (Cambridge, U.K, New York: Cambridge University Press, 2004), 5; D. N. Freedman, *Eerdmans Dictionary of the Bible* (Grand Rapids, Mich., Cambridge: W.B. Eerdmans, 2000), 426; S. J. Pfann, "A Table in the Wilderness: Pantries and Tables, Pure Food and Sacred Space at Qumran," in *Qumran, the Site of the Dead Sea Scrolls: Archaeological Interpretations and Debates*, ed. K. Galor, J. B. Humbert and J. Zangenberg, v. 57 (Leiden, Boston: Brill, 2006), 159, 161; J. C. Vanderkam, *The Dead Sea Scrolls and the Bible* (Grand Rapids, Mich: W.B. Eerdmans, 2012), 99-100; M. Broshi, "Qumran: Archaeology," in *Encyclopedia of the Dead Sea Scrolls*, ed. L. H. Schiffman and J. C. Vanderkam (New York, Oxford: Oxford University Press, 2000), 735. For the differences between the Essenes and the Qumran Community, W. S. Lasor, "Essenes," in *Baker Encyclopedia of the Bible*, ed. W. A. Elwell and B. J. Beitzel (Grand Rapids Mich: Baker Book House, 1988), 719;

also C. Hempel, "Qumran Community," in *Encyclopedia of the Dead Sea Scrolls*, ed. L. H. Schiffman and J. C. Vanderkam (New York, Oxford: Oxford University Press, 2000), 749-750.

[234] Bauer argues that this section from Josephus must have been influenced by some work of Philo on the Essenes which has not been excavated so far. Philo must have written in this lost work about the organization of the Essenes as a counterpart to the description of the *Therapeutae* in his work *'On the Contemplative Life.'* He calls this lost work of Philo, *On the Active Life*. As cited in J. Van der Ploeg, "The Meals of the Essenes," *Journal of Semetic Studies* 2, no. 2 (1957), 164.

[235] H. St. J. Thackeray, *Josephus: The Jewish War, Books I-III: With an English Translation*, 9 vols., LCL 2 (London, Cambridge, Massachusetts: William Heinemann; Harvard University Press, 1956).

[236] Cf. J. Van der Ploeg, "The Meals of the Essenes." 167.

[237] F. G. Martínez, *The Dead Sea Scrolls Translated: The Qumran Texts in English*, 2nd ed. (Leiden, New York, Grand Rapids: E.J. Brill; W.B. Eerdmans, 1996).

[238] As cited by S. J. Pfann, "A Table in the Wilderness: Pantries and Tables, Pure Food and Sacred Space at Qumran." 162.

[239] D. E. Smith, *From Symposium to Eucharist*, 155.

[240] S. J. Pfann, "A Table in the Wilderness: Pantries and Tables, Pure Food and Sacred Space at Qumran." 175.

[241] Philo, *Philo: trasl. F. H. Colson; G. H. Whitaker*, 12 Vls, Vol. 9, The Loeb Classical Library (London: William Heinemann, 1929-1991). Josephus too says, the Essenes did not bring wives into the community. The archaeological findings at the burial sites of the Essenes show bones only of men; around the site however, there were also bones of women to be found. Further Josephus tells in his Wars (J. *BJ.* 2.8.160), that there was another order of the Essenes who were married. Perhaps there existed a group of celibate Essenes and another group of married Essenes. Cf. T. S. Beall, *Josephus' Description of the Essenes Illustrated by the Dead Sea Scrolls*, 39.

[242] F. W. Danker and W. Bauer, *A Greek-English lexicon of the New Testament and other early Christian literature*, 453.

[243] J. E. Taylor and P. R. Davies, "The So-Called Therapeutae of "De Vita Contemplativa": Identity and Character," *The Harvard Theological Review* 91, no. 1 (1998), 5.

[244] B. Eckhardt, "Meals and Politics in the Yahad: A Reconsideration." 191; J. König, *Saints and Symposiasts: The Literature of Food and the Symposium in Greco-Roman and Early Christian Culture* (Cambridge: Cambridge University

Press, 2012) 135; for a contrasting perspective, cf. B. M. Bokser, *The Origins of the Seder*, 57.

[245] J. Van der Ploeg, "The Meals of the Essenes." 164; cf also S. J. Pfann, "A Table in the Wilderness: Pantries and Tables, Pure Food and Sacred Space at Qumran." 161-162; D. E. Smith, *From Symposium to Eucharist*, 158; T. S. Beall, *Josephus' Description of the Essenes Illustrated by the Dead Sea Scrolls*, 36; B. Eckhardt, "Meals and Politics in the Yahad: A Reconsideration." 191. J. E. Taylor and P. R. Davies, "The So-Called Therapeutae of "De Vita Contemplativa": Identity and Character." 6.

[246] J. E. Taylor and P. R. Davies, "The So-Called Therapeutae of "De Vita Contemplativa": Identity and Character.", 24.

[247] M. R. Niehoff, "The Symposium of Philo's Therapeutae: Displaying Jewish Identity in an Increasingly Roman World," *Greek, Roman, and Byzantine Studies* 50 (2010), 104.

[248] D. E. Smith, *From Symposium to Eucharist*, 19; also K. E. Corley, *Private Women, Public Meals*, 68.

[249] J. R. Bartlett, *Jews in the Hellenistic World*, Cambridge Commentaries on Writings of the Jewish and Christian World 200 BC to AD 200 vol. 1, part 1 (Cambridge: Cambridge University Press, 1985), 17; O. Murray, "Hellenistic Royal Symposia," in *Aspects of Hellenistic Kingship*, ed. P. Bilde, *Studies in Hellenistic civilization* 7 (Aarhus, Oakville, Conn: Aarhus University Press, 1996), 22; S. Honigman, *The Septuagint and Homeric Scholarship in Alexandria: A Study in the Narrative of the Letter of Aristeas* (London, New York: Routledge, 2003), 11.

[250] J. H. Charlesworth, ed., *The Old Testament Pseudepigrapha: Expansions of the "Old Testament" and Legends, Wisdom and Philosophical Literature, Prayers, Psalms, and Odes, Fragments of Lost Judeo-Hellenistic Works*, 2 vols., 2 (Garden City, New York: Doubleday, 1985).

[251] Mendels contrasts the theme of kingship at the table talk of the *Letter of Aristeas* with the chapter in the Temple Scroll of the Dead Sea Scrolls which also concentrates on the kingship. D. Mendels, "'On Kingship' in the "Temple Scroll" and the Ideological "Vorlage" of the Seven Banquets in the "Letter of Aristeas to Philocrates"," *Aegyptus* 59, 1/2 (1979), 127-136.

[252] J. Klawans, "Notions of Gentile Impurity in Ancient Judaism," *Association for Jewish Studies* 20, no. 2 (1995), 288, 297.

[253] B. Eckhardt, "Meals and Politics in the Yahad: A Reconsideration." 189.

[254] Cf. C. Burchard, "The Importance of Joseph and Aseneth for the Study of the New Testament: A General Survey and a Fresh Look at the Lord's Supper," *New Testament Studes* 33, no. 1 (1987), 103; R. Nir, ""It is not right for a man

who worships God to repay his neighbor evil for evil": Christian Ethics in Joseph and Aseneth (CHAPTERS 22–29)," *Journal of Hebrew Scriptures* 13 (2013), 2.

[255] E. M. Humphrey, *Joseph and Aseneth*, Guides to Apocrypha and Pseudepigrapha (Sheffield: Sheffield Academic Press, 2000), 14-15.

[256] C. Burchard, "The Importance of Joseph and Aseneth for the Study of the New Testament." 104; also R. S. Kraemer, *When Aseneth met Joseph: A Late Antique Tale of the Biblical Patriarch and his Egyptian Wife, Reconsidered* (New York: Oxford University Press, 1998), 238.

[257] Charlesworth, *The Old Testament Pseudepigrapha*.

[258] C. Burchard, "The Importance of Joseph and Aseneth for the Study of the New Testament." 109.

[259] R. D. Chesnutt, *From Death to Life: Conversion in Joseph and Aseneth*, Journal for the study of the pseudepigrapha. Supplement series 16 (Sheffield: Sheffield Academic Press, 1995), 178; cf. also the article from the same author, R. D. Chesnutt, "Perceptions of Oil in Early Judaism and the Meal Formula in Joseph and Aseneth," *Journal for the Study of the Pseudepigrapha* 14, no. 2 (2005), 120; and J. Klawans, "Notions of Gentile Impurity in Ancient Judaism." 295-296.

[260] S. Stein, "The Influence of Symposia Literature on the Literary Form of the Pesah Haggadah," *Journal of Jewish Studies* 8, 13-44 (1957), 13.

[261] Ibid., 15.

[262] H. Danby, *The Mishnah: Translated From the Hebrew With Introduction and Brief Explanatory Notes* (Oxford: Oxford University Press, 1933), 150-151.

[263] Bahr, "The Seder of Passover and the Eucharistic Words."188-192; B. M. Bokser, *The Origins of the Seder*, 52; D. E. Smith, *From Symposium to Eucharist*, 149-150; K. E. Corley, *Private Women, Public Meals*, 69.

[264] S. Stein, "The Influence of Symposia Literature on the Literary Form of the Pesah Haggadah." 31.

[265] Although in the *Pesachim* there is no mention of servants bringing water, it is safe to conclude this ceremony was there in every festive meal. Bahr talks about the "first water," which was given at the beginning of the main course and the "last water" at the end of it, and the "middle water" when someone went outside of the room and came in. cf. Bahr, "The Seder of Passover and the Eucharistic Words." 194.

[266] J. Neusner, *The Tosefta: Second Division: Moed: Translated from Hebrew* (New York: Ktav Publishing House, 1981). As translated in B. M. Bokser, *The Origins of the Seder*, 36.

[267] S. Stein, "The Influence of Symposia Literature on the Literary Form of the Pesah Haggadah." 33.

[268] Bahr, "The Seder of Passover and the Eucharistic Words." 199.

[269] B. M. Bokser, *The Origins of the Seder*, 31, 65. Danby makes a special care to differentiate the Passover from sympotic gatherings, in that he says, "the joy of the Passover meal with its solemn symbolism must not degenerate into an ordinary convivial gathering". Danby, *The Mishnah*, 151, no.9.

[270] B. M. Bokser, *The Origins of the Seder*, 62-66; Smith rejects the arguments of Bokser as unconvincing; for his arguments cf. D. E. Smith, *From Symposium to Eucharist*, no. 55, 334.

Chapter - 2

Table Fellowship and the Gospel of Luke

One of the unique insights of Luke-Acts is the way Luke handles the table fellowship of Jesus and of the early Christians. As Wanke rightly points out, no other Gospel writer narrates so frequently about Jesus enjoying meals at table.[1] There is "the aroma of food"[2] practically in each chapter of the third Gospel. Comparing the third Gospel with other two synoptic Gospels, we are immediately able to see the increase in the number the instances, where Jesus is narrated to be reclining at table with different sets of groups. The banquet scenes come at regular and important intervals. While some of the banquet scenes are taken from the earlier sources, some are unique to Luke himself. The following table gives an overview of the times, Jesus is seen participating at a meal in the third Gospel:

Banquets of Jesus in the Third Gospel

Texts	Host	Chief Guest	Other Guests	Uninvited Guest	Controversy (*fait divers*)	Final Proclamation of Jesus	Result of the Banquet
Luke 5:27-32 (Mark 2:13-17; Matt 9:9-13)	Levi	Jesus	Tax Collectors and Others	--	Jesus and his disciples eat with tax collectors and sinners	'I have come to call not the righteous but sinners to repentance.'	Levi leaves everything and becomes a disciple of Jesus
Luke 7:36-50 (Mark 14:3-9; Matt 26:6-13)	Simon the Pharisee	Jesus	--	A Sinful Woman?	Jesus allows himself to be touched and kissed by a sinful woman	'Your faith has saved you; go in peace.'	(Strained Relation of the Pharisee with Jesus)
Luke 10:38-42 (Lukan Special Material)	Martha	Jesus	--	--	Martha complaining about her sister, not helping her	'Mary has chosen the better part, which will not be taken away from her.'	--

Luke 11:37-54 (Mark 12:38-40; Matt 23:1-40)	Another Pharisee	Jesus	Other Pharisees and Lawyers	--	Jesus does not wash his hands before dinner	'Woe to you lawyers! For you have taken away the key of knowledge; you did not enter yourselves, and you hindered those who were entering.'	Pharisees are hostile to Jesus and wait to catch him
Luke 14:1-24 (Matt 22:1-10)	A Leader of the Pharisees	Jesus	--	A Man with dropsy?	Healing on the Sabbath day	'For I tell you, none of those who were invited will taste my dinner.'	(Strained relation of the Pharisee with Jesus)
Luke 19:1-10 **(Lukan Special Material)**	Zacchaeus, the chief tax collector	Jesus	--	Jesus?	'He has gone to be a guest of a sinner'	'For the Son of Man came to seek out and to save the lost.'	Zacchaeus and his Household has found Salvation.

Reference							
Luke 22:7-30 (Mark 14:12-26; Matt 26:17-30; John 13:21-30)	Jesus		Twelve Disciples		Dispute among the Disciples as to who among them is the greatest	'You will eat and drink at my table in my kingdom, and you will sit on thrones judging the twelve tribes of Israel.'	
Luke 24:1-35 (Lukan Special Material)	Emmaus Disciples	Resurrected Lord		--	--	--	The Eyes of the Disciples are opened and they go back to Jerusalem
Luke 24:36-42 (Lukan Special Material)	Eleven Disciples	Resurrected Lord		--	--	--	Disbelief and Joy after seeing the Resurrected Lord

It is evident from the foregoing table that some of the material which are found scattered in the Gospel of Mark and other sources, are brought together by Luke in the framework of a banquet, specially in the context of a sympotic meal. The anointing at Bethany which is narrated in Mark and Matthew in the context of the imminent death of Jesus (Mark 14:3-9; Matt 26:6-13) is taken out of the context of passion prediction and placed in Luke in the context of a *symposium*. In a similar way the condemnation of the Pharisees and Lawyers (Mark 12:38-40; Matt 23:1-40) are placed by Luke in the framework of a *symposium*. The parable of the great dinner too is placed within the framework of a *symposium* in Luke (cf. Matt 22:1-10). Furthermore, the characteristics of a sympotic meal, (i.e., the host, the chief guest, *fait divers* and the emerging table talk) are conspicuous in the banquets, in which Jesus participates with tax collectors and Pharisees. The Last Supper clearly points to a sympotic background, while in other banquets, sympotic framework is not so evident.

The two banquets of Jesus with tax collectors (Levi and Zacchaeus) are to be noted in the third Gospel. The fact that Jesus enjoyed table fellowship with the tax collectors is not a specific and focused theme in Mark and Matthew, apart from few references (cf. Mk 2:16; Matt 9:9-13); on the contrary it is apparent that Luke portrays Jesus as someone who enjoys table fellowship with this group (Luke 5:27-32; 7:34; 15:1-2; 19:1-10). Besides Luke seems to be conspicuously depicting the tax collectors as a group in a favourable light than the other two synoptic writers. The contrast between Mark and Matthew on the one hand and Luke on the other, would make this evident (Matt 5:46; 9:10; 18:17; 21:32; Luke 3:12; 7:29; 15:1; 18:9-14; 19:1-10). Through the banquet narrations of Jesus with the tax collectors, Luke's aim is conspicuous, that is, to portray Jesus as the man who entertains sinners, as a person who is happy in their company, as a person who enjoys table fellowship with them; because "sinners provide the target group, which Jesus attempts to reach."[3] However the Lukan Jesus reclines not only at the houses of the tax collectors; he also reclines with another group, which stands directly at the other end of the spectrum – the Pharisees.

We do not see anywhere in Mark or in Matthew that Jesus went to the house of a Pharisee for a meal; but in Luke, we have three instances of Jesus eating with Pharisees. One could see here almost a deliberate pattern that Luke follows in his banquet narrations, which is evident in the narration of Jesus' meal with the above-mentioned two groups. This paper contends that our study of Luke 19:1-10 would be complemented, if we are able to look at it in the larger background of the narration of Jesus' banquets with these two major groups in the Gospel of Luke. Even if we seclude the five meal narratives aloof and analyze them in the light of each other, we would be able to get a complete and an important message from the author of the third Gospel on the table fellowship of Jesus. This chapter aims to analyze this block of Jesus' table fellowship with the two groups - the tax collectors and the Pharisees; it is an attempt to understand the five banquet narratives of Jesus with tax collectors and Pharisees in the light of each other. The interweaving of the meal narrations of Jesus with both these groups heightens the plot of Luke; their placing one after another suggests to the readers that the one is to be understood in the light of another. In this way, they would perhaps give the reader a new twist of meaning to the phrase, "the tax collectors and sinners" and help one to understand the Pharisaic group / school as narrated in Luke.

Secondly, through the deliberate and periodical placing of meal scenes, we might be able to see how important the understanding and the practice of table fellowship would have been for the Lukan community. Just as the table fellowship in the Acts of the Apostles became a center of controversies as well as of new and trend-setting decisions, so is the table fellowship of Jesus in the third Gospel. Each of the table fellowship narrations in the Gospel looks to be an attempt by Luke to throw some more light on how the fellowship meals of the community have to be handled.

Jesus' Table Fellowship with Tax Collectors

The synoptic Gospels are unanimous in portraying Jesus' desire and initiative to dine with tax collectors. One of the main accusations of the opponents of Jesus against him was that he is 'glutton and drunkard and is the friend of tax collectors and sinners' (Luke 7:34) and that he shares table companionship with them. The table companionship of Jesus with tax collectors assumes significance, because, of all other professional groups, Jesus' association with tax collectors has been the target of the opponents. All the three Gospels narrate Jesus' dining with tax collectors – much to the murmur of the Pharisees and the scribes. This general consensus of the synoptic writers in depicting the table fellowship of Jesus with tax collectors suggests that it could be historically probable that Jesus indeed dined with tax collectors and felt at home in their company. We see that at least one of the apostles whom Jesus called to follow him was a tax collector (Mk 2:13-17; Matt 9:9-13; Luke 5:27-32). Since the term tax collectors comes more often in Luke than in other synoptic Gospels (Luke 3:12; 5:29, 30; 7:29, 34; 15:1), we need to understand how Luke perceives and depicts this important group in his Gospel. A prior analysis is needed to know about tax collectors in general in the Palestinian world view and how the collection of taxes functioned at the time of Jesus and understand the reason why the term 'tax collectors' was combined to 'sinners.'

The System of Taxation in Palestine

From the combination of τέλος ("tax") and ὠνέομαι ("I purchase"), a tax collector (τελώνης) could be understood in the ancient world as someone who purchased the right to collect one or a group of taxes on behalf of the state.[4] The rights to collect taxes were given for a year. Every year, the contract had to be renewed, even if the same contractor was selected to collect taxes also for the next year. Two types of taxes were levied upon the people apart from the tribute that had to be paid collectively to the conqueror nation – the direct tax and the indirect tax. Direct tax was levied on the land and the properties that a person possessed; it also consisted of head tax, poll tax, tax on his profits (profession or trade which one undertook) and crown tax. Indirect tax included other minor taxes like tax on buying or selling, transport tax and tax collected at the city entrances and at important bridges and ports, fruit tax and salt tax.⁵ From the *Zenon papyri* documents Herrenbrück exhibits that taxes were collected not only in the coastal and port cities but also in the interior cities.⁶ During the rule of Seleucids, Jews in Palestine were granted relief from paying some of the taxes. 1 Mac 10:25-45 as well as 1 Mac 13:36-40 narrate the concession given by the Seleucids. According to the letter of agreement sent by the king Demetrius, the Jews were given concession from paying some taxes like head tax, salt tax and crown tax. They were also given exemption to pay the one third of their grain produce and half of their fruit production. The arrival of Hasmonaean dynasty did not mean for the Jews that they would be exempted from paying taxes. The Jews continued to pay taxes, now to their new rulers, though priests were exempted from taxes.

Taxation at the Time of Herod

With the arrival of Pompey, Palestine witnessed not only the decline of Seleucid dynasty and the end of Hasmonean rule, but also the emergence of Roman Empire and the rise of Herod the Great. Once Herod was appointed king of the Jews by the Roman Senate, he continued levying taxes on his people, just as the Hasmonaeans did. We hear much about Herod´s mode of taxation from Josephus who sharply criticizes Herod´s obsession for taxing his people in order to fund his building projects. In his ambition for building constructions, Herod collected the much-needed resources to build his ambitious monuments though different taxes that he imposed on the people. It is said that Herod "drained the lifeblood of his subjects through high taxation rates,"⁷ so much so that the entire country became so poor to the situation of revolt. Rocca is however of a different view. He suggests that Herod´s rule should be divided into two parts, 37 – 31 BCE and 31 – till his death. Only at the first stage of his ruling career, Herod resorted to a heavy taxing of his people; since he was short of money, he even minted his personal possessions as coins in order to pay the tribute. At the second stage of his rule, once, after his victory over Cleopatra and Mark Antony, once Octavian gifted much of the territory belonging to Cleopatra and Mark Antony to Herod, Herod´s financial situation steadily improved so much that there was relief in paying taxes. Rocca tells that at least twice (20 BCE and 14 BCE) Herod cancelled the taxes of the Jews.[8] For Rocca, the hatred of Josephus against Herod the Great could be understandable from the fact that Herod taxed also the priests, which was not the case during the rule of Hasmonaeans and Seleucids.[9] After Herod the Great, taxation of Judaea, Samaria and Idumaea came under the direct rule of the Roman Procurators and it was undertaken in Galilee by Herod Antipas till his death. The collection of direct taxes in Judaea was then entrusted to the Sanhedrin, which was regulated by the Roman Procurator.

Roman administrators had an institution to collect taxes - *publicani* as they were called in the Roman Empire. In the cities, wealthy citizens owned the right to collect taxes. And in order to collect taxes, they made use of all possible means including violence and militia. Wealthy as they were, the tax collectors formed an association of their own, *'societas publicanorum'* which would take care of the welfare of the tax collectors and other administrative affairs in Rome; and the *pubilcani*, the tax collectors in different cities involved locals and slaves to collect taxes from the people. These men were called *portitores*.[10] The society of the tax collectors was so dangerously powerful and levied heavy taxes upon the people that there arose the feeling that the tax collectors had to be controlled.[11] The presence of the Roman *publicani* is also said to have been in Palestine, who acted as the brokers between the Roman administration and the local leaders in charge of tax collection.[12] It was Julius Caesar, who, much to the relief of the people put an end to the institution of the *publicani* in the year 47 BCE.

Tax Collectors and Toll Collectors
There has been a discussion whether τελῶναι in the Synoptics are to be understood as tax collectors or toll collectors - those who were responsible for the direct taxes and those who were collecting customs. Some scholars suggest that the τελῶναι in the Synoptics should not be understood as the normal tax collectors collecting direct taxes; rather they were only the toll collectors sitting at the city borders.[13] This means

they did not have the chance to enter the houses of the Jews as did the tax collectors who were incharge of direct taxes. Herrenbrück refutes this argument. He says, understanding the τελῶναι in the Synoptics merely referring to the toll collectors is an unreflected conclusion.[14] For him τελῶναι at the time of Jesus were in charge of collecting both direct as well as indirect taxes.

The collection of taxes was leased out to the one who bade the highest amount. Since the one who bought the right to collect taxes had to pay the entire amount of taxes that they would be collecting at the very beginning itself, only the wealthy of the land could become a τελώνης. It was, however also possible that the person, who bought the rights to collect taxes, could not collect the entire sum that he had initially paid, especially at times of drought, or due to the tax evasion by people. If there was a failure to collect the required sum of taxes, then the tax collector had to make up for it and spend the rest of the sum from his pocket. Hence the only way to see to it that he did not suffer from financial losses, was that he collected more than what was officially allowed to be collected; thereby the tax collector made sure, he made profit out of his job. Since the tax collector paid the entire amount already at the beginning, the government in general did not bother to see how much a tax collector collected from the people. This paved the way for a deceitful behavior from tax collectors. We should also note that attempts were made to reduce the cheating of the tax collectors in the interest of the ordinary people paying the taxes.[15]

Contempt against Tax Collectors

Despite attempts by the governments to curb dishonesty by the tax collectors, there was enormous corruption and abuse in collecting taxes. Throughout the Hellenistic world the tax and toll collectors were infamous for their cheating, and hence were hated and reproached. The negative mindset about the tax collectors could be seen already from writers like Xenophon, for whom "πάντες τελῶναι πάντες εἰσὶν ἅρπαγες"[16] linking thereby the tax collectors with robbers. Since the tax collectors had paid a huge sum for buying the right to collect taxes, and since they earned their livelihood from the commissions from the customs, they normally collected more than what was asked for from the state. Hence it is said that they were generally understood to be men with „*schrankenloser Habgier*."[17] As regards the customs, the Romans had installed toll stations at every entrance of the city and of important junctions. Hence if a businessman had to transport his goods from one city to another, he had to pay taxes at different times in different cities he passed through, for the same goods. The toll collector had also the right to check the person passing through the city, if he thought the person was cheating. In short the different toll stations were thought to be places of "institutionalized robbery"[18] where the traders and those who passed by, had to undergo manifold injustice and dishonesty and cheating.

It is said that in Palestine the image and the treatment of the tax collectors was even worse. Perrin says tax collectors in Palestine were understood to be "those Jews who made themselves as gentiles."[19] They were hated for their dishonesty at work and went about without any regard for morality or for the purity Laws. Rabbinic literature has classified the profession of tax collecting as despicable, since it involved cheating. The Rabbis categorized them along with dicers and money lenders. Because of their cheating and immoral lifestyle, they were also paired along with robbers, adulterers, murderers and cheats.[20] Secondly, apart from their dishonesty and deceit, which they were notorious for, they were all the more hated for their collaboration with the Roman authorities, the oppressors of the land.[21] For a patriotic Jew, paying taxes was a "painful symbol of conquest."[22] It is the nature of the tax collectors' job, which made it necessary to be constantly in contact with their superior authorities who ultimately were Romans. Hence those in whose houses the tax collectors entered were considered to be ritually so unclean, that the discussion among the Rabbis was, how far a house became unclean, due to the entry of a tax collector or a thief. Mishnah attests to conception of the Jews: "If tax gatherers entered a house [all that is within it] becomes unclean; … If thieves entered a house, only that part is unclean that was trodden by the feet of the thieves."[23] A tax collector could not become a judge and still worse, he could not be a witness in a case. The money touched by him could not be used even for charity purposes.[24] Since the tax collector was unclean because of his job, the money used by him is tainted and taints all those who come in contact with it.

Such an understanding of tax collectors is not without criticism. Herrenbrück for example, admits that there was hatred towards tax collectors in Palestine; this hatred however which is seen in Rabbinic sayings have been from the second and third century CE. Herrenbrück however suggests that the τελῶναι of Palestine at the time of Jesus, should have belonged not only to the financial but also to the social elite class of Jews.[25] Hence according to him it is wrong to take the second century CE Rabbinic sayings and apply them to the time of Jesus. If this was the case, then the question needs an answer as to why the Gospels should connect the tax collectors with sinners.

Οἱ Τελῶναι Καὶ οἱ Ἁμαρτωλοί in the Synoptics

One could find the conspicuous differences in the treatment of τελῶναι between the synoptic authors. In the call of Levi for example, Mark simply narrates, πολλοὶ τελῶναι καὶ ἁμαρτωλοί were eating with Jesus (Mk 2:15). Through the narrative comment by Mark himself who pairs the tax collectors with sinners, one could guess the moral status of the tax collectors at the time of writing the Gospel. Matthew in particular pairs the τελῶναι not only with the ἁμαρτωλοί (Matt 5:46-47) but also with πόρναι (Matt 21:31) and in fact with ἐθνικός (Matt 18:17). These sayings in Matthew could betray a Palestinian Jewish Christian worldview to which the Matthean community might have belonged.[26] Luke however, makes a conscious and deliberate change. He intentionally avoids pairing of tax collectors with sinners. This is clear through his redactional change in the story of Levi (compare ὄχλος πολὺς τελωνῶν καὶ ἄλλων in Luke 5:29 instead of πολλοὶ τελῶναι καὶ ἁμαρτωλοί in Mk 2:15; Matt 9:10). Unlike in Mark and Matthew, in Luke alone we find the tax collectors without being attached to other groups like prostitutes or gentiles. At the same time, he has elsewhere taken and used the Q formation of the phrase τελῶναι καὶ ἁμαρτωλοί (Luke 7:34).

In Luke, the use of the phrase "tax collectors and sinners" could be categorized into two parts. First the phrase with double article and second the phrase with a single article. We see the phrase with the double definite article, οἱ τελῶναι καὶ οἱ ἁμαρτωλοί in Luke 15:1. On the contrary there are also uses of the phrase with a single article or without a definite article. For example, we see instances where only one definite article is used for both the nouns διὰ τί μετὰ τῶν τελωνῶν καὶ ἁμαρτωλῶν ἐσθίετε καὶ πίνετε; (Luke 5:30b; Mk 2:16). In Luke 7:34 we see the phrase without a definite article, φίλος τελωνῶν καὶ ἁμαρτωλῶν. Herrenbrück suggests that the phrase with double use of the definite article is used to categorize both the professions in the „negativen Reihe."[27] He takes the definite article in these two words as referring to two different categories. One article refers to one particular category. In that sense, 'tax collectors' as a group are similar to 'sinners' as a group.

The phrase οἱ τελῶναι καὶ ἁμαρτωλοί (with a single article) is placed in the mouth of the opponents of Jesus. This single use of the definite article suggests that the phrase tax collectors and sinners has to be understood epexegetically. This would mean that the phrase οἱ τελῶναι καὶ ἁμαρτωλοί without the second definite article, would mean the sinful tax collectors.[28] This is similar to ἁμαρτωλός ἀνήρ of Luke 19:7.

Sinners in the Gospels could be a synonym for the Àm-hă-ăretz as it is in the Rabbinic traditions. The term which was a technical term for the Samaritans after the arrival of the Jews after their exile and was used by the Pharisaic groups to differentiate them from other ordinary Jews, who show little regard for the strict observance of the Law. Ebertz informs us how the Pharisaic circles used Àm-hă-ăretz as a derogatory term to brand all those Jews who ignored the purity laws as strictly followed by them. It became a technical term for all those who in the eyes of the Pharisees did not have concern for the purity laws and for those ordinary people who were ignorant of these laws.[29] The Rabbinic sayings categorize Jewish people into three categories, as Raney points out; they were "(1) the *bene torah* or students of the law; (2) the *Àm-hă-ăretz* or common people, and (3) the *borim* or very ignorant."³⁰ The people of the second category are understood to be those who have no concern for the Law. Not reciting the Shema, not paying the tithes and not eating his food with ceremonial cleanliness are some of the objections raised against the *Àm-hă-ăretz*.³¹ Since all of these objections suited also to the tax collectors, they were branded one with the *Àm-hă-ăretz*. Hence the combination of tax collectors with sinners, shows the thought pattern of the opponents of Jesus that the stigma of the *Àm-hă-ăretz* applies also to the tax collectors as a social group, who also belong to the *Àm-hă-ăretz* by having no regard for the law. Raney however rightly points out the major characteristic of this stigma attributed to the tax collectors and the *Àm-hă-ăretz*. Their stigma is not hereditary or based on their birth. Their stigma is because of their attitude towards the Law.³² This is the major differentiating factor between the self-righteous Pharisaic group and the tax collectors as socially inferior class on the one hand, and the elite *Brāhmaṇas* and the socially untouchable *Dalits* in India on the other, which will be studied later in our work.

Portrayal of the Tax Collectors in Luke

In Luke's Gospel we see many instances where tax collectors are in the presence of Jesus. They are portrayed as a group of people, who admit that they are sinners but in need of forgiveness. But they are shown to be willing to take steps to receive forgiveness from God. Right at the beginning of the Gospel, they are portrayed to have come to John the Baptist with the earnestness towards repentance (Luke 3:12); they are even positively contrasted with the Pharisees and are shown favorable in the eyes of God (Luke 18:9-14). Above all, Jesus feels at home in their company. One of the groups with whom Jesus happily reclines for meals in Luke's Gospel is the group of tax collectors. More than other Gospel writers, we see more instances of Jesus' dining with tax collectors in Luke (Luke 5:27-32; 15:1-2; 19:1-10). These instances betray the author's efforts to give specific importance to the group of tax collectors. The portrayal of the tax collectors in the third Gospel is significant since it shows the Lukan effort to contrast Jesus' teaching of the Kingdom of God which *includes* the socially and religiously outcasts of the society over against the ideology of the Pharisees for whom the tax collectors were sinners and hence *ipso facto excluded* from the Kingdom of God. Furthermore, it is important for us to understand the Lukan contrast between the tax collectors as those who eagerly *accept* Jesus and are ready to repent and the Pharisees who are portrayed as *rejecting* Jesus and who thought they were justified by their strict observance of the Law. Hence, we have here two contrasts in every fellowship meal of Jesus: the teaching of the Pharisees vs. the message of Jesus, the attitude of the Pharisees vs. the attitude of the tax collectors and sinners towards Jesus. The question that arises, however, is why, of all the seven despicable jobs the tax collectors alone are singled out by the opponents of Jesus? What could be the underlying aim of Luke in showing Jesus, dining with tax collectors? How are these table fellowship instances related to the Hellenistic literary *symposia*? What could be the reasons for Luke to narrate the table fellowship of Jesus similar to the Hellenistic *symposia*? Perhaps we find answers to these questions by going through the texts of Jesus' table fellowship with tax collectors and Pharisees.

The Banquet at the House of Levi (Luke 5:27-39)

With his first meal scene of Jesus, Luke introduces one of the most important controversies that Jesus had with the Pharisees and their scribes – his table fellowship with outcasts. The Levi Episode (Luke 5:27-39) could be divided into two parts: the call of Levi (Luke 5:27-29) and the banquet and emerging conversations that followed it (Luke 5:30-32, 33-39). With his redactional alterations Luke is able to synchronize the call of Levi together with the meal that followed and the question about fasting.[33] He does it so as to give an impression that all the three events (call, banquet and discussion) happen in the single framework of a fellowship meal of Jesus with Levi and thus he parallels this episode with the fellowship meal of another tax collector Zacchaeus (Luke 19:1-10). Thus the fact that Jesus engaged himself with the social outcasts of the society and enjoyed the company of the tax collectors gets a real picture with this episode. This would time and again resurface in the central section of the Gospel.

Call of Levi (Luke 5:27-28)

Luke chisels away the initial remarks found in Mark about Jesus passing along the lake and teaching the crowd (Mk 2:17) and focusses on Jesus' encounter with Levi. One is able to see the novelty in Luke as he changes the ordinary εἶδεν into a strong ἐθεάσατο. Jesus is not casually looking at Levi, as he passes by him, but he is observing Levi keenly; this reveals that it is Jesus who chooses Levi, and not the other way. This change of verb sharpens the picture of Jesus' initiative in inviting the tax collector to receive him.[34] Another difference which Luke makes from his Markan source is the absence of the name of Alphaeus, the father of Levi, which gives the readers a clue that for Luke, the importance is more on the profession of Levi than the name of his father.[35] By his editorial reconstruction of the story, Luke brings the story in connection with what has gone before and what comes after. It is interesting to note that, in contrast to Markan and Matthean parallels, the call of the first apostles in Luke, does not have this important command of Jesus δεῦτε ὀπίσω μου. Hence in Luke's Gospel, the command of Jesus "to follow" him (ἀκολούθει μοι) is first addressed to the tax collector Levi (cf. Luke 5:27; Mk 1:17; Matt 4:19; Luke 5:10). In the same way the response given by Levi in Luke (καὶ καταλιπὼν πάντα ἀναστὰς ἠκολούθει αὐτῷ) is similar to the response of the first apostles of Jesus. (Luke 5:11). Luke alone adds the redactional element of leaving everything - καταλιπὼν πάντα. Through this addition Luke connects the call of Levi with the call of the first Apostles at the Lake of Galilee.[36] This redactional connection is further strengthened at least partly remotely by the fact that the controversy of Jesus' association with the 'tax collectors and sinners' (Luke 5:33), has an echo in the narration of the call of Peter, wherein he says "Go away from me, Lord, for I am a sinful man!" (Luke. 5:8).

Banquet of Acceptance (Luke 5:29)

The response of Levi leads him to host a 'great banquet' in honor of Jesus. The vague construction in Mk 2:15 with third-person pronouns (Καὶ γίνεται κατακεῖσθαι αὐτὸν ἐν τῇ οἰκίᾳ αὐτοῦ) is corrected in Luke with the proper name of Levi (Luke 5:29). Luke thereby clarifies, what otherwise had caused an unending discussion on the question, who was intended by Mark in both the pronouns – whether it was Jesus who sat at table at *his* house, or it was Levi who sat at table in *his* house, or it was Jesus who sat at table at the house of Levi.[37] It is clear in Luke's Gospel that it is Levi who is the host of this great banquet and Jesus is the chief guest in his house. Furthermore, to add to what was a simple act of "κατακεῖσθαι" sitting or reclining at table to eat (Mk 2:14), Luke changes a normal meal into a "δοχὴν μεγάλην." Through this Luke evokes in his audience the flavor of a sympotic meal.[38] By portraying Levi as the one, who gave a great banquet, Luke has made Levi as the host of the *symposium* and Jesus is then the chief guest who is invited along with others.

Unlike Mark, Luke as the narrator does not portray those who sat with Jesus as 'tax collectors and *sinners*' (Mk 2:15), but substitutes it to a gentle "tax collectors and *others*" (πολὺς τελωνῶν καὶ ἄλλων Luke 5:29). On the one hand, it could mean that Luke does not want to brand tax collectors as sinners; rather he wants to distance himself from the Pharisaic thought that links tax collectors as a group that is despicable in the society. This seems to indicate on the one hand, as Nolland rightly points out, that in the Lukan perspective, those who are willing to be with Jesus can no longer be called as sinners.[39] It could also mean on the other, that Luke does not want to make a provocative statement about whom Jesus chose to be his table companions. According to Hotze, there is a christological and soteriological aim in the addition of the words "others."[40] The redaction of the evangelist, πολὺς τελωνῶν καὶ ἄλλων brings to light once again the all-inclusive nature of Jesus' mission. Luke wants to show that Jesus' ministry is not for one particular group of people – not only for the righteous but also for the sinners. He has come for everyone. He is guest to whomsoever, who accepts and invites him. This view is strengthened later by the fact that Jesus accepted the invitations of the Pharisees to dine with them.

Murmuring of the Pharisees (Luke 5:30)

The conflict of Jesus with the Pharisees, which began already during Jesus' healing of the paralytic (Luke 5:17-26), gets aggravated by this banquet scene. Historically it would have been unlikely for a Pharisee to be present at the dining venue, at the house of Levi. LaVerdiere suggests that the presence of Pharisees at the dining venue of Jesus with Levi could be paralleled to the self-righteous Christians among the Lukan Christian community who represent the Pharisaic thought pattern, whose attitude was similar to that of the self-righteous Pharisees, judging everyone else as sinners. This view, says LaVerdiere, is further strengthened by the fact that the criticism is not directed to Jesus himself but to the disciples.[41] In any case, Luke has been more successful than other synoptic writers in connecting the call of Levi (5:27-28) and the murmuring of 'the Pharisees and their scribes' together with the banquet scene. The word that Luke uses to denote the murmuring attitude of the Pharisees is ἐγόγγυζον. The verb γογγύζειν has a theological character in the LXX in that it points to the negative character of humans in relation to God's benevolence and parallels the Pharisees and the scribes to the Israelites who murmured against Moses and Aaron (Exod 15:24, 16:2). It is understood that Luke does not use the term in such a theological connotation but only in its secular meaning of showing displeasure and dissatisfaction about one's action.[42] It is interesting to note though, that Luke uses this word only thrice (Luke 5:29, 15:2, 19:7). In all these three times the word is used to denote the response of the opponents against Jesus eating with the tax collectors. The fact that Luke uses the word in three instances, which are similar in content - i.e. murmuring of the opponents of Jesus against the all-inclusive banqueting of Jesus and his all-embracing character of his message - leads one to think, that Luke uses the word perhaps in a theological connotation as it was in the LXX, as "the judgment and condemnation of God by the man whom God has bound to Himself."[43]

Table Talk

In Luke, the murmuring of the Pharisees and their questioning the apostles have been transformed have taken the form of a table talk during the Hellenistic συμπόσιον that follows the δεῖπνον. The content of the discussion in this table talk is derived from what is happening at the banquet - as was always the case in every Hellenistic *symposium*.[44] Luke has intentionally made this unity, by including the aspect of drinking in the question - "Why do you eat and *drink* with tax collectors and sinners?" (Luke 5:30). This combination of eating and drinking continues further in the second theme of table talk, about the fact that the disciples of John fast and pray whereas the disciples of Jesus eat and drink (5:33). Through this combination of eating and drinking, Luke cements the unity of the call of Levi and his fellowship meal with Jesus together with the two controversies. Scholars suggest that Luke does not invent this combination of eating and drinking but takes it from Q.[45] Besides, the Pharisees do not question the eating and drinking of Jesus as it is in Mark but question only the behavior of the disciples. This could very well refer to the Lukan community's "*Sitz im Leben* in which the early Church sought to defend its own associations with the outcasts of the Jewish society, perhaps even with gentile 'sinners.'"[46] This is strengthened by the fact that for the first time the term 'disciples' appear here. Perhaps the Lukan community had serious problems due to its all-inclusive nature of fellowship meal, which had to be addressed. This practice of the early Church has been justified by the evangelist from the very practice of Jesus himself.

The Solemn Pronouncement of Jesus (Luke 5:31-32)

Jesus' answer to the Pharisees and the scribes consists of two parts. The first statement about the physician and the sick has its parallels in Greek proverbs.[47] Through this imagery of a physician in v. 31, Jesus justifies his presence in the company of the tax collectors. In the second part (v. 32) Jesus enumerates for what he has been sent and what his mission is. He has come to "call" not the righteous but the sinners. The verb καλεῖν takes the connotation of the host who invites the guests to his banquet.[48] While the first part of Jesus' answer in v. 32 is similar to Mark and Matthew, Luke makes a significant addition in Jesus' answer - εἰς μετάνοιαν. While Mark and Matthew only write about Jesus calling the sinners, Luke explicitly states the purpose of his calling the sinners. Καλεῖν comes thus with a precondition which Luke alone presents in his Gospel, namely repentance. Through this unique word Luke sums up the aim of Jesus' table fellowship with tax collectors and sinners and succinctly answers his critics.

That the term repentance is very important for Luke is very clear from the fact that Luke uses it more often than the other synoptic writers.[49] Although Jesus takes up from John the Baptist the message of repentance (Luke 3:3-14), which for John the Baptist meant returning to God and thereby avoiding judgment, Jesus takes repentance to a higher perspective. "Conversion as Jesus understands is not just negative. It is more than a break with the old nature in face of the threat of eschatological judgment. It embraces the whole walk of the man who is claimed by the divine lordship. It carries with it the founding of a new personal relation of man to God."[50] Hence, repentance contains in it the unconditional invitation of God to return and the consequent joy on the part of the humans. The banquet that Levi offered to Jesus is the result of his repentance and the expression of his joy.

Feasting versus Fasting (Luke 5:33-39)

The controversy regarding the fasting of the disciples of John and of the Pharisees and feasting of the disciples of Jesus (Luke 5:33-39), is redactionally as well as thematically connected by Luke to this table talk, following the banquet of Levi. In Mark the controversy story begins anew with a narration by the writer, and those who question Jesus are not the Pharisees but the people (Mk 2:18). But Luke joins the controversy story together with the phrase, οἱ δὲ εἶπαν (Luke 5:33). Through this he suggests that the same Pharisees and scribes who questioned Jesus during the table talk continue to pose another question. Thus Luke has redactionally brought together under this table talk two controversy stories - Jesus´ eating and drinking with tax collectors and of the disciples feasting instead of fasting - thereby bringing a unity between the call of Levi, the great banquet and the controversies. It is also thematically connected with the theme of repentance (Luke 5:32).[51] The question for the Pharisees was that if Jesus calls sinners for repentance, why he does not encourage fasting - which is the sign of repentance, which is also what the disciples of John and the Pharisees observed. Jesus and his disciples are differentiated from the disciples of John and of Pharisees in that they do not fast but eat and drink. For Luke, "The message of Jesus concerning μετάνοια does not drive us to the torture of penitential works or to despair. It awakens joyous obedience for a life according to God's will."[52] This is why there is more joy over a repentant sinner not only in heaven (Luke 15:10) but also on this earth and this element of joy takes its form in the fellowship meals of Jesus.

The Banquet at the House of Zacchaeus (Luke 19:1-10)

The next chapter would be dedicated to an exegetical analysis of Luke 19:1-10 and hence it would perhaps suffice here, just to note how the story of Zacchaeus is interconnected with the story of Levi as well as the fellowship meals of Jesus with three Pharisees and how themes dear to Luke could be found in both texts. First of all, the similarities between the first banquet of Jesus with a tax collector (Levi) and the last banquet of Jesus with a tax collector (Zacchaeus) are apparent. From a structural point of view, it is interesting to note, that the meal narratives of Jesus with the tax collectors sandwich the meal narratives of Jesus with the Pharisees. There is a progression that could be clearly seen in all these meal narratives. Levi was an ordinary toll collector while Zacchaeus was the chief of the toll collectors. This progression is also seen in the meal narratives of Jesus with the Pharisees. Simon was an ordinary Pharisee; so was the case with another Pharisee who had invited Jesus to a festive lunch. But the final meal of Jesus with the leader of the Pharisees.

The story of Zacchaeus also goes a step further in the theme of sharing of wealth to the poor that ran through the preceding meal narrations. The question of being the followers of Christ and their handling of possession is dealt once again with the fact that Zacchaeus was a chief of toll collectors and therefore very rich (Luke 19:2). Although he does not leave everything to follow Jesus, as did Levi (Luke 5:28), Zacchaeus makes use of his wealth to secure his salvation, by willingly giving away half of his property to the poor (Luke 19:7) and thereby contrasts the negative model of the rich ruler who hesitated to share his riches with the poor (Luke 18:18-25) and other such negative models of the rich in the Gospel (Luke 6:24, 12:16, 14:12, 16:1, 19-22).

Table Fellowship of Jesus with Pharisees

Luke's Gospel has many instances where Pharisees appear in the presence of Jesus. They warn him about the possible threat to his life from Herod (Luke 13:31). Although they are cynical about Jesus that he enjoys table fellowship with tax collectors and sinners (Luke 5:30; 7:34; 15:1-2), they all the same invite Jesus to dine with them (Luke 7:36-50; 11:37-54; 14:1-24). These banquet scenes are significant and unique since no other Gospel writer narrates the willingness of the Pharisees to invite Jesus who constantly challenges their notion of purity.

The Banquet at the House of Simon (Luke 7:36-50)

The tension, which was already palpable at the banquet of Levi, namely Jesus' attitude towards sinners and the response of the Pharisees against Jesus' behavior, is taken by Luke to a higher level, in this first banquet of Jesus with a Pharisee. The overwhelming similarities between this banquet scene with that of Markan, Matthean and Johannine parallels (cf. Mk 14:3-9; Matt 26:1-13; Jn 12:1-8) cannot be ignored: Jesus is at a banquet, Simon is the host (except in John), a woman appears on the scene, anoints him with a costly oil; this action is criticized by those around, and Jesus justifies the woman's actions. Scholars find also similarities in the word usage in the narration.[53]

There are also, however, overwhelming contrasts between the Lukan version of the story and that of others.[54] In Luke the placing of the banquet is somewhere in the setting of Jesus' Galilean ministry, whereas in all the other Gospels the setting is in Bethany and the context is the ensuing passion of Jesus in Jerusalem. Luke has however placed the pericope in the context of and as the continuation of the previous pericope, where Jesus talks about the criticism about him by opponents as a glutton and drunkard and a friend of tax collectors and sinners (Luke 7:34-35). This time, though, these two aspects of eating and drinking and friendship with the sinners are displayed at the house of a Pharisee himself. The host of the banquet in the Lukan version is Simon the Pharisee where as in other Synoptics it is Simon the leper; in John it is at the house of Martha, Mary and Lazarus (cf. Mk 14:3; Matt 26:6; Jn 12:2-3). The criticism in the other Gospels is about the cost of the perfume, which could have been used to help the poor, whereas in the Lukan version the criticism is about the fact that the one who anoints Jesus is a sinful woman. In Mark and Matthew the woman pours out the oil on the head of Jesus whereas in Luke she anoints Jesus' feet with the costly perfume.[55] Since in other Gospels, the context of the anointing is the passion that Jesus has to undergo in Jerusalem, the action of the woman anointing the head / feet of Jesus is narrated by the evangelists, as the anticipation of the anointing of Jesus' dead body (Mk 14:8; Matt 26:12; Jn 12:7). This is completely left out by Luke, who renders a whole new meaning to the anointing. The context of the anointing in Luke is in the background of repentance of the woman which is shown by her tears and the expression of the consequent forgiveness of her sins.

These differences between the Lukan version of the story and the other Gospels have led some scholars to conclude that either there was one original tradition about anointing of Jesus which was probably worked out by different evangelists to suit their own theological orientation,[56] or there were two traditions which were connected together by Luke – anointing of Jesus on his head, which could be found in Mark and Matthew and anointing of Jesus by a woman on his feet and her wiping them with her hair, which would be found in Luke and John.[57] It is difficult to state conclusively whether Luke takes the anointing tradition from Mark[58] and adds the parable of the debtor in it (Luke 7:40-43), or Luke found the entire anointing story together with the parable already in his special Luke material;[59] one thing we could be sure of, is that Luke is responsible for its placement here, just after the Q sayings of Jesus, in which Jesus compares himself with John the Baptist, and accepting the criticism of the opponents as the friend of tax collectors and sinners. Luke 7:36-50 is hence a narrative explanation of the criticism about Jesus' intimacy with sinners in 7:34-35, and the sinful woman who approaches Jesus, plays the role of the 'tax collectors and sinners' as against Simon the Pharisee. Thereby Luke drives home very clearly the central theological theme that runs along the entire Gospel, namely, Jesus' acceptance of sinners and the joy of the sinners because of being accepted by Jesus and the resulting repentance, which is seen in their external deeds. Once again we see the Lukan connection of banquet, repentance of sin and the joy of conversion that is expressed in outward actions.

Sympotic Meal Setting

As stated earlier, no other Gospel writer, except Luke, narrates a banquet in which Jesus is invited by a Pharisee. Luke goes on to narrate not just one, but three banquets, in which Jesus is said to have partaken with Pharisees. All the three fellowship meals are narrated in the form of the Hellenistic *symposium*. Bendemann looks at all the three meals of Jesus, with Pharisees together with the banquet of Jesus with the Levi as belonging to the typical Hellenistic sympotic setting. Through the following table Bendemann throws light on the sympotic setting, which could be seen in the meals narratives in which Jesus is said to have participated with Pharisees:

Meal setting   (Luke 5:29, 7:36; 11:37; 14:1)

Fait Divers   (Luke 5:29; 7:37-38; 11:38; 14:2-6)

Reaction to the incident (Luke 5:30; 7:39; 11:38; 14:4,6)

The response of Jesus	(Luke 5:31-32; 7:40-48; 11:39-44; 14:7-14)
Further objection	(Luke 5:33; 7:49; 11:45; 14:15)
Final and solemn proclamation of Jesus	(Luke 5:34-39; 7:50; 11:46-52; 14:16-24).[60]

Among the three Pharisaic banquets, only in Luke 7:36-50 the name of the Pharisee is rendered. It is also interesting to note that at the beginning of the narration the host is being introduced without his name. The host Pharisee is only casually mentioned as τις τῶν Φαρισαίων (7:36). Only as the story unveils, the name Simon is revealed to the readers. Bovon believes that the framework of the banquet setting is not the invention of Luke; rather he has happily absorbed it from his special Lukan material.[61] Nolland too suggests something similar: "the meal setting here is too integral to the episode to have been created merely for the sake of this literary convention."[62]

Looking at the larger picture of all the banquet scenes of Jesus which are narrated in the central section of Luke, in which controversy stories are blended with the sympotic banquet framework, the possibility suggested by Nolland and others could be doubted since in all these banquet narrations, the Lukan redactional efforts are clear to be seen. His attempt to portray the meal scene as a *symposium* is evident from the usage of the words, κατεκλίθη and κατάκειται (7:36-37). Further, the sinful woman, standing ὀπίσω παρὰ τοὺς πόδας αὐτοῦ suggests a sympotic background, where the guests reclined, with their legs stretched outwards. This doubt is strengthened by the fact that Luke has summarized the entire banquet scene of the Greek *symposium* in just one verse (7:36). The host's invitation to the festive meal, the guest's acceptance and the act of reclining are narrated just in the preliminary remarks, so that the readers could concentrate on the controversy that follows. Since no other Gospel shows that a Pharisee invites Jesus to dine with him, it could be said that it is a redactional work of Luke himself. The fact that a Pharisee invites Jesus for a *symposium*, his previous understanding of Jesus as a prophet and his address of Jesus as διδάσκαλε, could be taken to believe that the Pharisees are portrayed here in a better light by Luke. One should however realize that every time Jesus enters into a fellowship meal with the Pharisees, they are either scandalized by the actions of Jesus and/or Jesus criticizes their actions.

With the phrase καὶ ἰδού Luke brings in the *fait divers*. Just as it was the case in the Greek literary *symposia*, in which, some intriguing event at the sympotic meal that occurred became the starting point of the sympotic discussion, so also here, Luke brings in the element of the unexpected which would introduce to the participants the theme for the table talk. This sudden and unexpected incident is well introduced by the phrase καὶ ἰδού. The house of a Pharisee who is known for his faithful observances of the Laws of purity, witnesses the entry of a woman who, by the nature of her profession, is sinful and unclean. Although it is not clearly stated that the woman was a prostitute, she is understood by the Pharisee to be sinner. Furthermore, since a Pharisee would not consider a formal wife of a Jew as a sinner, and this woman presents herself uninvited in the men-only sympotic room, she would have been understood by the readers of Luke as a prostitute.[63]

The woman weeps and as tears fall down the feet of Jesus, she "dries" them away with her unbound hair[64] and kisses them. Through the usage of imperfect tense here (ἐξέμασσεν καὶ κατεφίλει τοὺς πόδας αὐτοῦ καὶ ἤλειφεν), Luke reminds the readers that it was a continuous action. Her actions of unbinding her hair before the congregation of men and continuous kissing the feet of Jesus were nothing but "*Geste des Eros*," as Bovon calls it.[65] The erotic connotation continues with the anointing. The Lukan source varies from Mark and Matthew (Mk 14:3; Matt 26:7) in that, the woman pours the alabaster jar of ointment not on the head but on the feet of Jesus. It was understandable for Jews that someone is being anointed on the head. Such an action was loaded with theological meaning and hence Mk 14:3 would have been understood christologically by Markan community as the anointing of the suffering Messiah.[66] But washing of the feet of a person in the Jewish world was a personal affair in the house chambers, done either by wife of the man or his daughter.[67] Viewing from this point of view, one gets the feeling that Luke once again wants to portray the intimacy with which the woman serves Jesus. Thus the anointing of Jesus' feet once again confirms the literary motif, as Marshall points out.[68] As the diners at a *symposium* reclined, their legs are stretched outwards, it would have been easier for the woman to anoint Jesus' feet rather than his head. Wiefel makes an interesting comparison of the sinful woman in Luke with Aseneth in the Story of *Joseph and Aseneth*.[69] He compares the shedding of tears and the unbound hair of the sinful woman with the shedding of tears by the repentant Aseneth and her unbound hair as the sign of her repentance (Luke 10:14-17). When Joseph enters her house, Aseneth does not allow her maids to wash the feet of Joseph; instead she insists that she herself would wash his feet (*JosAs* 20:1-5). Seen from this perspective, more than rendering an erotic connotation, the actions of the sinful woman – her tears, her unbound hair, her kissing the feet of Jesus and anointing them – suggest an attitude and action of repentance on the part the woman who, in the view of Jesus, displays a better and more loving hospitality than the real host, the Pharisee. How was it possible that a woman of sinful nature could enter freely without any hindrance and without any invitation, at the house of a Pharisee whose meal is supposed to be eaten as though in the presence of the Holy Altar? This question remains unanswered in the text.

Sinful Woman - the Real Hostess

The host Pharisee has allowed the uninvited sinful woman to do what she pleased to his guest. But more than *her* actions, it is the behavior of Jesus and his silent acceptance of the actions of the woman, which irritate the Pharisee (Luke 7:38). What follows is a sympotic discussion following the *fait divers* in which Jesus is acknowledged as the teacher. By calling the Pharisee by his name, and giving a reply for his silent criticism, Jesus has already shown that he is a prophet, which the sinful woman had already understood. At the end of the parable, Jesus has emerged as one, having the final say in the sympotic discussion, just as Socrates through his argument makes Agathon accept his failure in Plato's *Symposium*. Yet another parallel between Jesus and Socrates is suggested by Plummer. "The ὀρθῶς ἔκρινας may be compared with the πάνυ ὀρθῶς of Socrates, when he has led the disputant into an admission which is fatal."[70] Already by now, the Pharisee, who is „*der Schüler gewordene Lehrer*"[71] has stepped down from his superiority complex by accepting his defeat in Luke 7:43. Jesus humiliates him further, by contrasting him with the sinful woman in the antithetic parallel: "you gave me no water for my feet, but she has bathed my feet with her tears and dried them with her hair. You gave me no kiss, but from the time I came in, she has not stopped kissing my feet. You did not anoint my head with oil, but she has anointed my feet with ointment" (Luke 7:44-46). Within the setting of the *symposium* Luke tries to intend his readers something deeper than mere love or repentance on the part of the sinful woman. Through the fact that she washes the feet of the guest and dries them and pours oil and kisses, Luke tells the reader, that the woman who comes into the sympotic setting uninvited, usurps from the Pharisee the role of the host. She fulfills the role of the host and so becomes the real hostess for the chief guest Jesus and Simon the Pharisee is for the Lukan community a '*Gegenmodell.*'[72] Although it is debatable whether a host of a banquet should anoint the guests with oil and kiss them as they enter,[73] the parallel actions and the lack of them by the sinful woman and the Pharisee are clearly contrasted by Jesus - which are to be understood as the expression of love and the lack of it with which they receive Jesus (Luke 7:47) Hence as Bovon says, the Pharisee who doubted the prophetic knowledge of Jesus and who had judged the woman as a sinner(Luke 7:39), has been given judgement by Jesus for his lack of hospitality,[74] whereas the sinful woman is gifted by Jesus forgiveness of sins (Luke 7:48) salvation and peace (Luke 7:50).

Positive Role of the Sinful Woman in the Banqueting Community of Luke

The *Sitz im Leben* of the Lukan community could be inferred through this narrative of the presence of the sinful woman at the banqueting house of a self-righteous Pharisee. Melzer-Keller thinks that the sinful woman could perhaps point to the women of the Lukan community, who perhaps belonged to the upper elite class and whose moral standards were low. The narrative is then a call for these women of the Lukan community for repentance as Melzer-Keller understands.[75] When we look at the pericope in relation to the meals of Jesus with "tax collectors and sinners" whose company Jesus happily cherished, Luke 7:29-34 once again brings in sharp focus, the contrast between the Pharisees on the one hand and the tax collectors and sinners on the other, with regard to their reception of Jesus. The sinful tax collector (Levi) and the sinful woman (Luke 7:36) could be seen as a positive role models of the Lukan community; they could represent those who eagerly accepted the way of Jesus, and ready to repent and mend their past lives of sin. The banquet room they entered into, could be the Lukan community who could be judgmental about their past. But Jesus, the chief guest lovingly accepts them, when they show their repentance through their actions. Through the contrasting parallel between the Pharisee and the sinful woman, the Lukan Jesus tells the community, that those who, in spite of their sinful nature, are ready to accept Jesus and willing to meet him are no more outsiders; because, „»in Frieden« gehen heißt, dass sie in eine Gemeinschaft hineingerufen sind."[76]

The Pharisees, on the contrary, are portrayed as negative role models for those who stand in the way of the sinful men and women, who are willing to repent. They oppose the fact that the sinners are accepted by the community of Jesus. Hence the text calls for a change of heart on the part of the sinful to accept Jesus; all the more it calls for a change of heart on the part of those who are already in the community to accept the sinful but repentant men and women, who are ready and willing to shed away from their past life and accept Jesus. In this way, the pericope serves as the narrative answer to the criticism about Jesus in Luke 7:34, as 'a glutton and a drunkard, a friend of tax collectors and sinners.'

The sympotic scenery has become a means for the Lukan Jesus to be in touch with sinners. The pericope has successfully shown the readers who can be the hosts for Jesus and his community. Luke brings the element of reversal of roles in this literary *symposium*. The self-righteous Pharisee is no more a host for the Lukan Jesus. On the contrary, the humbly weeping sinful woman who shows her repentance and love for Jesus through her actions of kissing and wiping his feet, has taken the role of the host for Jesus and his community. In the final sentence of the pericope, Luke once again brings up the change of roles in the literary *symposium*. As it was in the banquet of Levi, here too, Jesus does change his role at the *symposium*. He is no more the chief guest at the house of Simon the Pharisee. By having the final word in the συμπόσιον, and by his solemn forgiveness of sins of the woman, he takes upon himself the role of the host. In short, the banquet to which Simon the Pharisee invited Jesus to be the chief guest, ends up showing to the readers, who really the host of the fellowship meal is and who is not and what role repentance and self-righteousness play in accepting and rejecting Jesus.

Banquet at the House of another Pharisee (Luke 11:37-54)

Once again the Lukan Jesus is invited by a Pharisee for a festive meal. Closely following the heels of Simon the Pharisee, whom the Lukan Jesus had contrasted with the uninvited sinful woman and whom he criticized for not fulfilling the conditions of a host, and instead praised the woman as a better host, there comes another Pharisee who is willing to host an ἄριστον for Jesus. Jesus accepts the invitation but the hospitality of the Pharisee is reciprocated by Jesus with a series of woes addressed to the Pharisees and scribes, the participants of ἄριστον. The text which began with a cordial invitation to a meal, ends with the scribes and Pharisees very hostile to the one whom they had invited (Luke 11:53-54). The text does have its parallels in Matt 23, in its wordings and content; but there are also differences between the two.[77] The context of these woe sayings in Luke is the Travel Narrative while in Matthew Jesus addresses the woe sayings at the Temple in Jerusalem. There are some omissions of words and content in Luke from what is seen in Matthew. For example, Matthew has taken all the seven woes from Q, scattered all through the chapter (Matt 23:2, 13, 15, 23, 25, 27, 29) and these woes are addressed to the "scribes, Pharisees and hypocrites." Luke on the other hand, has taken these seven woes, but reduced them to six and packs them into two sets of three woes, the first three addressed to the Pharisees (Luke 11:42-44) and the second three to the lawyers (Luke 11:46-52). Besides, Luke does not have place for the Pharisees' neglect of the "weightier matters of the Law" as in Matt 23:23. Probably the Lukan audience did not need to be reminded about the observances of the Jewish Law.[78] The Lukan addition of Jesus' advice to the Pharisees to give alms (Luke 11:41) is not found in Matthew. Finally the most important difference between Matthew (Q) and Luke with regard to the context, is that Luke frames the entire woes in the context of a fellowship meal with a Pharisee. Hence one could clearly see the redactional addition of the author at the beginning (Luke 11:37-38) in the middle (Luke 11:45) and at the end (Luke 11:53-54).

This meal scene with the Pharisee goes hand in hand with the previous meal of Jesus with Simon the Pharisee (Luke 7:36-50). One could see the similarities between the two meal scenes through the (a). invitation by a Pharisee, (b). acceptance by Jesus, (c). the action of Jesus which induce astonishment on the part of the host and which leads the meal scene moving towards sympotic discussion. In both the scenes, the host responds only silently. However the difference between the two is that in Luke 7:36-50 Jesus' criticism was only towards Simon, an individual Pharisee, whereas in Luke 11:37-54 not only is the criticism directed to Pharisees in general; but the criticism is more brutal and vehement, compared to the politeness of the Pharisee, who invited him.

Sympotic Setting

Steele argues convincingly that the woe sayings of Luke 11:37-54 has been deliberately put by Luke in the literary form of a *symposium*, which could be seen in the redactional efforts of the author in Luke 11:37-38, 45, and 53-54.[79] Sympotic rules found in the literary *symposia* are followed here. The Pharisee is introduced by the narrator as the host who invites Jesus the chief guest, who immediately accepts the invitation and takes his seat at the table. The prominence given to the (chief) guest is seen from the fact that he is "the only one named and explicitly invited."[80] Jesus does not wash his hands before his meals which becomes the *fait divers* in this banquet scene. The host is astonished about the foregoing of the rules of meal etiquette by Jesus; this brings the participants to the discussion. One of the features of the Hellenistic *symposium* was the apparent wisdom of the chief guest who always wins at sympotic discussions. The wisdom of Jesus as the chief guest is seen here too, from the fact that the entire sympotic discussion is dominated by Jesus alone. The other guests make their appearance not at the opening of the scene but very gradually (Luke 11:45). Besides, as Steele points out,[81] the wisdom of Jesus as the guest is clearly linked with the phrase ἐν δὲ τῷ λαλῆσαι placed at the very beginning of the pericope; this phrase links the wisdom of Jesus during this sympotic discussion with the preceding verses regarding the wisdom of Jesus which is greater than that of Solomon (Luke 11:31).

The Polite Host

Looking at the laws of hospitality in the Mediterranean world, Pitt-Rivers observes that both the host and the guest have the duty to respect each other. The host is honored by the people whom he receives as guest and honors them, if he found them superior to him in wisdom. And the guest receives honor through the invitation he receives from the host and is duty bound to reciprocate that honor. Although the social positions of the host and the guests could differ from one another, especially in the sympotic context, they have one thing in common; both have to respect and honor each other through their actions.[82] Both of them breach the code of conduct and lose their honor when they fail to show respect for each other. The law of hospitality was breached in a *symposium* literature either by the host or by the guest. The host could breach the traditional code of *symposium* in three ways: (a). by insulting the guest, or by showing rivalry and hostility, (b). by failing to protect the honor of the guest before other guests (even if he does feel hatred towards his guest), and (c). by failing to offer what is best and most needed to the guest at his house. In turn the guest breaches the law of hospitality (a). by showing his hostility towards the host and insulting him, (b). by taking upon himself the role of the host, by ordering the servants what to do, and doing other things which only the host is supposed to do, and (c). by refusing to take what is offered by the host.[83] From this perspective of the breach of the sympotic rules, we need to look at the Pharisee, the host and Jesus, the chief guest in Luke 11:37-54.

The Pharisees, as we have seen in the first chapter, were a group of people who did not engage in table fellowship with everyone, except those who were willing to follow the rules of purity. Here, the Pharisee invites Jesus for a meal. The very fact that Jesus was invited by the Pharisee to dine with him is itself in the eyes of Luke and his readers, a sign of acceptance of Jesus by the Pharisees. We are not told that the Pharisee had any intention of putting Jesus to test or wanted to humiliate him. In all his good will he wants to be the host of Jesus. The phrase in the beginning, Ἐν δὲ τῷ λαλῆσαι does not point out to the Pharisee's interrupting Jesus as he speaks, but it points out to the politeness of the Pharisee. Further his politeness is once again attested by the fact that he 'requests' (ἠρώτα) Jesus to come to his house for meal.[84] Even at the end of the narration the author points out to the readers the politeness of the host from the fact that no offense is targeted at Jesus as long as he remains at the house of the Pharisee as a guest. Only after Jesus had left the house, the Pharisees and the scribes were hostile against Jesus. Hence the Pharisee fulfills his role as a host, without in any way breaching the code of hospitality in any way. (a). He does not show his hostility towards his guest. (b). Even when he is not satisfied with the actions of his guest, he does not say anything openly. (c). Till the guest leaves his house, the Pharisee sees to it that his guest is honored in his house.

The Rude Guest at the *Symposium*

On the contrary, it is Jesus the chief guest who is shown to be offending the host, the Pharisee, by not following the rules of hospitality. At a *symposium* it is the duty of the guest to comply with the rules of the community or group which has invited him for meals. But Jesus does not wash his hands before meals, which was an astonishment for the host Pharisee, who must have thought, Jesus would abide by the rules of a sympotic meal. Further he insults not only the host but also the other guests of the hosts, other Pharisees as well as lawyers. This insult is very vehement with many woes addressed to the Pharisees and the lawyers in general. The rudeness of Jesus was so conspicuous as to turn the host-guest relationship into enmity, as Gowler points out.

> Jesus' actions would be shameful for at least two reasons (1) He did not conform to his host's purity regulations, (2) His attack on the Pharisees goes beyond what his host's subsequent response ("astonishment") calls for. Because Jesus is a guest in the Pharisee's home, this show of hostility nullifies any possible positive ramifications of sitting down to dine together. The infringement of the hospitality code destroys the social roles of host and guest, incorporation from guest to friend does not occur, and Jesus, the Pharisees, and the lawyers all revert to a hostile relationship. They are no longer host and guest, they are enemies.[85]

Hence by breaking the hospitality code and by condemning the host and other guests, the Lukan Jesus has turned the meal setting of friendship into a setting of controversy and animosity. As a result both the host as well as the guest did not play their respective roles, corresponding to their character in the context of a *symposium*.

Rudeness Explained

A surprised reader might raise the following questions: why would the Lukan Jesus act in such a rude manner? What could have been the possible motive for Luke to show Jesus as the one who breaches the code of hospitality? Why should Luke portray the main character as the one who breaks the existing rules of *symposium*? From the literary point of view, a possible reason could be, that it is not uncommon in the literary *symposia* that the chief character breaks the sympotic rules. Socrates is unsympotic in the fact that he deliberately comes late. He says he does not know the method of making *encomium* on *eros* and going a step further, he even ridicules the host. It would not be erroneous to guess then, that Luke perhaps wanted his Gospel to comply with this characteristic of the literary *symposia*, so as to parallel Jesus with Socrates.

Hotze understands this pericope in contrast to the *symposium* at the house of Levi. For him Jesus' sympotic meal with the Pharisee is a „gescheiterte Einkehr."[86] To show that the visit of Jesus to the house of the Pharisee has been unsuccessful, Luke uses the compound verb ἔρχεσθαι – first, at the very beginning of the narrative to suggest the entry of Jesus into the house (Luke 11:37b) and right at the end to inform the readers that Jesus went out of the house (Luke 11:53). The verb ἔρχεσθαι, which for Luke is a theological pointer to show the nearness of salvation, has been used at the end to denote the 'Auszug' of Jesus, thereby showing the failure of this visit in bringing salvation to the house.[87] The reason for this failure is perhaps the intention with which the Pharisee had invited Jesus for the banquet, namely to see, if Jesus was following the rules of the Torah.

Making a narrative analysis of the text, Gowler points out that it is Jesus who is the main character. And the other characters in the text are understood in the light of the main character - Jesus who is always positively portrayed. In this text too, at the very beginning the narrator has introduced Jesus as ὁ κύριος (Luke 11:39). Other characters have to be judged only in so far as they accept the main character or reject him. Even "when Jesus performs some actions that seem to be shameful, the narrator implicitly declares that those actions are actually honorable (e.g. Jesus' violation of hospitality laws). For members of Jesus' group, his deviant actions are honorable, simply because he as κύριος (11:39) performs them."[88]

Finally Luke seems to have a purpose in portraying the polemics between Jesus and the Pharisees in this central Pharisaic meal. He wants to show his young Christian community, the contrast between the strict and dry observance of the purity laws, and the new way of life, which

Jesus brings, wherein *agape* has the central role (Luke 11:41). Luke wants to tell the readers that the chasm between the Christian community and Jewish community gets wider and wider.[89] Already with the life of Jesus and his practice of table fellowship, the process of breaking away of the Christian community from the official Judaism has begun. This breaking away which could have been very evident among the Christian community through their fellowship meals, has its roots already in the fellowship meals of Jesus with the Pharisees.

The Banquet with the Leader of the Pharisees (Luke 14:1-24)

For the third and final time Luke reports the banquet of Jesus with a Pharisee and the Lukan Jesus heals someone during the Sabbath for the fourth and final time (Luke 4:31-37; 6:6-11; 13:10-17; 14:1-6). This time the host of Jesus is the leader of the Pharisees (τινος τῶν ἀρχόντων [τῶν] Φαρισαίων). Of all the banquet texts in Luke, chapter 14 shows the sympotic character most conspicuously: Jesus accepts the invitation of the leader of the Pharisees to dine with him. The place is the house of the Pharisee; there are other guests too for this fellowship meal (φαγεῖν ἄρτον - v. 15).[90] In this pericope, which stands at the centre of the Travel Narrative (Luke 9:51-19:44), there are four different subunits (healing of the man with dropsy (Luke 14:1-6), the instruction of Jesus to the guests of the banquet regarding the preferences on the seating arrangement (Luke 14:7-11), his instruction to the host Pharisee on whom to invite for a dinner (Luke 14:12-14) and the parable of the Great Dinner (Luke 14:15-24). The form of subunits is different from each other. Luke 14:1-6 could be understood as the healing story and/or a controversy[91] while the two instructions are understood to be *chreia* / pronouncement stories[92] concluded with the parable in vv. 16-24. Although seen in different literary forms, these four episodes are well connected by the Lukan redactor with the overarching framework of sympotic meals and hence they form a single unified pericope.

Through the introductory verse where the day (Sabbath), the place (house of the leading Pharisee) and the context (meal) are introduced, Luke shows the change in the setting, in that he introduces among the guests, a man who has dropsy(Luke 14:1).⁹³ Similarly one could see at the end a new setting (Συνεπορεύοντο δὲ αὐτῷ ὄχλοι πολλοί - Luke 14:25); the Travel Narrative which has been so far interrupted, continues once again. In contrast to other two Pharisaic meals of Jesus, this Pharisee who invites Jesus is the leader of the Pharisees; here the relationship of other guest Pharisees with the chief guest Jesus is not one of receptive and friendly attitude but one of maintaining distance in order to find fault with him (v. 1). Pharisees´ criticism of Jesus also comes to a climax. Jesus has not made himself unclean, either by passively allowing himself to be touched by a sinner, as he did in Luke 7:38, or by not washing his hands before meals, as it was the case in Luke 11:38. He consciously breaks the third commandment of the Decalogue by doing what a Jew should not do on the Sabbath.⁹⁴ Hence, Luke intentionally creates a progression in the third and final συμπόσιον of Jesus with the Pharisees.

Sympotic Setting

A first glance of Luke 14:1-24 reveals that except for the healing story (Luke 14:2-6), all the other three episodes within the chapter are connected by a single theme of banquet. Although the healing of the man with dropsy does not seem to fit in the scene of a *symposium* and it seems to have come from a different tradition, Luke has masterfully blended it with Luke 14:7-24 with his redactional verse (Luke 14:1) to show that the healing had actually happened during the *symposium*; hence, taken in this way, the one who was healed could have been one of the invited guests or an uninvited person; and the lawyers and the Pharisees who were not able to answer Jesus were actually the other invited guests.

The setting of *symposium*, which is seen already in verse 1, continues to dominate the entire pericope. All through the chapter we hear about the host, chief guest, other invited guests, seating arrangement and the eagerness of the guests to get the desired seats. More than any other text that we have looked so far, Luke 14:1-24 revolves around the sympotic table. As Braun rightly perceives, from the beginning till the end of Luke 14:1-24 we encounter time and again "dining-room terminologies,"⁹⁵ –

words that refer to a typical sympotic banquet. Jesus is invited to the house of the leader of the Pharisees for a 'meal' (φαγεῖν ἄρτον) on the Sabbath day (v. 1). The setting directs its attention now to the 'invited guests' (κεκλημένους) who eye for the 'seats of honor' (πρωτοκλισίας - v. 7). Jesus advises the guests about the right table etiquette. An invited guest should not recline (κατακλιθῇς) right away at the place of honor but should take the lowest place; this humility would later give him honor among other guests who recline at table (συνανακειμένῳ - vv. 8-11). The Lukan Jesus advises the host, who in case invites the guests for ἄριστον ἢ δεῖπνον (v. 12), whom to invite and whom not to invite as guests. Similarly the parable of the great banquet (δεῖπνον μέγα - v. 16) is filled with sympotic character.[96] Similar terminologies all along suggest to Ernst that Luke 14:1-24 has most probably come to Luke from the special L source[97] which has been readily taken by the redactor. However, the sympotic terminologies present here, which have also occurred earlier, and the progression that the author shows in the portrayal of the characters shown in the last of the Pharisaic *symposium* suggest that the text has undergone a heavy redaction by Luke.

Sabbath Meal and Healing (Luke 14:1-6)

The healing of the man with dropsy seems to have been deliberately placed within the meal which the leader of the Pharisees hosted for Jesus. One could find a link between the introductory verse (14:1) with Luke 7:36 which also had a Pharisee as the host. While the Pharisee in Luke 7:36 was an ordinary one, it is the leader of the Pharisees who hosts Jesus in Luke 14:1. Thus Luke brings in this text, a gradual progression and brings the banquets of Jesus with Pharisees, to a climax. The initial story (14:1-6) contains all the aspects of the literary form of a healing story – although in a very short form – (entry of the healer, the condition of the sick person, the actual healing and the sending away of the healed). Scholars see the similarities between Luke 14:1-6 and Mk 3:1-6, which is also a healing story during a Sabbath. However there are more differences than similarities between the two.[98] In Mk 3:1-6 Jesus heals a man with a withered hand while in Luke the man suffers from dropsy. The healing controversy takes place in the synagogue in Mark, whereas Luke places it in the house of the Pharisee in the setting of a meal. The process of healing is also different. In Luke Jesus took him (ἐπιλαβόμενος) and hence touched him whereas in Mark Jesus asks the sick to stretch out his hand and heals him. The question of Jesus to the Pharisees and lawyers about what they would do if their son or ox fell into a pit is missing in Mark 3:1-6. These differences lead many to conclude that Luke does not take the pericope from Mark but has found it in his special L material which had a saying (14:5) which might have had a 'prior life' in Q.[99] The changes which Luke has added into what he received from Q, attest to the redactional efforts of Luke to fit this healing controversy within a *symposium* setting.

Apart from Luke 14:2-6, the entire pericope (14:1-24) looks to be united with one common theme of banquet. When one reads Luke 14:1 which is followed by 14:7, one is able to see clearly the continuity in the context as well as in the narration. Hence Luke 14:2-6 could seem to be an unnecessary addition to the material. The Lukan community must have been curious to know more about the man with dropsy at a sympotic setting. They would have probably understood the man to be healed, in two ways:

(a). He could be taken to be one of the ἄκλητοι, the presence of whom was normal at the houses where a *symposium* took place. The Lukan readers would have quickly remembered the literary *symposia* and hence could have paralleled the man with dropsy as an ἄκλητος who in every literary *symposium* interrupts the peaceful order of the banquet.[100] Or he could be tolerated by the banqueters as an entertainer, because through his physical ugliness he could bring laughter among the banqueters. From this perspective, Luke seems to link this man with the sinful woman in Luke 7:36-50 who also comes uninvited but was tolerated by the Pharisee; Luke also links this man with all the 'tax collectors and sinners' who are readily accepted by Jesus during his banquets.[101]

(b). The man with dropsy might be understood to be one of the invited guests, and hence probably belonged to the Pharisaic elite.[102] If the latter were to be the case, then Luke already makes a subtle criticism on the very contention of the Pharisees about their uprightness in observing the laws of purity; by inviting and including the unclean man into their banquet, the Pharisees who considered themselves as upright, now prove themselves as unclean.

Ὑδρωπικός

Luke suggests in his Gospel that the possibility of salvation is granted through the nearness of Jesus. Salvation is offered to every house, which Jesus enters into. At the house of Levi, it is Levi himself, who was saved and at the house of Simon the Pharisee, it was the sinful woman; here at the house of the leader of the Pharisee, it is the man suffering from dropsy. The sickness of the person who is found among the banqueting Pharisees is a point of interest to us. A curious question has been posed here, regarding the sickness of the man i.e. why the man to be healed was suffering from dropsy and not from any other disease. In Mk 3:1-6, the man had a withered hand – a disease which has something to do with 'dryness.' But here in the Lukan text the man has a disease which is connected with water. Perhaps it is not without any purpose the redactor has portrayed the man as suffering from dropsy. Klein sees the connection between the question of Jesus about saving a child or an ox from falling into a well (obviously filled with water) and Jesus' action of healing the man who has the addiction of falling in water.[103] However in the present context of the *symposium*, the disease of the man has more to it than meets the eye. The sickness of the man suggests more than mere literary connections between Jesus 'words and actions' a point very well explained by Braun.

Braun suggests that the placement of the dropsy disease in Luke serves as a metaphorical symbol for "the unquenchable craving for drink, though the body is inflated with fluid, a craving which, when indulged, serves not to ease but to feed the disease."[104] He brings up many examples from Hellenistic literature where dropsy as a disease was equated with avarice and greed. We have already seen in the first chapter, how the satirists had voiced against the never ending late night parties and the uncontrolled and drunken behavior of the partakers. Here the example of Polybius is given by Braun: "[Scopas, the strategus of the Aetolians] was unaware that as in the case of a dropsy (τῶν ὑδρωπικῶν) the thirst of the sufferer never ceases and is never allayed by the administration of liquids from without, unless we cure the morbid condition of the body itself, so it is impossible to satiate the greed for gain, unless we correct by reasoning the vice inherent in the soul."[105] Further he quotes the conversation between the Micyllus and the Cock (Pythagorus) in Lucian's *The Dream or the Cock*, where the Cock says "the rich, unhappy that they are - what ills are they not subject to through intemperance? Gout and consumption and pneumonia and dropsy are the consequences of those splendid dinners" (*The Dream or the Cock* 23). From such references in the Hellenistic literature comparing dropsy with avarice, Braun suggests that this connection between the "signifier (dropsy) and the signified (greed) would have been an "every day familiarity"[106] among the readers of Luke. Hence for Braun, the Lukan redaction and introduction of the man with dropsy in the banquet setting of the Pharisees is to direct the attention of the readers to the greedy character of the Pharisees and scribes who were partaking at the *symposium,* hosted by the leader of the Pharisees. Although such a comparison seems to be far-fetched in the text, I think this interpretation fits well with the pericope, which is filled with the sympotic vocabulary. This interpretation is also strengthened by the following pericope about the guests trying to acquire the best place of honor so that they could get not only the best honor, but also better portions of food than the rest of the guests.

New Rules for a New Sympotic Community (Luke 14:7-11)

Already in our first chapter we learnt through Plutarch's *Table Talk*, how Alexidemus one of the guests went away angry because he was not given proper seat at a *symposium*. This incident was the starting point of the table talk. We saw in the first chapter that, Plutarch enumerated different ways of looking at seating arrangement at a *symposium*.[107] The discussion was whether the guests should be seated according to the age or the rank that one held in the society, or whether the social status of a person should be completely disregarded at a *symposium*, or whether one should adopt to the middle position which Plutarch advises, namely, when the invited guests consist of officials of the land then it is better to arrange seats according to the rank of the person, so that no one is hurt, and if those gathered are friends, then the guests could be allowed to take up whichever seats they would like to have.

Similarly, we see in this Pharisaic banquet with Jesus, the fact that the guests were seeking the seats of honor, becomes the starting point of the discussion (14:7-11).[108] Luke is therefore not new to this discussion on the preference of seats at table. The advice of the Lukan Jesus as to where to sit at a *symposium*, looks similar to the discussion seen in the Deutero-Canonical Book of Sirach too: "Take care not to be led astray and humiliated when you are enjoying yourself. When an influential person invites you, be reserved, and he will invite you more insistently. Do not be forward, or you may be rebuffed" (Sir 13:8-10). The Book of Proverbs too has something similar: "Do not put yourself forward in the king's presence or stand in the place of the great; for it is better to be told, "Come up here," than to be put lower in the presence of a noble" (Prov 25:6-7). Hence the Lukan Jesus "taps into the everyday life of his audience that he knows so well, playing upon the feelings of honor and shame which run so deep."[109] In Luke 14:7-11, two ways of reclining behavior are contrasted - those who seek the best places of honor at table and those who are satisfied with the least. Pharisees are once again put in the negative light. The *fait divers* (Luke 14:7) of Jesus, observing the guests who were taking the places of honor suggests clearly that these guests would have surely been fellow Pharisees, who were already criticized in the previous meal narrative as loving the most important seats in the synagogues and in the marketplaces (Luke 11:43). Hence this contrast looks to show the difference between the Pharisaic community and the new community of Jesus' followers who are advised against the Pharisaic attitude.

In his advice to the new community the Lukan Jesus goes against the normal sympotic practices. To occupy the lowest place at a formal dinner was something the guests would avoid. All the same this is what the Lukan Jesus suggests to his community. The advice would have been looked at by the readers of Luke as very practical; because the invited guest of the highest rank usually came to the *symposium* after all the other guests had arrived.[110] If someone occupied the seat of honor, he had to move down in order to give place for the chief guest and was hence ashamed in front of all the invited guests. Besides, Dillersberger notes the difference in the gradation of relationship between the host and the guests. The command of the host to the person who sought the highest place, "Give this man your place" (Luke 14:9), suggests a cold relationship between the host and the guest, whereas "Friend, move up higher" (Luke 14:10) denotes a personal warmth of friendship between the host and the guest.[111] The final maxim about the exalted and the humbled (14:11) which has been part of the wisdom tradition of the Near East[112] has been rightly placed here by Luke to emphasize the theme of practicing humility at table.

Luke places the entire pericope as a 'parable' (14:7). This shows that Luke does not mean to give just a practical and moral advice to his Christian community which frequently reclined at table. Since Jesus starts the parable with the phrase, "When you are invited by someone to a wedding banquet" (14:8), this wedding banquet could also be understood to denote the messianic banquet that the readers would be reclining at the end-time as Kealy and Dillersberger suggest.[113] This is where perhaps Luke differs from Plutarch, Sirach and Proverbs.

New Guidelines for the Host (14:12-14)
As a follow-up to the advice to the guests the Lukan Jesus gives advice to the host as to whom the host should invite for a dinner. In the Hellenistic times being invited for a dinner not only means that one's friendship with the host is good; it also means that the guest has the obligation to invite the host for a dinner at his house. Hence only those who were wealthy enough to host a party were invited. The favors that one would

hope to receive by inviting persons of high social status and rank are not only reciprocating invitations for a banquet; it would also imply honor in the society as well as political favors, because of the social connections. This is why Rathje tells us, inviting someone for a dinner party was then an investment.[114] Apart from Jesus, the invited guests at the house of the leader of the Pharisees would have been understood by the readers of Luke as people of the same social rank – socially and religiously influential Pharisees. Against this background comes the new guideline of the Lukan Jesus to the Pharisee and through him to the new Christian community, as to who are to be invited to a banquet and who are not to be.

The Lukan Jesus speaks of "two alternatives of hospitality."[115] These alternatives are contrasted side by side, starting with a conditional statement, followed by an action one should do and end with the consequence of that action.

When you give a lunch or dinner (Luke 14:12 b)	But when you give a banquet (Luke 14:13 a)
Do not invite (Luke 14:12 b)	invite (Luke 14:13 a)
your friends or your brothers or your relatives or rich neighbors (Luke 14:12 c)	the poor, the crippled, the lame, and the blind (Luke 14:13 a).
in case they may invite you in return (Luke 14:12 c)	And you will be blessed, because they *cannot repay* you (Luke 14:13 b)
and you would be *repaid* (Luke 14:12 c).	for you will be repaid at the resurrection of the righteous. (Luke 14:14 b)

There are four types of people who are not to be invited: friends, brothers, relatives or rich neighbors. These are contrasted by four types of people who are to be invited: the poor, the crippled, the lame, and the blind. The difference between the two groups is their ability or the inability to repay. Finally, the contrasting parallels are summed up by the repayment, which the host would receive at the resurrection of the just. When the host invites those who cannot return the favor, then, Jesus says he would be repaid by God himself. Heil connects this advice with the healing of the man with the dropsy (Luke 14:2-6). Through this advice to the rich, "Jesus invites the host to cure his dropsical, selfish craving for social honor not only by humbling himself, like the guests, but also by demonstrating a selfless care and concern for those who are socially and economically unfortunate."[116] Does it reflect the view point of the historical Jesus? Commentators point out how well this statement goes hand in hand with the mission statement of Jesus at Nazareth, where Jesus announced his mission to proclaim the good news to the poor, to heal the blind, the lame and the crippled (Luke 4:16-19).[117] Braun thinks that Luke might have been influenced by the Greek satirists who were very vocal in criticizing the extravagance of the *symposia* of the elite. Especially the words of Luke echo the thought patterns of the cynic tradition in its contrasting of the rich and the poor and the final reversal of the prospects of the rich and the poor after one's death.[118] This notion of Braun is corroborated from the Acts of the Apostles, where we find the ideal banqueting community among whom there was no one who was hungry; there was no needy person among them (Acts 2:43-47; 4:32-35) Through the advice in Luke 14:12-14, Luke wants to tell his upper class readers that a meal should not be taken as a social contract or an investment. It should be a gift, gift that flows from the well-off's towards the have-not's. This gift would definitely be repaid by God.

Parable of the Great Dinner (Luke 14:15-24)
Though this book deals mainly with the biographical narratives in the third Gospel where Jesus is said to be dining with the Pharisees and the

tax collectors, all the same the parable of the Great Dinner is taken up in this work as an exception. This is because of two reasons: first, this parable comes within the narrative of Jesus' meal with the leader of the Pharisees; hence, it looks to be that Luke wants the readers to understand this parable as part of the table talk that followed the sympotic meal of Jesus. Second, the two groups of people that are compared in this parable, are very similar to the comparison that we are making in this chapter between the groups of Pharisees and the tax collectors.

The presence of a similar parable in the Gospel of Matthew (Matt 22:1-14) as well as in the Gospel of Thomas (64), suggests that Luke did not compose it; he rather works on what has been already available to him. Though there are the many differences between Luke's version and the other two, one could see in all the three Gospels, the original gist of the story, which would have been redactionally modified by the evangelists to suit their purposes.[119] The macarism by one of the participants of the *symposium* at the Pharisee's house is generally understood to be the work of Luke himself. Bailey looks at this verse in the background of the setting of the *symposium* in the Middle East.[120] The leaders of the village invite a new Rabbi or the preacher for a meal; during the meal they test him posing different questions. Through the macarism which comes from one of the guests, probably a Pharisee (Luke 14:15), a challenge is posed before Jesus, to express his view on the messianic banquet of the end-time, which has been an important theme of discussion from Isaiah onwards (Isa 25:6-9). However the answer which Jesus gives to this subtle test of the Pharisee targets his "self-congratulatory platitude"[121] and reverts „*das Recht der Sicherheit der Pharisäischen Hoffnung*"[122] into a warning against them.

The parable itself is a *symposium* within the *symposium*. The host invites his guests for a dinner. That it was not an informal *symposium*, is shown by Luke through his redactional δεῖπνον μέγα. This is all the more corroborated by the fact that the invitation for the first guests is two-fold.[123] The first invitation is issued not only because the host would want to know how many would turn up for the feast and cook accordingly, but also because a good amount of time should be given for the guests to prepare themselves for a good show-off during the dinner. The second invitation is issued on the day of the banquet. The guests who are invited for the banquet are shown to be economically powerful.[124]

Lame and Insulting Excuses (Luke 14:18-20)

The invited guests in the parable give three excuses for their decline to come to the banquet: one has purchased land, another has bought five pairs of oxen and another has just married. Many authors see a gradual progression in the three excuses (land, oxen and woman). Although the excuses contain a sense of regret and apology, the very fact that they do not decline the invitation on the first but do so on the second, must have been seen by the readers of the parable as a great public insult to the host. These excuses betray their priorities. Taking possession of the land, oxen and woman are preferred by the guests to the friendship with the host. But these excuses would have been understood by the listeners of the parable as very lame. Because, one does not buy a land or oxen before one thoroughly inspects them. Only after a careful inspection, one would normally buy anything. But here it is the other way round. The guests have already acquired them and only now they go to inspect them. The readers would have clearly understood these excuses as an insult to the host who had maintained his decorum by inviting them twice very formally. That it is more than just an insult is seen here with the addition of the phrase ἀπὸ μιᾶς which is a *hapax legomen*.

Plummer opines that this *hapax* used by Luke gives the impression that the excuses made by the invited guests were so unanimous and deliberate that they look like a "prearranged conspiracy."[125] This would then mean that the guests wanted to dump the image of the host in the society by their unanimous refusal to attend his banquet – although being very polite. Thus the decision of the elite of the society deciding to boycott a banquet offered by a host all at once, would have been aimed "to lower the honour grade of the host in the eyes of those who know him and thereby seriously impair his ability to maintain a positive social image in the minds of his fellow citizens."[126] It is indeed a grave damage to the social image of the host. The Lukan audience would have felt more sympathy for the host who has acted so far benevolently than the guests who were rude in unanimously rejecting the invitation. A sense of suspense is created in the readers, as to how the host would react now.

New Guest List (Luke 14:21-23)

The host is hurt; he is angry. His anger leads him to do something that is unheard of among the upper class elite. He not only rejects his usual social peers who have declined his invitation, but now has a new guest list. He asks his servant to go and invite "the poor, the crippled, the blind, and the lame" (14:21). The audience would have immediately seen a sharp contrast between those economically powerful guests, invited at first and the other extremes in the society. The audience would have also remembered at once the advice that Jesus gave to the host Pharisee in 14:13 to invite 'the poor, the crippled, the lame, and the blind' who cannot reciprocate the hospitality they receive. This is exactly what the host in the parable does. He does not give away food to the poor and the crippled as a Roman benefactor would do to gain honor, and yet "keep his social distance by not entering into the messy mesh of social interaction with them."[127] He invites them rather to partake in his table and to recline with him at his own house. When the servant tells him there is still room, he asks him to go out of the city to the roads and lanes and bring in people to recline with him for a banquet. Rohrbaugh renders a sketch of how the city looked like at the time of Luke. At the heart of the city lived the socially, economically and religiously powerful. Then there were internal walls that separated them from the poorest non-elite. Then there was the city wall outside of which prostitutes, beggars and outcasts lived.[128] The invitation of the poor is paralleled to the two-fold invitation given to the upper class elite. This way of invitation also suits well with this outline of the city as sketched out by Rohrbaugh. Through the second invitation, not only the poorest non-elite but also beggars and outcasts come to the heart of the city where they do not belong. This invitation is the 'conversion'[129] that the rich host has undergone after having been rejected by his social equals.

The text could be taken either as allegory as scholars point to. The banquet which is offered by the householder is taken by these authors as the "*eschatalogischen Freudenmahl*" which would be hosted by God.[130] The initial guests who had declined the gracious invitation of the κύριος would then have to be understood as people of Israel especially the Pharisees, who rejected the invitation of the servant Jesus[131] who came with the invitation from God. Not only this narrative, but all the three sympotic meals with the Pharisees, whose invitation Jesus willingly accepted, show to the Lukan readers that the invitation of Jesus towards Israel for its repentance has always been open. It depends on the response on the part of Israel to the call of Jesus. Jesus comes with an offer from God for the banquet at the Kingdom of God. The crippled and the blind are the 'people of the land'; the sinful, the ordinary and those living outside the city at the roads and hedges would be the gentiles who have willingly accepted the invitation. If the parable could have been from the historical Jesus himself, then it could be possible that Jesus understood his mission in terms of this parable. In this way "the parable becomes an interpretation of Jesus' own behavior in eating with tax collectors and sinners, and the point is basically the universal offer of the Gospel with a subsidiary warning not to refuse the offer."[132] The parable (Luke 14:16-23) has been sandwiched between two verses of the redactor, which strengthen this allegorical interpretation of the parable (Luke 14:15, 24). The only difference is the melting away of the roles of God as the κύριος and Jesus as the servant. Jesus here is not only the messenger; he is also the host of the eschatological banquet.[133]

Message to the Lukan Community

The question, however still remains as to what message the community of Luke would have taken home as it read and listened to this parable. Was it (only) an allegorical interpretation that Luke intended to give his audience? Or is there still something which Luke would have aimed to drive home to his audience? Two answers emerge:

Dropsical Character of the Invited Guests

At the very beginning of the *symposium* with the Pharisee, Luke presented a man with dropsy who needed a healing from Jesus. As discussed earlier, the illness would have been understood by the audience to imply the gluttonous and greedy behavior of the guests who were seeking the best places and the best food at the *symposium*. Dropsy as an illness is to be seen also, in the characters of the invited guests. As Heil puts it, the decline of the guests to attend the banquet is due to the "dropsical desire to acquire property and increase their wealth and social status."[134] He says that the Lukan audience would have understood the behavior of the guests at the house of the host Pharisee, whose preoccupation was to get the best seats of honor (Luke 14:7) in the metaphorical light of the man with dropsy. The final verse (Luke 14:24) is therefore a warning to the audience of Luke, to watch out for any dropsical behavior in their lives, lest they too be excluded from the eternal banquet that the Lord would host, just like the elite guests in the parable.

Host - A Model for the Christian Elite

The redundancy of the *symposium* material in the Gospel of Luke seems to suggest that the Lukan audience was very much aware of the *symposium* literature and perhaps even *symposium* would have been regular practice among the audience of Luke. Ernst is of the opinion that the sympotic framework of Luke 14 and the advice of Jesus towards a correct way of conducting a sympotic banquet is definitely a hint on the Lukan community, for whom it would have been customary to participate in such Hellenistic sympotic meals.[135] Hence the parable here intends to give an important lesson for the practice of *symposia* among the newly converted Christians. The host in the parable (apart from being understood in an allegorical manner to refer to God), could also be portrayed by Luke as the model to be imitated by the audience of Luke. The fact that the elite guests unanimously declined to participate in the *symposium* of the host, would have caused a humiliation in the society for the host. This was perhaps something that the Lukan audience were suffering in their real lives. Precisely because they became Christians, their wealthy peers with whom they had their businesses and who had so far reclined with them at *symposia*, would have refused to have anything to do with the newly converted Christians. The words of Rohrbaugh put it succinctly: "Elite Christians who participated in the socially inclusive banquet of the Christian community risked being cut-off from the prior social networks on which their positions depended... If becoming part of the Christian community provided a social haven for the poor, it occasioned a social disaster for the rich. For many rich Christians their social position in elite circles was no doubt shaky enough."[136] Through the example of the host in the parable, the elite Christians are called to "relinquish the quest for belonging to the circle of social elite;"[137] as hosts need conversion of heart from inviting only those who could invite them back towards inviting those who cannot repay them for their fellowship meals. It is not only because Jesus their master has preached and advocated them; but it was precisely what he practiced, by leaving the Pharisees, the religious elite of the time, and by making the tax collectors and sinners as his friends and table companions at his fellowship meals.

Λέγω γὰρ ὑμῖν of 14:24 is loaded with a double sense. It could either denote the host in the parable (vv. 15-24) who is hosting the dinner; it could also denote Jesus who as the chief guest has a final say in the real *symposium* at the house of the Pharisee. Taken in this way, then, it is Jesus who becomes the host himself. Although Jesus began his entry in the house of the Pharisee as a guest, he is now the host who is hosting a banquet where those who rejected his invitation would be excluded. This change of position – from being a guest to becoming the host is already anticipated here which would be seen clearly later in the Zacchaeus as well as in the Emmaus Narratives. From now on, the Lukan Jesus would no more recline with the Pharisees, the religious elite of the time, who were suffering from dropsy of a kind, seeking to acquire positions of honor. The next and the final *symposium* before the Last Supper that Jesus would partake in, would be with someone (Zacchaeus) who could never be part of the social and religious elite, instead who is one of the rejected classes of the society and therefore looked down upon.

Analysis of the Fellowship Meals: Final Remarks

Triangular Formation in the Meal Narratives of Luke

In the third Gospel, we frequently see a triangular formation of characters in relation to Jesus. The entire mid-section of the Gospel of Luke is about the Lukan Jesus coming in contact with two groups of people. At one end there are sinner characters, who are shown to be repentant; at the other end there are so called righteous, who resent this Jesus-sinners relationship. Pesonen too looks at the 'Lukan sinner triangle' as typical of the third Gospel. In his words, "The sinner figure longs for forgiveness and the presence of the representative of God; the criticizing figure heightens the tension by trying to separate the sinner and the representative of God discrediting their closeness. The climax is reached when the representative of God justifies the advances and presence of the sinner, teaching the critic a lesson."[138] Ebner and Heininger compare this triangle formation in the Gospel with two teams of players and their relation to one another and to the referee in the game.[139] Jesus stands in this *dramatisches Dreieck* as the main character. His relation to the repentant sinners and the pious critics and the tension it creates in the Gospel is described by Byrne in the following diagram:[140]

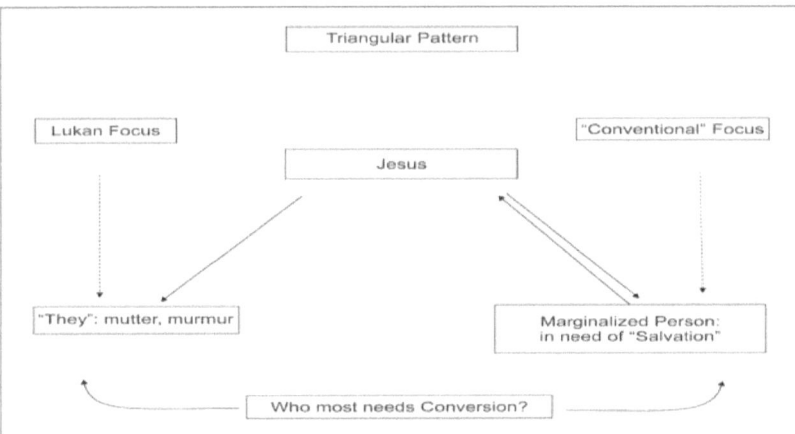

Pesonen points out that this sinner triangle occurs six times in the Gospel of Luke.[141] It begins with the Levi narrative (Luke 5:27-32); it is seen in the context of Jesus reclining at the house of Simon the Pharisee, where a sinful woman gets appreciated for her actions (Luke 7:36-50); Luke's summary statement of Jesus accepting tax collectors and sinners as his table companions (15:1-2) is done with a sinner triangle. It is seen in the parable of the Prodigal son (Luke 15:11-32), in the parable of the rich man and Lazarus (Luke 16:19-31) and in the parable of the tax collector and the Pharisee (Luke 18:9-14). Finally, one sees the sinner triangle in the story of Zacchaeus (Luke 19:1-10). Sinners and the righteous are not portrayed in an abstract manner in the third Gospel. Instead they are symbolized by two concrete groups. The tax collectors represent all the groups that are categorized as sinners and the Pharisees take the role of the righteous.

It is interesting to note that in such a triangular formation, the theme of food is present in almost all of the six narratives except in the parable of the tax collector and the Pharisee (Luke 18:9-14). More specifically the Lukan *Dreieckformation* concentrates on the table fellowship controversies of Jesus where Jesus is seen enjoying table companionship with tax collectors and sinners and justifies his actions (Luke 5:27-32; 7:36-50; 15:1-2; 19:1-10). Table fellowship controversies of Jesus, moulded in the triangular formation display the intention of the author; first of all, through this triangular formation, "Luke underlined that being a 'friend of toll collectors and sinners' was not just one small feature in the general overview of Jesus' words and actions, but a central and dominant aspect of his career."[142] Secondly, they show how Jesus is related to these groups; by showing that no one was excluded from the fellowship of Jesus, Luke intends to tell his audience, how they need to go about in their relation with others and how exclusive relationship of any kind should be avoided, especially in their practice of fellowship meals.

Jesus - Friend of Repentant Tax Collectors

At the center of Luke's Gospel is the criticism of the Pharisees, the so-called righteous, against Jesus, that he welcomes sinners and eats with them (Luke 15:1-2), for which Jesus gives the answer through the parables of the joy of finding the lost (Luke 15:3-32). The similar criticism was already directed at Jesus at his first meal with Levi the tax collector (Luke 5:30). The answer of Jesus to this criticism was that the main purpose of his calling was "not to call the righteous but sinners to repentance" (Luke 5:33).[143] This mission of Jesus which was emphasized at every meal narratives – his meal with Levi the tax collector (Luke 5:27-32), his acceptance of the sinful woman who touched and kissed Jesus during a *symposium* (Luke 7:37-38), and the presence of the man with dropsy who was accepted and healed by Jesus in the midst of the reclining members (Luke 14:1-6) - comes to the climax by Jesus being a guest at the house of the chief of the toll collectors. The criticism of Jesus as the friend of tax collectors and sinners, the unclean and outcasts climaxes with the Zacchaeus story, where the Lukan Jesus once again finally and emphatically proclaims to his adversaries, that "the Son of Man came to seek out and to save the lost" (Luke 19:10). It is noteworthy to look at the verbs that are used in the *chreia* at the end in both the tax collector narratives. In the first meal with the tax collector Levi, Luke writes about Jesus' arrival in the perfect tense (ἐλήλυθα) which indicates a prolonged and still continuing effect of Jesus' ministry. But in the final meal with the tax collector Zacchaeus, the verb used is ἦλθεν, which does show a definiteness and a sense of completion of the mission of Jesus in calling the sinners to repentance. This completion is also strengthened by the act of sharing their wealth. Levi the first tax collector left everything to follow Jesus and Zacchaeus is ready to sell half of his possessions and give them away to the poor. This action shows their willingness to repent.

Pharisees: A Double Portrayal

Over against tax collectors, the sinner-group, which is ready to repent, stands the group of Pharisees who understand themselves as self-righteous. Luke definitely has material that exonerates Pharisees and depicts them very positively. In the Acts of the Apostles, when the high priests want to kill the apostles who were boldly preaching about Jesus, Gamaliel the Pharisee makes a convincing speech that puts their decision to kill them on hold (Acts 5:33-40). In fact, the Jerusalem council attests to the fact that there were Pharisees who were sympathizers of the new Christian movement (Acts 15:5). The Pharisees side with Paul and with Christian ideology with regard to the Resurrection of the dead (Acts 23). The third Gospel too has its share in depicting the Pharisees in a better light. For example, the Pharisees do not appear in the passion narrative at all. While this could be also told about other synoptic writers, there are other things which only Luke has about the Pharisees. He makes them warn Jesus about the plot of Herod to kill him (13:31). Above all, through his redactional work, Luke has become the only evangelist who shows that Pharisees invited Jesus to dine with them, not just once but three times, as we have seen so far. Such newness in the Pharisee material prompts scholars like Ziesler to think of "a greater friendliness towards the Pharisees on the part of Luke than we find in Mark or Matthew."[144]

Pharisees – Friendly to Jesus?

At this juncture, the view of Finkel regarding the relation of Jesus with the Pharisees needs to be noted. Finkel observes that at least in the beginning, the Pharisees had understood Jesus as someone belonging to or in close connection with the Pharisaic school of thought. Anyone who shares the meal with an individual or a group, shares the worldview and philosophy of the individual and the group. Hence, only when the Pharisees observed that Jesus' ideas were closely resembling theirs, they could have invited and included him into their table-fellowship community. They would not have invited an unclean person (if they thought Jesus to be unclean), to their fellowship meals. For Finkel, "the Pharisaic masters recognized Jesus at first, as a colleague and the people address him with the title *Rabbi*. They did not reprimand his actions in the beginning, but rather directed his attention to the disciples' negligence of observance of the laws of purity and of the Sabbath."[145] If the Pharisees' invitation to Jesus for a fellowship meal were to be historical, the question then arises, whether the Pharisees invited Jesus alone, or also his disciples, whom they found to be negligent in their observance of the purity laws. If one assumes the historicity of the Pharisaic invitation to Jesus,[146] then one thing could be plausible. Pharisees found in Jesus and his school of thought an ideological ally. Because Jesus was not against the Roman rule altogether, he tolerated their rule, provided the Jews were allowed to follow their religious values as were the Pharisees (cf. Luke 20:20-26; Mk 12:13-17; Matt 22:15-22). But Jesus deliberately wants to show the Pharisees that his way is different from theirs, by intently partaking in the fellowship meals with those, whom Pharisees considered unclean.

Hillel School and the Lukan Community

For Smith, these invitations of Pharisees to Jesus for fellowship meals could not be historically probable. Together with other scholars he observes that the presence of the Pharisees at the time of Jesus was mostly in and around Jerusalem, and not in Galilee. Smith puts it bluntly, "the Synoptics' picture of a Galilee swarming with Pharisees is ... anachronism."[147] If Smith were to be true, then the presence of Pharisees in and around Galilee in Luke does not seem then to be historical. We need then to understand the positive portrayal of Pharisees towards Jesus in the Gospels as well as towards the early church from the perspective of the life and experience of the Lukan community or the early Church. If the invitations of the Pharisees to Jesus to dine with them is more a redactional work of Luke, then it betrays the relation / tension that might have existed between the Lukan community and the Pharisaic community, between the ideology of the new Christian Community and the Pharisaic ideals. Finkel makes a difference between Hillel school of Pharisees and its counterpart Shammai school in the early Church era. According to him, Hillel's school known for its "humbleness, restraint, clear argumentative reasoning and liberal stand – was close in spirit to that of the teacher of Nazareth."[148] While the Hillel school was peace loving, the Shammai school was the opposite. Hence for Finkel, those whom the Lukan Jesus opposed with strong words were not the Pharisees of Hillel school, but the disciples of Shammai. The reference to Gamaliel in the Acts of the Apostles could be seen as a further proof to this view, since Gamaliel who interceded for the Apostles in Acts 5:33-40, was the grandson of Hillel. Further positive references in the Acts of the Apostles, for example the reference to Paul as a Pharisee (Acts 23:6) and the subsequent support of the Pharisees to Paul (Acts 23:9-10) support the view that Luke, perhaps, would like to point out to this socially powerful group of Judaism that the early Church community is ideologically similar to the Pharisaic school of Hillel. At least, as Smith points out, they could be seen as "relics from the period of good relations under James"[149] between the Pharisaic school and early Christian community. One is immediately tempted to understand the reference to the name Zacchaeus which would have immediately induced the Lukan readers to connect the character of Zacchaeus with Johanan Ben Zakkai, one of the famous Pharisees from the school of Hillel. This very veiled reference could perhaps suggest the Lukan positivity towards the Pharisaic school of Hillel.

Tax Collectors and Pharisees: Contrasting Figures

Luke is the only evangelist to give a positive picture of Pharisees; this is seen in many of his special Pharisee material in the Gospel as well as in the Acts of the Apostles; all the same the Lukan Pharisees who are willing to host and to invite Jesus to their fellowship meals, are portrayed in every meal as a negative character, as we have seen above.

The way Luke has structured his meal narratives of Jesus with the Pharisees and the tax collectors helps one to understand that Luke wants the readers to understand the Pharisees not as positive role models to be followed, but as negative examples, whom the audience are not to imitate. In contrast to the Pharisees, the tax collectors are shown as the right examples whose lives of repentance the Lukan audience should emulate. This is evident in the contrasting parallels, which we see in the banquets of the tax collectors and the Pharisees.

There is a clear redactional similarity between the way, how Levi and Zacchaeus see, welcome and respond to Jesus as against the Pharisees: the way the characters are introduced, Jesus´ initiative to meet the tax collectors, their joyful reception of Jesus and the mention of the crowd that is not happy with Jesus going to the house of these tax collectors and the justification of Jesus for his actions could be seen both in Luke 5:27-32 as well as in Luke 19:1-10. On the other hand, one could also see parallels in all the three meal narratives of Jesus with the Pharisees.

> Mention of the invitation coming from the Pharisee (Luke 7:36; 11:37; in 14:1, however, an explicit invitation is missing).
>
> A sense of indifference and disdainful distance towards Jesus from the part of the Pharisees (Luke 7:39; 11:38, 53-54; 14:1-6).
>
> The disapproval of certain behaviors of the host Pharisees and other guest-Pharisees by Jesus (Luke 7:40-46; 11:38-44; 14-24).

When one begins to compare and contrast the meals of Jesus with the tax collectors Levi and Zacchaeus with the meal narratives of Jesus with the Pharisees, one could conspicuously see how the two types of hosts are contrasted against each other. There is a joyful acceptance on the part the tax collectors when Jesus wishes to relate with them. This joy results in a banquet at their home and is expressed further in the change they experience in their lifestyle, whereas there is no real welcome but a silent indifference on the part of the host Pharisees towards Jesus. The ´joy´ which was present in the host tax collectors (and literally shown in the texts) has been contrasted with ´indignance´ from the part of the host Pharisees towards Jesus. The end of the banquet at the house of the tax collectors leads to a long-lasting friendship with Jesus whereas the banquet with Jesus does not increase the friendship with Jesus for the Pharisees but every banquet of the Pharisees widens their relational gap between Jesus and Pharisees as a group, thus leading towards anger and enmity. Three negative example of banquets with the Pharisees are sandwiched by two positive examples of banquet scenes with the tax collectors. The result is the joy of Jesus in receiving the repenting sinners back into the house of the Father. This is also symbolized in the parables of the joy of finding the lost (Luke 15) and is especially evocative of the father's words as he pleads with his older son: 'but now we must celebrate and rejoice, because your brother was dead and has come to life again; he was lost and has been found' (15:32)"[150] Thus the author of the third Gospel has used the meal narratives of Jesus with the tax collectors to form an inclusion to arch the meal narratives of Jesus with the Pharisees and thereby tries to warn the behavior of the audience, and to check and correct their behavior in accordance with the behavior of the tax collectors. Though the tax collectors were largely understood at that time as negative characters symbolizing sinners and the Pharisees were the positive characters, Luke has turned it the other way around, by using the banquet scenes. This is also clearly seen from the parable of the Pharisee and the tax collector (Luke 18:8-14). The tax collector was indeed a sinner, and the Pharisee a righteous man. But at the end of the prayer, the one who goes justified is not the Pharisee but the tax collector.

Reversal of Characters

The criticism of the opponents, especially by the Pharisees is that Jesus is at home and relating with ease with tax collectors and sinners who are impure and thereby making himself impure. But the Lukan Jesus shows them, how due to their own practices the Pharisees are similar to the tombs of the dead people, which are the best symbol of uncleanness (Luke 11:44). The Pharisees think of themselves as self-righteous and of the tax collectors as sinners. But in reality they are full of wickedness and greed inside. In contrast to them the joyful reception of Jesus by the tax collectors at their homes would have been looked at by the audience of Luke as an act of their repentance for their misdeeds. Hence those who are understood so far to be the sinners are in fact becoming righteous by their acts of repentance and those who think of themselves as self-righteous are in fact shown to be sinners.

This reversal is once again brought in full force by the way both the groups handle wealth. The tax collectors were generally thought to be greedy and hoarders of money. But it is the Pharisees, who were advised by Jesus to give alms so that they might be clean (Luke 11:41); they are the ones, who are criticized by Jesus later as the "lovers of money" (Luke 16:14). In contrast to these lovers of money, Luke narrates that Levi has left everything and followed Jesus and Zacchaeus is willing to sell half of his possessions and give away to the poor and is willing to compensate four-fold for his mistakes committed in the past. In short the audience of Luke is asked to weigh between the characters of the tax collectors and that of the Pharisees. They are asked to make a personal choice between the behavior of the two groups and choose their role model accordingly.

Community of Luke: A Learned Community

The frequent participation of Jesus in sympotic banquets and his reclining at table are something very special for the writer of the third Gospel. The tax collectors and the Pharisees who host *symposia* for Jesus would not have been understood by the audience of Luke as belonging to the poor or middle class society; rather they would have been considered to be an "eminent and affluent people because of the resources required to entertain in this fashion."[151] Hence the frequency of the banquet narrations in Luke which imitate the Hellenistic atmosphere of *symposia* suggests that the community to which Luke wrote, must have been a learned community. Only to an intellectual community which is very much acquainted with the literary genre and nuances of *symposium* literature, could a writer display his art and brilliance of writing in the same genre; only before the intellectual elite could a writer place different nuances of the literature of his time. As Ziesler points out, "why should the evangelists go to the trouble of making a nice distinction which probably few or even none of their readers would spot?"[152] Hence the banquet scenes imply that the Lukan community would have been a learned group of people who were probably acquainted with the Hellenistic literature of the time.

Luke: The Evangelist of the Rich

The banquet narrations seem to suggest that apart from being a learned community the Lukan community was also an affluent and wealthy community. So much is written in the Gospel of Luke about wealth and possessions. Many characters are projected as rich. There is a rich but a foolish man who does not know what to do with his abundant crops (Luke 12:16-21). There is a rich man whose name we are not told along with a poor man, Lazarus whose reversal of fortune strikes the readers (Luke 16:19-31). There is a rich young man who wants to follow Jesus but hesitates to let go of his possessions and share them with the poor (Luke 18:18-25). We also have many rich characters who host *symposia* to Jesus. Why should Luke narrate so many instances where the rich are the key persons in the narratives? It could be perhaps Luke has in mind the rich people of his community. The frequency of the banquet meals in the third Gospel also adds further proof to the suggestion that a considerable amount of the intended audience of Luke might have been rich. Many of these rich characters in Luke are critiqued and contrasted as against the poorest of the poor. It is these rich characters in the Gospel whose way of handling money brings judgement to them, seem to be the models of life for the rich members of the Lukan community.

The third Gospel, hence, looks to be an advice or a warning to the rich of the community about the reversal of destinies if they do not mend their ways (Luke 6:17-49; 16:19-31). Hence the aim of talking about the poor in Luke's Gospel is not just to console the poor but mainly to challenge the rich. In this way, Cadbury is right when he says the Jesus of Luke spoke to the "possessors not to the dispossessed."[153] It is the conversion of the rich in sharing their wealth with the needy that Luke is aiming at through his Gospel. Only such handling of wealth would save them. This is the message, scattered all through the Gospel. We could therefore together with Schottroff confidently say that Luke is the "evangelist to the rich and the respected."[154] The disciples of Jesus left everything in order to follow him. But the members of the new community of disciples need not leave everything. It is even enough to sell half of one's possession and to share it among the poor as Zacchaeus does. This would make them as the 'sons of Abraham' (Luke 19:10) who would recline at the bosom of Abraham like Lazarus. If the readers who are rich, hesitate or fail to share their wealth with the needy, then "it is easier for a camel to go through the eye of a needle than for someone who is rich to enter the kingdom of God" (Luke 18:25).

The Segregation of the Rich Christians in the Society

The meal narratives of Jesus address also another important issue that his community was perhaps facing. The rich elite who newly became Christians were perhaps confronted with the sudden desertion of their non-Christian counterparts. The rich Christian elite are abandoned perhaps for following a new way of life and for allowing in their fellowship *symposia*, not only the elite and rich counterparts but also the poor, the slaves and even the gentiles whose presence is a disgrace to the elite Jewish circle. This segregation which the elite Christians faced at the society is what Luke tries to address in all of his meal narrations, especially in the *symposium* of Jesus with the leader of the Pharisees and the parable of the Great Dinner. The Pharisees who were objecting to Jesus' friendship with tax collectors and sinners might have represented the old elite class to which the elite Christians so far belonged. The rich elite Christians are invited to come out of the Pharisaic attitude of exclusivism and to embrace the ideology of the new community; in other words the believing Christian community is to be a community that does not operate with elite hospitality that is available only to those who would be able to reciprocate, rather it should be a community, whose hospitality is to be open to everyone without judging any one according to economic and social gradations.

Overview

We began by identifying the importance of fellowship meals for the third Gospel. The theme of meal has been understood to be very special for Luke. Although meal as a theme is narrated in different forms such as parables, controversy stories, etc., our study focused only on the biographical narratives in which Jesus is shown to be partaking in a banquet, the parable of the Great Dinner being an exception. Here too we concentrated only on five of them, though there are other meal narratives scattered in the mid-section of the Gospel. Among the five narratives two of the meal narratives – Jesus' banquet with the tax collectors had sandwiched the three banquets of Jesus, hosted by three Pharisees. By this sandwich formation, we have come to the conclusion that Luke tries to compare and contrast these two groups which offered banquet hospitality to Jesus in the light of one another. But Jesus' preference between these two contrasting models was clear. He was a friend of tax collectors and sinners, a group which was understood and judged negatively at the time of Jesus, which did not have any place in the elite circle of the time, but a group, which is shown by Luke, ready to repent and change. Precisely their willingness to repent has induced Jesus to be friendly with them and show them the openness of God in receiving them. The friendship of Jesus with the tax collectors and sinners and his offering of forgiveness of God had irritated the exclusive attitude of the Pharisees who were ready to accept Jesus as one among them, provided he shunned away from the friendship with the abominable people of the land. The banquet, which Jesus enjoyed with the social outcasts of the time, should be a model for the audience of Luke. This was the aim of Luke as he molded many of the controversies of Jesus within the banquet narrations.

The frequency of the banquet material in the Gospel of Luke and the use of the literary nuances of the Hellenistic *symposia* has led one to conclude that the Lukan community was not only an intellectual community, which was able to understand and enjoy the nuances of the literary *symposia;* the Lukan readers were also a well-to-do community, which was affluent enough to host sympotic banquets at regular intervals and be invited for such elite banquets; sadly this affluent Christian community would have had to suffer rejection from other elite of the society because of their acceptance of Christianity. Luke invites this socially elite group of Christians to embrace a new community, a community where there is no exclusivism involved, a community where the wealth of the elite rich is shared with the poor, a community whose fellowship meals embrace and include people of all sorts, especially "the poor, the crippled, the lame, and the blind" (Luke 14:13).

Endnotes

[1] J. Wanke, *Beobachtungen zum Eucharistieverständnis des Lukas auf Grund der lukanischen Mahlberichte*, Erfurter theologische Schriften 8 (Leipzig: St-Benno-Verlag, 1973), 54.

[2] R. J. Karris, *Luke, Artist and Theologian*, 47.

[3] D. A. Neale, *None But the Sinners*, 100.

[4] O. Michel, "τελώνης," in *Theologisches Wörterbuch zum Neuen Testament: Begründet von Kittel*, ed. G. Friedrich, Achter Band (Stuttgart, Berlin, Köln, Mainz: Kohlhammer Verlag, 1967), 89; W. Bauer, *Griechisch-Deutsches Wörterbuch*, 1619; H. G. Liddell and R. Scott, *A Greek-English Lexicon*, 1774; J. Bolyki, *Jesu Tischgemeinschaften*, Wissenschaftliche Untersuchungen zum Neuen Testament Reihe 2 96 (Tübingen: Mohr Siebeck, 1998), 109; W. Manson, *The Gospel of Luke*, The Moffatt New Testament Commentary (Great Britain: Hodder and Stoughton, 1963), 209; S. R. LLewelyn, "Tax Collection and the τελōναι of the New Testament," in *New Documents Illustrating Early Christianity: A Review of the Greek Inscriptions and Papyri*, ed. S. R. LLewelyn, 8 (Grand Rapids, Michigan: W. B. Eerdmans, 1998), 49.

[5] O. Michel, "τελώνης." 97; T. E. Schmidt, "Taxes," in *Dictionary of Jesus and the Gospels*, ed. J. B. Green, S. McKnight & I. H. Marshall (Illinois: InterVarsity Press, 1992), 804-807; F. Herrenbrück, *Jesus und die Zöllner: Historische und Neutestamentlich-exegetische Untersuchgen*, WUNT 41 (Tübingen: Mohr Siebeck, 1990), 32, 116-118; J. R. Donahue, "Tax Collectors and Sinners: An Attempt at Identification," *CBQ* 33, no. 1 (1971), 42.

[6] Herrenbrück, *Jesus und die Zöllner*, 166-173.

[7] Cf. S. Rocca, *Herod's Judaea: A Mediterranean State in the Classical World*, Texts and Studies in Ancient Judaism 122 (Tübingen: Mohr Siebeck, 2008), 204; similar view could also be found in T. Rajak, *Josephus: The Historian and His Society*, Classical Life and Letters (London: Duckworth, 1983), 213; J. Klausner, "The Herodian Period," in *World History of the Jewish People: The Herodian Period*, ed. M. Avi-Yonah (Jerusalem: Massada Publications, 1975), 204. For some of the building constructions of Herod the Great, cf. also J. Jeremias, *Jerusalem zur Zeit Jesu: Eine Kulturgeschichtliche Untersuchung zur Neutestamentlichen Zeitgeschichte*, 3rd ed. (Göttingen: Vandenhoeck & Ruprecht, 1962), 9-10.

⁸ Rocca, *Herod's Judaea*, 206.

⁹ Ibid., 207.

¹⁰ O. Michel, "τελώνης." 93; J. R. Donahue, "Tax Collectors and Sinners." 43; N. Hillyer, "τελώνιον," in *The New International Dictionary of New Testament Theology*, ed. C. Brown (Michigan: Zondervan Publishing House, 1981), 755.

¹¹ Herrenbrück, *Jesus und die Zöllner*, 186.

¹² Ibid., 186.

¹³ J. A. Fitzmyer, *The Gospel According to Luke I-IX*, The Anchor Bible 28 A (New Haven: Yale University Press, 2006), 470; P. Perkins, "Taxes in the New Testament," *The Journal of Religious Ethics* 12, no. 2 (1984), 184; H. Maccoby, "How Unclean were the Tax Collectors?," *BTB* 21, no. 2 (2001), 60-61; J. R. Donahue, "Tax Collectors and Sinners." 59; O. Michel, "τελ}νης." 89, 103.

¹⁴ Herrenbrück, *Jesus und die Zöllner*, 291.

¹⁵ Prohibition of the royal officials in collecting taxes, the government fixing the amount to be paid (cf. Luke 3:12-13), and regulation of the number of personell who were sent out to collect taxes were some of the attempts of the government to reduce cheating by a tax collector. Furthermore, if ~~some one~~someone had refused / was unable to pay taxes, the tax collector could not arbitrarily confiscate the properties of that person. All he could do was to inform the government about the amount, not paid by a particular person. Llewelyn says, it is here there is a possibility here for a tax collector for the abuse of συκοφαντία. LLewelyn, "Tax Collection and the τελόvαι of the New Testament." 53-57.

¹⁶ As quoted by F. W. Danker and W. Bauer, *A Greek-English lexicon of the New Testament and other early Christian literature*, 999; H. G. Liddell and R. Scott, *A Greek-English Lexicon*, 1774; O. Michel, "τελ}νης." 98-103.

¹⁷ O. Michel, "τελώνης.", 100; further about the greed of the tax collectors cf. also P. Perkins, "Taxes in the New Testament." 183; LLewelyn, "Tax Collection and the τελόvαι of the New Testament." 68-74.

¹⁸ T. E. Schmidt, "Taxes." 806.

¹⁹ N. Perrin, *Rediscovering the Teaching of Jesus* (New York: Harper & Row, 1967), 106; Herrenbrück, *Jesus und die Zöllner*, 227.

²⁰ Cf. J. Jeremias, "Zöllner und Sünder," *Zeitschrift Zeitschrift Für die Neutestamentliche Wissenschaft* 30, no. 3 (1931), 296-301; Herrenbrück, *Jesus und die Zöllner*, 206-208; O. Michel, "τελ}νης." 101.

²¹ W. Bauer, *Griechisch-Deutsches Wörterbuch*, 1619; F. W. Danker and W. Bauer, *A Greek-English lexicon of the New Testament and other early Christian literature*, 999; A. Brooks, "Salvation and Loss in the Story of Zacchaeus," *Exp Tim* XXXIII, no. 6 (1922), 287; N. Hillyer, "τελώνιον." 757; R. A. Horsley, *Jesus and the spiral*

of violence: Popular Jewish resistance in Roman Palestine (San Francisco: Harper & Row, 1987), 212; M. J. Borg, *Conflict, Holiness, and Politics in the Teachings of Jesus* (London, New York: Continuum International Publishing Group, 1998), 100.

[22] T. E. Schmidt, "Taxes." 806.

[23] *M. Tohoroth* 7.6 as in Danby, *The Mishnah*, 726.

[24] O. Michel, "τελώνης." 101; N. Hillyer, "τελώνιον." 756.

[25] Herrenbrück, *Jesus und die Zöllner*, 195.

[26] O. Michel, "τελώνης." 104; R. A. Horsley, *Jesus and the spiral of violence*, 214; W. O. Walker Jr., "Jesus and the Tax Collectors," *JBL* 92, no. 2 (1978), 225.

[27] Herrenbrück understands the ′negative Reihe′ as narrations of professions or persons with a negative judgment. In his words, "*Unter einer 'Negativen Reihe' verstehen wir Aufzählungen von Berufen oder Eigenschaften mit negativer Beurteilung, vergleichbar den Lasterkatalogen.*" Herrenbrück, *Jesus und die Zöllner*, 81.

[28] Ibid., 230-231.

[29] In his words, "*Àm-hă-ăretz wurde zu einem diskreditierenden Schlagwort, mit dem die pharisäisch-rabbinishcen Kreise den kampf gegen alle die die Verwirklichung ihres Zieles führen, die diesen Weg nicht mitgehen wollen, in offensiver Distanz zu ihm stehen, aber auch zum inferiorisierenden Stigma-Terminus an die Adresse derjenigen, die den verschärften religiös-nomistischen Liestungsanforderungen der Pharisäer nicht genügen können, sie schlechterdings ignorieren, ihnen indifferent, in defensiver Distanz gegenüberstehen oder schlicht unwissentlich- ohne ein spezifisches Normbewußtsein – von ihnen abweichen.*" M. N. Ebertz, *Das Charisma des Gekreuzigten: Zur Soziologie der Jesusbewegung* (Tübingen: Mohr Siebeck, 1987), 219; also 255-256.

[30] W. H. Raney, "Who Were the "Sinners"?," *JR* 10, no. 4 (1930), 580.

[31] Ibid., 581.

[32] Ibid., 581.

[33] W. Bösen, "Das Mahlmotiv bei Lukas: Studien in Lukanischen Mahlverständnis unter besonderer Berücksichtigung von Lk 22:12-20" (PHD Dissertation, Universität des Saarlandes, 1976) 272, W. Grundmann, *Das Evangelium nach Lukas*, Theologischer Handkommentar zur Neuen Testament 3 (Berlin: Evangelische Verlaganstalt, 1971), 272.

[34] H. I. Marshall, W. W. Gasque, and D. A. Hagner, *The Gospel of Luke: A Commentary on the Greek Text: The New international Greek Testament commentary*, 1st ed. (Grand Rapids: Eerdmans, 1978), 217-221; D. L. Bock, *Luke*, The IVP New Testament Commentary Series (Illinois: InterVarsity Press, 1994), 489–494; H. Schürmann, *Das Lukas Evangelium: Kommentar zu Kap. 9,51*

- *11,54*, Herders theologischer Kommentar zum Neuen Testament 3,2 (Freiburg: Herder, 1994), 288.

[35] Hotze, *Jesus als Gast*, 37.

[36] H. Klein, *Das Lukasevangelium*, Kritisch-exegetischer Kommentar über das Neue Testament (Göttingen: Vandenhoeck & Ruprecht, 2006), 225; J. F. Walvoord and R. B. Zuck, *The Bible Knowledge Commentary: An Exposition of the Scriptures* (Wheaton Ill.: Victor Books, 1985), 150; R. H. Stein, *Luke*, The New American commentary v. 24 (Nashville, Tenn.: Broadman Press, 1992), 181.

[37] R. Pesch, "Das Zöllnergastmahl (Mk 2:15-17)," in *Mélanges Bibliques: en Hommage au R.P. Béda Rigaux*, ed. B. Rigaux, A. L. Descamps and A. Halleux (Gembloux, Belgium: Duculot, 1970), 64; D. L. Bock, *Luke*, 494–501; R. C. Tannehill, *The Narrative Unity of Luke-Acts*, 105; J. Nolland, *Luke: 1-9:20*, Word biblical commentary 35 A (Dallas, Texas: Word Books Publisher, 1989), 245.

[38] J. Brumberg-Kraus, "Memorable Meals: Symposia in Luke's Gospel, the Rabbinic Seder,and the Greco-Roman Literary Tradition," http://www.wheatoncollege.edu/academic/academicdept/religion/MemorableMeals/mm_chptIV.pdf, chapter III, 12-17, accessed on 15.08.2015; also D. A. Neale, *None But the Sinners*, 116; Hotze opines that Luke has made this fellowship meal narrative as the base from which he moulds further meal narratives in his Gospel. Hotze, *Jesus als Gast*, 43.

[39] J. Nolland, *Luke*, 245. All the same, one finds the redactional comment in Luke 15:1, where the redactor combines the tax collectors with sinners. This combination however is done to show their positive attitude and eagerness to listen to the words of Jesus.

[40] Hotze, *Jesus als Gast*, 43.

[41] E. LaVerdiere, *Dining in the Kingdom of God*, 43.

[42] K. Rengstorf, "γογγύζω," in *ThWNT: Begründet von Kittel*, ed. G. Friedrich, Achter Band (Stuttgart, Berlin, Köln, Mainz: Kohlhammer Verlag, 1967), 733.

[43] Ibid., 731; similar view could be seen in W. Wiefel, *Das Evangelium nach Lukas* (Berlin: Evangelische Verlagsanstalt, 1988), 119, accessed on 24.01.2015.

[44] W. Grundmann, *Das Evangelium nach Lukas*, 132. Luke takes away the Markan participle (καὶ οἱ γραμματεῖς τὸν Φαρισαιων 0δγντες Ετι σθwει μετρ τὸν μαρτωλὸν καν τελωνὸν – Mk 2:16), which made clear that the Pharisees and the scribes were not present at the meal but only 'saw' that Jesus was at a *symposium*. Though this omission by Luke, does not mean that they were partaking at this *symposium*, rather betrays the Lukan attempt to connect the banquet with the discussion.

[45] W. Bösen, "Das Mahlmotiv bei Lukas." 277-278; S. Witetschek, "The Stigma of a Glutton and Drunkard," *Ephemerides Theologicae Lovanienses* 83, no. 1 (2007), https://doi.org/10.2143/ETL.83.1.2021745, 135-154, accessed on 24.01.2015.

[46] H. I. Marshall, W. W. Gasque, and D. A. Hagner, *The Gospel of Luke: A Commentary on the Greek Text*, 217; along the similar line of thought Hotze, *Jesus als Gast*, 45; D. L. Tiede, *Luke*, Augsburg commentary on the New Testament (Minneapolis, Minn.: Augsburg Publ. House, 1988), 127; H. Klein, *Das Lukasevangelium*, 225; N. Geldenhuys, *Commentary on the Gospel of Luke* (Michigan: W. B Eerdmans Publishing company, 1956), 290; R. H. Stein, *Luke*; J. A. Fitzmyer, *The Gospel According to Luke I-IX*, 588; E. LaVerdiere, *Dining in the Kingdom of God*, 43.

[47] Bock looks at the quotation from Antisthenes close to the saying of Jesus, "Doctors associate with the sick but do not contract fevers." Cf. D. L. Bock, *Luke*, 498.

[48] W. Wiefel, *Das Evangelium nach Lukas*, 120; H. I. Marshall, W. W. Gasque, and D. A. Hagner, *The Gospel of Luke: A Commentary on the Greek Text*, 220.

[49] Of the 16 usages of μετανοέω in the Synoptics, 9 usages are found in Luke; the noun form μετάνοια is stated 8 times in the Synoptics, of which 5 usages are found in Luke. Cf. J. Behm and E. Würthwein, "μετανοέω, μετάνοια," in *ThWNT: Begründet von Kittel*, ed. G. Friedrich, Achter Band (Stuttgart, Berlin, Köln, Mainz: Kohlhammer Verlag, 1967), 4, 999.

[50] Ibid., 1003.

[51] W. Grundmann, *Das Evangelium nach Lukas*, 133; H. Klein, *Das Lukasevangelium*, 226.

[52] Behm and Würthwein, "μετανοέω, μετάνοια." 1003.

[53] Cf. F. Bovon, *Das Evangelium nach Lukas: Lk 1,1-9,50*, Evangelisch-katholischer Kommentar zum Neuen Testament III/I (Zürich: Benziger, 1989), 388; W. Bösen, "Das Mahlmotiv bei Lukas." 301; J. A. Fitzmyer, *The Gospel According to Luke I-IX*, 683.

[54] W. Grundmann, *Das Evangelium nach Lukas*, 169.

[55] The similarity between John's account and that of Luke has to be noted here. In both the sinful woman / Maria anoints Jesus on the feet and wipes them with her hair. Cf. J. Nolland, *Luke*, 352; W. Grundmann, *Das Evangelium nach Lukas*, 170.

[56] F. Bovon, *Das Evangelium nach Lukas*, 387-388; K. E. Corley, *Private Women, Public Meals*, 122.

[57] H. Klein, *Das Lukasevangelium*, 294; J. Ernst, *Lukas: Ein Theologisches Portrait* (Düsseldorf: Patmos, 1985), 119.

⁵⁸ According to Bovon, the fact that Luke does not narrate the anointing of Jesus in Bethany, could be perhaps that Luke has taken it from the context of the passion narrative and placed it in the ministry of Jesus in Galilee. F. Bovon, *Das Evangelium nach Lukas*, 388.

⁵⁹ W. Grundmann, *Das Evangelium nach Lukas*, 170. Wiefel opines that Luke 7:36-47 should have been from the special material of Luke. Luke 7:48-50 could be a Lukan redaction; W. Wiefel, *Das Evangelium nach Lukas*, 153-154; also H. Leroy, "Vergebung und Gemeinde nach Lukas 7,36-50," in *Wort Gottes in der Zeit: Festschrift Karl Hermann Schelkle zum 65. Geburtstag*, ed. H. Feld, trans. Karl H. Schelkle (Düsseldorf: Patmos-Verl, 1973), 85.

⁶⁰ Bendemann however does not refer to the Zacchaeus narrative belonging to this sympotic banquet setting. R. Bendemann, "Liebe und Sündenvergebung: Eine Narrativ-traditions-geschichltiche Analyse von Lk 7,36-50," *BZ* 44 (2000), 164.

⁶¹ F. Bovon, *Das Evangelium nach Lukas*, 390.

⁶² J. Nolland, *Luke*, 353. Cf. also W. Bösen, "Das Mahlmotiv bei Lukas." 303.

⁶³ Bendemann sees the untied hair of the woman, her carrying of alabaster oil and her kissing shows that she was indeed a woman of sinful nature, one of the *hetairai* of the town. Bendemann, "Liebe und Sündenvergebung." 167ff.; cf. also W. Wiefel, *Das Evangelium nach Lukas*, 154; R. Dillmann and C. Mora Paz, *Das Lukas-Evangelium: Ein Kommentar fur die Praxis* (Stuttgart: Verlag Katholisches Bibelwerk, 2000), 146. Kilgallen is however of the view that the woman need not necessarily be a prostitute. He suggests that the Lukan placing of the words "in the city" between "a certain woman was" and "a sinner" could be understood to mean, the woman was in actuality not a sinner, but she was falsely understood *by the city* to be a sinner; J. J. Kilgallen, "Forgiveness of Sins (Luke 7:36-50)," *Novum Testamentum* 40, no. 2 (1998), 106; Another view is that any woman, whose husband was a sinner, was also called a sinner by the Pharisaic community, hence this woman need not necessarily be a *prostitute*. Cf. W. Grundmann, *Das Evangelium nach Lukas*, 170.

⁶⁴ One wonders, along with Klein, how the hair of a woman would have been useful to dry the watery substances like tears. H. Klein, *Das Lukasevangelium*, 294. Luke however wants the reader to understand the action of the woman of unbinding her hair in the presence of men, to show that she was of a sinful character, similar to the presence of the *hetairai* in the Hellenistic sympotic space. Hotze, *Jesus als Gast*, 141.

⁶⁵ F. Bovon, *Das Evangelium nach Lukas*, 390-391; with the similar view Hotze, *Jesus als Gast*, 141; K. E. Corley, *Private Women, Public Meals*, 125; M. J. Marshall, "Jesus and the Banquets: An Investigation of the Early Christian Tradition Concerning Jesus' Presence at Banquets with Toll Collectors and

Sinners" (Dissertation, Murdoch University, 2002), http://researchrepository.murdoch.edu.au/id/eprint/183/#?, 321, accessed on 20.03.2017. Some scholars say that her tears, the wiping away with her hair and her continuous kissing are not the erotic signs but signs of „Erniedrigung und metanoia"; others are of the opinion these actions are signs of gratitude for the forgiveness, she has already received. Regarding the discussion among the scholars with regard to the action of the woman, cf. H. Leroy, "Vergebung und Gemeinde nach Lukas 7,36-50." 87; J. A. Fitzmyer, *The Gospel According to Luke I-IX*, 686; on the contrary J. J. Kilgallen, "Forgiveness of Sins (Luke 7:36-50)." 114.

[66] F. Bovon, *Das Evangelium nach Lukas*, 388.

[67] Cf. R. Dillmann and C. Mora Paz, *Das Lukas-Evangelium*, 146; F. Bovon, *Das Evangelium nach Lukas*, 391; W. Radl, *Das Evangelium nach Lukas: Kommentar: Erster Teil: 1, 1-9, 50* (Freiburg: Herder, 2003), 496.

[68] Marshall, "Jesus and the Banquets." 321.

[69] W. Wiefel, *Das Evangelium nach Lukas*, 155.

[70] A. Plummer, *A Critical and Exegetical Commentary on the Gospel According to S. Luke*, 5th ed., International critical commentary (Edinburgh: T. & T. Clark, 1981), 212.

[71] F. Bovon, *Das Evangelium nach Lukas*, 386.

[72] Hotze, *Jesus als Gast*, 174, also 149. Hotze states further in p. 174 „indirekt hält Lukas damit jenen, die nach Ostern Gefahr laufen, Christus nur mit der Durchschnittsmentalität eines Simon 'bei sich aufzunehmen,' ein Gegenmodell vor. Vielleicht ist dieses Profil der Sünderin als exemplarische Jüngerin, obwohl erst beim tieferen Eindringen in den Text erkennbar, in seiner pragmatischen Dimension sogar die Hauptintention des Lukas."

[73] J. Ernst, *Das Evangelium nach Lukas*, Regensburger Neues Testament vl. 3 (Regensburg: Verlag Friedrich Pustet, 1993), 199; also J. Bolyki, *Jesu Tischgemeinschaften*, 114.

[74] In the words of Bovon, „Der verurteilende Pharisäer von V 39 soll sich jetzt verurteilt fühlen." F. Bovon, *Das Evangelium nach Lukas*, 387.

[75] H. Melzer-Keller, *Jesus und die Frauen: Eine Verhältnisbestimmung nach den Synoptischen Überlieferungen* (Freiburg im Breisgau: Herder, 1997), 228-229.

[76] F. Bovon, *Das Evangelium nach Lukas*, 396.

[77] For a parallel study cf. J. A. Fitzmyer, *The Gospel According to Luke X-XXIV*, Anchor Bible 28B (New Haven: Yale University Press, 2008), 942; H. I. Marshall, W. W. Gasque, and D. A. Hagner, *The Gospel of Luke: A Commentary on the Greek Text*, 491-492; H. Klein, *Das Lukasevangelium*, 425-426; D. L. Tiede, *Luke*, 221; M. J. Borg, *Conflict, Holiness, and Politics in the Teachings of Jesus*, 114.

⁷⁸ On the Lukan dropping of the Q phrase "the weightier matters of the law," J. A. Fitzmyer, *The Gospel According to Luke I-IX*, 42.

⁷⁹ S. E. Steele, "Luke 11:37-54 - A Modified Hellenistic Symposium?," *JBL* 103, no. 3 (1984), 379-394; also H. Klein, *Das Lukasevangelium*, 425; Hotze, *Jesus als Gast*, 188-190.

⁸⁰ S. E. Steele, "Luke 11:37-54 - A Modified Hellenistic Symposium?" 387.

⁸¹ Ibid., 389; again Kremer is of the opinion that the role of ν δr τ÷ λαλÆσαι is not to link the text with what goes before; it is used here to give the text the literary frame of a *symposium*. J. Kremer, *Lukasevangelium*, Die neue Echter-Bibel Kommentar zum Neuen Testament mit der Einheitsübersetzung (Würzburg: Echter Verlag, 1988), 131.

⁸² J. Pitt-Rivers, "The Stranger, the Guest and the Hostile Host: Introduction to the Study of the Laws of Hospitality," in *Contributions to Mediterranean Sociology*, ed. J. G. Peristiany, *Publications of the Social Sciences Centre Athens* 4 (Paris: Mouton, 1968), 26; also D. B. Gowler, "Hospitality and Characterization in Luke 11:37-54: A Socio-Narratological Approach," *Semeia* 1993, no. 63, 221.

⁸³ J. Pitt-Rivers, "The Stranger, the Guest and the Hostile Host." 27-28; D. B. Gowler, "Hospitality and Characterization in Luke 11:37-54: A Socio-Narratological Approach." 221.

⁸⁴ Apart from the meaning of asking, the verb ρωτάω is also used in the meaning of requesting. Luke uses the verb in many instances in the sense of requesting (cf. Luke 4:38; 7:3; 8:37; 14;18). Cf. F. W. Danker and W. Bauer, *A Greek-English lexicon of the New Testament and other early Christian literature*, 395; F. Bovon, *Das Evangelium nach Lukas*, 224-225.

⁸⁵ D. B. Gowler, *Host, Guest, Enemy, and Friend: Portraits of the Pharisees in Luke and Acts*, Emory studies in early Christianity vol. 2 (New York: P. Lang, 1991), 233; also his article D. B. Gowler, "Hospitality and Characterization in Luke 11:37-54: A Socio-Narratological Approach." 226.

⁸⁶ Hotze, *Jesus als Gast*, 212.

⁸⁷ In the words of Hotze, „Die von Jesu Gastgeber eingeforderte Torah-Regel schiebt sich zwischen den Besucher und die Besuchten und verhindert das Gelingen des Gastmahls – sonst stets Sinnbild der Heilbringenden Nähe Gottes. Damit ist dieser Hausbesuch des göttlichen Gastes zum Scheitern verurteilt. Das Gesetz in der Hand von Menschen stört die rettende Heimsuchung Gottes." ibid., 213.

⁸⁸ D. B. Gowler, "Hospitality and Characterization in Luke 11:37-54: A Socio-Narratological Approach." 223-224.

⁸⁹ In the words of Schürmann „es gibt zwischen Juden und der Jüngergemeinde keine 'ekklesiale' communio und keine Mahlgemeinschaft mehr." H. Schürmann, *Das*

Lukas Evangelium, 311; cf. also J. Ernst, *Das Evangelium nach Lukas*, 290. Klein too says, these woe sayings originate from the conflicting time and context of the early Christian community which had to deal with the law abiding powerful; H. Klein, *Das Lukasevangelium*, 428.

[90] φαγεÖν ρτον was a kind of *terminus technicus* for a fellowship meal. The meal was much more than eating bread. The dishes included also other items like cheese, meat and fish apart from bread. Cf. P. Billerbeck and H. L. Strack, *Kommentar zum Neuen Testament: Aus Talmud und Midrasch*, ed. Joachim Jeremias (München: Beck, 1956), 613.

[91] J. Ernst, "Gastmahlgespräche: Lk 14,1-24," in *Die Kirche des Anfangs: Für Heinz Schürmann*, ed. J. E. R. Schnackenburg and J. Wanke (Freiburg: Herder, 1978), 63; M. Wolter, *Das Lukasevangelium*, Handbuch zum Neuen Testament (Tübingen: Mohr Siebeck, 2008), 500; R. Dillmann and C. Mora Paz, *Das Lukas-Evangelium*, 269; H. Klein, *Barmherzigkeit Gegenüber den Elenden und Geächteten: Studien zur Botschaft des Lukanischen Sondergutes*, Biblisch-theologische Studien 10 (Neukirchen-Vluyn: Neukirchener Verl, 1987), 23; Willibraun looks at it as the initial pronouncement story that leads the text further to the discussion about banquets; W. Braun, *Feasting and Social Rhetoric in Luke 14*, 14.

[92] M. Wolter, *Das Lukasevangelium*, 500; Braun looks at them as antithetical parallel sayings: W. Braun, *Feasting and Social Rhetoric in Luke 14*, 15.

[93] Καν γsνeτο ν τ÷... has been generally understood as the typical Lukan formula for introducing a new episode.

[94] Hotze, *Jesus als Gast*, 243-244.

[95] W. Braun, *Feasting and Social Rhetoric in Luke 14*, 17.

[96] Ibid., 17; cf. also J. Ernst, "Gastmahlgespräche: Lk 14,1-24." 63; M. Wolter, *Das Lukasevangelium*, 500.

[97] J. Ernst, "Gastmahlgespräche: Lk 14,1-24." 65.

[98] Cf. H. Klein, *Barmherzigkeit Gegenüber den Elenden und Geächteten*, 24-25.

[99] W. Braun, *Feasting and Social Rhetoric in Luke 14*, 25; also J. Ernst, "Gastmahlgespräche: Lk 14,1-24." 63.

[100] J. Ernst, "Gastmahlgespräche: Lk 14,1-24.", 64.

[101] Again, in the words of Ernst, „Wir erfahren hier ...über das neue Verständnis von, 'Feier' und 'Fest: wenn Jesus feiert, sind die Außenstehenden, die Kranken und vom Schicksal Gezeichneten mit dabei. Es gibt keine exklusive Gesellschaft der Previlegierten... Die Vorliebe des Lukas für die Mahlgemeindschaft Jesu mit den Sündern unterstreicht diesen Gedanken mit Nachdruck." ibid., 66.

[102] Against this view, W. Braun, *Feasting and Social Rhetoric in Luke 14*, 41.

[103] H. Klein, *Barmherzigkeit Gegenüber den Elenden und Geächteten*, 28.

¹⁰⁴ W. Braun, *Feasting and Social Rhetoric in Luke 14*, 32; for a similar view J. P. Heil, *The Meal Scenes in Luke-Acts*, 100.

¹⁰⁵ Polybius as quoted in W. Braun, *Feasting and Social Rhetoric in Luke 14*, 36.

¹⁰⁶ Ibid., 39, 37. For the same comparison cf. also M. Wolter, *Das Lukasevangelium*, 502.

¹⁰⁷ Cf. Chapter II. 1.2.4

¹⁰⁸ Michaelis tells that πρωτοκλισία was allocated to the person high in social rank. After 300 CE, age played an important role in deciding who would get the seats of honor. W. Michaelis, "πρωτοκαθεδρία, πρωτοκλισία," in *TDNT*, ed. G. Kittel et al., 10 vols. (Grand Rapids, Michigan: W. B. Eerdmans, 1964-1976), 6, 870.

¹⁰⁹ B. Byrne, *The Hospitality of God: A Reading of Luke's Gospel* (Collegeville, Minn.: Liturgical Press, 2000), 123.

¹¹⁰ Cf. W. Grundmann, *Das Evangelium nach Lukas*, 294.

¹¹¹ J. Dillersberger, *The Gospel of Saint Luke* (Cork: The Mercier Press, 1958), 370-371.

¹¹² W. Braun, *Feasting and Social Rhetoric in Luke 14*, 47; D. L. Bock, *Luke*, 251.

¹¹³ J. P. Kealy, *Luke's Gospel Today: "That you may know the truth" - Luke - 1:4* (Denville: Dimension Books, 1979), 322-323; J. Dillersberger, *The Gospel of Saint Luke*, 371.

¹¹⁴ A. Rathje, "A Banquet Service from the Latin City of Ficana," *ARID* 12 (1983), 12.

¹¹⁵ H. Moxnes, *The Economy of the Kingdom: Social Conflict and Economic Relations in Luke's Gospel*, Overtures to biblical theology [23] (Philadelphia: Fortress Press, 1988), 129; cf. also H. Klein, *Barmherzigkeit Gegenüber den Elenden und Geächteten*, 88.

¹¹⁶ J. P. Heil, *The Meal Scenes in Luke-Acts*, 105.

¹¹⁷ Ibid., 105-106; similar suggestion is also rendered by E. LaVerdiere, *Dining in the Kingdom of God*, 104.

¹¹⁸ In Saturnalia 21 for example, Lucian narrates how indifferent the rich are towards the poor. He says it is "intolerable thing for such a man to lie in his purple clothes, and gorge himself on all these good things, belching, receiving his guest's congratulations and feasting without a break, while I and my sort dream where we can get four obols to be able to sleep after a fill of bread or barely, with cress or thyme or onion as relish." K. Kilburn, *Lucian: With an English Translation*, 8 vols., LCL 6 (London, Cambridge, Massachusetts: William Heinemann; Harvard University Press, 1959). Although here in the earth the rich enjoy sumptuous meals in their houses and the poor die of hunger, Lucian talks of, what Braun calls the "post-mortem judgement and reward." W. Braun,

Feasting and Social Rhetoric in Luke 14, 60. In the after-life both the rich and the poor would experience reversal of their fate after death. The poor would recline among the heroes after their life but the punishment for the rich would be the denial to drink the "water of Lethe" and thereby the constant remembrance of "what he was and how much power he had in the upperworld, and reviewing of his luxury" (*The Downward Journey of the Tyrant* 28). Cf. Harmon, *Lucian*.

[119] Braun is of the opinion that the parable of the Great Dinner has been taken from the Q Tradition; he gives the original form of the story common to the three texts. Jesus telling the story about a person preparing a dinner, inviting his guests through his servant, the decline of the guests, the host's anger, his anger leading to his invitation to the less fortunate to participate in his dinner and the final saying of Jesus about the invited not participating in his dinner are the common elements found in all the three narrations. W. Braun, *Feasting and Social Rhetoric in Luke 14*, 68-73; for identical view cf. also W. Grundmann, *Das Evangelium nach Lukas*, 296-297; J. A. Fitzmyer, *The Gospel According to Luke X-XXIV*, 1052. P. F. Esler, *Community and Gospel in Luke-Acts: The Social and Political Motivations of Lucan Theology*, Monograph series / Society for New Testament Studies 57 (Cambridge, New York: Cambridge University Press, 1989), 192. However, the important differences between Luke and Matthew are the following: the notice that the banquet is a wedding banquet (Matt 22:2), maltreatment and murder of the servants of the host by the invited guests (Matt 22:6), the anger of the host which is shown through the destruction of the cities of the invited guests (Matt 22:7) and the redactional addition of the man without the wedding garment (Matt 22:11). These unique differences make some authors doubt whether it was Q tradition, which Luke, Matthew and the Gospel of Thomas have as their common source. Cf. W. Grundmann, *Das Evangelium nach Lukas*, 296; H. I. Marshall, W. W. Gasque, and D. A. Hagner, *The Gospel of Luke: A Commentary on the Greek Text*, 584; J. P. Kealy, *Luke's Gospel Today*, 323.

[120] K. E. Bailey, *Jesus Through Middle Eastern Eyes: Cultural Studies in the Gospels* (Downers Grove, Ill.: IVP Academic, 2008), 307.

[121] J. P. Kealy, *Luke's Gospel Today*, 324.

[122] W. Grundmann, *Das Evangelium nach Lukas*, 298.

[123] The twofold invitation was not abnormal. It was in fact put to practice by the upper class elite of the time. Cf. J. Kremer, *Lukasevangelium*, 153; H. I. Marshall, W. W. Gasque, and D. A. Hagner, *The Gospel of Luke: A Commentary on the Greek Text*, 588; K. E. Bailey, *Jesus Through Middle Eastern Eyes*, 313.

[124] That the guests have bought land and oxen does not mean that they are village farmers but they are 'absentee landlords' who live in the cities, having entrusted their fields and oxen to stewards in the country yards. Getting a woman

as a wife was seen in the ancient as a possession. Cf. W. Braun, *Feasting and Social Rhetoric in Luke 14*, 75-79.

[125] A. Plummer, *A Critical and Exegetical Commentary on the Gospel According to S. Luke*, 361.

[126] W. Braun, *Feasting and Social Rhetoric in Luke 14*, 110-111.

[127] Ibid., 119-120.

[128] R. L. Rohrbaugh, "The Pre-industrial City in Luke-Acts: Urban Social Relations," in *The Social World of Luke-Actts: Models for Interpretation*, ed. J. H. Neyrey (Peabody, Mass.: Hendrickson Publishers, 1991), 135.

[129] The term is taken from Braun from his sixth chapter, "The conversion of a wealthy householder." W. Braun, *Feasting and Social Rhetoric in Luke 14*, 98-131; we have it also in J. P. Heil, *The Meal Scenes in Luke-Acts*, 109.

[130] W. Grundmann, *Das Evangelium nach Lukas*, 296; Hotze, *Jesus als Gast*, 233, 258; J. A. Fitzmyer, *The Gospel According to Luke X-XXIV*, 1053; D. L. Bock, *Luke*, 253; K. E. Bailey, *Jesus Through Middle Eastern Eyes*, 319. J. Dillersberger, *The Gospel of Saint Luke*, 375; J. P. Heil, *The Meal Scenes in Luke-Acts*, 106-107; W. Manson, *The Gospel of Luke*, 173; W. Bösen, "Das Mahlmotiv bei Lukas." 104-105. We hear also the opposite view. For example the phrase δεῖπνον μέγα need not necessarily imply an eschatological meal; it is used only to show how extraordinary and luxurious the banquet could have been arranged. R. L. Rohrbaugh, "The Pre-industrial City in Luke-Acts." 140.

[131] Another viewpoint would be to understand Jesus as the host; the servant who invite the guests are associated with the disciples who take the message of Jesus to the people. Cf. J. P. Heil, *The Meal Scenes in Luke-Acts*, 108.

[132] H. I. Marshall, W. W. Gasque, and D. A. Hagner, *The Gospel of Luke: A Commentary on the Greek Text*, 585.

[133] There is much discussion among the authors over the λεγω γρρ QμÖν in 14:24, whether it is told by the host in the parable or by Jesus himself. If it was the host in the parable, he had sent only one servant; hence QμÖν does not fit here. If it was the Lukan Jesus who had said to the partakers of the *symposium* at the house of the leader of the Pharisees, then once again it proves the eschatological dimension of the parable, which is upheld by many authors. A. Plummer, *A Critical and Exegetical Commentary on the Gospel According to S. Luke*, 361; H. I. Marshall, W. W. Gasque, and D. A. Hagner, *The Gospel of Luke: A Commentary on the Greek Text*, 590; J. A. Fitzmyer, *The Gospel According to Luke X-XXIV*, 1057. Braun thinks that the speaker of λεγω γρρ QμÖν is the host in the parable himself, addressing the audience of Luke. W. Braun, *Feasting and Social Rhetoric in Luke 14*, 125-126.

¹³⁴ J. P. Heil, *The Meal Scenes in Luke-Acts*, 107.

¹³⁵ Looking also at the eschatological overtones in the entire pericope, Ernst suggests, Luke 14:1-24 encompasses a three dimensional aspect of the fellowship meals, past, present and the future – the banquet at which the historical Jesus partook, the fellowship meals of the Lukan community and the anticipated eschatological meal. J. Ernst, "Gastmahlgespräche: Lk 14,1-24." 74-76.

¹³⁶ R. L. Rohrbaugh, "The Pre-industrial City in Luke-Acts." 146.

¹³⁷ W. Braun, *Feasting and Social Rhetoric in Luke 14*, 126.

¹³⁸ A. Pesonen, "Luke, The Friend of Sinners," https:// helda.helsinki.fi / bitstream/ handle/ 10138/ 21588/ lukethef.pdf ? sequence= 2, 104-105, accessed on 21.05.2017.

¹³⁹ M. Ebner and B. Heininger, *Exegese des Neuen Testaments: Ein Arbeitsbuch für Lehre und Praxis*, 3rd ed. (Paderborn: Verlag Ferdinand Schöningh, 2015), 76. Cf. also Hotze for the *Dreieckformation* in the Gospel of Luke. He concentrates on the meal of Jesus at the house of Simon the Pharisee where the actoinsactions of the sinful woman are contrasted with those of Simon the Pharisee. Hotze, *Jesus als Gast*, 134-135.

¹⁴⁰ B. Byrne, *The Hospitality of God*, 9.

¹⁴¹ Pesonen, "Luke, The Friend of Sinners." 105.

¹⁴² Ibid., 105.

¹⁴³ It is noteworthy to mention that already in Luke 3:12-13, the tax collectors are portrayed as sinners but who admit their sinfulness and are ready to repent.

¹⁴⁴ J. A. Ziesler, "Luke and the Pharisees," *NTS* 25, no. 2 (1979), 150.

¹⁴⁵ A. Finkel, *The Pharisees and the Teacher of Nazareth* (Leiden: E. J. Brill, 1964), 132.

¹⁴⁶ *Contra* M. Smith, *Jesus the Magician*, 1st ed. (San Francisco: Harper & Row, 1978), 153.

¹⁴⁷ Ibid., 157; J. Neusner, *Formative Judaism: Religious, Historical, and Literary Studies*, 57; J. Jeremias, *Jerusalem zur Zeit Jesu*, I, 122.

¹⁴⁸ A. Finkel, *The Pharisees and the Teacher of Nazareth*, 134.

¹⁴⁹ M. Smith, *Jesus the Magician*, 153. One should not forget the fact though, that it is the Pharisees, who around 100 CE, incorporated a curse against Christians in their daily prayer, which was to be recited in their synagogues.

¹⁵⁰ E. LaVerdiere, *Dining in the Kingdom of God*, 110.

¹⁵¹ P. J. Mullen, *Dining with Pharisees* (Collegeville, Minn.: Liturgical Press, 2004), 106.

¹⁵² J. A. Ziesler, "Luke and the Pharisees." 155.

[153] H. J. Cadbury and P. N. Anderson, *The Making of Luke-Acts*, 2nd ed. (Peabody, Mass.: Hendrickson Publishers, 1999), 262; also R. L. Rohrbaugh, "The Pre-industrial City in Luke-Acts." 146.

[154] L. Schottroff and W. Stegemann, *Jesus and the Hope of the Poor* (Maryknoll, N.Y.: Orbis Books, 1986), 91. Perhaps a word of caution is also to be noted in our understanding. I would like to point out here the warning that Moxnes gives about the "rich and the respected." In the Greco-Roman world, a person could be rich but not necessarily respected. "Rich men could be outsiders and make their money on non-elite occupations (e.g. as toll collectors and merchants) ... The 'ideal rich' in Luke, like the toll collector Zacchaeus (Luke 19:1-10), do not belong to the elite." Moxnes further states that through the different rich persons that we see in Luke-Acts, including Zacchaeus, we may understand the community of Luke "as a group of non-elite persons who are culturally and ethnically mixed but who also include among them some who come from the elite periphery." H. Moxnes, "The Social Context of Luke's Community," *Interpretation: A Journal of Bible & Theology* 48, no. 4 (1994), 387.

Chapter - 3

The Story of Zacchaeus: An Exegetical Analysis (Luke 19:1-10)

The biographical narration of Jesus' meals with different classes of people in Luke functions as an invitation of Jesus to accept his message. When Jesus is invited by Pharisees, tax collectors, or Martha, he changes his role from being a guest to being the actual host, entertaining his 'guests' with his message and offer of salvation. In Luke 19:1-10, Luke portrays the last meal of Jesus before his entry into Jerusalem. In this meal with Zacchaeus, which is the "penultimate supper"[1] before his Last Supper with his disciples, the Lukan Jesus sums up his entire ministry of table fellowship. Although Pharisees had invited Jesus to be his guest, they rejected his offer of salvation. On the contrary, Zacchaeus the host receives Jesus in his house, and having changed his role from the host to a 'guest' of Jesus, Zacchaeus receives the message of Jesus who would 'host' him with offer of salvation.

This chapter is an attempt to make an exegetical study of the story of Zacchaeus (Luke 19:1-10). The variant readings in the NA[28] would be analyzed into in order to find out the most preferred reading; we would begin by delimiting the story of Zacchaeus from the texts that precede and follow it. The immediate and its remote context of the story of Zacchaeus would help us understand the meaning of the pericope. The different redactional elements in Luke 19:1-10 help one to recognize not only the core text that has been received by Luke from his special L source but also the purpose of his redaction to suit his overarching theme and concern.

Word analysis of Luke 19:1-10 in this chapter, aims at understanding the nuances of the words and phrases used by Luke in this pericope, within the broader context of the third Gospel. Some of the words that are used in this pericope are nowhere else used except in Luke 19:1-10; this leads one to ascertain their meaning from the background of the particular story as well as from the general context of Luke's Gospel. Through this word analysis, we try to find answers to the following questions:

- Is the naming of the city of Jericho significant for the pericope? Does Jesus' going through the city (διήρχετο) mean more than just passing through (19:1)?

- Does Luke attach theological significance to the name of the main character Zacchaeus? How do the characteristics of Zacchaeus as the rich chief tax collector who is small in stature portray him before the readers of Luke? Is Zacchaeus' desire to see who Jesus is (19:2-3), just a matter of curiosity, or does Luke add a theological meaning to it?

- Why is it 'necessary' (δεῖ) for Jesus to 'stay' (μεῖναι) at the house of Zacchaeus? Does the joyful reception of Zacchaeus denote something more than just a stay (19:5-6)?

- Does the only sentence said by Zacchaeus portray him as a righteous man or as a sinner (19:8)? What is the theological significance of Jesus' reply to Zacchaeus in the light of the context of the third Gospel (19:9-10)?

1 Luke 19:1-10 as in NA[28]

1. Καὶ εἰσελθὼν διήρχετο τὴν Ἰεριχώ.
2. Καὶ ἰδοὺ ἀνὴρ ὀνόματι καλούμενος Ζακχαῖος, καὶ αὐτὸς ἦν ἀρχιτελώνης καὶ αὐτὸς πλούσιος·

3. καὶ ἐζήτει ἰδεῖν τὸν Ἰησοῦν τίς ἐστιν καὶ οὐκ ἠδύνατο ἀπὸ τοῦ ὄχλου, ὅτι τῇ ἡλικίᾳ μικρὸς ἦν.

4. καὶ προδραμὼν εἰς τὸ ἔμπροσθεν ἀνέβη ἐπὶ συκομορέαν ἵνα ἴδῃ αὐτὸν ὅτι ἐκείνης ἤμελλεν διέρχεσθαι.

5. καὶ ὡς ἦλθεν ἐπὶ τὸν τόπον, ἀναβλέψας ὁ Ἰησοῦς εἶπεν πρὸς αὐτόν· Ζακχαῖε, σπεύσας κατάβηθι, σήμερον γὰρ ἐν τῷ οἴκῳ σου δεῖ με μεῖναι.

6. καὶ σπεύσας κατέβη καὶ ὑπεδέξατο αὐτὸν χαίρων.

7. καὶ ἰδόντες πάντες διεγόγγυζον λέγοντες ὅτι παρὰ ἁμαρτωλῷ ἀνδρὶ εἰσῆλθεν καταλῦσαι.

8. σταθεὶς δὲ Ζακχαῖος εἶπεν πρὸς τὸν κύριον· ἰδοὺ τὰ ἡμίσιά μου τῶν ὑπαρχόντων, κύριε, τοῖς πτωχοῖς δίδωμι, καὶ εἴ τινός τι ἐσυκοφάντησα ἀποδίδωμι τετραπλοῦν.

9. εἶπεν δὲ πρὸς αὐτὸν ὁ Ἰησοῦς ὅτι σήμερον σωτηρία τῷ οἴκῳ τούτῳ ἐγένετο, καθότι καὶ αὐτὸς υἱὸς Ἀβραάμ ἐστιν·

10. ἦλθεν γὰρ ὁ υἱὸς τοῦ ἀνθρώπου ζητῆσαι καὶ σῶσαι τὸ ἀπολωλός.

Textual Critical Analysis

Ὀνόματι Καλούμενος (Luke 19:2)

The redundant usage of the phrase, ὀνόματι καλούμενος would have been looked at by the scribes who copied the text as something irregular. According to many scholars this pleonastic usage does not suit the literary characteristics of Luke.[2] Hence there is a variant without the word καλούμενος which is attested, among others, by the Codex Bezae (005), by some minuscules 892 and 1241, and few Latin and Sahidic manuscripts as well as Bohairic witnesses. The omission is understandable as an attempt to correct the redundancy of the expressions ὀνόματι and καλούμενος. Some scholars think, however, that the pleonasm here is not necessarily "a fault of style but may be deliberately employed for effect."[3] For Marshall the usage could be deliberate in order to "draw a special attention to the man's name."[4] Zacchaeus, whose name means "just" or "innocent," is, because of his trade, taken as someone who is not merely corrupt but also a sinner. Perhaps Luke uses the pleonastic ὀνόματι καλούμενος in order to highlight the irony in the name of the character and the view of the bystanders.[5] Since the pleonastic usage is attested by earlier manuscripts like Codex Vaticanus (003), as well as f^1 ^{13} among others, we intend to take the NA[28] phrase ὀνόματι καλούμενος as the primary reading.

Ἀρχιτελώνης (Luke 19:2)

Another important variant in v. 2 relates to the profession of the main character. Ψ changes the profession of Zacchaeus; instead of καὶ αὐτὸς ἦν ἀρχιτελώνης καὶ αὐτὸς πλούσιος, Ψ describes Zacchaeus as ἄρχων τῆς συναγωγῆς ὑπῆρχεν. Besides changing the profession of Zacchaeus as the leader of the synagogue, Ψ has also removed the last clause of v. 2, καὶ αὐτὸς πλούσιος. It is difficult, first of all, to imagine how a leader of the synagogue could have been considered by "all" in the city of Jericho as a notorious sinner (19:7). Text critically Ψ has very weak evidence in favor of naming Zacchaeus as the leader of the synagogue and for the removal of the richness of Zacchaeus. Apart from Ψ, which belongs to the Byzantine family, no other codex attests to this variant reading. The absence of such a reading in Alexandrian text type makes one doubt this variant reading. We need to take into consideration that ἀρχιτελώνης is a *hapax legomenon;* nowhere in the Greek literature the profession of chief tax collector (ἀρχιτελώνης) is mentioned. Hence it might be probable that the scribes wanted to avoid the difficulty and changed the difficult and unusual word into a more common expression. Altering ἀρχιτελώνης to ἄρχων τῆς συναγωγῆς ὑπῆρχεν is more probable than changing ἄρχων τῆς συναγωγῆς ὑπῆρχεν to ἀρχιτελώνης. Because of these above-mentioned reasons, we take the Ψ variant as secondary and go along with the NA[28] reading of Zacchaeus as chief of tax collectors and rich.

The Presence of Double Αὐτός

NA²⁸ follows the Codex Vaticanus, the important *papyri* families *f* ¹,¹³ and other later Codices like K, T to read the personal pronoun αὐτός twice in v. 2b. Some scholars believe that this double use of αὐτός is stylistically not a good composition.⁶ For them it might be probable, that "the evangelist retains his source without much change."⁷ The important witness Codex Sinaiticus (001), among others however reads αὐτός only once and reads καὶ ἦν πλούσιος. Plummer suggests that this reading of Codex Sinaiticus without the second αὐτός could be right.⁸ The presence of the phrase in other verses in Luke´s Gospel leads Plummer to believe that the phrase καὶ αὐτός is a favorite term of Luke to connect different clauses.⁹ The question then arises as to why Plummer favors a reading without the phrase as primary, if he views καὶ αὐτός a Lukan favorite connecting phrase.

5ᵗʰ century Codex W (without the phrase καί), 6ᵗʰ century Codex R (027), among others read οὗτος ἦν πλούσιος instead of καὶ αὐτὸς πλούσιος. The reason for this variant could be that the copyist tried to avoid the repetition of αὐτός. Since it is more probable that a copyist omitted that which is used twice, than that someone added it to create redundancy, I am of the opinion that the omission of αὐτός is a correction and therefore secondary. The double use of αὐτός is witnessed not only by Codices like Vaticanus, Cyprius (017) Borgianus (029) but also by *f* ¹, ¹³ among others. Besides, the double usage of αὐτός serve the purpose of creating a "dramatic style."¹⁰ Perhaps, the evangelist uses two different clauses with αὐτός in order to emphasize the two important characteristics of the main character, which, from the perspective of the readers are very important to the narration. On the one hand, Zacchaeus is the chief of the tax collectors who have been characterized all through the Gospel in a positive light. On the other hand, Zacchaeus belongs to the affluent group of the society, which is seen throughout the Gospel as negative examples. This raises the question for the readers / the listeners what the fate of the main character will be. The double use of αὐτός serves to shed light on the contrasting characteristics of Zacchaeus. Hence, here it is preferred to consider the variant which reads αὐτός twice as original.

Προδραμὼν εἰς τὸ Ἔμπροσθεν (Luke 19:4)

Once again, there is a pleonasm, this time in the phrase προδραμὼν εἰς τὸ ἔμπροσθεν,[11] which literally means "running *ahead* into the *front*"[12] and is retained among many others by important early manuscripts like Codex Sinaiticus and Vaticanus, which belong to Alexandrian family type.

Other manuscripts like W, R, L, G, Ψ read "running to" (προσδραμών). This is probably an attempt to create a smoother reading. Other manuscripts have only δραμών, perhaps to avoid the redundancy. Fifth century Codex Bezae (05) reads προλαβών. Another variant reading attested by important manuscripts like Codex Alexandrinus, Bezae, Nitriensis as well as the $f^{1,\,13}$ is without the phrase εἰς τό. Bovon understands this pleonasm as the Lukan attempt to explain the action of Zacchaeus, from the temporary and special perspective. He explains, „*Zacchäus ist zeitlich zuvorgekommen, indem er sich örtlich nach vorne bewegte.*"[13] Although this seems to be plausible, the better reason to accept the NA[28] reading could lie in the rule *lectio difficilior, lectio portior*. Other variant readings appear to be attempts to smoothen a difficult reading. Hence, the preference to the most difficult reading favours προδραμὼν εἰς τὸ ἔμπροσθεν. Since several manuscripts of the important Alexandrian text type attest to the difficult and pleonastic reading προδραμὼν εἰς τὸ ἔμπροσθεν, the reading as in NA[28] is preferred.

Καὶ Ὡς Ἦλθεν Ἐπὶ τὸν Τόπον, Ἀναβλέψας ὁ Ἰησοῦς (Luke 19:5)

The variant reading in verse 5 concerns the meeting of Jesus with Zacchaeus. Codex Bezae as well as *itala* versions read ἐγένετο ἐν τῷ διέρχεσθαι instead of ὡς ἦλθεν ἐπὶ τὸν τόπον, ἀναβλέψας ὁ Ἰησοῦς. The purpose of the scribes might have been to make the verse complement 'Jesus going through' Jericho in v. 1. A number of manuscripts read εἶπεν πρὸς αὐτόν before εἶδεν αὐτόν. (Ψ reads the verb οἶδα in a participial form, καὶ ἰδὼν αὐτόν). Marshall is right to note that εἶδεν αὐτόν καί after ἀναβλέψας looks to be redundant.[14] There is a similar word order in Luke 21:1 (Ἀναβλέψας δὲ εἶδεν). If one prefers the variant reading (with the phrase εἶδεν αὐτόν καί) as the original, then the absence of the phrase in Codices like 01 and 03 and other witnesses would have been a scribal error due to *homoioarcton*. I prefer to consider the shorter reading without the phrase εἶδεν αὐτόν καί as the more original reading. It is likely that the scribes added the phrase ἔιδεν αὐτόν in order to emphasize the fact that Jesus actually recognized Zacchaeus.[15] This intention is corroborated by the fact that Jesus calls Zacchaeus by name even though he is meeting him for the first time. The scribes through this addition wanted perhaps to emphasize the subtle theological significance noting that it is Jesus who actually "sees" Zacchaeus while Zacchaeus was seeking to "see" Jesus. Applying the rule of preference of the shortness of a reading, the reading preferred by NA[28] could be assumed as the original reading.

Καὶ Ἰδόντες Πάντες Διεγόγγυζον Λέγοντες (Luke 19:7)

The word λέγοντες is not read by Western texts – among others by Codex Bezae and the majority of the old Latin witnesses. Levinsohn suggests that in the third Gospel when the word λέγοντες precedes the word ὅτι, the author introduces a direct speech, which concludes a unit or subunit of a narrative.[16] Since Luke 19:1-10 does not end with vv. 7-8 but continues further with the pronouncement of Jesus in vv. 9-10, it might have been that the scribes who copied the text, recognized this nuance and attempted to modify the pericope. By omitting the word λέγοντες the scribes indicated that the narrative does not end with the murmuring of the crowd or the resolution of Zacchaeus but with the solemn acceptance of Zacchaeus by Jesus. The support for the reading without λέγοντες is not very strong; it is attested primarily by the Western text types. If we consider λέγοντες as probably having been received by Luke from his source, which Luke did not find necessary to remove it, one could surmise that the reading with λέγοντες, as it stands in NA[28], is closer to the original than the reading without λέγοντες.

Τὰ Ἡμίσια (Luke 19:8)

It is strange to note that the evangelist speaks of "the halves" (plural) of the properties of the rich man. Is Zacchaeus going to, or does he give *both halves* of his properties to the poor, as Jesus commanded the rich ruler in 18:22? This difficulty could have been the reason for the change of ἡμίσια into ἡμίση in some manuscripts. Ἡμίση was the preferred text in NA[26] which has now been replaced by ἡμίσια in NA[28], supported among others by Codices Sinaiticus and Vaticanus. Another variant is ἥμισυ. In a slight variation, 031 has τὸ ἡμίσυ. The genitive which is employed in v. 8 (τὰ ἡμίσιά μου τῶν ὑπαρχόντων) is a "classical reverse assimilation of gender and number."[17] Since ἡμίση is more common, it is more probable that the scribes attempted to change it to the regular usage than did the opposite; hence the difficult reading of ἡμίσια is to be preferred to the more usual one.[18]

Τοῖς Πτωχοῖς Δίδωμι (Luke 19:8)

The preferred word order in NA[28] τοῖς πτωχοῖς δίδωμι which is supported by Sinaiticus, Codex Bezae and other manuscripts, is not found in all the manuscripts. A first variant δίδωμι τοῖς πτωχοῖς is read by Codex Alexandrianus and others. Codex Vaticanus reads the dative noun πτωχοῖς without the definite article as πτωχοῖς δίδωμι. A plausible explanation for the reading by Codex Vaticanus could be that a scribe understood the poor not as a definite group of people but in more general terms. Moreover, the reading of πτωχοῖς without the definite article might be a harmonization with the similar reading διάδος πτωχοῖς (Jesus' command to the rich ruler in 18:22). For these reasons, the reading πτωχοῖς δίδωμι is probably secondary.

Σήμερον Σωτηρία Τῷ Οἴκῳ Τούτῳ Ἐγένετο (Luke 19:9)

Codex Alexandrianus, Codex Bezae and others read the preposition ἐν before the phrase τῷ οἴκῳ τούτῳ. This preposition ἐν gives the phrase τῷ οἴκῳ τούτῳ a locative meaning. It is in this locative understanding that NRSV translates v. 9 "Today salvation has come *to* this house."

Without the preposition ἐν, the phrase τῷ οἴκῳ τούτῳ is used as a "dative of advantage or possession, meaning, 'Salvation is for this house' or 'salvation belongs to this house.'"[19] Moreover, the reading ἐν is not supported by the Alexandrian text-type, and the clause καθότι καὶ αὐτὸς υἱὸς Ἀβραάμ ἐστιν, which follows immediately, fits better with a dative of possession than with dative of location. Hence τῷ οἴκῳ τούτῳ could be preferred to ἐν τῷ οἴκῳ τούτῳ.

Working Translation
1. And having entered, he was passing through Jericho.

2. And behold, (there was) a man called by name Zacchaeus, and he was a chief tax collector and he (was) rich.

3. And he was seeking to see Jesus, who he was, but he was not able to, on account of the crowd, because he was small for his age.

4. And having run ahead, to the front, he climbed up upon a sycamore tree so that he might see him; for he was about to pass by that way.

5. And as he came to the place, Jesus looked up and said to him: "Zacchaeus, come down immediately, for today it is necessary for me to stay in your house."

6. and he came down immediately and received him with joy.

7. But seeing (it), all were murmuring, saying, "he has gone in to stay with a sinful man."

8. But standing, Zacchaeus said to the Lord, "Behold, the half of my properties, Lord, I give to the poor, and if I have defrauded anyone of anything, I pay back fourfold."

9. And Jesus said to him; "Today salvation has come to this house, for he too is a son of Abraham.

10. For the Son of Man came to seek and to save the lost."

Delimitation of Luke 19:1-10

Luke 19:1-10 forms part of Jericho material and hence is connected to what has gone before - the healing of the blind beggar (Luke 18:35-43). The geographical reference at the beginning of the pericope however shows that Luke wants to show the story of Zacchaeus as a separate text from the healing of the blind beggar. Even though both happen around Jericho, the healing of the blind beggar takes place before Jesus entered Jericho, as he "approached Jericho" (Ἐγένετο δὲ ἐν τῷ ἐγγίζειν αὐτὸν εἰς Ἰεριχώ - Luke 18:35) while Zacchaeus story happens after Jesus "entered Jericho and was passing through it" (Καὶ εἰσελθὼν διήρχετο τὴν Ἰεριχώ - Luke 19:1).

We have however difficulties to define the end of the pericope. The clause "Ἀκουόντων δὲ αὐτῶν ταῦτα προσθεὶς εἶπεν" (Luke 19:11) points out that the addressees of Jesus are the very people who were murmuring (Luke 19:7) and with whom Jesus conversed (Luke 19:9-10). The pericope is thus not differentiated with a spatial difference; there is no change in the place of the happening for the following parable. For some scholars, since the parable seems to be told in Jericho "in or near the house of Zacchaeus"[20] and hence as the continuation of what has gone before (Luke 19:1-10), there seems to be no break between Luke 19:1-10 and the following parable.[21] Apart from the fact that the audience of Luke 19:1-10 and vv. 11-27 are the same and the place of happening is near the house of Zacchaeus in Jericho, both the pericopes are also thematically united.[22] Both the pericopes deal with the disciples' use of possessions.[23] The demonstrative pronoun ταῦτα in Luke 19:11 suggests that Luke wants to connect the parable with the theme of σωτηρία (Luke 19:9).[24] Luke might have been responsible for the linking of the parable of the Talents with the story of Zacchaeus. In the words of Miyoshi, Zacchaeus is the living example of those servants in the parable to whom the Lord entrusts his possessions, who have used in a better way what was entrusted to them.[25]

Though there are factors that unite the two pericopes, one is able to see a clear-cut separation between 19:1-10 and vv. 11-27. The following pointers could prove this:

- Luke 19:11 begins with the geographic reference about Jesus being 'near Jerusalem' (διὰ τὸ ἐγγὺς εἶναι Ἰερουσαλὴμ αὐτόν 19:11b), which is a pointer to the transition that Luke makes from one pericope to another (cf. Luke 9:51; 13:22; 17:11; 18:31; 19:28). Further the entire verse, as Jeremias says,[26] does not look like a continuation of v. 10. V. 11 serves as an introduction and setting for the parable that follows in vv. 12-27.

- As for the source, the Zacchaeus pericope is unique to Luke, as it comes from his special material, whereas the parable of the talents (vv. 12-27) has some similarities with Matt 25:14-30.

- As for the form, Luke 19:1-10 is a unified whole, since Luke makes a transition from a biographical narrative (19:1-10) to a parable (vv. 12-27).

- As for the theme, although both the pericopes concern about the theme of salvation, there is difference between the two pericopes. While Luke 19:1-10 talks about the "actuality of the Messianic salvation"[27] the parable that follows is a warning against those who think about the immediate arrival of this salvation.

Summing up we could say, though there are factors that unite Luke 19:1-10 with the parable that follows, it does not necessarily imply that Luke 19:1-27 is one unified pericope. Having seen the above-mentioned differences between the vv. 1-10 and vv. 11-27 one could agree with Marshall, that Luke 19:1-10 stands as a "unified composition"[28] different from the healing of the blind beggar (Luke 18:35-43) and the parable of the talents (Luke 19:11-27).

Literary Context of Luke 19:1-10

Immediate Context

Readers of the third Gospel would rightly recognize the placement of the story of Zacchaeus as the summation of what they have been reading in Luke 18. The parables and events that were narrated in the entire chapter provide a better understanding of the story of Zacchaeus. The hindrance by the crowd, the perseverance of Zacchaeus to see Jesus in overcoming the barrier of his short stature by climbing a sycamore tree– all these remind the readers about the widow in the parable of the unjust judge, who shows her perseverance in obtaining justice from the unjust judge (Luke 18:1-8). The ludicrous action of the rich and chief tax collector Zacchaeus of climbing a tree like a small child, takes the readers back to the advice of Jesus, to be like little children in order to enter the Kingdom of heaven (Luke 18:17). In a special way, Luke connects the Zacchaeus story with the other three events that are narrated in the 18th chapter. In the following pages we could see the thematic as well as word parallels with which Luke has very artistically connected the story of Zacchaeus with the parable of the Pharisee and the tax collector (Luke 18:9-14), with the parable of the rich ruler (Luke 18:18-30) and with the healing of the blind beggar (Luke 18:35-43).

Zacchaeus and the Blind Beggar (Luke 18:35-43)

The meaning and interpretation of Zacchaeus story would be complete if one sees it in the context of the healing of the blind beggar in Jericho (Luke 18:35-43).[29] Luke places the Zacchaeus story as well as the healing of the blind beggar around Jericho. While Mark places the blind Bartimaeus narrative as Jesus was leaving the city (Mk 10:6), Luke places it before Jesus entered the city (Luke 18:35). In this way, Luke tries to prepare the readers for what is coming ahead in the city of Jericho. It is significant to see that Luke avoids naming the blind beggar as Bartimaeus as is found in Mark. Luke Instead gives the character of the chief tax collector a name. Even if he found the name Zacchaeus in his original source, the deliberate removal of the name Bartimaeus from the previous incident, shows that the readers should understand the blind beggar incident before the arrival of Jesus in the city of Jericho as an introduction for the Zacchaeus story which would happen in the city of Jericho.[30] In the following table one could see very clearly how both the texts are connected not just geographically but also thematically:

• Jesus and Zacchaeus (Luke 19:1-10)	• Healing of the Blind Beggar (Luke 18:35-43)
• The main character, Zacchaeus is a social outcast	• The main character, blind beggar, is a social outcast
• Geographical reference of Jesus passing through Jericho (19:1)	• Geographical reference of Jesus approaching Jericho (18:35)
• Mention of the crowd going with Jesus (19:3)	• Mention of the crowd going with Jesus (18:36)
• Mention of the physical inability of Zacchaeus (short in stature 19:3)	• Mention of physical inability of the beggar (blindness 18:35)
• The hindrance Zacchaeus faces to reach Jesus (19:3)	• The hindrance the blind beggar faces to reach Jesus (18:39)
• The perseverance of Zacchaeus to see Jesus by climbing a tree (19:4)	• The perseverance of the blind beggar to encounter Jesus by shouting even more loudly (18:38-39)
• The initiative of Jesus to stop the travel and meet Zacchaeus (19:5)	• The initiative of Jesus to stop the travel and meet the blind beggar (18:40)

• The sole aim of Zacchaeus is to "see" who Jesus was (19:3)	• The sole aim of the blind beggar is to "see" (18:41)
• Zacchaeus addressing Jesus as κύριε (19:8)	• The blind beggar addressing Jesus as κύριε (18:41)
• Zacchaeus is rich but he receives salvation "σωτηρία" / "ζητῆσαι" (19:9-10).	• The beggar is poor but he receives the salvation "σέσωκέν" (18:42).

The above-mentioned table helps one to understand that these texts which follow one another have to be understood in the light of each other. In both the pericopes, the themes of blindness and seeing play an important role. The word, 'to see' occurs in the story of Zacchaeus at least four times - ἰδεῖν (19:3), ἴδῃ (19:4), ἀναβλέψας (19:5), ἰδόντες (19:7) - the recurrence of which displays the significance of the word for Luke. This goes very well with the longing of the blind beggar who wants to "see" (κύριε, ἵνα ἀναβλέψω 18:41). In this sense, the story of the blind beggar anticipates the story of Zacchaeus, who wants to see who Jesus is (19:3). The story of Zacchaeus no longer deals with physical blindness and seeing, as was the case with the blind beggar: it goes far deeper. It is about the healing of the spiritual blindness. The spiritually blind Zacchaeus who wanted to see who Jesus was, has received sight in the fact that he addresses Jesus as "κύριε" (19:8). There is also an attempt to understand the twin Jericho stories in the light of the overall theology of Luke, namely, the movement of the Gospel to the ends of the earth beginning from Israel; Creed cites Loisy, who understands the healing of the blind beggar symbolizing the salvation which is rendered to the Judeo-Christians and the arrival of Jesus at the house of Zacchaeus symbolizing the salvation reaching out to the gentile Christians.[31] Creed however is right in refuting this argument. The text as it stands does not warrant such an interpretation. The very pointer of Zacchaeus as the son of Abraham does suggest a Judeo-Christian worldview than a gentile Christian one. If we understand the character of Zacchaeus as symbolically, referring to a gentile Christian acceptance of Jesus, there is then the difficulty in understanding the phrase υἱὸς Ἀβραάμ (19:9). We will have to understand Zacchaeus only as a spiritual son of Abraham. The criticism of the onlookers however is not that Zacchaeus is a gentile, but that Zacchaeus is a sinner.

Zacchaeus and the Rich Ruler (Luke 18:18-27)

The story of Zacchaeus should also be seen in the background of the use of riches in obtaining salvation, the theme which is central to the Lukan theological purpose. In this sense, Luke 19:1-10 fits very well in the context of the story of the rich ruler who meets Jesus in search of salvation (Luke 18:18-27).[32] One could observe many parallels between Luke 18:18-27 and Luke 19:1-10. In both texts we repeatedly hear favorite themes of Luke like πλούσιος (18:23; 19:2), giving the riches to the πτωχοῖς (18:22; 19:8), and the theme of σωτηρία (18:26; 19:9). Both the characters are rich and have acquired possessions and both of them are rulers (ἄρχων -18:18 and ἀρχιτελώνης - 19:2). Both of them have the desire to come to Jesus. There are also contrasting parallels between the two characters. One has observed the commandments since his youth (18:21), the other has no respect for following the Law and hence is a sinner (19:7). Another important difference between the two is that the rich ruler is asked to sell his properties and give to the poor but he is not willing to do so (18:22-23), whereas Zacchaeus willingly announces that he would give away half of his properties to the poor without being asked by Jesus (19:8).

This confirms our view once again that Luke targets the upper middle class Christian readers. These narratives about the rich ruler and the rich chief of tax collector are portrayed as prototypes for his community. These two characters are to be seen as messengers to the upper middle class readers to show them whether or not riches and possessions play any role in acquiring salvation. The question of the onlookers in Luke 18:26, "who then can be saved?" gets the answer in the life and person of Zacchaeus the rich man, to whose house salvation has come (19:9) due to his readiness to let go of his dearly held possessions. Hence Zacchaeus who found joy in receiving Jesus in his heart and house (19:6), is shown to be the model of the rich Christians of the Lukan community; he is the positive counterpart of the rich ruler who went away sad and was not ready to share his riches as prompted by Jesus (18:23).

Zacchaeus and the Parable of the Pharisee and the Tax Collector (Luke 18:9-14)

Another important text, which enhances the meaning of the story of Zacchaeus, is the parable of the Pharisee and the Tax Collector (18:9-14). The very introduction to the parable (18:9) narrates the disdain, self-righteous people had against the social outcasts. The disdainful attitude of the self-righteous Pharisee is the same as that of the crowd that murmurs against Jesus going to the house of Zacchaeus who in their eyes is a "sinner" (19:7). As Ernst suggests, the parable of the Pharisee and the tax collector, the remorse with which the tax collector prayed in the Temple and the repentance he showed get actualized in the story of Zacchaeus.[33] This makes very much sense, in our study of Jesus' table fellowship with Pharisees and the tax collectors.

Remote Context of the Story of Zacchaeus

The Place of Luke 19:1-10 in the Travel Narrative

It is generally suggested that the third Gospel is geographically structured.[34] The first part of the Gospel, after the birth narratives, is seen as the mission of Jesus in Galilee (Luke 4:14-9:50). The last part of his Gospel concentrates on the mission of Jesus in Jerusalem (Luke 19:45-21:38) and his Death and Resurrection narratives are centered around Jerusalem (Luke 22:1-24:53). In the middle section of the Gospel (Luke 9:51-19:44) Luke focuses on the journey of Jesus 'on the way' setting his face from Galilee towards Jerusalem.[35] The story of Zacchaeus should be seen in the above broader background, since it falls practically at the end of the Travel Narrative (Luke 19:44).[36] Hence, the story of Zacchaeus encompasses practically all the themes which the Travel Narrative and the Lukan special material deal with: the theme of salvation, reversal of status, poverty and the use of riches, Jesus in search of the despised of the society and above all Jesus as guest.

The Story of Zacchaeus in 'the Gospel of the Outcasts'

Within the Travel Narrative, the story of Zacchaeus comes within a unit, which Manson terms as the Gospel of the Outcasts (ch. 15-19).[37] This section which is introduced by a summary statement of the murmuring of the Pharisees and scribes against the table fellowship of Jesus with tax collectors and sinners and which begins with the three parables in Luke 15, "show a deliberate attempt to show God´s concern for those human beings whom people tend to despise or condemn."[38] The characters in this Lukan special material (ch. 15-19) - in the three parables including the prodigal son, the parable of the rich man and Lazarus (Luke 16:19-31), the ten lepers (Luke 17:11-19), the parable of the Pharisee and the tax collector (Luke 18:9-14) and the story of Zacchaeus (Luke 19:1-10) - aim to show the readers that "it is God Himself who wills that the outcasts should be gathered in. The attitude of Jesus to publicans and sinners is not a mere humanitarian enthusiasm on his part: it is the manifestation of the will and purpose of God."[39] Zacchaeus is one among the many characters in this unit (ch. 15-19) who shows not only the divine option for and the gracious acceptance of the outcasts by God, but also the repentance of the outcasts and their joyful acceptance of Jesus.

Zacchaeus – Part of the Meal Narratives of Luke

Apart from the Travel Narrative, the story of Zacchaeus should also be seen in the context of the different meal narratives in the Gospel of Luke.[40] The second chapter analyzed important texts that showed Jesus being invited as the chief guest at sympotic meals. We began with Jesus at the house of the tax collector Levi (Luke 5:27-32) and how three Pharisees invited Jesus to their houses for fellowship meals (Luke 7:36-50; 11:37-54; 14:1-24). In these banquets Jesus was criticized for his active engagement with the social outcasts. The Lukan Jesus made use of these banquets to teach those who objected his behavior and his values. At the house of Levi, the Lukan Jesus proclaimed that he has come not to call the righteous but sinners (Luke 5:32); at the house of Simon the Pharisee the Lukan Jesus showed how the sinful woman became the model of repentance (Luke 7:36-50); at the house of another Pharisee Jesus invited the Pharisees to give alms in order to be clean (Luke 11:41) and at the house of the ruler of the Pharisees Jesus suggested that they should invite the poor and the crippled, the lame and the blind so that their actions would be repaid in the Kingdom of Heaven (Luke 14:13, 21). Hence all these meal narratives are intended by Luke to be "calls to conversion for those objecting to his meal fellowship with social outcasts and public sinners."[41] Zacchaeus comes as the climax of these fellowship meals of Jesus. The next meal that we would hear in the Gospel is the Meal *par excellence*, the Last Supper (Luke 22:14-23). Hence before the Last Supper, the story of Zacchaeus climaxes all the above-mentioned sympotic meals that Jesus partook in and sums up all the themes dealt with in the previous meal narratives.

The Story of Zacchaeus and of Levi: Parallel Encounters

The encounter of Jesus with Zacchaeus is very much connected to the encounter of Jesus with Levi the tax collector (Luke 5:27-32) and functions as the climax of all the tax collector material in Luke.[42] The similarities in the structure as well as content are clear to be seen:[43]

• Jesus' Encounter with Zacchaeus (Luke 19:1-10)	• Jesus' Encounter with Levi (Luke 5:27-32)
• Jesus is on the way (19:1).	• Jesus is on the way (5:27).
• The character is the chief tax collector by profession (19:2).	• The character is tax collector by profession (5:27).
• The character is given a name – Zacchaeus (19:2).	• The character is given a name – Levi (5:27).

• There is mention of the crowd (19:3).	• There is mention of large crowd (5:29).
• Initiative to meet Zacchaeus comes from Jesus (19:5).	• Initiative to meet Levi comes from Jesus (5:27).
• Zacchaeus is rich and receives Jesus joyfully in his house as guest.	• Levi is rich and receives Jesus joyfully to host his chief guest a great banquet (5:29).
• Zacchaeus stands up and is willing to give away (at least half of) his possessions to the poor (19:8).	• Levi gets up and leaves everything to follow Jesus (5:28).
• Objection is raised by all those around, who grumble against Jesus being the guest of the one who is considered to be a sinner (19:6).	• Objection is raised by Pharisees and scribes who grumble against Jesus reclining at table with the socially outcast (5:30).
• Jesus defends his action with a solemn pronouncement about his mission with the double *logion* (19:9-10).	• Jesus defends his action with a solemn pronouncement about his mission which the evangelist renders with a double *logion* (5:31-32).

As we have mentioned earlier, both the texts that deal with tax collectors form an inclusion.[44] These similarities lead one to the conclusion that Luke must have modified the call of Levi, which he found in Mark 2:13-17 and modified it intentionally to look similar to the story of Zacchaeus. As Kariamadam points out the redactional addition of εἰς μετάνοιαν in 5:32 clearly takes the story forward to the character of Zacchaeus who shows his repentance by his willingness to share his riches (19:8).[45] Hence, the story of Zacchaeus has to be seen within the broader context of the meal narratives and especially within the background of the call of Levi in Luke 5:27-32.

Hamm divulges how Luke 19:1-10 stands parallel not only to the call of Levi but also to Luke 15:1-32.[46] For him the following three texts have to be understood in the light of the theme of repentance - Luke 5:30; 15:2; 19:7. In all the three texts, Jesus is accused by his opponents for accepting / sharing hospitality with tax collectors and sinners. In all the three texts, the word that is used for murmuring of the opponents is the same (ἐγόγγυζον, διεγόγγυζον, διεγόγγυζον respectively). In all three we hear Jesus proclaiming that his mission is to save that which is lost (Luke 5:32; 15:3-32; 19:9-10). In all the three texts, there is a mention of rejoicing. In the call of Levi, joy is implied in his hosting a great banquet (Luke 5:29), while in the other two texts joy is explicit (Luke 15:5, 6, 7, 9, 10, 32; 19:6). The story of Zacchaeus comes therefore as the climax, not only of the theme of Jesus' reaching out to the despised of the society, despite the murmuring of the opponents but it also serves as the climax of the texts which display the willingness of the lost ones to repent and return.

The Story of Zacchaeus and the Story of the Sinful Woman (Luke 7:36-50)

Just as there were similarities between the character of Levi and Zacchaeus, we find also parallels between the story of Zacchaeus and Jesus' meal at the house of Simon the Pharisee. The following parallels could be seen.[47] Both pericopes begin with the indication that Jesus was on the way (Luke 7:36; 19:1). In both, names of the main characters are given (Simon the Pharisee and Zacchaeus, Luke 7:44; 19:2). In both, the characters, who are interested in Jesus, are seen as sinful in the eyes of the society (the sinful woman in 7:37, 39 and Zacchaeus in 19:7). There is a mention of grumbling against the behavior of Jesus in both the texts (Luke 7:39; 19:7). Repentance of the sinful woman is seen by her tears and in her action of washing the feet of Jesus (7:38), while Zacchaeus shows his repentance by his willingness to give away half of his possessions to the poor (19:8). Jesus defends his behavior of acceptance of the sinful woman (Luke 7:40-46) and Zacchaeus (Luke

19:9-10). Both the sinful woman and Zacchaeus (and his household) are saved (Luke 7:50; 19:9). From these parallels one is able to see that Luke intends to project Jesus as the friend of outcasts of the society, and that through the encounter with Jesus, salvation is possible for the socially despised. It is also very unique to observe that the encounter of Jesus with the despised of the society happens in Luke within the context of banquets. Zacchaeus should be seen in this context of persons of low status who gain their salvation through their encounter with Jesus, their table fellowship with him and their repentance, which is shown by their sharing of riches with the poor.

Structure of Luke 19:1-10

Ellis puts forward the following structure for Luke 19:1-10, which focuses on the conversion of Zacchaeus: the introduction (vv. 1-4), the encounter of Zacchaeus with Jesus (vv. 5-7), the conversion Zacchaeus, which happens at his house (vv. 8-9) and conclusion (v. 10). The introduction and the encounter happen at the wayside conversion while the response of Jesus takes place at the house of Zacchaeus.[48] La Verdiere suggests a similar structure: introduction (vv. 1-4), body (vv. 5-9) and conclusion (v. 10). The body of the text has word parallels that form an inclusion: the word σήμερον in v. 5 forms an inclusion with σήμερον of v. 9. The conclusion in v. 10 takes the specific mission of Jesus to save Zacchaeus and gives it a universal character.[49] The structure that Dillmann offers, is also similar to the above two proposals: the first part 19:1-3 is the initial situation; the second part vv. 4-10 could be divided further: Zacchaeus' encounter with Jesus which leads him to receive Jesus in his home (vv. 4-6) is followed by the murmuring of the crowd, the conversion statement by Zacchaeus and Jesus' final word about salvation (vv. 7-10). Dillmann takes the word ζήτει in v. 3 and 10 as an inclusion that gives the entire pericope its meaning.[50] Kariamadam divides the story into two: introduction (vv. 1-4) and the body (vv. 5-10).

I Introduction (Luke 19:1-4)

    A.

        a. The arrival of Jesus and *passing through* Jericho (19:1)

        b. Presentation of Zacchaeus with his qualifications (19:2)

    B.

        a. The search of Zacchaeus to *see* who Jesus is (19:3)

        b. Climbing the sycamore tree to *see* Jesus who is *passing through* the city (19:4)

II Body (Luke 19:5-10)

    A. Jesus meeting Zacchaeus and criticism of the bystanders (19:5-7)

    B. The response of Zacchaeus and his conversion (19:8)

    C. The response of Jesus to the criticism of the bystanders and to the conversion of Zacchaeus (19:9-10)[51]

Kariamadam sees many word parallels in the structure. For example, in the introduction vv. 1-4 geographical reference forms an inclusion with the use of the word διέρχεσθαι (vv. 1, 4); similarly, the verb ἰδεῖν forms a parallel in vv. 3-4. In the body section (vv. 5-10) the first and the last sections are made parallel by beginning and end with the saying of Jesus (vv. 5,10). The phrase καὶ εἶπεν ὁ Ἰησοῦς is the Lukan redaction. Further, the sayings of Jesus in A and C are connected with the use of the words σήμερον (vv. 5, 9). The use of ἦλθεν (vv. 5, 10) shows the mission of Jesus to save the lost. The middle section B constitutes the conversion of Zacchaeus. This conversion is seen very well by the fact that Zacchaeus addresses Jesus as κύριε (19:8). Meynet finds a chiastic structure in Luke 19:1-10 in which the conversion of Zacchaeus stands at the center.[52] But as O'Toole enumerates, Meynet's structure does not take into consideration the theme of "seeing" that is profound in the text.

Klein proposes a geographical structure.[53] Luke 19:1-10 falls into two parts:

Part I

1. Statement of place (on the street of Jericho) and introduction of the character (19:1)

2. The action of Zacchaeus (19:2-4)

3. The response of Jesus (19:5)

Part II

1. Statement of place (at the house of Zacchaeus) (19:6-7)

2. Action of Zacchaeus (19:8)

3. The response of Jesus (19:9-10)

The action of Zacchaeus overcoming the hurdle comes at the center of each part. And the response of Jesus climaxes each part. In both the responses of Jesus we find an appreciation of Jesus to the action of Zacchaeus.

Luke 19:1-10 – a Diptych

In our study we adopt the structure that is put forward by O'Toole. According to him, in Luke 19:1-10 we are able to see a Diptych. Just as in some of his previous texts, like the infancy narrative, in which Luke places complementary parallels side by side and tries to understand the parallel texts in the light of each other, Luke shapes Luke 19:1-10 in the Diptych structure. According to O'Toole, after the introduction (v. 1) the first part (vv. 2-5) is paralleled by the second part (vv. 6-10).[54]

The introduction (Luke 19:1)

• First Part of the Diptych (Luke 19:2-5)	• Second Part of the Diptych (Luke 19:6-10)
• Zacchaeus wants to see who Jesus is (19:2-3a)	• Zacchaeus wants to receive Jesus joyfully in his house σπεύσας κατέβη καὶ ὑπεδέξατο αὐτὸν χαίρω (19:6)

• He faces hindrance from the crowd (19:3b)	• Objection is raised by the crowd against Jesus being guest at a sinner's house (19:7)
• Zacchaeus attempts to overcome this hindrance by climbing a sycamore tree (19:4)	• Zacchaeus makes attempt to overcome this objection by doing reparation for the misdeeds he has committed (19:8)
• His quest is rewarded in the fact that Jesus wants to be guest in his house: σπεύσας κατάβηθι, σήμερον γὰρ ἐν τῷ οἴκῳ σου δεῖ με μεῖναι (19:5).	• His attempt is rewarded by the fact that his household has received salvation (19:9-10).

O'Toole frames the two parts of the Diptych in the framework of the quest of the main character Zacchaeus in relation to another character Jesus. In both the parts of the Diptych, Zacchaeus is the protagonist. In both parts, there is an effort by Zacchaeus. This effort is hindered by the crowd. Steps are taken to overcome the hindrance. Ultimately this is rewarded by Jesus through his words. From the structure we understand the story only from the perspective of Zacchaeus; because around him alone revolves the entire story. We see however, that Zacchaeus alone is not the sole character. Hence in this structure proposed by O'Toole the quest of Jesus does not get its due importance. An attempt is made in this work to modify the Diptych structure suggested by O'Toole, so that the quests of both the characters (Zacchaeus and Jesus) assume their due significance.

Introduction   Καὶ εἰσελθὼν διήρχετο τὴν Ἰεριχώ. (19:1)

First part of the Diptych	Second part of the Diptych
Quest of Zacchaeus (Luke 19:2-5a)	Quest of Jesus (Luke 19:5b-10)

Character of Zacchaeus shows his quest to see who Jesus is. Καὶ ἰδοὺ ἀνὴρ ὀνόματι καλούμενος Ζακχαῖος, καὶ αὐτὸς ἦν ἀρχιτελώνης καὶ αὐτὸς πλούσιος· καὶ ἐζήτει ἰδεῖν τὸν Ἰησοῦν τίς ἐστιν (19:2-3a).	Jesus expresses his quest to be the guest at the house of Zacchaeus, who upon hearing it, receives Jesus joyfully in his house. Σήμερον γὰρ ἐν τῷ οἴκῳ σου δεῖ με μεῖναι. καὶ σπεύσας κατέβη καὶ ὑπεδέξατο αὐτὸν χαίρων (19:5b-6)
He faces hindrance from the crowd as well as due to the shortness of stature. καὶ οὐκ ἠδύνατο ἀπὸ τοῦ ὄχλου, ὅτι τῇ ἡλικίᾳ μικρὸς ἦν (19:3b).	Objection is raised by the crowd against Jesus being guest at a sinner's house. καὶ ἰδόντες πάντες διεγόγγυζον λέγοντες ὅτι παρὰ ἁμαρτωλῷ ἀνδρὶ εἰσῆλθεν καταλῦσαι (19:7)
He attempts to overcome this hindrance by climbing a sycamore tree. καὶ προδραμὼν εἰς τὸ ἔμπροσθεν ἀνέβη ἐπὶ συκομορέαν ἵνα ἴδῃ αὐτὸν ὅτι ἐκείνης ἤμελλεν διέρχεσθαι (19:4).	Zacchaeus makes attempt to overcome this objection by doing reparation for the misdeeds he has committed. σταθεὶς δὲ Ζακχαῖος εἶπεν πρὸς τὸν κύριον· ἰδοὺ τὰ ἡμίσιά μου τῶν ὑπαρχόντων, κύριε, τοῖς πτωχοῖς δίδωμι, καὶ εἴ τινός τι ἐσυκοφάντησα ἀποδίδωμι τετραπλοῦν (19:8).

The quest of Zacchaeus is rewarded in the fact that Jesus calls him by name and commands him to come down quickly from the tree. καὶ ὡς ἦλθεν ἐπὶ τὸν τόπον, ἀναβλέψας ὁ Ἰησοῦς εἶπεν πρὸς αὐτόν· Ζακχαῖε, σπεύσας κατάβηθι (19:5a).	The quest of Jesus achieved its goal in that Zacchaeus and his household has received salvation. εἶπεν δὲ πρὸς αὐτὸν ὁ Ἰησοῦς ὅτι σήμερον σωτηρία τῷ οἴκῳ τούτῳ ἐγένετο, καθότι καὶ αὐτὸς υἱὸς Ἀβραάμ ἐστιν· ἦλθεν γὰρ ὁ υἱὸς τοῦ ἀνθρώπου ζητῆσαι καὶ σῶσαι τὸ ἀπολωλός (19:9-10).

At the outset it should be said that there are minor loopholes in the structure. For example the words of Jesus in v. 5 are dissected into two; one-half (Ζακχαῖε, σπεύσας κατάβηθι - 19:5a) is used to end the quest of Zacchaeus and the other half (Σήμερον γὰρ ἐν τῷ οἴκῳ σου δεῖ με μεῖναι - 19:5b) is used to begin the quest of Jesus. This dissection of a single verse belonging to two different Diptych could be viewed as artificial. Furthermore, the hindrance to the quest of Jesus is not overcome by the main character Jesus; the hindrance to the quest of Jesus is overcome by Zacchaeus (19:8). Nevertheless, both parts of the Diptych are "hooked" by the phrase σπεύσας κατέβη and σπεύσας κατάβηθι respectively. The command to come down is accepted by Zacchaeus who immediately comes down and joyfully receives Jesus at his house. Above all, this structure does justice to both personalities of the text - Zacchaeus and Jesus - and their quests. The actions and words of both Zacchaeus and Jesus get their due importance in this structure. Both parts of the Diptych climax in the words of Jesus. The quest of Zacchaeus to see who Jesus is, is finally fulfilled by the fact that he knows now that Jesus is "Lord" (19:8) and he is rewarded by Jesus (19:9). The Diptych makes sense against the background of the quest story. It is not only the quest of Zacchaeus that is addressed here. Parallel to the quest of Zacchaeus, the quest of Jesus should also be seen. As Zacchaeus tries to see who

Jesus is, it is Jesus, who actually seeks him because he 'must' stay in his house. This quest of Jesus to stay at the house of a man whom the entire city brands as a sinner is actually the mission of Jesus. "For the Son of Man came to seek out and to save the lost" (19:10). Through this structure, Luke has merged the two great quest stories – Zacchaeus seeking Jesus and Jesus seeking Zacchaeus – into one unified narrative.

Literary Form of Luke 19:1-10

There are different proposals for the literary form of Luke 19:1-10. We hope to study them here and propose the one that would do justice to the theme, dealt so far.

Biographical Apothegm

Bultmann proposes that the story of Zacchaeus is a biographical apothegm.[55] Using many rabbinic stories, Bultmann tries to understand the different texts of the New Testament. Many independent sayings of Jesus which were circulated in the early tradition, were in course of time joined to narrative traditions. This is how apothegm gets its origin. According to Bultmann a biographical apothegm is a 'terse saying' which comes at the end of a biographical note of the character. It is ideal in character and hence is "not intended to be actual historical reports but rather metaphorical presentations of a life."[56] Understood along this line, the story of Zacchaeus, is not a historical report, but a metaphorical one. Since normally an apothegm does not come with place and time, Bultmann posits that the mention of Jericho in Luke 19:1-10 might have been a later addition.

Pronouncement Story

Fitzmyer views Luke 19:1-10 as pronouncement story.[57] A pronouncement story is a brief narrative material in the Gospel tradition, which focusses on and climaxes in a pointed saying of Jesus. As Taylor points out, the salient feature of pronouncement stories is that "they culminate in a saying of Jesus which expresses some ethical or religious precept; the saying may be evoked by a question friendly or otherwise, or may be associated with an incident which is indicated in very few words."⁵⁸ The proposal of Zacchaeus story as a pronouncement story fits well, since as in many pronouncement stories, Luke 19:1-10 ends with a solemn and pointed pronouncement of Jesus. The entire pericope hangs on what Jesus is to say at the end in vv. 9-10, which is the climax of the story. Taylor nevertheless contends that the story of Zacchaeus looks more than just a pronouncement story. For him Luke 19:1-10 is a story about the historical Jesus;⁵⁹ this contention is because of the many minute details of the main character which are not really necessary for a pronouncement story. Furthermore, the interest of the evangelist is not just on the final words of Jesus as is customary in the pronouncement stories but his concentration on the entire incident as a whole.

A Personal Legend

Martin Dibelius looks at the story of Zacchaeus as a "genuine personal legend."⁶⁰ The many minute details in the story, such as the name of the main character, his shortness of stature, climbing the tree, Jesus spotting Zacchaeus and calling him by name articulate the character of a legend. Hence, Dibelius is implicitly going against Bultmann who viewed the story of Zacchaeus as the Lukan replication of Mk 2:13-17.

A Conflict Story

Talbert looks at Luke 19:1-10 as a conflict story.⁶¹ An encounter of Jesus with a notorious person of the society (Luke 19:1-6 = Luke 5:27-39) occasions a controversy and criticism against Jesus from those around (Luke 19:7 = 5:30). Jesus responds and justifies his action (Luke 19:9-10 = Luke 5:31-32). Hence, the story of Zacchaeus is very much connected with other conflict / controversy stories, especially with the call of Levi. This connection looks appealing, although Zacchaeus is portrayed to be playing a more active role than Levi. O'Toole however argues against this suggestion, pointing out to the placing of the narrative.⁶² Luke does not place the story along with other controversy stories (Luke 5:27-6:11) but at the end of the Travel Narrative. This shows that Luke aims at portraying the story of Zacchaeus more than a controversy story.

A Vindication Story

Already in the nineteenth century, Godet proposed that the verbs δίδωμι and ἀποδίδωμι in Luke 19:8 should not be taken in a futuristic sense, to imply repentance and conversion on the part of the main character Zacchaeus; Luke 19:8 is not a vow or promise of what Zacchaeus would henceforth be doing. The solemn declaration of Zacchaeus giving his possessions to the poor in v. 8 is not to be understood as something that will be done in the future but as that which Zacchaeus has been doing normally.[63] If ἀποδίδωμι is understood as futuristic, then the problem we face is that how a repentant and converted toll collector could allow himself the possibility of consciously using extortion and force to collect taxes in the future. Godet says that μου τῶν ὑπαρχόντων is to be translated not merely as a reference to the properties of Zacchaeus but also to his yearly income.[64] R. White too suggests that the story of Zacchaeus is a vindication story.[65] For him there is no conversion taking place on the part of Zacchaeus. The key characteristics of a conversion / salvation story, such as indication of the character as a sinner, his contrite heart and asking Jesus for mercy and the clear pronouncement of forgiveness by Jesus are not explicitly mentioned in the story of Zacchaeus. The words of Zacchaeus in v. 8 do not evoke a contrite heart. They show him as defending himself against the accusation of the public that he is a sinner. And hence Jesus through his solemn announcement with a third person reference to Zacchaeus does not confirm the conversion of the character by forgiving him; Jesus does not view Zacchaeus as a sinner but actually vindicates the "maligned but surprisingly just toll-collector"[66] before the grumbling crowd which falsely accuses him.

A Conversion Story

Understanding Luke 19:1-10 as a vindication story is under criticism by those scholars who understand the words of Zacchaeus as an act of repentance / conversion although the actual word μετανοεῖν does not occur.[67] The general meaning of the word ὑπάρχοντα is not yearly income as Godet points out,[68] but merely properties.[69] Besides, if δίδωμι and ἀποδίδωμι in 19:8 should be understood to be customary present, then a question arises as to how a person can customarily give away the half of his possessions. If Zacchaeus had given half of his riches to the poor twice, he himself would be one among the poor.[70] The verb ἐσυκοφάντησα denotes a deliberate act of injustice and extortion. And if ἀποδίδωμι is also understood to be customary present then the question arises on the possibility of a just tax collector involving every now and then in a deliberate act of injustice and extortion and, paying back fourfold as retribution. In other words, "is it likely that a man guilty of such acts would be so conscientious as habitually to make fourfold restitution?"[71] Further, the argument of White that Jesus in vv. 9-10 is actually vindicating Zacchaeus does not hold good. For, the words of Jesus at the end of the pericope exhibit that Zacchaeus is indeed one of the lost whom the Son of Man came to seek and save. Above all, if Zacchaeus is taken to be a just man, and this pericope is to be understood as a vindication of his righteousness, then the pericope falls out of the overall context of the third Gospel, which is showing Jesus, reaching out to the 'tax collectors and sinners' who are willing to accept him and undergo a conversion of heart and thereby receive the joy of salvation. What actually happens at the house and at the heart of Zacchaeus is parallel to what happens at the house of Levi in 5:27-32. In both houses, conversion was the aim. In fact, conversion was the primary aim of the "table fellowship ministry"[72] of Jesus. Both the texts emphasize the themes of conversion and joy. Hence, for Luke the story of Zacchaeus comes "as a climactic example of the same kind of *metanoia*"[73] that is seen not only in the context of Levi (5:27-32) but also in the context of the parables of the lost sheep, lost coin and the prodigal son (15:1-32).

A Quest Story

All of the above-mentioned proposals look attractive for the literary form of the story of Zacchaeus. One definitely sees the validity of these literary forms depending on the theme one wants to emphasize within the passage. Hence, Bovon is right in saying that Luke 19:1-10 cannot be put under a single category as far as its form is concerned. For him it has all the characteristics of *"Bekehrungs-, Vergebungs-, Heils-, und Streitgesprächsgeschichte."*[74]

Looking at Luke 19:1-10 however, from the background of the structure that we saw above we could say together with Tannehill and O' Toole that Luke 19:1-10 is a form of pronouncement story, but take it further to understand it as a quest story.[75] Quest story is a type of pronouncement story, which Luke commonly handles. A character approaches Jesus in quest for something. This quest of the character plays the central part of the pericope. "Its significance is shown by the fact that the episode does not end until we are told whether the quest is successful or not. The quest story, therefore, shows greater interest in the persons who encounter Jesus than do most pronouncement stories."[76] The quest story answers the question raised by Taylor about the presence of minute details about the main character. Tannehill suggests that the minute details found in this pronouncement story are for rhetorical purposes. At the same time, we need to understand Luke 19:1-10 in the context of the general thrust of the fellowship meals of Jesus that we have so far discussed; in the words of Bolyki, *„in den Tischgemeinschaften Jesu begegnen sich die einander-suchenden Partner."*[77] Hence Luke 19:1-10 is not only about Zacchaeus the main character seeking to know who Jesus is. Understanding the Zacchaeus pericope as a quest story throws light to another important theme prominent here and elsewhere; it shows Jesus rightly as one seeking to cure the sick (5:32) and save the lost (19:10).

Source and Redaction

Jericho material in the Gospel of Mark is limited to the story of the healing of the blind beggar; since Mark is unaware of the story of Zacchaeus in Jericho, one could make two inferences on the Lukan source of the Zacchaeus pericope. The first would be that Luke could have been responsible for creating a tax collector narrative, basing himself on Levi material in Mark 2:14-17. This conjecture would suggest, Luke 19:1-10 is only a Doublet or "an extended version"[78] of the Markan Levi narrative and hence an ideal scene without a historical element in it. The source of the story of Zacchaeus would then be the Markan narrative on the call of Levi. This proposal is refuted by many scholars. Bolyki for example, points out the various differences between the Markan Levi narrative and Luke 19:1-10.[79] The name of the tax collector, the place where the narrative happens, the difference in the hierarchy of their profession, Jesus´ calling of Levi to follow him as one of his disciples as against Zacchaeus who is not called to follow Jesus, and the difference with regard to those who murmur lead him to believe that Luke 19:1-10 is not a Doublet deriving from the Markan Levi narrative. Dibelius understands the minute details in the story of Zacchaeus as suggesting the historicity of what might have happened during Jesus´ visit to Jericho.[80] This proposal seems to validate the argument of some scholars who say that Luke 19:1-10 may have a historical core.[81] For them Luke is faithfully handing down a biographical memory of a tradition about a historical tax collector who welcomed Jesus in his home.

The second inference and perhaps the better one is that Luke 19:1-10 comes from the Lukan special L source. This answers the question, why the Zacchaeus story is different from the Levi narrative of Mark. Moreover, thematically viewed, the story of Zacchaeus fits very well with the Lukan special material that focuses on Jesus as the savior of the outcasts and Jesus as guest.[82] Although scholars see the redactional hand of Luke in the entire pericope, there is consensus in saying that the original core of the Zacchaeus pericope in the special L material must have been 19:2-7, 9. This would help one to study the redactional additions of the evangelist in Luke 19:1-10.

Lukan Redaction

Luke 19:1 is understood by some to be a redactional addition by Luke. Through this verse Luke connects this pericope with what has preceded.[83] Schramm suggests that the original introduction of the story of Zacchaeus would have been 18:35.[84] Luke would have replaced this introduction and used it as introduction to the story of the healing of the blind man and hence Luke 19:1 is the Lukan redaction. Luke might have been responsible for the placing of the Zacchaeus pericope of the special L material within the geography of Jericho.[85] The addition of 19:1 serves his purpose very well.

V. 8 seems to be a later insertion.[86] A strange element in this verse is the double use of κύριος in comparison to the rest of the pericope, which only speaks of "Jesus." The murmuring of the crowd in v. 7 is not about Zacchaeus but about the action of Jesus. Therefore, it is clear that the "answer" of Zacchaeus in v. 8 does not seem fit with the murmuring of the crowd. This objection of the crowd is better answered by v. 9b in which Jesus justifies his decision to be guest at the house of Zacchaeus. Furthermore, the justification of his action by Jesus (vv. 9-10) does not seem to pay attention to the words of Zacchaeus in v. 8 (even though these words form one of the important sayings of the pericope). V. 8 for most scholars seems to be a later addition, which disturbs the smooth flow of the text from v. 7 to v. 9.[87] Without v. 8 the story of Zacchaeus does make sense. Therefore, it appears that Luke has added v. 8 into the received tradition.

V. 10 too is understood as a Lukan addition into an already existing story.[88] This is clear by the fact that the pronouncement of Jesus does not directly allude to the character of Zacchaeus but is used as a generalizing statement. Since we understand the story of Zacchaeus not as a vindication story but as a story about someone being lost (ἀπολωλός) but willing to return, the verse is certainly meaningful within the pericope, but is not absolutely necessary as the pericope's concluding sentence. By this redactional addition, Luke brings to the climax the theme which is dear to him – salvation to the lost. The γάρ of v. 10 is unnecessary because of the word καθότι in v. 9.[89] This repetition is explainable when we take v. 10 as later redaction.

Hirsch suggests that the original answer of Jesus was only 9b, which states Zacchaeus in the third person. Hence, according to him, not only v. 10 but also v. 9a is to be understood as a later addition. To the original answer 9b, 9a and 10 were added by the Lukan redactor. Hirsch also proposes the original core of the story (vv. 2-7, 9b) to have originated and circulated in a Jewish Christian community. It advises the Jewish Christian community not to segregate fellow Jewish brethren from the community, since they all are sons of Abraham.[90] Who is then the redactor? Is it Luke or someone earlier to Luke? Hirsch advocates that Luke would have found the pericope as it stands, already in his L source. Others, however, find that the usage of words in v. 8 and in 9-10, especially κύριος, σταθείς, εἶπεν πρός with accusative and καθότι, which are dear to Luke, clearly shows the Lukan hand in the redacton.[91] Whether one holds vv. 8, 9a and 10 as a Lukan redaction or as redaction by the author of "L", we could safely say that it is Luke who is responsible for the placement of the pericope. Through this Luke definitely aims at portraying Zacchaeus as the positive counter-image to the character of the rich ruler who was not willing to give away his riches. In the words of Kariamadam, "for the evangelist, Zacchaeus' action is already a Christian act and may well prefigure the distribution of wealth narrated in the Acts of the Apostles."[92]

Exegetical Analysis of Luke 19:1-10

The background study of the story of Zacchaeus has shown Luke as a well-educated author, well-versed not just in the Jewish Scriptures, but also very much in the Hellenistic literature of *symposia* and in the cultural tradition relating to συμπόσιον. The third Gospel appears to be his attempt to bring the Gospel of Christ to an informed Christian audience. Although the story of Zacchaeus is a complete whole in itself, the author connects it not just with the call of Levi, another tax collector but also with all the preceding banquet narratives – linguistically as well as thematically. The way Luke artistically composes this quest story by combining the quest of Zacchaeus to see Jesus (19:2) with the quest of the Son of Man to seek and save the lost (19:10) and the Diptych structure that he employs for the purpose of the double quest story shows the author's eloquence. As it stands just before the ministry and passion of Jesus in Jerusalem, the story of Zacchaeus serves as the climax of Jesus' Travel Narrative, packed with all the important themes of hospitality, Jesus as guest, his mission of seeking the lost and the positive outlook of the tax collectors as the recipients of the saving mission of Jesus. Hence the story of Zacchaeus in 19:1-10 is merged within the entire Gospel narrative and stands as a unique masterpiece of Luke. The emphasis which Luke lays on the Hellenistic tradition of *symposia* would once again be confirmed as we make a word analysis of the story of Zacchaeus.

The Quest of Zacchaeus to See Jesus (Luke 19:1-5a)

Introductory Verse (v. 1)

The first verse begins with καί. Within the pericope there are as many as 14 instances of καί. Luke starts the first seven verses of this ten-verse episode with καί. Godet[93] understands such redundant use of καί could be a sign that Luke had an Aramaic text as his source.

Absence of the Name of Jesus

The introductory verse does not explicitly introduce or mention the name of the main character who is on the journey. Just as in the two previous pericopes, Jesus is introduced only through a third person pronoun (18:31, 35): "He entered Jericho and was passing through it" (19:1). Although it is not difficult to surmise who this ′he′ might be, as an introduction to a new pericope, Luke 19:1 seems to be conspicuously consise and ′laconic.′[94] From the background and the end of the previous pericope one could also think of other characters apart from Jesus, fitting to the personal pronoun (18:42), namely the blind man (vv. 35-43) or the λαός (18:43). From the context it is clear that Jesus is implied here, however the question is whether the "curious omission"[95] of the name Jesus at the beginning of this pericope has a purpose.

In the view of Yamasaki, the absence of name and details about the main character in verse one serves the purpose of creating a distance between the character and the audience. The narrator tries to keep "the audience from identifying this character as the point-of-view character of this new episode."[96] The purpose of the narrator is to indicate that, Jesus is not ′the point-of-view character′ of the story. As Tannehill puts it, "when Zacchaeus becomes the focus of attention, readers tend to look at events from his viewpoint and sympathize with his goals."[97] This is why perhaps Jesus is referred to with a simple third person pronoun. This is why Luke specifically avoids naming this character as Jesus. Through the absence of the name of Jesus there is an interest created in the audience to the character who would be entering the scene as the plot unfolds.

Εἰσελθών

The two verbs used in 19:1 here are typically Lukan. Luke uses εἰσελθών relatively often.[98] In the Travel Narrative Luke uses it in order to express Jesus' entrance to a town or a village, a synagogue or the Temple (Luke 9:52; 17:12; 19:45).[99] Εἰσέρχομαι is also used in the cultic context of one's entrance into a synagogue, the Temple, or the Kingdom of God and into the glory of God (Luke 11:52; 13:24; 14:23; 17:27; 18:17, 25; 24:26).[100] Luke uses the verb also in the travel narratives of the apostles in the Acts of the Apostles. Hence, the verb is important for Luke to denote the travel of both Jesus and the apostles.

In the third Gospel, the first appearance of Jesus in his public ministry is introduced with the verb εἰσέρχομαι (Luke 4:16). The usage of the verb in Luke 19:1 could also be understood to introduce the saving ministry of Jesus, apart from the locative meaning of the word, as was in Luke 4:16. The presence of this verb again in 19:7 brings another perspective. In Luke's Gospel, the aorist participle of εἰσέρχομαι is used (twice out of six instances), to denote Jesus going into a house for a meal (Luke 7:36; 11:37). Granted that the participle is in Luke 19:1 is used to denote Jesus going into the town of Jericho, at the same time it seems to anticipate the aorist use of the verb in Luke 19:7. Jesus' entering into the city of Jericho is to be seen in connection with his entering into the house of Zacchaeus to stay there for a meal.

Διέρχομαι

Mark uses the word διέρχομαι only once and Matthew twice; Luke on the other hand uses it as many as ten times in his Gospel and twenty times in the Acts of the Apostles (out of 42 references in the New

Testament).¹⁰¹ The verb is mostly used in the sense of passing through different regions and places: (e.g. 4:30; 8:22). Although used in many places in a locative sense, Luke uses it also in relation to Jesus´ preaching. This can be seen for instance in Luke´s summary statements about the earthly ministry of Jesus who went through villages and towns proclaiming the word (Luke 17:11; Acts 10:38); the verb is also used in relation to the ministry of the apostles (Luke 9:6; Acts 8:4, 40; 15:3).¹⁰² For Luke, the verb διέρχομαι could be understood as a technical term for the missionary activity of Jesus.¹⁰³ It should be also noted that in the New Testament, the combination of the two compound verbs εἰσέρχομαι and διέρχομαι is found only in Luke 19:1. What then is the meaning of this combination in Luke 19:1?

Through the combined use of the verbs εἰσέρχομαι and διέρχομαι in the first verse, Luke perhaps tries to situate the Zacchaeus episode within the larger frame of the preaching and healing ministry of Jesus. The coming of Jesus to Jericho is part of the overall plan of preaching the Kingdom of God by his travel through the cities and villages. Especially within the Travel Narrative, Luke points out to the readers, time and again that Jesus set his face to go to Jerusalem (Luke 9:51; 13:22; 17:11; 18:31; 19:11); Jesus´ passing through Jericho should also be understood in this context. The durative imperfect of διήρχετο indicates that Jesus originally did not intend to stay in Jericho, but only wanted to pass through the city on his way to Jerusalem.¹⁰⁴ According to Yamasaki, the imperfect διήρχετο is used to create a sense of distance between the main character and the audience (readers).¹⁰⁵ This distance is strengthened by another important characteristic in this verse – the absence of the name of Jesus as seen earlier.

Ἰεριχώ

The first verse also connects the Zacchaeus episode with the story of healing of the blind man (Luke 18:35-43). The connecting link is the city Ἰεριχώ. in the Gospel of Mark, Jericho is only mentioned in the narration of the healing of the blind Barthimaeus in Mk 10:46; the healing however takes place, not within the city limits, but while Jesus was leaving the city. Besides, as O'Hanlon points out, Markan Jesus goes mostly around villages; he goes to the 'country' of Gerasenes (Mk 5:1), to the 'region' of Tyre (Mk 7:24), and to the 'villages' of Caesaria Phillipi (Mk 8:27). O'Hanlon is right in pointing out that the synoptic Gospels do not mention anything at all about the very important cities at the time of Jesus, for example, Sepphoris, Can or Jotapata.[106] One can, however, clearly notice the difference between the Markan and the Lukan ways of reporting a location in their Gospels.

The Lukan Interest on Πόλις

It is important to note that half of the 160 occurrences of πόλις in the New Testament, are found in Luke-Acts. In the Acts of the Apostles we see that the preaching work of the apostles happens most of the time in big cities (cf. Acts 5:16; 7:58; 8:40; 14:13,19; 15:21, 36; 16:4; 20:23; 26:11). This "metropolitan viewpoint"[107] of the mission could also be recognized in Luke's Gospel. Luke places many of his narratives in the vicinity of the cities. Already in the infancy narrative the angel Gabriel is said to have gone to a πόλις called Nazareth (Luke 1:26). Zachariah and Elizabeth live in a πόλις (Luke 1:39). Bethlehem, the village where David lived (Jn 7:42), is for Luke the city of David (Luke 2:4, 11). The preaching and healing ministry of Jesus is not only in villages (Luke 9:6) but also in cities (Luke 7:11, 37; 9:10). For example, Luke has changed κωμοπόλεις of Mk 1:38 into πόλεσιν in Luke 4:43. Important places of Jesus' ministry like Capernaum, Bethsaida, Nain and Arimathea are understood in Luke to be cities. Mark places healing of the blind Barthimaeus in the periphery of Jericho (Mk 10:46). Luke on his turn goes beyond this "urban-rural bias"[108] of Mark. Jesus of Luke is not confined to villages alone. His message and ministry is extended to cities too. Although the word πόλις is not attested in Luke 19:1-10, the mention of Jericho in v. 1 could be better understood in this urbanizing context. Luke 19:1-10 is one more example of how the message of Jesus' salvation reaches out to those who live in cities like Jericho.

Grandeur of Ἰεριχώ

Jericho was an affluent city which was very much influenced by Hellenistic culture. Already before the time of Herod the Great, it was an important city. Mark Antony is said to have gifted the city to Cleopatra. At the time of Jesus, Jericho of the Old Testament might have already been in ruins. Once the Romans gave it to Herod the Great, he and his son Archelaus greatly modified the city with a winter palace, theater, hippodrome and other such aspects of Hellenistic culture.[109] This new city, which was an "oasis city in the Jordan valley, but a few miles away from the northern end of the Dead Sea at the point where the Roman Road began its steep climbing through the Judean desert to Jerusalem"[110] and filled with rose and balsam gardens and palm trees, lay in the important trade route between Judaea and the East, and so it was considered to be, as Mansion would say, "the emporium of a large trade."[111] As a border city where trades flourished, Jericho was an important city for taxes. Different taxes like land tax, road tax, and custom fees were collected in the city.[112] What could be the intention of the author in naming Jericho as the place of the incident, other than connecting it with the healing of the blind beggar?

Jesus and Zacchaeus, Joshua and Rahab?

When he mentions a city, Luke normally adds an introductory phrase as εἰς πόλιν τῆς Γαλιλαίας ᾗ ὄνομα Ναζαρὲθ (Luke 1:26) or as εἰς πόλιν Δαυὶδ ἥτις καλεῖται Βηθλέεμ (Luke 2:4). Nevertheless, in Luke 19:1 as well as in Luke 18:35, there is no introductory phrase for such a great city of Jericho. This means Luke understands that his readers are very familiar with the city. Drury renders an interesting interpretation. According to him, Luke must have taken the name Jericho from Mark 10 and used it here with the intention of connecting the Zacchaeus story with the Old Testament episode of Joshua entering Jericho as in Joshua 2 and 6. In the Book of Joshua and here in Luke 19:1-10 the two main characters go to Jericho on their way to Jerusalem. Just as the "first Jesus came and conquered Jericho, before entering the Promised Land,"[113] the second Jesus enters Jericho and 'conquers' it before entering Jerusalem. Another important parallel between the Jericho material in Joshua and Luke 19:1-10 is formed by the characters of Rahab and Zacchaeus. Both characters are pursuing a sinful trade in the eyes of the public. Both of them welcome Jesus - the first Jesus in Joshua and the second Jesus in Luke - in their respective houses and both are thereby saved. This hypothesis is convincing, given the fact that the Lukan Jesus is presented as the friend of tax collectors and sinners. The difficulty with this latter conjecture however, is that Luke does not connect tax collectors with prostitutes. The phrase "tax collectors and prostitutes" is not found in Luke, whereas it occurs in Matthew (cf. Matt 21:32). According to O'Hanlon, "it is difficult to understand why Luke should want to change the harlot into a tax collector."[114] All the same, Drury's proposal of linking Jericho of Luke with Jericho of Joshua and the characters of Zacchaeus and Rahab looks very attractive in the background of sinner material in Luke. It is plausible that the readers or hearers of the Zacchaeus story about Jesus entering Jericho and being welcomed by a sinner, saw a connection with the story of Joshua entering Jericho and being welcomed by the sinner Rahab.

Ministry and Message of John the Baptist Reminded

Jericho being situated in the Jordan valley, Luke perhaps wants the readers to remind here of John the Baptist, whose ministry was in "all the regions around the Jordan" (Luke 3:3). As Fitzmyer points out, Jericho was by that time part of the region where John the Baptist performed his ministry of repentance and where his message was popular.[115] Hence the mentioning of Jericho in the ministry of Jesus indicates that Jesus not only touches upon the geographical location where John the Baptist preached repentance; but the tax collectors who came to John the Baptist to be baptized in the region of Jordan (Luke 3:12-13) prefigure the chief tax collector Zacchaeus who would later turn to Jesus. Zacchaeus the chief tax collector in Jericho has actually understood the call of John the Baptist to turn to the one who would "gather the wheat in the granary" (Luke 3:16-17).

Zacchaeus: Introduction of the Character (v. 2)

Καὶ Ἰδοὺ Ἀνήρ

Luke uses καὶ ἰδού more often than the other evangelists do.[116] The phrase is frequently used to introduce a man, as ἀνήρ (Luke 5:12; 8:41; 9:38; 19:1; 23:50; Acts 10:30), καὶ ἰδοὺ ἄνθρωπος (Luke 2:25; 14:2), καὶ ἰδοὺ νομικός (Luke 10:25), or to introduce a woman, as καὶ ἰδοὺ γυνή (Luke 7:37; 13:11); with the phrase καὶ ἰδού Luke also introduces more than one person as καὶ ἰδοὺ ἄνδρες (Luke 5:18; 9:30; 24:4) or as καὶ ἰδοὺ δύο (Luke 24:13); through the usage in Luke we also find an introduction an important message (Luke 1:20, 31; 7:12; 9:39; 11:31, 32; 11:41; 13:30; 23:14, 15, 49; Acts 5:28; 27:24). The phrase καὶ ἰδού is usually taken as the LXX translation of the Hebrew $w^e hinneh$, and hence as an example of Semitic language in Luke.[117] In 19:2 the word is used in order to introduce the main character of the episode, hence it could be termed a "focusing device"[118] used by Luke to shift the focus from Jesus (v. 1), to the main character Zacchaeus (v. 2). Yamasaki understands the clause καὶ ἰδοὺ ἀνήρ as "nominal clause of exclamation,"[119] basing himself on Dana and Mantey, who define the nominal clause of exclamation as follows: "When it is desired to stress a thought with great distinctness, the nominative is used without a verb. The function of designation, serving ordinarily as a helper to the verb, thus stands alone and thereby receives greater emphasis."[120] Thus using the word in this format Luke wants to emphasize the introduction of Zacchaeus.

Ὀνόματι Καλούμενος

The phrase ὀνόματι καλούμενος is a pleonasm. While Mark and Matthew use the word ὀνόματι only once, Luke uses it in his Gospel seven times (of which four are from the special L source) and in the Acts of the Apostles twenty two times.[121] The use of καλούμενος is attested among the synoptic writers only in Luke. He uses it as many as eleven times in his Gospel and thirteen times in the Acts of the Apostles. In the third Gospel, the word is followed almost every time by a proper noun, except in one occasion (cf. Luke 1:36).[122] The combination of ὀνόματι καλούμενος is a *hapax* in the New Testament, though a similar combination of these two words occurs in Luke 1:61 ("...ὃς καλεῖται τῷ ὀνόματι τούτῳ"). Here in Luke 19:1, it might be deliberately pleonastic. While some regard the phrase as a pre-Lukan phrase,[123] others suggest, it might be a Lukan device to highlight the significance of the name of the character. According to Maier, ὀνόματι καλούμενος serves two possible purposes: It could have been used to give focus on the Jewish name of the person with its Jewish characteristics, or the phrase could also imply that the name Zacchaeus was a later addition into a well-established tradition by Luke. Maier believes the first to be true.[124] The phrase is used in order to show the Jewishness of the character. This *hapax* use of this redundant phrase ὀνόματι καλούμενος does indeed make the name of the character special.

Ζακχαῖος

One finds two tendencies in handling of the personal names in the Gospel of Luke. On the one hand, Luke at times removes the personal names of characters, which are attested, in his sources, and on the other hand, he adds new names where he did not find one. The blind Bartimaeus, whom we find in Mk 10:46, is in Luke anonymously called the blind beggar (Luke 18:35). In the parable of the rich man and Lazarus, Lazarus is given a name while the rich man stays anonymous (Luke 16:19-31). While it could be argued that the name 'Zacchaeus' was present only in the Lukan source, it could well be the case, that Luke added the name of the character to the story. It is striking that the name Zacchaeus comes in these ten verses three times (vv. 2, 5, 8).

Since we have no information about the person of Zacchaeus except from this text, we need to see whether the name itself throws light on the story's main character. In the Old Testament Ezra 2:9 and Neh 7:14 speak of the υἱοὶ Ζακχού. In 2 Mac 10:19 we hear about one Zacchaeus who along with Simon and Joseph is placed by Maccabaeus to guard the conquered strongholds of Idumea. Apart from these texts, the name is unique in the New Testament. There is no scholarly consensus as to the etymology of the name. Some scholars suggest the name derives from Zechariah, meaning 'YHWH has thought of': God has thought of Zacchaeus as he climbed on a tree and hence Jesus took the initiative to meet him.¹²⁵ Others, however, are of the opinion that the name derives from *Zakkai*, meaning "clean, innocent, a term often used in parallelism to ṣaddîq, righteous, upright."¹²⁶

It could also be that Luke is responsible for rendering the character this name¹²⁷ with the intention that the Jewish readers of his community would immediately be reminded of Rabbi Yohanan Ben Zakkai, who was an important figure before and after the Fall of Jerusalem.¹²⁸ As the leader of the Pharisees, and the leader of the Sanhedrin in the sixties CE, Yohanan Ben Zakkai was the one responsible for the continuation of Jewish thought which flourished through his school at Jabneh even after the destruction of the Temple.¹²⁹ If Luke is responsible for naming the main character as Zacchaeus, the name reminds the readers of the important and influential figure at the time of writing the Gospel, and thereby renders a positive image to the character Zacchaeus. Still others suggest that Luke would not have laid so much importance on the etymology of the name to throw light on the story of Zacchaeus, as the majority of the Lukan readers might not have known the meaning of the term. Hence, these authors think that Luke lays more emphasis on the profession of the main character than on the etymology of this name.¹³⁰ One cannot fail to see, however, the irony between the name of the character, his dubious profession and the bad reputation he has acquired from the people due to his profession. His name tells him to be pure and clean and yet "from many points of view he was neither clean nor a good Jew."¹³¹ Perhaps, as Nolland puts it, the name Zacchaeus points the readers to the future picture of the main character and "to the man's destiny beyond this encounter with Jesus."¹³²

It is questionable whether the information about Zacchaeus in other early Christian witness is reliable. From the writings of Clement of Alexandria, we are able to see that in the early Church there was a confusion as to whether Matthew the tax collector and Zacchaeus are one and the same.¹³³ The *Constitutions of the Holy Apostles* VII. 46

mentions Zacchaeus as appointed by Peter as the bishop of Caesarea of Palestine.[134] The Pseudo-Clementine Homilies write about the appointment of Zacchaeus:

> But of those who are present, whom shall I choose but Zacchaeus, to whom also the Lord went in and rested, judging him worthy to be saved?" And having said this, he laid his hand upon Zacchaeus, who stood by, and forced him to sit down in his own chair. But Zacchaeus, falling at his feet, begged that he would permit him to decline the rulership; promising, at the same time, and saying, 'Whatever it behoves the ruler to do, I will do; only grant me not to have this name; for I am afraid of assuming the name of the rulership, for it teems with bitter envy and danger' (3.63).[135]

Whether this information about Zacchaeus is reliable or not, we can safely presume that the Zacchaeus story was well known in the early Church. Tertullian for example, thought of Zacchaeus as a pagan, who because of his professional contacts with Jews had some knowledge of the Scriptures.[136] Zacchaeus' name and the fact that Jesus calls him son of Abraham (v. 9) are, however, strong indications that he was a Jew.

Two Characteristics of Zacchaeus

Luke introduces Zacchaeus with two characteristics that have so far played an important role in his Gospel: Zacchaeus is a tax collector and he is rich. Both characteristics are introduced with καὶ αὐτός. Fitzmyer divides the use of the phrase καὶ αὐτός in Luke-Acts into two categories: stressed and unstressed usage; he considers the use of the phrase in 19:2 among the twenty "unstressed" uses. He opines that by using καὶ αὐτός Luke imitates the language of the LXX.[137] On the contrary, Yamasaki advocates that the phrase καὶ αὐτός is employed by Luke as an emphasizing pronoun in order to articulate the two characteristics of Zacchaeus.[138] We tend to agree with this proposal. If καὶ αὐτός were to be unemphatic, then Luke would have brought the two characteristics of the character in one single clause. The double use of καὶ αὐτός separates the two characteristics and thereby emphasizes both of them. Seen from the overall theme of Luke, the two characteristics of Zacchaeus are in conflict with each other, as we will examine below. This could well be the reason why Luke was keen on rendering a separate καὶ αὐτός to each of the two characteristics of Zacchaeus. Hence this paper assumes that by the double use of καὶ αὐτός Luke wants to emphasize that the readers need to pay heed to both characteristics of Zacchaeus.

Ἀρχιτελώνης

The term ἀρχιτελώνης is a *hapax legomenon* in the NT. Interestingly enough, Luke is the only author who uses this word in the entire Greek literature. The absence of the word in the Greek literature till that time, makes us wonder, whether Luke specifically coins the word for the character of Zacchaeus. Fitzmyer thinks in the negative.[139] In the Roman system of administration, there were *publicani*, who purchased the right to collect taxes by paying the entire sum to the administration in advance. The *publicani* entrusted the task of collecting taxes to middle agents called *magistri* who would oversee the collection of taxes in a particular region and who would in turn appoint *portitores* who were directly involved in the task of tax collection. The *portitores* were native men. Zacchaeus is not one of the *portitores*: the use of ἀρχιτελώνης suggests that Zacchaeus was one of the *magistri,* who were accountable to the *publicani* on the one hand and who directed the work of tax collection to the *portitores* on the other.[140] Hence Zacchaeus is portrayed not as one among the tax collectors but as the "superintendent of taxes."[141]

Jericho, a city at the trade route, not only between the cities of East Jordan and Jerusalem, but also between cities like Damascus and Tyre in the north and Egypt in the south, was indeed a city for taxes. As a border city of Judaea under the direct rule of the Roman Procurator, it became an important place for collecting customs fees for goods that passed through Judaea and Perea. Hendriksen says, Jericho was "one of the three main Palestinian tax offices, the other two being located in Caesarea and Capernaum."[142] Hence Jericho would have been an ideal place for a profession of ἀρχιτελώνης.

In case Luke artificially coins the word ἀρχιτελώνης, then two comparisons could be probably understood as reasons for such this neologism by Luke. Luke could have used the word in order to make a comparison between Zacchaeus the ἀρχιτελώνης, the leader of the tax collectors and the ἀρχόντων [τῶν] Φαρισαίων (Luke 14:1) who also invites Jesus for the sabbath meal. Luke narrates about tax collectors six times (Luke 3:12; 5:27, 29, 30; 7:29, 34; 15:1; 18:10, 11, 13; 19:1-10). Zacchaeus as the chief of the tax collectors is surely to be understood as the climax or summing up of all the Lukan narrations on tax collectors.[143] In a similar way, the banquets of Jesus at the houses of the Pharisees come to a climax with the meal of the leader of the Pharisees.

O'Hanlon and others suggest that the description of Zacchaeus as the chief of tax collectors denotes the summation of the sinful character of all the tax collectors. For him Zacchaeus "is a chief, rich tax collector, a sinner supreme."[144] Given the Lukan context, it is doubtful to fully embrace the suggestion of O'Hanlon that Zacchaeus is a sinner supreme. I think that his suggestion is only partly right. It is true that at the time of Jesus, and in the synoptic Gospels, tax collectors were understood to be sinners *par excellence*. But Luke takes up the concept of tax collectors to another degree. Luke presents them not only as sinners but also as those who are willing to mend their ways and willing to repent. In the houses of both (chief tax collector and the chief of the Pharisees), Jesus stays for a meal; but the one receives him joyfully (Luke 19:6) and the another together with others watches keenly whether Jesus makes a mistake (Luke 14:1). Hence Zacchaeus forms the counterpart of the leader of the Pharisees. As already seen in the second chapter the three banquets for which Jesus was invited by the Pharisees climaxes with the banquet hosted by the leader of the Pharisees (Luke 14:1-24). This leader is not depicted favorably by Luke. In contrast we have Zacchaeus, the chief of tax collectors, whose behavior is in sharp contrast to the behavior of the leader of the Pharisees in ch. 14. Hence, the favorable picture of the tax collectors should not be left out of our sight. Viewed in this way, Zacchaeus, the ἀρχιτελώνης is because of his profession a 'sinner supreme,' but because of his reception of Jesus and his further actions is a 'penitent supreme.'

Another comparison could also be surmised as the reason for the use of ἀρχιτελώνης. Luke could have artificially coined the word ἀρχιτελώνης and could have used it to a person who is understood by all a sinner, in order to contrast him with the high priests ἀρχιερεῖς who would be playing an active role from the 19th chapter onwards. The ἀρχιτελώνης is not respected by everyone around him; but he has accepted Jesus joyfully in his house and his heart. On the contrary the ἀρχιερεῖς have the respect of the society; however they are the pioneers in rejecting Jesus and his message. This is seen from the fact that from now onwards till the passion of Jesus, the chief priests are shown actively involved in plotting against Jesus. Jesus prophesied in Luke 9:22 that the Son of Man would be rejected by the chief priests. Luke perhaps would like to contrast the rejection of the ἀρχιερεῖς against the warm reception of the ἀρχιτελώνης. In fact, once the Travel Narrative comes to an end, then the ἀρχιερεῖς are shown by Luke taking up the main role in conspiring against the death of Jesus (cf. Luke 19:47; 20:1,19; 22:2,4,52,66; 23:4,10,13;23; 24:20).

Favorable Picture of Tax Collectors in Luke

In the first instance, Luke portrays tax collectors as those who realize their weaknesses, who are ready to repent and who are really wanting to get baptized by John the Baptist (Luke 3:12-13). In the second instance, Levi the tax collector is portrayed, as someone who receives the person Jesus joyfully in his house and accepts his message of Jesus joyfully in his heart (Luke 5:27-32). Similar positive depictions of tax collectors can be found in other instances too. Hence although due to his profession as ἀρχιτελώνης, Zacchaeus could be understood as a sinner, yet there is joy in receiving Jesus and his message as it was with other tax collectors in Luke's Gospel. Tax collectors are portrayed in Luke as sinful but at the same time not as being condemned but as being welcomed by Jesus.

Πλούσιος

The word πλούσιος is used by Luke more often than by the other synoptic writers.[145] In Luke 19:1-10, the word is used to remind the readers, of the rich man who met Jesus in the previous chapter (Luke 18:18-25) and helps to contrast him with Zacchaeus. Both of them are ἄρχοντες; the readers would have clearly seen the similarities between the rich man as leader (ἄρχων) and Zacchaeus as the leader of tax collectors (ἀρχιτελώνης). Both characters are financially rich. But only the rich man is said to be πλούσιος σφόδρα (Luke 18:23). The absence of the word σφόδρα in the Zacchaeus account does not mean Zacchaeus was inferior to the rich ruler in his richness.[146] By mentioning that Zacchaeus was rich, Luke not only tries to show the financial success that Zacchaeus had achieved through his profession, but also tries to raise suspicion among the readers of his Gospel about his acquiring of so much wealth.

Among the synoptic writers, Luke is relatively more critical about rich men and riches.[147] In the infancy narrative Luke proclaims that the rich would be sent away empty (Luke 2:15) and in the Sermon on the Mount, he brings in specific woes against the rich (Luke 6:24). The rich are portrayed as fools (Luke 12:16-21) and as insensitive to the needs of the poor (Luke 16:19-31); they are so reluctant to accept the message of Jesus that it would be easier for a camel to go through the eye of a needle than for someone who is rich to enter the kingdom of God (Luke 18:25). At the same time, being rich is not, in principle, bad. Riches could also help one attain the Kingdom. Luke points at some rich women who used their riches to serve Jesus (Luke 8:1-3). Dishonest wealth can be an instrument to make friends (Luke 16:9). Hence one's handling of riches would define one's destiny as in the Parable of the Talents (Luke 19:11-27). Therefore, the readers and the hearers of Luke's Gospel would have wondered what the destiny of the rich man Zacchaeus would be. Most likely they would have been reminded in the first place of the rich man who became sad because he was not ready to part from his riches (Luke 18:23).

Two Contrasting Characteristics
Tannehill is right to point out the 'ambiguous' nature of the character of Zacchaeus for the readers of Luke.[148] On the one hand the tax collectors

have been portrayed favorably by Luke all along: they have been willing to receive Jesus and his message and Jesus has been happy to be in their company (Luke 5:30; 7:34; 15:1-2). But ambiguity sets in once Zacchaeus the chief tax collector is also portrayed as rich. All along the Gospel, the rich are portrayed as fools whose riches and earthly cares do not allow God's word to grow (Luke 8:14). A rich character in the third Gospel should be seen with caution. Hence on the one hand Zacchaeus could be understood positively as tax collector; on the other he could be viewed as a negative character as a rich man. Zacchaeus could be seen as an "ambiguous figure at this point having both favorable (as chief tax collector) and unfavorable (as rich man) connections to the previous narrative."[149] This ambiguity heightens the dramatic narration as well as the expectations on the audience as to how the story would end.

VV. 1-2: Concluding Remarks

Through the use of the verb διήρχετο Luke points out to his readers, that Jesus' aim is not just to pass through Jericho, but to bring good news of salvation to the inhabitants of the city. Zacchaeus the main character is portrayed as a bundle of contradictions. His name which literally means "clean" or "just," is the opposite of what his profession as the chief tax collector would allow him to be. The attention of the audience is wrapped well by the double but contrary characteristics of Zacchaeus as a tax collector and as a rich man. Readers could view him sympathetically because of his profession as a tax collector, but also with aversion because of his wealth. In this way, Luke has been successful in dramatizing the introduction of this main character.

The Quest and the Hurdles (v. 3)

Ἐζήτει

After introducing the main character, Luke now turns towards the action of Zacchaeus. We have in this verse two verbs that are important to Luke - ἐζήτει and ἰδεῖν. Luke uses the verb form of ζητέω as many as 26 times. He uses it a few times in the sense of seeking a person (Luke 2:45, 48), but mainly in the sense of searching for truth, for meaning of life, for healing, and for salvation (cf. 4:42; 11:10; 12:31; 13:24; 15:8; 17:33; 24:5).¹⁵⁰ Sometimes the subject of the word ζητέω is God himself.¹⁵¹ Through the parable of the barren fig tree (Luke 13:6-9) Luke shows God's seeking of fruits in the lives of humans. God's search is also portrayed in the three parables of the lost sheep, lost coin and the lost son (Luke 15:1-32). However, mostly the subject of the verb ζητέω is a human person. In Luke 19:1-10 Luke creates an inclusion with the verb ζητέω: just as Zacchaeus seeks Jesus (v. 2), so does the son of Man seek what is lost (v. 10). As Johnson puts it, "Zacchaeus seeks to see and does not know that he is being sought after and saved."¹⁵² Hence there is a mutual seeking in this pericope. There is however a difference: while Jesus knows, who Zacchaeus is (Luke 19:5, 10), the quest of Zacchaeus is precisely to see who Jesus is. This is what Luke wants to inform the readers with the aorist infinitive ἰδεῖν.

Ἰδεῖν

The verb ὁράω is an important verb for the third evangelist. Right from the infancy narrative we see that there is an effort on the part of different people to see Jesus. The shepherds hurry to see Jesus (Luke 2:15-17). The crowd is looking for Jesus (Luke 4:42); further Jesus tells the apostles, 'many prophets and kings wanted to see what you see but did not see it, and to hear what you hear but did not hear it' (Luke 10:24). Here and in many other instances Luke goes along with other New Testament writers in using the verb in its general meaning. But there is more to ἰδεῖν than just seeing. It could also be used figuratively. "The one who sees is able to perceive particular persons in their individuality."¹⁵³ Hence, the quest of Zacchaeus to see Jesus goes beyond the physical aspect of seeing. In both instances, Luke uses the verb ζήτει with the aorist infinitive ἰδεῖν (Luke 9:9; 19:3). Luke uses this combination in order to indicate the search of someone "to understand the mystery of Jesus, the Kingdom of God and one's salvation."¹⁵⁴

Herod and Zacchaeus: Two Seekers of Jesus

It is interesting to see the similarities between the seeking of Herod (Luke 9:7-9) and that of Zacchaeus. Just as Zacchaeus is seeking for Jesus, Herod too is seeking to see him. The search of Herod and the search of Zacchaeus show several parallels.[155] Both Herod and Zacchaeus have not seen Jesus but have heard about him, and want to see him. Is their seeking merely out of sheer curiosity? Some authors believe that the seeking of Herod is out of sheer curiosity whereas Zacchaeus' seeking is out of a "deep yearning."[156] Another difference between the seeking of Zacchaeus and of Herod is that Herod does not show any personal effort or perseverance in his effort to see Jesus, whereas Zacchaeus does. The fact that the chief tax collector Zacchaeus, an important social figure, climbs a tree in order to see Jesus, is more than just a curiosity: Luke has gradually revealed Jesus up unto this point as the "friend of tax collectors and sinners." It is this friend of tax collectors and sinners whom Zacchaeus wants to see.

A further difference between Herod and Zacchaeus is that in Luke 9:9 it is merely stated that Herod sought to see him (ἐζήτει ἰδεῖν αὐτόν); whereas in 19:3 Zacchaeus is said to seek *who Jesus is,* puts the desire of Zacchaeus in this verse more strongly (ἐζήτει ἰδεῖν τὸν Ἰησοῦν τίς ἐστιν). Through the phrase τίς ἐστιν, Luke strongly suggests that the quest of Zacchaeus is a quest to see the identity of Jesus. O'Toole[157] advocates that τίς ἐστιν in v. 3, forms a chiasm with verse 10. Zacchaeus seeks to understand the mystery of the person of Jesus, who he is. He gets the answer and understands him as κύριος (Luke 19:8), but Jesus reveals himself as ὁ υἱὸς τοῦ ἀνθρώπου (Luke 19:10).

Another difference between the seeking of Herod and of Zacchaeus to see Jesus is the response of Jesus to the seeking. Luke mentions Herod's search for Jesus twice (Luke 9:9; 23:8). Jesus is indifferent in his response to this desire of Herod. Even when the two met, Jesus deliberately maintains silence, since the desire of Herod to meet Jesus is only to see some signs performed in front of his eyes. By contrast Jesus not only responds to the desire of Zacchaeus positively, but also rewards this seeking with his stay in the house of Zacchaeus, which took everyone by surprise – including Zacchaeus.

We agree with scholars who connect the desire of Zacchaeus to see Jesus with the desire of the blind man to see in Luke 18:41.[158] Just as the desire of the blind man is fulfilled with the coming of Jesus, the desire of Zacchaeus is fulfilled with the arrival of Jesus. Zacchaeus' desire to see Jesus is for Luke very important, which is shown by the fact that the verb 'see' comes twice within vv. 3-4.

Ὄχλος: The First Obstacle for Zacchaeus

Two obstacles hinder the search of Zacchaeus to see Jesus: the crowd and the shortness of the stature of Zacchaeus. The crowd could be seen in the third Gospel playing different roles: first of all they are the witness to the miracles of Jesus. Ascough, who views the third Gospel along the lines of ancient novels,[159] suggests that Luke has molded the character of the crowds as witnesses of the mighty deeds of Jesus, the main character (Luke 5:19; 8:42, 45, 47; 9:10-17, 34-43). Secondly, the mention of the crowd indicates the reputation that Jesus enjoys among the masses. Just as in ancient novels, Luke has portrayed the crowd as an indication of the popularity of Jesus. In Luke 4:42, the crowd wants Jesus to be with them. The crowd tries to "prevent" Jesus from leaving them. In Luke 5:1, 15-16, 6:17-19 the crowds gather around Jesus, want to hear from him and be healed of their diseases. As Jesus returns from the country of Gerasenes, the crowd, which was waiting for him, welcomes him (Luke 8:40). Again we see in Luke 12:1 the presence of a large number of people - so large that the people trampled on one another. Thirdly the crowd also plays a positive role of safeguarding the main character from his opponents. The chief priests and the scribes could not do anything to Jesus because the crowd was spellbound at the teaching of Jesus (Luke 19:47-48). This positive portrayal of the crowd in Luke-Acts is however only one side of the coin, when it comes to the understanding of the crowd in the Gospel of Luke.

Crowd: A Hindrance for Jesus and the Disciples

Another important characteristic of the crowd in Luke-Acts as suggested by Ascough as in the ancient novels is that the crowd is shown in Luke-Acts as an unruly and unpredictable mob which could be easily incited against the main characters Jesus as well as the apostles (Luke 23:18-23; Acts 17:8,13).[160] Meyer too, looking at the use of the word ὄχλος in classical Greek concludes that the word is frequently used to denote, "leaderless and rudderless mob, … politically and culturally insignificant mass… where the people is said to have no power of judgment."[161] Citron rightly says, "the third Evangelist is conscious of the derogatory meaning of the word in classical Greek where it denotes 'the mob.'"[162] We see the word ὄχλος in Luke´s Gospel first at the baptism scene, where John the Baptist addresses the crowd as "brood of vipers" (Luke 3:7). Luke gives here a negative picture of the crowd. Just as John the Baptist calls them a brood of vipers, Jesus too later calls the crowd an evil generation (Luke 11:29) and hypocrites (Luke 12:56).[163] At the very beginning of Jesus´ ministry, the crowd prevented Jesus from his mission of preaching the Gospel to the entire region. The crowd has been a hindrance not only to Jesus but also to individuals to come closer to Jesus. The faithful who bring the paralytic in 5:19 are hindered by the crowd. The kindred of Jesus are not able to approach Jesus because of the crowd (Luke 8:19). The crowd is also there at the healing of the blind man near Jericho: it hinders the blind man who is sternly ordered to stop calling out to Jesus (Luke 18:36-39). The same crowd follows Jesus as he walks through Jericho. In Luke 19:3 too the crowd is portrayed as a hindrance.[164] Crowd is hence portrayed by Luke as a group which either hinders Jesus, or prevents others to see Jesus.

We are able to see remarkably well "Luke´s aversion to the crowds,"[165] particularly in the response of Jesus towards the pressing crowds. Citron compares the Sermon on the Mount (Matt 5:1-7:29) with the Sermon on the Plain (Luke 6:17-49) and highlights the point that the addressees of Jesus in the Sermon on the Plain were the disciples, whereas for Matthew it was the crowd. "Though the Sermon on the Mount is not directly addressed to the multitude it is spoken with an eye on the multitude, while the Sermon in the Plain is preached with his eyes fixed on the disciples alone."[166] Similarly when Luke reports the presence of a crowd of thousands of people (Luke 12:1), Jesus addresses not the crowds but his disciples. Another important reaction of Jesus to the crowds that could be seen in Luke is that Jesus leaves the crowd to be alone or to be with his disciples (Luke 5:15-16). Even when the crowd is present, Jesus directs his attention and focus either on the disciples or on the individuals in the particular scene. This is seen in the healing of the blind man. A large crowd is around Jesus but Jesus directs his attention to the request of the blind beggar. Similarly, a large crowd is following him on his way through the city of Jericho, but Jesus leaves the crowd, directs his attention on the lone man sitting on the branch of a sycamore tree, and tells him that he wants to be guest at his house (Luke 19:5). Above all, the compassion of Jesus towards the multitudes, which is an important theme in both Mark and Matthew (Mk 6:34; 8:2; Matt 9:36; 14:14; 15:32) is entirely missing in Luke. Such a response of Jesus towards the crowds show that for Luke, the disciples of Jesus are to be distinguished from the ὄχλος. Luke perhaps wants his reader to choose between Zacchaeus (a model for the disciples) and the crowds and decide for oneself whom to imitate.

Ἡλικίᾳ Μικρός: the Second Obstacle for Zacchaeus

Zacchaeus has another hindrance: his shortness of stature. Μικρός means "small in outward or physical size."[167] But in the synoptic usage of the word, there is much more to the meaning of μικρός than the physical size. In Luke 17:2 and its parallels we have Jesus issuing a warning against those who cause on of these little ones (τῶν μικρῶν τούτων ἕνα) to stumble. Furthermore, the Lukan Jesus advises the little flock (τὸ μικρὸν ποίμνιον) not to fear (Luke 12:32). These instances suggest that μικρός is used to denote the followers of Jesus who are considered as small in the eyes of others.

The word ἡλικία is used in classical Greek either to denote age or point to the physical growth and maturity of a person. In the LXX, too the word is mostly used to designate the age. The two places where ἡλικία is used in LXX meaning the physical size or stature are Sir 26:17 and Ezek 13:18. Schneider suggests that the word in Luke 19:3 "indisputably" means stature and not age.[168] We too would like to understand the word not as referring to the age of Zacchaeus, but to his physical size. Zacchaeus was probably an adult man; he has a high profession, holding the office presumably for a considerable period of time. The word suggests that he is too small for his age, that is, he is an adult with the stature of a non-adult. If ἡλικία were to mean that Zacchaeus was young of age, then the question arises, how it was possible for him to attain such a high profession as chief tax collector at such a young age. Secondly if Zacchaeus was ready to give half of his properties to the poor and to compensate fourfold for the wrongdoings of his past, that impels one to assume, that he was not new to his job, but has been in the job for a considerable period of time so as to amass wealth through his job. Therefore, Luke gives a picture he would have relatively been a middle aged man, if not old enough to acquire the job, but not definitely a young man - so young that he has not grown up to see in a crowd a grown up man. For these reasons, we along with others[169] would like to take ἡλικίᾳ μικρός as denoting the physical size of Zacchaeus.

Since v. 3 says, "*he* was small in stature" a question might be asked as to whom the third person pronoun refers. Since in the previous two verses Zacchaeus and Jesus are mentioned, the third person pronoun could refer either to Jesus (v. 4) or to Zacchaeus. Together with Fitzmyer[170] we could safely assume that it refers to Zacchaeus. Already in the infancy narrative Luke has denoted that Jesus grew [ἐν τῇ] σοφίᾳ καὶ ἡλικίᾳ (Luke 2:52). Besides from the narrative point of view, the clause ὅτι τῇ ἡλικίᾳ μικρὸς ἦν suits Zacchaeus more than Jesus, because Luke wants to portray Zacchaeus as someone lacking something in order to receive Jesus. Being short of stature adds to this ´lack.´ Perhaps Luke wants to make of Zacchaeus as a comic character before the public;[171] although a powerful official, he is forced to climb a tree in order to see Jesus. Hence being short of stature suits well to the character of

Zacchaeus than to Jesus. If Jesus were to be short, not just Zacchaeus, but also many of the onlookers would have climbed the tree in order to have a glance at him.

But there is more to the meaning of the phrase ἡλικίᾳ μικρός, than a mere description of the physical stature of Zacchaeus. The physical description of the shortness of the man is not absolutely necessary for the story or for the final pronouncement of Jesus.[172] What then would be the motive of Luke to point out the shortness of stature of Zacchaeus? At a time when physical defects were understood to be the result of sinfulness (cf. Jn 9:2), the shortness of stature could have reminded to the readers about the sinful nature of Zacchaeus. It could then be plausible, that Luke wanted to link the physical deficiency of Zacchaeus with his inner or moral deficiency. Taken so, τῇ ἡλικίᾳ μικρός would mean to the readers of Luke that Zacchaeus was a small-minded person.[173] Referring to Chrysostom, Parsons tries to understand the small-mindedness of Zacchaeus as pointing to his pettiness and greed. This goes well with the amount of wealth Zacchaeus had amassed through his job as the chief tax collector. The phrase τῇ ἡλικίᾳ μικρός points now to a dual nature of sinfulness: "He was born a sinner, as evidenced by his physical size, and he lived as a sinner, as evidenced by his cheating fellow country folk out of their money."[174]

Shortness of Stature – a Positive Trait?

There could definitely be a theological significance to the phrase τῇ ἡλικίᾳ μικρός which the third evangelist wants to evoke. Apart from suggesting a moral aptitude of the main character through the phrase, Luke also prefers that the readers see τῇ ἡλικίᾳ μικρός with the lens of the LXX. The word μικρός in LXX denotes the humility of those whom God chooses for his service. When Gideon is called by God to redeem his folk, his answer is: καὶ ἐγώ εἰμι μικρὸς ἐν τῷ οἴκῳ τοῦ πατρός μου (Judg 6:15). Solomon prays to God, as he is allowed to ask for a favor, καὶ ἐγώ εἰμι παιδάριον μικρόν (1 Kgs 3:7). Hence as Michael rightly notes, showing oneself or others as μικρός is a pointer towards modesty, and "this trait of modesty is typical of election and calling. It displays a right attitude on the part of the elect and called."¹⁷⁵ More than pointing out the physical shortness of stature as something that is humiliating before the public, Luke wants to show Zacchaeus in the right attitude to be accepted by Jesus. Michel has this to say:

> Whereas the term "the small" is used disparagingly in the Rabbis (the immature, those who are not yet great and old), and whereas μέγας has a particular glory in the Greek and Hellenistic world, and μικρός is usually disdained (at best it is only a means and way for the μέγας), the saying on the lips of Jesus seems to point paradoxically to a secret, a concealed inner or future dignity.¹⁷⁶

Zacchaeus: One Among the Little Ones

Scholars see the link between μικρός and the phrase "the little ones" which is attested by all synoptic writers.¹⁷⁷ Légasse suggests that Jesus used this phrase not to refer "to children but to the outcasts of his nation, who were despised and scorned by the leading religious groups."¹⁷⁸ Hence Zacchaeus who is portrayed as τῇ ἡλικίᾳ μικρός is not only physically but also socially "short" in stature. But precisely because of their insignificance in the society, the little ones are preferred by God. Portrayed as τῇ ἡλικίᾳ μικρός, Zacchaeus is outwardly understood to be insignificant, but actually "in the term 'little' (קָטֹן, μικρός) there may be implied … the sign of conversion (הַבּוּשֶׁת, μετάνοια), the battle against the Pharisaic or general striving to be great."¹⁷⁹ This is the twist that Luke brings to the story and to the main character. Zacchaeus is introduced as a despicable character. He is a tax collector, he is rich; and he is physically short. But he would soon have his dignity once Jesus acknowledges his quest for him and comes towards him to remain in his house as a guest. The readers of Luke would not only have understood τῇ ἡλικίᾳ μικρός as pointing to Zacchaeus' shortness of stature, and to his social insignificance of the character, but as a phrase that indirectly points to the future dignity of Zacchaeus as one whom God cares about. The socially insignificant Christian community, which was looked down upon by the society as 'small' would have recognized Zacchaeus as one among them because of the phrase; because he too belonged to the τὸ μικρὸν ποίμνιον (Luke 12:32). Hence, the smallness of stature was a hindrance for Zacchaeus to see Jesus, but his being small becomes a reason for Jesus to seek him. Hence the phrase τῇ ἡλικίᾳ μικρός points to the reversal of tables that would soon happen to the main character.

The Hurdles Overcome (v. 4)

Just like the blind beggar had to overcome the pressing crowd that was hindering him to reach Jesus (Luke 18:36-39), Zacchaeus too had to overcome the hindrance of the crowd. But he cleverly overcomes both hurdles that were on his way to 'see' Jesus. By climbing a tree, he avoids both the external hindrance of being trampled by the crowd and the internal hindrance of being short of stature. His attempt shows his resoluteness in his quest to see Jesus.

Προδραμών

The verb τρέχω literally means "the rapid forward movement of the feet of humans ... and animals."[180] The compound verb προτρέχω is used in the third Gospel only here. προδραμών εἰς τὸ ἔμπροσθεν is understood to be pleonastic.[181] The phrases "running ahead" and "to the front" seem to be redundant and hence "tend to dull the sense of evident eagerness in Zacchaeus"[182] to see Jesus. However, some do not understand the phrase as redundant. Wolter and Bovon for example suggest that προδραμών could imply the time factor. It could mean Zacchaeus ran ahead before Jesus and the crowd came there.[183] In this sense the phrase εἰς τὸ ἔμπροσθεν together with προδραμών could imply the double perspective of the movement of Zacchaeus, temporary as well as spacious. This explanation of spatial and temporary meaning of the phrase, indeed seems to be an attempt to explain the redundancy of the phrase. Hence, the difficulty of redundancy is still there. Black tries to explain this redundancy. The phrase προδραμών εἰς τὸ ἔμπροσθεν is understood by him to be a common biblical phrase having a Semitic origin.[184] Black suggests that the Aramaic source of Luke 19:4 would have contained also the phrase "to meet him" along with προδραμών, which would have been inspired by Gen 29:13, where Laban is shown as running ahead to meet his sister's son Jacob.[185] Although it might have been taken from an Aramaic source, one wonders as to why Luke should suddenly bring in the context of Jacob and Laban in the story of Zacchaeus. It could be safely admitted that through the use of this phrase, Luke prompts once again the readers about the progression of the Travel Narrative and about the movement of Jesus with the crowd as he was about to enter Jericho (Luke 18:36). It is also possible that the placing of the word προδραμών at the end of the Travel Narrative narrates the story of Zacchaeus as the climax of all the texts regarding the rich in the Gospel and it is our opinion that Luke wishes that the readers understand Zacchaeus as the forerunner (πρόδρομος) of all the rich men who would be saved because of their repentance.

Συκομορέα

The συκομορέα tree, is a *hapax* in the New Testament. Although we have a mulberry tree in Luke 17:6, which sounds similar (συκαμίνος), a sycamore tree is unique to the story of Zacchaeus. It belongs to the family of ficus which covers over 1000 species.[186] But it differs from the mulberry trees which could be seen in the West.[187] The tree grows in the coastal plains and in the tropical countries. It grows 10-15 meters high and it is known for its fruits and wood used for construction. The tree has a short stem but long, easy to climb branches. This makes it easy for a short man like Zacchaeus to climb on.

It has been argued, that the naming of the sycamore tree does not have any special significance.[188] It is said that Luke's focus is not on the type of the tree but on the fact that Zacchaeus climbed on a tree in order to see Jesus. Apart from the fact that the shortness of the trunk of sycamore tree makes it possible for a short man like Zacchaeus to climb on it, it does not seem however, to be a matter of coincidence that there is a word parallel between the συκομορέαν (v. 4) and the verb ἐσυκοφάντησα in v. 8. Bolyki suggests that Luke makes a deliberate connection between the two words, since the literal meaning of the verb συκοφαντέω suggests „*die, die Feigenausfuhr Betreibenden anzeigen.*"[189]

According to him, Zacchaeus's climbing upon the sycamore tree alludes to the economic oppressions (ἐσυκοφάντησα) he was inflicting upon others.

Ἀνέβη

The verb ἀναβαίνω is generally understood in a literal as well as in a cultic sense. Among the nine usages within his Gospel, Luke uses the verb as many as three times within a short space of two chapters (Luke 18:31; 19:4, 28). In the first and the third, we find it in the cultic meaning of Jesus going up to Jerusalem.[190] But Luke uses ἀναβαίνω in the story of Zacchaeus just in the ordinary, spatial meaning of climbing up. Kariamadam points out the similarities between the use of ἀναβαίνω in the story of Zacchaeus and in the story of the healing of the paralyzed man (Luke 5:19). In both the pericopes the verb is used with the preposition ἐπί. Just as Zacchaeus wants to see Jesus, the men in Luke 5:17-26 also want to meet Jesus. Just as the crowd hinders the view of Zacchaeus, so does the crowd hinder the men to carry the paralyzed man to Jesus. Just as Zacchaeus climbs upon the tree in order to see Jesus, these men who carry the paralyzed man climb up the roof. Both the paralyzed man and Zacchaeus get to meet. In both the cases there is a murmur against what Jesus says /does. At the end in both the texts Jesus justifies his actions, invoking the authority of the Son of Man.[191] Just as Jesus accepts and heals the paralytic who was carried up on a roof (ἀναβάντες Luke 5:19) in order to get to Jesus, Zacchaeus who climbs up a tree (ἀνέβη) is accepted by Jesus. The climbing of Zacchaeus upon a tree mirrors the absolute faith of the men in Luke 5:17-26, who carried the paralytic upon the roof.

Vv. 3-4: Concluding Remarks

Luke's interest to portray Zacchaeus positively is clearly seen in vv. 3-4. He shows the desire of Zacchaeus to see Jesus. He faces hindrances and resolves to overcome them. His desire to see Jesus is not out of sheer curiosity like that of Herod. The interest is evoked in the audience as to whether the quest of Zacchaeus to see Jesus would be fulfilled. Through the theological ramifications of the words that have been used, Luke does not point to the mere physicality of seeing. ἰδεῖν ... τίς ἐστιν shows that Zacchaeus wants to understand and perceive the personality of Jesus. The two hindrances actually portray Zacchaeus positively and in a favourable position to encounter Jesus, since he belongs to the class of τὸ μικρὸν ποίμνιον. Hence Zacchaeus, who is eager to see Jesus should get ready to expect the unexpected.

Quest Fulfilled (v. 5a)

One of the important verses in the Zacchaeus pericope is v. 5. This is the linking verse between the two main characters of the passage. The sycamore tree is the meeting point for the two main characters who are seekers in their own way. The quest of Zacchaeus to see Jesus (v. 2) and the quest of Jesus to seek the lost (v. 10) blend at the foot of the sycamore tree. The longing of Zacchaeus to see Jesus has finally been fulfilled, when Jesus comes on his way. "Hoping to see Jesus, he is seen by him."[192] The initiative of Jesus to meet Zacchaeus and to have personal contact with him merges with the initiative of Zacchaeus to see Jesus.

Ὡς Ἦλθεν ἐπὶ τὸν Τόπον

For the third time within this passage, Luke denotes the movement of Jesus, though it does not seem to have any theological implications in it. Ὡς ἦλθεν ἐπὶ τὸν τόπον connects the verse with ἐκείνης ἤμελλεν διέρχεσθαι of the previous verse. Luke uses the word τόπος more than other synoptic writers.[193] He uses it sometimes as a substitute for cities (Luke 4:37; 10:1), and other times just in the normal meaning of place (cf. Luke 2:7; 23:33). Even when his Markan source does not have the word, Luke employs it (e.g. Luke 4:37 = Mk 1:28; Luke 22:40 = Mk 14:32). Just as in the beginning of the Travel Narrative Luke has words like ἔρχομαι and ἤμελλεν and τόπος (Luke 10:1), so also he employs these words in Luke 19:4-5. This shows that the Travel Narrative is coming to an end. Bovon suggests that by writing this phrase ἐπὶ τὸν τόπον, Luke points out that the plan of Jesus seems to suddenly change.[194]

The reason why Jesus passes through Jericho is not just because he is on his way to Jerusalem, but because he has a divine plan to fulfill in Jericho. This becomes clear when Jesus expresses the necessity for him to stay with Zacchaeus.

Ἀναβλέψας ὁ Ἰησοῦς Εἶπεν Πρὸς Αὐτόν

The word ἀναβλέψας is used in the Synoptics with two different meanings. The subjects of the verb are shown 'to look up' (e.g. Luke 19:5; 21:1); sometimes they look up to heaven in prayer (Luke 9:16). In Mark and Matthew, the subject of the verb ἀναβλέπω is sometimes person(s) other than Jesus (cf. Mk 8:24; 16:4); Luke sometimes uses the word for Jesus (Luke 9:16; 19:5; 21:1). The verb is also used in the sense of seeing again. This 'seeing again' is always used in references to the saving mission of Jesus. This meaning is clear from the following verses: Jesus reads in Nazareth a passage from Isaiah about the blind recovering their sight (Luke 4:18); he repeats it to the disciples of John the Baptist (Luke 7:22); the blind beggar requests Jesus, that he wants to see again (Luke 18:41-43). That the blind recover their sight from Jesus is an important sign of the time of messianic salvation.[195] Receiving sight could also be metaphorically or spiritually interpreted.[196] This notion is brought out by the deliberate link between the blind man and Zacchaeus. Both want to see Jesus, and both regain their sight – the former physically and the latter the interior vision. Hence the verb makes a direct link between the physically blind beggar and the spiritually blind Zacchaeus.

Ζακχαῖε

Compared to the Synoptics, it is John, who portrays Jesus with a superhuman knowledge about persons. It is the Johannine Jesus who knew about Nathaniel before he came to Jesus (Jn 1:47). But the Lukan Jesus too calls Zacchaeus by his name at the very first time. Without having met him before, Jesus seems to have known not only his name, but also that he had a house in the city. It is often taken for granted that Jesus had supernatural knowledge about the character with whom he was going to stay.¹⁹⁷ Luke does not mention how Jesus came to know the name of the rich man, but he does bring to our notice that Jesus knew Zacchaeus at their very first meeting. Especially by the use of words important to him, like, σήμερον, δεῖ, ζητῆσαι καὶ σῶσαι …, Luke has made Jesus' knowledge about the person of Zacchaeus as supernatural.¹⁹⁸ Other commentators are of the opinion that one does not need to understand it from a supernatural perspective. For them, Jesus' knowledge of Zacchaeus could be explained in mere human terms. Perhaps Jesus would have learnt from his disciples – who had gone ahead of Jesus in different villages and towns to preach the Gospel (Luke 10:1). The disciples would have told him as to who among the locals would eagerly welcome a nomadic preacher like Jesus. They might have told Jesus about this rich man who was seen to be receptive to the message of Jesus.¹⁹⁹ Or perhaps Jesus might have inquired from others about the rich man who was strangely sitting upon a tree; or he might have overheard others calling Zacchaeus by his name.²⁰⁰

As Fitzmyer and Summers rightly suggest, it is not the intention of Luke to show the fact that Jesus knew the name of Zacchaeus: "The details of how Jesus knew Zacchaeus is not part of Luke's story."²⁰¹ The significance of the story lies in what happens after Jesus meets Zacchaeus. Maier brings in the concept of relationship between the two characters.²⁰² The very addressing of a character by name implies a close connection between the two persons. Hence Jesus' calling of the rich man by his name makes the relationship smoother. Calling Zacchaeus by his name, Luke tries to show Jesus as someone who does not bother about attributes of Zacchaeus as a tax collector or sinner. For Jesus, Zacchaeus is just an individual who is in the need of God.

Κατάβηθι

καταβαίνω as the opposite of ἀναβαίνω is used in the New Testament as many as 80 times. In the synoptic Gospels we see it around 30 times. Among the synoptic writers, it is Luke who uses it more than others.²⁰³ In the synoptic Gospels it is not used in a cultic or religious sense of gods coming down to the world of humans, but in a spatial or geographic sense.

Usually the verb καταβαίνω comes with a place, from / to which one should move. Zacchaeus should come down from a tree. Kariamadam[204] rightly sees the connection between Jesus' command to Zacchaeus to come down (κατάβηθι) and the command of the Holy Spirit to Peter to come down (κατάβηθι) (Luke 19:5; Acts 10:20). Both texts are about being given lodging (ἐξένισεν, Acts 10:23) and staying (ἐπιμεῖναι, Acts 10:48) in the house of a controversial character. Luke connects the verb καταβαίνω with an adverbial aorist participle. Zacchaeus should come down from the tree hurriedly.

Σπεύσας

Σπεύδω in the classical intransitive sense of hurrying, making haste, is within the New Testament used only by Luke (Luke 2:16; 19:5, 6; Acts 20:16; 22:18). It is mostly used in combination with another verb. The other book that uses σπεύδω in its transitive sense of striving / desiring for something is used in 2 Pet 3:12.[205] This "descriptive participle of manner"[206] is combined with an aorist imperative. Making haste indicates a divine intervention and plan.[207] After the angel tells Mary about the conception of Elisabeth, Mary makes haste to meet her relative (Luke 1:39).[208] The shepherds make haste to see the new born savior, after having been informed by the angels (Luke 2:16). Paul goes in haste to Jerusalem to be there before Pentecost (Acts 20:16). He says that he is on the way to Jerusalem because of the divine command from the Holy Spirit; he is going to Jerusalem as a captive of the Spirit (Acts 20:22). After his arrest in Jerusalem, Paul tells in his defense, that Jesus commanded him, as it is seen in Acts 22:18-19 to "make haste" and get out of Jerusalem (σπεῦσον καὶ ἔξελθε ἐν τάχει ἐξ Ἰερουσαλήμ), so that he would go out and preach the Gospel to the gentiles. The command of Jesus to Zacchaeus to make haste and come down is similar to the divine imperative to hurry. Zacchaeus should make haste, because it is a divine necessity. This divine imperative is clear from what Jesus says further to Zacchaeus.

The First Quest: Concluding Remarks

After an introductory statement about Jericho, Luke introduces the main character of the story: Zacchaeus as having two contrasting characteristics. On the one hand he belongs to the group of tax collectors, a group which has a yearning to repent (Luke 3:12-14), throngs to Jesus and is eager to listen to him (Luke 15:1-2); on the other hand he is a very rich man, for whom, as we have seen earlier in the Gospel, it would be difficult to enter into the Kingdom of heaven (Luke 18:18-25). In addition to the two hindrances which he faces in his quest to see Jesus (his shortness of stature and the hindrance of the crowd), his exceeding richness would be viewed by the readers of Luke as the major hindrance to "see" Jesus. While Zacchaeus overcomes the hindrances by climbing on a sycamore tree, it remains to be seen whether he will overcome the major hurdle to his longing to "see" Jesus (being exceedingly rich). Whether and how Zacchaeus will overcome this main hindrance will be explained in Luke in the following verses. The first quest of Zacchaeus to see Jesus has already come to a climax in v. 5. He has not only seen Jesus; But Jesus not only makes a contact with him but calls him by his name.

Quest of Jesus in Search of Zacchaeus (Luke 19:5b-10)

Jesus' Wish and the Joyful Reception by Zacchaeus (vv. 5b-6)

Just as Zacchaeus wanted to see Jesus, there is another seeking from the part of Jesus. The first quest leads to the second. While Jesus seems to have known about the quest of Zacchaeus, Zacchaeus seems to have taken by surprise by the quest of Jesus. Surprise of Zacchaeus accompanied by joy, results in receiving Jesus in his home and offering him hospitality. This would in turn bring about the change of heart by Zacchaeus. It remains to be seen however, who offers hospitality to whom, since the second quest culminates in Jesus gifting of salvation to the household of Zacchaeus.

Σήμερον

In the New Testament, one finds 41 occurrences of σήμερον and once again it is Luke who uses it more often than others. While Matthew and the author of the Letter to the Hebrews use it 8 times each, Paul thrice and Mark and James just once, Luke has more than 20 occurrences in his double work.[209] The word is used in the New Testament in two different ways: in an ordinary, non-theological way as with regard to the dream of Pilate's wife about Jesus in Matt 27:19, and in a theological way. Luke does use σήμερον in the temporal sense (Luke 2:11; 5:26; 12:28; 13:33; 22:34; 23:43), but he also closely follows the LXX meaning of the word, where it is understood to denote that, what is happening today, comes from God. "To-day, what is decisive comes about or comes to light ... 'To-day' is fulfilment, revelation, whether as salvation or disaster ... Thus 'to-day' can be the means as well as the content of revelation."[210] Σήμερον in Luke 19:5 seems to have both a temporal and a theological meaning. On the one hand, it indicates the particular day Jesus wants to stay as a guest in Zacchaeus' house[211] and on the other, it points to the decisive work of God in history and in the world, which is at work today at Zacchaeus' house. Hence σήμερον should be understood here from both perspectives.

At the birth of Jesus, the angels announce to the shepherds that today the savior is born (Luke 2:11); already at the very birth of Jesus the word σήμερον is used in a soteriological connotation together with the word σωτήρ. The first utterance of Jesus in his public ministry (apart from his reading of Isaiah 61) is his proclamation that today the Scripture is being fulfilled (Luke 4:21). After the healing of the paralytic, which is similar to the story of Zacchaeus in many aspects, the crowd praises God saying, "we have seen strange things today" (Luke 5:26). Luke combines the two words σωτήρ and σήμερον also at the time of Jesus' death: Oberlinner points out how beautifully Luke shows soteriological motive of "today" through the interplay of the two words σήμερον and σωτήρ at the cross.[212] The leaders mock at Jesus saying "He saved others; let him save himself if he is the Messiah of God, his chosen one!"

(ἄλλους ἔσωσεν, σωσάτω ἑαυτόν, εἰ οὗτός ἐστιν ὁ χριστὸς τοῦ θεοῦ ὁ ἐκλεκτός, Luke 23:35) The soldiers were next, to mock at Jesus with similar words, "If you are the King of the Jews, save yourself!" (εἰ σὺ εἶ ὁ βασιλεὺς τῶν Ἰουδαίων, σῶσον σεαυτόν, Luke 23:37). Finally, one of the crucified laughs at him contemptuously and says, "Are you not the Messiah? Save yourself and us!" (οὐχὶ σὺ εἶ ὁ χριστός; σῶσον σεαυτὸν καὶ ἡμᾶς. Luke 23:39). Finally, it is to another of the crucified, who accepts Jesus, that salvation is promised with the word σήμερον. Jesus assures him, that 'today' he would be with Jesus in Paradise (σήμερον μετ' ἐμοῦ ἔσῃ ἐν τῷ παραδείσῳ. Luke 23:43). What was pointed out at the birth of Jesus, all along his ministry and very forcefully at the time of his death, is also seen in σήμερον of Luke 19:5 as well as in Luke 19:10. The saving ministry of Jesus is once again understood with the usage of σήμερον in the story of Zacchaeus. Just as in Luke 4:21, Luke solemnly announces here "God's Kingdom having come in Jesus' ministry with the offer of salvation to the outcasts."[213] The σήμερον in Luke 19:5 also tries to "heighten the immediacy of salvation which becomes effectively present with Jesus."[214] When we look at the other words, that Luke uses in 19:5, like δεῖ and μεῖναι, it is clear that for Luke, today is here in 19:5 "the salvific today"[215] that Zacchaeus encounters.

Jesus utters this important word σήμερον twice within this short pericope (Luke 19:5, 9). Jesus' desire to stay for the fellowship meal today (Luke 19:5) should be understood in the context of the salvation that has come to the house of Zacchaeus today (Luke 19:9).[216] This goes well with the meaning of 'today' all along the Gospel of Luke. Just as with the blind who see and the deaf who hear, and the kingdom that is preached to the sinners "today" (Luke 4:21), the arrival of Jesus at the house of Zacchaeus and his fellowship meal with Zacchaeus 'today' is linked with the arrival of salvation to the household of Zacchaeus. This is the divine plan, which Jesus has come to carry out in Jericho.

Δεῖ

Why does Jesus say that he 'must' stay in the house of Zacchaeus? Is there an external force that pushes Jesus to stay in Jericho? What does Luke want to say his audience by the use of δεῖ in the story of Zacchaeus? In the Hellenistic literature, δεῖ is understood to refer to fate, as something inevitable in the life of humans, as "divinely ordained necessities of destiny"[217] which humans cannot bypass. Schulz points out that the traditional view of the Lukan salvific history in its three constitutive parts of the time i.e., the time of the Old Testament, the time of Jesus and the time of the Church should be understood in the light of the divine providence, or the destiny which God has in store for the world. For Schulz God's choosing Israel should not be understood in the light of the theology of election; election theology fathoms a two-way agreement of the parties concerned. God chooses Israel and Israel fulfils the conditions which God places before it. For Luke, in the opinion of Schulz, God predestined Israel's election. Israel cannot but be elected.[218] It has no other chance but to comply with the will of God. This understanding is more Hellenistic than Jewish. A better understanding of Israel's election could be that it is a free gift from God himself. Even when the people of Israel murmured, even when they went astray from him, God is steadfast in his covenant with them. The saving of Israel is a free gift of God. Jesus's life as well as the history of the Church should be understood in a similar way. The words which Luke uses in his double work enlighten the readers how salvation offered by God through the person of Jesus is a free gift to all and how no human can come against or hinder the divine providence which has to be fulfilled in the salvific history of the world.[219] Hence the life and the ministry of Jesus in Luke's Gospel should be viewed in this perspective.

In Luke-Acts we find different words that are used to symbolize the divine necessity in the history of salvation: Gosgrove points to some of the words that Luke uses to denote the divine necessity: they are προ-composite verbs (e.g. in Acts 1:16; 2:25,31; 3:18 and 7:52), and other words like ὁρίζειν ("to determine"), τίθενμαι ("to destine"), ἱστάναι ("to establish"), τάσσειν ("to appoint"), μέλλειν ("to be about to"), βουλή ("purpose"), and θέλημα ("will").[220] One other word used by Luke to point to the undeniable plan of God is δεῖ ("it is necessary"). All these words denote that the life and actions of Jesus and of the Christian community are more according to the divine plan of God, than as a fulfillment of the Old Testament prophecies (which is the case for the Gospel of Matthew). All what Jesus does is divinely ordained; every action of his is in accordance with the already determined divine plan of God. According to this plan the child Jesus "must" be in his house (Luke 2:49); he "must" proclaim the Kingdom of God in cities (Luke 4:43); he "must" be on the way to Jerusalem in order to give his life there (Luke 13:33); above all the passion prediction of Jesus is denoted with the use of this "must." "The Son of Man ´must´ undergo great suffering, and be rejected by the elders, chief priests, and scribes, and be killed, and on the third day be raised." (Luke 9:22).[221] Once again we see the importance of the element of "must" in the mouth of the resurrected Christ, that it was necessary (ἔδει) that the Messiah should suffer in order to enter into his glory (Luke 24:26). Hence δεῖ denotes the "character of necessity or compulsion in an event."[222] While Schulz understands the Lukan use of the verb from this Hellenistic perspective of divine *fatum*-theology,[223] against which humans have no choice, Fascher understands the verb from the Jewish perspective and says that Luke uses the verb along the line of the Old Testament, in order to show Jesus´ actions as the fulfillment of the Scriptures. According to Grove, these two perspectives on are in a way ´pigeonholing´[224] the Lukan use of the word, either with the Hellenistic understanding of the word or the Old Testament understanding. Grove says that one should see the word δεῖ from the stylistic nuances of Luke himself. What does then Luke mean by using δεῖ?

Δεῖ is an important word that Luke employs to denote the history of salvation. Luke "uses it to designate important turning points in the story as directed by God (Luke 2:49; 4:43; 9:22; 13:16,33; 17:25; 21:9; 22:37; 24:7, 26, 47 and often in the Acts of the Apostles)."[225] The significance of the word δεῖ in Luke-Acts can be understood from the word count. Among the hundred and two occurrences of the word,

Matthew uses it eight times and Mark six times, but Luke uses it in his double work as many as forty-four times, of which nineteen are found in the third Gospel and as many as ten times the word is seen in the Lukan special material.[226] At the outset, we should clarify that Luke has made use of the expression from his Markan source too; besides, not all the uses of δεῖ in Luke denote the divine necessity. As Cosgrove points out, some uses of δεῖ are ordinary, i.e., to mean an ethical valuation (cf. Luke 13:14). In other usages, it has theological connotation; however δεῖ, "even where it has the divine will in view, should not be regarded as a *terminus technicus* for divine necessity."[227] Cosgrove divides those occurrences, where δεῖ implies a divine necessity, into three categories:

a. Fulfillment of the Old Testament

First, δεῖ is used to denote the fulfillment of the Old Testament prophecies. Especially the passion predictions of Jesus are portrayed as a necessity based on the Scriptures (Luke 9:22; 13:33; 17:25; 22:37; 24:7; 24:26; 24:44). These δεῖ statements of the fulfillment of the Scriptures are for Cosgrove not just a "prophetic *ex post facto*" statements as in Matthew but they are used "both as a proof of divine endorsement and as an imperative to be obeyed."[228] Does this mean that the divine necessity forces Jesus to do what the Scriptures tell him, so that Scriptures could be fulfilled in and through the life of Jesus (Luke 22:37 – "The Scripture must be fulfilled in me")?

b. Personal Initiative of Jesus

One could also see a personal initiative in the actions of Jesus to fulfill the divine necessity through his life. In the words of Cosgrove again, "Jesus' messianic self-consciousness with regard to Scripture fulfillment … provides the framework in which specific 'musts' of his life are best understood."[229] Hence there is no compulsion in Jesus; but Jesus willingly goes forward to fulfill the Scripture regarding him. "Jesus is no passive pawn of divine necessity in Luke's Gospel; he is the executor of that necessity."[230] The choices that he makes to be in his Father's house, or his going to the wilderness to be tempted, or to incur the wrath of his own village people, are according to this self-consciousness of Jesus.

c. Choice of the Divine Providence

Δεῖ implies that the divine providence chooses the right persons to fulfill its plans for the world. This choice sometimes involves a coercion that induces a reversal in the lives of those, chosen. Saul for example, who was persecuting the church is all of a sudden encountered by the divine and he has to change his entire way and lifestyle. This coercion does not mean that the person has no other choice but to obey. "God's rule need not always override the desires of his servants; the two generally coincide."[231] Hence δεῖ implies also the cooperation from the part of the humans to the divine plan.

When we look at the word δεῖ in Luke 19:5 in the light of the above-mentioned views, we are able to see that Jesus goes to Jericho as part of the larger divine plan of going to Jerusalem. Just as his preaching is in accordance with the divine plan of God, just as his going to Jerusalem and his forthcoming passion are according to the pre-designed salvific plan of God, so too his going through the city of Jericho, his stopping at the tree on which Zacchaeus is sitting, and his desire to go to his house are all part of God's saving plan.[232] The δεῖ in Luke 19:5 should not be taken to mean that Jesus is passive, that Jesus is someone through whom the divine will is acted upon to save Zacchaeus. As Cosgrove says, "The δεῖ of Luke 19:5 is a specific example of the choices Jesus makes all through the Gospel regarding the accomplishment of his mission."[233] Luke has placed the word δεῖ in the mouth of the father who, after seeing the return of the prodigal son and the reversal of his attitude, feels that he must celebrate his return (Luke 15:32). Perhaps we should understand the δεῖ in Luke 19:5 also in this light of divine reversal that is at play, as God, through Jesus, wants to save individuals as well as the world. In Luke 19:5 and the necessity of Jesus going to the house of Zacchaeus recalls the δεῖ in Luke 15:32, where the prodigal father talks of the necessity of celebration of the return of the younger son. In this way, it anticipates the reversal of life and the joy over the return of Zacchaeus.

Ἐν τῷ Οἴκῳ Σου ... Με Μεῖναι

The general meaning is 'to remain in a place' or 'to stay in a house;' in Hellenistic times it meant staying in a house overnight. When in the Old Testament, the word has God as the subject, it is used in contrast to the transitory element of humanity. The righteousness of God (Ps 111:9), his wisdom (Wis 7:27), or his counsel (Isa 14:24) remains and endures forever. Such an understanding is found in John's Gospel (Jn 1:32; 6:56; 12:34; 14:10; 15:4-7).[234] Hübner citing Bultmann says that "in reference to humankind 'abide in' designates 'loyalty'; in reference to the revealer or God, it designates 'the eternal validity of the divine act of salvation for the believer'."[235] Does Luke use it in a theological sense? Or is it just to say Jesus is going to have an overnight stay in the house of Zacchaeus? When Luke uses the combination of μένω with οἰκία (Luke 8:27; 10:7), it means "to dwell" or "to stay in the house." This is a strong indication that in 19:5 Luke uses the word μένω to mean Jesus' intention of staying or lodging in the house of Zacchaeus. Luke does not say how long Jesus stayed at the house of Zacchaeus. Μένω could mean a "stay of unspecified duration,"[236] sometimes more than a day. From the word σήμερον, one could guess that Jesus intended to stay at the house of Zacchaeus at least that night. It is more significant to ask what happens at the house of Zacchaeus "today" than to ask how long Jesus' journey to Jerusalem is interrupted by the stay at the house of Zacchaeus.

Meaning of Οἶκος in NT

Luke uses the term οἶκος in its normal sense of house, a physical living space.[237] The word οἶκος could also be used to mean household, and all those who live in the house as a family (see Luke 10:5; 19:9; Acts 10:2; 11:14; 16:31; 18:8). In the LXX οἶκος θεοῦ is used for the sanctuary of God (e.g. בֵּית אֱלֹהִים Gen 28:17, 19). Along the similar lines, it is used sometimes in the New Testament to show the reverence for Israel as the earthly abode of God (cf. Mk 2:26; Heb 3:6; 1 Pet 4:17).[238] There is a distinction between οἶκος and οἰκία. The word οἶκος is "more comprehensive and could represent entire possessions, while οἰκία designated only one's dwelling."[239] In the New Testament, we see that οἶκος and οἰκία are used interchangeably. Like Paul, Luke also uses these words side by side to denote a house (Luke 15:6, 8; 1 Cor 11:22, 34). However, οἶκος is more common than οἰκία. Among 115 usages of the word οἶκος in the New Testament, Luke uses it the most.[240] When Luke uses both terms in the same context, he means a single house (Luke 7:6, 10, 36, 37, 44; 8:27, 39; 8:41, 51; 10:5a, b, 7a). In Luke 19:5 and 19:9, only one word οἶκος is used to refer to house as well as household.[241]

As many as nineteen times Luke uses οἶκος in the narrative portion of his Gospel. It is always used in the sense of someone visiting a house of someone and staying there as a guest. This guest motif is seen in Luke's Gospel time and again, especially in the combination of words οἶκος and μένειν, which is very significant for Luke.[242] Already at the beginning of his Gospel Luke uses these two words together. Mary remains at the house of Elisabeth as a guest and returns to her house (Luke 1:56). From the words of Elisabeth, the readers come to know that the presence of Mary brought joy not only to Elisabeth but also to the entire household including the child in the womb. Jesus enters the house of Simon Peter as a guest, which brings healing to the mother in law of Simon, who starts to serve him afterwards (Luke 4:38-39). To the house of Levi, Jesus goes as a guest to partake in a banquet (Luke 5:27). He goes to the house of Simon the Pharisee as a guest for the meal for which he has been invited and reclines there (Luke 7:36); although there is no mention of a meal, Jesus enters the house of Jairus as a guest; his entrance gives healing to the daughter of Jairus (Luke 8:41). To the house of the chief of the Pharisees Jesus is invited to partake in the meal (Luke 14:1). At the end of the Gospel we see Jesus again as a guest who remains with the two disciples of Emmaus (Luke 24:29) where there is a note on the breaking of bread. As Jesus remains with them and breaks the bread, the eyes of the disciples are opened and they see who he is. As we have seen so far, in houses where Jesus entered, there had been either a banquet, or some kind of deliverance. When Jesus enters into the houses of the Pharisees, there is a banquet but no deliverance for the hosts: in the houses of those who accept Jesus, however, there is deliverance. Jesus' stay at the house of Zacchaeus should be looked at in the light of Luke 5:27-32, where Jesus enters the house of Levi who offers him a great banquet. Since being a guest at someone's house implied sharing and enjoying the table hospitality, it is likely and it is implied in Luke 19:5 that Zacchaeus arranged a banquet for his hero, whom he wanted to see by all means. Hence the combination of the words οἶκος and μένειν would have invoked in the audience of Luke a *symposium*-like banquet.

Self-Invitation of Jesus

In all the *symposium*-like meals in which Jesus previously participated (Luke 5:27-32; 7:36-50; 11:37-54; 14:1-24), the hosts invite Jesus and Jesus accepts the invitation and enters the house of the host as a guest. But in the story of Zacchaeus it is entirely different from the banqueting culture of the time. Here it is Jesus who takes the initiative to get himself invited. He calls Zacchaeus and asks him to take him to his house as a guest (Luke 19:5). Hotze suggests that the self-invitation of Jesus displays „*eine signifikante Anreicherung*" over against the Levi pericope, since Jesus who was invited by the tax collector Levi, is now the one who invites himself to be the guest at the house of Zacchaeus.[243] Moreover, this self-invitation of Jesus displays a progression in the reason for the murmuring of the onlookers. At the house of Levi, Jesus is passive and it is Levi who invites him for a great party in his house; hence the murmuring of the Pharisees and the scribes is only indirectly pointed to Jesus; the question of eating and drinking with tax collectors and sinners is not addressed to Jesus but only to his disciples (Luke 5:30). In Luke 19:7 however, the criticism is that Jesus goes to be the guest at the house of a sinner. The murmuring in Luke 5:30 was from the Pharisees and the scribes but in the Zacchaeus incident, there is once again a progression, in that, those who murmur are not just a particular group like Pharisees and scribes but "*all*" the onlookers murmur against Jesus (καὶ ἰδόντες πάντες διεγόγγυζον). The question that should be addressed now is, why Jesus should invite himself to the house of Zacchaeus.

Jesus: An Ἄκλητος?

Marshall suggests an interesting insight into the reason for the self-invitation of Jesus. She enumerates that Jesus' excitement to get himself invited by Zacchaeus shows that "the historical Jesus had the reputation for attending banquets as an uninvited guest."[244] Marshall begins by analyzing the texts of the missionary sending out of the disciples of Jesus. Jesus is portrayed by the evangelists, as an itinerant preacher influenced by the Cynic philosophers who were wandering mendicants, preaching to different villages and towns and depending on the generosity of the people to whom they preached. Along the similar line, the Lukan Jesus imparts his disciples as he sends them to different towns and villages (cf. Mk 6:7-15; Matt 10:5-15; Luke 9:1-6). Luke narrates not only the sending out of the twelve but also the sending of other seventy disciples of Jesus (Luke 10:1-12, 16), which probably could have been the Lukan creation of a "doublet" derived from the one and the same Q source similar to Mk 6:7-15.[245] That the disciples are asked not to carry purse, bag or sandals, shows that Luke wants to portray them as similar to their master, who was depending on the generosity and hospitality of the people to whom he preached. The combination of εἰσέρχομαι with οἰκία in Mk 6:10, Matt 12:10-13; Luke 9:4; 10:5-6 suggests for Marshall that the disciples were not waiting to be invited by a householder but they are shown to be entering directly into the dining area of the house, without even being invited.[246]

Marshall also looks at Luke 7:34 (Matt 11:19) where Jesus answers the criticism against him that he is an ἄνθρωπος φάγος καὶ οἰνοπότης. Looking at the usage of the word φάγος in Homer for Odysseus who comes uninvited, Marshall suggests that the combination of the two words glutton and a drunkard suits a parasite who wants to come to a dinner party uninvited. Jesus too would have gone to dinner parties without being invited. This is why he has been given the same attributes used normally for an ἄκλητος.[247] Further looking at Luke 7:36-50, Marshall says that the refusal of Simon the Pharisee who had failed to do the duties of a host (by not giving Jesus water to wash the feet, not kissing him, not anointing his head with oil) would have been because Jesus was not a guest at all; he would have been a mere ἄκλητος.

While in Luke 7:36-50, Marshall´s view does not hold valid, since in the very first verse (Luke 7:36) it is explicitly told that Jesus was invited,[248] her view nevertheless seems to be justified at least on this occasion in Luke 19:5, where Jesus suddenly invites himself and comes as an uninvited guest at the house of Zacchaeus. However, this self invitation of Jesus should also be understood from the light of the soteriological mission of Jesus. From the very beginning of his Gospel Luke tries to say, that the savior comes to the abode of humans in order to save them (2:11). In the summary statement of his ministry at Nazareth, the Lukan Jesus proclaims that his arrival would be Good News for the powerless and the outcasts. The role models for his mission are the great prophets Elijah and Elisha whose mission was to save those who were viewed by the society as gentiles and outcasts. Similarly seeking to save the 'lost' was the mission of the Son of Man all along. This is the answer that Jesus gives, when he is asked why he eats with tax collectors and sinners (cf. 5:31-32). When Jesus is criticized for eating with sinners (15:1-2), he answers the critics through three parables, in which the main characters make a great effort to search and save the lost. The joy of finding back the lost one is so great, that they invite others to rejoice with them. Jesus´ self-invitation has to be understood along this soteriological perspective. The Lukan Jesus hence is like the father of the prodigal son, who, with compassion ran up to the younger son to embrace him, when the younger son was still far off (Luke 15:20). The great banquet at the house of the father is in honor of the prodigal son, who has returned.

Jesus: The Host

If the self-invitation of Jesus at the house of Zacchaeus could point to Jesus an ἄκλητος, from the very argument of Marshall, Luke 19:5 could also point towards the Lukan interest in showing the reversal of roles played by the participants at a sympotic meal. Taken in this way, Luke 19:5 could be understood as an attempt by Luke to show Jesus not as an uninvited guest but as the host himself. Normally it is the host who invites the guests to partake in the banquet at his house; since the Lukan Jesus takes upon himself the task of inviting who should come to the house of Zacchaeus, it could be said that Luke tries to play with the traditional characters of a literary *symposium* here. Though Zacchaeus is the host, the Lukan Jesus takes upon himself the role of the host by fulfilling the task of sending invitation to be guest at the house of Zacchaeus. The question that remains then is, why should Jesus take upon the role of the host here? The words of Jesus in v. 10, "the Son of Man came to seek out and to save the lost" express succinctly why Jesus invites himself to the house of Zacchaeus.

As already seen, there are two seekers in this text: Zacchaeus is in search of seeing Jesus; Jesus is on his way, seeking the lost. It is because of his search for the lost, and his eagerness to save, not only the rich, sinful chief tax collector but also his entire household, that Jesus invites himself to the house of Zacchaeus. By gifting the household with salvation, Jesus himself becomes the host. In this sense, the Lukan Jesus is like the father who gives a great banquet for the one who is returning. He is offering hospitality to the sinners who are ready to welcome him. As Kariamadam says, Luke 19:5 shows Jesus´ willingness to extend his hospitality with all those who are socially marginalized. This verse is "one of the significant parabolic actions. The feasts for publicans are prophetic signs, more significant than words, silent proclamations that the messianic age is here, the age of forgiveness. Jesus' common meal with publicans and sinners is indeed a sign or forgiveness of sins as baptism was a sign of forgiveness for John the Baptist."[249] The word analysis of verses 9-10 would later confirm this view that Jesus indeed plays the role, not of an ἄκλητος, but of the host of the banquet, through his self-invitation.

Zacchaeus an ἄκλητος?

We saw in the first chapter that the presence of a person at a *symposium* with a physical deformity, his ugliness or his weakness could be a sign that this person came to the party as an entertainer. He could be a parasite / shadow, who is tolerated by the banqueters as someone who could be made fun of because of his physical ugliness. The very sight and the size of a man with dropsy could bring laughter to the banqueters. In a similar way the character of Zacchaeus could be viewed. Luke's narration of Zacchaeus as physically short of stature and his effort to climb a tree makes one wonder, whether Luke had the intention of projecting Zacchaeus as an entertainer. If this proposal is right, Zacchaeus could then be understood, not as a host but as an entertainer, who seems to be uninvited / unwelcomed in this large crowd (v. 3).

The self-invitation of Jesus proves once again that Zacchaeus could be understood as an ἄκλητος in the great banquet of the Kingdom of God (cf. Luke 13:29). His sinful way of living and his unjust methods of amassing wealth show that he does not merit to be invited to the banquet of the Kingdom of God. But this ἄκλητος who displays his moral weakness is not only accepted and allowed in the Kingdom of God by the host Jesus; Jesus would also save him (cf. v. 10), as he once healed the man with dropsy (Luke 14:4). That people will come from east and west, from north and south, and will eat in the kingdom of God (Luke 13:29) is actualized in the person of Zacchaeus.

Καὶ Σπεύσας Κατέβη

There is a deliberate parallel between v. 5 and v. 6. The verb which came in the previous verse in the aorist imperative (σπεύσας κατάβηθι) comes once again in this verse, though now in the indicative mood (σπεύσας κατέβη), thus making a deliberate link between the first quest of the story and the second. Luke aims to achieve not only the literary link, but also tries to drive home a message to the audience, that Zacchaeus does exactly what Jesus tells him to do.[250] The progressive development that Luke makes in vv. 5-6 with the link words of σπεύσας and κατέβη seems to suggest for Kariamadam, a link between the story of Zacchaeus and the story of the blind beggar (Luke 18:46-52). The desire of the blind man to see Jesus (vv. 47-48), Jesus command and his healing (vv. 49, 52) resemble the desire of Zacchaeus to see Jesus (Luke 19:3), the command of Jesus (v. 5) and his saving Zacchaeus (vv. 9-10). While agreeing with Kariamadam with regard to the connecting parallels between the two stories, one should not overlook differences between the Zacchaeus pericope and the healing of the blind beggar. In the Markan version of the healing of the blind Bartimaeus, the joy of the blind man is explicitly given. Bartimaeus throws off his cloak, springs up and comes to Jesus (Mk 10:50). Luke leaves out in his version this verse for some purpose (Luke 18:40). But this element of joy, which was not there at the healing of the blind beggar is inserted in the character of Zacchaeus. His coming down quickly, tells the readers of his eagerness to receive Jesus.

We also find parallel between the hurried reaction of Zacchaeus as he came down from the tree, and the hurry of the shepherds to see the new-born savior (Luke 2:16).[251] In both stories, the verb is used as an aorist participle, but there is a slight difference.[252] While the participle in 2:16 is used after the main verb, saying "they went with haste" (ἦλθαν σπεύσαντες), 19:6 puts the participle before the verb, saying "hurrying, he came down" (σπεύσας κατέβη), thereby giving the emphasis on the hurried manner of Zacchaeus.

Ὑπεδέξατο

The word δέχομαι is used in the New Testament with the meaning of offering hospitality to Jesus and his disciples. Jesus tells his disciples, "Whoever welcomes (δέξηται) one of these little ones in my name, welcomes me and whoever welcomes me, welcomes the one who sent me." (Mk 9:37; Matt 10:40; Luke 9:48). The word comes in the mission of the twelve (Luke 9:5) and again in the sending of the seventy-two (εἰς ἣν ἂν πόλιν εἰσέρχησθε καὶ δέχωνται ὑμᾶς, ἐσθίετε τὰ παρατιθέμενα ὑμῖν - 10:8). The word, as seen above, explicitly deals with hospitality in the sense of meals given to the disciples. The word ὑποδέχομαι, which is used in Luke 19:6, has the meaning of welcoming, receiving or entertaining someone as guest in one's home and giving him complete hospitality. There is a difference between Levi who gave a great banquet to Jesus and Zacchaeus who received Jesus in his house. Luke wants to show through the word ὑποδέχομαι, much more than just hosting a meal. Zacchaeus goes a step further from Levi, in that he gives Jesus accommodation, which includes, among other things, services like offering the guest food.

The verb ὑποδέχομαι occurs only four times in the New Testament and among the four instances, once in James 2:25 and thrice in Luke-Acts (Luke 10:38; 19:6; Acts 17:7).[253] All the three usages of Luke are about Jesus or his apostles being accepted as guests. In the Acts of the Apostles it is Jason who is reported to have entertained Paul and Silas as his guests. In the third Gospel both occurrences are about Jesus being received as guest. It is interesting to note that in both instances the wordings used, are exactly the same (ὑπεδέξατο αὐτὸν). At the first instance it is a woman (Martha) who takes Jesus in her home and hosts him. At the second it is a man (Zacchaeus). At the first instance it is a village where Jesus is received by his host (κώμη), at the other it is a city (Jericho). The first usage is placed at the beginning of the Travel Narrative (10:38), the second right at the end (19:6). Together with these interesting comparisons, we also find many word parallels in both the texts. Brutscheck finds as many as ten word parallels between the two texts.[254]

Luke 19:1-10	Luke 10:38-42
19:1 Jesus enters Jericho (εἰσελθὼν)	10:38 Jesus enters a village (εἰσῆλθεν)
19:2 A man named Zacchaeus (ἀνὴρ ὀνόματι καλούμενος)	10:38-39 A woman named Martha (τις ὀνόματι... καλουμένη

19:6 Welcomed him (ὑπεδέξατο αὐτὸν)	10:39 Welcomed him (ὑπεδέξατο αὐτόν)
19:5 "at your house" (ἐν τῷ οἴκῳ σου)	10:39 In her house (εἰς τὸν οἶκόν αὐτῆς)[255]
19:8 Standing he said (σταθεὶς δὲ... εἶπεν)	10:40 Standing she said (ἐπιστᾶσα δὲ εἶπεν)
19:8 To the Lord (πρὸς τὸν κύριον)	10:40 at the foot of the Lord (πρὸς τοὺς πόδας τοῦ κυρίου)
19:8 "Lord" (κύριε,)	10:40 "Lord" (κύριε,)
19:10 "salvation" (σωτηρία) "to save" (σῶσαι)	10:42 "Better part" (ἀγαθὴν μερίδα)[256]

These word parallels and the placing of the texts at the beginning and at the end of the Travel Narrative need not be a matter of coincidence.[257] Luke might have deliberately placed it at the beginning and at the end of the Travel Narrative in order to drive home to the readers not only the point of the Lordship of Jesus but also to portray that the followers of Jesus receive him joyfully in their house. The phrase ὑπεδέξατο αὐτόν clearly exposes in both the pericopes the theme of table hospitality. That Martha was busy preparing many things, suggests to readers that there was a great feast prepared for Jesus at her house. We do not find anything explicit that would imply a great feast at the house of Zacchaeus, but since ὑποδέχομαι encompasses in it all the nuances of hospitality in the then known world, which also includes a feast, we could say with Bovon and others that Luke implies that there was a banquet at the house of Zacchaeus.[258] This assumption is corroborated by 15:1-2 where Jesus is portrayed as enjoying fellowship meals with tax collectors and sinners.

Χαίρων

While the first action of Zacchaeus, coming down from the tree was narrated with an adverbial participle before the verb (σπεύσας κατέβη), the second action of Zacchaeus is in the same way described with an adverbial participle but this time after the verb (ὑπεδέξατο χαίρων). Such a usage at the end of the sentence is typically Lukan and the word is theologically significant for Luke.[259] There are 74 uses of the verb χαίρω in the New Testament and among them the use of the verb is more significant for Luke than for the other synoptic writers. The element of joy is to be found from the beginning to the end of the Gospel. In the infancy narrative the angel tells Zechariah that there will be joy at the birth of John the Baptist and that many will rejoice (χαρήσονται Luke 1:14). The angel greets Mary also with this verb χαῖρε (Luke 1:28). Then the angel tells the shepherds about the birth of the child, it is news of great joy (χαρὰν μεγάλην, Luke 2:10).

After the infancy narrative, we find Jesus in the Sermon on the Plain telling the disciples to rejoice and be glad (χάρητε ... καὶ σκιρτήσατε Luke 6:23) at the time of the Son of Man. Within the Travel Narrative, there are as many as twenty instances of joy.[260] What is significant here is the joy of finding the lost. At the center of the Gospel, the three parables come as the result of the criticism that Jesus eats with tax collectors and sinners. In these parables, the main character invites his friends and others to rejoice with him (συγχάρητέ μοι, Luke 15:6; 9), since he / she has found what has been lost. And the father tries to convince his elder son to rejoice with him saying, it was necessary that they rejoice, since he has found the younger son (εὐφρανθῆναι δὲ καὶ χαρῆναι ἔδει Luke 15:32, 23). The joy of Zacchaeus perhaps could be understood in this fashion. As Jesus says in Luke 15:7, there is more joy in heaven over one repented sinner than all the righteous ones, the joy of Zacchaeus can be understood as the joy of the one who is lost and returns. But the nuance of the joy of Zacchaeus in receiving Jesus is different from the joy of the Father, who sees his son repenting. His joy is not the joy of others about the lost and found. It is different. Hence the χαίρων of Luke 19:6 should not be equated with the χαρά of Luke 15. The meaning should be seen elsewhere. The meal of Jesus with the tax collector Levi leads the readers to a better understanding the joy of Zacchaeus.

Joy of Levi and Zacchaeus

Joy of Zacchaeus could be compared with the joy of Levi in Luke 5:27-32. Once Levi hears the words of Jesus to follow him, he leaves everything he owns and follows Jesus. Leaving everything and following displays the repentance of Levi indirectly. This repentance was the aim of Jesus seeking the lost (Luke 5:32). Similar kind of repentance is shown by Zacchaeus through his immediate coming down from the tree. From the perception of Hotze, the fact that Zacchaeus comes down immediately from the tree and accepts Jesus in his house joyfully is a sign of his repentance which is a precondition for the „Heimsuchung Jesu." Already in this action of coming down from the tree Hotze finds a parallel to Levi´s leaving everything to accept and follow Jesus.[261] The joy of Levi is displayed by the fact that the tax collector organizes a great banquet for Jesus. It was out of gratitude for Jesus' invitation to follow him; it was out of gratitude for Jesus who came in search of him who was considered as an outcast; it was out of gratitude for Jesus who accepted his friendship. Hence the Levi´s hosting of a δοχὴν μεγάλην has to be understood in the background of joy of the one who has returned to God. Zacchaeus´ joy in 19:6 should be understood in this manner too. Zacchaeus comes down from the tree in haste and receives Jesus joyfully, not only because he is very much impressed by Jesus, for his openness towards the outcasts, as Bock would point out,[262] but receives Jesus with joy also because through Jesus, God has come in search of the outcasts. It is "a joy that springs from an expectation or reception of salvation."[263] Does this joy show an eschatological character in it, or at least faith in Jesus? While Stein and others[264] assume it to be so, others doubt it.[265] One thing, however is certain: Luke wants the readers to understand the joy of the rich Zacchaeus in contrast to the sadness of the rich man in 18:23.²⁶⁶ The difference between the two would be more evident in the following verses in their response to Jesus and his words.

Vv. 5b-6: Concluding Remarks

Through the use of δεῖ Luke has introduced the quest of Jesus to see Zacchaeus. Verse 5b has also introduced the theme of hospitality and banquet. That Jesus invites himself to the house of Zacchaeus, does not show him as someone who like a parasite who shamelessly went to the banquet uninvited. It is theologically loaded with meaning. The willingness of Jesus to enter into the οἰκία of Zacchaeus should be understood to be one of the many instances of the „*Heimsuchung*" ²⁶⁷ of Jesus in the lives of people. Through this willingness, the Lukan Jesus shows himself as the one who plays the role of the host, who has something to offer and who indeed offers the much needed salvation to the house of Zacchaeus (v. 10). Verse 6 illustrates the two actions of Zacchaeus with two participial adverbs which are theologically significant for the entire third Gospel. Σπεύσας and χαίρων connect the story of Zacchaeus with the theme of human response to the invitation of God. Just as the shepherds went with haste to see the savior and the younger son went with haste to his father´s house, Zacchaeus too comes down from the tree with haste. Just as Levi received Jesus with joy and gave him a great meal, Zacchaeus too receives Jesus with joy. In the words of Hendriksen, "never had Zacchaeus climbed down from a tree more quickly than now, and never with greater joy."²⁶⁸ Through his response to Jesus which is with haste and with joy, Zacchaeus is no longer an outsider but an insider.²⁶⁹ This is what makes him a contrasting figure not only to the rich ruler in Luke 18:23 but also to the crowd that murmurs against Jesus in Luke 19:7. The participial adverbs which express the human joy of finding God could also indirectly point to the Lukan theme of God´s joy over the returning; one should admit, however, that God´s joy over the return of the lost is not so explicitly stated in Luke 19:1-10 as in Luke 15:1-32. By the phrase ὑπεδέξατο αὐτόν Luke proceeds further and brings a change in the narrative. It is time now to change the setting and actors on the scene.

Bystanders as Hindrance (v. 7)

The joy of Zacchaeus is, however, immediately countered by the murmuring of the bystanders. Just as the joy of Zacchaeus was because of the presence of Jesus at his house, the criticism too is because of the willingness of Jesus to go to the house of Zacchaeus and to dine with him. It is an important verse for Luke as far as the table fellowship of Jesus with the outcasts is concerned. It also stands at the important place in the narrative, as an introduction to the words of Zacchaeus on the one hand and to the final proclamation of Jesus on the other. Since similar murmuring of the Pharisees and the scribes are placed at regular intervals in the Gospel of Luke against Jesus´ outreach towards the tax collectors (Luke 5:30; 15:1-2), v. 7 is understood to be the redactional work of Luke.

From the joyful reception of Jesus by Zacchaeus Luke takes the narrative forward to the house of Zacchaeus. Luke changes the scene from the streets of Jericho to the house of Zacchaeus.[270] Luke shows that the people grumble against Jesus after having "seen" how Jesus was received by Zacchaeus, perhaps at the entrance of his house, though it is not explicitly stated. Klein understands that the people have walked with Jesus till Jesus was warmly received at the entrance of the house of Zacchaeus.[271] If Klein is right, then the situation reminds the readers of the setting of a grand reception at a Hellenistic *symposium*, where the guests were accorded at the entrance of the host´s house before entering the *symposium*. Although the text does not explicitly state that Zacchaeus offered Jesus a grand feast (δοχὴν μεγάλην), similar to what the tax collector Levi offered for Jesus (Luke 5:29), the murmur of the people around, reveals indirectly that it was for a banquet and a stay that Jesus goes into the house of Zacchaeus.

Καὶ Ἰδόντες Πάντες

In the previous instances where Jesus was criticized for enjoying table fellowship with tax collectors and sinners, the groups that grumbled against Jesus´ actions were οἵ Φαρισαῖοι καὶ οἱ γραμματεῖς (Luke 5:30;

15:2). But in Luke 19:7 it is "all" who murmur against Jesus. Does this "all" include also Jesus' disciples?[272] From the previous texts we know that those who follow Jesus on his way are not just the crowd (Luke 18:9:3-4) but also his disciples. The addressees of Jesus in the Travel Narrative are not only the Pharisees, scribes and the crowd, but also his disciples. Hence "all" seems to be all-inclusive. Gotze is right in suggesting that the clause ἰδόντες πάντες διεγόγγυζον could be translated in two ways – not only as "all those who saw it, murmured ..." but it could also be translated as "all saw it and murmured." According to him, through the second translation, one could surmise that the people of the entire city of Jericho saw it and murmured.[273] This shows the steady increase in the number of people who are against the actions of Jesus. As Jesus nears the end of his ministry, the number of those who oppose his way of proclaiming God's kingdom increases.

As scholars point out, πάντες is used by Luke in many places in a hyperbolic sense.[274] There are as many as 44 uses of the word in the third Gospel, where Luke exaggerates the number of the onlookers and their reaction over what happens at a particular point of time in the salvific history.[275] Luke uses this hyperbolic "all" to refer to the people who normally praise God for what Jesus does (Luke 18:43) and eagerly wait to hear Jesus speak (Luke 8:40). There is, also however, the reference to "all" (πάντες) who are furious over what Jesus says (Luke 4:28). Luke's use of πάντες with its positive and negative reactions to the events of salvific history is similar to the use of crowd in his Gospel. Just like the crowd, the actions of "all" are also unpredictable. They, who praised God for the actions of Jesus (Luke 18:43) show all of a sudden their murmuring character against Jesus. The response of Jesus to the behavior of all is the same as it was for the crowd.

Διεγόγγυζον
Luke uses here one of the important verbs in the Bible, γογγύζω which means to express dissatisfaction over the action of someone. The verb describes, for instance, the complaining attitude of the Israelites against Moses and Aaron, and thereby against YWHW himself, during their

wandering through the desert (Exod 15-17; Num 14-17). Through the 25 uses of the verb (including fifteen uses of the composite verb διαγογγύζω) the LXX seems to describe the "ungodly attitude on the part of man and not merely dissatisfaction at an unfulfilled promise."[276] In the New Testament usage (e.g. Matt 20:11; Luke 5:30; Jn 6:41, 43, 61; 7:32; 1 Cor 10:10), Matthew, for instance, uses the verb in the parable where the workers grumble against the generous landowner. Paul uses the verb to quote the grumbling of the Israelites against YHWH. The negative usage of the verb is taken up also by Luke in the third Gospel. His use of the word is important for us, since it is used to portray the grumbling of the Pharisees and scribes against Jesus. The reason for their murmuring is the table fellowship of Jesus with the tax collectors and sinners, specifically with the tax collector Levi (Luke 5:30). The composite verb διαγογγύζω, which occurs ten times in the LXX just as an alternative to γογγύζω, is used in the New Testament only by Luke, who uses it only twice (Luke 15:2; 19:7). It is interesting to note that Luke uses the verb γογγύζω and its alternative διαγογγύζω only in the context of the fellowship meal of Jesus with the tax collectors and sinners. Since Mark does not use the word γογγύζω in his narration of the call of Levi, Luke's use of the word γογγύζω in the Levi story (Luke 5:30) assumes significance. The fact that Luke uses διαγογγύζω always in combination with the eating and drinking of Jesus with the tax collectors and sinners shows how important this word is for Luke with regard to the theme of fellowship meal.

Those who murmur against Jesus' practice of table fellowship for the first two instances (Luke 5:30; 15:2) are the Pharisees and scribes. The composite verb διεγόγγυζον in the imperfect in Luke 19:7 reminds of the grumbling of the Pharisees against Jesus' practice of table fellowship with tax collectors and sinners.[277] Subject of the verb in Luke 19:7 are, however, not the Pharisees and scribes but it is the πάντες who murmur against Jesus' fellowship with Zacchaeus. As the last usage of the verb in the Gospel, the grumbling by "all" shows the gradual increase in the rejection of Jesus and his message by the people. Perhaps Luke wants his readers to understand that as Jesus is nearing his goal of being glorified in Jerusalem, the number of people who find fault with Jesus is increasing. "The force of πάντες adds to the impending gloom ... the verse takes on the quality of a depressing summary, the total failure to understand the nature and extent of the divine pity."[278] Wolter is of the opinion that Luke changes the story into a controversy story with the use of the word διεγόγγυζον, just as he did for Luke 5:27-32 and 15:1-2.[279] Through the murmuring of 'all' two things are evident:

a. First, Zacchaeus as a tax collector was considered to be a sinner. Already in 19:2, we saw how the Jews looked at tax collectors at the time of Jesus. Because of their profession which involved fraudulence and cheating and because of their cooperation with the oppressors of Israel they were regarded to be traitors of the nation and thus robbers and extortionists. Even though Jericho was a strongly hellenized city due to the presence of foreigners,[280] the view about the tax collectors in Jericho was overall the same as in other Jewish cities.

b. Secondly and more importantly, the verb διεγόγγυζον in 19:7 indicates strongly the table fellowship character of Jesus' stay at the house of Zacchaeus. Jesus willingly invites himself to be a guest of such a sinner and enters into table fellowship with him. We have already seen how the word γογγύζω is used by Luke only in the two places where there is a reference to Jesus' presence with the tax collectors and that this presence is a joyful presence of table fellowship (Luke 5:30; 15:1-2). By using διεγόγγυζον in 19:7, Luke connects the Zacchaeus story with these two texts on the theme of table fellowship. Luke seems to imply that Jesus enjoys table fellowship also with Zacchaeus. This assumption is confirmed by the use of καταλῦσαι in 19:7.

Καταλύω

Καταλύω, apart from the principal meaning of destroying or dissolving, has also the meaning of taking rest. Literally it could mean freeing the animals from their yokes with the reference to rest on a journey.²⁸¹ Out of 14 usages of the verb in the synoptic Gospels, only Luke uses it in the sense of resting (Luke 9:12; 19:7). In the first usage, the disciples ask Jesus to dismiss the crowd so that "they might find lodging." Here finding lodging (καταλύω) is used together with finding food. Such a combination of finding lodging and food help one to assume that the aorist infinitive καταλῦσαι in Luke 19:7 is also about Jesus' „gastliche Einkehr"²⁸² at the house of Zacchaeus involving a fellowship meal.

Another interesting pointer to the use of the word καταλύω with regard to a fellowship meal could be found in the LXX in Gen 19:2, where Lot sees the two angels and requests them to take rest in his house (καταλύσατε). Once they entered his house, he makes a feast for them. It is interesting to note that Lot and his household are saved because of their table hospitality to the strangers, while the entire city is destroyed. We could assume that Luke might have had the LXX connotation in mind when he used the word καταλύω to express Jesus' staying at the house of Zacchaeus. By reminding the readers of what went earlier in his Gospel (Luke 9:12), and by invoking the LXX reference of the word (Gen 19:2) Luke convincingly suggests the readers what Zacchaeus offers Jesus, is not only a night stay but also a meal. On the other hand, all those who murmur against Jesus' stay at the house of Zacchaeus are like those inhabitants of Sodom, who were not saved during the destruction.

Maier sees a link between the verb καταλύω in Luke 19:7 and the noun κατάλυμα in Luke 2:7.²⁸³ He notes that, in the Gospel of Luke, Jesus needs a lodging place (*Herberge*) twice: in Bethlehem and in Jericho. In Bethlehem, there was no one to give the child Jesus a lodging place and hence he had to stay in a manger. In contrast, Zacchaeus joyfully provides Jesus a place to stay. He prepares his house for the stay of the Lord.²⁸⁴

Relationship with a tax collector was scandalous for a pious Jew. A Jewish religious leader would not normally entertain himself at the house of a tax collector; but Jesus not only stays at the house of a tax collector but also has table fellowship with him. This eating with Zacchaeus has, in the eyes of the people, brought upon Jesus "ceremonial defilement and social ostracism."[285] Precisely this is what angers the public. Through the murmur of all, the readers are able to recognize the people's judgment of Zacchaeus as a sinner and their rejection of Jesus because he went to stay with a sinner. By condemning Zacchaeus and judging Jesus, the people take upon the mantle of the Pharisees and scribes who till now played the role of the righteous ones (cf. Luke 18:1). Through this grumbling the readers are once again reminded of the constant criticism against Jesus as the glutton and drunkard (Luke 7:34).

Concluding Remarks

In the previous verse (v. 6) Zacchaeus received Jesus. In this verse (v. 7) "all" the people reject Jesus and condemn him for his action of going to the house of Zacchaeus. In the previous verse "joy" was expressed by Zacchaeus. In this verse there is disdain, which is expressed through the "murmur." The joy of Zacchaeus on the one side and the murmur of the people on the other, recalls the joy of the younger son who was able to come once again back into the embracing arms of his father and the murmur and resentment of the elder son upon the return of his younger brother (Luke 15:11-32). Just as the Israelites murmured against Moses and Aaron and YHWH, the crowd murmurs against Jesus. Just as the elder son murmurs against the father who has accepted his younger brother again into the family, the people murmur against Jesus who accepts Zacchaeus into the family of Abraham (Luke 19:9).

By portraying the acceptance of Jesus by an outcast Zacchaeus and the rejection by the Jews who thought of themselves as righteous, Luke connects instantly with his readers, who witness in their own community rejection by the Jewish authorities on the one hand and the joyful reception of the message of Jesus by the gentiles.[286] The Acts of the Apostles is filled with illustrations how the Gospel moves from the Jewish world to the ends of the earth. Zacchaeus serves as an example of the acceptance of Jesus and his message by the Lukan community, as against self-proclaimed righteous people.

Hindrance Overcome by Zacchaeus (v. 8)

Jesus' initiative and his self-invitation to be the guest of Zacchaeus have prompted two reactions: the crowd reacted to it negatively by murmuring, and Zacchaeus responded positively. From the content wise, as Bock says, verse 8 stands at the important place. For him, the legal aspects of the verse can't just be ignored as an insertion.[287] The resolution of Zacchaeus to compensate for his wrongdoings is very important for Jesus' applauding Zacchaeus. Hence for Bock, verse 8 belonged to the original source. One finds however, verse 8 is a little awkward as it stands. The murmur of the people in verse 7 is against Jesus. And the readers expect Jesus to reply to this murmur of the people. But the reply of Jesus comes only in verse 9. In this reply Jesus does not seem to answer to what Zacchaeus has just said; his answer seems to have been directed to those who murmur in verse 7. Hence the flow of the narrative is disturbed by a saying of Zacchaeus, who speaks not to those who murmur but to Jesus. Besides the double presence of κύριος in this single verse, as against the use of ὁ Ἰησοῦς in verses 3, 5, 9 makes many scholars assume a later insertion of the verse in the already circulated Zacchaeus story.[288] Most probably the redactor, who, in the final verse of the Levi narrative added an important phrase εἰς μετάνοιαν (Luke 5:32) and thereby tried to emphasize the aspect of repentance of the sinners, has tried to do the same in the Zacchaeus narrative by adding verse 8 which shows the repentance of Zacchaeus before Jesus promises salvation to his household. Thereby he has successfully shown the readers the *"komplementäre Verantwortlichkeit"*[289] of the sinners towards their salvation.

Zacchaeus: A Just Man or A Repentant Sinner?

Verse 8 poses an important problem. Does it show the main character Zacchaeus as someone who repents about his past actions or are we "to understand Zacchaeus' statement as a bristling protest of self-righteousness"?[290] White argues for the latter based on form-critical grounds. In normal salvation stories,[291] or stories of forgiveness in Luke and in the Synoptics, one finds almost always the following features:

indication of the character as a sinner and mention of the character's sinfulness by Jesus, contrite behavior of the sinful person, his petition for mercy from Jesus, a solemn pronouncement of Jesus forgiving sins, finally the crowd's reaction either marveling or complaining. None of these features are to be found in the story of Zacchaeus. First of all, Zacchaeus is not explicitly called a sinner by the narrator. Secondly the interest of Zacchaeus to see Jesus is not to acknowledge his sinfulness before Jesus and to ask him forgiveness. Only the critics of Jesus identify Zacchaeus as a sinner. When the critics say that he is a sinner, Zacchaeus does not admit to his sinfulness, instead what he says seems to be "a defense of his accustomed generosity and honesty."[292] Jesus does not utter words of forgiveness in vv. 9-10. There is no mention of the final response of the onlookers marveling / complaining of what has just happened. Instead, there is only a solemn pronouncement of Jesus about his mission, which is understood by many to be redactional work by the narrator. For all these reasons White and others conclude that the story of Zacchaeus is not about a man in need of forgiveness from Jesus. Zacchaeus is just defending himself against the critics who do not know about his generous practices; he is a just man whose just practices are accepted by Jesus and who defends Zacchaeus as being a son of Abraham. Although it is difficult to deny these arguments outright, they do not hold good, when we look at the context of Luke's Gospel in general and this text in particular. The form critical argument of White about the salvation stories in Luke has been validly refuted by Hamm, who points out that not all stories of forgiveness have all the elements, laid down by White.[293] Scholars also point out the linguistic details employed by Luke, which portray the character of Zacchaeus not as a just man but as a man who seems to be penitent of his past. What he says to Jesus are not words of defense but words of repentance. This has happened, just because of the arrival of the unique guest at his house.

Place of Zacchaeus' Utterance

As to the question where exactly Zacchaeus is shown to be uttering these words, there are different opinions among scholars. Some propose that what Zacchaeus says, happens at his house, while the murmuring takes place outside the house. While Fitzmyer and others suggest that Zacchaeus might have uttered the words while he and Jesus were still on their way to his house,[294] Ellis is of the opinion that the words of Zacchaeus come during or after the dinner that he hosted for Jesus.[295] Geldenhuys thinks that Zacchaeus might have uttered these words "probably when they again left his house and the Lord was about to rejoin the multitude to go to Jerusalem."[296] Since Luke gives so much importance to the theme of food and *symposium*-like table fellowship in his Gospel we tend to disagree with Stein, for whom Luke does not focus on the question where exactly Zacchaeus uttered his words.[297] But since, in the third Gospel, there is almost always a controversy when Jesus reclines at table, it might well be that Luke molded the story of Zacchaeus too in the same fashion. Luke 19:6 has already pointed out, that Zacchaeus has welcomed Jesus in his house. Understanding the sentence in the light of the word ὑποδέχομαι in v. 5, we could say that it is when Jesus is at table, that the controversy and the answers to the controversy take place. The word σταθείς is perhaps a help to understand where Zacchaeus uttered these words.

Σταθείς

Luke is the only New Testament writer, who uses the word σταθείς (Luke 18:11, 40; 19:8; Acts 2:14; 17:22, 27:21). Apart from Luke 18:40, in all the instances where σταθείς is used, Luke uses it as an introduction to a formal statement. Hence we could understand Luke 19:8 as a formal statement by Zacchaeus. Standing implies the formality of what Zacchaeus says.[298] It could also be looked at in "religious and quasi-liturgical character" as Kariamadam and Maier suggest.[299] In this way, Zacchaeus could be understood to be a servant of God, exactly in the same way, how the tax collector stood before God in the temple (Luke 18:13).

The word σταθείς could also be understood literally as some would argue; and it is also tempting to adopt such a position. According to Lagrange Zacchaeus utters these words during the second part of the dinner; once the δεῖπνον part of the banquet was over, in which the participants eat silently, and once the συμπόσιον part of the dinner had begun, in which extended discussion and the table talk would have taken place, Zacchaeus is shown to have talked to Jesus.[300] This would mean Zacchaeus stands to raise the toast for the chief guest and at this time, he utters these words. Although we admit that Luke is not very clear in saying where exactly Zacchaeus utters these words, given the fact that Luke all along shows Jesus' conflict with the religious authorities especially due to his eating habits, it would not be an exaggeration, if we postulate that Luke creates a *symposium* scenery, where Zacchaeus formally stands up to utter his life-decision before Jesus and others present at the banquet and at least who observe banquet from outside.

Εἶπεν Πρὸς τὸν Κύριον

The vocabulary here is a little awkward according to some scholars, but definitely Lukan.[301] The narrative designation κύριος, when it is used for Jesus is normally a post-resurrectional attribute for the risen Christ. But Luke uses the word not only for the Resurrected Christ (Luke 24:3, 34), but also at the earthly ministry of Jesus of Nazareth, which is typical for the third Gospel.[302] Jesus is addressed as Lord, not only by the characters in the Gospel (Luke 5:8, 12; 7:6; 9:54, 59, 61; 10:17, 40; 11:1; 12:41; 13:23; 17:37; 18:41; 19:8, 34; 22:33, 49), but also the narrator addresses the historical Jesus as κύριος (Luke 7:13, 19; 10:1, 39, 41; 11:39; 12:42; 13:15; 17:5, 6; 18:6; 19:8a, 31, 34; 22:61). The fact that Luke calls Jesus Lord, shows that he wants his readers to understand the earthly Jesus as Lord.

The Words of Zacchaeus

We come now to the words proper, which Zacchaeus utters. Luke begins the sentence with ἰδού. In a similar way as in v. 2, the word ἰδού is used by Luke again in v. 8 as a focusing device, this time to indicate that something important is about to be uttered by Zacchaeus.[303] Godet understands the word ἰδού in the sense of an unexpected revelation about Zacchaeus which the critics are going to find out for the first time.[304] The use of both the expressions σταθείς and ἰδού show that

Luke wants his readers to understand that what Zacchaeus is going to say is crucial to the understanding of the entire text. Zacchaeus tells two things in his address to Jesus.

Τὰ Ἡμίσιά μου τῶν Ὑπαρχόντων, Κύριε

How do we understand the neuter plural participle μου τῶν ὑπαρχόντων in v. 8? Does it mean properties or income? Among the 60 uses of the verb ὑπάρχω in the New Testament, Luke uses it in his third Gospel 15 times and in the Acts of the Apostles 25 times. The usual meaning of the verb ὑπάρχω is 'to belong to.' The numerous occurrences of the plural participle in Luke reveal that the evangelist uses the word in the meaning of what one possesses or owns.[305] The women provided for Jesus and his mission ἐκ τῶν ὑπαρχόντων αὐταῖς (Luke 8:3). A strong man arming himself protects τὰ ὑπάρχοντα αὐτοῦ (Luke 11:21). One's life does not consist of the abundance of one's ὑπάρχοντα (Luke 12:15) and hence those who would like to follow Jesus should sell τὰ ὑπάρχοντα and give alms (Luke 12:33; 14:33). In all these instances and others, the participle is used in the sense of possessions and properties. Luke uses them in order to enumerate his views on possessions and properties, rather than saying something about one's income. Luke does not use the participle in the meaning of income. Taking the global use of the participle in Luke, the genitive μου τῶν ὑπαρχόντων is probably to be understood as belongings, possessions or properties,[306] not as income.

Zacchaeus' Address of Jesus as Κύριος

The word κύριος comes within this verse for the second time. First Luke as the narrator acknowledged Jesus as Lord. Now it is Zacchaeus who calls him Lord, this time in the vocative case. It is not in the general and secular meaning of the term as "lord, the owner, the one who has full authority"[307] that the narrator has used the κύριος for Jesus. That Luke describes Jesus as κύριος not in a secular but in a theological sense, is clear from his statement in Acts 2:36. There Peter proclaims that through the Resurrection God has made Jesus κύριος and Χριστός. Hence the narrator's description of Jesus in Luke 19:8 as κύριος originates from the post-Resurrection faith of the evangelist and his community.

A question however remains, whether the first use of κύριος by the evangelist and the second, vocative use of κύριε by Zacchaeus have a same meaning. One could surmise that perhaps Zacchaeus addresses Jesus as κύριος from a secular perspective, as 'lord.' This seems to be logical from a narratological perspective; because Zacchaeus sees Jesus for the first time and hence would not be able to share in the faith of the Christian community through his address of Jesus as lord. When we look at the references of κύριε in the third Gospel, we get a different picture. One should admit that the vocative use of 'lord' appears in Luke in the secular sense of Master or the rightful owner of a property including slaves. This sort of use, however, pops up only in the parables of Jesus, in which the owner is addressed as κύριε (cf. Luke 13:8, 25; 14:22; 19:16,18, 20, 25). Apart from the parables of Jesus, κύριε once is addressed to God by Jesus (Luke 10:21); other than that the word is directed only to Jesus; the word is put in the mouth of Peter to address Jesus (Luke 5:8; 12:41; 22:33); it is also used by other disciples of Jesus, including the women disciples of Jesus (Luke 9:54, 59, 61; 10:17, 40; 11:1; 13:23; 17:37; 22:38, 49), or those who see Jesus for the first time and yet show complete faith in Jesus (Luke 5:12; 7:16; 18:41). Zacchaeus' address of Jesus as κύριε in Luke 19:8 suits in this category better. Through this usage, Luke shows the faith of Zacchaeus in Jesus. As Yamasaki rightly points out, "In the narrator's account of Jesus' ministry, the designation 'Lord' is most often found as a phraseological trait of characters who exhibit at least some degree of faith in Jesus, as they either address him or refer to him."[308] Another important pointer to note is the connection of v. 8 with v. 3. Zacchaeus wanted to see who Jesus is (τίς ἐστιν - v. 3). Now he has found out and acknowledges him as Lord. Zacchaeus' address of Jesus as Lord, shows that by recognizing Jesus as Lord, Zacchaeus has already been part of the believing community, of which Luke and his community are members.

Questions on Δίδωμι

The meaning of the present tense of δίδωμι looks to be, for some, similar to that of ἀποδεκατῶ in 18:12, where the Pharisee says it is his custom to give one tenth.[309] Hence this present tense in 19:8, according to some scholars, should be understood as an iterative / customary present. Zacchaeus' concern for, and his daily practice of almsgiving to the poor show his actions "a true sign of righteousness."[310] But reading δίδωμι and the entire verse 8 as customary present "raises as many problems as it appears to solve."[311] For a question arises in our minds as to how long one could customarily give half of his properties.[312] Another clue to the understanding of the verb could be from the attitude of the bystanders regarding Zacchaeus. Elsewhere, in the case of the centurion whose beloved slave is sick, the Jewish elders come to Jesus and plead him to help the centurion, saying, "He is worthy of having you do this for him, for he loves our people, and it is he who built our synagogue for us" (Luke 7:4b-5). Similarly, if Zacchaeus with half of his properties had been practicing almsgiving on a regular basis, how then could the onlookers consider such a generous man as Zacchaeus to be a sinner? Besides, if the present tense of δίδωμι in 19:8 is to be understood in connection with the present tense ἀποδεκατόω in Luke 18:12, then as Plummer rightly argues, is Zacchaeus not equally boasting before Jesus, just as the Pharisee was boasting before God?[313] Through the above-mentioned arguments, one could conclude that the verb δίδωμι, though in the present, should be understood in a futuristic sense of resolution to do something from now on.

Τοῖς Πτωχοῖς

The rich Zacchaeus talks for the first time about giving alms to the poor. In Greek the word πτωχός "designates the person wholly without possessions who must acquire the necessities of life through petition, hence those poor as beggars."[314] However, in the Old Testament the meaning of the word evolves and gets a religious coloring. A poor man (πτωχός) is used many times in LXX to denote someone who is economically disadvantaged and who is under the protection of

YHWH.³¹⁵ Hence Deut 15:11 gives the command of YHWH, that Israel should open her hand to the poor and needy in her land; because the poor are dependent on other people for their livelihood. The prophets during the monarchic period were strongly against the oppression of the poor and the needy (Amos 8:4-14). In the post-exilic period, Israel is regarded as poor and in need of the saving help of YHWH. Almsgiving attains the highest pedestal in the Wisdom Literature. The Book of Tobit, for example says that prayer with fasting is good, but with almsgiving and righteousness are best (Tob 12:8).

According to Billerbeck it was possible for a family to become poor just because of extensive almsgiving. This is why the rabbinic rules regarding almsgiving prescribe that when one spends money for charity for the first time, one could spend only one fifth of one's entire property and in the coming years he had to spend one fifth of his yearly income.³¹⁶

In the New Testament the word πτωχός has an important place, especially in the Gospels. Luke uses it more often than Mark and Matthew. For Mark the word has a literal meaning, while Matthew extends the meaning also to its spiritual sense (οἱ πτωχοὶ τῷ πνεύματι in Matt 5:3). In Luke we see the theme of rich and poor already in the infancy narrative (Luke 1:53). Jesus' ministry begins with his official proclamation of the motto of his coming – with his quoting of Isa 61:1-2: the proclamation of the good news to the poor is the aim of his ministry (Luke 4:18-19). Out of the ten occurrences of the word in Luke, five are coming from the special L source. In all of them Luke depicts the poor in a positive light. In contrast, the rich are portrayed negatively (Luke 6:24; 8:14; 12:15, 21, 33; 14:33; 16:10–12; 18:25). If at all he is moderate in his description of rich, it is done with the condition that the rich are asked to sell their possessions and give to the poor (Luke 16:9; 18:22; 19:8).

These references of advice for the rich are understood by Bammel to show, that "Luke neither thinks from the standpoint of the poor nor really seeks to address them ... The partial or total renunciation he demands is less for the sake of the poor than for that of the salvation of the owner."³¹⁷ Such an understanding leads one to surmise that the third Gospel is not the Gospel for the poor but the Gospel for the rich. This work agrees with it, though partially; it is true that the third Gospel has more material about, and for the rich. All the same, one cannot say that Luke does not explain the Gospel message from the standpoint of the poor. In fact, for Luke, every follower of Christ belongs to the class of the poor. Already in the beginning of his preaching, the Lukan Jesus identifies his followers as πτωχοί (Luke 6:20).³¹⁸ What Bammel rightly points out is that Luke intends to show the pathway for the rich towards their salvation. This is precisely the opportunity which Zacchaeus has grabbed. He has understood almsgiving to the poor as pivotal for being saved. But the offer of Zacchaeus to give away half of his properties to the poor is far more than the legal bindings. It is more than what the critics would have hoped for. Through this Zacchaeus shows the radical change that he has undergone due to the arrival of Jesus.

Ἐσυκοφάντησα

The aorist active indicative of συκοφαντέω in Luke 19:8 is understood by scholars differently. For Fitzmyer, the aorist verb in combination with εἴ implies that Zacchaeus did not deliberately involve in extortion. In other words, Zacchaeus does not admit to have committed extortions. But he is ready to make compensations for the extortions which he might have committed without his knowledge.³¹⁹ But such an understanding does not suit the usage in Luke. The verb συκοφαντέω, which occurs as many as ten times in the LXX occurs only twice in the New Testament and that too, only in Luke (Luke 3:14; 19:8). It is used to mean the attitude of intentional force that the economically and politically powerful used upon the powerless.³²⁰ Etymologically coming from the two words σῦκον and φαίνω the verb literally means to make an illegal smuggling of figs out of Greece. Later it became to mean to make a false statement or to extort someone through falsehood and slander. Juridically the word was used in the sense of speaking evil of someone. ³²¹ It could also mean to cheat or to defraud someone and extort falsely something from someone or to oppress someone with false accusations as in Luke 19:8. Hence through the phrase εἴ τινός τι ἐσυκοφάντησα Luke does not suggest, that Zacchaeus has *not* extorted anyone, but is ready to compensate for wrongdoing he has committed unknowingly. On the contrary, εἴ τινός τι ἐσυκοφάντησα, should be understood "as a delicate way of referring to past injustices to which the speaker admits guilt."[322] Bovon says, when a tax collector could not collect from someone what he intended, he could take him before the legal procedures, whereby tax collectors oftentimes made false accusations to win the course.[323] The first time in Luke's Gospel when the word is used by John the Baptist, it is not used to address tax collectors but soldiers. John the Baptist asks them not to extort money from anyone by threats (Luke 3:14). Luke might have used the word for both the soldiers (Luke 3:14) and the tax collectors (Luke 19:8) because he might have been aware that soldiers assisted tax collectors often with violence in collecting taxes from the people. These soldiers could have been those Jewish men who were appointed by Herod to protect the tax collectors.[324] Because of the use of the word in relation to the baptism by John the Baptist, Ravens thinks that the readers of Luke would have understood Zacchaeus to be one of the tax collectors who had been baptized by John the Baptist.[325] The mere use of the word in both the places however, does not validate such a proposal.

For scholars like Bock the word 'if' (εἴ) should be understood in the sense of 'since.'[326] The possible unconscious extortion of Zacchaeus would have made sense, if συκοφαντέω was used a perfect tense. The aorist shows the readers that Zacchaeus admits that he has indeed committed extortion in collecting taxes. The if clause does not mean that Zacchaeus doubts whether he extorted money during tax collection. As Plummer and others suggest, the clause should be understood to mean, "if, as I know, is the case, I have…"[327] extorted anybody of anything.

Ἀποδίδωμι - Futuristic or Present?
Godet does not have problems with understanding δίδωμι in a futuristic sense; it could express a vow that Zacchaeus makes then and there

to give half of his wealth.³²⁸ The futuristic understanding of the verb ἀποδίδωμι, however, poses a problem for him. According to Godet, restoring fourfold to those whom he has done wrong should be taken as a general practice Zacchaeus has been used to. If one takes the fourfold restitution of Zacchaeus as futuristic, then one sets in for a problem. He says, "It is unnatural to apply it to a measure which would relate to only some special cases of injustice to be repaired in the future."³²⁹ Fitzmyer thinks along the same line and asks if the fourfold retribution is to be understood in a futuristic resolve, then "would a repentant sinner foresee so clearly his new lapses?"³³⁰ However a similar question could also be asked against the customary understanding of the present ἀποδίδωμι. If this statement is a justification of what Zacchaeus customarily does, then it is indeed a funny justification; for, by the very fact he is justifying himself, that he is customarily paying fourfold, to everyone, whom he has cheated, Zacchaeus has accepted the fact, that it is customary for him to cheat everyone in his job and he has no plan to shun away this evil habit.³³¹ For, when we suppose that it has been his custom to compensate fourfold retribution to those whom he extorted, we should also assume that he has been customarily extorting from his clients. We are of the opinion that a futuristic understanding of compensating fourfold for the wrongs committed in the past suits not only the repentant Zacchaeus but also the Lukan context of salvation entering the house of a repentant sinner (v. 9).

Τετραπλοῦν

Τετραπλοῦν is a *hapax* in the New Testament. This word indicates that Luke shows Zacchaeus as someone following the Old Testament regulations for a repentant person. According to Exod 22:1-4, a thief, who has stolen a sheep or an ox and has either slaughtered or sold it, should make a restitution by paying fourfold to the victim, if stolen yet alive, then twofold (cf. also 2 Sam 12:6). In Lev 6:1-5 and Num 5:7 by contrast, the law of restitution is less strict. We see there that the one who has robbed his neighbor should give back what he has unjustly obtained and add one fifth to it. Zacchaeus offers to take up the highest penalty which the Law prescribes to do. Though his fraudulent behavior in his job as the chief tax collector is not like the killing of a stolen sheep, which is then irreversible, Zacchaeus "observes the most stringent demands of the law in this regard."[332] There are some who suggest that the offer of Zacchaeus to compensate fourfold for his wrongdoings, does not follow the Jewish Law but Roman legal procedures, which could have been the rule of the time.[333] More important here is the resolve of Zacchaeus to be willing to go an extra mile in compensating for his previous dishonest behavior. He does not cling to his riches as did other rich men in Luke´s Gospel (cf. Luke 12:13-21; 16:19-31; 18:18-27), but is ready to compensate his dishonest behavior.

Proposed Actions of Zacchaeus

When we look at the proposal of Zacchaeus from the perspective of the Jewish rules for charity, Zacchaeus goes far beyond the requirements of the rules. Zacchaeus does not give away just one fifth of his properties; he is ready to give away half of his properties. Through this Luke wants to show the generosity of Zacchaeus. He, unlike the rich ruler does not ask Jesus how much he should give to the poor.[334] Even though Jesus does not give any instruction regarding the sharing of wealth, Zacchaeus is spontaneous in his decision of giving half of his possessions to the poor, so spontaneous as the willingness of Herod to give away half of his kingdom to the dancing daughter of Herodias (Mk 6:23).[335]

One should however, note a slight change in the sharing of wealth by the rich Zacchaeus here. When we look at the actions of Zacchaeus from the demands of the Lukan Jesus, his actions do not qualify to be a follower of Jesus. The demands of the third Gospel over the rich are more stringent. The rich should sell *all* their properties and give everything to the poor if they want to enter the Kingdom (Luke 12:33; 18:22). Zacchaeus does not sell everything he has. He is ready to give away only half of his properties. Hence he is "falling short of what was required of the rich man."[336] The rich ruler was asked to sell everything he had, and to follow Jesus (Luke 18:22). Jesus does not demand such a stringent action from Zacchaeus (and his household). For the readers the question may arise what would happen to Zacchaeus, who does not sell everything, but only half of his properties. There are some who say,[337] Luke is very much aware of the Jewish Law of retribution. A sinner who wanted to repent had to show his repentance by compensating for the wrongdoings he had committed. Perhaps Zacchaeus gives away only half of his possessions to the poor, because he needs the other half for the retribution he has to make. The action of Zacchaeus could also be understood as the future mandate for the readers of Luke. While following Jesus involves selling one's properties (Acts 2:45; 4:34; 5:1-11), Luke shows that there is also another way: "Zacchaeus provides an example that whereas the demand to sell all (Luke 12:33; 18:22) is not obligatory for all believers; generosity is."[338] In the words of Green,

> Luke's almsgiving is neither charity in the modern sense, nor an ascetic ideal; rather it has to do with including in one's circle of kin those who are unable to reciprocate (e.g., 14:1-24) to make friends via giving without expectation of return (cf. 6:35-36; 16:9). Unlike the rich ruler, Zacchaeus does not employ his wealth so as to procure honor and friends; rather he is a social outcast, who puts his possessions in the service of the needy and of justice.[339]

In this way, as Löning[340] rightly points out, Luke has answered the question that bothered the Apostles as well as the readers of the Gospel, "who then can be saved?," and the answer, which Jesus gave to his disciples, "What is impossible for mortals is possible for God" (Luke 18:27), suits the household of Zacchaeus.

There is another question which v. 8 raises in the minds of the readers - namely the relation between the human readiness towards repentance and the response and reward of God towards this readiness. We have already seen that v. 8 could be the result of the redactor to the already existing story. Could it be possible that the redactor, through his addition of v. 8 before Jesus' solemn gift of salvation to the house of Zacchaeus (vv. 9-10), wanted to address an ideological issue that perhaps was very much alive at the time of writing? In other words, does the salvation gifted to humans by God, need a *prior* repentance? Or is it a free gift from God? From the pericope of Luke 19:1-10, it is difficult to decide, which comes first, whether it is the human readiness to repentance and the subsequent reward of salvation by God, or whether God´s unconditional offer of salvation for the lost, and the subsequent joyful acceptance of this offer by humans through their readiness to repent. The Lukan Jesus decides to be the guest of Zacchaeus, *not because* Zacchaeus took steps to see him. On the contrary, it is the plan of God that Jesus *must* stay in the house of Zacchaeus. The words of Zacchaeus in v. 8 should also be understood along the similar line. Luke is very clear to show that Zacchaeus and his household is offered salvation, *not because* of Zacchaeus´ proposed actions of compensation to his unjust actions. His proposed actions are not at all referred to, as the reasons for Jesus´ solemn gift of salvation to the household of Zacchaeus. This shows that God´s offer of salvation is unconditional regardless of the human response.[341] However the redactor´s inclusion of v. 8 before vv. 9-10 shows the existing tension that might have existed in the theology of relation between the God´s offer of salvation and the human response and emphasis the importance of repentance as the human response towards God´s offer of salvation.

Quest of Jesus: Concluding Remarks

Through the words σταθείς and ἰδού we are able to understand the weight and importance that Luke wants to give to this statement of Zacchaeus. Moreover, σταθείς would make the reader surmise that Zacchaeus has been all along sitting at the δεῖπνον part of the dinner and gets up at the beginning of the *symposion* part of the dinner, to raise the toast for his unique guest. The arrival of Jesus in his house has pushed Zacchaeus to make "a mighty revolution"[342] in his life. First of all, he has recognized Jesus as κύριος and thereby has become part of the believing community. Secondly his handling of his riches will be completely changed. The one-half of his riches will be spent to provide for the poor; with the other half he will probably compensate for the wrongdoings he had committed in the past. Thereby Luke tries to imbibe in his community that the sharing of wealth, even partial, should not be out of compulsion; it should be out of free will and as an expression of gratitude for the salvation received from God.

Quest of Jesus Fulfilled (vv. 9-10)

Luke brings the controversy and the conversion of Zacchaeus to a climax with the words of Jesus. As it was in healing-controversy stories of Luke, Jesus has the final word, so also here he makes a solemn proclamation, with which he justifies his coming to the house of Zacchaeus. The double *logion* of vv. 9-10 is a clear parallel to the solemn proclamation of Jesus at the banquet of Levi in Luke 5:31-32. The coming of the physician to heal the sick gets concrete example in the coming of Jesus to the house of Zacchaeus. The wordings the evangelist uses here are very dear to him. They have been used all along the Gospel specially in Jesus´ Galilean ministry and his Travel Narrative and find their climax at this story.

Εἶπεν δὲ Πρὸς Αὐτὸν ὁ Ἰησοῦς

The question that arises at first is to whom Jesus speaks these final words. Is it to Zacchaeus or to those who murmur? This question arises because Jesus speaks about Zacchaeus in the third person. Since it is not clear, scholars like Fitzmyer state that originally this verse might have been Jesus´ answer to the critics. Hence πρὸς αὐτόν should be translated not as "to him" but "about him" or "with regard to him." This goes along with the Lukan use of πρὸς αὐτούς in Luke 20:19 (taken from the Markan parallel 12:12).[343] If we understand πρὸς αὐτόν in v. 9 as in Luke 20:19, then it means that Jesus, looking at Zacchaeus, spoke these words *to* those who were murmuring *concerning* Zacchaeus. Summers rightly points out however that only v. 9b states Zacchaeus in the third person and hence speaks *about* Zacchaeus, while v. 9a seems to have been spoken to Zacchaeus.[344] This shows the redactional hand of Luke[345] in molding the statement of Jesus which might have been earlier part of a controversy story.[346] As Luke has placed it, we could understand the first part of v. 9 as Jesus´ saying to Zacchaeus and the second part as Jesus´ saying to the murmurers. The first part justifies

Zacchaeus and the second part justifies the actions of Jesus, coming to the house of Zacchaeus.

Σήμερον

Jesus uses the word 'today' twice in the pericope (Luke 19:5, 9). The emphasis on "today" in 19:9 is evident from the placement of the word σήμερον at the very beginning of the clause. It is to be noted that also in v. 5 the word is placed right at the beginning of the clause. Such placement suggests the redactional hand of the evangelist and the significance he attaches to the word. The redactional nature of the verse is seen particularly in the fact that in v. 5 as well as in v. 9a the word σήμερον comes together with τῷ οἴκῳ. Such doubling of words is not uncommon in the third Gospel.[347] Hence the "today" of v. 9 could be seen as a counterpart to the "today" of v. 5. Through this the evangelist wants to say to his readers, Jesus' wish to stay at the house of Zacchaeus is fulfilled now.

Σωτηρία ... Ἐγένετο

The word σωτηρία could be understood from two different perspectives. From the physical sense, σωτηρία is understood as delivering an individual or a group or as preserving someone from illness, from the dangers of the sea, delivering from enemies at war or even from legal convictions. It could also mean to stay in good health. In the religious meaning, σωτηρία brings in the concept of deliverance from the gods.[348] In the LXX too we see the word used in both meanings. Σωτηρία could mean deliverance acquired through humans either legally or through military mediation. Though salvation is brought by men, ultimately it comes from God. It is God who helps through men, whom he appoints to deliver his people (Judg 2:16; 3:9, 15). It is the Lord who delivers his people from the enemies (Exod 15:2; Deut 33:29).

In the synoptic Gospels, Luke is the only writer who uses this word. The noun is used by Luke ten times in his double work.[349] In Luke 1:71, 73 it is used in the sense of the deliverance of Israel from its enemies (σωτηρίαν ἐξ ἐχθρῶν ἡμῶν καὶ ἐκ χειρὸς πάντων τῶν μισούντων ἡμᾶς). Further, the verb form σῴζω is used in Luke to denote the physical healing from illnesses or the preservation of life (Luke 6:9; 8:36, 48; 17:19; 18:42). In Luke 1:77 σωτηρία means deliverance from sins (τοῦ δοῦναι γνῶσιν σωτηρίας τῷ λαῷ αὐτοῦ ἐν ἀφέσει ἁμαρτιῶν αὐτῶν). Similarly, the phrase "your faith has saved you," which Jesus utters at the end of many healings, is attested, for instance, in Luke 7:50, where Jesus talks of the deliverance of the woman from her sins. Hence both the noun and the verb forms are used in Luke in the sense of physical as well as spiritual deliverance.

Luke uses the noun σωτηρία four times: thrice in the infancy narrative (Luke 1:69, 71, 77), and once in Luke 19:8. Hahn suggests that σωτηρία is the central word around which the entire pericope revolves.[350] For Fitzmyer too, with this verse "the primary Lukan effect of the Christ event surfaces in the lips of Jesus."[351] It is not in the sense of healing the physical illnesses but it is the deliverance of Zacchaeus from his sins. More precisely, σωτηρία in Luke 19:8 means on the one hand coming back to the life of the community[352] and on the other, "restored relationship that one has with God."[353] This restored relation of an individual with the divine and the community is a recurrent theme in the New Testament (e.g. Luke 10:5-7, 21-24; 23:43; Acts 13:26-27; 2 Cor 6:2). The words of Jesus show that Zacchaeus is brought back into the community and into the relationship with God. Johnson translates ἐγένετο with 'happened.'[354] According to him salvation has happened at the house of Zacchaeus in and through the presence of Jesus; Jesus' coming to the house of Zacchaeus has made salvation possible for him. In the words of Godet, "Jesus is the living salvation. Received as he was into the house, he brought into it by his very presence this heavenly blessing."[355] While salvation is the free gift of God through Jesus' presence, the Lukan redactor also wants to say that salvation was possible because of Zacchaeus' reception of Jesus and his handling of his riches.

Τῷ Οἴκῳ Τούτῳ

Salvation of the household is something unique to Luke-Acts. In the Acts of the Apostles we see the household of Cornelius (Acts 10:1-11:18), the household of the jailer (Acts 16:25-34), and the household of Crispus the official of the Synagogue (Acts 18:1-11) receiving Jesus and his message and becoming believers of the Lord. For Green and others, the salvation of these households is anticipated in Luke's Gospel by the story of Zacchaeus. The significance of the salvation of the entire household is clear from both the ministry of Jesus in the Gospel and from the ministry of the apostles.[356] House could be understood in two ways here, as Ray Summers points out.[357] When 'house' is understood literally, then we may say that salvation has entered in this house and made Zacchaeus' home its abode, just as Jesus made Zacchaeus' house his abode. Jesus would leave the house next day. Salvation, however, would remain in that house permanently. When we understand 'house' as family then the action of the *paterfamilias* transforms the entire family and makes the members of the entire family recipients of salvation. The salvation of the individual is contagious and has spread from Zacchaeus to his entire household.

Salvation: Gift of the Host

The participants at a Hellenistic *symposium* were given something at the end of the party, so that they might take home something, which they have been enjoying at the house of the host. Generally, the guests were given part of the food as a nourishment for their way home; sometimes it also included expensive plates on which the guests ate their food. Such gifts not only displayed the richness and generosity of the host but also helped to cement his status and position in the society. Understood from the background of the gift-giving tradition of the Hellenistic *symposium*, the final verses of the text, which show Jesus solemnly gifting salvation to Zacchaeus and his household, enlighten the readers, that the Lukan Jesus is not a guest any more at the house of Zacchaeus. He indeed plays the role of the host, not only because he invites himself; rather as a true host, he gifts the household of Zacchaeus with an unfathomable gift at the end of the *symposium*. The gift however is not just food or plates or vases, which would be temporary; what Jesus offers to Zacchaeus is salvation for the entire household. Inviting himself to the *symposium*, having the final say at the banquet, gifting the guest with salvation... with all these characteristics, Luke moulds and changes the role of Jesus from being an ἄκλητος, to the chief guest at the banquet and finally as the one taking upon himself the role of the host himself, who takes charge of the entire proceedings of the *symposium* from inviting to the final sending away of the guests with gifts.

Καὶ Αὐτὸς γίὸς Ἀβραάμ Ἐστιν

The character of Abraham is attested in the Gospel of Luke fifteen times and in the Acts of the Apostles seven times. Mark mentions him only once, Matthew seven times and John eleven times.[358] For Luke Abraham is an important figure as far as the salvation history is concerned. At the beginning of the Gospel, the childless couple Elisabeth and Zechariah with the reference to their old age (Luke 1:7) and in Zechariah´s questioning the angel about the promise of the son (Luke 1:18) the story of Abraham and Sarah is alluded to. In the infancy narrative the major theme of Abraham concerns God´s promise to Abraham. This promise is attested both in the Magnificat (Luke 1:54-55) and in the Benedictus (Luke 1:73-74). Abraham is also seen in the genealogy (Luke 3:34). Luke describes him in heaven in the afterlife (Luke 13:28; 16:22-31). Apart from this, Luke also speaks about the children of Abraham (Luke 3:8; 13:16; 19:9; Acts 13:26,33).

In all these citations one finds that Luke´s understanding of the character of Abraham is different from what Paul talks about him. Pauline understanding of Abraham concentrates on his trust in the saving power of God (cf. Gal 3:6-9, 29; Rom 4:1-3). John also talks about Abraham in the context of the pre-existence of Jesus (Jn 8:58). But Luke shows Abraham differently. In Siker´s opinion, Luke brings in the character of Abraham in his double work, in order to show the salvific inclusion of those who are outside – not only gentiles but also those within Judaism, who were considered unworthy, due to their lowly status of social and economic poverty. The Gospel of Luke focuses on the inclusion of lowly Jews, whereas the Acts of the Apostles focuses on the inclusion of gentiles in the salvific plan of God.[359] This is why in Luke, Abraham is seen as the father of the people of Israel. In this portrayal of Luke, "one sees his underlying concern to show the priority of Israel in the plan of God's salvation-history."[360] Salvation starts from Israel, though it has an all-inclusive character. Jesus´ reaching out to the crippled woman on the one hand and to Zacchaeus on the other is precisely because both of them are daughter and son of Abraham respectively (Luke 13:16, 19:9). The Lukan Jesus concentrates at first on the lost sheep of Israel.

Luke´s reference to Zacchaeus as the son of Abraham should not be merely understood in a biological / genealogical sense, since for Luke, Abrahamic blessing is not always linked with the biological heritage. That Zacchaeus is a descendant of Abraham cannot be the only reason for him to be saved. Luke´s earlier sayings do not substantiate such an understanding. As Godet says, "Jesus could not make the possibility of salvation dependent on the naked characteristic of being a member of Israelitish nation. The idea would be in contradiction to his whole teaching, and to the very saying which concludes this verse."[361] Some suggest that sonship of Abraham should be understood spiritually. The Abrahamic faith (cf. Rom 4:12; Gal 3:6-9) with which Zacchaeus has received Jesus and accepted him as Lord would show him that he is the spiritual descendant of Abraham.[362] It seems doubtful whether Luke would have understood sonship of Abraham in a pure spiritual sense. First of all, we need to ask how far Luke would have taken this Pauline way of understanding in his Gospel. Paul brings in the concept of sonship of Abraham in his defense of the inclusion of gentiles into the Christian faith. To show that the gentiles also form part of God´s people, Paul says, "Abraham believed God, and it was reckoned to him as righteousness, so, you see, those who believe are the descendants of Abraham." (Gal 3:6-7). Whenever Abraham is referred to in the third Gospel, Luke does not bring him in the context of faith of gentiles, but in the context of the Jews. Hence as Bovon suggests,[363] the Pauline sense of spiritual descendancy of Abraham might not be applicable to the texts of Luke, especially in the context of Zacchaeus.

What would then be the understanding with which Luke uses the concept of the children of Abraham? An interesting parallel is brought forth by Hotze between Abraham and Zacchaeus. Just as Abraham hosts the heavenly messengers of God a sumptuous meal and thereby his household is rewarded by the three angels, Zacchaeus hosts Jesus and thus is rewarded by him.[364] Although it is tempting to accept this parallel, we are of the opinion that the sonship of Abraham in the third Gospel is to be linked with the Lukan portrayal of salvation that has been offered in the person and the ministry of Jesus. Siker finds two patterns in Luke´s descriptions of the character of Abraham. The first pattern deals with God´s action of rendering salvation to the poor and the lowly, while the second pattern involves the action of God bringing salvation to those who repent.[365]

Apart from the reference to Abraham in the infancy narrative, the inclusion of the lowly and the poor in the salvific plan of God could be seen especially in Luke 13:10-17, where a crippled woman is healed by Jesus. Jesus justifies his action against those who question her healing on the Sabbath day and says she is a daughter of Abraham (θυγατέρα Ἀβραάμ Luke 13:16). The crippled woman seems to form the counterpart to Zacchaeus who is proclaimed by Jesus as the son of Abraham.

In the parable of rich man and Lazarus (Luke 16:19-31), Jesus gives the same message. It is the poor Lazarus (who is a social outcast), who sits at the bosom of Abraham, whereas the rich man, who calls on to Abraham as πάτερ Ἀβραάμ (Luke 16:24) and portrayed as Abraham´s child (τέκνον v. 25), does not get a positive reply from Abraham for any of his requests. The similarities between the crippled woman and Lazarus are that both are considered lowly by the majority of the Jews because of their social and economic conditions. Precisely because of their lowly condition salvation reaches out to them.

The second pattern, which, according to Siker, is found in Luke's portrayal of Abraham, is that those who repent from their sinful ways are considered to be υἱοί / τέκνα of Abraham. The message of John the Baptist is very striking in this regard: What Jews need at the time is not their pride that they are the descendants of Abraham; what they need to do, is to bear fruits worthy of their repentance. Because God could turn stones into τέκνα τῷ Ἀβραάμ (Luke 3:8). Through this text Luke has at the very beginning of his Gospel rightly connected the theme of children of Abraham and repentance. According to Bovon, the Jewish nation "had to show itself worth of its status, if not it would lose its privilege."[366] In order to remain descendants of Abraham they had to do repentance. Zacchaeus as the υἱὸς Ἀβραάμ should be understood along this line. Through his response Zacchaeus shows Jesus and his murmurers that he has repented and thereby is a true heir of Abraham.[367]

While Siker suggests that Zacchaeus belongs to this second pattern, one could also understand him fitting exactly with those social outcasts of the society. As Green points out, "since Lukan narrative has redefined status as a 'child of Abraham' with reference to lowly position and faithful practices, Jesus' assertion vindicates Zacchaeus as one who embodies the qualities of those fit for the kingdom of God."[368] Zacchaeus' shortness, his climbing a tree and above all his job as the chief of tax collectors are all elements with which Luke portrays Zacchaeus as a marginalized outcast, precisely someone, whom Jesus wants to reach out to. This means, just like the lowly Jewish woman, who is regarded by other Jews as unclean due to her illness, finds favour with God (Luke 13:16) so also does Zacchaeus, who, in the eyes of others, is a social outcast due to his profession, finds favour with Jesus who accepts him.

If we understand the words of repentance and resolve of Zacchaeus as the sole reason for Jesus' acknowledgement of Zacchaeus' sonship of Abraham, then the salvation of an individual seems to be heavily dependent on the personal effort of the individual. But this is not the idea of salvation as elucidated in the New Testament, especially in the Gospel of Luke. As Foerster points out, salvation in the New Testament "has to do solely with man's relationship to God. Hence salvation is accomplished neither by man's self-mastery through autonomous reason ... nor by perfect contrition, i.e. the absolute acceptance of the heteronomously understood Torah ... No man can effect salvation for himself."[369] This is similar to the story of Zacchaeus too. Jesus´ answer to Zacchaeus in vv. 9-10 does in no way refer to the repentance of Zacchaeus. Godet rightly points out, "without allowing the least meritorious value to those restitutions and those extraordinary almsgivings, He (Jesus) declares that Zacchaeus is the object of divine grace as much as those can be, who accuse him."[370] Salvation hence, is the free gift of God in the person of Jesus, who is responsible for the blessings that Zacchaeus would receive as the son of Abraham. This is further corroborated in the previous chapter of Luke, where Jesus answers the question who would then be saved, "What is impossible for mortals is possible for God" (Luke 18:26). At the same time, humans are not passive receivers of salvation. What the individual needs to do is to be ready to receive the offer of blessing that comes with the arrival of Jesus. Zacchaeus was not only seeking to see Jesus but immediately received him in his house. Zacchaeus´ reception of Jesus has induced him to repent his ways and thereby made him worthy to be the host of Jesus. This in turn has brought him back to the blessings of sonship of Abraham. Acceptance and reception of Jesus then would go hand in hand with repentance and the subsequent salvation.

Ἦλθεν γὰρ ὁ γἰὸς τοῦ Ἀνθρώπου Ζητῆσαι καὶ Σῶσαι τὸ Ἀπολωλός
Marshall suggests that if we want to have just one verse that could sum up the entire ministry of Jesus in the Gospel of Luke, then it is Luke 19:10 – the saving mission of the Son of Man.[371] The placement of the story of Zacchaeus shows that this statement of Marshall is very significant. Luke climaxes the entire ministry of Jesus in Galilee and Judaea outside Jerusalem with the story of Zacchaeus. After the parable of the pounds (Luke 19:11-27) Jesus´ entry into Jerusalem begins with his subsequent passion, death and glorification. Hence the climax of the entire ministry of Jesus, which began with the proclamation in Nazareth

(Luke 4:14-16), is his assertion that salvation of humans is his ultimate mission. This is why the word σωτηρία is significant in Luke 19:9.

There is, however, a question about the redactional nature of this verse. The discussion ranges from whether such a proclamation could have come from the historical Jesus himself, or whether the verse was originally pre-Lukan tradition but Luke is responsible for its insertion in the story of Zacchaeus, or whether this verse was altogether a Lukan invention. Those who suggest that the verse is part of a pre-Lukan tradition point to the fact that the phrase υἱὸς τοῦ ἀνθρώπου is not typically a Lukan phrase and the combination of this phrase with ἦλθεν has been already in the pre-Lukan tradition (cf. Mk 10:45; Matt 20:28; Matt 11:19; Luke 7:34).[372] Others who do not see this verse as part of the original story but as a redactional work of Luke[373] suggest the following arguments:

- Verse 10, which gives a general statement about the mission of Jesus is not intricately connected to the Zacchaeus episode. It may well be applied and placed in any other stories in the Gospel as well.

- The statement of Jesus with the conjunction γάρ seems to render a Christological framework for the entire story.

- The verse which is possibly taken from Ezek 34:16 is only one of the two references which Luke has kept in his Gospel, the other one being Luke 15:3-4.

Because of these reasons Kariamadam believes Luke 19:10 must have been originally a "free-floating *logion*" which Luke has made to fit at the end of the Zacchaeus pericope.[374] Though it is probable that this *logion* might have been edited and placed by Luke at this place, verse 10 could also be understood as a pre-Lukan verse or even as a statement which was actually uttered by the historical Jesus himself.

Ὁ γιὸς τοῦ Ἀνθρώπου

The Son of Man is one of the terms in the New Testament that has led to unending discussions among the New Testament scholars. The 'Son of Man' problem seems to be insoluble.[375] Vögtle, the eminent Professor emeritus of Freiburg University, who has contributed so much to the understanding of this important phrase of the New Testament,[376] rightly points out that the discussion on the Son of Man problem would go a long way. Although it is difficult to do justice to all the material on the Son of Man problem, we shall attempt, nevertheless, in the following few pages to outline the problem in a nutshell and then proceed to understand the meaning of the phrase ὁ υἱὸς τοῦ ἀνθρώπου in the Zacchaeus pericope.

Origin of the Term

The term ὁ υἱὸς τοῦ ἀνθρώπου occurs in the Synoptics sixty nine times.[377] The meaning of the term ὁ υἱὸς τοῦ ἀνθρώπου, which literally means 'the son of the man' or 'the man's son,' is usually translated in the Gospels with "the Son of Man." It is generally accepted that there lie behind this Greek concept one or more semitic terms, since at the time of Jesus, there was no specific term like this in the Greek language.[378] Vögtle sees it as the literal transliteration of the "*bar nasha*" which has a generic meaning, denoting a human being or man in general.[379]

Titular Use of Bar Nasha by the Historical Jesus?

The Son of Man occurrences in the Gospel traditions have been traditionally divided into three major categories. The first category deals with those Son of Man sayings that speak of the earthly ministry of Jesus.[380] The second is about predictions of Jesus as the Son of Man enduring suffering and death and rising again to life, and the third situates the exaltation of the Son of Man and his future coming in glory to judge the world.[381] But the big question is, whether the historical Jesus ever used the word *bar nasha* as a title and, if he used it, whether he understood and used the term to refer to himself or to someone else. Before looking for an answer to these questions, it is helpful to look at the usage of the term ὁ υἱὸς τοῦ ἀνθρώπου in the Gospel traditions. Some of the general observations made by Walker are here worth mentioning:

> (1) The title, Son of Man, is almost completely absent from early Christian literature other than the canonical Gospels. (2) The title occurs in all four of the canonical Gospels, and, indeed, in all of what are commonly taken to be the various strata of the Gospel traditions: the triple tradition, the various double traditions, Special Matthew, Special Luke, and John. (3) With only one exception, and this in the Fourth Gospel, the title is found in the Gospels only on the lips of Jesus himself. (4) The references to the Son of Man on the lips of Jesus are always in the third person, never the first, and, in some cases, a rather clear distinction between Jesus and the Son of Man seems to be implied.[382]

This observation about the Son of Man usage in the Gospel traditions, especially in the Synoptics, leads to various hypotheses as to whether and how Jesus used the title ὁ υἱὸς τοῦ ἀνθρώπου and if they are really coming from Jesus himself, which Son of Man sayings are authentic and which could have been secondary, and hence coming from the post-Resurrection faith of the Christian believers. The following points are the three major suggestions put forward by scholars:

1. All, or at least some of the Son of Man sayings in all the three groupings could have been authentic self-designations of Jesus himself.

2. At least some of the Son of Man sayings in all the three groups are from the historical Jesus, but he might have used the term not as a title or as a self-designation, but might be referring to someone other than himself.

3. "Son of Man" as a christological title has its origin in the post-Resurrection faith of the Christian community.

Authenticity of the Titular Son of Man Sayings

Those who regard the Son of Man sayings as authentic,[383] contend that there is no reason to doubt that the historical Jesus indeed referred to himself as the Son of Man. The absence of the title in the New Testament books other than the Gospel traditions and the absence of the title in the lips of other people, apart from Jesus could be proofs that Jesus understood himself as the Son of Man. Within the Gospel tradition, these sayings are central to the understanding of Jesus about his mission and identity. Besides, since John the Baptist thought of himself as the last messenger before the Son of Man, Jesus might have understood himself and his mission as the Son of Man. Since in Jewish thought Son of Man was a technical term for the one with God-given authority, Jesus would have found the term as the perfect choice to explain his God-given authority. Hence the historical Jesus might have found this term very apt in contrast to the title Messiah, which was misleading. Son of Man as a title would have been "a perfect vehicle for expressing the divine self-consciousness of Jesus while at the same time preserving the secrecy of his self-revelation from those who had blinded their eyes and closed their ears."[384]

Jesus might have also used the title ´Son of Man´ to describe his imminent humiliation and rejection and also his elevation by the Father. Jesus might have preferred this term "on the one hand because it was no customary title and could design a humble ´man´ as well as an ´eschatological´ figure, on the other, perhaps, because in Daniel 7 the Son of Man is the representative of the suffering and finally exalted Israel."[385] Jesus might have expected that after his life and death he would be elevated to the presence of God and would be given the power to judge the world. Hence for him the Son of Man is "not a personal figure but a symbolic description of his own expected dignity, status and function as judge."[386]

Authenticity of Non-Titular Son of Man Sayings

Others like Vermès take the Son of Man sayings as a circumlocution for the first person pronoun.[387] Fitzmyer thinks Jesus might not have used the term in a titular sense; he might have used it in an indefinite or generic sense of any "mortal human being."[388] Since Jesus used it in a generic sense, to include each and every person, it would also include himself in the secondary place.

Scholars like Bultmann, who accept the authenticity of the sayings, reject that Jesus identified himself with this title. Bultmann[389] takes only those Son of Man sayings that refer to the eschatological role of the Son of Man as authentic, but posits that, when Jesus spoke of the Son of Man, he used it to refer to someone other than himself, who would take up the role of the end-time judge.

Post-Resurrection Faith of the Early Christians

Those who argue that the titular use of the Son of Man sayings is of post-Resurrection origin, raise valid questions against those, claiming that the Son of Man sayings authentically originate from Jesus: If Jesus understood himself as the Son of Man, as the Synoptics portray, why then does none of his disciples or followers address him with the title, or ask him about the implications or the meaning of this indirect self-given title? Why is it that not even the Pharisees and scribes ask about the meaning of such a term? Besides, the absence of the term in the Pauline Corpus is for them an indication that the Son of Man title is a Post-Resurrection title and it has its origin in the Parousia expectations of the community.[390] "Son of Man" would have evolved into a title in different stages. For Perrin, the belief in the resurrection of Jesus has helped the early Christians to interpret the Psalm 110, where the 'One sitting at the right hand of God' is referred to. This understanding of Ps 110:10 was combined with Dan 7:13 to interpret the resurrection of Jesus as the ascension of Jesus to the right hand of God. In the later stages Dan 7:13 was interpreted against the background of the suffering of Jesus. The third phase unfolds in the Parousia sayings of the Son of Man as in Mk 13:26. Perrin assumes that there was no concept of the Son of Man in first century Judaism.[391] Christian exegetes took up the term from Dan 7:13 and combined with 1 Enoch where Enoch is said to have taken up to heaven. By combining these two texts they tried to interpret the resurrection of Jesus and his elevation to the right hand of God as the Son of Man.

Possible Conjectures from the Discussion

The above-mentioned arguments about the origin and use of the Son of Man sayings in the Synoptics show how difficult it is to understand the Son of Man problem. The following is an attempt to deduce at least some of the probabilities from what has been said in the foregoing pages. First of all, the point of reference for everything that has been spoken and written about Jesus is the faith of the believers on the resurrection of Christ. Vögtle, who originally in his habilitation work understood the Son of Man sayings (especially Luke 12:8-9) as authentically originating from the historical Jesus corrects his view in his later work and argues that the Son of Man sayings (including Luke 12:8-9), have their origin in the post-Resurrection faith of the Christian community. It is on this faith that the early Christology got rooted and developed. Hence one has to agree that any title referring to Jesus, including the 'Son of Man,' is influenced by this Easter faith of the Christian community.

This, however, does not mean that the term the Son of Man had its origin purely from the Easter faith of the believing community. The fact that the title appears nowhere else in the early Christian literature than in the Gospels and only on the lips of Jesus, shows that Jesus might have used the term at least in some instances. The fact that it is always in the third person singular, one gets the feeling that Jesus might have used the term, either to refer to himself or to someone else other than himself. In contrast to Χριστός, a term which is used in the earliest Christian literature to denote Jesus but never uttered by Jesus to refer to himself, the term Son of Man is never uttered by anyone except Jesus to refer to himself, though Jesus uses it always in the third person singular. In fact, the term disappears from the Christian literature outside the Gospels. The fact that the term is a translated phrase of the Aramaic language, the *lingua franca* of the time, and since the evangelists have tried to represent it by their – clumsy – translation into ὁ υἱὸς τοῦ ἀνθρώπου, one could probably understand the honest effort of the Gospel traditions in handing down the exact words which Jesus might have spoken. Hence as Oberliner observes, the development of Christology should not stay disconnected from the public ministry of Jesus.[392] This close relationship between the public ministry of Jesus and the formation of the christological titles should be taken into account when one analyses the title Son of Man.

One cannot adequately prove whether the historical Jesus really used this term, and yet one cannot outrightly reject it as purely the formation of the early Christian community. The early Christian community could not have taken from the Jewish literature to apply to Jesus out of the blue, unless and until Jesus himself used the title at one point of time or another. Since the apocalyptic world view was already prevalent in Jewish literature like Daniel and Enoch, the Son of Man concept was not foreign to the Jews of the first century. It would have been a prevalent thought at least among some apocalyptic Jewish groups. Since the historical Jesus was baptized by John the Baptist, who was preaching with an apocalyptic background, Prostmeier rightly observes that the historical Jesus would probably have definitely known about such apocalyptic imageries and hence the usage of the term by the historical Jesus need not be thought to be improbable.[393] Understood in this way, one could say together with Prostmeier, „Die Anwendung der Menschensohnbezeichnung auf die Logienüberlieferung verleiht diesem Glauben der Gemeinden einen personalen Haftpunkt in ihren Erinnerungen an Worte und Taten des historischen Jesus."[394]

However, as we have noted earlier, Jesus in the Synoptics does not directly talk of himself as the Son of Man, instead reports about the Son of Man always in the third person. This feature is very evident in Luke 12:8-9 where Jesus makes a clear separation between himself and the Son of Man. This could mean one of the following: a. Jesus used the first-person pronoun 'I' and the term Son of Man interchangeably; b. the historical Jesus did not understand himself and his mission in the apocalyptic person of the Son of Man but thought of someone other than himself as the Son of Man who would take up the role of the eschatological judge in the end-time; or c. The attribution of the title Son of Man to the words and actions of Jesus was a result of the believing community, which found appropriate to use the term for Jesus, whose second coming the community was eagerly waiting for, with the invocation, 'Maranatha.'

It is not easy to come to a satisfactory conclusion, whether or not Jesus used the term Son of Man in reference to his mission as a title – a title which is "both revealing as well as hiding."[395] This paper is too short and too humble to give an answer to a crucial question as this. However, since the title Son of Man is uttered only by Jesus and not by anyone else in the Synoptics, this work assumes the following: it is probable that the historical Jesus talked about the Son of Man in his preaching; this term in the Synoptics would have come from the eyewitnesses who would have recalled Jesus using the term in his preaching[396] whether Jesus through the use of the term referred to himself or to a person other than himself as the eschatological judge. This unique expression of the historical Jesus in his mother tongue has perhaps been preserved and handed over and expanded by the Gospel traditions. The believing community, expecting the return of the Resurrected Lord, happily embraced the title and used it convincingly to refer to the life and mission of the earthly Jesus.

Luke's Use of 'the Son of Man'

Out of the twenty-five occurrences of the phrase in Luke,[397] seven are taken from Mark (Luke 5:24; 6:5; 9:22, 26, 44; 18:31; 22:22), eight from Q (Luke 7:34; 9:58; 11:30; 12:10, 40; 17:24, 26, 30) and others are attributed to the special L source (Luke 17:22; 18:8; 19:10; 21:36; 22:48, 24:7; Acts 7:56), or to a Lukan redaction: for example in the Matthean version of the Sermon on the Mount, we see Jesus praising those who suffer on *his* account (Matt 5:11), whereas the Lukan Jesus praises the disciples for their sufferings on the account of the Son of Man (Luke 6:22). Further in Matt 10:32-33 Jesus tells his disciples that he will acknowledge or deny before the Father in Heaven, those who acknowledge or deny him; whereas in Luke 12:8-9 we see that the Son of Man will acknowledge or deny those who acknowledge or deny Jesus. This change raises doubts as to who is responsible for the change. One could understand that Luke has altered the first person pronoun into the Son of Man; or one could take it as a pre-Lukan material.[398] Some scholars think that Luke does not use the Son of Man title independently.[399] Since, by the time of Luke's reception it might have well been a full-fledged title for Jesus, Luke perhaps faithfully hands down his sources. Though it could be possible that Luke faithfully hands down what he found in his sources, one should not neglect the redactional hand of Luke in using the term 'Son of Man.' When we try to see the Lukan use, we could indeed detect in the Son of Man sayings of Luke a new element.

A New Dimension of the Lukan Son of Man Sayings

Even if one maintains that Luke is faithfully handing down from his sources about the earthly authority and passion as well as the eschatological role of the Son of Man, one is able to see a new thrust to the Son of Man concept in Luke's Gospel. It is interesting to see that some of those Son of Man sayings in reference to the earthly ministry of Jesus are placed directly or indirectly in the context of table fellowship controversies.

Ὁ υἱὸς τοῦ ἀνθρώπου sayings that refer to the earthly ministry of Jesus are used either with the connotation of dignity and authority (Luke 5:24; 6:5; 11:30; 12:10; 19:10) or with the connotation of service (Luke 6:22; 7:34; 9:58). In Luke 5:24 however the context is the forgiving and healing of a paralytic. This immediately precedes the controversy of Jesus having table fellowship with Levi (Luke 5:27-32). The Son of Man reference in Luke 7:34 comes in the context of a comparison between John the Baptist and Jesus and the controversy once again is about the Son of Man who feels at home with eating and drinking. Though Luke is dependent here on Q, this reference fulfills his aim to present Jesus as the Son of Man in a new perspective. The Son of Man is a friend of outcasts such as tax collectors and sinners and his ministry to them is referred to in terms of his table fellowship with them. As Lindars rightly points out, the Son of Man for Luke "is a self-designation which Jesus used when speaking of his ministry to the outcasts and the tax-collectors as well as in apocalyptic contexts. He thinks of it as a special feature of Jesus' style-as indeed it was ..."[400] The Son of Man reference in Luke 19:10 has to be understood in this Lukan aim of showing Jesus as the one whose mission is to save a sinner (similar to Luke 5:24) through his eating and drinking with tax collectors (similar to Luke 7:34).

The Son of Man in Luke 19:10

It could be assumed from the above discussion that the historical Jesus used the term Son of Man and that the possibility cannot be denied that he could have understood and expressed himself in terms of 'the Son of Man' at least in some contexts if not in all the references attributed to him by the evangelists. The question which then arises is about the authenticity of the Son of Man in Luke 19:10. Should we value it as an authentic saying from Jesus or a saying faithfully handed down by Luke from his sources?

It is helpful to recall at this stage, our earlier discussion regarding the Lukan redaction of Luke 19:10,[401] where we took note of the arguments by scholars who understood Luke 19:10 as not absolutely necessary to complete the story of Zacchaeus[402] and that the story could very well end with verse 9 itself. Hence it is seen as a "christological appendage"[403] to the Zacchaeus pericope and hence later addition to the already existing story.

Hahn, who suggests that the titular usage of the Son of Man in the Gospel tradition cannot be traced back to the historical Jesus but originates from the christological conception of the early community, argues that Luke 19:10 is a free-floating saying which would have had a later origin.[404] For him Luke 19:1-10 could have been of Jewish-Hellenistic origin (and not of Palestinian origin like the Son of Man sayings about the earthly ministry of Jesus in Q and in Mark), since the story talks about Jesus' ministry of saving the lost sheep of Israel. He understands that it could have been the only Son of Man saying that was incorporated into the Gospel tradition from the Hellenistic soil. [405]

Vermès, on the other hand, posits that Luke 19:10 comes from authentic sayings of Jesus, who refers himself as the Son of Man in a circumlocutional form.[406] Marshall too observes "there is no good reason why Jesus should not have understood his mission in terms of the bringing of salvation and made the creative link between the coming of the Son of Man and the advent of salvation."[407] This argument is indeed valid. Jesus might have understood his mission as one bringing salvation to the lost. Hence the argument for the authenticity of this verse still holds good.

Some argue that Luke found the Zacchaeus pericope in his source together with v. 10,[408] while others understand that it might have been a free-floating logion, but an authentic saying of Jesus which was placed by Luke at the end of the Zacchaeus story in Luke 19:10. Lindeskog, for example, distinguishes between authenticity of form and authenticity of content. While Mk 2:17 (Luke 5:32) could be authentic both in form and in content, Lindeskog suggests Luke 19:10 is authentic only in content.[409] It is clear from the life and preaching of Jesus that he understood himself and his mission from the perspective of bringing back the people who went astray. The content of Luke 19:10 just summarizes the life of Jesus. In this way the suggestion of Lindeskog does justice to the historical Jesus and his ministry.

The question regarding the authenticity of the content however, whether the Son of Man expression in Luke 19:10 authentically coming from Jesus himself, or whether Luke found the verse in his special L source and faithfully handed down, or whether Luke added this free-floating logion together with the term Son of Man to the existing story, is difficult to answer. As Colpe says, "this much debated question hinges finally on the principle of identity and hence it is hardly possible to give an answer either way, whether Yes or No."[410] Since Luke 19:1-10 is stemming from the Lukan special L source, it is probable that Luke found the final verse of the Zacchaeus pericope together in its present form in his special L source and he faithfully passes on the story to his readers.

To understand the meaning of the phrase here, we should compare Luke 19:10 first of all with other pronouncement stories where Luke has a solemn concluding proclamation of Jesus' mission either in the first person pronoun as in the Levi narrative ("I have come to call not the righteous but sinners to repentance" Luke 5:32),[411] or with the reference to the Son of Man ("when the Son of Man comes, will he find faith on earth?" Luke 18:8). The variant text of Luke 9:56 forms a close parallel with Luke 19:10: "the Son of Man has not come to destroy the lives of human beings but to save them."[412] The similarities betray the redactional effort of the evangelist to provide a fitting climax to a particular narrative with a solemn proclamation of Jesus about his mission; above all they betray the kind of mission that the Son of Man has come for: to call and save the sinners who are lost, and were thought to be beyond the hope of redemption. The verb ἦλθεν shows that he has been sent by God with a heavenly mission. Tödt rightly points out the presence of ἦλθεν in Luke 7:34, where the Son of Man is accused of eating with tax collectors and sinners, in Luke 19:7, where the Son of Man is accused of going to be the guest of Zacchaeus the sinner and in Luke 19:10, which states his mission as precisely to seek and save the lost. This „*Gekommensein*" of the Son of Man in both texts is according to Tödt, – and rightly so – not coincidental.[413] It is deliberately paralleled by Luke in order to remind the readers about Jesus' ministry to the tax collectors and sinners, especially through his ministry of table fellowship.

This adds a new dimension to the earthly mission of the Son of Man. Son of Man has come to seek and save the rejected and the hopeless. But what is new in it is that, this saving activity of the Son of Man is deliberately emphasized by Luke through Jesus' willingness to enter into a table fellowship with the outcasts and sinners. This is what the '*Gekommensein*' of the Son of Man in Luke 5:32, 7:34 and 19:10 points out. The difference between the '*Gekommensein*' of Jesus in Luke 5:32 and in Luke 19:10 is significant. In the Levi narrative, Luke shows Jesus as having come to "call sinners to repentance." In the Zacchaeus narrative however there is no calling to repentance, but importance is given to seek and save. As Hotze says, there is a sense of urgency involved here. In this verse, one could see the nearness of Calvary and the sense of urgency in the mission of Jesus – „ein Klima der Definität, des sich nahenden Endes."⁴¹⁴ Just as Jesus as the Son of Man had the power to forgive sins (Luke 5:24), he also has the power to save the sinners and outcasts through his table fellowship (Luke 19:10). The forgiveness of sins in the third Gospel is administered in and through the person of Jesus, although it is administered in the passive voice by Jesus (ἀφέωνταί in Luke 5:20, 23; 7:47, 48). All the same the person gets forgiveness of his / her sins through his nearness to Jesus. This is the highlight of the third Gospel. The sins of the paralytic are forgiven, through the fact that he is made to come near the person of Jesus. Similarly the sinful woman is forgiven her sins, due to the fact that she comes near Jesus. The saving of Zacchaeus should be seen along the similar line. Zacchaeus is saved together with his household, due to the fact that he and his household come closer to Jesus.

The nearness to Jesus is actualized in the third Gospel through the table fellowship. It is through his table fellowship, that the saving grace of the Son of Man is expressed in the third Gospel. This fact could be corroborated with Luke 15:1-2, where Jesus is once again accused of welcoming tax collectors and sinner and eating with them. The three parables, which Jesus narrates in response to the criticism against his opponents [the parable of the lost sheep (Luke 15:3-7), lost coin (Luke 15:8-10) and the lost son (Luke 15:11-32)] climax with the joyful celebration of finding them back. A great feast is organized for the sinner-son, who has returned to the prodigal Father's house. His coming back to the father is celebrated with a feast; hence feast becomes the symbol of healing the estranged relationships between God and humans and this feast of grace is offered through the mission of the Son of Man. The table fellowship of Jesus in the third Gospel thus becomes a symbol. It is a symbol of forgiveness of sins for all those who make effort to come near Jesus. The sinful woman takes pain to meet Jesus (Luke 7:37-38). Zacchaeus takes pain to see Jesus (Luke 19:3) and further he is happy to take him to his house (Luke 19:6). Thus forgiveness and saving mission of the Son of Man through his table fellowship with sinners and outcasts has been given a fitting climax in the Zacchaeus narrative.

Ζητῆσαι καὶ Σῶσαι τὸ Ἀπολωλός

Luke 19:10 succinctly sums up at the end of the Travel Narrative the entire ministry of Jesus upto now. The Son of Man showed the onlookers that he has the power to heal and to forgive (Luke 5:24). The Son of Man showed himself and his ministry to be different from that of John the Baptist by the fact that he ate and drank and was a friend of the tax collectors and sinners (7:34; 15:1-2) and the Son of Man now shows ultimately what his mission is. His mission of coming to the house of Zacchaeus is a divine mandate; ultimately his mission of seeking and saving the lost is indeed a symbol of God's own mission of shepherding the flock.

Saving the Ἀπολωλός: the Lukan Concern

The abundant use of the word in the Gospel shows Luke's deep-seated interest in those in the house of Israel who are considered to be lost.[415] We saw earlier that the work of shepherds was considered menial among the Jews. But right from the infancy narrative onwards Luke portrays shepherds in a very positive light. It is to them that the message of the birth of the savior is first announced. By showing the shepherds as the first receivers of the Good news of the birth of the Messiah, Luke has shown right from the beginning that there is a reversal of favors. God reaches out not to those who consider themselves righteous but to the outcasts of society. At the end of the Travel Narrative, before his entry into Jerusalem Jesus once again announces that his mission is seeking and saving the lost (as prophesied by Ezek 34:16).[416] This important mission of a shepherd is stated already indirectly in the controversy story of Jesus eating at the house of Levi (Luke 5:32). In response to the same question by his adversaries, why he eats with tax collectors and sinners, Jesus answers with three parables, one of which shows the joy of a shepherd in finding the lost sheep (Luke 15:3-7). The basic structure of all the three parables is losing something, finding it back and a joyful celebration. The use of the word ἀπόλλυμι in this chapter is noteworthy (Luke 15:4, 6, 8, 9, 17, 24, 32). In Jesus God encounters his people as a good shepherd. What was told in the parables about God seeking the lost ones (Luke 15:1-32), is being actualized in the story of Zacchaeus. Zacchaeus is one of the lost sheep of Israel who is found by the shepherd God, who rejoices over his return. Jesus fulfils God's role of saving the lost through his table fellowship with Zacchaeus.

We find however, a significant difference between Ezek 34:16 and Luke 19:10. Luke has added the word σῶσαι. With this addition Luke shows that the mission of Jesus involves not just bringing back the lost sheep but also saving them. This recalls the previous verse, where Jesus spoke of σωτηρία that has come to the house of Zacchaeus. The birth of the savior (σωτήρ in Luke 2:11) was proclaimed to the shepherds (the outcasts of the society) who were guarding their flock (ἐπὶ τὴν ποίμνην αὐτῶν in Luke 2:8). What has been proclaimed to them that day (σήμερον in Luke 2:11) has been actualized in the household of Zacchaeus. God as a shepherd in the person of Jesus visits his sheep especially those who were stranded astray (Ezek 34:16). The mission of the Son of Man is to seek and save the lost sheep of Israel and to bring them back to the sonship of Abraham.

Vv. 9-10: Concluding Remarks

The words used in the final verses have been carefully selected by Luke with the clear intention to link the 'saving' of Zacchaeus by Jesus with the joy of finding the lost sheep (Luke 15:3-7), lost coin (Luke 15:8-10) and the lost son (Luke 15:11-32); it is also connected with the saving of the "daughter of Abraham" (Luke 13:16) and with the tax collector Levi (Luke 5:27-32). The sonship of Abraham is dependent not only on the biological heritage of Zacchaeus; it depends much more on the Abrahamic faith with which Zacchaeus wanted to see Jesus; the sonship of Abraham is also to be seen from his joyful reception of Jesus, just like Abraham received the heavenly guests in his tent. The salvation that is offered to Zacchaeus is not just to the individual but also to the household; its effects would reach out to the poor as well as to those who have been affected by the dishonest behavior of the chief tax collector. The mission of the Son of Man in saving the lost is once again accomplished in Luke 19:10 through his table fellowship with the outcasts as it was in Luke 7:34 and 15:1-2.

Overview

Luke 4:16-21 begins with the kerygmatic proclamation of Jesus and Luke 19:1-10 sums up the Galilean ministry of Jesus and the vibrations that it created in the Jewish society at the time. The character of Zacchaeus "prefigures the course of Christian history in which religious outcasts would repent, give to the poor and be saved, over the objections of those who deemed themselves righteous."[417] It is therefore a paradigm for the Lukan community, the way, through which the community could be saved. The importance of the story of Zacchaeus is seen from the fact that Luke has tried to squeeze in these ten verses all the themes, which he thought very important to the Gospel. This is seen from the fact that all the important words dear to Luke are put together in this pericope like δεῖ, χαίρων, and that too, some of them twice – σήμερον, σωτηρία, σπεύσας.

From the perspective of the word analysis, we could divide significant words which Luke has used in to three main categories:

1. First of all, there are four words / phrases in this story, that are *hapax* in the New Testament:

    a. The phrase ὀνόματι καλούμενος points out to the fact that the character in question – Zacchaeus – is important for Luke. Whereas all other rich men in the Gospel are not given a proper name, this rich man has been given a name. That itself shows that the character is essential for the episode as well as for the entire Gospel.

    b. Apart from the proper name Ζακχαῖος, the profession of the character ἀρχιτελώνης is a *hapax* in the New Testament too. This ἀρχιτελώνης forms the summation of all the tax collector material in the third Gospel. Through this *hapax* use, Luke perhaps wants to make a comparison between the joyful acceptance of Jesus by the ἀρχιτελώνης over against the rejection of Jesus shown by the ἀρχόντων [τῶν] Φαρισαίων on the one side, and by the ἀρχιερεῖς on the other. While Zacchaeus was a social and religious outcast the other two were renowned men of the society and religion. By accepting Jesus, Zacchaeus becomes the climax character of all those who accept Jesus' message. Through his repentance Zacchaeus shows himself worthy of his name, and is ready to make himself 'clean' and 'righteous.'

c. The tree on which Zacchaeus climbs is also a *hapax* in the New Testament. The συκομορέα tree, belonging to the family of figs, similar to the one found in 17:6 (συκαμίνος), has its connection with the dishonesty (ἐσυκοφάντησα, Luke 19:8) with which Zacchaeus prospered in his profession. Similarly, τετραπλοῦν is a *hapax* in the New Testament. Through the use of many *hapax* words in a small pericope like 19:1-10, Luke has conclusively shown the significance of the pericope for his entire Gospel.

2. Secondly, apart from the *hapax* words, the words which are central to Luke's Gospel message, are cited twice within this short narrative of ten verses: the mention of Jesus entering into Jericho (εἰσελθών, v. 1) and going into the house of Zacchaeus (εἰσῆλθεν, v. 7); his passing through Jericho (διήρχετο v. 1, - διέρχεσθαι v. 4); the command of Jesus to come down immediately (σπεύσας κατάβηθι v. 5) and the faithful obedience of Zacchaeus (σπεύσας κατέβη v. 6), the narrator's mention of Jesus as κύριος and Zacchaeus' recognition and address of Jesus as κύριε (v. 8), the mention of ἰδοὺ in v. 2 and in v. 8, the reference to the salvific σήμερον in verse 5 and in verse

9, the reference in vv. 9-10 to the saving act of Jesus (σῶσαι), salvation (σωτηρία), which has come to the house (τῷ οἴκῳ) of Zacchaeus (v. 5, 9) and the seeking of Zacchaeus (ἐζήτει v. 3) to see Jesus and Jesus' seeking of the lost (ζητῆσαι v. 10). These words show the readers that the themes of "salvation" that is granted "today" to the "house" of Zacchaeus are actually the themes which are spread throughout the entire Gospel. Hence the entire ministry of Jesus so far has been summed up in this important episode through these words.

3. There are also other distinctive words put together in Luke 19:1-10, which are central to the message of the third Gospel. The phrase ἡλικίᾳ μικρός has reminded the reader of the inner lack (moral shortness) that Zacchaeus suffers from and his effort to remedy this lack by climbing a tree and trying to seek Jesus. This shortness of Zacchaeus and his consequent acceptance by Jesus also takes one right back to the Magnificat where the lowly are said to be exalted (Luke 1:52).[418] In the mention of the ὄχλος we see the distance the evangelist keeps from the crowd. As it was elsewhere in the Gospel, especially for the blind beggar (Luke 18:39), the crowd becomes hindrance not only for Zacchaeus to see Jesus, but also a hindrance for Jesus to enter into the house of Zacchaeus. But it has been a divine mission for Jesus (δεῖ), that he stays at the house of Zacchaeus (μεῖναι) who actually is the υἱὸς Ἀβραάμ because of his reception of Jesus and his faith in him. In the words of Craddock, "Jesus' visit in Zacchaeus' house was not a delay or a detour on his journey to Jerusalem. This was and is the very purpose of his journey"[419] – to save the lost son of Abraham. Through the use of the words central to the entire Gospel in this episode, which stands right at the doorsteps of Jerusalem, where Jesus would be glorified, Luke climaxes Jesus' Travel Narrative and his Galilean and Judean ministry with the episode of Zacchaeus.

Salvation through a Meal

There are two important words that take the Zacchaeus story to another level: μεῖναι and ὑπεδέξατο. The study of μεῖναι has substantiated that Jesus wanted to stay at least that night by Zacchaeus, if not for a longer period of time. The use of the word ὑπεδέξατο which relates to a meal in 10:38 has led the reader to understand that Luke refers to a meal scene also in 19:6 although indirectly. Hence Jesus´ intention to stay at the house of Zacchaeus and Zacchaeus' joyful reception of Jesus lead both to solemn meal – a meal similar to the meal of Levi (Luke 5:28-32). It has helped to compare the meal of Jesus with the meal narratives of Jesus with three Pharisees (Luke 7:36-50; 11:37-54; 14:1-24). Although Jesus was at the house of these three Pharisees, the household did not receive either salvation or healing except the lowly and the sinful woman who expressed her remorse and thankfulness by her tears and the man with a dropsy (7:36-50; 14:2-4). In contrast to the reception of the Pharisees, who considered themselves to be righteous, Zacchaeus shows his remorse and thankfulness not only by what he is going to do, but also through a meal to which he welcomes Jesus joyfully. The discussion in 19:7-10 could actually be understood as the συμπόσιον part of the meal. The criticism of the Pharisees and the scribes that he eats and drinks with tax collectors gets actualized in the episode of Zacchaeus. Precisely this gesture of Jesus and his participation at a meal with the chief tax collector brings Zacchaeus nearer to Jesus, makes him realize the Lordship of Jesus and obtain salvation not just for himself but for his entire household.

Jericho, the industrial city of the time, which was thriving in economy, had a rare sight on the day when Jesus came to it. In this affluent city, the rich tax collector wants to see who Jesus is and is able to recognize him as κύριος, which is the same title which the evangelist and his community use, to address Jesus. In this way, Zacchaeus is already shown to be part of the believing community. From the part of Jesus, he goes through the city and seeks to stay at the house of Zacchaeus because it is his divinely-ordained mission "to seek and save the lost."

Hence Zacchaeus, whose profession as the chief tax collector brands him as the 'sinner supreme' in the eyes of the Jews, whose affluence brands him in the eyes of the readers of the Gospel as someone *unsaveable*, actually receives salvation. This was possible because of the arrival of Jesus in Jericho, his willingness to stay with Zacchaeus on the one hand, and because of the joyful acceptance of Jesus by Zacchaeus and his willingness to repent his previous ways on the other. The words used by Luke in this episode have conclusively shown that what was impossible has indeed been possible for God (18:27); a rich man could be saved, provided he receives Jesus and handles his riches prudently (cf. 12:33-34; 16:1-9; 19:11). For Zacchaeus, it was possible with his meeting with Jesus and with his table fellowship.

Endnotes

[1] A. McGowan, "The Meals of Jesus and the Meals of the Church: Eucharistic Origins and Admission to Communion," in *Studia Liturgica Diversa: Essays in Honor of Paul F. Bradshaw*, ed. P. F. Bradshaw, M. E. Johnson and L. E. Phillips, *Studies in church music and liturgy* (Portland, Or.: Pastoral Press, 2004), 105.

[2] F. Bovon, *Das Evangelium nach Lukas*, Evangelisch-katholischer Kommentar zum Neuen Testament III/3 (Düsseldof, Zürich: Benziger, 2001), 271; cf. also his English commentary, F. Bovon, H. Koester, and D. S. Deer, *Luke 2: A Commentary on the Gospel of Luke 9:51—19:27*, Hermeneia - A Critical and Historical Commentary on the Bible (Minneapolis, MN: Fortress Press, 2013), 586; J. Reiling and J. L. Swellengrebel, *A Translator's Handbook on the Gospel of Luke* (Leiden: E. J. Brill, 1971), 615; J. O'Hanlon, "The Story of Zacchaeus and the Lukan Ethic," *JSNT* 4, no. 12 (1981), 4; M. Zerwick and M. Grosvenor, *A Grammatical Analysis of the Greek New Testament* (Roma: Editrice Pontificio Istituto Biblico, 1993), 257.

[3] P. Kariamadam, *The Zacchaeus Story (Lk 19:1-10): A Redaction-Critical Investigation* (Kerala: Pontifical Institute of Theology and Philosophy, 1985), 7. Godet is of the opinion that Luke faithfully hands down an Aramaic source. F. L. Godet, *A Commentary on the Gospel of St. Luke*, 2 Volumes in 1 (Michigan: Zondervan Publishing House, 1887), 2, 216.

[4] H. I. Marshall, W. W. Gasque, and D. A. Hagner, *The Gospel of Luke: A Commentary on the Greek Text*, 696; similar view could also be found in D. A. S. Ravens, "Zacchaeus: The Final Part of a Lucan Triptych?," *JSNT*, no. 41 (1991), 29.

[5] J. O'Hanlon, "The Story of Zacchaeus and the Lukan Ethic." 12.

[6] F. Bovon, *Das Evangelium nach Lukas*, 272; A. Plummer, *A Critical and Exegetical Commentary on the Gospel According to S. Luke*, 433; P. Kariamadam, *The Zacchaeus Story (Lk 19:1-10)*, 7.

[7] P. Kariamadam, *The Zacchaeus Story (Lk 19:1-10)*, 7.

[8] A. Plummer, *A Critical and Exegetical Commentary on the Gospel According to S. Luke*, 433. The 9th cent codex Θ, and a few Italian manuscripts actually extend the second clause of v. 2b καν αΡτχς πλο{σιος as καν αΡτχς ἦν πλο{σιος.

[9] In fact, one finds numerous places where the phrase appears: the following uses of καν αΡτγς in the third Gospel alone could convince us about the interest of Luke for this term. Luke 1:17, 22; 2:28; 3:23; 4:15; 5:1,14, 17, 34; 6:20; 8:1, 22; 9:51; 15:14; 16:24; 17:11, 16; 19:2; 19:9; 22:41; 24:15, 25, 28; cf. ibid., 149.

[10] M. M. Culy, M. C. Parsons, and J. J. Stigall, *Luke: A Handbook on the Greek Text*, Baylor handbook on the Greek New Testament (Waco, Tex.: Baylor University Press, 2010), 587.

[11] J. Nolland, *Luke: 18:35-24:53*, Word biblical commentary 35 C (Dallas, Texas: Word Books Publisher, 2002), 905; H. I. Marshall, W. W. Gasque, and D. A. Hagner, *The Gospel of Luke: A Commentary on the Greek Text*, 696; F. Bovon, *Das Evangelium nach Lukas*, 273; P. Kariamadam, *The Zacchaeus Story (Lk 19:1-10)*, 18.

[12] J. A. Fitzmyer, *The Gospel According to Luke X-XXIV*, 1223, the emphasis is mine; also M. M. Culy, M. C. Parsons, and J. J. Stigall, *Luke*, 588.

[13] F. Bovon, *Das Evangelium nach Lukas*, no. 50, 273; J. A. Fitzmyer, *The Gospel According to Luke X-XXIV*, 1223-1224; For Kariamadam the phrase has an Aramaic source which has been used by the evangelist. P. Kariamadam, *The Zacchaeus Story (Lk 19:1-10)*, 18.

[14] H. I. Marshall, W. W. Gasque, and D. A. Hagner, *The Gospel of Luke: A Commentary on the Greek Text*, 697.

[15] W. Willker, "A Textual Commentary on the Greek Gospels," *Luke*, last modified 2015, http://www-user.uni-bremen.de/~wie/ TCG/TC-Luke.pdf, 456, accessed on 30.05.2015.

[16] Levinsohn as cited in M. M. Culy, M. C. Parsons, and J. J. Stigall, *Luke*, 25.

[17] F. Blass, A. Debrunner, and R. W. Funk, *A Greek Grammar of the New Testament and Other Early Christian Literature* (Chicago: University of Chicago Press, 1961), 91.

[18] Cf. U. Kellermann, "%μισυς," in *Exegetical Dictionary of the New Testament*, ed. H. Balz and G. Schneider (Grand Rapids, Mich.: Eerdmans, 1990-1993), 122.

[19] M. M. Culy, M. C. Parsons, and J. J. Stigall, *Luke*, 591.

[20] A. Plummer, *A Critical and Exegetical Commentary on the Gospel According to S. Luke*, 438.

²¹ J. B. Green, *The Gospel of Luke*, The new international commentary on the New Testament (Grand Rapids, Mich.: W.B. Eerdmans Pub. Co., 1997), 677; J. A. Fitzmyer, *The Gospel According to Luke X-XXIV*, 1233; J. Dillersberger, *The Gospel of Saint Luke*, 443; J. M. Creed, *The Gospel According to St. Luke* (London: Macmillan, 1942), 233; J. P. Kealy, *Luke's Gospel Today*, 360; W. Manson, *The Gospel of Luke*, 212; R. Summers, *Commentary on Luke: Jesus, the Universal Savior* (Waco, Tex.: Word Books, 1972), 225.

²² For Bovon Luke 19:1-10 and vv. 11-27 are thematically connected, since both the pericopes deal with the theme of salvation and in both the texts the main character is on the journey. Cf. F. Bovon, *Das Evangelium nach Lukas*, 283.

²³ J. A. Fitzmyer, *The Gospel According to Luke X-XXIV*, 1228.

²⁴ M. Miyoshi, *Der Anfang des Reiseberichts Lk 9,51-10,24: Eine Redaktionsgeschichtliche Untersuchung*, Analecta Biblica 60 (Rome: Biblical Institute Press, 1974), 145; also A. Plummer, *A Critical and Exegetical Commentary on the Gospel According to S. Luke*, 438.

²⁵ M. Miyoshi, *Der Anfang des Reiseberichts Lk 9,51-10,24*, 146.

²⁶ J. Jeremias, *The Parables of Jesus*, 3rd ed. (London: S.C.M. Press, 1972), 58. Ernst too suggests that 19:11-27 is independent from the story of Zacchaeus: J. Ernst, *Das Evangelium nach Lukas*, 512; Hotze, *Jesus als Gast*, 49.

²⁷ W. Manson, *The Gospel of Luke*, 212; cf. also H. I. Marshall, W. W. Gasque, and D. A. Hagner, *The Gospel of Luke: A Commentary on the Greek Text*, 703.

²⁸ H. I. Marshall, W. W. Gasque, and D. A. Hagner, *The Gospel of Luke: A Commentary on the Greek Text*, 695.

²⁹ J. B. Green, *The Gospel of Luke*, 666-667; W. Manson, *The Gospel of Luke*, 209; E. Arens, *The Hlthon-Sayings in the Synoptic Tradition: A Historico-Critical Investigation*, OBO 10 (Freiburg, Schweiz: Universitätsverlag, 1976), 161; C. F. Evans, *Saint Luke*, TPI New Testament commentaries (London, Philadelphia: SCM Press; Trinity Press International, 1990), 660; J. Ernst, *Das Evangelium nach Lukas*, 512; J. M. Creed, *The Gospel According to St. Luke*, 228; F. B. Craddock, *Luke*, Interpretation, a Bible commentary for teaching and preaching (Louisville, Ky.: John Knox Press, 1990), 218; M. Miyoshi, *Der Anfang des Reiseberichts Lk 9,51-10,24*, 146; A. Plummer, *A Critical and Exegetical Commentary on the Gospel According to S. Luke*, 432; P. Kariamadam, *The Zacchaeus Story (Lk 19:1-10)*, 62-63; E. LaVerdiere, *Dining in the Kingdom of God*, 109.

³⁰ E. LaVerdiere, *Dining in the Kingdom of God*, 110.

³¹ As cited in J. M. Creed, *The Gospel According to St. Luke*, 229.

³² Hotze, *Jesus als Gast*, 52; Arens, *The Çlthon-Sayings in the Synoptic Tradition*, 161; J. B. Green, *The Gospel of Luke*, 666-667; C. F. Evans, *Saint Luke*, 660; J. Ernst, *Das Evangelium nach Lukas*, 512; F. B. Craddock, *Luke*, 218; J. P. Kealy, *Luke's Gospel Today*, 360; W. Grundmann, *Das Evangelium nach Lukas*, 358; W. Wiefel, *Das Evangelium nach Lukas*, 326.

[33] J. Ernst, *Das Evangelium nach Lukas*, 512.

[34] J. A. Fitzmyer, *The Gospel According to Luke I-IX*, 134-142; L. T. Johnson, *The Gospel of Luke: ed. Harrington, J. Daniel*, Sacra pagina series 3 (Collegeville, Minn.: Liturgical Press, 1991), 14-15; D. L. Bock, *Luke*, 20.

[35] This research does not go into details about the artificiality and 'geographical insensitivity' of Luke that scholars find in the Lukan Travel Narrative. The different travel indicators (9:51-53, 56-57; 10:1, 17, 38; 13:22, 31-33; 14:25; 17:11; 18:31, 35; 19:1, 11, 28, 41), illustrate that Luke intends to connect the material in the middle section of his Gospel into one single travel unit. For a general overview of the discrepancies in the Travel Narrative, cf. C. C. McCown, "The Geography of Luke's Central Section," *JBL* 57, 51-66 (1938), 51-66; D. P. Moessner, *Lord of the Banquet: The Literary and Theological Significance of the Lukan Travel Narrative* (Minneapolis: Fortress Press, 1989), 13ff.

[36] F. Bovon, *Das Evangelium nach Lukas*, 266; D. Gill, "Observations on the Lukan Travel Narrative and Some Related Passages," *The Harvard Theological Review* 63, no. 2 (1970), 199; J. Dillersberger, *The Gospel of Saint Luke*, 440.

[37] T. W. Manson, *The Sayings of Jesus: As Recorded in the Gospels According to St. Matthew and St. Luke* (London: SCM Press, 1971), 282; cf. also J. A. Fitzmyer, *The Gospel According to Luke X-XXIV*, 1072; F. Bovon, *Das Evangelium nach Lukas*, 266.

[38] J. A. Fitzmyer, *The Gospel According to Luke X-XXIV*, 1072.

[39] T. W. Manson, *The Sayings of Jesus*, 282.

[40] J. Ernst, *Das Evangelium nach Lukas*, 512; J. P. Heil, *The Meal Scenes in Luke-Acts*, 162.

[41] J. P. Heil, *The Meal Scenes in Luke-Acts*, 161.

[42] W. Wiefel, *Das Evangelium nach Lukas*, 326; J. A. Fitzmyer, *The Gospel According to Luke X-XXIV*, 1219; J. P. Heil, *The Meal Scenes in Luke-Acts*, 16; F. Bovon, *Das Evangelium nach Lukas*, 266. C. F. Evans, *Saint Luke*, 661; looking at the similarities, Bultmann suggests that the story of Zacchaeus might have been an "imaginary, and extended version" of Mk 2:14. R. Bultmann, *The History of the Synoptic Tradition* (New York: Harper & Row, 1963), 32. Other scholars like J. M. Creed posit the same. "The hospitality of Zacchaeus is to the hospitality of Levi what the healing of the ten lepers is to the healing of the leper of Mark i.40f." J. M. Creed, *The Gospel According to St. Luke*, 229.

[43] The comparison that is presented here is a modified version of the one found in Kariamadam's redactional analysis of the story of Zacchaeus. P. Kariamadam, *The Zacchaeus Story (Lk 19:1-10)*, 50-51. Similar comparison could also be seen in Hotze, *Jesus als Gast*, 55; C. H. Talbert, *Reading Luke: A Literary and Theological Commentary on the Third Gospel*, [Reading the New Testament series] (New York: Crossroad, 1982), 176.

⁴⁴ Tannehill too suggests that table fellowship of Jesus with the two tax collectors form an inclusion to the three banquet narratives, where Jesus is said to have reclined with ~~Pharices~~Pharisees. Cf. R. C. Tannehill, *The Narrative Unity of Luke-Acts*, 107.

⁴⁵ P. Kariamadam, *The Zacchaeus Story (Lk 19:1-10)*, 52.

⁴⁶ Cf. D. Hamm, "Luke 19:8 Once Again: Does Zacchaeus Defend or Resolve?," *JBL* 107, no. 3 (1988), 436-437.

⁴⁷ The parallels are again a modified form of what Kariamadam presents to us: P. Kariamadam, *The Zacchaeus Story (Lk 19:1-10)*, 32. Kariamadam takes it from Schneider. F. Schneider, *Jesus, der Prophet*, Orbis biblicus et orientalis 2 (Freiburg/Schweiz, Göttingen: Universitätsverlag; Vandenhoeck & Ruprecht, 1973), 118. For a similar view, cf. also J. Ernst, *Das Evangelium nach Lukas*, 512; B. Byrne, *The Hospitality of God*, 152; J. P. Heil, *The Meal Scenes in Luke-Acts*, 161.

⁴⁸ E. E. Ellis, *The Gospel of Luke*, The Century Bible (London: Nelson, 1966), 221.

⁴⁹ E. La Verdiere, *Luke* (Wilmington, Delaware: Michael Glazier, 1980), 225.

⁵⁰ R. Dillmann and C. Mora Paz, *Das Lukas-Evangelium*, 324-325.

⁵¹ P. Kariamadam, *The Zacchaeus Story (Lk 19:1-10)*, 54-56.

⁵² For the chiastic structure of Meynet and for the loopholes in it cf. R. F. O'Toole, "The Literary Form of Luke 19:1-10," *JBL* 110, no. 1 (1991) 111.

⁵³ H. Klein, *Barmherzigkeit Gegenüber den Elenden und Geächteten*, 69-70.

⁵⁴ R. F. O'Toole, "The Literary Form of Luke 19:1-10." 113.

⁵⁵ R. Bultmann, *The History of the Synoptic Tradition*, 57. Further on biographical apothegm cf. J. Kremer, *Lukasevangelium*, 183; Herrenbrück, *Jesus und die Zöllner*, 228.

⁵⁶ R. Bultmann, *The History of the Synoptic Tradition*, 57.

⁵⁷ J. A. Fitzmyer, *The Gospel According to Luke X-XXIV*, 1219.

⁵⁸ V. Taylor, *The Formation of the Gospel Tradition* (London: Macmillan and co. limited, 1957), 63.

⁵⁹ Ibid., 76.

⁶⁰ Dibelius opines that though the historicity of the character cannot be guaranteed, one cannot doubt the historicity of the incident. M. Dibelius, *From Tradition to Gospel* (New York,: Charles scribner's Sons, 1935), 118; O'Hanlon also observes there are no reasons, which are convincing to reject the historicity of the event. J. O'Hanlon, "The Story of Zacchaeus and the Lukan Ethic." 8.

⁶¹ C. H. Talbert, *Reading Luke*, 176; also P. Kariamadam, *The Zacchaeus Story (Lk 19:1-10)*, 53.

⁶² R. F. O'Toole, "The Literary Form of Luke 19:1-10.", 109.

⁶³ For Godet, the word 0δοæ has to be understood as to present something unexpected; through the use of this word, Zacchaeus reveals something that was till now unknown to the bystanders. F. L. Godet, *A Commentary on the Gospel*

of St. Luke, 2, 217. Fitzmyer too understands the words of Zacchaeus not as a futuristic but a customary action. J. A. Fitzmyer, *The Gospel According to Luke X-XXIV*, 1225. For a similar argument cf. R. F. O'Toole, "The Literary Form of Luke 19:1-10." 108.

[64] F. L. Godet, *A Commentary on the Gospel of St. Luke*, 2, 218.

[65] R. C. White, "Vindication for Zacchaeus?," *Exp Tim* 91 (1979), 21; also D. A. S. Ravens, "Zacchaeus.", 19-32.

[66] The words are from Hamm who holds it is NOT a vindication story but a conversion story. D. Hamm, "Luke 19:8 Once Again." 433. For a similar view A. C. Mitchell, "Zacchaeus Revisited: Luke 19,8 as a Defense," *Biblica* 71 (1990), 153-176.

[67] Plummer says, if one takes v. 8 as a defense, then it projects Zacchaeus as boasting himself for his good works. A. Plummer, *A Critical and Exegetical Commentary on the Gospel According to S. Luke*, 435; Ellis too thinks the story revolves around the conversion of Zacchaeus. E. E. Ellis, *The Gospel of Luke*, 221; also H. I. Marshall, W. W. Gasque, and D. A. Hagner, *The Gospel of Luke: A Commentary on the Greek Text*, 698; J. Ernst, *Das Evangelium nach Lukas*, 512-513; D. Hamm, "Luke 19:8 Once Again." 431-437; cf. also his later article, D. Hamm, "Zacchaeus Revisited Once More: A Story of Vindication or Conversion?," *Biblica* 72 (1991), 249-252.

[68] F. L. Godet, *A Commentary on the Gospel of St. Luke*, 218.

[69] Cf. N. M. Watson, "Was Zacchaeus Really Reforming?," *Expository Times* 77 (1965-1966), 282.

[70] T. Zahn, *Das Evangelium des Lucas*, 1st ed., Kommentar zum Neuen Testament Bd. 3 (Leipzig: Deichert, 1913), 622.

[71] N. M. Watson, "Was Zacchaeus Really Reforming?" 282-283.

[72] D. Hamm, "Luke 19:8 Once Again." 436.

[73] Ibid., 437.

[74] F. Bovon, *Das Evangelium nach Lukas*, 269.

[75] R. C. Tannehill, *The Narrative Unity of Luke-Acts*, 111; also his article, R. C. Tannehill, "The Story of Zacchaeus as Rhetoric: Luke 19:1-10," in *The Rhetoric of Pronouncement*, ed. V. K. Robbins, *Semeia* 64 (Atlanta, GA: Scholars Press, 1994), 201-202; R. F. O'Toole, "The Literary Form of Luke 19:1-10." 108; also Hotze, *Jesus als Gast*, 56-57.

[76] R. F. O'Toole, "The Literary Form of Luke 19:1-10." 108.

[77] J. Bolyki, *Jesu Tischgemeinschaften*, 112; cf. for a similar view, J. P. Heil, *The Meal Scenes in Luke-Acts*, 205.

[78] R. Bultmann, *The History of the Synoptic Tradition*, 34.

[79] J. Bolyki, *Jesu Tischgemeinschaften*, 109-110.

[80] In his words, „Eimalige Nennung eines Mannes als Hauptperson einer Legende verdächtigt die Geschichtlichkeit der Figur nicht ... Das gilt auch für die Geschichte von Zachäus, Luke 19, 1-10." Elsewhere regarding the story of Zacchaeus he says „manche von ... Legenden sind nur in besonderer Verehrung frommer Personen ausgeformt, haben aber gewiß ihren letzten Grund in geschichtlicher Wirklichkeit." M. Dibelius, *Die Formgeschichte des Evangeliums*, 6th ed. (Tübingen: Mohr Siebeck, 1971), 115, 293.

[81] E. Hirsch, *Die Vorlagen des Lukas und das Sondergut des Matthäus*, Frühgeschichte des Evangeliums 2 (Tübingen: Mohr, 1941), 232; Grundmann and others agree with Hirsch in this point. W. Grundmann, *Das Evangelium nach Lukas*, 359. Also F. Bovon, *Das Evangelium nach Lukas*, 271; J. A. Fitzmyer, *The Gospel According to Luke X-XXIV*, 1219; H. I. Marshall, W. W. Gasque, and D. A. Hagner, *The Gospel of Luke: A Commentary on the Greek Text*, 695; J. O'Hanlon, "The Story of Zacchaeus and the Lukan Ethic." 9.

[82] W. Grundmann, *Das Evangelium nach Lukas*, 358; W. Wiefel, *Das Evangelium nach Lukas*, 326; J. Ernst, *Das Evangelium nach Lukas*, 388; Hotze, *Jesus als Gast*, 53.

[83] F. Bovon, *Das Evangelium nach Lukas*, 269; J. A. Fitzmyer, *The Gospel According to Luke X-XXIV*, 1219; P. Kariamadam, *The Zacchaeus Story (Lk 19:1-10)*, 11.

[84] T. Schramm, *Der Markus-Stoff bei Lukas: Eine Literarkritische und Redaktionsgeschichtliche Untersuchung*, Society for New Testament Studies. Monograph series. no. 14. (Cambridge: University Press, 1971), 143-144; cf. also H. I. Marshall, W. W. Gasque, and D. A. Hagner, *The Gospel of Luke: A Commentary on the Greek Text*, 695.

[85] H. I. Marshall, W. W. Gasque, and D. A. Hagner, *The Gospel of Luke: A Commentary on the Greek Text*, 695.

[86] Bovon takes v. 8 as part of the original tradition. He says, the word order in v. 8 – the placing of μου in between the two nouns (τρ !μωσιq μου τὸν Qπαρχγντων), is foreign to Luke. F. Bovon, *Das Evangelium nach Lukas*, 270. Klein has a different opinion: for him it is v. 7 that seems to be secondary rather than v. 8. He says it is Luke who has added the murmuring of all, as he also did in 7:49 and 15:1. This murmuring is the human response to Jesus´ acceptance of sinners. H. Klein, *Barmherzigkeit Gegenüber den Elenden und Geächteten*, 69.

[87] R. Bultmann, *The History of the Synoptic Tradition*, 33-34; E. Hirsch, *Die Vorlagen des Lukas und das Sondergut des Matthäus*, 231; J. Ernst, *Das Evangelium nach Lukas*, 388; W. Grundmann, *Das Evangelium nach Lukas*, 358; W. Wiefel, *Das Evangelium nach Lukas*, 326; J. A. Fitzmyer, *The Gospel According to Luke X-XXIV*, 1219; H. I. Marshall, W. W. Gasque, and D. A. Hagner, *The Gospel of Luke: A Commentary on the Greek Text*, 695; C. H. Talbert, *Reading Luke*, 176; P. Kariamadam, *The Zacchaeus Story (Lk 19:1-10)*, 38.

[88] R. Bultmann, *The History of the Synoptic Tradition*, 34; F. Bovon, *Das Evangelium nach Lukas*, 269; W. Wiefel, *Das Evangelium nach Lukas*, 326; H. Klein, *Barmherzigkeit Gegenüber den Elenden und Geächteten*, 69; P. Kariamadam,

The Zacchaeus Story (Lk 19:1-10), 48; B. Lindars, *Jesus Son of Man: A Fresh Examination of the Son of Man Sayings in the Gospels in the Light of Recent Research* (London: SPCK, 1983), 137; W. Schenk, *Das biographische Ich-Idiom "Menschensohn" in den frühen Jesus-Biographien: Der Ausdruck, seine Codes und seine Rezeptionen in ihren Kotexten*, Forschungen zur Religion und Literatur des Alten und Neuen Testaments 177 (Göttingen: Vandenhoeck & Ruprecht, 1997), 180. Fitzmyer suggests that although v. 10 is a secondary addition, it could not have come from Luke himself. He says Luke must have found it already added in the pre-Lukan tradition. V. 10 would have been uttered by Jesus himself at some point of time, which has been incorporated in this section by Luke. Its original context is unknown to us. J. A. Fitzmyer, *The Gospel According to Luke X-XXIV*, 1219-1220.

[89] E. Hirsch, *Die Vorlagen des Lukas und das Sondergut des Matthäus*, 231; W. Grundmann, *Das Evangelium nach Lukas*, 359.

[90] E. Hirsch, *Die Vorlagen des Lukas und das Sondergut des Matthäus*, 232; Along the similar line Hotze also suggests that the presence of σημερον in v. 5 and 9a is from the hand of the redactor (as in 2:11; 4:21; 5:26; 23:43), and hence not from the original story; cf. Hotze, *Jesus als Gast*, 54.

[91] P. Kariamadam, *The Zacchaeus Story (Lk 19:1-10)*, 34.

[92] Ibid., 39.

[93] F. L. Godet, *A Commentary on the Gospel of St. Luke*, 2, 216.

[94] F. Bovon, H. Koester, and D. S. Deer, *Luke 2*, 592.

[95] Ibid., 592.

[96] G. Yamasaki, "Point of View in a Gospel Story: What Difference Does It Make?: Luke 19:1-10 as a Test Case," *JBL* 125, no. 1 (2006), 97-98.

[97] R. C. Tannehill, "The Story of Zacchaeus as Rhetoric." 202.

[98] Luke uses the word as many as 50 times in his Gospel and 32 times in Acts, while we find the word 30 times in Mark and 36 times in Matthew. Cf. P. Kariamadam, *The Zacchaeus Story (Lk 19:1-10)*, no. 9, 2.

[99] Cf. J. Schneider, "εισέρχομαι," in *Theological Dictionary of the New Testament*, ed. G. Kittel, G. W. Bromiley & G. Friedrich, 10 vols. (Michigan: Grand Rapids; Eerdmans, 1964-1976), 2, 677; H. Weder, "εισέρχομαι," in *Exegetical Dictionary of the New Testament*, ed. H. Balz and G. Schneider, 3 vols. (Grand Rapids: Eerdmans, 1990-1993), 1, 400-401.

[100] J. Schneider, "εισέρχομαι." 676-678; also P. Kariamadam, *The Zacchaeus Story (Lk 19:1-10)*, 3.

[101] Cf. U. Busse, "διέρχομαι," in H. Balz and G. Schneider, *Exegetical Dictionary of the New Testament*, 1, 322-323; also J. O'Hanlon, "The Story of Zacchaeus and the Lukan Ethic." 2; P. Kariamadam, *The Zacchaeus Story (Lk 19:1-10)*, 4.

[102] Luke's preference for the verb διέρχομαι becomes even more clear, when

we note that in Luke 9:6 he adds διυρχοντο to his Markan source (cf. Mk 6:12), perhaps to parallel their preaching ministry of the disciples with the preaching and healing ministry of Jesus.

[103] U. Busse, "διέρχομαι." 323; also P. Kariamadam, *The Zacchaeus Story (Lk 19:1-10)*, 4.

[104] J. Reiling and J. L. Swellengrebel, *A Translator's Handbook on the Gospel of Luke*, 615; also J. Dillersberger, *The Gospel of Saint Luke*, 440; J. Ernst, *Das Evangelium nach Lukas*, 389; L. Morris, *Luke: An Introduction and Commentary*, The Tyndale New Testament commentaries 3 (Leicester, England, Grand Rapids, Mich.: Inter-Varsity Press; William. B. Eerdmans Pub. Co., 1990), 297; J. O'Hanlon, "The Story of Zacchaeus and the Lukan Ethic." 11.

[105] G. Yamasaki, "Point of View in a Gospel Story: What Difference Does It Make?" 89-105.

[106] J. O'Hanlon, "The Story of Zacchaeus and the Lukan Ethic." 11. Also H. Strathmann, "πόλις," in G. Kittel, G. W. Bromiley & G. Friedrich, *Theological Dictionary of the New Testament*, 6, 529-530; U. Hutter, "πόλις," in H. Balz and G. Schneider, *Exegetical Dictionary of the New Testament*, 3, 129.

[107] H. J. Cadbury and P. N. Anderson, *The Making of Luke-Acts*, 246.

[108] J. O'Hanlon, "The Story of Zacchaeus and the Lukan Ethic." 12; similar idea is also expressed in H. J. Cadbury and P. N. Anderson, *The Making of Luke-Acts*, 246-247.

[109] Cf. J. B. Green, J. K. Brown, and N. Perrin, eds., *Dictionary of Jesus and the Gospels: A Compendium of Contemporary Biblical Scholarship*, 2nd ed. (Nottingham: InterVarsity Press, 2013), 52.

[110] E. LaVerdiere, *Dining in the Kingdom of God*, 224.

[111] W. Manson, *The Gospel of Luke*, 209.

[112] More on the city Jericho, cf. D. Dormeyer, *Das Lukas-evangelium: Neu übersetzt und kommentiert* (Stuttgart: Verlag Katholisches Bibelwerk, 2011), 213; W. Wiefel, *Das Evangelium nach Lukas*, 326; P. Kariamadam, *The Zacchaeus Story (Lk 19:1-10)*, 6; A. Stöger, *Das Evangelium nach Lukas*, 3rd ed., Geistliche Schriftlesung Erläuterungen zum Neuen Testament für die geistliche Lesung 3,2 (Düsseldorf: Patmos-Verl., 1985), 143; R. Summers, *Commentary on Luke*, 222; W. Manson, *The Gospel of Luke*, 209; T. Zahn, *Das Evangelium des Lucas*, 620.

[113] J. Drury, *Tradition and Design in Luke's Gospel: A Study in Early Christian Historiography* (Atlanta: John Knox Press, 1977), 73; for a similar argument cf. J. O'Hanlon, "The Story of Zacchaeus and the Lukan Ethic." 6.

[114] J. O'Hanlon, "The Story of Zacchaeus and the Lukan Ethic.", 7-8.

[115] J. A. Fitzmyer, *The Gospel According to Luke I-IX*, 170.

[116] In the third Gospel we find the phrase as many as 26 times. Cf. ibid., 121;

also J. A. Arthur Jr., "Table fellowship and the Eschatological Kingdom in the Emmaus Narrative of Luke 24," Ph.D. Thesis, http:// etheses.dur.ac.uk / 10486/ 1/ 10486_ 7283.PDF ? UkUDh:CyT, 56, accessed on 20.07.2015.

[117] J. A. Fitzmyer, *The Gospel According to Luke I-IX*, 121; P. Kariamadam, *The Zacchaeus Story (Lk 19:1-10)*, 6; G. Yamasaki, "Point of View in a Gospel Story: What Difference Does It Make?" 98-99.

[118] G. Yamasaki, "Point of View in a Gospel Story: What Difference Does It Make?", 99; for a similar view cf. also J. Reiling and J. L. Swellengrebel, *A Translator's Handbook on the Gospel of Luke*, 615.

[119] G. Yamasaki, "Point of View in a Gospel Story: What Difference Does It Make?" 99.

[120] H. E. Dana and J. R. Mantey, *A Manual Grammar of the Greek New Testament* (New York: Macmillan, 1967), 70. Cf. also G. Yamasaki, "Point of View in a Gospel Story: What Difference Does It Make?" 99.

[121] Cf. J. C. Hawkins, *Horae Synopticae: Contributions to the Study of the Synoptic Problem* (Oxford: Clarendon Press, 1909), 21; also P. Kariamadam, *The Zacchaeus Story (Lk 19:1-10)*, 7.

[122] J. C. Hawkins, *Horae Synopticae*, 19, 42.

[123] F. Bovon, *Das Evangelium nach Lukas*, 271; also F. Bovon, H. Koester, and D. S. Deer, *Luke 2*, 596; J. Nolland, *Luke*, 904; J. O'Hanlon, "The Story of Zacchaeus and the Lukan Ethic." 12.

[124] G. Maier, *Lukas-Evangelium: 2. Teil*, Edition C 5 (Neuhausen-Stuttgart: Hänssler, 1992), 425.

[125] Cf. T. Zahn, *Das Evangelium des Lucas*, 620; P. G. Müller, *Lukas-Evangelium*, Stuttgarter kleiner Kommentar Neues Testament 3 (Stuttgart: Verlag Katholisches Bibelwerk, 1984), 147; W. Manson, *The Gospel of Luke*, 208. For Bock and Zahn, *Zakkai* itself is the abbreviated form of Zacharia. D. L. Bock, *Luke: 9:51-24:53*, 2 vols., Volume 2 (Grand Rapids, Mich.: Baker, 1996), Baker Exegetical Commentary on the New Testament, 1516.

[126] J. A. Fitzmyer, *The Gospel According to Luke X-XXIV*, 1223; other scholars who think along the similar line are F. Bovon, *Das Evangelium nach Lukas*, 272; F. Bovon, H. Koester, and D. S. Deer, *Luke 2*, 396; J. Kremer, *Lukasevangelium*, 182; R. H. Stein, *Luke*, 467; J. P. Kealy, *Luke's Gospel Today*, 360; J. O'Hanlon, "The Story of Zacchaeus and the Lukan Ethic." 12. The following authors hold that the name could be the short form of *either* Zechariah *or* it could have come from the name *Zakkai*: cf. W. Grundmann, *Das Evangelium nach Lukas*, 359; G. Maier, *Lukas-Evangelium*, 425; G. Schneider, *Das Evangelium nach Lukas: Kapitel 11-24*, Ökumenischer Taschenbuchkommentar zum Neuen Testament 3/2 (Gütersloh: Gütersloher Verlagsh. Mohn, 1984), 326.

[127] W. O. Walker Jr., "Jesus and the Tax Collectors." 234; Marshall, "Jesus and the Banquets." 193.

¹²⁸ A. Schlatter, *Die Evangelien nach Markus und Lukas*, Erläuterungen zum Neuen Testament 2 (Stuttgart: Calwer, 1979), 249; J. A. Fitzmyer, *The Gospel According to Luke X-XXIV*, 1223; G. Maier, *Lukas-Evangelium*, 425.

¹²⁹ R. Hirschel, "Johanan Ben Zakkai," in *The Universal Jewish Encyclopedia: An Authoritative and Popular Presentation of Jews and Judaism Since the Earliest Times*, ed. I. Landman, 10 vols. (New York: Universal Jewish Encyclopedia, 1948), 6, 164-166; also A. Batya and C. Roth, eds., *The Standard Jewish Encyclopedia* (London: Allen, 1959), 1054-1055.

¹³⁰ R. H. Stein, *Luke*, 467; D. L. Bock, *Luke*, 1516; J. Ernst, *Das Evangelium nach Lukas*, 389; Bovon thinks that for Luke, the etymology of names is not important at all. F. Bovon, *Das Evangelium nach Lukas*, 272.

¹³¹ D. L. Tiede, *Luke*, 320. The irony is rightly seen also by J. O'Hanlon, "The Story of Zacchaeus and the Lukan Ethic." 12; Creed too says that Luke only here uses names with a symbolic purpose. J. M. Creed, *The Gospel According to St. Luke*, 230.

¹³² J. Nolland, *Luke*, 904.

¹³³ *Strom. IV, 6,35;* cf. Clément d'Alexandrie and Otto Stählin, *Des Clemens von Alexandreia ausgewählte Schriften aus dem Griechischen ubersetzt. 4: Stromateis, Buch 4-6*, 19 vols., Bibliothek der Kirchenväter: 2. Reihe 4 (Munchen: Kösel, 1937), 31.

¹³⁴ Cf. A. Roberts et al., eds., *Ante-Nicene Fathers: The Writings of the Fathers Down to A.D. 325*, 10 vols., 7 (Peabody, Mass.: Hendrickson Publishers, 1995), 477-478.

¹³⁵ A. Roberts, J. Donaldson, and A. C. Coxe, eds., *Ante-Nicene Fathers: The Writings of the Fathers Down to A.D. 325*, 10 vols., 8 (Peabody, Mass.: Hendrickson Publishers, 1995), 250.

¹³⁶ *Adv. Marc.* IV, 37,1; Tertullian, *Adversus Marcionem, Books 4-5: Ed. and trsl. by Evans, Ernest*, Oxford Early Christian Texts (Oxford: Clarendon Press, 1972), 473.

¹³⁷ J. A. Fitzmyer, *The Gospel According to Luke I-IX*, 120; Luke absorbs in his Gospel the *LXX* translation of *whû* as καν αPτxς. This unstressed and – in the words of Kariamadam – "unemphatic usage" of καν αPτxς is to be contrasted with the intensive use of the phrase as in Luke 24:15. P. Kariamadam, *The Zacchaeus Story (Lk 19:1-10)*, 8; also W. L. Knox, *The Sources of the Synoptic Gospels: Vol. 2, St. Luke and St. Matthew: ed. Chadwick, Henry* (Cambridge: Cambridge U.P, 1957), 112; J. P. Kealy, *Luke's Gospel Today*, 360; A. R. C. Leaney, *A Commentary on the Gospel According to St. Luke*, Harper's New Testament commentaries (New York: Harper, 1958), 241.

¹³⁸ G. Yamasaki, "Point of View in a Gospel Story: What Difference Does It Make?" 99; cf. also R. C. Tannehill, "The Story of Zacchaeus as Rhetoric." 202.

¹³⁹ J. A. Fitzmyer, *The Gospel According to Luke X-XXIV*, 1223. Fitzmyer suggests that the indirect taxes like customs were auctioned to the one who paid the highest bid. The one who had the right to collect the direct tax was called ρχιτελ}νης and had officers who worked under him. Cf. J. A. Fitzmyer, *The Gospel According to Luke I-IX*, 470.

¹⁴⁰ N. Hillyer, "τελώνιον." 758.

¹⁴¹ M. Zerwick and M. Grosvenor, *A Grammatical Analysis of the Greek New Testament*, 257; cf. also H. G. Liddell and R. Scott, *A Greek-English Lexicon*, 1774; R. Summers, *Commentary on Luke*, 222;

¹⁴² W. Hendriksen, *Exposition of the Gospel According to Luke*, New Testament Commentary (Grand Rapids, Mich.: Baker Academic, 2007), 855; also D. L. Bock, *Luke*, 1516; N. Hillyer, "τελώνιον." 758; Bovon however, questions the presence of an organized tax system in Jericho. He says, "To my knowledge we are unaware of the organization of taxes and duties in this city." F. Bovon, H. Koester, and D. S. Deer, *Luke 2*, 1223; also F. Bovon, *Das Evangelium nach Lukas*, 272. It is however difficult to accept the position of Bovon in doubting the presence of an organized system of taxation in Jericho. I am of the opinion that at the time of Jesus in big cities like Jericho there would surely have been an orderly system to collect taxes. This is even more confirmed by the fact that Jericho is a city in Judaea´s border and an important way to the region of Perea, which belonged to tetrarchy of Herod Antipas.

¹⁴³ D. A. S. Ravens, "Zacchaeus." 21; J. P. Heil, *The Meal Scenes in Luke-Acts*, 151.

¹⁴⁴ J. O'Hanlon, "The Story of Zacchaeus and the Lukan Ethic." 9; cf. also J. Nolland, *Luke*, 905; J. Gillman, *Possessions and the Life of Faith: A Reading of Luke-Acts*, Zacchaeus studies: New Testament (Collegeville, Minn.: Liturgical Press, 1991), 89.

¹⁴⁵ While Mark uses it twice and Matthew thrice, Luke uses the word as many as eleven times. Apart from two occurrences (6:24, 21:1), the word appears only in the Travel Narrative. In Acts, we do not find the usage of the word. Cf. J. O'Hanlon, "The Story of Zacchaeus and the Lukan Ethic." 2; also P. Kariamadam, *The Zacchaeus Story (Lk 19:1-10)*, 9.

¹⁴⁶ J. O'Hanlon, "The Story of Zacchaeus and the Lukan Ethic." 12.

¹⁴⁷ Check H. Merklein, "πλοætoς," in H. Balz and G. Schneider, *Exegetical Dictionary of the New Testament*, 3, 114-117; also F. Hauck and W. Kasch, "πλοætoς," in G. Kittel, G. W. Bromiley & G. Friedrich, *Theological Dictionary of the New Testament*, 6, 318-332.

¹⁴⁸ R. C. Tannehill, "The Story of Zacchaeus as Rhetoric." 202.

¹⁴⁹ J. P. Heil, *The Meal Scenes in Luke-Acts*, 151; cf. also R. C. Tannehill, "The Story of Zacchaeus as Rhetoric." 202.

¹⁵⁰ F. Bovon, *Das Evangelium nach Lukas*, 272-273; F. Bovon, H. Koester, and D. S. Deer, *Luke 2*, 596; P. Kariamadam, *The Zacchaeus Story (Lk 19:1-10)*, 11.

¹⁵¹ H. Greeven, "ζητέω," in G. Kittel, G. W. Bromiley & G. Friedrich, *Theological Dictionary of the New Testament*, 2, 892-896; also E. Larsson, "ζητέω," in H. Balz and G. Schneider, *Exegetical Dictionary of the New Testament*, 2, 102-103.

¹⁵² L. T. Johnson, *The Gospel of Luke*, 285.

¹⁵³ J. Kremer, "Αράω," in H. Balz and G. Schneider, *Exegetical Dictionary of the New Testament*, 2, 526-529, 527; Michaelis also says that the active form of Αράω with the accusative would mean not just seeing but perceiving. "To see is to take part in life itself." W. Michaelis, "Αράω," in G. Kittel, G. W. Bromiley & G. Friedrich, *Theological Dictionary of the New Testament*, 5, 315-370, 316; also F. Bovon, H. Koester, and D. S. Deer, *Luke 2*, 597; J. O'Hanlon, "The Story of Zacchaeus and the Lukan Ethic." 13.

¹⁵⁴ P. Kariamadam, *The Zacchaeus Story (Lk 19:1-10)*, 11.

¹⁵⁵ F. Bovon, *Das Evangelium nach Lukas*, 272.

¹⁵⁶ G. B. Caird, *Saint Luke*, Westminster Pelican commentaries (Philadelphia: Westminster Press, 1978), 217; cf. also M. Wolter, *Das Lukasevangelium*, 612; R. H. Stein, *Luke*, 467; R. Dillmann and C. Mora Paz, *Das Lukas-Evangelium*, 326; N. Geldenhuys, *Commentary on the Gospel of Luke*, 470; P. G. Müller, *Lukas-Evangelium*, 147; J. Kremer, *Lukasevangelium*, 182; E. Schweizer, "The Son of Man," *Journal of Biblical Literature* 79, no. 2 (1960), 291.

¹⁵⁷ R. F. O'Toole, "The Literary Form of Luke 19:1-10." 111.

¹⁵⁸ A. Stöger, *Das Evangelium nach Lukas*, 143; R. Dillmann and C. Mora Paz, *Das Lukas-Evangelium*, 326.

¹⁵⁹ Ascough suggests, Luke must have written his double work along the lines of ancient novels. His comparison of the crowd scenes in Luke-Acts with one of the ancient novels *Chaereas and Callirhoe* tries to prove this. R. S. Ascough, "Narrative Technique and Generic Designation: Crowd Scenes in Luke-Acts and in Chariton," *Catholic Biblical Quarterly* 58, no. 1 (1996), 69-81.

¹⁶⁰ Ibid., 78-79.

¹⁶¹ R. Meyer, "Dχλος," in G. Kittel, G. W. Bromiley & G. Friedrich, *Theological Dictionary of the New Testament*, 583.

¹⁶² B. Citron, "The Multitude in the Synoptic Gospels," *SJT* 07, no. 04 (1954), 410.

¹⁶³ Citron points out that of all the synoptic writers, Matthew is more sympathetic in his portrayal of the crowd. In all three instances, Matthew avoids calling the crowds with these names. He gives these names not to the crowds but only to the Pharisees and Sadducees and Scribes. If both Luke and Matthew have taken a common source, who has altered the source? In the narrative of the healing of the paralytic (Mk 2:1-12; Matt 9:1-8; Luke 5:17-26, we see at the, Matthew changes the πqντας of Mk 2:12 into οι Dχλοι who glorify God, while Luke retains the word παντας (Luke 5:26). One could see that Matthew wants to soften his stand on the Dχλος. Nevertheless, the Lukan redactional effort to show his aversion to them is seen in his Gospel. For example, in Mark, the Dχλος would speak

for the relatives of Jesus who have come to see him (Mk 3:32), whereas in the third Gospel, the Dχλος becomes a hindrance for the mother and the brothers of Jesus to reach him. ibid., 416.

[164] M. Wolter, *Das Lukasevangelium*, 612; P. Kariamadam, *The Zacchaeus Story (Lk 19:1-10)*, 14-15; J. B. Green, *The Gospel of Luke*, 669; M. C. Parsons, "'Short in Stature': Luke's Physical Description of Zacchaeus," *NTS* 47 (2001), 51.

[165] B. Citron, "The Multitude in the Synoptic Gospels." 412.

[166] Ibid., 415.

[167] O. Michel, "μικρxς," in G. Kittel, G. W. Bromiley & G. Friedrich, *Theological Dictionary of the New Testament*, 4, 648.

[168] J. Schneider, "!λικία," in G. Kittel, G. W. Bromiley & G. Friedrich, *Theological Dictionary of the New Testament*, 2, 941-943, 942; also T. Schramm, "!λικία," in H. Balz and G. Schneider, *Exegetical Dictionary of the New Testament*, 2, 117. However, this is not without criticism. Green for example questions this view. He understands !λικία in Luke 19:3 as referring to the relative youthfulness of Zacchaeus than to the shortness of his stature. J. B. Green, *The Gospel of Luke*, 669. However, the use of the word in LXX denoting the stature or the physical size of someone does allow to translate it as physical stature.

[169] O'Hanlon suggests that Luke is the only author who uses !λικw³ in the physical sense of the word. J. O'Hanlon, "The Story of Zacchaeus and the Lukan Ethic." 2. Others who look at !λικw³ μικργς as the physical disability of shortness of the main character are: F. Bovon, *Das Evangelium nach Lukas*, 273; D. L. Bock, *Luke*, 1517; R. C. Tannehill, "The Story of Zacchaeus as Rhetoric." 201.

[170] J. A. Fitzmyer, *The Gospel According to Luke X-XXIV*, 1223; also J. P. Kealy, *Luke's Gospel Today*, 381.

[171] Cf. S. H. Ringe, *Luke*, Westminster Bible companion (Louisville, Ky.: Westminster John Knox Press, 1995), 232; M. C. Parsons, "'Short in Stature': Luke's Physical Description of Zacchaeus." 55.

[172] Cf. F. Bovon, *Das Evangelium nach Lukas*, 273; J. M. Creed, *The Gospel According to St. Luke*, 229; Tannehill compares it with another pronouncement story where he quotes from Hock und O Neil, "Damon the gymnastic teacher whose feet were deformed, when his shoes had been stolen, said "may they fit the thief." The final pronouncement of the character depends on the physical disability that was narrated earlier. But this is not the case in the story of Zacchaeus. R. C. Tannehill, "The Story of Zacchaeus as Rhetoric." 201-202.

[173] Parsons states that from the time of Homer till the third century CE it was customary to equate the 'physiognomic' characteristics of a person with his inner disposition or his small mindedness. M. C. Parsons, "'Short in Stature': Luke's Physical Description of Zacchaeus." 52-54.

[174] Ibid., 55. Further he states in page 57, "His occupation, his greed, and his physical stature combine to convince Luke's audience that this man was a sinner

indeed." Liefeld too says that Luke, through the phrase τÇ !λικw³ μικργς indicates the moral degradation of Zacchaeus. W. L. Liefeld and D. W. Pao, *Luke - Acts*, The expositor's Bible commentary 10 (Grand Rapids, Mich.: Zondervan, 2007), 286; also E. LaVerdiere, *Dining in the Kingdom of God*, 113.

[175] O. Michel, "μικρχς." 649.

[176] Ibid., 652; for the theological ramifications of the word cf. S. Légasse, "μικρός," in H. Balz and G. Schneider, *Exegetical Dictionary of the New Testament*, 2, 427-428.

[177] O. Michel, "μικρχς." 651; S. Légasse, "μικρός." 427-428.

[178] S. Légasse, "μικρός.", 427.

[179] O. Michel, "μικρχς." 652.

[180] O. Bauernfeind, "τρέξω," in G. Kittel, G. W. Bromiley & G. Friedrich, *Theological Dictionary of the New Testament*, 8, 226.

[181] P. Kariamadam, *The Zacchaeus Story (Lk 19:1-10)*, 18; J. O'Hanlon, "The Story of Zacchaeus and the Lukan Ethic." 13; J. Reiling and J. L. Swellengrebel, *A Translator's Handbook on the Gospel of Luke*, 616.

[182] J. O'Hanlon, "The Story of Zacchaeus and the Lukan Ethic." 13.

[183] M. Wolter, *Das Lukasevangelium*, 612; F. Bovon, *Das Evangelium nach Lukas*, 273.

[184] M. Black, *An Aramaic Approach to the Gospels and Acts* (Oxford: Clarendon Press, 1967), 116; also P. Kariamadam, *The Zacchaeus Story (Lk 19:1-10)*, 18.

[185] P. Kariamadam, *The Zacchaeus Story (Lk 19:1-10)*, 18.

[186] M. Zohary, *Plants of the Bible: A Complete Handbook to all the Plants with 200 Full-Color Plates Taken in the Natural Habitat* (Cambridge: Cambridge University Press, 1982), 68-69.

[187] D. L. Bock, *Luke*, 1517; F. Bovon, *Das Evangelium nach Lukas*, 274; M. Strauss, "Luke," in *The Illustrated Bible Backgrounds Commentary*, ed. C. E. Arnold, 1 (Zondervan: Grand Rapids, 2002), 463; there is a double opinion among the scholars regarding the identity of the tree. While the above-mentioned authors hold that sycamore is different from a mulberry tree, some do hold that it comes under the family of mulberry tree. Check D. Dormeyer, *Das Lukas-evangelium*, 213; L. Morris, *Luke*, 297; A. Plummer, *A Critical and Exegetical Commentary on the Gospel According to S. Luke*, 433; R. Summers, *Commentary on Luke*, 222. R. Dillmann and C. Mora Paz, *Das Lukas-Evangelium*, 326. In this way, the translation of the word συκομορsα as *'Maulbeerfeigenbaum'* in many German Bible translations (for example, *Die Einheitsübersetzung, Die Luther Bibel, Gute Nachrichte Bibel and Menge Bibel*) makes sense. Further on the discussion of the sycamore tree G. Maier, *Lukas-Evangelium*, 427; W. Hendriksen, *Exposition of the Gospel According to Luke*, 855, J. Ernst, *Das Evangelium nach Lukas*, 389; P. Kariamadam, *The Zacchaeus Story (Lk 19:1-10)*, 18; W. Wiefel, *Das Evangelium nach Lukas*, 326-327.

[188] J. Reiling and J. L. Swellengrebel, *A Translator's Handbook on the Gospel of Luke*, 616.

[189] J. Bolyki, *Jesu Tischgemeinschaften*, 110. Similar view is rendered also in P. Kariamadam, *The Zacchaeus Story (Lk 19:1-10)*, 18.

[190] In the parable of the Pharisee and the tax collector (18:10), the word is used in the sense of going up to Jerusalem: the two characters are portrayed as going up to the Temple to pray.

[191] P. Kariamadam, *The Zacchaeus Story (Lk 19:1-10)*, 19.

[192] J. B. Green, *The Gospel of Luke*, 670; also W. Hendriksen, *Exposition of the Gospel According to Luke*, 855.

[193] The frequency of the use of the word could be, in the opinion of Köster, because of the influence of LXX in Luke. Cf. H. Köster, "τόπος," in G. Kittel, G. W. Bromiley & G. Friedrich, *Theological Dictionary of the New Testament*, 8, 203.

[194] F. Bovon, *Das Evangelium nach Lukas*, 274.

[195] Cf. P. G. Müller, "ναβλέπω," in H. Balz and G. Schneider, *Exegetical Dictionary of the New Testament*, 1, 76; more on ναβλέπω cf. also F. W. Danker and W. Bauer, *A Greek-English lexicon of the New Testament and other early Christian literature*, 50.

[196] F. W. Danker and W. Bauer, *A Greek-English lexicon of the New Testament and other early Christian literature*, 50.

[197] Bovon says, Jesus knows the name because of his superhuman omniscience - „mit seiner übermenschlinschen Allwissenheit." F. Bovon, *Das Evangelium nach Lukas*, 274; also F. Bovon, H. Koester, and D. S. Deer, *Luke 2*, 598; also J. P. Kealy, *Luke's Gospel Today*, 361; J. Nolland, *Luke*, 905; T. Zahn, *Das Evangelium des Lucas*, 621; H. Klein, *Das Lukasevangelium*, 601; A. Stöger, *Das Evangelium nach Lukas*, 144.

[198] J. O'Hanlon, "The Story of Zacchaeus and the Lukan Ethic." 14.

[199] W. Manson, *The Gospel of Luke*, 210.

[200] A. Plummer, *A Critical and Exegetical Commentary on the Gospel According to S. Luke*, 434; H. I. Marshall, W. W. Gasque, and D. A. Hagner, *The Gospel of Luke: A Commentary on the Greek Text*, 696; C. A. Evans, *Luke*, NIBC (Peabody, Massachusetts: Hendrickson Publishers, 1990), 283.

[201] J. A. Fitzmyer, *The Gospel According to Luke X-XXIV*, 1224; R. Summers, *Commentary on Luke*, 222.

[202] G. Maier, *Lukas-Evangelium*, 427.

[203] While Mark uses it 6 times and Matthew 11, Luke has used the word 13 times in the third Gospel and 19 times in the Acts of the Apostles. Cf. J. Feindrich, "καταβαίνω," in H. Balz and G. Schneider, *Exegetical Dictionary of the New Testament*, 2, 254; J. Schneider, "βαίνω," in G. Kittel, G. W. Bromiley & G. Friedrich, *Theological Dictionary of the New Testament*, 1, 522.

204 P. Kariamadam, *The Zacchaeus Story (Lk 19:1-10)*, 22.

205 F. W. Danker and W. Bauer, *A Greek-English lexicon of the New Testament and other early Christian literature*, 762; N. Walter, "σπεύδω," in H. Balz and G. Schneider, *Exegetical Dictionary of the New Testament*, 3, 264; P. Kariamadam, *The Zacchaeus Story (Lk 19:1-10)*, 22; J. O'Hanlon, "The Story of Zacchaeus and the Lukan Ethic." 3.

206 D. L. Bock, *Luke*, 1518.

207 Cf. J. O'Hanlon, "The Story of Zacchaeus and the Lukan Ethic." 14; F. Bovon, *Das Evangelium nach Lukas*, 274; F. Bovon, H. Koester, and D. S. Deer, *Luke 2*, 598.

208 The word that is used in Luke 1:39 is, however, not σπε{δω but the nominal form μετρ σπουδÆς.

209 Among these twenty occurrences, at least eight are unique to Luke: 2:11; 4:21; 5:26; 13:32-33; 19:5,9; 22:61; 23:43. Cf. M. Völkel, "σήμερον," in H. Balz and G. Schneider, *Exegetical Dictionary of the New Testament*, 3, 241; J. Drury, *Tradition and Design in Luke's Gospel*, 70; P. Kariamadam, *The Zacchaeus Story (Lk 19:1-10)*, 22. For further understanding of the word cf. E. Fuchs, "σήμερον," in G. Kittel, G. W. Bromiley & G. Friedrich, *Theological Dictionary of the New Testament*, 7, 269-275; F. W. Danker and W. Bauer, *A Greek-English lexicon of the New Testament and other early Christian literature*, 749.

210 E. Fuchs, "σήμερον." 270; cf. also Hotze, *Jesus als Gast*, 66.

211 Marshall tells that συμερον in Luke 19:5 should be taken literally. All the same, he does not exclude the possibility that "it may convey the idea that the time has come for the fulfilment of God's plan of salvation." H. I. Marshall, W. W. Gasque, and D. A. Hagner, *The Gospel of Luke: A Commentary on the Greek Text*, 697.

212 L. Oberlinner, "Das Jesusbild des Lukasevangeliums: Eine soteriologische Alternative?," in *Verantwortete Exegese: FS. F. G. Untergaßmair*, ed. G. Hotze and E. Spiegel (Berlin: LIT, 2006), 168.

213 R. H. Stein, *Luke*, 468.

214 P. Kariamadam, *The Zacchaeus Story (Lk 19:1-10)*, 23.

215 Ibid., 23; Gerhard Maier talks about it as „messianische Heute" or „Heute der Heilszeit." G. Maier, *Lukas-Evangelium*, 428. Hotze too looks at the συμερον of Luke 19:5 as „das mit dem Besuch Jesu einbrechende endzeitliche Heilszeit." Hotze, *Jesus als Gast*, 66. For a similar view cf. also P. G. Müller, *Lukas-Evangelium*, 147; G. Schneider, *Das Evangelium nach Lukas*, 377; L. T. Johnson, *The Gospel of Luke*, 285.

216 W. Grundmann, *Das Evangelium nach Lukas*, 359; J. P. Kealy, *Luke's Gospel Today*, 361.

217 W. Grundmann, "δεÖ," in G. Kittel, G. W. Bromiley & G. Friedrich, *Theological Dictionary of the New Testament*, 2, 21.

[218] The individual patriarchs in the history of the Old Testament are only the instruments of the one and unchanging will of God. In this way Schulz understands the time of the Old Testament. S. Schulz, "Gottes Vorsehung bei Lukas," *ZNW 54* 54 (1963), 104-116.

[219] Again in the words of Schulz, „*gegen die personifizierte Ananke kann kein Sterblicher — eingeschlossen Christen, Apostel und Jesus — etwas ausrichten. Widerstand ist zwecklos, wir alle sind nur Werkzeuge dieses unmißverständlichen und unwiderstehlichen Gotteswillens.*" ibid., 109.

[220] Cf. C. H. Cosgrove, "The Divine ΔεÖ in Luke-Acts: Investigations into the Lukan Understanding of God's Providence," *Novum Testamentum* 26, no. 2 (1984), 109.

[221] ΔεÖ and μέλλειν are used by Luke in the passion predictions in order to denote the necessity of Jesus' passion: Mark uses the word "must" only in the first passion prediction (Mk 8:31), while Luke brings in the element of "must" in all the three passion predictions; in the first passion prediction he uses δεÖ, in the other two, however, he uses the verb μέλλειν.

[222] W. Grundmann, "δεÖ." 2, 21; also W. Popkes, "δεÖ," in H. Balz and G. Schneider, *Exegetical Dictionary of the New Testament*, 1, 279-280; F. W. Danker and W. Bauer, *A Greek-English lexicon of the New Testament and other early Christian literature*, 172.

[223] S. Schulz, "Gottes Vorsehung bei Lukas." 112.

[224] C. H. Cosgrove, "The Divine ΔεÖ in Luke-Acts.", 171.

[225] L. T. Johnson, *The Gospel of Luke*, 285; also F. Bovon, *Das Evangelium nach Lukas*, 274; F. Bovon, H. Koester, and D. S. Deer, *Luke 2*, 598; D. L. Bock, *Luke*, 1518; A. Stöger, *Das Evangelium nach Lukas*, 144; P. Kariamadam, *The Zacchaeus Story (Lk 19:1-10)*, 24.

[226] L. Oberliner, ""Der Menschensohn muss leiden..." (Mk 8,31): Das Bekenntnis zur Auferweckung Jesu als theologische Voraussetzung des Christologischen Bekenntnisses," in *Jesus im Glaubenszeugnis des Neuen Testaments: Exegetische Reflexionen zum 100. Geburtstag von Anton Vögtle*, ed. L. Oberlinner and F. R. Prostmeier, *Herders biblische Studien Herder's biblical studies* Band 80 (Freiburg im Breisgau: Herder, 2015), 52; also J. O'Hanlon, "The Story of Zacchaeus and the Lukan Ethic." 3; E. Fascher, "Theologische Beobachtungen zu δεÖ," in *Neutestamentliche Studien für Rudolf Bultmann: Zu seinem 70. Geburtstag am 20. August 1954*, ed. W. Eltester, *Beihefte zur Zeitschrift für die neutestamentliche Wissenschaft und die Kunde der älteren Kirche* 21 (Berlin: A. Töpelmann, 1954), 246, 248; C. H. Cosgrove, "The Divine ΔεÖ in Luke-Acts." 173.

[227] Cosgrove quotes as many as eleven instances in Luke-Acts where δεÖ is ordinarily used to mean, what one should say before the authorities (Luke 12:12), the open accusation of the leader of synagogue and his command that the people should not come to Jesus on the day of the Sabbath for healing (Luke 13:14),

the custom of slaughtering the Passover Lamb (Luke 22:7) and many others. C. H. Cosgrove, "The Divine ΔεÖ in Luke-Acts.", 173.

²²⁸ Ibid., 174.
²²⁹ Ibid., 175.
²³⁰ Ibid., 180.
²³¹ Ibid., 190.

²³² Cf. M. Wolter, *Das Lukasevangelium*, 612; R. H. Stein, *Luke*, 467; J. P. Kealy, *Luke's Gospel Today*, 361; E. LaVerdiere, *Dining in the Kingdom of God*, 114-115.

²³³ C. H. Cosgrove, "The Divine ΔεÖ in Luke-Acts." 175.

²³⁴ Of all the 118 occurrences of the verb μένω in the New Testament, the Johannine literature has the highest number of usages. While Matthew uses it thrice and Mark twice, Luke uses it 7 times in his Gospel and 13 times in the Acts of the Apostles. H. Hübner, "μένω," in H. Balz and G. Schneider, *Exegetical Dictionary of the New Testament*, 407; for the meaning of the word cf. also F. Hauck, "μένω," in G. Kittel, G. W. Bromiley & G. Friedrich, *Theological Dictionary of the New Testament*, 574-575; F. W. Danker and W. Bauer, *A Greek-English lexicon of the New Testament and other early Christian literature*, 503-504.

²³⁵ H. Hübner, "μένω." 408.

²³⁶ D. L. Bock, *Luke*, 1518; G. Maier, *Lukas-Evangelium*, 428; E. Schweizer, *The Good News According to Luke: trsl. David E. Green* (London: SPCK, 1984), 298.

²³⁷ Cf. Luke 1:56; 7:10; 8:39; 9:61; 11:17; 15:6; Acts 7:20; 8:3; 10:30; 11:13; 16:34; 19:16; 20:20.

²³⁸ O. Michel, "о6коς," in G. Kittel, G. W. Bromiley & G. Friedrich, *Theological Dictionary of the New Testament*, 5, 121.

²³⁹ P. Weigandt, "о6коς," in H. Balz and G. Schneider, *Exegetical Dictionary of the New Testament*, 2, 501.

²⁴⁰ In Luke-Acts we find о6коς more often than о0кíα (Mark and Matthew use о0кíα more often). While in the Gospel о6коς comes 33 times, о0кíα could be seen 24 times. Hence the term 'house' is used by Luke altogether 57 times. Both the words denoting house, appear in the Lukan double work 94 times. ibid., 2, 500; cf. also Hotze, *Jesus als Gast*, 23.

²⁴¹ Cf. Acts 10:22; 11;12 (house) and Acts 10:2; 11:14 (household of Cornelius).

²⁴² The exception is Luke 8:27, where both the words о6коς and μένειν are used; but they mean the Gerasene Demoniac who does not 'live in his house' but in the tombs.

²⁴³ Hotze, *Jesus als Gast*, 66.
²⁴⁴ Marshall, "Jesus and the Banquets." 271.
²⁴⁵ J. A. Fitzmyer, *The Gospel According to Luke X-XXIV*, 842.
²⁴⁶ Marshall, "Jesus and the Banquets." 280-281.
²⁴⁷ Ibid., 298-299.

[248] Ibid., 327. According to Marshall, although it is said in Luke 7:36, that the Pharisee had asked Jesus to dine with him, the verb ρωτάω is a weak verb in the sense of requesting, or asking. The Lukan host does not use καλεὉν which is the traditional word for a formal invitation of a banquet. Marshall understands however, that this argument is very weak, since the verb καλεὉν is indeed used in the pericope and the host is mentioned as Α καλσας in Luke 7:39.

[249] P. Kariamadam, *The Zacchaeus Story (Lk 19:1-10)*, 25; Müller also says that the action of Jesus is sign of "God´s communion and acceptance of a believer who is a sinner." P. G. Müller, *Lukas-Evangelium*, 147.

[250] J. O'Hanlon, "The Story of Zacchaeus and the Lukan Ethic." 15; R. Dillmann and C. Mora Paz, *Das Lukas-Evangelium*, 326; D. L. Bock, *Luke*, 1518.

[251] D. L. Bock, *Luke*, 1518; J. Ernst, *Das Evangelium nach Lukas*, 514.

[252] Cf. G. Yamasaki, "Point of View in a Gospel Story: What Difference Does It Make?" 102.

[253] Cf. F. W. Danker and W. Bauer, *A Greek-English lexicon of the New Testament and other early Christian literature*, 1037; H. Giesen, "Ǫποδέχομαι," in H. Balz and G. Schneider, *Exegetical Dictionary of the New Testament*, 3, 402; D. Hamm, "Luke 19:8 Once Again." 435.

[254] J. Brutscheck, *Die Maria-Marta-Erzählung: Eine Redaktionkritische Untersuchung zu Lk 10, 38-42*, Bonner biblische Beiträge Bd. 64 (Frankfurt am Main: P. Hanstein, 1986), 102-104; P. Kariamadam, *The Zacchaeus Story (Lk 19:1-10)*, 26; One finds however number of differences between the two narratives. For example, Martha and Maria who receive and host Jesus at their house, are not newly repentant sinners just as Zacchaeus is portrayed. For further differences between the two narratives, cf. Hotze, *Jesus als Gast*, 88.

[255] Although this phrase is omitted in the NA[28], because of its absence in manuscripts like P[45], P[75], B, the phrase εὈς τtv οὈκίαν is found in some of the important manuscripts like P[3], ℵ*, C*, L, Ξ. Some other manuscripts like A, D, K, P, W, Δ have εὈς τxν ο6κyν αΡτÆς. Fitzmyer doubts whether the omission of the phrase is closer to the original. J. A. Fitzmyer, *The Gospel According to Luke X-XXIV*, 893.

[256] It is doubtful whether this could be considered a correct parallel here.

[257] J. Brutscheck, *Die Maria-Marta-Erzählung*, 72, 100-107; P. Kariamadam, *The Zacchaeus Story (Lk 19:1-10)*, 26.

[258] F. Bovon, *Das Evangelium nach Lukas*, 274-275; F. Bovon, H. Koester, and D. S. Deer, *Luke 2*, 598; also J. P. Heil, *The Meal Scenes in Luke-Acts*, 154; L. T. Johnson, *The Gospel of Luke*, 285.

[259] Bovon, Wolter and others suggest that Luke might have taken this construction from the Hellenistic writers. F. Bovon, *Das Evangelium nach Lukas*, 275; F. Bovon, H. Koester, and D. S. Deer, *Luke 2*, 598; M. Wolter, *Das Lukasevangelium*, 613; R. Dillmann and C. Mora Paz, *Das Lukas-Evangelium*, 326;

D. L. Bock, *Luke*, 1518; R. H. Stein, *Luke*, 468; D. L. Tiede, *Luke*, 321; G. Maier, *Lukas-Evangelium* 429; L. T. Johnson, *The Gospel of Luke*, 285; D. Dormeyer, *Das Lukas-evangelium*, 213.

[260] P. Kariamadam, *The Zacchaeus Story (Lk 19:1-10)*, 27-28.

[261] In his own words, "Zachäus ... erfüllt ... in dem sprechenden Akt des 'Nach-unten-Steigens' die für die Heimsuchung Jesu notwendige Bedingung der Umkehr." Hotze, *Jesus als Gast*, 67.

[262] D. L. Bock, *Luke*, 1518.

[263] J. O'Hanlon, "The Story of Zacchaeus and the Lukan Ethic." 15.

[264] R. H. Stein, *Luke*, 468; D. L. Tiede, *Luke*, 321; J. Nolland, *Luke*, 905; J. Ernst, *Das Evangelium nach Lukas*, 389.

[265] J. A. Fitzmyer, *The Gospel According to Luke X-XXIV*, 1224; Wolter says it is a „überinterpretation," because Luke does not say anything beyond simply stating that Zacchaeus received Jesus with joy. M. Wolter, *Das Lukasevangelium*, 613.

[266] F. Bovon, *Das Evangelium nach Lukas*, 275; Evans, *Luke*, 283.

[267] Hotze, *Jesus als Gast*, 66.

[268] W. Hendriksen, *Exposition of the Gospel According to Luke*, 856.

[269] J. Nolland, *Luke*, 905; D. L. Bock, *Luke*, 1518.

[270] M. Wolter, *Das Lukasevangelium*, 613; also K. Löning, *Der Weg Jesu*, Das Geschichtswerk des Lukas Bd. 2 (Stuttgart: Kohlhammer, 2006), 192; J. M. Creed, *The Gospel According to St. Luke*, 230. Manson thinks the opposite. For him the scene is still at the roadside. Jesus and Zacchaeus are still in the street with the people. W. Manson, *The Gospel of Luke*, 210. For Wolter, the question whether there was a fellowship meal at the house of Zacchaeus is very much open. For him, one can argue for and against such a presumption. M. Wolter, *Das Lukasevangelium*, 613.

[271] H. Klein, *Das Lukasevangelium*, 601.

[272] Cf. J. A. Fitzmyer, *The Gospel According to Luke X-XXIV*, 1224 and J. B. Green, *The Gospel of Luke*, 671.

[273] Hotze, *Jesus als Gast*, 67.

[274] J. A. Fitzmyer, *The Gospel According to Luke X-XXIV*, 1224; P. Kariamadam, *The Zacchaeus Story (Lk 19:1-10)*, 29; R. H. Stein, *Luke*, 468.

[275] Cf. Luke 1:63, 66; 2:3, 18, 47; 4:22, 28, 40; 5:26; 8:40; 52; 9:15, 17, 43; 13:3, 5,1 7, 27; 14:29; 15:1, 19:7; 20:38; 21:15; 22:70; 23:48-49.

[276] K. Rengstorf, "γογγύζω," in G. Kittel, G. W. Bromiley & G. Friedrich, *Theological Dictionary of the New Testament*, 1, 730; cf. also A. J. Hess, "γογγύζω," in H. Balz and G. Schneider, *Exegetical Dictionary of the New Testament*, 1, 256; F. W. Danker and W. Bauer, *A Greek-English lexicon of the New Testament and other early Christian literature*, 204.

[277] J. B. Green, *The Gospel of Luke*, 671; R. Dillmann and C. Mora Paz, *Das Lukas-Evangelium*, 326; D. Dormeyer, *Das Lukas-evangelium*, 214; W. L. Liefeld and D. W. Pao, *Luke - Acts*, 286; W. Wiefel, *Das Evangelium nach Lukas*, 327; D. A. S. Ravens, "Zacchaeus." 24. Kariamadam finds many similarities between the murmuring of "all" in 19:7 and the murmuring of Simon the Pharisee (7:39). In both texts Jesus enjoys table fellowship. In both grumblings, Jesus´ acceptance of a sinner is referred to. And in both grumblings, the woman / man is called a "sinner." Cf. P. Kariamadam, *The Zacchaeus Story (Lk 19:1-10)*, 32-33.

[278] J. O'Hanlon, "The Story of Zacchaeus and the Lukan Ethic." 15-16; cf. also D. L. Bock, *Luke*, 1519.

[279] M. Wolter, *Das Lukasevangelium*, 613.

[280] J. B. Green, *The Gospel of Luke*, 671.

[281] F. Büchsel, "καταλύω," in G. Kittel, G. W. Bromiley & G. Friedrich, *Theological Dictionary of the New Testament*, 4, 338; H. Hübner, "καταλύω," in H. Balz and G. Schneider, *Exegetical Dictionary of the New Testament*, 2, 264; F. W. Danker and W. Bauer, *A Greek-English lexicon of the New Testament and other early Christian literature*, 522.

[282] W. Grundmann, *Das Evangelium nach Lukas*, 359; cf. W. Wiefel, *Das Evangelium nach Lukas*, 327.

[283] G. Maier, *Lukas-Evangelium*, 430.

[284] This connection seems to be <u>farfetched</u> and it is not very sure, whether this is intended by Luke.

[285] M. Strauss, "Luke." 463.

[286] F. Bovon, *Das Evangelium nach Lukas*, 275; F. Bovon, H. Koester, and D. S. Deer, *Luke 2*, 598.

[287] D. L. Bock, *Luke*, 1521.

[288] F. Hahn, *Christologische Hoheitstitel: Ihre Geschichte im frühen Christentum*, 5th ed., Uni-Taschenbücher 1873 (Göttingen: Vandenhoeck & Ruprecht, 1995), no. 5, 270; in the words of Hotze, „Die Umkehr des Zachäus liegt dem Redaktor zwar irnmerhin so am Herzen, dass er V. 8 eingefügt hat." Hotze, *Jesus als Gast*, 71; also W. Grundmann, *Das Evangelium nach Lukas*, 359; J. Ernst, *Das Evangelium nach Lukas*, 390; A. R. C. Leaney, *A Commentary on the Gospel According to St. Luke*, Harper's New Testament commentaries (New York: Harper, 1958), 241; P. Kariamadam, *The Zacchaeus Story (Lk 19:1-10)*, 34; W. Wiefel, *Das Evangelium nach Lukas*, 327; J. Nolland, *Luke*, 905.

[289] Hotze, *Jesus als Gast*, 72.

[290] J. A. Fitzmyer, *The Gospel According to Luke X-XXIV*, 1220.

[291] R. C. White, "Vindication for Zacchaeus?" 21; also J. Gillman, *Possessions and the Life of Faith*, 90.

[292] R. C. White, "Vindication for Zacchaeus?" 21.

[293] First of all, White has put together different forms of narratives like parables (Luke 15:11-32), healing narratives (Luke 5:17-27; 9:37-43) and Jesus' forgiving narratives (Luke 7:36-50). Secondly in mentioning the different elements that these salvation stories have, White himself is not able to show that these stories have all the elements which he thought fitting to be salvation stories. ibid., 21. For further references, cf. D. Hamm, "Luke 19:8 Once Again." 434.

[294] J. A. Fitzmyer, *The Gospel According to Luke X-XXIV*, 1225; A. Plummer, *A Critical and Exegetical Commentary on the Gospel According to S. Luke*, 425; Bock is also of the same opinion; D. L. Bock, *Luke*, 1519. For Johnson, the word σταθεως suggests that on the way to his house, Zacchaeus stopped to proclaim something about his future life. L. T. Johnson, *The Gospel of Luke*, 285. Dillersberger too says something similar. J. Dillersberger, *The Gospel of Saint Luke*, 441.

[295] E. E. Ellis, *The Gospel of Luke*, 222. Other scholars who are of the same opinion are D. Hamm, "Luke 19:8 Once Again." 435; R. Summers, *Commentary on Luke*, 223; G. Maier, *Lukas-Evangelium*, 430; W. Hendriksen, *Exposition of the Gospel According to Luke*, 856.

[296] N. Geldenhuys, *Commentary on the Gospel of Luke*, 470; Godet suggests that the redactional comments in v. 11 and in 28 support such a proposition. F. L. Godet, *A Commentary on the Gospel of St. Luke*, 2, 217.

[297] R. H. Stein, *Luke*, 468.

[298] M. Wolter, *Das Lukasevangelium*, 613; L. Morris, *Luke*, 298; D. Hamm, "Luke 19:8 Once Again." 435; the word could also mean the resoluteness of Zacchaeus in what he says. He stands firm and ready to do what he proclaims to Jesus. Cf. also R. Summers, *Commentary on Luke*, 223; D. A. S. Ravens, "Zacchaeus." 26. Godet on the other hand looks at the standing posture of Zacchaeus, as "a firm and dignified attitude such as suits a man whose dignity is attacked." F. L. Godet, *A Commentary on the Gospel of St. Luke*, 2, 217.

[299] P. Kariamadam, *The Zacchaeus Story (Lk 19:1-10)*, 34; G. Maier, *Lukas-Evangelium*, 430.

[300] As stated by J. A. Fitzmyer, *The Gospel According to Luke X-XXIV*, 1225; That Zacchaeus spoke these words during a meal is supported also by F. L. Godet, *A Commentary on the Gospel of St. Luke*, 2, 217; E. E. Ellis, *The Gospel of Luke*, 221; J. Dillersberger, *The Gospel of Saint Luke*, 441; R. Summers, *Commentary on Luke*, 223; Marshall also states that Zacchaeus utters these words during the meal, but that the murmurers are still present. H. I. Marshall, W. W. Gasque, and D. A. Hagner, *The Gospel of Luke: A Commentary on the Greek Text*, 697.

[301] It is awkward because the answer for the criticism from the murmurers is not from Jesus against whom the criticism was directed but from Zacchaeus. It is Lukan, because of the words that Luke uses here like ε6πεν with πρиς + accusative, together with other words. Cf. J. Nolland, *Luke*, 905; also J. A. Fitzmyer, *The Gospel According to Luke X-XXIV*, 1219.

[302] J. A. Fitzmyer, "κύριος," in H. Balz and G. Schneider, *Exegetical Dictionary of the New Testament*, 2, 331; P. Kariamadam, *The Zacchaeus Story (Lk 19:1-10)*, 34; O'Hanlon too says, using πρχς τxν with κ{ριον is typical of Luke. J. O'Hanlon, "The Story of Zacchaeus and the Lukan Ethic." 16.

[303] G. Maier, *Lukas-Evangelium*, 430; P. Kariamadam, *The Zacchaeus Story (Lk 19:1-10)*, 35.

[304] F. L. Godet, *A Commentary on the Gospel of St. Luke*, 2, 217.

[305] Cf. H. Probst, "Qπάρχω," in H. Balz and G. Schneider, *Exegetical Dictionary of the New Testament*, 3, 395-396.

[306] J. P. Louw, E. A. Nida, and R. B. Smith, *Greek-English Lexicon of the New Testament based on Semantic Domains*, 2nd ed. (New York: United Bible Societies, 1989), 1, 558; H. G. Liddell and R. Scott, *A Greek-English Lexicon*, 1857; also, N. M. Watson, "Was Zacchaeus Really Reforming?" 282; D. Hamm, "Luke 19:8 Once Again." 434; M. Wolter, *Das Lukasevangelium*, 613; R. C. Tannehill, "The Story of Zacchaeus as Rhetoric." 468; P. Kariamadam, *The Zacchaeus Story (Lk 19:1-10)*, 35.

[307] W. Foerster, "Κύριος," in *TDNT*, ed. G. Kittel et al., 10 vols. (Grand Rapids, Michigan: W. B. Eerdmans, 1964-1976), 1046.

[308] G. Yamasaki, "Point of View in a Gospel Story: What Difference Does It Make?" 103.

[309] Cf. A. Plummer, *A Critical and Exegetical Commentary on the Gospel According to S. Luke*, 435.

[310] L. T. Johnson, *The Gospel of Luke*, 286; J. A. Fitzmyer, *The Gospel According to Luke X-XXIV*, 1219.

[311] D. Hamm, "Luke 19:8 Once Again." 434.

[312] Cf. N. M. Watson, "Was Zacchaeus Really Reforming?" 282-283; also M. Wolter, *Das Lukasevangelium*, 613.

[313] A. Plummer, *A Critical and Exegetical Commentary on the Gospel According to S. Luke*, 435.

[314] H. Merklein, "πτωχός," in H. Balz and G. Schneider, *Exegetical Dictionary of the New Testament*, 3, 193.

[315] Ibid., 193-194; F. Hauck and E. Bammel, "πτωχός," in G. Kittel, G. W. Bromiley & G. Friedrich, *Theological Dictionary of the New Testament*, 6, 887-888; F. W. Danker and W. Bauer, *A Greek-English lexicon of the New Testament and other early Christian literature*, 896. We do not go into the political connotation of the term, where the people of Israel after exile are collectively understood to be the poor and the afflicted ones (cf. Isa 51:21; 54:11; 61:1-11).

[316] P. Billerbeck and H. L. Strack, *Kommentar zum Neuen Testament*, IV, 547; also W. Wiefel, *Das Evangelium nach Lukas*, 327; M. Strauss, "Luke." 463.

[317] F. Hauck and E. Bammel, "πτωχός." 6, 907.

[318] H. Merklein, "πτωχός." 194.

[319] J. A. Fitzmyer, *The Gospel According to Luke X-XXIV*, 1225; L. T. Johnson, *The Gospel of Luke*, 286.

[320] M. Wolter, *Das Lukasevangelium*, 614.

[321] C. H. Hunzinger, "συκοφαντέω," in G. Kittel, G. W. Bromiley & G. Friedrich, *Theological Dictionary of the New Testament*, 7, 759; O. Hofius, "συκοφαντέω," in H. Balz and G. Schneider, *Exegetical Dictionary of the New Testament*, 3, 285; F. W. Danker and W. Bauer, *A Greek-English lexicon of the New Testament and other early Christian literature*, 955; E. Nestle, "Sykophantia im biblischen Griechisch," *ZNWÿþ* 4 (1903), 271; D. Hamm, "Luke 19:8 Once Again." 434.

[322] D. Hamm, "Luke 19:8 Once Again.", 434.

[323] F. Bovon, *Das Evangelium nach Lukas*, 276; F. Bovon, H. Koester, and D. S. Deer, *Luke 2*, 599.

[324] J. Nolland, *Luke*, 150.

[325] D. A. S. Ravens, "Zacchaeus." 22.

[326] Bock looks at similar usage of ε4 in Pauline Corpus, where the word is used in the sense of since (Rom 5:17; Col 2:20; 3:1). D. L. Bock, *Luke*, 1520-1521; authors with similar thoughts are R. Summers, *Commentary on Luke*, 223; W. L. Liefeld and D. W. Pao, *Luke - Acts*, 286; E. E. Ellis, *The Gospel of Luke*, 221; J. Reiling and J. L. Swellengrebel, *A Translator's Handbook on the Gospel of Luke*, 618.

[327] A. Plummer, *A Critical and Exegetical Commentary on the Gospel According to S. Luke*, 435.

[328] For Godet, the word Qπαρχυντων should be understood not as properties but his (yearly) income. F. L. Godet, *A Commentary on the Gospel of St. Luke*, 2, 217.

[329] Ibid., 217.

[330] J. A. Fitzmyer, *The Gospel According to Luke X-XXIV*, 1221.

[331] Cf. M. Wolter, *Das Lukasevangelium*, 614, also G. Schneider, *Das Evangelium nach Lukas*, 378; J. Nolland, *Luke*, 906.

[332] L. T. Johnson, *The Gospel of Luke*, 286; cf. also F. Bovon, *Das Evangelium nach Lukas*, 276; G. B. Caird, *Saint Luke*, 208; A. Stöger, *Das Evangelium nach Lukas*, 145; D. L. Bock, *Luke*, 1520; W. Grundmann, *Das Evangelium nach Lukas*, 360; A. Schlatter, *Die Evangelien nach Markus und Lukas*, 250.

[333] K. Löning, *Der Weg Jesu*, 185; R. Dillmann and C. Mora Paz, *Das Lukas-Evangelium*, 326; F. Bovon, H. Koester, and D. S. Deer, *Luke 2*, 599; J. P. Kealy, *Luke's Gospel Today*, 361.

[334] D. L. Tiede, *Luke*, 321.

[335] R. Summers, *Commentary on Luke*, 468; G. Maier, *Lukas-Evangelium*, 431.The context of the generosity of these two men is entirely different from each other. Herod generously offers the half of his kingdom in response to the enthralling dance performed by the daughter of Herodias, whereas Zacchaeus offers to let go half of his possessions as a sign of showing repentance. It is however interesting

to note, that both the offers / promises are made in the context of a banquet.

[336] S. H. Ringe, *Luke*, 232.

[337] F. Bovon, *Das Evangelium nach Lukas*, 276; R. C. Tannehill, "The Story of Zacchaeus as Rhetoric." 203.

[338] R. H. Stein, *Luke*, 468.

[339] J. B. Green, *The Gospel of Luke*, 672.

[340] K. Löning, *Der Weg Jesu*, 185.

[341] Hotze puts it succinctly when he says in p. 69, „beides" ist „*in etwa gleichgewichtet, die zuvorkommende (heimsuchende) Gnade Gottes ebenso wie die Umkehr des Menschen.*" He states further, „*Wichtig ist dass Jesus in 9c eine solche Heilsgeschichtliche und keine andere Begründung gibt, etwa: „weil Zachaus sich von seinen Sünden Iosgesagt hat" o.ä. Nicht die Umkehr des Menschen, so unverzichtbar sie auch ist, sondern Gottes Heilsplan bildet den tiefsten Grund fur die eschatologische Rettung.*" Hotze, *Jesus als Gast*, 70.

[342] N. Geldenhuys, *Commentary on the Gospel of Luke*, 470.

[343] J. A. Fitzmyer, *The Gospel According to Luke X-XXIV*, 1225; F. L. Godet, *A Commentary on the Gospel of St. Luke*, 2, 218; H. Klein, *Das Lukasevangelium*, 602; D. L. Bock, *Luke*, 1522; P. Kariamadam, *The Zacchaeus Story (Lk 19:1-10)*, 39; similar use of πρχς could is seen in 12:41 (πρὸς ἡμᾶς and πρχς πqντας). Cf. T. Zahn, *Das Evangelium des Lucas*, 623.

[344] R. Summers, *Commentary on Luke*, 223-224; *Contra*, R. Bultmann, *The History of the Synoptic Tradition*, 33.

[345] The redactional hand of Luke is also seen in the fact that the phrase ε6πεν δr is typically Lukan. It is used as many as 59 times in Luke and 15 times in Acts. Cf. P. Kariamadam, *The Zacchaeus Story (Lk 19:1-10)*, 39.

[346] M. Wolter, *Das Lukasevangelium*, 615.

[347] Kariamadam gives many examples within Luke where such doubling could be seen (e.g. Luke 7:38, 44, 46; 14:21, 23; 15:18-19, 21; 15:24, 32; 18:2, 4). P. Kariamadam, *The Zacchaeus Story (Lk 19:1-10)*, 40.

[348] W. Foerster and W. Fohrer, "σὀζω," in G. Kittel, G. W. Bromiley & G. Friedrich, *Theological Dictionary of the New Testament*, 7, 966-969; also K. H. Schelkle, "σωτηρία," in H. Balz and G. Schneider, *Exegetical Dictionary of the New Testament*, 3, 327; F. W. Danker and W. Bauer, *A Greek-English lexicon of the New Testament and other early Christian literature*, 985-986.

[349] Apart from the Lukan double work we see the word fourteen times in Paul, four times in Deutero Pauline letters, six times in the pastoral letters and seven times in the Letter to the Hebrews. Cf. K. H. Schelkle, "σωτηρία." 3, 327.

[350] F. Hahn, *Christologische Hoheitstitel*, no. 6, 45.

[351] J. A. Fitzmyer, *The Gospel According to Luke X-XXIV*, 1225.

[352] J. B. Green, *The Gospel of Luke*, 673.

[353] D. L. Bock, *Luke*, 1522.

[354] L. T. Johnson, *The Gospel of Luke*, 286.

[355] F. L. Godet, *A Commentary on the Gospel of St. Luke*, 2, 218.

[356] J. B. Green, *The Gospel of Luke*, 673; also T. Zahn, *Das Evangelium des Lucas*, 623-624; D. L. Bock, *Luke*, 1522; W. Grundmann, *Das Evangelium nach Lukas*, 360; F. B. Craddock, *Luke*, 220; N. Geldenhuys, *Commentary on the Gospel of Luke*, 472.

[357] R. Summers, *Commentary on Luke*, 224.

[358] Cf. P. Kariamadam, *The Zacchaeus Story (Lk 19:1-10)*, 41.

[359] J. S. Siker, "From Gentile Inclusion To Jewish Exclusion: Abraham in Early Christian Controversy with Jews," *Biblical Theology Bulletin: A Journal of Bible and Theology* 19, no. 1 (1989), https://doi.org/10.1177/014610798901900105, 32, accessed on 15.03.2016.

[360] H. I. Marshall, *Luke: Historian and Theologian* (Milton Keynes, UK: Paternoster, 1970), 188; also W. Wiefel, *Das Evangelium nach Lukas*, 327; D. L. Bock, *Luke*, 1522.

[361] F. L. Godet, *A Commentary on the Gospel of St. Luke*, 2, 218; also D. L. Bock, *Luke*, 1522.

[362] Cf. W. Hendriksen, *Exposition of the Gospel According to Luke*, 29; L. Morris, *Luke*, 299; P. Billerbeck and H. L. Strack, *Kommentar zum Neuen Testament*, 251; A. Stöger, *Das Evangelium nach Lukas*, 146; E. E. Ellis, *The Gospel of Luke*, 221; R. H. Stein says, not only by his repentance, but also through his reception of Jesus in faith, Zacchaeus has shown himself as the son of Abraham. R. H. Stein, *Luke*, 469.

[363] F. Bovon, *Das Evangelium nach Lukas*, 277.

[364] Hotze, *Jesus als Gast*, 70. Hotze however says, it is difficult to decide whether Luke was aware of and deliberately made this parallel between Abraham and Zacchaeus.

[365] J. S. Siker, "From Gentile Inclusion To Jewish Exclusion." 30-36.

[366] F. Bovon, H. Koester, and D. S. Deer, *Luke 2*, 600; also F. Bovon, *Das Evangelium nach Lukas*, 277.

[367] G. B. Caird, *Saint Luke*, 208; L. T. Johnson, *The Gospel of Luke*, 286;

[368] J. B. Green, *The Gospel of Luke*, 672.

[369] W. Foerster and W. Fohrer, "σόζω." 7, 1002.

[370] F. L. Godet, *A Commentary on the Gospel of St. Luke*, 2, 218. The word within brackets is not in the original.

[371] H. I. Marshall, *Luke*, 116.

[372] R. Bultmann, *The History of the Synoptic Tradition*, 34; C. Colpe, "Ἀ υιxς τοæ νθρώπου," in G. Kittel, G. W. Bromiley & G. Friedrich, *Theological Dictionary of the New Testament*, 453.

[373] P. Kariamadam, *The Zacchaeus Story (Lk 19:1-10)*, 43; Conzelmann looks at 19:10 as a later formulation of the Christian community about the earthly ministry of Jesus. H. Conzelmann, *Grundriss der Theologie des Neuen Testaments*, 5th ed., UTB (Tübingen: Mohr, 1992), 108.

[374] P. Kariamadam, *The Zacchaeus Story (Lk 19:1-10)*, 43.

[375] The very titles of the articles of A. J. B. Higgins and Morna Hooker show how challenging the understanding of 'the Son of Man´ is for the scholars. M. D. Hooker, "Is the Son of Man Problem Really Insoluble?," in *Text and Interpretation: Studies in the New Testament presented to Matthew Black*, ed. Matthew Black, Ernest Best and Robert M. Wilson (Cambridge: Cambridge University Press, 1979), 155-168.

[376] Vögtle´s seminal contribution, *Die Gretchenfrage des Menschensohn-Problems* is an attempt to revise his earlier understanding of the Son of Man problem in his habilitation work. A. Vögtle, *Die "Gretchenfrage" des Menschensohn-Problems: Bilanz und Perspektiven*, Quaestiones disputatae 152 (Freiburg im Breisgau: Herder, 1994).

[377] Ibid., 10.

[378] A. Y. Collins, "The Origin of the designation of Jesus as "Son of Man," *The Harvard Theological Review* 80, no. 4 (1987), 394.

[379] In his words „Bar bezeichnet das zum Kollektiv 'Mensch´ (enascha) gehörige Individuum." There is no essential difference between the definite *bar nasha* and the indefinite *bar enash*. Hence for Vögtle and others, the different Aramaic terms like "*bar nasha*" / "*bar nash*" or "*bar enasha*" / "*bar enash*" mean the same thing – a man or someone. A. Vögtle, *Die "Gretchenfrage" des Menschensohn-Problems*, 11. Earlier in the twentieth century, M. Black too attests to this generic understanding of the aramaic *bar enash(a)*. M. Black, "The 'Son of Man' in the Teaching of Jesus," *Exp Tim* 60 (1948), 32-36, esp. 35.

[380] For Schweizer, the references to the Son of Man in this group of sayings might well go back to the historical Jesus, who "takes up the term Son of Man, on the one hand because it was no customary title and could design a humble "man" as well as an "eschatological" figure, on the other, perhaps, because in Daniel 7 the Son of Man is the representative of the suffering and finally exalted Israel." E. Schweizer, "The Son of Man." 122.

[381] H. I. Marshall, "The Synoptic Son of Man Sayings in Recent Discussion," *NTS* 12 (1966), 327; Hooker states that this traditional grouping, though convenient, is 'misleading,´ since one cannot strictly divide the sayings of Jesus between the sufferings and the Resurrection, hence between the "Suffering Son of Man" and the "Eschatological Son of Man." M. D. Hooker, "Is the Son of Man Problem Really Insoluble?" 159-160. Moloney too holds a similar view saying these groupings are "highly unsatisfactory" though very practical. F. J. Moloney, "Constructing Jesus and the Son of Man," *CBQ* 75, no. 4 (2013), 735. Scholars

attempt other ways of grouping the Son of Man sayings in the Synoptics. Vermès lays out another way of grouping than the above-mentioned: (a). those Son of Man sayings which have direct allusions to Daniel 7, (b). those which have an indirect allusions to Daniel and (c). those sayings with no reference to the text in Daniel. Cf. G. Vermès, *Jesus the Jew: A Historian's Reading of the Gospels* (London: Collins, 1973), 180-186. Bock divides the Son of Man sayings into two categories: (a). those sayings which refer directly or indirectly to Daniel and (b). those which refer to the authority of the Son of Man and others which refer to his sufferings. For Bock Luke 19:10 does not come under either of the two, since 19:10 does not talk about the authority but about the mission of the Son of Man. Cf. D. L. Bock, "The Son of Man in Luke 5:24," *Bulletin for Biblical Research* 1 (1991), 112.

[382] W. O. Walker Jr., "The Son of Man: Some Recent Developments," *CBQ* 45, no. 4 (1983) 589-590.

[383] E. Schweizer, "The Son of Man." 119-129; E. Schweizer, "The Son of Man Again," *NTS* 9 (1962-63), 256-261; H. I. Marshall, "The Synoptic Son of Man Sayings in Recent Discussion." 327-351; R. N. Longenecker, "'Son of Man' as a Self-Designation of Jesus," *Journal of the Evangelical Theological Society* 12, no. 3 (1969) 151-158.

[384] H. I. Marshall, "The Synoptic Son of Man Sayings in Recent Discussion." 350-351.

[385] E. Schweizer, "The Son of Man." 122; cf. also E. Schweizer, "The Son of Man Again." 259.

[386] A. J. B. Higgins, *The Son of Man in the Teaching of Jesus* (Cambridge: Cambridge University Press, 1980), 125.

[387] Vermès gives many examples of Aramaic texts wherein the phrase *hahu gabra* is used as a circumlocution. G. Vermès, *Jesus the Jew*, 163-164.

[388] J. A. Fitzmyer, *The Gospel According to Luke I-IX*, 210. Though Fitzmyer accepts the authenticity of these sayings, he doubts whether Jesus used the phrase to refer to himself. He proposes Jesus "probably used *bar înâś* in the generic sense (a human being, a mortal); and that this was later understood in the early tradition in a titular sense and applied to him. J. A. Fitzmyer, *The Gospel According to Luke I-IX*, 210, 681.

[389] R. Bultmann, *The History of the Synoptic Tradition*, 151-152; also A. Y. Collins, "The Origin of the designation of Jesus as "Son of Man." 406. *Contra* Vögtle. Vögtle is right in saying that the belief that Jesus understood himself as the end-time judge is as equally unthinkable as the belief that Jesus thought of a third person between God and him as the end-time judge. In his words, „*Dass Jesus außer Gott sich selbst als Endrichter verstand und ankündigte, ist nicht ganz aber annähernd so unwahrscheinlich wie die Annahmen, er habe einen anderen, also einen zwischen Gott und sich tretenden Dritten als über Heilserlangung und*

Verwerfung entscheidende Größe erwartet." A. Vögtle, *Die "Gretchenfrage" des Menschensohn-Problems*, 24-25.

[390] A. Vögtle, *Die "Gretchenfrage" des Menschensohn-Problems*, 174. Vögtle further states „*der Glaube an das Kommen des erhöhten Herrn zu Gericht und Heilsvollendung („Maranatha") vorausging der Artikulierung dieses Glaubens mittels der MS-Bezeichnung.*" The word *'vorausging'* is placed in a different word order in the original.

[391] N. Perrin, *Was Lehrte Jesus Wirklich?: Rekonstruction und Deutung* (Göttingen: Vandenhoeck und Ruprecht, 1972), 184, 225.

[392] In Oberliner's words, *"zwei Aspekte der die Evangelien prägenden Jesustradition sind ... miteinander verschmolzen. Es ist zum einen die Art der Formulierung, die vom nachösterlichen Bekennnis zum Auferweckten bestimmt ist; und ist zum anderen der Jesus in der Zeit seines öffentlichen wirkens zugeschriebene Ausblick auf einen gewaltsamen Tod in Jerusalem, den Jesus im kleineren Kries seiner Jünger ankündigt und der dann ... in der Passionerzählung geschildert wird."* L. Oberliner, ""*Der Menschensohn muss leiden...*" (Mk 8,31)." 53.

[393] In the words of Prostmeier, *"Sofern für die geistig-sozialen Milieus im Judentum, in denen der historische Jesus auftrat, die Vertrautheit mit den virulenten apokalyptischen Vorstellungen nicht ausgeschlossen werden kann, wäre es nicht unplausibel, wenn in seiner Verkündigung auch vom Menschensohn in dem Sinne die Rede gewesen wäre, dass diese himmlische Gestalt als Gottes Vollmachtsträger bald zum eschatalogischen Gericht kommen und alle retten wird, die an Gott glauben und nach seinem Willen gerecht leben."* F. R. Prostmeier, "Thesen zur "Gretchenfrage"," in L. Oberlinner and F. R. Prostmeier, *Jesus im Glaubenszeugnis des Neuen Testaments*, 241.

[394] Ibid., 242; similar view is also rendered by Moloney; cf. F. J. Moloney, "Constructing Jesus and the Son of Man." 738. Collins <u>understands</u> that Jesus might have meant some other person when he talked about the Son of Man. A. Y. Collins, "The Origin of the designation of Jesus as "Son of Man." 406.

[395] E. Schweizer, "The Son of Man." 128; cf. also R. Morton, "Son of Man," in *Encyclopedia of the Historical Jesus*, ed. Craig A. Evans (London: Routledge, 2008), 593-598.

[396] To quote further from Prostmeier, es „*ist nicht auszuschließen, dass neben oder vor der Signierung des Osterglaubens mit maranatha die Erinnerung , der historische Jesus habe vom kommenden Menschensohn im Sinn der apokalyptischen Theozentrik gesprochen, einen Anhalt für die Applikation und Entfaltung der Menschensohnlogien geboten hat.*" F. R. Prostmeier, "Thesen zur "Gretchenfrage"." 242.

[397] Schenk categorizes the Son of Man sayings in Luke according to the geographical ministry of Jesus: a. seven references to the Son of Man in the Galilee ministry of Jesus (5:24; 6:5, 22; 7:34; 9:22, 26, 44); b. twelve Son of Man

references in the Travel Narrative (9:58; 11:30; 12:8, 10, 40; 17:22, 24, 26, 30; 18:8; 19:10); c. six Son of Man references in the Jerusalem ministry (21:27, 36; 22:22, 48, 69; 24:7). Since in all three phases (Galilee ministry, Travel Narrative and Jerusalem ministry) there are references to the earthly ministry of Jesus, his suffering, his death and his coming in glory, Schenk is of the opinion that the traditional grouping of the references as seen in the previous page is not compatible with Luke's use of phrase A υlxς τοæ νθρώπου. W. Schenk, *Das biographische Ich-Idiom "Menschensohn" in den frühen Jesus-Biographien*, 177.

[398] The question is, though, as to which usage is was originally found in Q whether it was 'I' or whether it was the Son of Man, and who has redacted the source; whether Matthew found the Son of Man in Q and changed it into the first person pronoun in these two verses or whether Luke changed the first person pronoun found in Q into the Son of Man. Schenk argues for the authenticity of "I" in Q, which was changed to the 'Son of Man.' ibid., 179.

[399] C. Colpe, "A υlxς τοæ νθρώπου.", 458.

[400] B. Lindars, *Jesus Son of Man*, 143.

[401] Cf. Chapter IV. 8.1.

[402] Lindars rightly sees a thematic connection between the Levi narrative and the Zacchaeus narrative. While Luke 5:32 was essential to the narrative, Luke 19:10 is not absolutely essential to complete the story of Zacchaeus. B. Lindars, *Jesus Son of Man*, 137.

[403] A. J. B. Higgins, *The Son of Man in the Teaching of Jesus*, 25.

[404] In the words of Hahn „Luke 19,10 ist relativ selbständiger, jedenfalls später zugewachsener Spruch." F. Hahn, *Christologische Hoheitstitel*, no. 5, 270.

[405] Hahn states „Dabei stoßen wir auf ein vom AT abhängiges, aber nicht spezifisch palästinisches Denken, weswegen die Herkunft aus dem hellenistischen Judenchristentum am wahrscheinlichsten ist." ibid., 45.

[406] Vermès states the following regarding the Son of Man sayings of Jesus including Luke 19:10: "there is no reasonable doubt why Jesus would not have uttered them. If fact, if only half of these sayings are authentic, it would still be justifiable, to infer that the Son of Man circumlocution belonged to the stylistic idiosyncracies of Jesus himself." G. Vermès, *Jesus the Jew*, 182; *contra* J. A. Fitzmyer, "Another View of the 'Son of Man' Debate," *JSNT* 2, no. 4 (1979), 59.

[407] H. I. Marshall, "The Synoptic Son of Man Sayings in Recent Discussion." 343.

[408] H. E. Tödt, *Der Menschensohn in der Synoptischen Überlieferung*, 4th ed. (Gütersloh: Mohn, 1978), 124.

[409] G. Lindeskog, "Das Rätsel des Menschensohnes," *Studia Theologica* 22, no. 2 (1968), no. 68, 167.

[410] C. Colpe, "A υlxς τοæ νθρώπου." 439.

[411] It is to be noted that Luke adds the word 'repentance' to the Mk source (Mk 2:8).

⁴¹² Codices like Κ, Γ, Θ, f ¹,¹³ have an additional reading for Luke 9:56, which renders the reason for Jesus' rebuking the disciples. Καν ε6πεν ... Α γpp υ1οΒς τοæ νθρώπου οΡκ &λθεν ψυχρς νθρώπων πολέσαι λλρ σöσαι.

⁴¹³ H. E. Tödt, *Der Menschensohn in der Synoptischen Überlieferung*, 125.

⁴¹⁴ Hotze, *Jesus als Gast*, 71.

⁴¹⁵ Luke's interest in the word πόλλυμι and its variants could be seen from the fact that in the third Gospel the word is found as many as 27 times, while in Matthew it is employed in 19 times and in Mark 10 times. Cf. P. Kariamadam, *The Zacchaeus Story (Lk 19:1-10)*, 44.

⁴¹⁶ Scholars point out the similarities in wordings between Ezek 34:16 and Luke 19:10. Just like Luke, Ezekiel talks of seeking the lost and bringing back the strayed. The wordings of 34:16a, Τx πολωλxς ζητυσω are also similar to Luke 19:10: M. Wolter, *Das Lukasevangelium*, 615; J. A. Fitzmyer, *The Gospel According to Luke I-IX*, 1226; A. Stöger, *Das Evangelium nach Lukas*, 146; D. L. Tiede, *Luke*, 322; R. Summers, *Commentary on Luke*, 224; G. Maier, *Lukas-Evangelium*, 434; D. L. Bock, *Luke*, 1523; R. Dillmann and C. Mora Paz, *Das Lukas-Evangelium*, 326; P. Kariamadam, *The Zacchaeus Story (Lk 19:1-10)*, 44.

⁴¹⁷ E. LaVerdiere, *Dining in the Kingdom of God*, 225.

⁴¹⁸ Dillmann too suggests that through this episode of Zacchaeus, the pronouncement of the infancy narrative has become actualized. God has visited his people as it is proclaimed in the Magnificat: "for he has looked favorably on his people and redeemed them" (Luke 1:68). R. Dillmann and C. Mora Paz, *Das Lukas-Evangelium*, 326.

⁴¹⁹ F. B. Craddock, *Luke*, 220.

Chapter - 4

Casteism in the Light of Zacchaeus Story

As an Indian Christian, one cannot but look at the story of Zacchaeus in the context of caste system in India. There is much in common between the narration of the tax collectors in Jewish society at the time of Jesus and the plight of social outcasts like and their counterparts in the Indian society at present. In the following pages, we try to understand casteism in India from a historical background, the absorption of casteism in Christianity and its evil ramifications even to the present generation. Over against this background, the initiative of Jesus to have table fellowship with Zacchaeus shows what model of relationship the Indian Christians need to embrace in our effort to follow Jesus.

Caste: A Hierarchical Structure

Caste system is millennium year old social order, through which the Indian society has been organized and maintained as a hierarchical structure.[1] Mill defines the caste system in India in the following way:

> The classification and distribution of the members of a community into certain classes or orders, for the performance of certain functions, with the enjoyment of certain privileges or the endurance of certain burdens, and the establishment of hereditary permanence in these orders, the son being ordained to perform the functions, to enjoy the privileges, or

sustain the burdens of the father, and to marry only in his own tribe, without mixture of the classes, in regular succession, through all ages.[2]

Caste has been one of the indelible characteristics of the Indian culture. Speaking of Indian society one cannot and should not avoid caste system; because, caste in India has broken the barriers of languages, religions and races; it has spread its roots in the deepest layers of the Indian society.

Class and Caste - *Varna and Jāti*

The Hindu society is divided into four classes, which are called *varnas* (which literally means *color*). It has its origin from the Laws of *Manu* (*Manu Dharma*), the ancient Hindu Code of Conduct for religious and social life, which tries to explain the origin of humans, as being formed from the primordial human being, the *Purusha*. Out of his mouth sprang forth the *Brāhmaṇas*, the priestly class; out of his arms the *Kṣatriyas*, the warrior class came into existence. The *Vaiśyas*, the merchant class, tradesmen and artisans came from the thighs of the *Purusha* and out of his feet came forth the *Śūdrās*, the commoners and the working class (*Laws of Manu* I. 31). In this explanation we are able to see clearly the basic hierarchical structure of the caste system; the *Brāhmaṇas* are said to be the most powerful and most intelligent race in comparison to the people of other *varnas*, since they were formed from the head of the *Purusha*. The *Manu Dharma* states categorically who the best of creations is: "A *Brāhmaṇa* coming into existence, is born as the highest on earth, the lord of all created beings, for the protection of the treasury of the law. Whatever exists in the world is the property of the *Brāhmaṇa*" (*Laws of Manu* I. 99-100).[3] The arms being the symbol of strength, the *Kṣatriyas* who were formed from the arms of the Purusha are to be the warrior class and are to be inferior to the *Brāhmaṇas*. In contrast, the *Śūdrās* are considered to be lowly, since they were formed from the feet of the *Purusha*. In this way even the human body itself does not escape the concept of purity-pollution, since some parts of the body are said to be pure and other parts are said to be polluting. This purity-pollution seeps through the caste identity of the Hindu society. These four classes (*varnas*) in India are further divided into innumerable caste groups called *jātis*. Encyclopedia Britannica notes, there are around three thousand castes (*jātis*) under which there are 25000 sub-castes.[4]

Jāti could be understood as formation of a group based on the genealogical lineage. Within a *jāti* there could be different ancestral groups (*Gotra*). These ancestral groups intermarry within the *jāti* but not outside. Hence, a *jāti* is an endogamous system. A person marrying someone outside of his *jāti*, was normally thrown out of his caste. The names of the most of the *jātis* denote a profession. In that sense, a *jāti* could be paralleled to different family names in Germany, for example, *Zimmermann, Schneider, Wagner, Bäker* or *Müller*. Hence, it looks to be that the classification of the society into different *jātis* – at least originally – emerged due to the division of labor in the society. It is to be noted, however, that a *jāti* in principle is hereditary; a person belonging to carpenter *jāti* could not wish that his son takes up the job of officiating religious services at a temple. He had to remain within his borders and perform only what his *jāti* allows him to do. The Laws of *Manu* are clear in saying that performing the job which one's *jāti* stipulates one to do – this alone would liberate a man from the clutches of this life.

Oppressive Nature of Caste

Group identity or group pride could be seen all over the world. When, however, this pride is displayed as to project oneself superior to others and thereby showing the other as inferior to oneself, then the *group identity* becomes an instrument of *group oppression*. Nevertheless, with regard to the system of caste, there is no clear-cut distinction between "caste as a form of group identity and caste as a form of social oppression."[5] Over the millennia, caste has become an unconquerable monster through which different groups try to show their superiority over others in the social ladder and try to oppress other groups which are down, not just economically but also socially and culturally. As a social structure which is said to have been originated in the Vedic Period,[6] caste system in India divides the whole society into a large number of hereditary groups, distinguished from one another and connected together by three characteristics: *separation* in matters of marriage and contact, whether direct or indirect (food); *division of labour*, each group having, in theory or by tradition, a profession from which their members can depart only within certain limits; and finally *hierarchy*, which ranks the groups as relatively superior or inferior to one another.[7]

Many of the Hindu intelligentsia in India support caste system. Bhattacharya for example, refutes the claims of authors who talk about the oppressive nature of the caste system. In his view, caste system has played an important role in unifying the entire Hindu society and "provided bonds of union between races and clans that had nothing in common before its introduction."[8] It is true, that, as Bhattacharya says, the people of India were not united back then as one nation or religion. In fact, the notion of India as a nation is a development after the arrival of the colonial powers. One wonders, however, whether this way of uniting people of different culture and language and even different schools of religion into one single Hindu society through caste system, has not done more harm in creating enmity between different groups of people than uniting them. That people belonging to one caste would abhor sharing table hospitality with another, does not seem to be creating bonds of union but creating dissidence and hatred among one another, while upholding the supremacy of the *Brāhmaṇas*.

Another argument which Bhattacharya brings up in advocating for and upholding the caste system is that by assigning different castes hereditary rights for different jobs or professions in the society, caste system has helped to maintain the smooth running of the society. According to him, if not for caste system,

> There could not possibly have been… any great attraction either for military service or for intellectual pursuits. The resources of the country were then too limited for adequately rewarding either the soldier or the scholar, and as any able-bodied man could, in those times, earn his living without any difficulty, either in agricultural pursuits or by breeding cattle; the only way to induce any class of man to adopt a more ambitious or risky career, lay in giving them a superior status by hereditary right.[9]

In this sense, a *Kṣatriya* cannot but go for war. Otherwise, he brings his caste and his family to shame. A *Brāhmaṇa* cannot but learn the *Vedas* and teach others. A *Vaiśya* has to pursue a trade and it is the duty of a *Śūdrā* to see to it that the menial works of the society are performed. Bhattacharya upholds and justifies caste system from this perspective of the smooth running of the society. In this way, the society has people for every job; there are people to go for battle in times of difficulties and people to offer worship to the gods for the welfare of all and people to do trade and those who take care of other works of the society. One should however note that a *Śūdrā*, his children and his children´s children did not have the opportunity to learn *Vedas*, or officiate sacrifices in temples; much worse, for thousands of years they were denied entry into a Temple. The hereditary imposing of works upon a caste could be a blessing for *Brāhmaṇas* and *Kṣatriyas*. Iit is definitely an eternal curse, especially for the lowest castes of the Indian society. Here we need to point out the existence of another group of in India, which forms the backbone of the entire Indian society.

Dalits

Apart from the four *varnas* or classes, there is also another group in the Indian society, called *Dalits*,[10] the *panchamas* (which means people belonging to the fifth group) or *avarnas* (which means color-less) as they sometimes called: they stand away from the four classifications of the society. Their role in the society was to serve the above-mentioned four classes of people and to make sure that the streets and houses of the people of the upper caste remain clean. In particular manual scavenging and removing the dead bodies of humans and animals were the only jobs, which the fifth group could do in the society. It is this group of people who suffers the most in the Indian society. Mahatma Gandhi shows glaringly how the untouchables suffer in all aspects of life:

> Socially they are lepers. Economically they are worse than slaves. Religiously they are denied entrance to places we miscall ´houses of God.´ They are denied the use, on the same terms as the caste men, of public roads, public schools, public hospitals, public wells, public taps, public

parks and the like and in some cases their approach within a measured distance is a social crime and in some other rare enough cases, their very sight is an offence. They are relegated for their residence to the worst quarters of cities and villages where they practically get no social service. Caste Hindu lawyers and doctors will not serve them as they do other members of society.[11]

What Gandhi wrote in the middle of the last century, is still a reality in the rural areas of Indian subcontinent. It is saddening to say that even in the 21st century that the situation has only partially improved. There are innumerable examples of how the basic rights are often denied to the *avarnas*, the casteless people. They were and are still to some extent, understood to be "ritually impure and untouchable by birth."[12] Because, their occupation dealt with dead bodies of animals and humans and with the disposal of the body wastes of humans – an occupation that is seen, polluting and defiling others in the society.

For generations remaining as servants of the above-mentioned four classes, *Dalits* were and are considered till today to be untouchables in the society. Their dwelling place is literally outside the residence of the people of four castes, so that their presence does not contaminate the caste people. The *Brāhmaṇas* and other higher caste groups denied the untouchables entry into their streets; if at all the *Dalits* had to pass through or enter the streets for the household chores, they needed to remove the sandals off their feet (if at all they had sandals); they were, and are even now in some places not allowed to draw water from the same well used by the caste people,[13] much less, to use the same utensils used by the *Brāhmaṇas* or other *upper caste Hindus* in *cafés* and restaurants. A former Chief Minister of the ruling *Bharatiya Janata Party* got the media attention recently as he went to a *Dalit* house and ate with them in their house. Just within a day, it was exposed by the media that this person did not eat the meals that were prepared for him at the house of *Dalits*. He actually bought meals from a Restaurant and took along with him and ate it at the *Dalit* house.[14] Another incident got the attention of the media recently, when the officers of the Chief Minister of Uttar Pradesh in the central India distributed soaps and shampoos to a group of people belonging to *Dalit* community and asked them to take bath, before meeting the Chief Minister.[15] This shows the mentality of a common Indian, to brand *Dalit* community as unclean and impure.

At this time, it is important to note how Mahatma Gandhi viewed untouchability and the different *varnas*. In his magazine *Young India*, Gandhi wrote, that "untouchability is a sin, a grievous crime and will eat up Hinduism, if the latter does not kill the snake in time."[16] For him untouchability due to the differences in birth is unacceptable; because we are all equal in the spiritual sense of the word. Gandhi however maintains that *varna*, the division of people according to four classes is correct. He says, "I do however believe in *varna* which is based on hereditary occupations. *Varnas* are four to mark four universal occupations, — imparting knowledge, defending the defenceless, carrying on agriculture and commerce and performing service through physical labour."[17] In his reply to Ambedkar's undelivered speech, "The Annihilation of caste," Gandhi gives a similar reply. In favour of the *varna* system, Gandhi says, "The law of *varna* teaches us that we have each one of us to earn bread by following the ancestral calling. It defines not our rights but our duties. It necessarily has reference to callings that are conducive to the welfare of humanity and to no other. It also follows that there is no calling too low and none too high. All are good, lawful, and absolutely equal in status."[18] Such justification of caste system - maintaining the social order - is taken up once again very strongly by the social and religious elite of Hinduism of today. This has been, of late, vehemently proposed by the supporters and organizers of the *Hindutva*[19] whose representatives are ruling the country for three years under the political banner *BJP (Bahratiya Janata Party)*. But sadly enough, these supporters of the caste system are against the upward movement of other castes. This would mean that a *Brāhmaṇa* remains always a *Brāhmaṇa*, enjoying the service of the people of the lower castes and that a *Dalit* would always remain a *Dalit*, without respect and dignity, economically and socially dependent on others. He can and should never move upward in the social order. A *Dalit* can never become a *Brāhmaṇa*. The reply of Ambedkar to Gandhi's justification on *varna* system of the division of labour in the society is very poignant. While Ambedkar agrees with Gandhi, that the society needs the division of labour for a smooth functioning, he however points out, "Caste system is not merely division of labour but it is also a division of labourers ... it is a hierarchy in which the divisions of labourers are graded one above the other."[20] Ambedkar further asks Gandhi, why Gandhi as a person belonging to *Vaiśya* class, chose the profession of lawyer instead of being a merchant, which was his ancestral calling according to his *varna*. He goes on to ask whether one should faithfully observe one's ancestral calling even if one finds it morally unacceptable. "If everyone must pursue his ancestral calling, then it must follow that a man must continue to be pimp because his grandfather was a pimp and a woman must continue to be a prostitute because her grand-mother was a prostitute. Is the Mahatma prepared to accept the logical conclusion of his doctrine?"[21]

Annihilation of Caste: A Possibility?

The caste of a person is determined by one's birth and hence it is often asked in the western world, if it is possible to eradicate this caste system which has its roots in the deepest cells of the Indian society. An important tool against this millennium-old oppressive structure is perhaps the mixture of peoples of different castes through intermarriage; because the essence of caste system, according to Ambedkar goes back to the "prohibition, rather the absence of intermarriage - endogamy, to be concise."[22] When partners of two different castes are allowed to intermarry, and when such marriages are supported and encouraged, then in the long run, there would be a new society, in which birth of a child does not determine its caste. Although it is practiced here and there, it is still not the rule of the day in India. Nripendra Kumar Dutt attests to this most apparent feature of the present day caste system:

> The members of the different castes cannot have matrimonial connections with any but persons of their own caste; that there are restrictions, though not so rigid as in the matter of marriage, about a member of the caste

eating and drinking with that of a different caste; that in many cases there are fixed occupations for different castes; that there is some hierarchical gradation among the castes.[23]

Even those attempts of intermarriage by the young literates of the Indian society is immediately thwarted with gruesome aggression and dreadful violence instigated by the people of the upper castes. The year 2012 witnessed a shocking event in the state of Tamil Nadu. A father of a high caste girl committed suicide out of humiliation, since his daughter eloped with and married a *Dalit* boy. Shortly after this incident, a mob of 2500 upper caste Hindus ransacked and burnt down around 148 houses of *Dalits* in the surrounding three villages.[24] After months of ordeal for the *Dalit* communities, the *Dalit* boy who married the higher caste girl was found dead on the railway tracks. Just one single intermarriage between a *Dalit* and a person of a higher caste was the cause for the loss of the hard-earned properties and houses of 148 *Dalit* families. It is just one of many incidents, through which the caste forces try to instill fear among the *Dalit* communities, to show what sort of ordeals awaits those *Dalits* and their families, if they dare to marry a person of a higher caste.

Towards the end of his life Ambedkar decided to convert to Buddhism, since he felt that in Hinduism abolition of caste would not be a reality. He titled his undelivered speech, "Annihilation of Caste," and said that as a religion, Hinduism does not offer a universal set of principles which are applicable to all. Instead all what Hinduism is able to offer is a set of rules containing do's and don't's. All what it tries to do is to divide people of same culture into different hereditary groups. "What the Hindus call religion is really Law or at best legalized class-ethics. Frankly, I refuse to call this code of ordinances, as religion ... and I say, there is nothing irreligious in working for the destruction of such a religion."[25] He further suggests, Hinduism as of now needs drastic religious reforms, which include the removal of the authenticity and the sacredness of many of Hindu literature like *Vedas* and *Puranas* and *Shastras* which prohibit common table fellowship with all the caste groups and intermarriage between them.

Efforts of the Indian Government and the Fate of Dalits

There are some characteristics of the caste system, which have changed over the millennia. The Constitution of India has tried to give some privileges to *Dalits* in the society. In the Articles especially 330-341 of the Indian Constitution, it is stated that out of 545 seats in the *Lok Sabha* (Lower House of the Indian Parliament), 78 seats should be reserved for *Dalits* and out of 3997 seats in the State Assemblies, 540 seats are to be allotted for them. The Parliament also asks the State Governments to make sure that 15% of the posts in the Municipal Bodies, District Councils and Village Administrative Bodies is reserved for them. All along these seventy years of independence, the country has passed several laws in the Parliament for the protection of the people of the *Scheduled* castes. This means, a son or a daughter of the lowest caste in the Indian society, need not necessarily do the same job, which his / her father was destined to do two generations ago. He / she can indeed become the judge in the Supreme Court of India or become a Chief Minister of the State or even the Head of the State. While such changes have resulted in the financial betterment of the people of the lowest class of India, the mere financial prosperity alone has not been enough to eradicate the social oppressions of the lowest class of the Indian society.

Caste and Christianity

The *Brāhmaṇas*, the highest class of the Indian society, amount to 3.5% of the entire population of Tamil Nadu. The untouchables however constitute as many as 20% of the entire population of the state. The minority 3.5% of the population owns majority of the agricultural lands and properties and occupy important jobs offered by the central and state governments. The other 75% population of the state are non-*Brāhmaṇas* and non-*Dalits*.[26] Interestingly enough, the behavior and the attitude of this non-*Brāhmaṇa* and non-*Dalit* castes towards the *Dalits* is the same as the *Brahmiṇic* outlook towards them.

Religiously, it is told with pride that Christianity in India has its origins from the Apostle Thomas. It is from the arrival of the colonial powers in the sixteenth century, however, that Christianity has become one of the main religions of the country. It is estimated that approximately 2.32% of the entire population of India are Christians. In Tamil Nadu, the majority of the people (as many as 88.67%) belong to Hinduism; while Muslims in Tamil Nadu amount to 5.47% of the population, the Christians are around 5.69%. Christians in Tamil Nadu as elsewhere in India are divided into different castes, just as their Hindu counterparts. And in this meagre population of Christians, around 65% of the entire Christians in Tamil Nadu are *Dalits*.[27] This statistic tells categorically that the majority of the Christians in Tamil Nadu are *Dalits*. But the privileges enjoyed by them were and are till today minimal.

Missionaries and the Dalits of India

For foreign missionaries who risked their lives with a goal of evangelizing the Indian masses with the ministry and message of Jesus, every Indian was equal - illiterate and without culture - at least in the beginning of their arrival to India. They did not look at some Indians as high caste and others belonging to lower caste and untouchable. Hence, the arrival of the missionaries in the colonial period was thought to bring many social changes in the Indian society, especially for the lower castes Hindus and *Dalits*. One needs to say, however, that the primary concern of the missionaries was to baptize as many Indians as possible and convert them to Christianity. Number of Baptism, they administered was understood to be the pointer of success to their missionary activity. In their effort to "win souls" for Christ, they tried to adapt or even compromise the Christian message of equality and common brotherhood of humanity to the hierarchical structure of the Indian society.

Pandara Swamis and *Sannyasis*

The experiment of the Jesuit missionaries in the process of evangelization needs to be mentioned here. As the Jesuits learnt the cultures of the Indian society and some, even the language, they understood that there is an innate difference between different groups of the society. Hence, they divided themselves into different groups in order to target and evangelize different layers of the society. Many concentrated on and evangelized the lower class of the Indian society people and they were called *Pandaraswamis* (a term, which meant wandering mendicants); some of the missionaries targeted the elite and creamy layer of the Hindu society and tried to evangelize the *Brāhmaṇas* of India. These missionaries were called *Sannyasis* (meaning ascetic priests). They tried to incorporate and imitate the lifestyle of the *Brāhmaṇa* priests. They embraced the lifestyle of the *Brāhmaṇas*. Avoiding eating meat, these foreign missionaries ate only vegetarian food, clothed like the *Brāhmaṇa* priests, and adapted their lifestyle to parallel to that of the *Brāhmaṇa* priests.

Robert De Nobili

The pioneering work along this way of life was accomplished by the Jesuit priest Robert De Nobili, who was successful in learning both Sanskrit as well as the local language Tamil; De Nobili went on to shave off his head as did the *Brāhmaṇa* priests, took off his black cassock and wore saffron attire, put on the sacred thread around his chest, as did the *Brāhmaṇas*, and when he was challenged and opposed by the *Brāhmaṇas* about his way of life, he called himself to be a "Roman *Brāhmaṇa*"[28] and tried to explain Christianity in the way *Brāhmaṇas* could understand it. This effort had indeed born fruit; De Nobili and his successors had attracted many *Brāhmaṇas* so much so that by the year 1644 they could convert as many as 1208 *Brāhmaṇas* to Christianity. This effort of bringing Jesus in the culture of the natives was and is indeed to be commended, the harsh criticism however against the Christian missionary activities is that, the missionaries and the arrival of Christianity in India could not succeed in eradicating the hereditary inequality and its subsequent social oppression that was innate Indian society in the name of caste system. As a consequence, Indians who were converted to Christianity brought along their caste identity into Christianity.

Conversion, only in Name?

Just as Jesus attracted tax collectors in his company and just as the social outcasts at the time of Jesus were eager to come and listen to him (Luke

15:1), Christianity in India attracted the economically and culturally oppressed lower castes in huge numbers. Numerous lower caste Hindus, *Dalits* as well as those from *Śūdrā* community, the fourth group in the Hindu caste ladder, who were in search of freedom from oppression in the social as well as economical fields, who were in search of better way of living with equal rights and dignity, were eager to embrace Christianity. Hence, it is mainly the *Śūdrās* and untouchable fifth class who became converts to Christianity; their conversion however did not abolish their caste identity. They brought their caste identity along as they converted. The caste Christians (mainly from the fourth class of the *varna* system and some *Brāhmaṇa* Christians) continued to look at *Dalit* Christians still as untouchables. As Fr Jerome D´Souza spoke in the Parliament of India regarding the plight of the converted Christians, conversion as a "mere change of religion … does not make any difference in social and economic conditions"[29] among the *Dalits*. Although, through the schools of the missionaries, the children of the newly converted Christians got education and slowly moved up in the economic ladder of the society, one should however say that culturally, the only major change the newly converted Christians had obtained, was a foreign name, unknown and unfamiliar to them. Apart from that, culturally they were still Hindus in their roots. Hence, a *Dalit* who converted to Christianity was seen as a *Dalit*-Christian. His plight as a *Dalit* continued to be the same even in Christianity; it became actually all the more acute, since his oppression continued not only by *upper caste Hindus*, but also by other upper caste Christians.

Ambedkar writes about the predominance of casteism in Indian Christianity: "There are *Brahmin* Christians and non-Brahmin Christians. Among non-*Brahmin* Christians there are *Maratha* Christians, *Mahar* Christians, *Mang* Christians, and *Bangi* Christians. Similarly there are *Paraiah*[30] Chrsitans, *Mala* Christians, and *Madiga* Christians. They would not intermarry, they would not inter-dine. They are as much caste ridden as the Hindus are."[31] Even the churches that were built in the colonial period for Christians were built in the structure of the cross, and were useful for segregating the untouchable Christians from mingling in the side of the *Śūdrā* Christians, who are now the 'high caste' within the Church. Kananaikil attests to this tension between caste Christians and *Dalit* Christians in the seating arrangement in the church already in 1937 in Tamil Nadu in South India.[32] The cross of Jesus which is a binding factor for all Christians, has become a symbol of division in the Church in India. The arrival of Christianity could not succeed in bringing back their common identity as brothers and sisters of one common human race.

It is not to be understood, that the missionaries did not do anything to ward-off the social evil of casteism in the Church. There were many missionaries who struggled to instill the notion of equality and brotherhood among Christian converts from different castes. But as the missionaries taught the Indian Christians to mix with the Christians of the lower castes in the churches, the Christians coming from the high castes understood and described this effort of the missionaries as a disgrace to their status and to their castes. Hence many of the missionaries had to yield to the aggressive demands of the caste Christians to build partition walls inside the churches so that they could participate in the same Eucharist but would not see or sit near each other, so that they could partake in the same Eucharistic Meal but could maintain distance from the lower caste Christians.

Dalit Christians Today

Today's India has changed a lot. The partition walls within the churches between the untouchables and other caste members have been long ago demolished. One should not however think that the untouchability is abolished. Even today *Dalit* Christians suffer more than other caste Christians. Stanislaus is right in saying that even now the *Dalit* Christians suffer a six-fold oppression. "i. discrimination by the Government, ii. by the *upper caste Hindus*, iii. by the Caste Christian community, iv. by the hierarchical Church, v. by fellow Hindu *Dalits* and vi. by the subgroups of *Dalit* Christians themselves."[33] In some places there are still separate churches for *Dalits* if they happen to live in the same village along with other caste Christians. In some villages, the *Corpus Christi* procession or other religious processions would not go through the streets of the *Dalits,* because caste Christians do not want to be polluted by going through the streets of *Dalits,* or they do not want the statues of Jesus, Mother Mary or the saints to be polluted by their presence in the streets of the untouchables; the financial contributions of *Dalits* for a village religious festival would not be accepted, so that they do not have the right to ask for equal right in the celebration and participation of the festivals. The participation of *Dalits* in the administrative bodies of the local parishes or in the dioceses is minimum, unless the majority of the diocese comprises of *Dalit* Christians. Even in the recruitment to the priesthood, *Dalits,* at least in the beginning, were denied access to enter seminaries. There was even an unwritten law at the time of the missionaries, that no one from the *Dalit* Community was recruited to become priests. In some cases, even those *Dalit* Christians who, with much struggle, were ordained as priests, were not able to administer the duties as a priest, as the upper caste Christians protested vehemently against them. Not being allowed to read the Scriptures in the church, denial to do altar service during the Eucharistic celebration or to join the choir, not being allowed to go as procession through the church street either for the funeral or for the wedding celebrations are some of the many oppressions that *Dalit* Christians were and are undergoing in many rural parts of Tamil Nadu, where the caste consciousness is very evident.[34]

Not only during their lifetime, but also after their death, *Dalits* are segregated. Even now in some Christian villages, there is a separate graveyard for *Dalit* Christians. If the graveyard is the same, there could be a wall or a path that would divide the cemeteries of *Dalits* from those of Caste Christians. There are separate vehicles to carry the dead bodies from the church to the cemeteries. In an open letter to the catholic bishops of India, *Dalit* Christians voice their grievances: "Even in our death we are not spared. Cemeteries are divided and one part is assigned for us with an impregnable wall dividing us from the so-called high caste Catholics. Is it to prevent our corpses walk past their area and contaminate it?"[35] In a parish called Eraiyur, in Tamil Nadu, the tension between the upper caste Christians and *Dalits* came to the limelight in the year 2008, as the body of a *Dalit* Christian, whose son is a priest of that diocese, was not allowed to be taken to the church for the funeral mass and was not allowed to be buried together with other upper caste Christians. This unrest was just a tip of the iceberg of the oppressions, which the *Dalit* Christians are undergoing in many of the parishes.

Impact of Modernity in the Caste-ridden Society

Development in the society and technological advancements have brought a sigh of relief to the untouchables of India in the 21st century. Especially in the cities, if a caste Hindu or Christian goes to a restaurant or any shop, he does not know who cooks for him or who serves him his food or who is the owner of the restaurant;[36] he would not know who sits near him in the cafés, restaurants or cinema halls. Almeida talks about it as the "erosion of casteism in the changing world."[37] This is the change which every person is forced to face due to his exposure to the media and to the world culture. The urban culture is a little more open and receptive to the otherness. However, it is also true, when one comes to know that the person next to him is a *Dalit*, then one tends to avoid him than to relate with him. Besides, the profession of cleaning the streets, removing the human waste on the roads and removing the dead bodies of humans and animals, which are to be done in the cities are still done only by *Dalits* who are stationed in the city slums, adjacent to the city. The danger has always been there in the cities, that the politicians and economically powerful make use of the men and youngsters who live in these slums as their goondas for their illegal purposes, since most of the youngsters in the slums have either not gone to school or have become school drop-outs because of the deplorable family conditions. We could be sure, that those youngsters who are jailed for their lawless behavior are more often those in the slum areas, since their political goondas entice them with easy cash for their unlawful behavior. In the rural areas however, the caste identity plays an important role; since it is very evident in the villages who belongs to which caste, the sense of 'we' against the 'others' is very strong in the villages. In this background of oppression, indifference and exploitation of the untouchables, the behavior of Jesus towards the tax collectors in general and towards Zacchaeus in particular assumes its significance.

Zacchaeus a Representative of *Dalit* Christians in India

It is not difficult to recognize the similarities between the predicament of *Dalits* in India and the plight of Zacchaeus and other tax collectors at the time of Jesus, who had the similar fate which modern day *Dalits* in India are undergoing; both were needed for the smooth running of the society, all the same they were never considered part of the society. In the Zacchaeus story as well as in the context of the Indian *Dalits*, equality and inequality should be seen from different elements of the society. Zacchaeus is considered to be one of the few members of the group which the Jews have considered impure, but who actually overcame the hurdles of economic oppression of other Jews. Although he might have been richer than many of the Israelites in Jericho, he still carries the stigma of being an outcast. His entry into the house of an Israelite or the entry of a pure Jew into the house of Zacchaeus was considered unclean and impure. He remained excluded from the common worship in the synagogue. Hence, although Zacchaeus attained economic freedom or status, he had to still face social inequality from the fellow Jews.

This is also true of the modern day *Dalits* in India. There is a slow but steady increase in the economic empowerment of the *Dalits* (Christians as well as Hindus). There are different measures taken by the Indian Government as well as the Church in India, which ensure equal opportunities for *Dalits* in terms of education, equal opportunities in jobs or even in the administrative bodies. The Government policy of Reservation, which we had already mentioned, entitles the *Dalits* to enjoy a certain percentage of preference over others in education and job opportunities. All the same, to a large extent, the oppressive ill-treatment, which they undergo, has not been changed. Economic betterment alone is not able to bring the desired social equality and betterment. In 2014, a shocking incident occurred in Bihar, one of the states in the northern India where the Chief Minister was a *Dalit* at the time. Jitan Ram Manjhi who was holding the highest office of the state, revealed, that the entire temple precinct which he visited as the Chief Minister, including the statues in the temple were ritually cleansed after he left the temple premises, because the temple authorities considered that the temple had become ritually impure and unclean, because of the visit of a *Dalit*.[38] This clearly attests to the fact that if a *Dalit* has gone up in the social ladders of the society, even if he is able to obtain important portfolios in the society, even if he is able to enjoy economic prosperity, he remains and is seen by others as a *Dalit*, as someone, whose contact, proximity and touch make everything – even gods in the temple – unclean and impure. Just as Zacchaeus underwent social segregation in an urban area, *Dalits*, like the Chief Minister of Bihar, like the Bishop of the diocese of Cuddapah in Andhra Pradesh, suffer humiliation not only in the rural India but also in urban areas, when their identity is known.

Zacchaeus: a Jewish-Dalit

The Zacchaeus story makes an instant appeal to the *Dalit* Christians of today since Zacchaeus is the best example of the social condition of the outcasts like the *Dalits* (Christians) in India. He was a Jew and like all other Jews, he too belonged to a race, which understood itself as especially chosen by God. At the same time because of his profession as a tax collector, he is despised by the members of his own race and considered a sinner, the dealings with whom would pollute other Jews. Although Zacchaeus was a chief tax collector and his job earned him enough income, he was not able to entertain fellow Jews in his house, since it would make other Jews impure.

Dalit Christians are at par with Zacchaeus as regards the cultural segregation they undergo. Just like the tax collectors, *Dalit* Christians are despised not only from the society at large, but also by their fellow Christians within the church, whose ideal is to treat everyone as children of the one and the same Father God. There is however one major difference between Zacchaeus and tax collectors at the time of Jesus who were religiously impure and culturally set aside, and *Dalit* Christians in India who are segregated now. Because of their profession tax collectors, shepherds and prostitutes were considered impure by Israelites at the time of Jesus, whereas for *Dalits* in India, it is not only because of his profession, but because of one's birth, a *Dalit* is considered impure and untouchable. Despite having a job that assures a good income, despite even owning a firm, despite being the head of a state, a *Dalit* who has embraced Christianity with the longing of being accepted and treated equally, is even now considered unequal. The Church as of now has a long way to go towards embracing the *Dalit* Christians who form a major chunk of Christianity in India.

Food and Caste

"Caste is only a question of food." This age-old saying in India sums up succinctly the interconnectedness of food and caste system. Food is understood in India as elsewhere as the means of binding together the people belonging to the same thought and same community. Since "it is a communion bringing together selected people who, by birth, have the right to eat certain foods prepared according to traditional rites,"[39] upper caste Hindus take utmost care to avoid the food pollution. Hence "to eat with, or even in the presence of a stranger, or worse, to eat food which he has touched, are … unpardonable sins."[40] This echoes the archaic practice of *symposium* where it was the custom to share meals, only with equals in status.

In order to avoid these "sins of the mouth"[41] Indians of high caste made sure, that they did not touch food or even utensils that have been prepared or even touched by untouchables and which hence are 'polluted.' A Punjabi proverb even states, "a *Bisnoi* mounted on a camel followed by a score more, will immediately throw away his food if a man of another caste happens to touch the last animal."[42] Bouglé points out to the fact that for a caste Hindu food is an important element of purity: "It is above all from food that contamination is feared. It can only be eaten amongst caste-fellows: it should not even be touched by a stranger, whose glance is sometimes sufficient to pollute it. If a *Paraiah* so much as looks into a kitchen all the utensils should be broken."[43] Such a conservative and rigid ideology, although proverbial in use, tells very clearly, the people of the 'higher' caste do not feel at home in participating in meals with the untouchable *Dalits*. The same was, and in some cases is true in the Indian society. Senart observes, "No superior tribe will eat or drink from the hands or vessels of an inferior one."[44] While in earlier days, only people belonging to the four castes could buy tea or coffee, later however accommodations and adjustments were made for *Dalits* to buy drinks at shops. The glasses which the *Dalits* were given tea or coffee were marked, so that these glasses were not served for caste people. Although such methods of segregation have been long back abolished, it shows all the same how brutally the *Dalits* were sidelined from the mainstream of the society.

The joy of Zacchaeus to receive Jesus and offer him table fellowship makes sense from the background of the caste system, where fellowship meal is not possible between higher and lower caste people. Zacchaeus could not invite and entertain people other than the tax collectors, though he was rich enough; similarly, a higher caste *Brāhmaṇa* would not dare to enter into the house of a *Dalit* to have a shared meal. Hence, the plight of Zacchaeus is similar to that of the *Dalits* of India.

Jesus the Minority: A Model for Instilling Change

The positive ending of the story of Zacchaeus challenges the Christians of India to be effective instruments of bringing about the much needed change in the mindset, recognizing the essential equality and fraternity not only between *Dalit* Christians and other Christians but also *Dalits* in general and others in the society. The joy of Jesus in the company of tax collectors and the other social outcasts and his initiative to enter into the house of Zacchaeus to be his guest and have meal with him are examples of how even an individual person could make a positive change in the thought patterns of the people around him, instilling in their mindset that no one is superior or inferior by his birth or profession. The ministry of Jesus as the friend of tax collectors and sinners challenges Indian Christians (and especially the Christian priestly 'class' which is all the more obsessed with caste consciousness), to go bravely against the oppressive structures and mindset of the society. There are numerous people in India – Christians and others - who live the way of Jesus, playing their role in changing the society's consciousness and thought patterns which discriminate one section of the society. Zacchaeus story induces the Indian readers to follow their footsteps.

Jesus' Revolt against the Purity-Pollution of the Pharisees

In ancient societies like India, even some of the body parts of a human being are considered unclean. For example, the left hand is considered impure compared to the right hand, since in some societies, it is being used to cleanse the waste of the human body. Similarly, in the earlier days, the first thing a man would do after coming home, is to wash his feet. Since one normally did not wear sandals when he went out, he needed to wash the unclean foot in order to enter the house. In comparison to the unclean feet, head is thought to be superior. We could understand now the ramifications of the Laws of *Manu*, which explain how different castes are understood to be emerging from the different body parts of the *Purusha*, the primordial human being. The *Brāhmaṇ as* are said to be coming from the head, hence automatically superior, and the fourth group, which emerges from the feet is automatically inferior and unclean.

The idea of Brahminism – 'anything impure should be separated - is similar to the Pharisaic ideology of purity, following Lev 20:26, "you should be holy for I the Lord am holy." The holiness for the Pharisees as well as the Essenes is not only in the sense of moral purity, but also in the sense of separation from everything and everyone unclean and impure. Finkel rightly points this out in the following words:

> In the Pharisaic schools 'holiness' the key word of the Priestly Codes is identified with the word 'separation': separation from the heathens and foreigners in order to preserve the identity of the Jewish people; separation or classification among its own members, segregating the priests and the

strict observers of the code from the non-observers, the boorish and the common folk (the so called *Àm-hă-ăretz*).⁴⁵

While Pharisees tried to live in the unclean society and tried to maintain their purity, Essenes went further in their zeal for purity, and separated themselves from this world of impurity to live alone in the wilderness. We saw in the first chapter, that the meals of both the groups are eaten with a great regard for ritual purity. Borg writes about the fellowship meals of the Pharisees that "they were committed ... to eating every meal in that degree of purity observed by officiating priests in the Temple."⁴⁶ Just like the Pharisaic group kept itself separated from everything it thought to be impure, so also, the *Brāhmaṇa* priestly class wanted to keep itself pure from the proximity of the lower caste, which is said to be impure. Jesus' actions of mingling with the tax collectors and sinners and his table fellowship with them break away this concept of purity-pollution, which was very essential to the Pharisaic way of life. In this sense Daube rightly understands the table fellowship of Jesus with tax collectors and sinners as one of the revolutionary actions of Jesus, through which he wanted to show that the Kingdom of God has already arrived.⁴⁷ The eagerness of Jesus to dine with the tax collectors and sinners could be understood as a revolt against the exclusivity of the Pharisaic school of thought, which excludes the ordinary and the ignorant of the society.

Dalits: Preferential Option of Jesus

The option of Jesus for the poor and the oppressed classes of the society is very evident in the Gospels. Especially Luke begins the ministry of Jesus with this preferential option for the poor (Luke 4:16-21). The poor in the Gospel are not just the economically poor and those whose situation forces them to beg for their livelihood. By the term 'poor' Jesus meant in the Gospels, especially in Luke "the *Àm-hă-ăretz* ('the peoples of the land') – a contemptuous designation by which the religious and social elite of his time labeled the 'rabble ignorant of the Law,' that is, the poor, the unschooled, the socially unacceptable, the religiously defiled, the sick."⁴⁸ In the Palestinian context it would comprise the tax collectors including Zacchaeus (though he was rich), and in the Indian context Jesus´ option for the poor means it is the option for the *Dalits* who are outcasts in the literal sense of the word. This option of Jesus for the poor and the outcasts is apparent in Luke already at the very beginning of the Gospel. As Stanislaus understands "Jesus identifies with the *Dalits*. He is born like a *Dalit* and dies like a *Dalit*. Jesus is *Dalit* from the cradle to the Cross."[49] Just like the *Dalits* in India do not have a place in the city but only outside the city, Jesus has no place in Bethlehem. He has to be born outside the city. His death too shows how Jesus was understood to be an outcast, who did not fit in the society and hence hung outside the city. This preferential option of Jesus for the ´poor´ which Luke shows very graphically in his ´On the Way´ narratives, is also to be the norm for the new community which is characterized as the ´Way´ (Acts 9:2, 19:23, 24:14,22). This is the Way that Indian Christians are advocated to follow.

Fellowship Meal: An Effective Instrument of Change

The preferential option of Jesus towards the poor, the tax collectors and sinners, does not mean that he excludes himself from the elite of the society, the Pharisees. Luke has made this very clear in the way he sandwiches the fellowship meals of Jesus with the Pharisees in between the meals of Jesus with tax collectors. The Lukan Jesus does not exclude Pharisees when he includes tax collectors in his company. His meals with the Pharisees and tax collectors, back and forth shows that the love of God does not exclude anyone. Having seen the exclusivism of the Pharisees, in special regard to the fellowship meals, Jesus takes a radical, all-inclusive approach. Soares Prabhu rightly observes that Jesus brings out a new understanding of Holiness. In comparison to the Pharisaic understanding of 'be holy as I am holy,' Jesus' understanding of holiness is totally new in that he suggests, 'be merciful just as your heavenly Father is merciful' (Luke 6:36; Matt 5:48).[50] This mercy, which Jesus speaks out, is actualized in his actions of table fellowship. He took fellowship meals as an instrument to sow the seeds of change in the society regarding the newness in the concept of purity-pollution. The table fellowship of Jesus is "not a proclamation in words at all, but an acted parable."[51] Jesus used it as a symbolic weapon to fight against the narrow mindset of his time. The fact that tax collectors and sinners were the fellow diners with Jesus shows that Jesus "actually took his stand among the pariahs of his world."[52] His table fellowship with tax collectors and sinners "challenges the Pharisaic and the Essenic ideal of Israel as a holy community, whose holiness is to be maintained by preserving a state of complete separation from all that is ritually unclean. It implies instead a radically new understanding of holiness, of community and of God."[53] At the same time his meals with the Pharisees invites the group to understand the all-embracing love of God and his invitation to all to repentance. Although his actions were misunderstood and he was branded as glutton and drunkard, Luke shows that through the meals in which he participated, Jesus gave his disciples an alternative vision of an equal society. Ordinary meals became for him a medium through which he imparted and instilled in the disciples as well as his society, that as God's children, there is and should never be a barrier between people. We could see in the third Gospel the tension, present in the table fellowship of Jesus with the Pharisees on the one hand and the tax collectors and sinners on the other; this tension should not only be seen as a pointer to the tension in the Lukan community's all-inclusive table fellowship against the exclusive Pharisaic table fellowship; it should also be seen as an invitation towards those people in every society with the Pharisaic ideology of exclusivism to understand the truth about the all-inclusive nature of the love of God and about the power of ordinary meals, which could become a powerful symbol of change for this all-embracing character of God's love.

Overview

We looked briefly at the caste system in India with its debilitating structures, which keep a major group of Indian citizens under the grip of hereditary social ostracization. We saw how even in the twenty first century there are *Dalits* and there are people who hold other humans as inherently polluting. It is clear that the random voices of agitation by *Dalits* and their attempts against the caste system and towards an egalitarian society are thwarted with so much brutality. The everyday newspapers in India are a witness to the brutality and hatred with which the social upcoming of the *Dalits* and how their shrill voices of longing for liberation are treated. Apart from the initiatives of the Government, Christianity too has done a lot for the upliftment of the *Dalits* in India. We saw however, that Indian Christian Church has a long way to go in making everyone realize equal sonship of all of us before one and the same Father God.

For the Indian Christian community, which wants to emulate Christian values of equality of the children of God, Jesus' entry into the house of Zacchaeus and his dining with his household in Jericho are a symbolic actions. Zacchaeus too is a son of Abraham, similar to all those who chastise him as a sinner. This realization would help the upper caste Christians to come to the realization that *Dalits* (Christians and Hindus and Muslims alike), who were so far kept at a distance both mentally as well as literally are indeed children of God, equal to everyone else in human dignity. The table fellowship of Jesus with Zacchaeus is a symbol in action to show that God has not shut his door on anyone, including sinners, and that everyone is welcome to dine in his Kingdom. The challenges, which the table fellowship of Jesus posed to the Pharisaic concept of purity-pollution is a sign for everyone in the Indian society to upset the existing barriers of pure and impure, higher and lower, holy and unholy. Ordinary meals could be taken up by the Indian Christians to show that there is no difference between *Dalit* Christian and caste Christian but all are equal. Those who are said to be following Jesus cannot have walls of separation between each other based on castes. Those who are said to be following Jesus cannot have two burial grounds for 'higher' and 'lower' caste Christians. Because being a Christian and at the same time to belong to an 'upper caste,' being a Christian and at the same time to be a *Dalit*, who is an untouchable, is a contradiction in itself. As Soares Prabhu says, "the fact that Christian *Dalits* do exist (and suffer) among us is a sign of how little Christian we are, and how much we stand in a state of serious, and one suspects, unrepentant sin."[54] Table fellowship was a bold step of Jesus to point out to the people of his time, that no one, regardless of one's race, gender and profession is far from the love of God. This table fellowship among the Indian Christians could be also a powerful symbol to show that we are all equal before the eyes of God, and that no one is higher or lower because of his birth, status or profession.

Endnotes

[1] The word *caste* is of Portuguese and Spanish origin. Derived from the Latin root *castus* meaning chaste, the word has been understood by Portuguese and Spanish people who had witnessed the division of Indian society, to mean and refer to the purity of blood which was held by every clan / tribe of India to be of utmost importance. Cf. L. Dumont, *Homo Hierarchicus: The Caste System and its Implications* (Oxford: Oxford University Press, 1999), 21; also M. Klass, *Caste: The Emergence of the South Asian Social System* (Philadelphia: Institute for the study of Human Issues, 1980), 20; L. Stanislaus, *The Liberative Mission of the Church among Dalit Christians* (Delhi: ISPCK, 1999), xxiii.

[2] As quoted in C. Bouglé and D. F. Pocock, *Essays on the Caste System*, The European Understanding of India (London: Cambridge University Press, 1971), p. 10.

[3] F. M. Müller, ed., *The Laws of Manu: transl. G. Bühler*, The Sacred Books of the East XXV (Oxford: Clarendon Press, 1886).

[4] T. Pappas, *Britannica Concise Encyclopedia* (Chicago, London, New Delhi: Encyclopaedia Britannica, 2003), 347.

[5] J. Kananaikil, *Christians of scheduled Caste Origin*, Monograph series / Indian Social Institute 10 (New Delhi: Indian Social Institute, 1983), p. 2.

[6] *Vedic* period is roughly understood to be from 1500 BCE, when people of *Indo-European* origin settled from nomadic life to agricultural life. The period is said to have lasted until 500 BCE.

[7] C. Bouglé and D. F. Pocock, *Essays on the Caste System*, 4; along the similar lines L. Dumont, *Homo Hierarchicus* 21.

[8] J. N. Bhattacharya, *Hindu Castes and Sects: An Exposition of the Origin of the Hindu Caste System and the Bearing of the Sects Towards Each Other and Towards Other Religious Systems* (New Delhi: Munshiram Manoharlal, 1995), 4.

[9] Ibid., 5.

[10] The word *Dalit* comes from the Sanskrit root *dal*, which means to crack, open or split. "When used as a noun or adjective it means burst, split, broken, or torn asunder, downtrodden, scattered, crushed, destroyed..." L. Stanislaus, *The Liberative Mission of the Church among Dalit Christians*, 2. This word was first coined by the most prominent person from the untouchable community,

Bhimrao Ramji Ambedkar (1891-1956) in order to represent the brokenness of the untouchables of the Indian society. Having studied in New York as well as in London, Ambedkar was instrumental in writing the Constitution of the Republic of India. Mahatma Gandhi introduced another word to call the fifth class of the Indian social ladder. He called them *Harijans*, a word which means ´children of God.´ This word however, was not liked and preferred by *Dalits* themselves. Because *Harijan* could also mean the children of the temple prostitutes. The Indian Government names them as the people of the *Scheduled* Castes.

[11] M. K. Gandhi, *The Collected Works of Mahatma Gandhi*, 100 vols., 51 (Ministry of Information and Broadcasting: New Delhi, 1972), 347.

[12] J. Kananaikil, *Christians of scheduled Caste Origin*, 7.

[13] Recently in the month of May 2016, Indian media recounted an incident about a *Dalit* man in North India, Bapurao Tajne, who singlehandedly toiled night and day for forty days to dig a well for his wife, who was denied access to fetch water from the public well that was in the area of upper caste Hindus. Thanks to him, all the *Dalits* can now draw water from the well, which he dug without suffering any humiliation from the upper caste Hindus. Cf. PTI, "Dalit woman denied water access, husband digs own well in drought-hit Maharashtra village," http:// indianexpress.com / article/ india/ india- news- india/ dalit- woman- denied- water- access- husband- digs- own- well- in- drought- hit- maharashtra- village- 2790466/ , accessed on 28.10.2016. Similarly, in the year 2013, a 11 year old *Dalit* boy was forced to carry his sandals on his head for the pure reason that he was wearing them on the street of upper caste Hindus. This happened in the state of Tamil nNadu, which is called to be one of the progressive states of India. S. Dorairaj, "Stripped of Dignity," http:// www.frontline.in / social- issues/ stripped- of- dignity/ article4840220.ece, accessed on 31.05. 2016.

[14] PTI, "Yeddyurappa in Controversy again, this time by eating 'Hotel food' at Dalit's home," http:// www.bhatkallys.com / state/ yeddyurappa- controversy- time- eating- hotel- food- dalits- home/ , accessed on 25.05.2017.

[15] ANI, "Dalits Given Soap, Shampoo; Asked to Take Bath before Meeting Yogi," http:// www.rediff.com / news/ report/ dalits- given- soap- shampoo- asked- to- take- bath- before- meeting- yogi/ 20170528.html, accessed on 28.05.2017.

[16] M. K. Gandhi, *The Collected Works of Mahatma Gandhi*, 100 vols., 46 (Ministry of Information and Broadcasting: New Delhi, 1971), 303.

[17] Ibid., 302.

[18] M. K. Gandhi, *The Collected Works of Mahatma Gandhi*, 100 vols., 63 (Ministry of Information and Broadcasting: New Delhi, 1976), 153.

[19] It is one of the many groups of Hindu fundamentalists, which "represents a palpable resurgent, united and increasingly militant movement of Hindu revivalism." L. Stanislaus, *The Liberative Mission of the Church among Dalit Christians* 33-34. This group is notorious for its organized crimes against the

minorities throughout the country. It is very discouraging to see that such Hindu fanatic groups make their presence and impart their fanatic ideologies even in the schools and colleges in India and they go largely unpunished for their fanatic and gruesome activities.

[20] B. R. Ambedkar, *Annihilation of Caste: An Undelivered Speech: Edited by M. R. Anand* (New Delhi: Arnold Publishers, 1990), 47.

[21] Ibid., 120-121.

[22] B. R. Ambedkar, "Writings and Speeches," http:// drambedkarwritings.gov.in / upload/ uploadfiles/ files/ Volume_ 01.pdf, 8, accessed on 01.11.2017.

[23] N. K. Dutt, *Origin and Growth of Caste in India*, 2nd ed. (Calcutta: K. L. Mukhopadhyay, 1968), 3.

[24] Cf. K. A. Shaji, V. Senthil Kumaran, and S. Karthick, "Inter-Caste Marriage Sparks Riot in Tamil Nadu District: 148 Dalit Houses Torched," http:// timesofindia. indiatimes.com / india/ Inter- caste- marriage- sparks- riot- in- Tamil- Nadu- district- 148- Dalit- houses- torched/ articleshow/ 17151170.cms, accessed on 30.10.2016.

[25] Ambedkar, *Annihilation of Caste*, 96-97.

[26] For the wholistic statistic cf. M. Amaladoss, *A Call to Community* (Gujarat: Gujarat Sahitya Prakash, 1994), 57.

[27] This is from the census taken from the Government of India in 1991. Cf. L. Stanislaus, *The Liberative Mission of the Church among Dalit Christians*, 47.

[28] S. J. Stephen, *Caste, Catholic Christianity, and the Language of Conversion: Social Change and Cultural Translation in Tamil Country, 1519-1774* (Delhi: Kalpaz Publications, 2008), 59, 76, 95. Therampil calls De Nobili as the "hero among the champions of indigenization." J. Therampil, "How can the Church in India be redeemed from Casteism?," in *Caste Culture in Indian Church: The Response of the Church to the Problem of Caste within the Christian Community*, ed. S. L. Raj S.J and G. F. Xavier Raj (New Delhi: Indian Social Institute, 1993), 51.

[29] As cited in J. Kananaikil, *Christians of scheduled Caste Origin*, 17.

[30] *PParaiah* is one of the dominant castes which come under the untouchable *Dalits*, in the state of Tamil Nadu.

[31] As quoted in L. Stanislaus, *The Liberative Mission of the Church among Dalit Christians*, 54.

[32] J. Kananaikil, *Christians of scheduled Caste Origin*, 20-21.

[33] L. Stanislaus, *The Liberative Mission of the Church among Dalit Christians*, 62.

[34] Mosse studies in the impacts of the caste system specially from the background of Tamil Nadu. D. Mosse, *The Saint in the Banyan Tree: Christianity and Caste Society in India*, The Anthropology of Christianity 14 (Berkeley: University of California Press, 2012).

[35] Cf. J. Kananaikil, *Christians of scheduled Caste Origin*, 21.

³⁶ There are here and there in Tamil Nadu some shops whose names show that they are indeed owned and run by and for the high caste people alone. For example, there is a Coffee and Backery shop only for *Brāhmaṇas*, with an additional information given on the board outside, "100% cooked and served by *Brāhmaṇas*."

³⁷ L. J. Almeida, "The Indian Church and the Invincible Virus of Casteism," in S. L. Raj S.J and G. F. Xavier Raj, *Caste Culture in Indian Church*, 32-33.

³⁸ Cf. Thomson, "Indian Temple 'purified' after Low-Caste Chief Minister Visits," http:// www.reuters.com / article/ us- foundation- india- caste- idUSKCN0HP1DE20140930, accessed on 20.10.2016; also R. A. Krishna, "Temple Cleaned after Visit, Reiterates Bihar CM," http:// www.hindustantimes. com / india/ temple- cleaned- after- visit- reiterates- bihar- cm/ story-IP7e87GDCM6tHz5RxmDbZN.html, accessed on 20.10.2016.

³⁹ C. Bouglé and D. F. Pocock, *Essays on the Caste System*, 149.

⁴⁰ Ibid., 149.

⁴¹ Ibid., 149.

⁴² Cf. E. Senart and E. D. Ross, *Caste in India: The Facts and the System* (Delhi: Ess Ess Publications, 1975), 43.

⁴³ C. Bouglé and D. F. Pocock, *Essays on the Caste System*, 23.

⁴⁴ E. Senart and E. D. Ross, *Caste in India*, 40.

⁴⁵ A. Finkel, *The Pharisees and the Teacher of Nazareth*, 43; for a similar view, cf. also G. M. Soares-Prabhu, *The Dharma of Jesus*, 121-122.

⁴⁶ M. J. Borg, *Conflict, Holiness, and Politics in the Teachings of Jesus*, 80-81.

⁴⁷ D. Daube, *The New Testament and Rabbinic Judaism*, Jordan Lectures in Comparative Religion 2 (London: University of London Athlone Press, 1956), 174.

⁴⁸ G. M. Soares-Prabhu, *The Dharma of Jesus*, 237.

⁴⁹ L. Stanislaus, *The Liberative Mission of the Church among Dalit Christians*, 222.

⁵⁰ G. M. Soares-Prabhu, *The Dharma of Jesus*, 122.

⁵¹ N. Perrin, *Rediscovering the Teaching of Jesus*, 102.

⁵² G. Vermès, *Jesus the Jew*, 224.

⁵³ G. M. Soares-Prabhu, *The Dharma of Jesus*, 122; similar thought is shared also by M. Amaladoss, *A Call to Community*, 110-111.

⁵⁴ G. M. Soares-Prabhu, *The Dharma of Jesus*, 130.

General Conclusion

The aim of this book was to understand the story of Zacchaeus and his encounter with Jesus (Luke 19:1-10) from the background of meal narratives in Luke. Although there is no explicit indication that Zacchaeus gave a banquet for Jesus, as it is with Levi the tax collector (Luke 5:27-32), this work concludes on the basis of the literary nuances found in Luke 19:1-10 that Luke actually describes the table fellowship of Jesus with Zacchaeus. Since the table fellowship of a first century Jewish family embraced and adopted the Hellenistic cultural customs and meal practices, we began our study of the encounter of Zacchaeus with Jesus with the analysis of Greco-Roman fellowship meals.

Overview of the Chapters

Chapter I: Hellenistic Symposia

In the first chapter we learnt about the Greco-Roman practice of holding a *symposium*, which was a feast of the 'aristocracy of leisure,' where the society's elite came together not just for recreation, entertainment and communal meals, but also to maintain the status quo and their influence in the society. We learnt that the sympotic space is not for the common public. The following characteristics were learnt through the study of Greco-Roman *symposia*:

- A Hellenistic *symposium* was an all-male event; women, who were present in the space of ἄνδρων were mainly entertainers and hence, of promiscuous character.

- Only socially equals, who were able to reciprocate the invitation for a *symposium*, were invited for such banquets. The aim of sympotic banquets as an institution was to encourage equality among the participants; everyone who came together to participate in a *symposium* was theoretically equal.

- In actuality, however, sympotic banquets were a place where strict hierarchy was maintained. Not only with regard to the seating arrangement of the participants, but also with regard to the differences in the portions of food given to the participants a *symposium* reinforced the social distinctions that existed in the outer society. It created a sense of competition among the participants as to who was greater among the ´equals.´ Hence instead of creating and strengthening the bond of friendship, a *symposium* could become an occasion where heavily drunk participants involved in fights and revelry as well as sexual indulgences.

- Philosophers and writers of the Hellenistic period who were captivated with the theme of *symposia* created a literary genre, out of this practice of sympotic banquets. Two groups of authors can be categorized clearly, using this literary genre: on the one hand, authors like Plato who elevated the genre of *symposium* as to make it a place where philosophical debates and dialogues were carried out and on the other hand authors like Lucian, who made satires out of the *symposium* genre to mock the existing behavior of drunkenness and fighting between the participants of *symposia*.

We then shifted our focus from the Hellenistic to the Jewish banquet tradition, and saw that, although there were tensions in Judaism in accepting the Hellenistic culture, Judaism was broadly in agreement with the banquet tradition of the time. Study of the meal practices of groups like the Essenes and Pharisees threw light on the response of different Jewish groups reacting to the Hellenistic banquet system to which Jews were attracted. Different Jewish groups wither adopted of

Hellenistic *symposia* or adapted to the Hellenistic banqueting culture. In any way this important cultural phenomenon of *symposium* was practiced in Jewish circles. In the literary field too, the *symposium* genre continued to attract Jewish authors. The Book of Sirach in the Old Testament and the Passover Seder in the Tannaitic period are clear examples of the fact how the assimilation of Hellenistic *symposia* was very successful in Jewish circles.

Chapter II: the Lukan Symposia

The above study on the Hellenistic *symposium* led us towards the questions as to whether the historical Jesus felt at home with the Greco-Roman sympotic meal culture of the day? Did he freely participate in such banquets? From the literary point of view, which type of authors does Luke belong to? Does he belong to the set of authors like Plato, who glorify the literary genre of *symposia*? Or does he go along with authors like Lucian, who would ridicule the practice of *symposia* and the way it was conducted? The study of different meal narratives (the Passover meal aside) gave the indication that

- Jesus as portrayed by Luke enjoyed sympotic meals with Jewish groups with different ideologies.

- Luke as a Hellenistic writer is fond of the literary genre of *symposium* and has tried to adapt his meal narratives to the *symposium* genre. This has become clear from the references to characteristics of Hellenistic *symposia* scattered in different meal material in Luke:

    - The reference to the host who invites Jesus for a meal
    - The mention of Jesus as the Socrates-like chief guest at meals
    - The presence of a sinful woman at the banquet
    - The apparent competition of the partakers of the meal to get to the πρῶτος, the seat of honor

- The discussion that emerges time and again out of the banqueting situation in which Jesus participates

All these characteristics attest to the interest that Luke shows on the literary adaptation of the *symposium* genre in his Gospel.

- By narrating various sympotic meals of Jesus, Luke is indirectly showing his readers to what kind of community he addresses his Gospel. It is a community where the presence of an elite social group is evident; only to those who could understand literary *symposia*, Luke could write one. Only to those who could participate in and host a *symposium*, he could advise how one should host a *symposium*. Hence, these sympotic meals tell that Luke is actually the evangelist of the rich, challenging them to use their wealth for the service of all. At the same time, he uses the symposium genre to underscore the drawbacks of the banqueting culture of the time. The Lukan Jesus is presented to be given new sets of rules for an ideal banqueting community.

- Luke has brought a sharp contrast between the two major banqueting groups in the middle section of his Gospel: the tax collectors on the one side and the Pharisees on the other - the sinners on the one side and the so-called righteous on the other. This contrast was very clear as we learnt that the three Pharisaic *symposia* in which Jesus partook, were deliberately and beautifully arched by the two *symposia* in which Jesus partook with tax collectors - Levi at the one end (Luke 5:27-32) and Zacchaeus at the other (Luke 19:1-10).

- By contrasting the behavior of one group with that of another, with regard to the reception of Jesus and his disciples, Luke is admonishing against the exclusive and self-righteous attitude of his community and advocating repentance, being the key to receive and host Jesus, who is actually the host, bestowing everyone with salvation.

Chapter III: Symposium with Zacchaeus

In the light of the fondness of Luke for Hellenistic *symposia* and against the background of meal narratives so far in his Gospel, we analyzed the Zacchaeus pericope in the third chapter. Zacchaeus is the sixth reference to tax collectors in the third Gospel and sums up all the tax collector material in Luke. It also sums up all the *symposia* materials. There is only one more banquet in which Jesus would participate before his death and Resurrection in the third Gospel, namely, the Last Supper, the *symposium par excellence*. Luke 19:1-10, being the climax of all the *symposia* material brings together all the important words and themes that Luke has used so far in the four preceding *symposia*. Although in every meal narrative there is some kind of a hidden controversy, we saw that the structure as well as the word parallels of the Zacchaeus narrative shows itself rather as a 'Quest Story' which aims at showing the two main characters – Jesus and Zacchaeus – seeking each other.

The references to Jericho and the 'rich' Zacchaeus led us to recognize the Lukan concern for cities and rich men. Besides, the mention of Jericho reminds the readers of the Old Testament incident where Joshua, 'the first Jesus,' enters Jericho and is instrumental in saving the household of Rahab, whose profession of prostitution is connected in the Synoptics with the profession of the tax collectors and other sinful trades. Jericho therefore gives a hint, in which direction the story will go. Jesus is now 'the second Joshua' who has entered Jericho in order to save Zacchaeus who, like Rahab, is practicing a dubious trade in the eyes of fellow Jews.

While on the one hand tax collectors are shown by Luke in a positive light in the Gospel, the rich, on the other, are almost always negative characters in the third Gospel. These two contrasting characteristics of Zacchaeus brought out the main thrust of every banquet narrative, in fact of the entire Gospel of Luke – what a sinner should do and what a rich man should do in order to receive Jesus. We were able to observe that the characteristics of a sinner and of a rich man blend in the person of Zacchaeus. We also saw that the very name Zacchaeus, coming from the word *Zakkai* – meaning 'pure and innocent' – shows the irony between how the character of Zacchaeus is viewed by those around him and how he is treated by Jesus. The longing of this character to see Jesus parallels him with the character of Herod who also wanted to see Jesus. Nevertheless, the additional phrase τίς ἐστιν makes the quest of Zacchaeus different from the sheer curiosity of Herod. The longing of Zacchaeus is to get to know Jesus. As the story progresses the readers come to realize that Zacchaeus indeed succeeds in his search. He recognizes Jesus as the κύριος.

Verses 3–4 narrate the hindrances of Zacchaeus in his seeking of Jesus, and his perseverance to overcome these obstacles. Just as the two characteristics of Zacchaeus – being a tax collector and a rich man – evoked among the readers both a positive and a negative reaction about his character, the two hindrances help to understand the character of Zacchaeus as well as his surroundings. Although in the Gospel a large crowd follows Jesus all along his journey, even trampling on one another (12:1), ὄχλος is also often presented negatively in the sense that it either hinders Jesus' ministry or hinders an individual's search for Jesus. The Lukan community is in a way contrasted against the crowd which is but a hindrance to come to Jesus. The theological significance that is attributed to the shortness of the main character as μικρός shows Zacchaeus as a socially insignificant person and therefore belonging to the group of the 'little ones' whom God takes care, and whose destiny changes with the arrival of Jesus. This theme, which runs through the entire Gospel gets once again prominence in the character of the 'little' Zacchaeus. The name of the συκομορέα tree evokes what Zacchaeus says about his oppressive behavior (ἐσυκοφάντησα), which he would promise to change in v. 8. The advice of John the Baptist in Luke 3:14 to the soldiers and tax collectors, who came to be baptized (μηδὲ συκοφαντήσητε) is once again brought to the reminder of the readers by the reference to the συκομορέα tree in v. 8.

Verse 5–6 present the central point of the pericope; Jesus must stay at the house of Zacchaeus as a guest. Through the portrayal of

Jesus as a guest, Luke has cleared our doubts whether Luke 19:1-10 has anything to do with fellowship meals. The combination of the words μένω, οἰκία and the verb ὑπεδέξατο have exposed the Lukan interest of showing Jesus as a guest at someone's house. In every house that Jesus enters, we have seen him enjoying banquets with the host; here too this is probably the case. Jesus as a guest at the house of Zacchaeus calls into mind and sums up all the previous narratives in which Jesus was a guest – at the houses of Levi the tax collector and at the houses of Pharisees. The significance of this verse was clear in the analysis:

- The seeking of Zacchaeus is fulfilled in this verse. He not only sees Jesus but Jesus actually gives him a chance to have close acquaintance with him.

- The command to make haste to come down from the tree as well as the reaction of Zacchaeus to come down hurriedly blends with the Lukan emphasis of making haste and its connection with the divine plan of salvation which is seen throughout the Gospel.

- The divine plan and necessity is seen also from the use of the word δεῖ. It is the destined plan of God that Jesus stays as a guest at the house of Zacchaeus and thereby becomes the host for Zacchaeus in rendering salvation to his household. But we have seen that by using δεῖ Luke does not intend to say that Jesus has no freedom and must be a guest at the house of Zacchaeus, but that the Lukan δεῖ shows the self-consciousness of Jesus in accepting the will of God for his life, which becomes the instrument to bring salvation to the household of Zacchaeus. Jesus conducts his whole life up until the cross according to the divine will of the Father. Going to the house of the religiously hopeless man is part of this larger plan of the Father. Hence Jesus' journey to Jericho is not a deviation from his goal to Jerusalem. As O'Hanlon suggests, going to the sycamore tree to find Zacchaeus, going to the house of Zacchaeus and "the searching out of the lost is part of the journey. Indeed, it is the whole point of the journey."[1]

- The double use of σήμερον in this short pericope helps to realize (as in Luke 2:14) that it is the presence of Jesus that brings the decisiveness of salvation. What Jesus expected to happen ʹtodayʹ (v. 5) has become reality ʹtodayʹ (v. 9). The presence of Jesus in Jericho and at the house of Zacchaeus has made it happen. The salvation is rendered to the household of Zacchaeus that day because Jesus has been joyfully accepted as the guest of that house.

- Just as in the literary *symposia* where the rules are there to be broken, here too there is a reversal of sympotic rules. Without being invited to be a guest, Jesus invites himself to the house of Zacchaeus. Thereby Luke shows that Jesus, the main character of his work, is the chief guest of the *symposium*, like Socrates, who, going to a house as a guest of a *symposium*, in fact usurps the role of the host. Though Zacchaeus as the host offers hospitality to Jesus at his house, it is actually Jesus who is the real host, who has come to offer the household of Zacchaeus the true hospitality of God and salvation. This reversal of role is once again confirmed in v. 10 through the final words of the Lukan Jesus the real host who has come to the house of Zacchaeus to give him the gift of salvation.

- The haste with which Zacchaeus comes down from the tree and the joy with which he receives Jesus in his house shows his unexpected surprise that Jesus comes to stay in his house. These two reactions of haste and joy with which Zacchaeus welcomes Jesus are important for the reception of salvation in Luke. They are actually the Lukan specific words with which Luke instructs his community how the human response should be in the face of the invitation from God. The joy with which Zacchaeus receives Jesus is definitely to be contrasted with the sadness of the rich ruler upon hearing the message of Jesus (Luke 18:23).

The word καταλύω in verse 7 confirms once again what Luke tries to instruct the reader through the words μένω with οἰκία: here at the house of Zacchaeus there is a banquet scene. The analysis has also shown that Luke makes a sharp contrast between the joy of Zacchaeus at the words of Jesus and the murmur of the people around him at what Jesus thinks of doing. The very purpose of Jesus to seek that which is lost, is not understood by the people even just before his passion and the cross. As O'Hanlon says, "After so much, so little is understood."[2] Till now only the Pharisees and scribes were murmuring when they saw that Jesus eating with tax collectors and friends. Now 'all' (πάντες) around Jesus murmur against him. Hence at the doorsteps of Jerusalem Luke shows graphically the heightening and increase of this murmur against Jesus. After Jesus is arrested, the same πάντες would pass judgement on Jesus, condemn him to death (Luke 22:70), and shout that he should be crucified. After his death once again the same πάντες would beat their breasts, looking at what has happened (Luke 23:48). Their murmuring reminds the readers not only of the murmur of the Pharisees and scribes against Jesus but also of the murmuring of the elder brother in the parable of the lost son (Luke 15:25-30). This would later take the Gospel story forward, as is clear from the events in the Acts of the Apostles, where the message of Jesus Christ is rejected by Israel and hence reaches out to the gentiles.

In verse eight, we saw that Zacchaeus comes once again in the foreground and 'answers' Jesus against the criticism of the crowd, although their criticism targets Jesus. We understood Zacchaeus standing up to answer as an action that resembles that of a host who actually stands up during the *symposion* to raise a toast to his guests and say something. Zacchaeus' address of Jesus as Lord (κύριε) means that he has become a member of the believing community, similar to the narrator (note that Luke as the narrator calls Jesus as κύριος). The presence of δίδωμι and ἀποδίδωμι is to be understood not as durative presence but as futuristic presence, indicating the future resolve of the character. This shows Zacchaeus ready to fulfill the conditions of a rich man who wants to enter into the Kingdom of heaven, and that even though Jesus does not ask him to do, as was the case with the rich man In Luke 18:22.

As it is in all the Lukan banquet narratives, Jesus has the final word. His words justify the acceptance of Zacchaeus and also the actions of Jesus in going into the house of Zacchaeus. The ΄today΄ in this verse which recalls the word in v. 5 states categorically that the arrival and the imminence of salvation which has been offered by Jesus in v. 5 has been actualized by the actions of both Zacchaeus and Jesus. Finally, the purpose for which Jesus ΄must stay΄ at the house of Zacchaeus has come to the fulfillment. That ΄today΄ in Luke 19:9 is the ΄salvific today΄ is clear from the fact that σήμερον comes together with σωτηρία, the combination of which we find only in the infancy narratives (Luke 2:11) apart from Luke 19:9. As in the infancy narrative here too the arrival and the presence of Jesus *is* salvation not only for Zacchaeus but also for his entire household. The acceptance of Jesus has resulted in the repentance of Zacchaeus which in turn brought salvation to the house. The advice of John the Baptist to the people of Israel, that they should show their sonship of Abraham through their repentance (Luke 3:12-14) has been actualized by Zacchaeus. Hence the acceptance of Jesus, the subsequent conversion of Zacchaeus and his salvation all three are closely interlinked.

Luke has summed up the entire life and mission of Jesus in v. 10. The parables of seeking the lost (ch. 15) get a concrete life example in the person of Zacchaeus. At the beginning of the narrative Zacchaeus seeks Jesus but later on it turns out that Zacchaeus is actually being sought after by Jesus, who, like the shepherd in Ezek 34:16, aims at seeking the lost ones of Israel in order to save them. Hence verse 10 summarizes for the readers the entire Gospel upto this point. It brings the memories of Jesus who heals a woman and upholds her daughtership of Abraham (13:16); it calls one΄s attention to the parables of the lost, where coin, sheep and the son are lost, found and saved, thus resulting in the joy of the master (15:1-32). Zacchaeus as the lost one has been found by Jesus whose mission is nothing but to seek and save the lost.

Chapter IV: Fellowship Meal and the Outcasts in India

We tried to see the story of Zacchaeus from the background of the caste system in India, which divides and segregates from their birth onwards some as pure and others as impure. Zacchaeus could be understood as a Jewish *Dalit*, one in whose house the 'pure' Pharisees would not dare to enter, with whom they would not dare to have table fellowship. We saw however, that there are main differences between Zacchaeus the tax collector and *Dalits* in India. Firstly, Zacchaeus does not remain in the permanent state of pollution from his birth onwards. It was his profession as a tax collector that kept him outside the social boundaries of the religious elite of the time, whereas the entire *Dalit* community is said to be impure because of their being born in this group of *panchama* – the casteless community. This is why, we saw, that the *Dailt* community is kept literally outside of other caste villages, in the fear of contamination. Secondly, Luke tells that Zacchaeus – the Jewish *Dalit* – was rich (19:2). At least economically he was free. Although there is a steady growth in the number of *Dalits* who come up in life and economically succeed, in an increasingly hostile environment – thanks to the effort of the Government as well as social works done by innumerable social institutions, this economic freedom is still a dream for most of the *Dalit* families.

The fourth chapter concluded with the call to all the Christians of India to look at the table fellowship of Jesus with Zacchaeus as a sign that shows that everyone is equal before God. Just as Pharisees understood themselves as sons of Abraham, so too was Zacchaeus a son of Abraham. Similarly, we are all the children of the one Father God, irrespective of which caste one belongs to. Jesus' partaking at a *symposium* at the house of Zacchaeus, despite the fierce criticism, is a proclamation in action; it is a call to all the caste groups against judging others as impure and untouchable. It is an invitation for the Indian Christians to take up food as a weapon to break down the narrow-minded barriers of caste, just as Jesus did.

The Lukan Message: Then and Now

The study of the Zacchaeus encounter does not end with analyzing the story for its own sake. It urges the present reader to understand the purpose of Luke behind writing such an encounter. Through his life, Zacchaeus conveys the message of discipleship not just to the community of Luke. His message is universal and eternal for all those who are fascinated by his character. At the end of our analysis, having studied his life in ten verses of Luke, we could gather a few nuances from the study of the encounter of Zacchaeus with Jesus and these will be enumerated in the following pages:

Diverse Models of Discipleship

One is able to see in the double work of Luke-Acts a tension between two forms of discipleship. The disciples including Levi the tax collector, who left everything in order to follow Jesus (Luke 5:11,28), the young man wanting to follow Jesus who is commanded by him to sell all his belongings and follow him (Luke 18:18-30), the story of Ananias and Sapphira in the Acts of the Apostles who are punished for keeping some of their properties for themselves (Acts 5:1-11) – these stories are advocating one type of discipleship through which individuals and families of the Christian community are called for total abandonment of their properties in solidarity with the entire Christian brethren. While such type of discipleship does not seem to have lasted very long (perhaps because of the delay of the imminent Parousia), there emerges a second type of discipleship. Already in the third Gospel, we see examples of such discipleship. The women who followed Jesus and provided for Jesus and his disciples out of their possessions (Luke 8:1-3) are models for those who want to follow Jesus and spend their fortunes for the poor as well as for the growth of the new movement. Zacchaeus is an example of this way of following Jesus. By being silent on whether Zacchaeus left his profession as chief tax collector and whether he continued to follow Jesus on his way to Jerusalem, and by not portraying him as selling everything he owns, Luke opens up to the readers a new model of discipleship. Just like those women who out of their belongings provided for the Jesus-community (Luke 8:1-3) and thereby were followers of Jesus, Zacchaeus too using his wealth to care for the poor, has become a true follower of Jesus. Through this Luke offers his community different models of following Jesus. One could follow the footsteps of Levi the tax collector by leaving everything and follow Jesus. One could also follow the footsteps of Zacchaeus. One need not give away one's entire property; one need not become a wandering mendicant to be a follower of Jesus. One could be a true disciple of Jesus being in his own house, doing his own job. In fact, his properties could be useful in this way of following Jesus, namely by spending them rightly and using to help the poor and the needy.

Righteous and Sinner: Breaking of Barriers

In the context of communities, which are busy creating boundaries between outsiders and insiders, this new alternative Jesus-community dissolves all the barriers between the concepts of rich and poor, man and woman, sinner and just, leader and the member. Zacchaeus' story states the fact that before the loving offer of God everyone is equal. There is no distinction between a sinner and a just in this community, in which the love of the Father is poured on to each child equally. In fact, there is a preference in the community for the lost and weak ones – literally as well as symbolically. This means that the rich and the strong within this community should care for the poor and the weak and behave in such a way, that the barrier between the rich and the poor is completely eradicated. The morally upright 'elder brothers' should care for the morally weak 'little ones,' the μικρότεροι, so that they are once again led to experience their sonship of the one loving Father.

Jesus the Host and his All-inclusive Invitation and Offer

Although there is murmur and indifference from the part of people in receiving and accepting Jesus there is always a sense of reception on the part of Jesus towards the Pharisees as well as towards the murmuring crowd. This is seen in the way Luke portrays Jesus willingly accepting any opportunity for a communal meal and chat with the Pharisees. His openness to dining with the Pharisees as well as his eagerness to interact with them shows the extension of his invitation even to the Pharisees whose narrow and closed ideology resist change.

In the same way, though there is a murmur from the people of Jericho, just before entering the city of Jerusalem, the 'City of Peace,' which will fail to recognize and hence reject and kill him, Jesus the bearer of peace is open to anyone in Jericho as well as anyone in Jerusalem who welcomes him. It reminds us of the parable of the lost son, which is a response to the criticism of the Pharisees and scribes to the fact that Jesus welcomes and eats with tax collectors and sinners (Luke 15:1-2) and ends with the invitation of the father to the "respectable but unsympathetic older brother"[3] to come in to the house and join the celebration of the return of the sinful but repentant younger son (Luke 15:28, 31-32). Hence the Lukan Jesus does not shut his door on anyone. The only prerequisite to be a member of this banqueting community and thereby to obtain salvation, is to accept the invitation offered by Jesus and rejoice in his company. If at all one finds oneself outside the community of Jesus, it is because the person has chosen to shut the door against the Kingdom, despite the invitation of Jesus and his community. Because, "the joy in heaven over one repentant sinner is something which the impeccable and long-standing observer of commandments can never understand."[4]

Two Banqueting Groups: A Contrast
The only Jewish group in the third Gospel, which invites Jesus to dine with them, is the group of Pharisees. The only Jewish group, which warns Jesus against the plot of Herod to kill him is the group of Pharisees. All the same, the study of Luke 19:1-10 in the light of the previous banquet narratives suggests to us, that one need not look at the Lukan portrayal of Pharisees either as friendly or as accepting the school of thought from Jesus. We understood that the very aim of Luke in arching the three pharisaic *symposia* within the two *symposia* of the tax collectors is to contrast the Pharisees and their idea of purity and pollution with that of Jesus and his community, especially with regard to the banqueting

culture. These two groups assume their significance in the Gospel in the way they contrast each other in their relation with Jesus. There is, on the one hand, a joyful reception of Jesus by the tax collectors, while on the other there is disapproval and murmuring from the part of the Pharisees about the way Jesus behaves at banquets and about the way he relates with the religious 'sinners' of the time. Hence, the effects of their *symposia* with Jesus is quite different. While the *symposia* of the tax collectors Levi and Zacchaeus are the symbols of the mutual acceptance and subsequent joy, the *symposia* of the Pharisees are used as an instrument by Luke to show how Jesus' community is completely different from the thought patterns of the Pharisees. Hence a growing distance has emerged through these banquets between the 'Jesus group' and the group of the Pharisees.

An Alternative Banqueting Community

The negative portrayal of Pharisaic banquets exhibit the real purpose of Luke, namely to show to his community, how a Christian *symposium* should *not* be celebrated, who in this *symposium* are *not* to be excluded and how the partakers in such a *symposium* should *not* behave. Luke does not use the *symposium* genre to glorify the Hellenistic as well as the Pharisaic practice. On the contrary, like Lucian of Samasota, Luke mocks at the sympotic behavior of the Greeks as well as of the Jews who had adopted this practice from the Hellenists. Through the positive banquet scenes of Jesus with tax collectors - Levi and Zacchaeus - Luke tries to point out how Christians, the new sympotic community *should* behave, when they gather. Hence, the study on Zacchaeus help the readers to conclude that Luke through these narratives aims at creating an alternative banqueting community, which bestows a universal offer upon everyone to dine in the Kingdom regardless of where one stands in the community, regardless of whether one observes the rules of the community strictly or not.

Eucharistic Community: A Banqueting Community

If the banquets of Jesus upto this point in Luke's Gospel are to show how a banqueting community should *not* behave, there is one particular meal, through which Jesus the host advises how the Jesus community *should* celebrate it. One does not do justice to the study of Jesus' meals in the Gospel of Luke, or in the other Gospels, if one bypasses the meal of Jesus *par excellence* - the Last Supper, which Jesus celebrated with his disciples. Our study of Jesus' meal with Zacchaeus too, would not be complete, if we would not look at the connections it has with the final banquet of Jesus with his disciples. The Last Supper is a subject of study in its own right; a deeper and a thorough analysis of the connection between the Last Supper and the story of Zacchaeus would definitely enrich the analysis on Luke 19:1-10; it would also open up new possibilities to understand the *symposium*-like banquet narratives in the third Gospel. Due to the limits of the present study, we would like to merely touch upon the basic connections of Zacchaeus' story with the Last Supper. We want to acknowledge that Jesus' meal with Zacchaeus has been in a way not just an ending to all the previous banquets in the Gospel narrative. It is also used by Luke as a hinge, as a connecting factor to the Last Supper that is coming ahead; indeed it anticipates all the meals of the early Christians in the Acts of the Apostles.[5] There are similarities as well as the differences between the meals of Jesus before the Last Supper and the Last Supper itself. In the following pages we would like to present a few of them. These similarities and differences between the banquets of Jesus (*Jesusmahl*) and the Last Supper (*Eucharistisches Mahl*) would perhaps be the impetus to bring the study of the *symposium*-like banquets of the Lukan Jesus further.

The Last Supper: A Passover Seder

The aim here is not to go into historical debate of whether Jesus' Last Supper was in fact celebrated on the 15th of Nisan (on the day of the Passover) or on the 14th of Nisan (a day before the Feast of the Passover), as the Gospel of John puts it.[6] This work confines itself to the account of the Last Supper itself as it is chronicled in Luke. Among the other

Synoptics, it is Luke who points out very clearly that the Last Supper was indeed celebrated on the day of the Passover. He hints this more than once.

- Luke 22:1: Now the festival of Unleavened Bread, which is called the Passover, was near.

- Luke 22:7-8: Then came the day of Unleavened Bread, on which the Passover lamb had to be sacrificed. So Jesus sent Peter and John, saying, "Go and prepare the Passover meal for us that we may eat it."

- Luke 22:14-15: When the hour came, he took his place at the table, and the apostles with him. He said to them, "I have eagerly desired to eat this Passover with you before I suffer."

These introductory verses clearly point out the aim of Luke – to present the Last Supper of Jesus as a Passover meal, as in Mark and Matthew. Secondly, the structure of the Last Supper as described by the Synoptics is similar to the Passover Seder, which is well described in *M. Pesachim* 10:1-9. And the Jewish Passover festival during the Tannaitic period of the first two centuries CE (any Jewish festive banquet for that matter) was similar to the existing Greco-Roman festive meals of the time. Bahr suggests that apart from the religious additions to the Jewish banquets, the festive meals of Jews even prior to the Tannaitic period were similar to the Greco-Roman banquets.[7] Hence it would not be wrong to see the Last Supper of Jesus as a Passover Seder which itself is structured along the Greco-Roman *symposia*.

The Lukan Last Supper: a "Christian *Symposium*"[8]?

At the outset it should be checked how Luke handles his Markan source. Although we see Luke follows his source in its narrative sequence (e.g. the plot to kill Jesus and the role of Judas in it, the preparation of the Passover, the Institution of the Last Supper and the foretelling of Peter's denial), Luke clearly tries to pinpoint what he thinks to be important in the section. Reading the Lukan Passover narration against the background of Markan Passover description from the perspective of the meal, we find the following conspicuous enhancements made by Luke:

- In Luke it is Jesus who takes the initiative by sending the disciples for preparing for the Passover meal, which he would eat with the twelve (Luke 22:8), whereas in Mark it is the disciples who ask Jesus, where they should prepare the Passover meal which "he" would eat (Mk 14:12).

- The Lukan Jesus expresses the longing to celebrate this meal with his disciples (Luke 22:15). In fact, Luke makes the δεῖπνον / συμπόσιον difference evident in the two special verses which we do not find in Mark (Luke 22:16-18).

- Luke deliberately brings in a new element of *'Rangstreit'* between the disciples during this meal (Luke 22:24-27).

Mark uses the story of the Passover meal to explain the institution of the Eucharist. The Lukan deviations from the Markan source, however reveal that Luke takes the Passover meal to a new height. The Passover meal that Jesus celebrated with his disciples is not only important for the Institution of the Last Supper. As a meal that comes as a climax of all the meals in which the earthly Jesus partook in, the Passover meal is of special importance to Luke. It is this *symposium* in which Jesus partakes that forms the climax of all the *symposia* in Luke – a Christian *symposium*, which Luke sets as an ideal for the followers of Jesus.

Sympotic Setting in the Lukan Passover Narration

a. First of all, the Last Supper is described as an all-male event. Beginning from those who prepared the Passover meal to those who participate in the meal, all characters are men.

b. Second, not only Jesus (ἀνέπεσεν Luke 22:14) but also the other participants including perhaps his disciples reclined at the meal.

c. Third, the distinct parts of a sympotic meal are more clearly alluded to in Luke than in Mark. Luke brings in the difference between the eating part of the meal and the drinking part in the short passage (Luke 22:16-18). The way Luke structures the Last Supper is different from how Mark does. In the Last Supper a three-part structure seems to emerge: first, the preliminary courses (Luke 22:15-18), which comprise of the talk about the paschal lamb (Luke 22:15-16), the cup of wine and the blessing before the meal (Luke 22:17-18); second the δεῖπνον, the meal proper (Luke 22:19, 20b) where the bread is blessed and meal is shared; finally, after the meal (μετὰ τὸ δειπνῆσαι Luke 22:20a) begins drinking part of the meal, the συμπόσιον, in which wine is blessed and shared after which the table talk emerges (Luke 22:20-38). Kraus[9] understands this structure to have emerged from the Passover Seder, which has been inspired by Greco-Roman sympotic meals.

d. The table talk during the *symposion* part of the meal revolves mainly around the incidents and themes that came up during the banquet. It centers around the meal aspects (what and how they eat and drink). It also focuses on the end-time banquet (Luke 22:30).

e. The characters which are typical of *symposium* literature are found also in the story of the Last Supper. Jesus plays the role of the host; although there is also a house owner, in whose house the banquet takes place, he does not come into the scene, thereby giving Jesus the role of the host; he blesses the meal and the drink and distributes them among the participants. "Jesus the teacher's usurpation of host's role is typical both of Luke's particular characterization of Jesus and generally of hosts/teacher relations in the symposium literary tradition."[10]

f. Just as in the Greco-Roman literary *symposia*, the death of the main character Jesus looms large at the Last Supper.

g. In the Lukan Last Supper we have yet another important sympotic setting that is conspicuous. Luke is the only evangelist who inserts into the Passover narrative the conflict of the disciples as to who is greater among them (Luke 22:24-27). Just as there were conflicts of getting higher places among the participants of Greek literary *symposia* and just as Luke portrays the dispute among the guests for the seats of honor at the *symposium* hosted by the leader of the Pharisees (Luke 14:7), Luke colors also the Passover meal of Jesus with a similar dispute among the disciples as to who among them is the greatest. This dispute among the apostles gains significance especially in the context of a *symposium*. This conflict gives rise to a table talk about the ideal behavior of a disciple of Jesus. Since the conflict is within a *symposium*-like meal, the Lukan Jesus differentiates between the one who reclines at table and the one who serves at the table (Luke 22:27).

With the above-mentioned observations one could see the aim of Luke to project the Passover meal in the form of a literary *symposium*. In this Christian ideal meal there is continuity as well as discontinuity in comparison to the existing meal practices of Greco-Roman and Jewish religious associations, including the Pharisaic group. The commonality between the Jesus community and the Pharisaic community is that both embrace the sympotic tradition and mold their identity in the form of a banqueting community. However, there is also discontinuity. The presence of the Pharisees in various *symposia* in which Jesus partakes throughout the Gospel of Luke, and their absence in the Last Supper suggest an important nuance. Through the contrast Luke seems to differentiate the Jesus community from the thought patterns of other schools especially the Pharisaic school. "Luke emphasizes that Christian communal ethics are both continuous and discontinuous with Pharisaic tablic ethics, by contrasting the Last Supper implicitly with his three prior scenes of Pharisaic *symposia*. This point is underlined when Luke casts his Last Supper as *the* paradigmatic Pharisaic *symposium*, the Passover Seder, from which Pharisees are conspicuously absent."[11]

The Meal with Zacchaeus and the Last Supper

The placement of the Zacchaeus' encounter with Jesus right at the doorsteps of Jerusalem is not only from the geographical point of view that Jericho lies near Jerusalem; it is the contention of this paper that Luke might have purposefully placed the Zacchaeus encounter and his meal with Jesus as the last of the Meals of Jesus, prior to the Last Supper. If this contention is valid, then there could be specific connections between Luke 19:1-10 and Luke 22:7-28. An attempt is made in the following pages to find these connections and the possible reasons for Luke for making such connections.

One of the differences between the five *symposia* of Jesus before the Jerusalem entry and the Last Supper *symposium* in Jerusalem is that the former was an occasion for a controversy between Jesus on the one side and the religious rulers of the day on the other. Not only in the Zacchaeus' encounter with Jesus, but in every meal of Jesus in the Gospel of Luke, Jesus would always court a controversy. While the form of the meal is similar to the Greco-Roman *symposia*, which is familiar to the Pharisees, the controversy is about the fact, with whom Jesus and his followers recline at *symposia*. Zacchaeus belongs to one of the social groups, with whom the religious rulers of the day would have no connection whatsoever; but Jesus has been seen and understood as a friend of such social outcasts. While the Pharisees were preoccupied with the purity of their meal and the purity of the participants, Jesus feels at home and enjoys his meals with the outcasts of the society. This creates the occasion for the meal controversies in the Gospel of Luke. The participants of the Last Supper should be understood in this background. In the Last Supper however, the opponents of Jesus, the Pharisees are completely absent, and the meal once again is an occasion for Jesus to teach his disciples, about the ethos of this new school of thought. The disciples of Jesus belong to the group of socially, if not, economically powerless. By entertaining and hosting such powerless people in this specific, *symposia*-like Passover meal, the Lukan Jesus perhaps wants to instruct his followers, to welcome the socially powerless and make them feel at home in their banquet community.

Secondly, all along the meals of Jesus (including the banquet with Levi, and the meals with the three Pharisees) Jesus is invited for a meal and he accepts the invitation. Hence he is a passive guest of the hosts who have invited him – at least initially; whereas in the Zacchaeus encounter, it is Jesus who takes initiative and invites himself at the house of Zacchaeus. This happens also at the Last Supper. We do not know anything about the house owner, in whose house Jesus celebrated the Last Supper, except that he is the owner of the upper room. The house owner vanishes from the scene after giving the room to Jesus and his disciple; then on Jesus takes the role of the host; he gives instructions how the room is to be arranged and how the meals are to be prepared. Through this Luke perhaps wants to show the following:

- Both Zacchaeus and the house owner at the Last Supper would have been taken by surprise by the self-invitation of Jesus to be at their house. But there is joy in welcoming Jesus and his disciples in their house. Luke wants to suggest to his community, this joy of the sudden reception and welcoming of the followers of Jesus at their houses.

- No matter in whose house the Christian community gathers together for fellowship meal, the host and the chief guest is always Jesus. It is he who has invited himself into the banqueting presence of the Jesus community. It is he who has become the host and the chief guest of the banqueting community.

There is an important deviation in the Last Supper of Jesus from all the other meals of Jesus. It is the absence of the critics of Jesus at the Last Supper. In every meal of Jesus so far, Jesus is always surrounded by his critics who question his controversial behavior of meal practices. The Last Supper however is a closed banquet of Jesus only with his disciples. There is no room for his critics. From the Last Supper onwards, the meals which Luke would narrate in the rest of the Gospel as well as in the Acts of the Apostles, would always be meals of the new community of Jesus. The ideal banquet would be celebrated and eaten by an ideal group, where Jesus is the host. The imagery for these ideal banquets is something new which Luke uses – "he took a loaf of bread, and when he had given thanks, he broke it and gave it to them..." (λαβὼν ἄρτον εὐχαριστήσας ἔκλασεν καὶ ἔδωκεν αὐτοῖς Luke 22:19). Such imagery of breaking the bread would come again not only in the rest of the Gospel but also in the Acts of the Apostles (Luke 24:30; Acts 2:42,46).

Hence we could say the meal of Jesus with Zacchaeus operates for Luke as a hinge through which Luke, on the one side, closes up all meals of Jesus, which courted a controversy, and on the other opens up a new banqueting ideology. The meals of Jesus-community take a definite turn from the Last Supper onwards. The breaking of the bread becomes symbolic for the followers of Jesus, because it is what Jesus did at the Last Supper; it is what Jesus commanded them to do in remembrance of him (Luke 22:19). 'Breaking of Bread' becomes the new identity for the followers of Jesus. The focus of this community is not any more the critics who find fault with their way of banqueting. It is on building up of the community itself. Everyone who does not divide humanity according to their social and economic status, is now welcome into the community of the followers of Jesus. When the Christian community does not show any inhibition or disdain towards others, when the Christian community in its behavior as well as in its table fellowship does not show differences between men and women, sinners and the just, slaves and freemen, then this community understands that Jesus their Lord himself is host and chief guest for the common banquets they partake in.

Barrier-Breaking Christian Banquets – A Need of the Time for India
Christianity did not come into existence in India with the arrival of the colonial powers. According to Indian tradition, the Apostle Thomas came to India to sow the seeds of Christianity and preach Jesus' message of love among the Indian people. Hence India has an almost 2000-year-

old Christian tradition. There exists a group of so-called 'pure blood Christians' in the southern state of Kerala, which is an endogamous community of Christians, who claim to have an almost 2000-year old Christian heritage and who like to keep up their identity and the purity of their race through their endogamy, so that they do not get contaminated by mingling with other Christians. The very notion that they are 'pure blood' Christians, betrays the ideology that there are other Christians who are not of pure blood. Among those of us, who were evangelized by the missionaries who came along with the colonial powers, the majority consists of former Hindus, who belonged either to the *Śūdrā* class – the fourth class in the caste structure – or they were *Dalits* – the untouchable class. Our ancestors eagerly embraced Christianity with the hope that their children and children's children would one day live with equal dignity and equal opportunity in life. We would not be wrong, however, to say that culturally Christians in India are still Hindus, although they bear Christian names. They have brought into Christianity their caste identity. Many of the Christians of the *Śūdrā* class still consider the Christian *Dalits* as the group with whom one should have a very limited relationship. The caste struggle among Christians – at least in the state of Tamil Nadu – is not between the *Dalit* Christians and the *Brāhmaṇa* Christians who are but a handful; the struggle is mainly between the Christian *Śūdrās* and Christian *Dalits*; these were the two classes, who, in their longing for freedom and equal rights came away from Hinduism.

The Eucharist, which Christians celebrate is a symbol of oneness to which all are called for. Sadly enough, this very celebration of the Eucharist has become the starting point for a fierce fight for asserting the caste identity as we saw in the fourth chapter. As said earlier, meals have the strength either to divide or to unite. Jesus' table fellowship with Zacchaeus invites the Indian Christians to value and make use of our everyday meal as a symbol of breaking the barrier between caste identities. We do not need to wait for Christianity as an institution to free itself from the oppressive clutches of the caste system. Change could and should begin from the individual, from one's own household.

Just a small thing like one's every day meal could play a pivotal role in bringing up change in the society, which does not look and judge anyone upon his caste identity. The Lukan Jesus not only 'welcomes' tax collectors and sinners and 'receives' them (Luke 15:1-2), he even invites himself to the house of Zacchaeus (Luke 19:5). He deliberately goes to the house of Zacchaeus, who was a sinner in the eyes of all. Such an attitude would perhaps ease the tension that exists between the different caste communities towards *Dalits*. Just as the table fellowship of Jesus was a proclamation in action, every meal that an Indian Christian eats with the members outside of his caste community, especially with members of the *Dalit* community, would be a powerful sign of change among the Christians as well as the Hindu brethren.

Challenge of Luke 19:1-10 for the Indian Christians

One's every day meal is such an ordinary event. It is the persons with whom we take this ordinary meal that gives it an extraordinary meaning. It can become a great inducement for change, as was the table fellowship of the historical Jesus, described by Luke. Christianity has done a lot for the alleviation of the sufferings of the *Dalits* as well as the *Śūdrās* of Hindus. It has brought them up the ladder of life, by giving them education and thereby assuring them of a decent job and life. With regard to the social acceptance of *Dalits* and with regard to the equal dignity of all, Christianity in India has also contributed a lot. Looking at the present day situation of Christianity in India, however, one is sure to see that there is a long, long way ahead to go towards this model of social acceptance of *Dalits* in general and especially of *Dalit* Christians. This is very evident from the hard and blunt questions, posed by Fr. Francis Xavier SJ, the former Jesuit Provincial of Madurai Province who is named after the famous missionary saint Francis Xavier. As a present day *Dalit* Christian, even though he has enjoyed a high position in the Society and was the Provincial of a Jesuit Province, Fr Fancis Xavier still faces enormous social inequalities in the mentality of the Christians. His words show the pain of being a *Dalit* and a Christian:

> Being a *Dalit* is more than original sin, because baptismal water can wash

the original sin but cannot remove the stigma of being a *Dalit*. You say all human beings are made in the image and the likeness of God, but is there a *Dalit* God? You bury the dead separately; is there going to be a *Dalit* heaven and a non-*Dalit* heaven? Or do we need a messiah who should be born as a *Dalit*? ... My question is, when a *Dalit* priest celebrates Mass, is a *Dalit* Christ coming or a regular Christ? Because some people do not want to receive Communion from a *Dalit* Priest.[12]

This sadly is the reality of the Indian Church. Jesus' initiative to dine with Zacchaeus is a prophetic call for the Christians of India to eradicate this evil called ´caste´ from one´s mindset. Jesus´ all-embracing and all-inclusive meal with Zacchaeus is a clear pointer in which direction we should go. A Church full of people, who work shoulder to shoulder, intermarry without looking at which caste one belongs to, and, above all, eat together with the sense of common brotherhood – this is our goal. The normal and ordinary meal that we share and eat in common, will play a decisive role in making that dream of common brotherhood a reality.

Endnotes

[1] J. O'Hanlon, "The Story of Zacchaeus and the Lukan Ethic." 15.

[2] Ibid., 15.

[3] H. J. Cadbury and P. N. Anderson, *The Making of Luke-Acts*, 259.

[4] Ibid., 259.

[5] Bösen divides the entire meals of Jesus into three classifications: „*Jesusmahl, Eucharistisches Mahl, Endzeitmahl.*" These meals go along the line of Conzelmann´s division of the history of Salvation. The meals of Jesus prior to the Last Super, i.e. the meals in which Jesus was a guest at the houses of tax collectors, Pharisees and others characterize the *Jesusmahl*. With the Last Supper, which Jesus celebrated with his apostles, begins the Meal of the in-between-time, the second phase of the salvation history. The post resurrection meals of Jesus then characterize the end-time meal. For Bösen, Luke understands the different meal accounts as the means to accomplish the continuity between the different divisions of the history of Salvation. Cf. the second chapter, *Das Mahl als Kontinuität-schafendes Symbol*, in W. Bösen, *Jesusmahl, Eucharistisches mahl, Endzeitmahl*, 78-117.

[6] While scholars perceive the problem of the Johannine difference from the Synoptics, there are also some who suggest that historically the Last Supper of Jesus was celebrated on the 14th of Nisan as John puts it. This means, what Jesus celebrated was not a Passover meal but an ordinary meal before the Passover. J.

Marcus, "Passover and Last Supper Revisited," *NTS* 59, no. 03 (2013), 303-324.

[7] Bahr, "The Seder of Passover and the Eucharistic Words." 181-182.

[8] The phrase is taken from J. Brumberg-Kraus, ""Not By Bread Alone...": The Ritualization of Food and Table Talk in the Passover Seder in the Last Supper," in *Food and Drink in the Biblical Worlds*, ed. A. Brenner and J. W. van Henten, *Semeia* 86 (Atlanta, GA: Society of Biblical Literature, 1999), 167; also in the fourth chapter of his unpublished book, Brumberg-Kraus argues how the Last Supper of Jesus could be paralleled to the Passover Seder. J. Brumberg-Kraus, "Memorable Meals." 1-67.

[9] J. Brumberg-Kraus, "Memorable Meals.", 11-12.

[10] Ibid., 12.

[11] Ibid., 17.

[12] As quoted in Mosse, *The Saint in the Banyan Tree*, 1-2.

Bibliography

Primary Sources

Biblical Sources

E. Nestle, B. Aland, K. Aland, ed. *Novum Testamentum Graece*. Stuttgart: Deutsche Bibelgesellschaft, 2013.

The Holy Bible, The New Revised Standard Version (Catholic Edition). Bangalore: Theological Publications in India, 2010.

Classical and Non-Biblical Sources

Athenaeus. *The Deipnosophists: With an English translation by Charles Burton Gulick*. [Loeb Classical Library.]. London, New York: William Heinemann; G. P. Putnam's Sons, 1957.

Bury, R. G. *Plato IX: The Laws: With an English Translation*. 2 vols. LCL 1. Cambridge, Massachusetts, London: Harvard University Press; William Heinemann, 1961.

Charlesworth, J. H. ed. *The Old Testament Pseudepigrapha: Expansions of the "Old Testament" and Legends, Wisdom and Philosophical Literature, Prayers, Psalms, and Odes, Fragments of Lost Judeo-Hellenistic Works*. 2 vols. 2. Garden City, New York: Doubleday, 1985.

Clément d'Alexandrie, and Otto Stählin. *Des Clemens von Alexandreia ausgewählte Schriften aus dem Griechischen ubersetzt. 4: Stromateis, Buch 4-6*. 19 vols. Bibliothek der Kirchenväter: 2. Reihe 4. Munchen: Kösel, 1937.

Danby, H. *The Mishnah: Translated From the Hebrew With Introduction and Brief Explanatory Notes*. Oxford: Oxford University Press, 1933.

Foster, B. O. *Livy: Books I and II: With an English Translation*. 13 vols. LCL 1. London, Cambridge, Massachusetts: William Heinemann; Harvard University Press, 1939.

Gulick, C. B. *Athenaeus: The Deipnosophists: With an English Translation*. 7 vols. LCL 204 3. London, Cambridge, Massachusetts: William Heinemann; Harvard University Press, 1967.

———. *Athenaeus: The Deipnosophists: With an English Translation*. 7 vols. LCL 5. London, Cambridge, Massachusetts: William Heinemann; Harvard University Press, 1963.

Harmon, A. M. *Lucian: With an English Translation*. 8 vols. LCL 1. London, Cambridge, Massachusetts: William Heinemann; Harvard University Press, 1961.

———. *Lucian: With an English Translation*. 8 vols. LCL 2. London, Cambridge, Massachusetts: William Heinemann; Harvard University Press, 1960.

Homer. *The Odyssey: trasl. A. T. Murray; G. E. Dimock*. The Loeb Classical Library. Cambridge, Mass: Harvard University Press, 1995.

Horace. *Satires, Epistoles, Ars Poetica: trasl. H. R. Fairclough*. Loeb Classical Library 194. Cambridge, Mass, London: Harvard University Press; W. Heinemann, 1978.

Hunter, R. L. *Plato's Symposium*. Oxford approaches to classical literature. Oxford, New York: Oxford University Press, 2004.

Kilburn, K. *Lucian: With an English Translation*. 8 vols. LCL 6. London, Cambridge, Massachusetts: William Heinemann; Harvard University Press, 1959.

Lamb, W. R. M. *Plato: Lysis, Symposium, Gorgias: With an English Translation*. LCL. London, New York: William Heinemann; G. P. Putnam's Sons, 1925.

Martínez, F. G. *The Dead Sea Scrolls Translated: The Qumran Texts in English*. 2nd ed. Leiden, New York, Grand Rapids: E.J. Brill; W.B. Eerdmans, 1996.

Melmoth, W. *Pliny: Letters: With an English Translation*. LCL 55. London, New York: William Heinemann; Macmillan, 1931.

Minar, E. L., JR., F. H. Sandbach, and W. C. Helmbold. *Plutarch's Moralia: With an English Translation*. 15 vols. LCL 9. Cambridge, Massachusets, London: Harvard University Press; William Heinemann, 1961.

Müller, F. M., ed. *The Laws of Manu: transl. G. Bühler*. The Sacred Books of the East XXV. Oxford: Clarendon Press, 1886.

Murray, A. T. *Homer: The Odyssey: With an English Translation*. 2 vols. LCL 2. Cambridge, Massachusetts, London: Harvard University Press; William Heinemann, 1919.

Neusner, J. *The Tosefta: Second Division: Moed: Translated from Hebrew*. New York: Ktav Publishing House, 1981.

Petronius Arbiter. *Satyrica: trasl. R. B. Branham; D. Kinney*. London: J.M. Dent, 1996.

Philo. *Philo: trasl. F. H. Colson; G. H. Whitaker.* 12 Vls, Vol. 9. The Loeb Classical Library. London: William Heinemann, 1929-1991.

Plutarque, and B. Perrin. *Plutarch's Lives*. The Loeb Classical Library 98. London, Cambridge (Mass): W. Heinemann; Harvard University Press, 1970.

Plutarque, P. A. Clement, and H. B. Hoffleit. *Plutarch's Moralia*. The Loeb Classical Library. London, Cambridge: Heinemann; Harvard Un. Press, 1986.

Roberts, A., J. Donaldson, A. C. Coxe, and A. Menzies, eds. *Ante-Nicene Fathers: The Writings of the Fathers Down to A.D. 325*. 10 vols. 7. Peabody, Mass.: Hendrickson Publishers, 1995.

―――. eds. *Ante-Nicene Fathers: The Writings of the Fathers Down to A.D. 325*. 10 vols. 8. Peabody, Mass.: Hendrickson Publishers, 1995.

Rogers, B. B. *Aristophanes*. [Loeb Classical Library.]. 3 vol. William Heinemann: London; G. P. Putnam's Sons: New York, 1930.

Tertullian. *Adversus Marcionem, Books 4-5: Ed. and trsl. by Evans, Ernest*. Oxford Early Christian Texts. Oxford: Clarendon Press, 1972.

Thackeray, H. St. J. *Josephus: The Jewish War, Books I-III: With an English Translation*. 9 vols. LCL 2. London, Cambridge, Massachusetts: William Heinemann; Harvard University Press, 1956.

Williams, W. G. *Cicero: The Letters to His Friends: With an English Translation*. 3 vols. LCL 2. London, Cambridge, Massachusetts: William Heinemann; Harvard University Press, 1952.

Secondary Sources

Lexicons, Dictionaries and Encyclopedia

Batya, A., and C. Roth, eds. *The Standard Jewish Encyclopedia*. London: Allen, 1959.

Bauer, W. *Griechisch-Deutsches Wörterbuch: Zu den Schriften des Neuen Testaments und der übrigen Urchristlichen Literatur*. Berlin, Newyork: Walter de Gruyter, 1965. herausgegeben von Kurt Aland und Barbara Aland.

Bauernfeind, O. "τρέξω." In *Theological Dictionary of the New Testament*. Edited by G. Kittel, G. W. Bromiley & G. Friedrich. 10 vols., 226–33. Michigan: Grand Rapids; Eerdmans, 1964-1976.

Behm, J., and E. Würthwein. "μετανοέω, μετάνοια." In *ThWNT: Begründet von Kittel*. Edited by G. Friedrich. Achter Band, 972–1004. Stuttgart, Berlin, Köln, Mainz: Kohlhammer Verlag, 1967.

Bosman, H. L. "Marzēaḥ." In *New International Dictionary of Old Testament Theology & Exegesis*. Edited by W. A. VanGemeren. 5 vols., 1102–3. Grand Rapids, Michigan: Zondervan Publishing House, 1997.

Broshi, M. "Qumran: Archaeology." In *Encyclopedia of the Dead Sea Scrolls*. Edited by L. H. Schiffman and J. C. Vanderkam, 733–39. New York, Oxford: Oxford University Press, 2000.

Büchsel, F. "καταλύω." In *Theological Dictionary of the New Testament*. Edited by G. Kittel, G. W. Bromiley & G. Friedrich. 10 vols., 338. Michigan: Grand Rapids; Eerdmans, 1964-1976.

Busse, U. "διέρχομαι." In *Exegetical Dictionary of the New Testament*. Edited by H. Balz and G. Schneider. 3 vols., 322–23. Grand Rapids: Eerdmans, 1990-1993.

Colpe, C. "ὁ υἱὸς τοῦ ἀνθρώπου." In *Theological Dictionary of the New Testament*. Edited by G. Kittel, G. W. Bromiley & G. Friedrich. 10 vols., 400–477. Michigan: Grand Rapids; Eerdmans, 1964-1976.

Danker, F. W., and W. Bauer, eds. *A Greek-English lexicon of the New Testament and other early Christian literature*. 3rd ed. Chicago, London: University of Chicago Press, 2000.

Fabry, H.-J. "מִרְזַח." In *ThWAT*. Edited by G. J. Botterweck, G. W. Anderson and H. Ringgren. 10 vols. 5, 11–16. Stuttgart: W. Kohlhammer, 1986.

Feindrich, J. "καταβαίνω." In *Exegetical Dictionary of the New Testament*. Edited by H. Balz and G. Schneider. 3 vols., 254. Grand Rapids: Eerdmans, 1990-1993.

Fitzmyer, J. A. "κύριος." In *Exegetical Dictionary of the New Testament*. Edited by H. Balz and G. Schneider. 3 vols., 328–31. Grand Rapids: Eerdmans, 1990-1993.

Foerster, W. "Κύριος." In *TDNT*. Edited by G. Kittel et al. 10 vols., 1039–98. Grand Rapids, Michigan: W. B. Eerdmans, 1964-1976.

Foerster, W., and W. Fohrer. "σῴζω." In *Theological Dictionary of the New Testament*. Edited by G. Kittel, G. W. Bromiley & G. Friedrich. 10 vols., 965–1024. Michigan: Grand Rapids; Eerdmans, 1964-1976.

Freedman, D. N. *Eerdmans Dictionary of the Bible*. Grand Rapids, Mich., Cambridge: W.B. Eerdmans, 2000.

Frey, J. "Essenes." In *The Eerdmans Bible Dictionary*. Edited by A. C. Myers, 599–602. Grand Rapids, Mich.: Eerdmans, 1987.

Fuchs, E. "σήμερον." In *Theological Dictionary of the New Testament*. Edited by G. Kittel, G. W. Bromiley & G. Friedrich. 10 vols., 269–75. Michigan: Grand Rapids; Eerdmans, 1964-1976.

Giesen, H. "ὑποδέχομαι." In *Exegetical Dictionary of the New Testament*. Edited by H. Balz and G. Schneider. 3 vols., 402. Grand Rapids: Eerdmans, 1990-1993.

Glare, P. G. W. *Oxford Latin Dictionary*. Oxford, New York: Clarendon Press; Oxford University Press, 1982.

Green, J. B. , J. K. Brown, and N. Perrin, eds. *Dictionary of Jesus and the Gospels: A Compendium of Contemporary Biblical Scholarship.* 2nd ed. Nottingham: InterVarsity Press, 2013.

Greeven, H. "ζητέω." In *Theological Dictionary of the New Testament.* Edited by G. Kittel, G. W. Bromiley & G. Friedrich. 10 vols., 892–96. Michigan: Grand Rapids; Eerdmans, 1964-1976.

Grundmann, W. "δεῖ." In *Theological Dictionary of the New Testament.* Edited by G. Kittel, G. W. Bromiley & G. Friedrich. 10 vols., 21–25. Michigan: Grand Rapids; Eerdmans, 1964-1976.

Hauck, F. "μένω." In *Theological Dictionary of the New Testament.* Edited by G. Kittel, G. W. Bromiley & G. Friedrich. 10 vols., 574–79. Michigan: Grand Rapids; Eerdmans, 1964-1976.

Hauck, F., and E. Bammel. "πτωχός." In *Theological Dictionary of the New Testament.* Edited by G. Kittel, G. W. Bromiley & G. Friedrich. 10 vols., 885–915. Michigan: Grand Rapids; Eerdmans, 1964-1976.

Hauck, F., and W. Kasch. "πλοῦτος." In *Theological Dictionary of the New Testament.* Edited by G. Kittel, G. W. Bromiley & G. Friedrich. 10 vols., 318–32. Michigan: Grand Rapids; Eerdmans, 1964-1976.

Hempel, C. "Qumran Community." In *Encyclopedia of the Dead Sea Scrolls.* Edited by L. H. Schiffman and J. C. Vanderkam, 746–51. New York, Oxford: Oxford University Press, 2000.

Hess, A. J. "γογγύζω." In *Exegetical Dictionary of the New Testament.* Edited by H. Balz and G. Schneider. 3 vols., 256. Grand Rapids: Eerdmans, 1990-1993.

Hillyer, N. "τελώνιον." In *The New International Dictionary of New Testament Theology.* Edited by C. Brown, 755–59. Michigan: Zondervan Publishing House, 1981.

Hirschel, R. "Johanan Ben Zakkai." In *The Universal Jewish Encyclopedia: An Authoritative and Popular Presentation of Jews and Judaism Since the Earliest Times.* Edited by I. Landman. 10 vols., 164–66. New York: Universal Jewish Encyclopedia, 1948.

Hofius, O. "συκοφαντέω." In *Exegetical Dictionary of the New Testament.* Edited by H. Balz and G. Schneider. 3 vols., 285. Grand Rapids: Eerdmans, 1990-1993.

Hübner, H. "καταλύω." In *Exegetical Dictionary of the New Testament.* Edited by H. Balz and G. Schneider. 3 vols., 264. Grand Rapids: Eerdmans, 1990-1993.

_____. "μένω." In *Exegetical Dictionary of the New Testament.* Edited by H. Balz and G. Schneider. 3 vols., 407–8. Grand Rapids: Eerdmans, 1990-1993.

Hunzinger, C. H. "συκοφαντέω." In *Theological Dictionary of the New Testament*. Edited by G. Kittel, G. W. Bromiley & G. Friedrich. 10 vols., 759. Michigan: Grand Rapids; Eerdmans, 1964-1976.

Hutter, U. "πόλις." In *Exegetical Dictionary of the New Testament*. Edited by H. Balz and G. Schneider. 3 vols., 129. Grand Rapids: Eerdmans, 1990-1993.

Johnston, P. S. "Marzēaḥ." In *The New Interpreter's Dictionary of the Bible*. Edited by K. D. Sakenfeld. 5 vols., 828. Nashville: Abingdon, 2006-2009.

Kellermann, U. "ἥμισυς." In *Exegetical Dictionary of the New Testament*. Edited by H. Balz and G. Schneider, 122. Grand Rapids, Mich.: Eerdmans, 1990-1993.

Köster, H. "τόπος." In *Theological Dictionary of the New Testament*. Edited by G. Kittel, G. W. Bromiley & G. Friedrich. 10 vols., 187–208. Michigan: Grand Rapids; Eerdmans, 1964-1976.

Kremer, J. "ὁράω." In *Exegetical Dictionary of the New Testament*. Edited by H. Balz and G. Schneider. 3 vols., 526–29. Grand Rapids: Eerdmans, 1990-1993.

Larsson, E. "ζητέω." In *Exegetical Dictionary of the New Testament*. Edited by H. Balz and G. Schneider. 3 vols., 102–3. Grand Rapids: Eerdmans, 1990-1993.

Lasor, W. S. "Essenes." In *Baker Encyclopedia of the Bible*. Edited by W. A. Elwell and B. J. Beitzel, 719. Grand Rapids Mich: Baker Book House, 1988.

Légasse, S. "μικρός." In *Exegetical Dictionary of the New Testament*. Edited by H. Balz and G. Schneider. 3 vols., 427–28. Grand Rapids: Eerdmans, 1990-1993.

Liddell, H. G., and R. Scott. *A Greek-English Lexicon*. Oxford: Clarendon Press, 1968.

Longenecker, R. N. "'Son of Man' as a Self-Designation of Jesus." *Journal of the Evangelical Theological Society* 12, no. 3 (1969): 151–58.

Louw, J. P., E. A. Nida, and R. B. Smith. *Greek-English Lexicon of the New Testament based on Semantic Domains*. 2nd ed. New York: United Bible Societies, 1989.

Merklein, H. "πλοῦτος." In *Exegetical Dictionary of the New Testament*. Edited by H. Balz and G. Schneider. 3 vols., 114–17. Grand Rapids: Eerdmans, 1990-1993.

———. "πτωχός." In *Exegetical Dictionary of the New Testament*. Edited by H. Balz and G. Schneider. 3 vols., 193–95. Grand Rapids: Eerdmans, 1990-1993.

Meyer, R. "ὄχλος." In *Theological Dictionary of the New Testament*. Edited by G. Kittel, G. W. Bromiley & G. Friedrich. 10 vols., 582–90. Michigan: Grand Rapids; Eerdmans, 1964-1976.

Michaelis, W. "ὁράω." In *Theological Dictionary of the New Testament*. Edited by G. Kittel, G. W. Bromiley & G. Friedrich. 10 vols., 315–70. Michigan: Grand Rapids; Eerdmans, 1964-1976.

———. "πρωτοκαθεδρία, πρωτοκλισία." In *TDNT*. Edited by G. Kittel et al. 10 vols., 870–71. Grand Rapids, Michigan: W. B. Eerdmans, 1964-1976.

Michel, O. "μικρὸς." In *Theological Dictionary of the New Testament*. Edited by G. Kittel, G. W. Bromiley & G. Friedrich. 10 vols., 648–59. Michigan: Grand Rapids; Eerdmans, 1964-1976.

———. "οἶκος." In *Theological Dictionary of the New Testament*. Edited by G. Kittel, G. W. Bromiley & G. Friedrich. 10 vols., 119–31. Michigan: Grand Rapids; Eerdmans, 1964-1976.

———. "τελώνης." In *Theologisches Wörterbuch zum Neuen Testament: Begründet von Kittel*. Edited by G. Friedrich. Achter Band, 89–106. Stuttgart, Berlin, Köln, Mainz: Kohlhammer Verlag, 1967.

Morton, R. "Son of Man." In *Encyclopedia of the Historical Jesus*. Edited by Craig A. Evans, 593–98. London: Routledge, 2008.

Müller, P. G. "ἀναβλέπω." In *Exegetical Dictionary of the New Testament*. Edited by H. Balz and G. Schneider. 3 vols., 75. Grand Rapids: Eerdmans, 1990-1993.

Pappas, T. *Britannica Concise Encyclopedia*. Chicago, London, New Delhi: Encyclopaedia Britannica, 2003.

Popkes, W. "δεῖ." In *Exegetical Dictionary of the New Testament*. Edited by H. Balz and G. Schneider. 3 vols., 279–80. Grand Rapids: Eerdmans, 1990-1993.

Probst, H. "ὑπάρχω." In *Exegetical Dictionary of the New Testament*. Edited by H. Balz and G. Schneider. 3 vols., 395–96. Grand Rapids: Eerdmans, 1990-1993.

Race, W. H. "Paean." In *Princeton Encyclopedia of Poetry and Poetics*. 3rd ed. Edited by A. Preminger and T. V.F. Brogan, 874. Princeton: Princeton University Press, 1993.

Rengstorf, K. "γογγύζω." In *Theological Dictionary of the New Testament*. Edited by G. Kittel, G. W. Bromiley & G. Friedrich. 10 vols., 727–37. Michigan: Grand Rapids; Eerdmans, 1964-1976.

———. "γογγύζω." In *ThWNT: Begründet von Kittel*. Edited by G. Friedrich. Achter Band, 727–37. Stuttgart, Berlin, Köln, Mainz: Kohlhammer Verlag, 1967.

Sacks, D., O. Murray, and L. R. Brody. *Encyclopedia of the Ancient Greek World*. New York: Facts On File, 2005.

Schelkle, K. H. "σωτηρία." In *Exegetical Dictionary of the New Testament*. Edited by H. Balz and G. Schneider. 3 vols., 327–29. Grand Rapids: Eerdmans, 1990-1993.

Schmidt, T. E. "Taxes." In *Dictionary of Jesus and the Gospels*. Edited by J. B. Green, S. McKnight & I. H. Marshall, 804–6. Illinois: InterVarsity Press, 1992.

Schneider, J. "βαίνω." In *Theological Dictionary of the New Testament*. Edited by G. Kittel, G. W. Bromiley & G. Friedrich. 10 vols., 518–23. Michigan: Grand Rapids; Eerdmans, 1964-1976.

———. "εἰσέρχομαι." In *Theological Dictionary of the New Testament*. Edited by G. Kittel, G. W. Bromiley & G. Friedrich. 10 vols., 676–78. Michigan: Grand Rapids; Eerdmans, 1964-1976.

———. "ἡλικία." In *Theological Dictionary of the New Testament*. Edited by G. Kittel, G. W. Bromiley & G. Friedrich. 10 vols., 941–43. Michigan: Grand Rapids; Eerdmans, 1964-1976.

Schramm, T. "ἡλικία." In *Exegetical Dictionary of the New Testament*. Edited by H. Balz and G. Schneider. 3 vols., 117. Grand Rapids: Eerdmans, 1990-1993.

Strathmann, H. "πόλις." In *Theological Dictionary of the New Testament*. Edited by G. Kittel, G. W. Bromiley & G. Friedrich. 10 vols., 515–34. Michigan: Grand Rapids; Eerdmans, 1964-1976.

Völkel, M. "σήμερον." In *Exegetical Dictionary of the New Testament*. Edited by H. Balz and G. Schneider. 3 vols., 241. Grand Rapids: Eerdmans, 1990-1993.

Walter, N. "σπεύδω." In *Exegetical Dictionary of the New Testament*. Edited by H. Balz and G. Schneider. 3 vols., 264. Grand Rapids: Eerdmans, 1990-1993.

Watson, D. F. "Greece and Macedon." In *Dictionary of New Testament Background*. Edited by C. A. Evans and S. E. Porter. The IVP Bible Dictionary Series, 421–26. Downers Grove, Ill: InterVarsity Press, 2000.

Weder, H. "εἰσέρχομαι." In *Exegetical Dictionary of the New Testament*. Edited by H. Balz and G. Schneider. 3 vols., 400–401. Grand Rapids: Eerdmans, 1990-1993.

Weigandt, P. "οἶκος." In *Exegetical Dictionary of the New Testament*. Edited by H. Balz and G. Schneider. 3 vols., 500–503. Grand Rapids: Eerdmans, 1990-1993.

Commentaries

Billerbeck, P., and H. L. Strack. *Kommentar zum Neuen Testament: Aus Talmud und Midrasch*. Edited by Joachim Jeremias. München: Beck, 1956.

Bock, D. L. *Luke*. The IVP New Testament Commentary Series. Illinois: InterVarsity Press, 1994.

———. *Luke: 9:51-24:53*. 2 vols. Volume 2. Grand Rapids, Mich.: Baker, 1996. Baker Exegetical Commentary on the New Testament.

Boling, R. G. *Judges*. The Anchor Bible v. 6A. New Haven, CT, London: Yale University Press, 2008.

Bovon, F. *Das Evangelium nach Lukas*. Evangelisch-katholischer Kommentar zum Neuen Testament III/3. Düsseldof, Zürich: Benziger, 2001.

———. *Das Evangelium nach Lukas: Lk 1,1-9,50*. Evangelisch-katholischer Kommentar zum Neuen Testament III/I. Zürich: Benziger, 1989.

Bovon, F., H. Koester, and D. S. Deer. *Luke 2: A Commentary on the Gospel of Luke 9:51--19:27*. Hermeneia - A Critical and Historical Commentary on the Bible. Minneapolis, MN: Fortress Press, 2013.

Caird, G. B. *Saint Luke*. Westminster Pelican commentaries. Philadelphia: Westminster Press, 1978.

Coggins, R. J. *Sirach: Guides to Apocrypha and Pseudepigrapha*. Sheffield: Sheffield Academic Press, 1998.

Collins, A. Y., and H. W. Attridge. *Mark: A Commentary*. Hermeneia. Minneapolis: Fortress Press, 2007.

Craddock, F. B. *Luke*. Interpretation, a Bible commentary for teaching and preaching. Louisville, Ky.: John Knox Press, 1990.

Creed, J. M. *The Gospel According to St. Luke*. London: Macmillan, 1942.

Dillersberger, J. *The Gospel of Saint Luke*. Cork: The Mercier Press, 1958.

Dillmann, R., and C. Mora Paz. *Das Lukas-Evangelium: Ein Kommentar fur die Praxis*. Stuttgart: Verlag Katholisches Bibelwerk, 2000.

Dormeyer, D. *Das Lukas-evangelium: Neu übersetzt und kommentiert*. Stuttgart: Verlag Katholisches Bibelwerk, 2011.

Ellis, E. E. *The Gospel of Luke*. The Century Bible. London: Nelson, 1966.

Ernst, J. *Das Evangelium nach Lukas*. Regensburger Neues Testament vl. 3. Regensburg: Verlag Friedrich Pustet, 1993.

Evans, C. A. *Luke*. NIBC. Peabody, Massachusetts: Hendrickson Publishers, 1990.

Evans, C. F. *Saint Luke*. TPI New Testament commentaries. London, Philadelphia: SCM Press; Trinity Press International, 1990.

Fitzmyer, J. A. *The Gospel According to Luke I-IX*. The Anchor Bible 28 A. New Haven: Yale University Press, 2006.

———. *The Gospel According to Luke X-XXIV*. Anchor Bible 28B. New Haven: Yale University Press, 2008.

Geldenhuys, N. *Commentary on the Gospel of Luke*. Michigan: W. B Eerdmans Publishing company, 1956.

Godet, F. L. *A Commentary on the Gospel of St. Luke*. 2 Volumes in 1. Michigan: Zondervan Publishing House, 1887.

Green, G. L. *The Letters to the Thessalonians*. Pillar New Testament commentary. Grand Rapids, Michigan: W.B. Eerdmans Pub.; Leicester, 2002.

Green, J. B. *The Gospel of Luke*. The new international commentary on the New Testament. Grand Rapids, Michigan.: W.B. Eerdmans Pub. Co., 1997.

Grundmann, W. *Das Evangelium nach Lukas*. Theologischer Handkommentar zur Neuen Testament 3. Berlin: Evangelische Verlaganstalt, 1971.

Hamlin, E. J. *At Risk in the Promised Land: A Commentary on the Book of Judges*. ITC. Grand Rapids, Michigan: W. B. Eerdmans, 1990.

Hendriksen, W. *Exposition of the Gospel According to Luke*. New Testament Commentary. Grand Rapids, Michigan.: Baker Academic, 2007.

Johnson, L. T. *The Gospel of Luke: ed. Harrington, J. Daniel*. Sacra pagina series 3. Collegeville, Minn.: Liturgical Press, 1991.

Klein, H. *Das Lukasevangelium*. Kritisch-exegetischer Kommentar über das Neue Testament. Göttingen: Vandenhoeck & Ruprecht, 2006.

Kremer, J. *Lukasevangelium*. Die neue Echter-Bibel Kommentar zum Neuen Testament mit der Einheitsübersetzung. Würzburg: Echter Verlag, 1988.

La Verdiere, E. *Luke*. Wilmington, Delaware: Michael Glazier, 1980.

Leaney, A. R. C. *A Commentary on the Gospel According to St. Luke*. Harper's New Testament commentaries. New York: Harper, 1958.

Liefeld, W. L., and D. W. Pao. *Luke - Acts*. The expositor's Bible commentary 10. Grand Rapids, Michigan: Zondervan, 2007.

Maier, G. *Lukas-Evangelium: 2. Teil*. Edition C 5. Neuhausen-Stuttgart: Hänssler, 1992.

Manson, W. *The Gospel of Luke*. The Moffatt New Testament Commentary. Great Britain: Hodder and Stoughton, 1963.

Marshall, H. I., W. W. Gasque, and D. A. Hagner. *The Gospel of Luke: A Commentary on the Greek Text: The New international Greek Testament commentary*. 1st ed. Grand Rapids: Eerdmans, 1978.

Morris, L. *Luke: An Introduction and Commentary*. The Tyndale New Testament commentaries 3. Leicester, England, Grand Rapids, Mich.: Inter-Varsity Press; William. B. Eerdmans Pub. Co., 1990.

Müller, P. G. *Lukas-Evangelium*. Stuttgarter kleiner Kommentar Neues Testament 3. Stuttgart: Verlag Katholisches Bibelwerk, 1984.

Nolland, J. *Luke: 1-9:20*. Word biblical commentary 35 A. Dallas, Texas: Word Books Publisher, 1989.

———. *Luke: 18:35-24:53*. Word biblical commentary 35 C. Dallas, Texas: Word Books Publisher, 2002.

Plummer, A. *A Critical and Exegetical Commentary on the Gospel According to S. Luke*. 5th ed. International critical commentary. Edinburgh: T. & T. Clark, 1981.

Radl, W. *Das Evangelium nach Lukas: Kommentar: Erster Teil: 1, 1-9, 50*. Freiburg: Herder, 2003.

Ringe, S. H. *Luke*. Westminster Bible companion. Louisvile, Ky.: Westminster John Knox Press, 1995.

Schlatter, A. *Die Evangelien nach Markus und Lukas*. Erläuterungen zum Neuen Testament 2. Stuttgart: Calwer, 1979.

Schneider, G. *Das Evangelium nach Lukas: Kapitel 11-24*. Ökumenischer Taschenbuchkommentar zum Neuen Testament 3/2. Gütersloh: Gütersloher Verlagsh. Mohn, 1984.

Schürmann, H. *Das Lukas Evangelium: Kommentar zu Kap. 9,51 - 11,54*. Herders theologischer Kommentar zum Neuen Testament 3,2. Freiburg: Herder, 1994.

Schweizer, E. *The Good News According to Luke: trsl. David E. Green*. London: SPCK, 1984.

Skehan, P. W., and A. A. Di Lella. *The Wisdom of Ben Sira*. Anchor Bible. 39. New York: Doubleday, 1987.

Stein, R. H. *Luke*. The New American commentary v. 24. Nashville, Tenn.: Broadman Press, 1992.

Stöger, A. *Das Evangelium nach Lukas*. 3rd ed. Geistliche Schriftlesung Erläuterungen zum Neuen Testament für die geistliche Lesung 3,2. Düsseldorf: Patmos-Verl., 1985.

Summers, R. *Commentary on Luke: Jesus, the Universal Savior*. Waco, Tex.: Word Books, 1972.

Talbert, C. H. *Reading Luke: A Literary and Theological Commentary on the Third Gospel*. [Reading the New Testament series]. New York: Crossroad, 1982.

Tiede, D. L. *Luke*. Augsburg commentary on the New Testament. Minneapolis, Minn.: Augsburg Publ. House, 1988.

Walvoord, J. F., and R. B. Zuck. *The Bible Knowledge Commentary: An Exposition of the Scriptures*. Wheaton Ill.: Victor Books, 1985.

Wiefel, W. *Das Evangelium nach Lukas*. Berlin: Evangelische Verlaganstalt, 1988.

Wolter, M. *Das Lukasevangelium*. Handbuch zum Neuen Testament. Tübingen: Mohr Siebeck, 2008.

Zahn, T. *Das Evangelium des Lucas*. 1st ed. Kommentar zum Neuen Testament Bd. 3. Leipzig: Deichert, 1913.

Monographs and Dissertations

Adkins, L., and R. A. Adkins. *Handbook to Life in Ancient Greece*. Facts on File Library of World History. New York, Oxford: Oxford University Press, 2005.

Amaladoss, M. *A Call to Community*. Gujarat: Gujarat Sahitya Prakash, 1994.

Ambedkar, B. R. *Annihilation of Caste: An Undelivered Speech: Edited by M. R. Anand*. New Delhi: Arnold Publishers, 1990.

Arens, E. *The Ēlthon-Sayings in the Synoptic Tradition: A Historico-Critical Investigation*. OBO 10. Freiburg, Schweiz: Universitätsverlag, 1976.

Bailey, K. E. *Jesus Through Middle Eastern Eyes: Cultural Studies in the Gospels*. Downers Grove, Ill.: IVP Academic, 2008.

Balsdon, J. P. V. D. *Life and Leisure in Ancient Rome*. London: Bodley Head, 1969.

Bartlett, J. R. *Jews in the Hellenistic World*. Cambridge Commentaries on Writings of the Jewish and Christian World 200 BC to AD 200 vol. 1, part 1. Cambridge: Cambridge University Press, 1985.

Beall, T. S. *Josephus' Description of the Essenes Illustrated by the Dead Sea Scrolls*. Society for New Testament Studies monograph series 58. Cambridge, U.K, New York: Cambridge University Press, 2004.

Benko, S. and J. J. O'Rourke, eds. *The Catacombs and the Colosseum: The Roman Empire as the Setting of Primitive Christianity*. Valley Forge: Judson Press, 1971.

Bhattacharya, J. N. *Hindu Castes and Sects: An Exposition of the Origin of the Hindu Caste System and the Bearing of the Sects Towards Each Other and Towards Other Religious Systems*. New Delhi: Munshiram Manoharlal, 1995.

Black, M. *An Aramaic Approach to the Gospels and Acts*. Oxford: Clarendon Press, 1967.

Blass, F., A. Debrunner, and R. W. Funk. *A Greek Grammar of the New Testament and Other Early Christian Literature*. Chicago: University of Chicago Press, 1961.

Bokser, B. M. *The Origins of the Seder: The Passover Rite and Early Rabbinic Judaism*. Berkeley: University of California Press, 1984.

Bolyki, J. *Jesu Tischgemeinschaften*. Wissenschaftliche Untersuchungen zum Neuen Testament Reihe 2 96. Tübingen: Mohr Siebeck, 1998.

Borg, M. J. *Conflict, Holiness, and Politics in the Teachings of Jesus*. London, New York: Continuum International Publishing Group, 1998.

Bösen, W. 'Das Mahlmotiv bei Lukas: Studien in Lukanischen Mahlverständnis unter besonderer Berücksichtigung von Lk 22:12-20.' PHD Dissertation, Universität des Saarlandes, 1976.

_____. *Jesusmahl, Eucharistisches mahl, Endzeitmahl: Ein Beitrag zur Theologie des lukas.* Stuttgart: Katholisches bibelwerk GmbH, 1980.

Bouglé, C., and D. F. Pocock. *Essays on the Caste System.* The European Understanding of India. London: Cambridge University Press, 1971.

Braun, W. *Feasting and Social Rhetoric in Luke 14.* Monograph series / Society for New Testament Studies 85. Cambridge: Cambridge Univ. Press, 1995.

Brutscheck, J. *Die Maria-Marta-Erzählung: Eine Redaktionkritische Untersuchung zu Lk 10, 38-42.* Bonner biblische Beiträge Bd. 64. Frankfurt am Main: P. Hanstein, 1986.

Bultmann, R. *The History of the Synoptic Tradition.* New York: Harper & Row, 1963.

Byrne, B. *The Hospitality of God: A Reading of Luke's Gospel.* Collegeville, Minn.: Liturgical Press, 2000.

Cadbury, H. J., and P. N. Anderson. *The Making of Luke-Acts.* 2nd ed. Peabody, Mass.: Hendrickson Publishers, 1999.

Campbell, D. A., ed. *Greek Lyric: Sappho and Alcaeus.* The Loeb Classical Library 142. Cambridge Mass, London: Harvard Univ. Press; W. Heinemann, 1982.

Carcopino, J. *Daily Life in Ancient Rome: The People and the City at the Height of the Empire.* Peregrine Books. S.l: Penguin, 1964.

Chesnutt, R. D. *From Death to Life: Conversion in Joseph and Aseneth.* Journal for the study of the pseudepigrapha. Supplement series 16. Sheffield: Sheffield Academic Press, 1995.

Collins, J. J. *Jewish Wisdom in the Hellenistic Age.* The Old Testament library. Louisville, Ky: Westminister John Knox Press, 1997.

Conzelmann, H. *Grundriss der Theologie des Neuen Testaments.* 5th ed. UTB. Tübingen: Mohr, 1992.

Corley, K. E. *Private Women, Public Meals: Social Conflict in the Synoptic Tradition.* Peabody, Massachusetts: Hendrickson, 1993.

Culy, M. M., M. C. Parsons, and J. J. Stigall. *Luke: A Handbook on the Greek Text.* Baylor handbook on the Greek New Testament. Waco, Tex.: Baylor University Press, 2010.

Dalby, A. *Empire of Pleasures: Luxury and Indulgence in the Roman World.* London, New York: Routledge, 2005.

Dana, H. E., and J. R. Mantey. *A Manual Grammar of the Greek New Testament.* New York: Macmillan, 1967.

Daube, D. *The New Testament and Rabbinic Judaism.* Jordan Lectures in Comparative Religion 2. London: University of London Athlone Press, 1956.

Davidson, J. N. *Courtesans & Fishcakes*. London: Fontana Press, 1998.

Davis, W. S. *A Day in Old Athens*. Boston, New York etc: Allyn and Bacon, 1914.

Dibelius, M. *Die Formgeschichte des Evangeliums*. 6th ed. Tübingen: Mohr Siebeck, 1971.

———. *From Tradition to Gospel*. New York,: Charles scribner's Sons, 1935.

Donahue, J. F. *Epula Publica: The Roman Community at Table During the Principate*. Ann Arbor, MI: UMI, 2002.

Drury, J. *Tradition and Design in Luke's Gospel: A Study in Early Christian Historiography*. Atlanta: John Knox Press, 1977.

Dumont, L. *Homo Hierarchicus: The Caste System and its Implications*. Oxford: Oxford University Press, 1999.

Dunbabin, K. M. D. *The Roman Banquet: Images of Conviviality*. New York: Cambridge University Press, 2003.

Dutt, N. K. *Origin and Growth of Caste in India*. 2nd ed. Calcutta: K. L. Mukhopadhyay, 1968.

Ebertz, M. N. *Das Charisma des Gekreuzigten: Zur Soziologie der Jesusbewegung*. Tübingen: Mohr Siebeck, 1987.

Ebner, M., and B. Heininger. *Exegese des Neuen Testaments: Ein Arbeitsbuch für Lehre und Praxis*. 3rd ed. Paderborn: Verlag Ferdinand Schöningh, 2015.

Ernst, J. *Lukas: Ein Theologisches Portrait*. Düsseldorf: Patmos, 1985.

Esler, P. F. *Community and Gospel in Luke-Acts: The Social and Political Motivations of Lucan Theology*. Monograph series / Society for New Testament Studies 57. Cambridge, New York: Cambridge University Press, 1989.

Evans, J. A. S. *Daily Life in the Hellenistic Age: From Alexander to Cleopatra*. Daily life through history series. Westport, Conn: Greenwood Press, 2008.

Finkel, A. *The Pharisees and the Teacher of Nazareth*. Leiden: E. J. Brill, 1964.

Gandhi, M. K. *The Collected Works of Mahatma Gandhi*. 100 vols. 46. Ministry of Information and Broadcasting: New Delhi, 1971.

———. *The Collected Works of Mahatma Gandhi*. 100 vols. 51. Ministry of Information and Broadcasting: New Delhi, 1972.

———. *The Collected Works of Mahatma Gandhi*. 100 vols. 63. Ministry of Information and Broadcasting: New Delhi, 1976.

Garland, R. *The Greek way of death*. London: Duckworth, 1985.

Garnsey, P. *Food and Society in Classical Antiquity*. Key themes in ancient history. Cambridge: Cambridge University Press, 1999.

Gillman, J. *Possessions and the Life of Faith: A Reading of Luke-Acts*. Zacchaeus studies: New Testament. Collegeville, Minn.: Liturgical Press, 1991.

Gowers, E. *The Loaded Table: Representations of Food in Roman Literature*. Oxford: The Clarendon Press, 1993.

Gowler, D. B. *Host, Guest, Enemy, and Friend: Portraits of the Pharisees in Luke and Acts*. Emory studies in early Christianity vol. 2. New York: P. Lang, 1991.

Hahn, F. *Christologische Hoheitstitel: Ihre Geschichte im frühen Christentum*. 5th ed. Uni-Taschenbücher 1873. Göttingen: Vandenhoeck & Ruprecht, 1995.

Hawkins, J. C. *Horae Synopticae: Contributions to the Study of the Synoptic Problem*. Oxford: Clarendon Press, 1909.

Heidel, A. *The Gilgamesh Epic and Old Testament Parallels*. Phoenix books. Chicago: University of Chicago Press, 1967.

Heil, J. P. *The Meal Scenes in Luke-Acts: An Audience-Oriented Approach*. Monograph series. Atlanta, Ga.: Soc. of Biblical Literature, 2004.

Hengel, M. *Judaism and Hellenism: Studies in their Encounter in Palestine During the Early Hellenistic Period*. 1st ed. Philadelphia: Fortress Press, 1974.

Herrenbrück, F. *Jesus und die Zöllner: Historische und Neutestamentlich-exegetische Untersuchgen*. WUNT 41. Tübingen: Mohr Siebeck, 1990.

Higgins, A. J. B. *The Son of Man in the Teaching of Jesus*. Cambridge: Cambridge University Press, 1980.

Hirsch, E. *Die Vorlagen des Lukas und das Sondergut des Matthäus*. Frühgeschichte des Evangeliums 2. Tübingen: Mohr, 1941.

Hobden, F. *The Symposion in Ancient Greek Society and Thought*. Cambridge: Cambridge University Press, 2013.

Honigman, S. *The Septuagint and Homeric Scholarship in Alexandria: A Study in the Narrative of the Letter of Aristeas*. London, New York: Routledge, 2003.

Horsley, R. A. *Jesus and the spiral of violence: Popular Jewish resistance in Roman Palestine*. San Francisco: Harper & Row, 1987.

Hotze, G. *Jesus als Gast: Studien zu einem Christologischen Leitmotiv im Lukasevangelium*. Würzburg: Echter Verlag, 2007.

Humphrey, E. M. *Joseph and Aseneth*. Guides to Apocrypha and Pseudepigrapha. Sheffield: Sheffield Academic Press, 2000.

Jeremias, J. *Jerusalem zur Zeit Jesu: Eine Kulturgeschichtliche Untersuchung zur Neutestamentlichen Zeitgeschichte*. 3rd ed. Göttingen: Vandenhoeck & Ruprecht, 1962.

———. *The Parables of Jesus*. 3rd ed. London: S.C.M. Press, 1972.

Kananaikil, J. *Christians of scheduled Caste Origin*. Monograph series / Indian Social Institute 10. New Delhi: Indian Social Institute, 1983.

Kariamadam, P. *The Zacchaeus Story (Lk 19:1-10): A Redaction-Critical Investigation*. Kerala: Pontifical Institute of Theology and Philosophy, 1985.

Karris, R. J. *Eating Your Way Through Luke's Gospel*. Collegeville, Minnesota: Liturgical Press, 2006.

―――――. *Luke, Artist and Theologian: Luke's Passion Account as Literature*. Theological inquiries. New York: Paulist Press, 1985.

Kealy, J. P. *Luke's Gospel Today: "That you may know the truth" - Luke - 1:4*. Denville: Dimension Books, 1979.

Kirk, O. *Controlling Desires: Sexuality in Ancient Greece and Rome*. Praeger series on the ancient world. Westport, Conn: Praeger, 2009.

Klass, M. *Caste: The Emergence of the South Asian Social System*. Philadelphia: Institute for the study of Human Issues, 1980.

Klein, H. *Barmherzigkeit Gegenüber den Elenden und Geächteten: Studien zur Botschaft des Lukanischen Sondergutes*. Biblisch-theologische Studien 10. Neukirchen-Vluyn: Neukirchener Verl, 1987.

Knox, W. L. *The Sources of the Synoptic Gospels: Vol. 2, St. Luke and St. Matthew: ed. Chadwick, Henry*. Cambridge: Cambridge U.P, 1957.

König, J. *Saints and Symposiasts: The Literature of Food and the Symposium in Greco-Roman and Early Christian Culture*. Cambridge: Cambridge University Press, 2012.

Kraemer, R. S. *When Aseneth met Joseph: A Late Antique Tale of the Biblical Patriarch and his Egyptian Wife, Reconsidered*. New York: Oxford University Press, 1998.

LaVerdiere, E. *Dining in the Kingdom of God: The Origins of the Eucharist in the Gospel of Luke*. Chicago, IL: Liturgy Training Publications, 1994.

Lindars, B. *Jesus Son of Man: A Fresh Examination of the Son of Man Sayings in the Gospels in the Light of Recent Research*. London: SPCK, 1983.

Lissarrague, F. *The Aesthetics of the Greek Banquet: Images of Wine and Ritual; translated by Andrew Szegedy-Maszak*. Princeton, N.J., Oxford: Princeton University Press, 1990.

Löning, K. *Der Weg Jesu*. Das Geschichtswerk des Lukas Bd. 2. Stuttgart: Kohlhammer, 2006.

MacMullen, R. *Enemies of the Roman order: Treason, Unrest, and Alienation in the Empire*. London: Routledge, 1992.

Manson, T. W. *The Sayings of Jesus: As Recorded in the Gospels According to St. Matthew and St. Luke*. London: SCM Press, 1971.

Marquardt, J. *Das Privatleben der Römer*. Darmstadt: Wissenschaftliche Buchgesellschaft, 1975.

Marshall, H. I. *Luke: Historian and Theologian*. Milton Keynes, UK: Paternoster, 1970.

Martin, J. *Symposion. Die Geschichte einer Literarischen Form*. Paderborn: Verlag Ferdinand Schöningh, 1931.

Matz, D. *Daily Life of the Ancient Romans*. The Greenwood Press "Daily life through history" series. Indianapolis IN: Hackett Pub. Co, 2008.

McLaughlin, J. L. *The Marzēaḥ in the Prophetic Literature: References and Allusions in Light of the Extra-Biblical Evidence*. Supplements to Vetus Testamentum v. 86. Leiden, Boston: Brill, 2001.

Melzer-Keller, H. *Jesus und die Frauen: Eine Verhältnisbestimmung nach den Synoptischen Überlieferungen*. Freiburg im Breisgau: Herder, 1997.

Menghini, S. ed. *Symposion: La cultura del vino nei valori della conoscenza storica e nelle strategie di mercato*. Firenze: Firenze Univ. Press, 2012.

Miyoshi, M. *Der Anfang des Reiseberichts Lk 9,51–10,24: Eine Redaktionsgeschichtliche Untersuchung*. Analecta Biblica 60. Rome: Biblical Institute Press, 1974.

Moessner, D. P. *Lord of the Banquet: The Literary and Theological Significance of the Lukan Travel Narrative*. Minneapolis: Fortress Press, 1989.

Mosse, D. *The Saint in the Banyan Tree: Christianity and Caste Society in India*. The Anthropology of Christianity 14. Berkeley: University of California Press, 2012.

Moulton, C., ed. *Ancient Greece and Rome: An Encyclopedia for Students*. New York: Scribner, 1998.

Moxnes, H. *The Economy of the Kingdom: Social Conflict and Economic Relations in Luke's Gospel*. Overtures to biblical theology [23]. Philadelphia: Fortress Press, 1988.

Mullen, P. J. *Dining with Pharisees*. Collegeville, Minn.: Liturgical Press, 2004.

Neale, D. A. *None But the Sinners: Religious Categories in the Gospel of Luke*. Journal for the study of the New Testament. Supplement series 58. Sheffield: JSOT Press, 1991.

Neusner, J. *Formative Judaism: Religious, Historical, and Literary Studies: Fifth Series: Revisioning the Written Records of a Nascent Religion*. Brown Judaic studies 91. Chico, Calif.: Scholars Press, 1985.

_____. *From Politics to Piety: The Emergence of Pharisaic Judaism.* New York: Ktav Pub. House, 1979.

_____. *The Idea of Purity in Ancient Judaism.* The Haskell lectures, 1972-73 1. Leiden: Brill, 1973.

Nickelsburg, G. W. E. *Jewish Literature Between the Bible and the Mishnah: A Historical and Literary Introduction.* 2nd ed. Minneapolis: Fortress Press, 2005.

Perrin, N. *Rediscovering the Teaching of Jesus.* New York: Harper & Row, 1967.

_____. *Was Lehrte Jesus Wirklich?: Rekonstruction und Deutung.* Göttingen: Vandenhoeck und Ruprecht, 1972.

Rajak, T. *Josephus: The Historian and His Society.* Classical Life and Letters. London: Duckworth, 1983.

Reiling, J., and J. L. Swellengrebel. *A Translator's Handbook on the Gospel of Luke.* Leiden: E. J. Brill, 1971.

Robinson, C. E. *Every Day Life in Anicient Greece.* Oxford: The Clarendon Press, 1934.

Rocca, S. *Herod's Judaea: A Mediterranean State in the Classical World.* Texts and Studies in Ancient Judaism 122. Tübingen: Mohr Siebeck, 2008.

Roebuck, C. *Corinth: Vol 14, The Asklepioion and Lerna.* Princeton, N.J: The American School Classical Studies at Athens, 1951.

Schenk, W. *Das biographische Ich-Idiom „Menschensohn" in den frühen Jesus-Biographien: Der Ausdruck, seine Codes und seine Rezeptionen in ihren Kotexten.* Forschungen zur Religion und Literatur des Alten und Neuen Testaments 177. Heft. Göttingen: Vandenhoeck & Ruprecht, 1997.

Schneider, F. *Jesus, der Prophet.* Orbis biblicus et orientalis 2. Freiburg/Schweiz, Göttingen: Universitätsverlag; Vandenhoeck & Ruprecht, 1973.

Schottroff, L., and W. Stegemann. *Jesus and the Hope of the Poor.* Maryknoll, N.Y.: Orbis Books, 1986.

Schramm, T. *Der Markus-Stoff bei Lukas: Eine Literarkritische und Redaktionsgeschichtliche Untersuchung.* Society for New Testament Studies. Monograph series. no. 14. Cambridge: University Press, 1971.

Senart, E., and E. D. Ross. *Caste in India: The Facts and the System.* Delhi: Ess Ess Publications, 1975.

Smith, D. E. "Social Obligation in the Context of Communal Meals: A Study of the Christian Meal in 1 Corinthians in Comparison with Graeco-Roman Communal Meals." Harvard University, 1980.

———. *From Symposium to Eucharist: The Banquet in the Early Christian Wrld.* Minneapolis: Fortress Press, 2003.

Smith, M. *Jesus the Magician.* 1st ed. San Francisco: Harper & Row, 1978.

Soares-Prabhu, G. M. *The Dharma of Jesus: ed. F. X, D´Sa.* Maryknoll, N.Y.: Orbis Books, 2003.

Stanislaus, L. *The Liberative Mission of the Church among Dalit Christians.* Delhi: ISPCK, 1999.

Stephen, S. J. *Caste, Catholic Christianity, and the Language of Conversion: Social Change and Cultural Translation in Tamil Country, 1519-1774.* Delhi: Kalpaz Publications, 2008.

Székely, J. *Structure and Theology of the Lucan 'Itinerarium': (Lk 9,51-19,28).* Budapest: Szent Jeromos Katolikus Bibliatársulat, 2008.

Tannehill, R. C. *The Narrative Unity of Luke-Acts: A Literary Interpretation.* Philadelphia: Fortress Press, 1986.

Taylor, V. *The Formation of the Gospel Tradition.* London: Macmillan and co. limited, 1957.

Tödt, H. E. *Der Menschensohn in der Synoptischen Überlieferung.* 4th ed. Gütersloh: Mohn, 1978.

Vanderkam, J. C. *The Dead Sea Scrolls and the Bible.* Grand Rapids, Mich: W.B. Eerdmans, 2012.

Vermès, G. *Jesus the Jew: A Historian's Reading of the Gospels.* London: Collins, 1973.

Vögtle, A. *Die „Gretchenfrage" des Menschensohn-Problems: Bilanz und Perspektiven.* Quaestiones disputatae 152. Freiburg im Breisgau: Herder, 1994.

Wanke, J. *Beobachtungen zum Eucharistieverständnis des Lukas auf Grund der lukanischen Mahlberichte.* Erfurter theologische Schriften 8. Leipzig: St-Benno-Verlag, 1973.

West, M. L. *Studies in Greek Elegy and Iambus.* Berlin, New York: De Gruyter, 1974.

Wilkins, J., and S. Hill. *Food in the Ancient World.* Ancient Cultures. Oxford: Blackwell Publishing, 2006.

Zerwick, M. and M. Grosvenor. *A Grammatical Analysis of the Greek New Testament.* Roma: Editrice Pontificio Istituto Biblico, 1993.

Zohary, M. *Plants of the Bible: A Complete Handbook to all the Plants with 200 Full-Color Plates Taken in the Natural Habitat.* Cambridge: Cambridge University Press, 1982.

Journal Articles

Ackerman, S. "A Marzēaḥ in Ezekiel 8:7-13?" *The Harvard Theological Review* 82, no. 3 (1989): 267–81.

Albenda, P. "Landscape Bas-Reliefs in the Bit Hilani of Ashurbanibal." *The American Schools of Oriental Research* 224 (1976): 49–72.

Appadurai, A. "Gastro-Politics in Hindu South Asia." *American Ethnologist* 8, no. 3 (1981): 494–511.

Ascough, R. S. "Narrative Technique and Generic Designation: Crowd Scenes in Luke-Acts and in Chariton." *Catholic Biblical Quarterly* 58, no. 1 (1996): 69–81.

Bahr, G. J. "The Seder of Passover and the Eucharistic Words." *NT* 12, no. 2 (1970): 181–202.

Bendemann, R. "Liebe und Sündenvergebung: Eine Narrativ-traditionsgeschichltiche Analyse von Lk 7,36-50." *BZ* 44 (2000): 161–82.

Black, M. "The 'Son of Man' in the Teaching of Jesus." *Exp Tim* 60 (1948): 32–36.

Bock, D. L. "The Son of Man in Luke 5:24." *Bulletin for Biblical Research* 1 (1991): 109–21.

Bowie, E. L. "Early Greek Elegy, Symposium and Public Festival." *The Journal of Hellenistic Studies* 106 (1986): 13–35.

Brooks, A. "Salvation and Loss in the Story of Zacchaeus." *Exp Tim* XXXIII, no. 6 (1922): 286–88.

Burchard, C. "The Importance of Joseph and Aseneth for the Study of the New Testament: A General Survey and a Fresh Look at the Lord's Supper." *New Testament Studes* 33, no. 1 (1987): 102–34.

Chan-Hie, K. "The Papyrus Invitation." *JBL* 94 (1975): 391–402.

Chesnutt, R. D. "Perceptions of Oil in Early Judaism and the Meal Formula in Joseph and Aseneth." *Journal for the Study of the Pseudepigrapha* 14, no. 2 (2005): 113–32.

Citron, B. "The Multitude in the Synoptic Gospels." *SJT* 07, no. 04 (1954): 408–18.

Collins, A. Y. "The Origin of the designation of Jesus as "Son of Man." *The Harvard Theological Review* 80, no. 4 (1987): 391–407.

Cosgrove, C. H. "The Divine Δεῖ in Luke-Acts: Investigations into the Lukan Understanding of God's Providence." *Novum Testamentum* 26, no. 2 (1984): 168–90.

Damon, C. "Greek Parasites and Roman Patronage." *Harvard Studies in Classical Philology* 97 (1995): 181–95.

Donahue, J. R. "Tax Collectors and Sinners: An Attempt at Identification." *CBQ* 33, no. 1 (1971): 39–61.

Eckhardt, B. "Meals and Politics in the Yahad: A Reconsideration." *Dead Sea Discoveries* 17, no. 2 (2010): 180–209.

Fitzmyer, J. A. "Another View of the 'Son of Man' Debate." *JSNT* 2, no. 4 (1979): 58–68.

Gill, D. "Observations on the Lukan Travel Narrative and Some Related Passages." *The Harvard Theological Review* 63, no. 2 (1970): 199–221.

Gowler, D. B. "Hospitality and Characterization in Luke 11:37-54: A Socio-Narratological Approach." *Semeia* 1993, no. 63: 213–52.

Hamm, D. "Luke 19:8 Once Again: Does Zacchaeus Defend or Resolve?" *JBL* 107, no. 3 (1988): 431–37.

———. "Zacchaeus Revisited Once More: A Story of Vindication or Conversion?" *Biblica* 72 (1991): 249–52.

Harmon, R. "Plato, Aristotle and Women Musicians." *Music & Letters* 86, no. 3 (2005): 351–56.

Harvey, A. E. "The Classification of Greek Lyric Poetry." *The Classical Quarterly* 5 (1955): 157–75.

Jeremias, J. "Zöllner und Sünder." *Zeitschrift Zeitschrift Für die Neutestamentliche Wissenschaft* 30, no. 3 (1931): 293–300.

Kilgallen, J. J. "Forgiveness of Sins (Luke 7:36-50)." *Novum Testamentum* 40, no. 2 (1998): 105–16.

Klawans, J. "Notions of Gentile Impurity in Ancient Judaism." *Association for Jewish Studies* 20, no. 2 (1995): 285–312.

Kurke, L. "Inventing the "Hetaira": Sex, Politics and Discursive Conflict in Archaic Greece." *Classical Antiquity* 16, no. 1 (1997): 106–50.

Lindeskog, G. "Das Rätsel des Menschensohnes." *Studia Theologica* 22, no. 2 (1968): 149–74.

Luke, J. "The Krater, 'Kratos,' and the 'Polis.'" *Greece and Rome* 41, no. 1 (1994): 22–32.

Lynch, K. M. "More Thoughts on the Space of the Symposium." *British School at Athens Studies* 15 (2007): 243–49.

Maccoby, H. "How Unclean were the Tax Collectors?" *BTB* 21, no. 2 (2001): 60–63.

Marcus, J. "Passover and Last Supper Revisited." *NTS* 59, no. 03 (2013): 303–24.

Marshall, H. I. "The Synoptic Son of Man Sayings in Recent Discussion." *NTS* 12 (1966): 327–51.

McCown, C. C. "The Geography of Luke's Central Section." *JBL* 57, 51-66 (1938).

McKeon, R. "Symposia." *Proceedings and Addresses of the American Philosophical Association* 25 (1971): 18–41.

Mendels, D. "'On Kingship' in the "Temple Scroll" and the Ideological "Vorlage" of the Seven Banquets in the "Letter of Aristeas to Philocrates"." *Aegyptus* 59, 1/2 (1979): 127–36.

Mitchell, A. C. "Zacchaeus Revisited: Luke 19,8 as a Defense." *Biblica* 71 (1990): 153–76.

Moloney, F. J. "Constructing Jesus and the Son of Man." *CBQ* 75, no. 4 (2013): 719-38.

Moxnes, H. "The Social Context of Luke's Community." *Interpretation: A Journal of Bible & Theology* 48, no. 4 (1994): 379–89.

Nestle, E. "Sykophantia im biblischen Griechisch." *ZNW* 4 (1903): 271–72.

Niehoff, M. R. "The Symposium of Philo's Therapeutae: Displaying Jewish Identity in an Increasingly Roman World." *Greek, Roman, and Byzantine Studies* 50 (2010): 95–116.

Nir, R. ""It is not right for a man who worships God to repay his neighbor evil for evil": Christian Ethics in Joseph and Aseneth (CHAPTERS 22-29)." *Journal of Hebrew Scriptures* 13 (2013): check page.

Nock, A. D. "The Historical Importance of Cult-Associations." *The Classical Review* 38, 5/6 (1924): 105–9.

O'Hanlon, J. "The Story of Zacchaeus and the Lukan Ethic." *JSNT* 4, no. 12 (1981): 2–26.

O'Toole, R. F. "The Literary Form of Luke 19:1-10." *JBL* 110, no. 1 (1991): 107–16.

Parsons, M. C. "'Short in Stature': Luke's Physical Description of Zacchaeus." *NTS* 47 (2001): 50–57.

Perkins, P. "Taxes in the New Testament." *The Journal of Religious Ethics* 12, no. 2 (1984): 182–200.

Raney, W. H. "Who Were the "Sinners"?" *JR* 10, no. 4 (1930): 578–91.

Rathje, A. "A Banquet Service from the Latin City of Ficana." *ARID* 12 (1983): 7–29.

Ravens, D. A. S. "Zacchaeus: The Final Part of a Lucan Triptych?" *JSNT*, no. 41 (1991): 19–32.

Relihan, J. C. "Rethinking the History of the Literary Symposium." *Illinois Classical Studies* 17, no. 2 (1992): 213–44.

Schulz, S. "Gottes Vorsehung bei Lukas." *ZNW 54* 54 (1963): 104–16.

Schweizer, E. "The Son of Man." *Journal of Biblical Literature* 79, no. 2 (1960): 119–29.

———. "The Son of Man Again." *NTS* 9 (1962-63): 256–61.

Smith, D. E. "Table Fellowship as a Literary Motif in the Gospel of Luke." *JBL* 106, no. 4 (1987): 613–38.

Sparkes, B. A. "Kottabos:: An Athenian After-Dinner Game." *Archaeology* 13, no. 3 (1960): 202–7.

Steele, S. E. "Luke 11:37-54 - A Modified Hellenistic Symposium?" *JBL* 103, no. 3 (1984): 379–94.

Stein, S. "The Influence of Symposia Literature on the Literary Form of the Pesah Haggadah." *Journal of Jewish Studies* 8, 13-44 (1957).

Taylor, J. E. and P. R. Davies. "The So-Called Therapeutae of "De Vita Contemplativa": Identity and Character." *The Harvard Theological Review* 91, no. 1 (1998): 3–24.

Van der Ploeg, J. "The Meals of the Essenes." *Journal of Semetic Studies* 2, no. 2 (1957): 163–75.

Van der Valk, M. "On the Composition of the Attic Scolia." *Hermes* 102 (1974): 1–20.

van der Veen, M. "When Is Food a Luxury?" *World Archaeology* 34, no. 3 (2003): 405–27.

Walker Jr, W. O. "Jesus and the Tax Collectors." *JBL* 92, no. 2 (1978): 221–38.

———. "The Son of Man: Some Recent Developments." *CBQ* 45, no. 4 (1983): 584–607.

Watson, N. M. "Was Zacchaeus Really Reforming?" *Expository Times* 77 (1965-1966): 282–85.

Węcowski, M. "When did the Symposion Rise?: Some Archaeological Considerations Regarding the Emergence of the Greek Aristocratic Banquet." *ΑΡΧΑΙΟΓΝΩΣΙΑ*, no. 16 (2012): 19–48.

White, R. C. "Vindication for Zacchaeus?" *Exp Tim* 91 (1979): 21.

Yamasaki, G. "Point of View in a Gospel Story: What Difference Does It Make?: Luke 19:1-10 as a Test Case." *JBL* 125, no. 1 (2006): 89–105.

Ziesler, J. A. "Luke and the Pharisees." *NTS* 25, no. 2 (1979): 146–57.

Articles from Edited work

Almeida, L. J. "The Indian Church and the Invincible Virus of Casteism." In *Caste Culture in Indian Church: The Response of the Church to the Problem of Caste within the Christian Community*. Edited by S. L. Raj S.J and G. F. Xavier Raj, 31–36. New Delhi: Indian Social Institute, 1993.

Aloni, A. "Elegy: Forms, Functions and Communication." In *The Cambridge Companion to Greek Lyric*. Edited by F. Budelmann, 168–88. Cambridge, New York: Cambridge University Press, 2009.

Bergquist, B. "Sympotic Space: A Functional Aspect of Greek Dining-Rooms." In *Sympotica: A Symposium on the Symposion*. Edited by O. Murray, 37–65. Oxford: Clarendon Press, 1990.

Boardman, J. "Symposion Furniture." In *Sympotica: A Symposium on the Symposion*. Edited by O. Murray, 122–31. Oxford: Clarendon Press, 1990.

Bremmer, J. M. "Adolescents, Symposion, and Pederasty." In *Sympotica: A Symposium on the Symposion*. Edited by O. Murray, 135–48. Oxford: Clarendon Press, 1990.

Broekaert, W. and A. Zuiderhoek. "Food and Politics in Classical Antiquity." In *A cultural history of food in Antiquity*. Edited by P. Erdkamp, 75–93. London: Berg, 2012.

Brumberg-Kraus, J. ""Not By Bread Alone…": The Ritualization of Food and Table Talk in the Passover Seder in the Last Supper." In *Food and Drink in the Biblical Worlds*. Edited by A. Brenner and J. W. van Henten. Semeia 86, 165–91. Atlanta, GA: Society of Biblical Literature, 1999.

Bruns, G. "Kuchenwesen und Mahlzeiten." In *Archaeologia Homerica*. Edited by F. Matz and H.G. Buchholz, 57-58. Göttingen: Vandenhoeck & Ruprecht, 1967-.

Burkert, W. "Oriental Symposia: Contrasts and Parallels." In *Dining in a Classical Context*. Edited by W. J. Slater, 7–24. Ann Arbor: University of Michigan Press, 1991.

Campbell, D. A. "Monody." In *The Cambridge History of Classical Literature: Vol 1. Greek Literature*. Edited by P. E. Easterling and B. M. W. Knox, 202–21. Cambridge: Cambridge University Press, 1985.

Carey, C. "Iambos." In *The Cambridge Companion to Greek Lyric*. Edited by F. Budelmann, 149–67. Cambridge, New York: Cambridge University Press, 2009.

Cooper, F. and S. Morris. "Dining in Round Buildings." In *Sympotica: A Symposium on the Symposion*. Edited by O. Murray, 66–85. Oxford: Clarendon Press, 1990.

Corner, S. "Bringing the Outside In: The Andrōn as Brothel and the Symposium's Civic Sexuality." In *Greek Prostitutes in the Ancient Mediterranean, 800 BCE-200 CE*. Edited by A. Glazebrook and M. M. Henry, 60–85. Madison, Wis: University of Wisconsin Press, 2011.

D'Arms, J. 'The Roman Convicium and the Idea of Equality.' In *Sympotica: A Symposium on the Symposion*. Edited by O. Murray, 308–20. Oxford: Clarendon Press, 1990.

Davidson, J. "Making a Spectacle of Her(self): The Greek Courtesan and the Art of the Present." In *The Courtesan's Arts: Cross-Cultural Perspectives*. Edited by M. Feldman and B. Gordon, 29–51. New York: Oxford University Press, 2006.

Dolansky, F. "Celebrating the Saturnalia: Religious Ritual and Roman Domestic Life." In *A Companion to Families in the Greek and Roman Worlds*. Edited by B. Rawson. Blackwell companions to the ancient world, 488–503. Malden, Mass. [u.a.]: Wiley-Blackwell, 2011.

Donahue, J. F. "Toward a Typology of Roman Public Feasting." In *Roman Dining*. Edited by B. K. Gold and J. F. Donahue, 95–113. Baltimore, Maryland: The Johns Hopkins university press, 2005.

Dunbabin, K. M. D. "Triclinium and Stibadium." In *Dining in a Classical Context: Symposium on Symposia*. Edited by W. J. Slater, 121–48. Ann Arbor: University of Michigan Press, 1991.

Erdkamp, P. "Introduction: Food and Commensality in the Ancient Near East." In *A Cultural History of Food in Antiquity*. Edited by P. Erdkamp. 6 vols. 1, 1–19. London: Berg, 2012.

Ernst, "J.Gastmahlgespräche: Lk 14,1-24." In *Die Kirche des Anfangs: Für Heinz Schürmann*. Edited by J. E. R. Schnackenburg and J. Wanke, 57–78. Freiburg: Herder, 1978.

Fascher, E. "Theologische Beobachtungen zu δεῖ." In *Neutestamentliche Studien für Rudolf Bultmann: Zu seinem 70. Geburtstag am 20. August 1954*. Edited by W. Eltester. Beihefte zur Zeitschrift für die neutestamentliche Wissenschaft und die Kunde der älteren Kirche 21, 228–54. Berlin: A. Töpelmann, 1954.

Fehr, B. "Entertainers at the Symposion: The Akletoi in the Archaic Period." In *Sympotica: A Symposium on the Symposion*. Edited by O. Murray, 185–95. Oxford: Clarendon Press, 1990.

Gardner, E. A. and D. Litt. "Food and Drink, Meals, Cooking and Entertainments." In *A Companion to Greek Studies*. 4th ed. Edited by L. Whibley, 541-546. Cambridge Eng: Cambridge University Press, 1931.

Gilliam, J. F. "Invitations to the Kline of Sarapis." In *Collectanea papyrologica: Texts publ. in honor of Herbert Chayyim Youtie*. Edited by A. E. Hanson. Papyrologische Texte und Abhandlungen 19, 315–24. Bonn: Habelt, 1976.

Griffith, M. "Greek Lyric and the Place of Humans in the World." In *The Cambridge Companion to Greek Lyric*. Edited by F. Budelmann, 72–94. Cambridge, New York: Cambridge University Press, 2009.

Grignon, C. "Commensality and Social Morphology: An Essay of Typology." In *Food, Drink and Identity: Cooking, Eating and Drinking in Europe since the Middle Ages*. Edited by P. Scholliers, 23–36. Oxford, New York: Berg, 2001.

Hooker, M. D. "Is the Son of Man Problem Really Insoluble?" In *Text and Interpretation: Studies in the New Testament presented to Matthew Black*. Edited by Matthew Black, Ernest Best and Robert M. Wilson, 155–68. Cambridge: Cambridge University Press, 1979.

Jameson, M. "Private Space and the Greek City." In *The Greek city: From Homer to Alexander*. Edited by O. Murray and S. R. F. Price, 171–95. Oxford: Clarendon, 1990.

Leroy, H. "Vergebung und Gemeinde nach Lukas 7,3-50." In *Wort Gottes in der Zeit: Festschrift Karl Hermann Schelkle zum 65. Geburtstag*. Edited by H. Feld. Translated by Karl H. Schelkle, 85-94. Düsseldorf: Patmos-Verl, 1973.

Lill, A. "The Social Meaning of Greek Symposium." In *Studien zu Ritual und Sozialgeschichte im Alten Orient: Studies on Ritual and Society in the Ancient Near East: Tartuer Symposien, 1998-2004*. Edited by T. R. Kämmerer, 171-86. Berlin, New York: Walter de Gruyter, 2007.

Ling, R. "The Decoration of Roman Triclinia." In *In Vino Veritas*. Edited by O. Murray and M. Tecuşan, 239–51. Oxford: The Alden Press, 1995.

Lissarrague, F. "Around the Krater: An Aspect of Banquet Imagery." In *Sympotica: A Symposium on the Symposion*. Edited by O. Murray, 196–209. Oxford: Clarendon Press, 1990.

LLewelyn, S. R. "Tax Collection and the τελῶναι of the New Testament." In *New Documents Illustrating Early Christianity: A Review of the Greek Inscriptions and Papyri*. Edited by S. R. LLewelyn. 8, 47–76. Grand Rapids, Michigan: W. B. Eerdmans, 1998.

Lukinovich, A. "The Play of Reflections between Literary Form and the Sympotic Theme in the Deipnosophistae of Athenaeus." In *Sympotica: A Symposium on the Symposion*. Edited by O. Oswyn, 263–71. Oxford: Clarendon Press, 1990.

McGowan, A. "The Meals of Jesus and the Meals of the Church: Eucharistic Origins and Admission to Communion." In *Studia Liturgica Diversa: Essays in Honor of Paul F. Bradshaw*. Edited by P. F. Bradshaw, M. E. Johnson and L. E. Phillips. Studies in church music and liturgy, 101–16. Portland, Or.: Pastoral Press, 2004.

Miller, M. "Foreigners at the Symposion?" In *Dining in a Classical Context: Symposium on Symposia*. Edited by W. J. Slater, 59–81. Ann Arbor: University of Michigan Press, 1991.

Morgan, J. "Drunken Men and Modern Myths: Reviewing the Classical Andron." In *Sociable Man: Essays on Ancient Greek Social Behaviour in Honour of Nick Fisher*. Edited by S. D. Lambert, N: R. E. Fisher and D. L. Cairns, 267-290. Swansea: Classical Press of Wales, 2011.

Morgan, T. "Ethos: The Socialization of Children in Education and Beyond." In *A companion to families in the Greek and Roman worlds*. Edited by B. Rawson. Blackwell companions to the ancient world, 504-20. Malden, Mass. [u.a.]: Wiley-Blackwell, 2011.

Moscato, F. "The Symposium." In *Symposion: La Cultura del Vino nei Valori Della Conoscenza Storica e Nelle Strategie di Mercato*. Edited by S. Menghini, 61-92. Firenze: Firenze Univ. Press, 2012.

Murray, O. "Hellenistic Royal Symposia." In *Aspects of Hellenistic Kingship*. Edited by P. Bilde. Studies in Hellenistic civilization 7, 15-27. Aarhus, Oakville, Conn: Aarhus University Press, 1996.

———. "Histories of Pleasures." In *In Vino Veritas*. Edited by O. Murray and M. Tecuşan, 1-17. Oxford: The Alden Press, 1995.

———. "Nestor's Cup and the Origin of the Greek Symposion." In *Annali di archeologia e storia antica*, 47-54. Napoli: [s.n.], 1994.

———. "Sympotic History." In *Sympotica: A Symposium on the Symposion*. Edited by O. Murray, 3-13. Oxford: Clarendon Press, 1990.

———. "The Affair of the Mysteries: Democracy and the Drinking Group." In *Sympotica: A Symposium on the Symposion*. Edited by O. Murray, 149-61. Oxford: Clarendon Press, 1990.

———. "The Culture of the Symposion." In *A Companion to Archaic Greek World*. Edited by K. Raaflaub and H. Wees. Blackwell Companion to the Ancient World, 508-23. Malden, MA: Blackwell, 2006.

———. "The Greek Symposion in History." In *Tria corda*. Edited by E. Gabba and A. Momigliano. Biblioteca di Athenaeum 1, 257-72. Como: Ed. New Press, 1983.

———. "The Symposion as Social Organization." In *The Greek Renaissance of the Eighth Century B C: Tradition and Innovation*. Edited by R. Hägg, 195⊠99. Stockholm: Skrifter utgivna av Svenska Instituten i Athen, 1983.

Nijboer, A. J. "Banquet, Marzeah, Symposion and Symposium During the Iron Age: Disparity and Mimicry." In *Regionalism and Globalism in Antiquity: Exploring their Limits*. Edited by F. De Angelis. Colloquia Antiqua 7, 95-126. Leuven: Peeters Publishers, 2013.

Oberliner, L. "„Der Menschensohn muss leiden..." (Mk 8,31): Das Bekenntnis zur Auferweckung Jesu als theologische Voraussetzung des Christologischen Bekenntnisses." In *Jesus im Glaubenszeugnis des Neuen Testaments: Exegetische Reflexionen zum 100. Geburtstag von Anton Vögtle*. Edited by L. Oberlinner and F. R. Prostmeier. Herders biblische Studien Herder's biblical studies Band 80, 49–85. Freiburg im Breisgau: Herder, 2015.

———. "Das Jesusbild des Lukasevangeliums: Eine soteriologische Alternative?" In *Verantwortete Exegese: FS. F. G. Untergaßmair*. Edited by G. Hotze and E. Spiegel, 167–82. Berlin: LIT, 2006.

Pantel, P. S. "Sarificial Meal and Symposion, Two Models of Civic Institutions in the Archaic Society?" In *Sympotica: A Symposium on the Symposion*. Edited by O. Murray, 14–36. Oxford: Clarendon Press, 1990.

Paul, G. "Symposia and Deipna in Plutarch's Lives and in Other Historical Writings." In *Dining in a Classical Context: Symposium on Symposia*. Edited by W. J. Slater, 157–70. Ann Arbor: University of Michigan Press, 1991.

Pellizer, E. "Outlines of a Morphology of Sympotic Entertainment." In *Sympotica: A Symposium on the Symposion*. Edited by O. Murray, 177–84. Oxford: Clarendon, 1990.

Pesch, R. "Das Zöllnergastmahl (Mk 2:15-17)." In *Mélanges Bibliques: en Hommage au R.P. Béda Rigaux*. Edited by B. Rigaux, A. L. Descamps and A. Halleux, 63–87. Gembloux, Belgium: Duculot, 1970.

Pfann, S. J. "A Table in the Wilderness: Pantries and Tables, Pure Food and Sacred Space at Qumran." In *Qumran, the Site of the Dead Sea Scrolls: Archaeological Interpretations and Debates*. Edited by K. Galor, J. B. Humbert and J. Zangenberg. v. 57, 159–78. Leiden, Boston: Brill, 2006.

Pitt-Rivers, J. "The Stranger, the Guest and the Hostile Host: Introduction to the Study of the Laws of Hospitality." In *Contributions to Mediterranean Sociology*. Edited by J. G. Peristiany. Publications of the Social Sciences Centre Athens 4, 13–30. Paris: Mouton, 1968.

Prostmeier, F. R. "Symposion - Begegnung - Rettung: Lukas und Seine Narrative Theologie." In *Jesus als Bote des Heils: Heilsverkündigung und Heilserfahrung in Frühchristlicher Zeit*. Edited by C. Georg-Zöller, F. R. Prostmeier and L. Hauser. Stuttgarter biblische Beiträge 60, 95-121. Stuttgart: Katholisches Bibelwerk, 2008.

———. "Thesen zur „Gretchenfrage"." In *Jesus im Glaubenszeugnis des Neuen Testaments: Exegetische Reflexionen zum 100. Geburtstag von Anton Vögtle*. Edited by L. Oberlinner and F. R. Prostmeier. Herders biblische Studien Herder's biblical studies Band 80, 229–46. Freiburg im Breisgau: Herder, 2015.

Rathje, A. "The Adoption of the Homeric Banquet in Central Italy in the Orientalizing Period." In *Sympotica: A Symposium on the Symposion*. Edited by O. Murray, 279–88. Oxford: Clarendon Press, 1990.

Robertson, N. "The Betrothal Symposium in Early Greece." In *Dining in a Classical Context: Symposium on Symposia*. Edited by W. J. Slater, 25–58. Ann Arbor: University of Michigan Press, 1991.

Rohrbaugh, R. L. "The Pre-industrial City in Luke-Acts: Urban Social Relations." In *The Social World of Luke-Actts: Models for Interpretation*. Edited by J. H. Neyrey, 125–50. Peabody, Mass.: Hendrickson Publishers, 1991.

Roller, M. "Horizontal Women: Posture and Sex in the Roman Convivium." In *Roman Dining*. Edited by B. K. Gold and J. F. Donahue, 49–97. Baltimore (Md): The Johns Hopkins university press, 2005.

Rositter, J. "Convivium and Villa in Late Antiquity." In *Dining in a Classical Context: Symposium on Symposia*. Edited by W. J. Slater, 199–214. Ann Arbor: University of Michigan Press, 1991.

Rösler, W. "Wine and Truth in the Greek Symposion." In *In Vino Veritas*. Edited by O. Murray and M. Tecuşan, 106–12. Oxford: The Alden Press, 1995.

Scholliers, P. "Meal, Food Narratives and Sentiments of Belonging in Past and Present." In *Food, Drink and Identity: Cooking, Eating and Drinking in Europe since the Middle Ages*. Edited by P. Scholliers, 3–22. Oxford, New York: Berg, 2001.

Strauss, M. "Luke." In *The Illustrated Bible Backgrounds Commentary*. Edited by C. E. Arnold. 1, 318–515. Zondervan: Grand Rapids, 2002.

Tannehill, R. C. "The Story of Zacchaeus as Rhetoric: Luke 19:1-10." In *The Rhetoric of Pronouncement*. Edited by V. K. Robbins. Semeia 64, 201–12. Atlanta, GA: Scholars Press, 1994.

Tecuşan, M. "Logos Sympotikos: Patterns of the Irrational in Philosophical Drinking." In *Sympotica: A Symposium on the Symposion*. Edited by O. Murray, 238–60. Oxford: Clarendon Press, 1990.

Therampil, J. "How can the Church in India be redeemed from Casteism?" In *Caste Culture in Indian Church: The Response of the Church to the Problem of Caste within the Christian Community*. Edited by S. L. Raj S.J and G. F. Xavier Raj, 45–52. New Delhi: Indian Social Institute, 1993.

Tomlinson, R. A. "The Chronology of the Perachora Hestiarorion and its Significance." In *Sympotica: A Symposium on the Symposion*. Edited by O. Murray, 95–101. Oxford: Clarendon Press, 1990.

Touliatos, D. "The Traditional Role of Greek Women in Music from Antiquity to the End of the Byzantine Empire." In *Rediscovering the Muses: Women's Musical Traditions*. Edited by K. Marshall, 111–23. Boston: Northeastern University Press, 1993.

Vössing, K. 'Family and Domesticity.' In *A Cultural History of Food in Antiquity*. Edited by P. Erdkamp. 6 vols. 1, 133–43. London: Berg, 2012.

Węcowski, M. "Homer and the Origins of the Symposion." In *Omero Tremila Anni Dopo*. Edited by P. Ascheri and F. Montanari. 210, 625–37. Roma: Edizioni di Storia e Letteratura, 2002.

Yatromanolakis, D. "Ancient Greek Popular Song." In *The Cambridge Companion to Greek Lyric*. Edited by F. Budelmann, 263–76. Cambridge, New York: Cambridge University Press, 2009.

Internet Articles

Ambedkar, B. R. "Writings and Speeches." Accessed November 1, 2017. http://drambedkarwritings.gov.in/upload/uploadfiles/files/Volume_01.pdf.

ANI. "Dalits Given Soap, Shampoo; Asked to Take Bath before Meeting Yogi." Accessed May 28, 2017. http://www.rediff.com/news/report/dalits-given-soap-shampoo-asked-to-take-bath-before-meeting-yogi/20170528.htm.

Arthur Jr., J. A. "Table fellowship and the Eschatological Kingdom in the Emmaus Narrative of Luke 24." Ph.D. Thesis. Accessed 20-07.2015. http://etheses.dur.ac.uk/10486/1/10486_7283.PDF?UkUDh:CyT.

Brumberg-Kraus, J. "Memorable Meals: Symposia in Luke's Gospel, the Rabbinic Seder,and the Greco-Roman Literary Tradition." Accessed May 30, 2016. http://www.wheatoncollege.edu/academic/academicdept/religion/MemorableMeals/mm_chptIV.pdf.

Dorairaj, S. "Stripped of Dignity." Accessed May 31, 2016. http://www.frontline.in/social-issues/stripped-of-dignity/article4840220.ece.

Krishna, R. A. "Temple Cleaned after Visit, Reiterates Bihar CM." Accessed October 20, 2016. http://www.hindustantimes.com/india/temple-cleaned-after-visit-reiterates-bihar-cm/story-IP7e87GDCM6tHz5RxmDbZN.html.

Marshall, M. J. "Jesus and the Banquets: An Investigation of the Early Christian Tradition Concerning Jesus' Presence at Banquets with Toll Collectors and Sinners." Dissertation, Murdoch University, 2002. Accessed March 20, 2017. http://researchrepository.murdoch.edu.au/id/eprint/183/#?

Pesonen, A. "Luke, The Friend of Sinners." Accessed May 21, 2017. https://helda.helsinki.fi/bitstream/handle/10138/21588/lukethef.pdf?sequence=2.

PTI. "Dalit woman denied water access, husband digs own well in drought-hit Maharashtra village." Accessed October 28, 2016. http://indianexpress.com /article/india/india-news-india/dalit-woman-denied-water-access-husband-digs-own-well-in-drought-hit-maharashtra-village-2790466/.

PTI. "Yeddyurappa in Controversy again, this time by eating 'Hotel food' at Dalit's home." Accessed May 25, 2017. http://www.bhatkallys.com/state/ yeddyurappa-controversy-time-eating-hotel-food-dalits-home/.

Shaji, K. A., V. Senthil Kumaran, and S. Karthick. "Inter-Caste Marriage Sparks Riot in Tamil Nadu District: 148 Dalit Houses Torched." Accessed October 30, 2016. http://timesofindia.indiatimes.com/india/Inter-caste-marriage-sparks-riot-in-Tamil-Nadu-district-148-Dalit-houses-torched/articleshow/ 17151170.cms.

Siker, J. S. "From Gentile Inclusion To Jewish Exclusion: Abraham in Early Christian Controversy with Jews." *Biblical Theology Bulletin: A Journal of Bible and Theology* 19, no. 1 (1989): 30–36. Accessed March 15, 2016. https://doi.org/10.1177/014610798901900105.

Thomson. "Indian Temple 'purified' after Low-Caste Chief Minister Visits." Accessed October 20, 2016. http://www.reuters.com/article/us-foundation-india-caste-idUSKCN0HP1DE20140930.

Voloshin, B. R. "Literary Banquets." *Pacific Coast Philology* 45 (2010): 1–11. Accessed March 3, 2014. http://www.jstor.org/page/info/about/policies/terms.jsp.

Willker, W. "A Textual Commentary on the Greek Gospels." *Luke*. Last modified 2015. Accessed May 30, 2015. http://www-user.uni-bremen.de/~wie/ TCG/ TC-Luke.pdf.

Witetschek, S. "The Stigma of a Glutton and Drunkard." *Ephemerides Theologicae Lovanienses* 83, no. 1 (2007): 135–54. Accessed January 24, 2015. https://doi.org/10.2143/ETL.83.1.2021745.

www.ingramcontent.com/pod-product-compliance
Lightning Source LLC
Chambersburg PA
CBHW020329240426
43665CB00043B/137